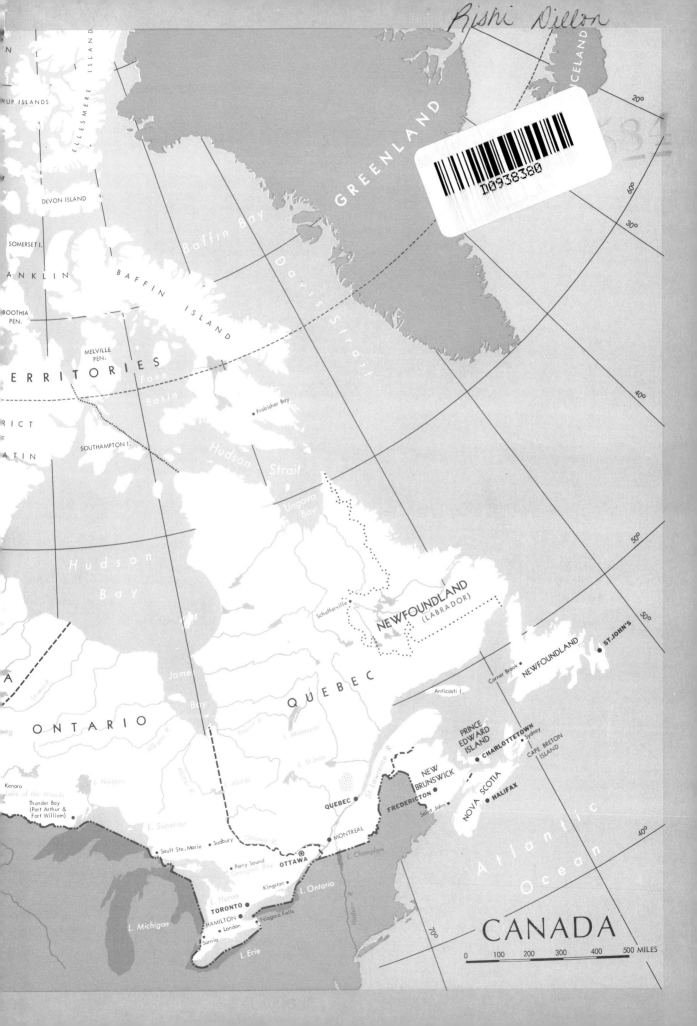

GREENLAND

ICELAND

20°

60°

30°

RUP ISLANDS

ELLESMERE ISLAND

DEVON ISLAND

Baffin Bay

40°

SOMERSET I.

ANKLIN

BAFFIN ISLAND

BOOTHIA PEN.

Davis Strait

MELVILLE PEN.

ERRITORIES

Foxe Basin

Hudson Strait

50°

RICT

ATIN

SOUTHAMPTON I.

• Frobisher Bay

Ungava Bay

Hudson

Bay

NEWFOUNDLAND
(LABRADOR)

50°

• Schefferville

• St. John's

A

Serven R.

Jame

Bay

ONTARIO

Albany R.

QUEBEC

Corner Brook •

NEWFOUNDLAND

Anticosti I.

Kenora

L. Nipigon

Abitibi R.

Rupert R.

L. Mistassini

L. St. Jean

St. Lawrence R.

PRINCE
EDWARD
ISLAND

CHARLOTTETOWN •
• Sydney

CAPE BRETON
ISLAND

Lake of the Woods

Thunder Bay
(Port Arthur &
Fort William)

L. Abitibi

NEW
BRUNSWICK

NOVA SCOTIA

L. Superior

QUEBEC •

FREDERICTON •

Saint John •

HALIFAX •

40°

• Sault Ste. Marie

• Sudbury

Ottawa R.

MONTREAL •

Atlantic

• Parry Sound
Georgian Bay

OTTAWA ⊙

L. Champlain

Ocean

L. Huron

Kingston •

L. Ontario

Hudson R.

TORONTO •

HAMILTON •
• London
Sarnia •

• Niagara Falls

CANADA

L. Michigan

L. Erie

70°

0   100   200   300   400   500 MILES

CHALLENGE & SURVIVAL:

The History of Canada

CHALLENGE & SURVIVAL:

The History of Canada

H. H. HERSTEIN
B.Sc., B.A., B.Ed., M.Ed., M.C.I.C.
History Department, St. John's High School, Winnipeg

L.J. HUGHES
B.A., B.Ed.
Formerly Vice-Principal, St. Paul's High School, Winnipeg

R. C. KIRBYSON
B.A., B.Ed., M.A.
Head of History Department, West Kildonan Collegiate, Winnipeg

Ph

PRENTICE-HALL OF CANADA, LTD.

Scarborough Ontario

PRENTICE-HALL, INC., ENGLEWOOD CLIFFS, NEW JERSEY
PRENTICE-HALL INTERNATIONAL, INC., LONDON
PRENTICE-HALL OF AUSTRALIA, PTY., LTD., SYDNEY
PRENTICE-HALL OF INDIA PVT., LTD., NEW DELHI
PRENTICE-HALL OF JAPAN, INC., TOKYO

Library of Congress Catalog Card No. 70-91954
13-125088-4
5 74 73

PRINTED IN CANADA

APPRECIATION

Challenge and Survival is the product of four years of intensive research and often frustrating work. In the preparation of such a book many people were involved in varying degrees. To our many colleagues and friends who offered constant encouragement and useful suggestions, we wish to express our deep gratitude.

From the inception of the idea for *Challenge and Survival,* we have been fortunate in enjoying the unwavering trust and limitless co-operation of Prentice-Hall of Canada Limited. We are especially grateful to Mr. Paul Hunt for his continued support and encouragement.

We wish to acknowledge the contribution of Father V. J. Jensen, S.J., of St. Paul's College of The University of Manitoba and Dr. Cornelius Jaenen of the University of Ottawa. Words cannot adequately express our sincere appreciation of the many hours they spent poring over hundreds of pages of unrefined manuscript. Their interest remained high, their advice was sound, their guidance sure and their criticism gentle. For this we shall be forever thankful.

The selection of illustrations in *Challenge and Survival* is the work of Mr. Richard Huyda, M.A., Head, Historical Photographs Section, Public Archives of Canada. To him the selection of illustrative material was not a random collection of photographs but rather a research project aimed at enhancing and fortifying the manuscript. We were fortunate, indeed, in having one so knowledgeable and so committed to excellence involved in the preparation of the text.

Special thanks are extended to Miss Gladys Hector for reading the manuscript and improving its construction through helpful suggestions. Acknowledgement is also made to the staffs of the Manitoba Archives and Provincial Library, Mr. George Goodman, Mr. Larry Herstein, Mr. John Lough and Mr. George Melnyk for their assistance.

Finally, we are deeply indebted to our wives and families for their continuous support, unending patience and sympathetic encouragement. Their appreciation of our efforts encouraged us to persist and to continue in spite of many setbacks and disappointments.

H.H.H.

L.J.H.

R.C.K.

TABLE OF CONTENTS

MAPS

(Drawn by Cyril Finch of Langridge, Ltd.)

LIST OF ILLUSTRATIONS

Threshing in Western Canada, 1910; photo (PAC). 294 — G.T.R. Engine 618 and Train, c. 1910; photo (PAC). 295 — A Prospector and Companion, 1898; photo (PAC). Paying with Gold Dust, 1899; photo (PAC). 299—Erecting an Elevator for Storing Grain; photo (PAC). 301 — Labour Day Parade, Winnipeg, 1914; photo (PAC).

PROGRESS TOWARDS NATIONAL STATES: "Lip-Loyalty vs. Loyalty that Acts" Cartoonist's view of Imperial Preference, by J. W. Bengough in *The Globe*, Oct. 25, 1900, p. 11 (PAC). 205 — Canadian Contingent Ready to Board the Milwaukee, Halifax, and Leave for South Africa; from the *Illustrated London News*, April 28, 1900, p. 575 (PAC). 309 — Street Scene in Scagway, Alaska, 1897; photo (PAC). 311 — H.M.C.S. Rainbow; photo (PAC). H.M.C.S. Niobe: Canada's First Battleship; photo (PAC). 313 — Sir Wilfrid Laurier in Mission City, B.C., Aug. 16, 1910; photo (PAC).

A NATION ON TRIAL, 1911-1939

CANADA AND WORLD WAR I: 319 — Sir Robert Borden; photo (PAC). Henri Bourassa; photo (PAC). 320 — Recruiting Poster, World War I; from an original in the Archives (PAC). 322 — Tank Advancing with Infantry, Vimy, April, 1919; photo (PAC). 324 — Soldering Fuses in the British Munitions Company, Verdun, P.Q., during World War I; photo (PAC).

CANADA IN THE TWENTIES: 327 — Moving Camp on the Provincial Highway, North of Parry, Saskatchewan, 1923.; (PAC). 328—Log Pile: Laurentide Pulp Co., Grandmere, P.Q., 1926; photo (PAC). 329—Mail is transferred from a plane to dogtrain at Fort Smith, N.W.T. First regular flight, 1929; photo (PAC). 331 — General Strike, Winnipeg, Manitoba, June 21, 1919, photo (PAC). 333 — Mackenzie King; photo (PAC). Arthur Mieghen; photo (PAC). 336—C.P.R. Ladies' Lounge in the New Solarium Car, 1920's; photo (PAC). 337 — Broadcast of Madge Macbeth's Play *Superwomen* from Radio Station CNRO, Ottawa, 1920's; photo (PAC).

THE GREAT DEPRESSION OF THE 1930's: 340 — The Globe Front Page; photo (PAC). 341 — Drifting Soil Covering Shrubbery Around a Settler's House, Saskatchewan; photo (PAC). 341 — Men Lined up For Food, 1930's photo (PAC). 342 — The Hon. R. B. Bennett and his Sister; photo (PAC). 342 — A Bennett Buggy; photo, Manitoba Archives. 343 — Unemployed men participating in "March on Ottawa" board train in Alberta, June 1935.; photo (PAC). 346 — James S. Woodsworth; photo (PAC). William S. Aberhart Addressing a Rally in St. George's Island Park, Calgary, June 1937; photo (PAC). Maurice Duplessis in the 1930's; photo (PAC). 350 — Single Men's Unemployed Association Parading in Toronto, 1930's; photo (PAC).

CANADA AND THE BRITISH COMMONWEALTH, 1918-1939: 355 — League of Nations, Geneva, Aug.-Sept. 1928; photo (PAC). 358 — The Original Group of Seven; from Macdonald, T., *The Group of Seven*, Toronto, 1944; photo (PAC). 359 — Canadian Pavillion at British Empire Exhibition, Wembley, England, 1924; photo (PAC).

THE INTER-WAR YEARS: CANADA AND INTERNATIONAL RESPONSIBILITY: 363 — Dominion Bureau of Statistics Computer in Operation, Ottawa, 1930's; photo (PAC). 366 — A Section of Halifax Harbour, Nova Scotia, 1930; photo (PAC).

THE MODERN NATION: CANADA, 1939-1968

CANADA AND WORLD WAR II: 373 — Hon. C. D. Howe, Minister of Munitions and Supply, accepts the 500,000th Canadian military vehicle at the General Motors Plant, Oshawa, Ontario, June 21, 1943.; photo (PAC). 374 — Churchill Addressing the House of Commons during Visit to Canada, 1941; photo (PAC). 275—Canadian troops, enroute to Britain, sail from Halifax, December 1939.; photo (PAC). 376—Royal Canadian Air Force Recruiting Poster; photo (PAC). 378—Dieppe, France, August, 1942; photo (PAC). 380—Canadian Armoured Column enroute to Gothic Line; photo (PAC). 381 — General de Gaulle Visiting Ottawa, July 11, 1944; photo (PAC). 384 — Wartime Prices and Trade Board window display urges people to save fat and bones for munitions.; photo (PAC).

CANADIAN GOVERNMENT AND THE ECONOMY, 1945 TO THE PRESENT: 389 — Operating a Drill Jumbo: Uranium Mine, Elliott Lake, Ontario; photo (National Film Board). Workmen Setting Drilling Bit at Imperial Oil Co. Oilwell; photo (NFB); Aerial View of the International Minerals and Chemicals Corp. Potash Mine, Esterhazy, Saskatchewan; photo (NFB). 390 — Two Freighters on the Welland Canal; photo (NFB). People walk along the Trans-Canada Highway in Glacier Park, B.C., to attend the opening ceremonies of the Rogers Pass Section.; photo (NFB). 392 — Entrance to Canada Pension Plan Office; photo (National Health & Welfare). 397 — Corporal Jim Davis, during 1100 mile journey, registers Eskimos for Family Allowance, at Great Whale, Quebec; photo (NFB).

POLITICAL LIFE IN CANADA, 1945 TO THE PRESENT: 400 — Welcoming Ceremonies for Newfoundland: Peace Tower, Ottawa, April 1, 1949; photo (Newton Photographers, Ottawa). 403 — John Diefenbaker, 1957; photo (Capital Press Photographers). 404 — T. C. Douglas; photo (NFB). 407 — Procession on the way to Burning of the Outhouses; photo (The Winnipeg Tribune). Canoe Race; photo (PAC). Expo '67; photo (PAC). 410—Pierre Elliott Trudeau; photo by Karsh (NFB). 412—General Assembly First Meeting, April-June, 1945; photo (PAC).

CANADA AND FOREIGN AFFAIRS: 413 — Canadian Food for Ghana: photo (Capital Press Photographers). 413 — Canadian Artillery in Korea Shelling Enemy Positions in Support of Infantry; photo (Canadian Armed Forces). 414 — UNEF Jeep in the Desert, Gaza; photo (Canadian Armed Forces). 416 — Hon. Lester B. Pearson; photo (Ashley-Crippen, Toronto). 418 — Canadian Nato Forces in Germany; photo (Canadian Armed Forces). 419 — A Canadian teacher trains a student at Uganda College of Commerce, Kampala.; photo (C.I.D.A.). 422 — DEW-line (Distant Early Warning) Radar Installation; photo (Canadian Armed Forces). 423 — A sergeant works on a radar console, part of the SAGE warning system, near North Bay.; photo (Canadian Armed Forces). 424—RCAF CF-104 Landing in Germany; photo (Canadian Armed Forces). 425 — President John F. Kennedy addresses the Canadian Parliament, May 17, 1961.; photo (NFB).

THE LATEST CHALLENGE: 428 — RIN Demonstraters; photo (PAC). 429 — Visit of General Charles de Gaulle to Canada, City Hall, Montreal, 1967; photo (PAC). 436 — Ukranian Festival; photo (NFB). 437 — An Eskimo *Komatic* drives towards the Midnight Sun: Aberdeen Lake, Keewatin District, west of Baker Lake, N.W.T.; photo (NFB).

CHALLENGE & SURVIVAL:

The History of Canada

INTRODUCTION

"HISTORY IS BUNK..."

The oft-quoted statement attributed to Henry Ford, the American auto-maker, that "history is bunk" probably sums up the attitude of a great number of students. For many students of Canadian history a more accurate statement would be "History is *dull* bunk!" A majority of adults would probably agree. Why? One reason, certainly, is that many think of history as a collection of stories about past persons and events having no relevance to the present. Also, many feel that Canadians have not experienced much in the way of heroes and glorious events, compared to the British, the French, or even the Americans.

What is history, then, if it is not folklore, to be judged merely by its entertainment value? History is many things — dates, places, past events, the record of past events, a method of looking at human affairs, even the writing of material about history. Moreover, history is concerned with studying the past to gain insights into the present.

So history is really about the present. History is a continuous process. History is being made by people even now, as these lines are being read. Are Canadians really aware of the ingredients that are making their history? Imagine the following man-in-the-street interview; are these not the issues that are making history now in Canada?

INTERVIEWER: What do you think are the most important problems facing
                Canada today? Inflation? NATO? The United Nations?
                Relations with the United States? The plight of the Indians
                and Eskimos?

RESPONDENT: I guess those are all important. I hear commentators talking
                about those things on television.

INTERVIEWER: What do you think about biculturalism, which many believe
                is the number one problem facing Canada?

RESPONDENT: I don't know much about it, but I think everybody in
                Canada should have to speak English.

INTERVIEWER: Why?

RESPONDENT: Well, English-speaking Canadians are in the majority and the French are in the minority. In a democracy, the majority rules. Therefore everybody should be forced to speak English.

INTERVIEWER: Then you think it would be a good thing if everybody spoke English.

RESPONDENT: Yes, it would simplify everything if we all spoke the same language.

INTERVIEWER: Do you think Canada will break up as a result of the difficulties in Quebec?

RESPONDENT: Oh, no!

What do you think of our respondent's attitudes? Do they reflect an informed, thoughtful, realistic point of view about the meaning of Canadianism? Do you think this imaginary interview illustrates the thinking of the average Canadian outside Quebec? If it does, should we be optimistic or pessimistic about the future of Canadian democracy? What are the possibilities for the endurance of the Canadian nation and the survival of its cultural diversity?

"I don't know much about it . . ."

If our respondent had stopped at this point and had stated that lack of information prevented him from discussing the problem, we could perhaps forgive him. Too many such people, however, are willing, even anxious, to express their prejudices. And so the press, radio and television often disseminate views based on ignorance or on superficial analyses of problems.

Citizens in a democractic society should not be denied the right to hold opinions on matters of national concern. To preserve free and democratic institutions it is essential that people be prepared to speak out. Public opinion often has a profound impact on a nation's leaders. However, it is important that citizens form their opinions only as a result of thorough and open-minded investigation of all facets of a problem.

Understanding a current problem is not fully possible without referring to its past. We cannnot meet the latest challenge to the survival of Canada without first acquiring insight into the historical forces which have shaped biculturalism and which have brought it into focus in the last decade. An individual who has lost his memory lacks frames of reference to guide his actions. He may be afraid to go forward in life because of insecurity about his past. Similarly, a nation ignores its history at its own peril, if only because it may repeat past mistakes.

Our respondent recommends Anglicization as a national policy. He does not realize that Canadian history records more than once the failure of such an approach. He does not realize that Canada was built and made prosperous by men who faced challenges with imagination, who rejected the illusion of simple solutions. He does not know of great leaders, such as

Macdonald and Laurier, Borden and King, St. Laurent and Pearson, who saw that simple solutions often do violence to men and groups, their ideas, values and practices.

"In a democracy, the majority rules."

Because English-speaking Canadians outnumber those who speak French, there is a temptation to think that English should prevail. Such a position, however, invites the Quebecker to put forward the reminder that French is the natural language of some four-fifths of the people of his province.

It is prudent to consider rather carefully, then, the implications of majority rule. It does not mean domination by a capricious majority. It does not give the majority a license to carry out unjust or immoral acts. Some years ago former Prime Minister Louis St. Laurent said:

The will of the majority must be respected and it must prevail. But I trust that, here in Canada, the majority will always, as it is doing in this case [conscription], assert that will only after giving due consideration to the feelings and views of the minority and to the reasons for such feelings and views, and then only to the extent to which the majority is sincerely convinced that the general interests of the whole body politic require that it be thus asserted.

HOUSE OF COMMONS DEBATES,
Nov. 29, 1944, p. 6860

The majority must rule, but it must do so for the general benefit of all, including the minority. In a pluralistic country such as Canada, it is not enough to say, "The majority so wishes, and hence it is good." Indeed, it is not at all certain that the majority of Canadians see one common language as any more desirable than one common religion or one common race.

". . . it would simplify everything if we all spoke the same language."

Unilingualism would mean no need for simultaneous translation in Parliament, no French language network in the CBC, and many other simplifications in Canada's public life. On the surface the proposition is attractive, not the least because of the likely financial saving. However, such a solution smacks of a dull uniformity that Canadians have rejected throughout their history. Canada has not been a melting pot, reducing peoples from many lands to some common denominator. Rather, Canada has recognized and welcomed cultural differences. The Canadian mosaic that has survived for more than a century has drawn much of its strength from the unrepressed energies and talents of diverse peoples.

To assert that unity and vigour come from uniformity is to ignore the lessons of Canada's past. For the lack of uniformity is surely one of the most distinctive elements in our national character — a quality that marks us as different from our cousins south of the border. The creative accommodation of French and English has sustained a cultural balance within which many nationalities have been encouraged to retain their traditions and customs. It is not possible to have unilingualism and, at the same time, to keep Canada alive as it has existed for more than one hundred years. To support the idea of one language only is to support separatism, which might "simplify everything" without solving anything.

"Oh, no!"

Whether or not our respondent represents Canadian thinking in his earlier remarks, he certainly echoes the feelings of most Canadians in his reply to the final question. It really is inconceivable to the majority that Canada might fail to survive as a nation from sea to sea. Though we see federations in other parts of the world being torn apart by violence, we cannot imagine Canada falling prey to bloody internal strife.

Intuitively, Canadians know that their nation shall survive its latest crisis. Though challenges abound — biculturalism and multiculturalism, American economic penetration, the rising expectations of Indian, Métis and Eskimo, the alienation of some young people — Canadians have an instinctive faith in the future of their land.

Many would argue that instinctive faith is really blind faith, that it means ignoring problems in the hope that they will eventually resolve themselves. Canadian history is reassuring in that Canadians have not stampeded into rash action when faced by problems. But Canadians have not ignored problems, either. There have been many challenges; there have been many appropriate responses. Perhaps if they look, Canadians can find in their history the bases for current optimism and the reasons for cautious approaches to the issues of the day.

The following excerpt is from the Canadian History syllabus of the Manitoba Department of Education:

. . . Canada today [is] a nation North American in environment, British in political tradition, multi-ethnic in social pattern, bilingual by law.

It is a nation divided physically into distinct regions with differing geographical features and economic interests; which accommodates different cultures and languages with differing attitudes and sets of values. Yet it is bound together with a common government, common traditions, common problems and a common citizenship.

It is a nation that is not artificial, although it seems to fly in the face of nature and the pull of natural forces. Although decisions made outside the country and incidents far removed from its shores helped shape its destiny, it is not an accident of history. It is rather a deliberate creation of people responding to challenges of geography and economics, overcoming divisions of language and race, adjusting to environment and learning to honour differences.

It is a nation that achieved nationhood in a way unique to the Americas — the slow road of evolution and compromise; a nation with a unique form of government, welding together the British principles of the Parliamentary system and the American principle of federalism; a nation without a common literature or language, without a common race or religion, without even a common civil law, yet with a unique basis of nationhood arising out of accepted differences and shared experience. It is a nation with its own destiny; the product of its own history. To understand Canada today one must understand how it came to be. Only with such understanding can there be direct interest and practical involvement in the political life of our nation.

To some, Canadian history is dull, and so it is, if one is looking for revolution, extremism and war. In a world torn by violence and bloodshed, Canadians can look with pride upon their generally peaceful and moderate past. If such "dullness" could become the way of the future for all nations, the world would surely be a better place in which to live. Twentieth-century man is coming to realize that his problems must be solved by means other than the sword. The alternatives — reason and compromise — are predominant throughout the Canadian historical experience.

Canadians, nevertheless, have no reason for smugness, since their circumstances have favoured a non-violent tradition. If Canada is to continue to meet its challenges, its citizenry must strive to be informed, enlightened and humane. Canadians can look for inspiration to their history of past challenges and imaginative responses. There the key may lie to Canada's meaningful survival.

1
THE EARLY FOUNDATION

Many of the voyages of the pre-Columbian era were clouded in mystery. By the end of the fifteenth century, however, the rise of strong national states, the emergence of an ambitious commercial class, advancement in the science of navigation and the desire for a short waterway to the East spurred large-scale explorations which somewhat replaced the individual adventures of earlier explorers. A shorter route to India, which would replace the risky and costly land route to the commercial centres of the Mediterranean, would bring greater profits on spices and luxury goods.

Columbus' discovery made it possible for Spain to build an empire in Central and South America and to emerge as a great European power, thriving on colonial gold, sugar and slaves. Portugal's and Spain's voyages around the southern tips of Africa and South America, respectively, spirited a search for a similar passage to Asia around the northern extremity of the New World. When this northern passage was not readily found, the searchers concentrated on finding a passage *through* the northern part of the New World.

However, such explorations technically would trespass Spanish territory as designated by the Treaty of Tordesillas.* Spain was annoyed by these voyages but was not too alarmed by them. Ever since the discovery of the New World, Spain seemed to have shown disinterest in North America, especially in the northern part. Spanish penetration into what is now the United States was only slight, and only in southern Florida, Texas, and California was there any sign of Spanish activity. The main concentration was on the wealthy countries of Central America and northern South America. Spain enjoyed the fruits of discovery in these areas and seemed reluctant to dissipate wealth and energy in the uncertainties of exploration farther north. This attitude

---

* On May 4, 1493, Pope Alexander VI divided the New World between the kings of Spain and Portugal. The demarcation line was 100 leagues (between 300 and 400 miles) west of the Azores and Cape Verde Islands. On June 7, 1494, in the Treaty of Tordesillas, the line of demarcation was moved 270 leagues farther west. Portugal was to have exclusive rights of all lands east of this line, and Spain of the lands west of it. This brought Brazil into Portuguese possession.

enabled others to trespass in North America. Later, when Spain resented English and French instrusions, the weakened country, no match for the rapidly ascending naval powers of England and France, could only protest.

Geographic barriers have always been a formidable challenge to Canadians. In the East, the mountains of the Appalachian Region, though only gentle plateaus, were obstacles to the westward movement of the early explorers, fur traders and settlers. The Canadian Shield, a plateau of bare rock, timberland, rivers and lakes, delayed the western and northern movement of the frontier. The Cordilleran Region with its rugged mountain ranges was so formidable a barrier that the Pacific Coast area remained isolated from the rest of Canada until the completion of the railroad in the late nineteenth century.

In spite of its size, Canada is not really landlocked. In the East, the Atlantic washes Canadian shores and offers ice-free ports. On the West Coast, several ice-free harbours give access to the Pacific Ocean. In the North, Hudson Bay and the Arctic Ocean provide ports which are used part of the year. The many rivers that drain into these large bodies of water are navigable part of the year and bring parts of Canada's heartland within reach of ocean highways.

When Europeans first set foot on Canada's soil, no more than 220,000 Indians claimed virtually all parts of Canada's 4 million square miles. It is generally assumed that Canada's aboriginal* population (Indians and Eskimos) came from Asia by way of the Bering Strait and the Aleutian Islands. Gradually, they migrated to all parts of the continent. This theory is reinforced by the fact that the Strait is only 36 miles across at its narrowest point — a distance of no great consequence even to a people with little navigational knowledge and crude means of transportation. This assumption gains more credibility when the physical characteristics of the Canadian Indian are considered. The coarse black hair, copper-coloured skin, oblique eyes, and protruding cheek bones, general to all Canadian Indians, mark them as members of the Asiatic Mongolian peoples.

With the coming of the Europeans, the Indian was forced to share his land with the intruders. In spite of a degree of mutual adaptation, the Canadian Indian became a stranger in his ancestral home.

---

* Aboriginal people are the first inhabitants of a country.

1

CANADA DISCOVERED

A

NORSE VOYAGES TO NORTH AMERICA

The presence of the Norsemen in North America is unquestioned. However, the point of contention about their sojourn is the extent of their exploration along the coast as well as their penetration into the North American continent. Some insist that Norsemen reached inland as far as Colorado, as evidenced by the Heavener Rune Stone, and farther north into Minnesota, as evidenced by the Kensington Rune Stone. Historians have found it difficult to come to concrete conclusions about the rune stones.* However, what is important is the Norse exploration along the Atlantic Coast of North America.

VIKING TRADE IN NORTHERN REGIONS[1]

The Norsemen in Greenland found valuable articles of trade — falcons, polar bears and ivory tusks — in the Canadian Arctic regions. The great demand for these luxury items can be gathered from the following description of Baffin Island, written by an Arab writer:

. . . . The island Harmûsa, which lies in the northernmost part of the inhabited world is almost 12 days' journeys in length and at the centre, ca. 4 days' journeys in breadth. From it, men get the good falcons. Its centre is: longitude 28° and latitude 58°. Around it lie small islands, which have falcons, and to the west of it is the white falcon island, which is almost 7 days' journeys in length from west to east, and almost 4 days' journeys in breadth. To it, and to the little northern island, men go to obtain the white falcons which are brought thence to the Sultan of Egypt, and the price of them, which is usually entered among the expenditures in his treasury, is a thousand denarii, but if they bring dead falcons, they get 500 denarii.

There is also found the polar bear. He walks out into the sea, swims, and catches fish, and what he cannot eat, or what he has no appetite for, these falcons take, and this is their food, for no birds are found there on account of the great cold. The pelts of these bears are soft, and it frequently happens that such pelts are brought to the royal residence in Egypt (or: to the Egyptian lands).

The compelling reason for Norse migration was the need for farmland. This search took the Vikings all over Europe and westward to the Shetlands, the Orkneys, the Hebrides and Iceland. From Iceland, Eric the Red established a colony in Greenland in 985. Among the first settlers was one called Herjulf. His son Bjarni, learning of his father's migration from Iceland, set out for Greenland in 986. Storms carried his ships off course and he sighted land that was hilly and wooded, probably northern Newfoundland. Realizing that this was not Greenland, he navigated northward. He passed the flat and wooded shore lines of Labrador, the mountainous and glacial Baffin Island and finally reached Greenland.

Eric's son Leif heard Bjarni's story and was very interested in the description of the timberlands in those far-away places. Lumber was an article that Greenland lacked. The profits to be gained by importing lumber motivated Leif to make his voyage of 1001.

* Runes are the straight-line letters of an alphabet used by ancient northern European nations. Stones having runic inscriptions on them are known as rune stones. The presence of rune stones has been advanced as evidence of the early presence of Vikings in the interior of the United States. Modern historical opinion, however, doubts the authenticity of the rune stones, and the Kensington Rune Stone has long since been discredited.

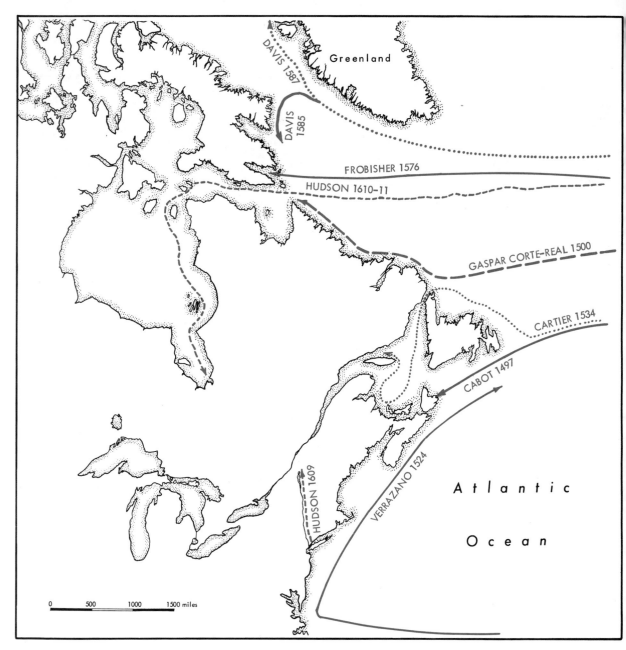

The Discovery of North America

Leif retraced Bjarni's route southward. The first land he sighted was the coast of Labrador, which he named Helluland (Flat Rock Land). He navigated the east side of Newfoundland and then headed southward where he came upon heavily forested lands. He called this area Markland (Forest Lands). After a brief stop, Leif continued southward. After sailing over an open sea for two days, he came upon land with a growth of grape vines and wild wheat. Leif named this land, which is believed to be Nova Scotia,* Vinland (Land of Wine).†

Leif returned to Greenland in the summer of 1002. His ships, laden with lumber and grapes, headed south and brought back riches from Markland and Vinland.

No doubt exaggerated tales of the riches of the distant lands whetted the appetites of explorers, adventurers and profit-seekers. It was not long before the route to Vinland became well-known

* Historians are uncertain about the exact locations of Helluland, Markland and Vinland. Helluland is said to be Labrador, northern Newfoundland or rocky Baffin Island; Markland — Newfoundland, wooded areas of the coast of Labrador or the forests of Nova Scotia; and Vinland — Newfoundland, Nova Scotia or New England.

† Some modern historians interpret Vinland as "grasslands."

and well-traveled. Numerous Norse expeditions headed south and brought back riches from Markland and Vinland.

Thorfinn Karlsefni, a prosperous merchant, realized the advantage to be gained from a permanent settlement in Vinland. In 1011, he undertook an expedition with settlers to start a colony there.* Skraelings† came and traded with the Norsemen. The friendly relations with the natives came to an end, however, when a Skraeling was killed. A band of natives retaliated by attacking the settlement. Subsequent encounters with the natives prompted Karlsefni's abandonment of the settlement. In 1013 he returned to Greenland.

The voyages of the Norsemen indicate that the route to Vinland, after a time, was well known and sailors had no difficulty reaching it. The Norsemen knew very little of the nature and extent of the new land, however, since they confined their explorations to the coastal areas and did not venture inland. Very little is known of their attempted settlements. Of their explorations and settlements only the famous Norse sagas are left.

B

ENGLISH VOYAGES TO NORTH AMERICA

The English, after being expelled from the Iceland cod fisheries in 1478, began to look westward for new fishing stations. Later, the news of Columbus' voyages and the benefits Spain obtained from them aroused great interest in England.

Henry VII, the frugal English monarch, gave John Cabot, a Venetian sailor, royal authorization to undertake a journey in search of a northern passage to Asia. In May 1497, Cabot set sail from Bristol, in the ship *Mathew* with a crew of eighteen men. Fifty-two days later he sighted some undetermined Atlantic coastal area which he believed to be the northeastern extremity of Asia. He found no people, but he saw snares set for game and noticed notches in trees, indications that the area was inhabited. Around the islands of St. Pierre and Miquelon, Cabot discovered the great fishing wealth of North America.

Cabot returned to Bristol and reported to Henry VII that 700 leagues beyond Ireland he reached the country of the Grand Khan. He also reported that fish were so plentiful in the distant waters that England would no longer need to rely on Iceland. He was royally received, honoured and rewarded, and assumed the title of Great Admiral.

AN ACCOUNT OF JOHN CABOT'S JOURNEY, 1497[2]

Lorenzo Pasqualigo wrote from London to his brothers in Venice:

That Venetian of ours who went with a small ship from Bristol to find new islands has come back and says he has discovered mainland 700 leagues away, which is the country of the Grand Khan, and that he coasted it for 300 leagues and landed and did not see any person; but he has brought here to the king certain snares which were spread to take game and a needle for making nets, and he found certain notched (or felled) trees so that by this he judges that there are inhabitants. . . . The king has promised him for the spring ten armed ships as he [Cabot] desires, and has given him all the prisoners to be sent away, that they may go with him, as he has requested; and has given him money that he may have a good time until then, and he is with his Venetian wife and his sons at Bristol. His name is Zuam Talbot and he is called the Great Admiral and vast honour is paid to him and he goes dressed in silk, and these English run after him like mad, and indeed he can enlist as many of them as he pleases, and a number of our rogues as well. The discoverer of these things planted on the land which he has found a large cross with a banner of England and one of St. Mark, as he is a Venetian, so that our flag has been hoisted very far afield.

In May 1498, Cabot sailed westward with two ships and three hundred men. On the western side of Greenland, icebergs forced him to steer a southerly course down the coast of Labrador, which he believed to be the Asiatic mainland. There he met some Indians who offered him furs and fish. Believing the Strait of Belle Isle to be a bay, he turned eastward along the coast of Newfoundland, then southward along the coast of Nova Scotia and New England. Hopes of reaching Japan, which he believed to be near the equator, may account for his prolonged southward course. Finding no sign of Eastern civilization, he terminated his voyage near Chesapeake Bay. He returned to England with only fish and furs — a great disappointment to Bristol merchants.

---

* His wife Gudrid gave birth to a son in Vinland. It was probably the first white child born in North America.

† It is believed that the Norsemen called the Labrador and Newfoundland Eskimos, as well as the Indians, Skraelings.

John Cabot Sighting North America, 1497

parts of North America. In 1577 Sir Francis Drake sailed around the southern tip of South America and along the west shore of North America. He claimed the Pacific Coast of the northern part of North America for England. This claim proved important to England in the eighteenth century in negotiations with Spain and Russia regarding the sea-otter trade in the northern Pacific waters.

Sir Humphrey Gilbert, another of Elizabeth's freebooting "sea dogs," laid claim to Newfoundland in 1583. Although an attempted settlement by Sir Walter Raleigh failed, the English claim proved to be so firm that England's sovereignty over Newfoundland lasted until 1949, when it joined Canada as a province.

The search for the elusive Northwest Passage continued, and English efforts to find the Passage resulted in explorations in the northern reaches of the Western Hemisphere. In 1576 Martin Frobisher's search ended in Frobisher Bay. John Davis, in 1586, ventured farther north into the strait that bears his name. In 1602 George Weymouth discovered Hudson Strait. Henry Hudson, in 1610, followed Weymouth's route and, continuing westward, discovered Hudson Bay.

Hudson was an accomplished English mariner. In 1609, while in the employ of the Dutch East India Company, he discovered and explored the Hudson River and thus established Dutch claim to a part of North America. The following year Hudson sailed from England in the *Discovery* with a crew of twenty-three men in search of the Northwest Passage. Following Weymouth's route, he entered what is now known as Hudson Bay. He followed the eastern shore of Hudson Bay and James Bay to its southern extremity. He realized, to his great disappointment, that the wide expanse of Hudson Bay was not the Passage but a huge inland sea. By this time winter had overtaken the expedition, and Hudson and his men were forced to spend the long arduous winter on the shores of James Bay. The supplies ran dangerously low, and the crew mutinied. Hudson, his son and eight loyal crew members were set adrift in the ship's boat. Nothing was ever heard of their fate. The tragic tale of the expedition was brought back to England by four surviving mutineers who managed to reach their homeland.

While Henry Hudson's efforts to find the Northwest Passage resulted in disappointment and tragedy, his explorations established English claim to the land surrounding Hudson Bay. The significance of this claim became apparent sixty years later when England realized that Hudson Bay and James Bay provided a direct water route to the great fur regions of the Canadian Shield.

Although the results of Cabot's voyages did not meet the expectations of his backers, nevertheless they were of considerable importance. Cabot failed to find a short trade route to the Orient, but he did establish England's claim to the northeastern coast of North America. He opened the fishing areas off Newfoundland for England when the country needed such a source of supply. Fish became an important article of English commerce in the European market. The fishing trade led to later development of dry fisheries and to rivalries for the North American mainland. Furthermore, fishing and the hauling of the bulky cargoes of fish across the Atlantic provided good training for sailors and promoted the development and expansion of the English navy. The furs that were brought back caused very little stir; Europe was not quite ready for them. In time they became valuable commodities, and rivalry between France and England for the fur regions in North America flared into open warfare.

During the reign of Elizabeth I, renewed interest in a Northwest Passage set off a wave of exploration which resulted in additional English claims to

C

PORTUGUESE VOYAGES TO NORTH AMERICA

Like Bristol in England, the Azores islands off the coast of Portugal were the starting point for expeditions across the Atlantic. In 1500 Gaspar Corte Real sailed to the east coast of Greenland and southwestward to the shores of North America.

Upon his return to Portugal, he reported that most of the land was covered with snow and ice, but also that there were large timber stands. Apparently, he brought back seven Indians with him. The king was pleased because he would have a relatively close and abundant supply of timber for masts and ships. The land Corte Real discovered also held promise of supplying Portugal with slaves.

In May 1501, Corte Real set out with another expedition for Greenland. Ice forced him to sail westward and then southward into an inlet where he came upon a band of Indians. He captured sixty of them and then proceeded southward to the Strait of Belle Isle. He mistook it for a bay, so he turned eastward and sailed along the coast to the south shore of Newfoundland, which he named Cabo de Boa Vista (Cape Bonavista). Two of his ships were sent back to Lisbon, while

he proceeded farther south to ascertain the connection between this continent and the island discovered by Columbus. Nothing was heard of him thereafter. A similar fate befell his brother Michael, who set out in 1502 in search of him.

Other Portuguese explorers scouted the shores of North America, but a major Portuguese expedition was not undertaken until 1521. In that year, Joam Alvarez Fegundes was instructed to explore and discover islands within the Portuguese sphere of influence without encroaching upon Spanish territory. Fegundes crossed the Atlantic and sailed along the coast of Cape Breton Island where he met fishermen from Brittany. He proceeded to the south coast of Newfoundland, past St. Pierre and Miquelon and to Portugal. Fegundes may have moved south to Nova Scotia, perhaps to the Bay of Fundy. The land Fegundes discovered was called Cabo Bretao; early accounts indicate that he established cod fisheries there, which became a large source of profit to Portugal. Although there is evidence that a Portuguese colony existed in Newfoundland between 1520 and 1525, Portugal seemed to have abandoned North America for more profitable enterprises elsewhere.

D

FRENCH VOYAGES TO NORTH AMERICA

At the beginning of the sixteenth century, French vessels made frequent voyages to the fishing grounds off Newfoundland. King Francis I, envious of the wealth Spain and Portugal were accumulating from their ventures in Central and South America, displayed interest in the exploitation of the New World. In 1523 he financed an expedition headed by Giovanni da Verrazano, which crossed the Atlantic and reached the eastern coast of America near present-day South Carolina. Verrazano then turned northward to Newfoundland. He reported to Francis I his conviction that the land he had reached was not Asia but a land block that obstructed the way to Asia. He discounted firmly-held beliefs that by following the Atlantic Ocean one could reach the East.

Several years later, Francis I decided to support another expedition to the New World, this time in search of gold and other riches. Jacques Cartier, a river pilot of St. Malo who had possibly sailed with Verrazano in 1523, was appointed to head the expedition.

In April 1534, two ships and sixty men left

St. Malo; after a rather fast Atlantic crossing of twenty days, they reached Newfoundland. Cartier followed the shore line northward and then sailed south through the Strait of Belle Isle. He remarked that the bleak infertile land of Labrador must have been the land "God gave to Cain." He proceeded southward along the western shore of Newfoundland, then across the open waters towards Prince Edward Island and along the New Brunswick coast. He thought the Bay of Chaleur might lead to a westward passage but soon found it was only a bay. The land of New Brunswick impressed him more favourably; there he met Indians who were friendly and eager to trade furs for trinkets. On the banks of the Gaspé Peninsula Cartier erected a cross and claimed the land for the King of France.

Cartier returned to France and reported the abundance of fish, timber stands, furs and fertile lands. He also introduced the possibility of discovering a passageway *through* the land mass to the East. Francis I, satisfied with the limited success of the expedition and impressed with future

The Arrival of Jacques Cartier at Quebec, 1535

prospects in the new land, ordered the preparation of another expedition.

In May 1535, Cartier's expedition of three boats followed the route of 1534 through the Strait of Belle Isle. He passed Anticosti Island and sailed into the wide gulf which he called St. Lawrence. He continued his westward course in the hope of reaching lands the Indians had spoken of as being rich in gold and copper. Where the St. Lawrence River narrows at present-day Quebec City, Cartier came upon the Indian village of Stadacona under the rule of Chief Donacona. Cartier sailed up the river to Hochelaga, where he terminated his journey because the rapids of Lachine obstructed the way up the St. Lawrence.

Near Hochelaga, a fortified Iroquois town, rose the mountain which Cartier named Mount Royal. He erected a cross on the mountain, marking French ownership of the surrounding land. With the approach of winter, Cartier returned to Stadacona. During his absence, his crew had built enclosures to protect their ships since an uneasy relationship had developed between the Indians and the Frenchmen. During the difficult winter that followed, twenty-five of Cartier's men died of scurvy. The expedition was somewhat of a disappointment to Cartier. Since the St. Lawrence was a fresh-water river, it was not likely to provide a passage to the East. Moreover, the Lachine rapids seemed to be a formidable barrier. Talk and promises were more evident than riches.

AN INDIAN CURE FOR SCURVY[3]

In the winter of 1535-36 at Stadacona, Cartier learned of a cure for scurvy:

. . . Dom Agaya [an Indian] whom he [Cartier] had seen ten or twelve days previous to this, extremely ill with the very disease his own men were suffering from; for one of his legs about the knee had swollen to the size of a two-year old baby, and the sinews had become contracted. His teeth had gone bad and decayed and the gums had rotted and become tainted . . . the Captain inquired of him what had cured him of his sickness. Dom Agaya replied that he had been healed by the juice of the leaves of a tree and the dregs of these, and that this was the only way to cure sickness . . . two squaws with our Captain . . . brought back nine or ten branches. They showed us how to grind the bark and the leaves and to boil the whole in water. Of this one should drink every two days, and place the dregs on the legs where they were swollen and affected. . . .

The Captain at once ordered a drink to be prepared for the sick men. . . . As soon as they had drunk it, they felt better . . . after drinking it two or three times, they recovered health and strength and were cured of all the diseases they had ever had. When this became known . . . in less than eight days a whole tree as large and as tall as any I ever saw was used up, and produced such a result, that had all the doctors of Louvain and Montpellier been there, with all the drugs of Alexandria, they could not have done so much in a year as did this tree in eight days. . . .

Nevertheless, his report in the court was impressive. He had forcibly taken Donacona and four other Indians with him to France so that they might relate the tales of the immense riches of the Saguenay country. Donacona proved to be a great storyteller. He described the abundant riches of the Saguenay country and spoke of the great wealth he had seen in other countries he had visited. His description of a great inland sea renewed hopes of finding a passage to the East.

Another expedition was not undertaken until 1541. This was to be a voyage of settlement and had been planned for over three years, but France's preoccupation with war against Spain had delayed it. Francis I appointed Roberval leader of the expedition and Lieutenant-General of the new land and gave him complete feudal rights. In May 1541, Cartier, the captain of the expedition, left with five of his own ships, 460 men, settlers, livestock, ammunition and food and supplies for three years. Roberval was to follow later. At Newfoundland, Cartier waited in vain for Roberval and then proceeded to Stadacona. He docked his ships nine miles upstream from Stadacona at Cap Rouge, where the settlement was to be located. Donacona and the other four Indians were conspicuously absent, and Cartier concealed the fact that they had died in France.

The colonists settled down to cultivate the land and build fortifications. The difficult winter, the increasing hostility of the Indians and Roberval's failure to arrive disheartened the settlers. In June 1542, Cartier abandoned the settlement and set sail for France. On the way, near Newfoundland, he unexpectedly met Roberval's three ships with 130 men, 200 colonists, supplies and provisions. Roberval ordered Cartier to return to Stadacona, but Cartier, as captain of the expedition, refused and returned to St. Malo. Roberval proceeded to Stadacona to revive the abandoned settlement.*

In spite of Cartier's apparent failure, the achievements of the Captain of St. Malo should not be minimized. Cartier discovered and explored Canada's great arterial highway, the St. Lawrence. His search for the Saguenay country and for the Northwest Passage produced the first attempt at settlement on the St. Lawrence. He brought to light the opportunity for missionary work among the Indians. His contact with the Indians revealed the abundance in Canada of furs, which later became the economic basis of the French empire in North America.

For the next half century, France was preoccupied with religious civil wars. With the return of stability under Henry IV, France once again attempted to establish settlements in North America. In 1598, the Marquis de La Roche landed a group of settlers, mainly convicts, on the barren shores of Sable Island. This undertaking was short-lived and ended in tragedy. After five years of hardship and privation, only a few survived; they were rescued and returned to France.

The sixteenth century was the age of North American discovery, but it produced no permanent settlement. Faint, undefined areas of interest in North America were marked out by European powers. Not until the seventeenth century were conditions in Europe favourable for the establishment of permanent French and English colonies in North America.

* Roberval, like Cartier, seemed to have encountered difficulties which were further accentuated by his unruly colonists. His attempt also ended in failure, in 1543.

"FALSE AS A CANADA DIAMOND"[4]

Near Stadacona, Cartier discovered some stones that appeared to be diamonds and gold. He stored them in barrels aboard ship. When he returned to France, word spread of the riches he had brought back, and there was excitement about the wealth of the New World. This, however, was short-lived. The glistening gold stones proved to be iron-pyrite; the diamonds were only quartz crystals. The phrase, "false as a Canada diamond," became part of the European vocabulary.

2

THE LAND AND ITS PEOPLE

A

PHYSIOGRAPHIC DIVISIONS

Canada is a vast land mass, stretching over 5,000 miles from the Atlantic to the Pacific and over 2,750 miles from the United States border to the North Pole. Canada occupies this whole area except Alaska on the Pacific Coast and the small islands of St. Pierre and Miquelon off the shores of Newfoundland. It covers an area of approximately 3,850,000 square miles, slightly larger than Europe (3,775,000 square miles) and larger than the United States including Alaska (3,615,000 square miles); only the Soviet Union (8,570,000 square miles) occupies a larger land mass. Yet, only 10 to 20 per cent of Canada has been regarded as suitable for habitation. This factor may account for Canada's population density of approximately 6 inhabitants per square mile as compared with 58 per square mile in the continental United States.

CANADA'S CLIMATE[5]

In 1663 Father Francois du Creux, in his history of Canada from 1625 to 1658, wrote the following about Canada's climate:

Many people will ask what is the cause of such long and such severe cold in a country whose situation is so similar to the situation of France. It will be enough to say, first, that the country is full of lakes and rivers and that the abundance of water is the cause of continuous dense and cold vapours; secondly . . . that since the rays of the sun never reach the ground except after penetrating tall and dark forests, the ground is very slow in receiving the warmth. . . . If the trees were cut down and the forest cultivated and inhabited, the exhalations from the continual fires burning in the houses would be warmer and dryer, and the open ground would receive the heat of the sun much sooner. Certainly experience has taught those who

have lived there that the snow melts and the vapours disappear earlier in the vicinity of cultivated fields than in the woods. . . .

The five physiographic divisions of Canada, from east to west, are generally referred to as the Appalachian Region (the Acadian Region, the Canadian Appalachians or the Maritime Region), the St. Lawrence Lowlands, the Canadian Shield (the Laurentian Plateau, the Laurentian Shield, or the Archaean Shield), the Great Central Plains (the Prairies, the Interior Continental Plain, the Central Plain or the Interior Plains) and the Cordilleran Region (the Western Cordillera or the Cordillera).

The Appalachian Region includes the Atlantic provinces of Prince Edward Island, Nova Scotia and New Brunswick; insular Newfoundland; the Gaspé Peninsula; and parts of Eastern Quebec south of the St. Lawrence River. This distinct region, also referred to as the Canadian Appalachians, is a medium-altitude plateau with narrow ridges and deep valleys, gentle rolling country, fertile lowlands, cliffs, large wooded areas, bare rock denuded by glacial action, inlets that serve as ports, and glacial lakes. This is what is left of old mountains worn down by millions of years of erosion. However, there are some heights that can be considered mountain peaks — Mount Jacques Cartier, 4,200 feet high, in Central Gaspé and some heights of over 2,000 feet in the long Range Mountains in the western part of Newfoundland.

The St. Lawrence Lowlands, which project southward to form the Central Lowlands of the United States, are a small but very important part of Canada. This triangular region situated between Lake Huron, Lake Erie and Lake Ontario, with a narrow neck extending eastward, was first mapped out by Champlain. The extension from the eastern

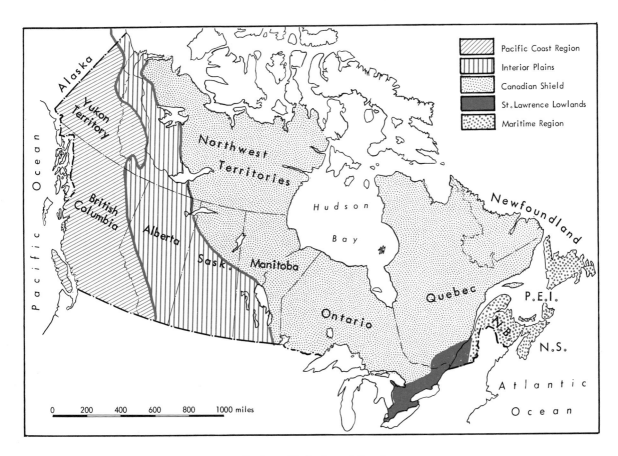

Physiographic Regions of Canada

tip of Lake Ontario is a narrow strip on either side of the St. Lawrence River, continuing beyond Quebec City, It is wedged between the Appalachians to the south and the Canadian Shield to the north. The level plains in the south of Ontario and Quebec form this area, which was the original Canada. The Niagara Peninsula, the waterways and canals connecting the St. Lawrence River with the Great Lakes, and the spectacular Niagara Falls lie within this region.

The largest physical division is the Canadian Shield, a vast plateau of Pre-Cambrian igneous rock that covers almost half of Canada. It forms a semi-circular collar around Hudson Bay from the coast of Labrador westward to the Mackenzie River Valley, extending over the northern parts of Quebec, Ontario, Manitoba, Saskatchewan and Alberta. It continues north of these provinces to engulf the Arctic Archipelago, a series of Arctic islands. It extends as far south as the Appalachians, the St. Lawrence Lowlands, Georgian Bay and Lake Superior; on the west it is bounded by the Great Central Plain. The Shield is made up of exposed rock, stripped of its topsoil by advancing glaciers of the Great Ice Age. It has a rugged rocky terrain interspersed with tundra forests, areas of muskeg and infertile land. For the most part, the

Shield is a series of monotonous stretches of barren lands, strewn with countless lakes and slashed by numerous rivers. In the nineteenth century this area was an obstacle to westward expansion and the agricultural development of Canada.

From the edge of the Canadian Shield westward to the foothills of the Rockies lie the Great Central Plains. This region funnels out from a relatively narrow area at the mouth of the Mackenzie River southward in an ever-widening expanse to the forty-ninth parallel and from there continues as the Great Plains and Central Lowlands of the United States to the Gulf of Mexico. During the Ice Age, part of the Plains was covered by Lake Agassiz. The deposits at the bottom of this lake became the rich soil of the Prairies. The Plains are flatlands with a gradual westward rise in elevation — from 800 feet above sea level at Lake Winnipeg to 3,400 feet at Calgary. Generally, this region is flat and treeless, but gentle rolling hills and deep river valleys provide relief from the uniformity of the land surface.

West of the Great Plains to the Pacific Coast stretches the Cordilleran Region. Here are mountain ranges averaging over 400 miles in width that run the whole length of the North American continent; some of these rugged snow-capped

mountains reach heights of over 13,000 feet. The Rocky Mountains on the eastern side and the Coast Ranges along the West Coast wall in the interior plateau of central British Columbia. The deep canyons with their rushing rivers, the cascading waterfalls, the wooded mountain slopes and the fiords offer magnificent scenery but also create formidable barriers.

B

WATERWAYS

Although great natural barriers hindered east-west development in Canada, this circumstance was mitigated by the mighty river and lake systems that provided avenues for the fur trader, missionary, soldier and settler. Canada's rivers and lakes allowed and, indeed, invited our venturesome forefathers to explore the interior of the continent and, in spite of natural barriers, to tap its great wealth. The rivers and lakes were essential to the great fur empire and the men in canoes who brought furs from the farthest extremity of the Canadian Shield to Montreal for exportation to Europe. The first settlements spread along the rivers, since only the rivers provided easy transportation and communication. Militarily, rivers and lakes were of prime importance; whoever controlled the St. Lawrence and its entrance, also controlled Canada.

With some knowledge of the importance of Canadian waterways, it is useful to divide these roughly into four categories: the St. Lawrence-Great Lakes system, the Hudson Bay system, the rivers of the Pacific Northwest, and the Ohio-Mississippi system.

The St. Lawrence–Great Lakes waterway system stretches over 2,000 miles from the Atlantic Ocean into the heart of North America. This system is made up of the Gulf of St. Lawrence, the St. Lawrence River, Lake Ontario, Lake Erie, Lake Huron, Lake Superior, Lake Michigan and three historically important tributaries of the St.

Lawrence River — the Saguenay River and the Ottawa River from the northwest and the Richelieu River from the south.

THE ST. LAWRENCE RIVER[6]

Father François du Creux described the St. Lawrence River in this way:

The St. Lawrence is not only the largest river in this region, but it rivals the famous rivers of the world in its volume and perennial flow. . . . It is supposed to flow from an immense lake known as Lake Huron . . . whose circumference is said to be five hundred leagues. The St. Lawrence flows out of the south-east corner of this lake in one direction, and from the north-west corner of this sea or lake another river flows, by which it is said to be possible to reach the Chinese Sea. . . . But this passage . . . is interrupted by what the French call *saults* or cataracts; and the *saults* are of frequent occurrence in making the passage to the Hurons. . . .

. . . the water plunges over precipices with a terrifying crash into an abyss below, just as it does in the Nile. It is impossible to descend these *saults* without great danger, and it is quite impossible to ascend them. . . .

The St. Lawrence remains salt ten leagues below Quebec; the tide reaches forty leagues below that place. . . . At Quebec the channel

North American Waterways

of the river is contracted to a quarter of a league, but elsewhere as far as the rapids of St. Louis, sixty leagues above Quebec, it is wider.

To the north, the Hudson Bay waterway system, the historic competitor of the St. Lawrence–Great Lakes system, provides a second great artery into the heart of the continent. This system essentially consists of Davis Strait, Hudson Strait, Hudson Bay, James Bay and the many rivers that flow into Hudson Bay. Of prime importance are those rivers and lakes which drain the Canadian Shield and the southern portion of the Central Plains. Some of the rivers draining the Shield are the Churchill, Nelson, Albany and Abitibi. The Saskatchewan River, flowing from the west, by emptying into Lake Winnipeg which in turn empties into Hudson Bay by way of the Nelson River, drains the southern plain.

The waterways of the Pacific Northwest do not constitute a system as such, since some of the rivers flow into the Arctic Ocean while others flow into the Pacific. These rivers have not been so much a means of entry into Canada as avenues of exit to the Pacific. Their turbulence made transportation along them difficult and trade routes impossible. The Pacific Northwest waterways of importance are, in the south, the Columbia and Fraser rivers flowing into the Pacific and, in the north, the Mackenzie, Peace and Athabaska rivers emptying into the Arctic.

Although the Ohio–Mississippi system is not really a Canadian waterway, it has had a profound effect on the history of Canada. The two great rivers, the Mississippi rising out of the north-central United States and the Ohio out of the eastern United States, come together to form the fertile Ohio Valley and then flow approximately 800 miles south to the Gulf of Mexico. The mighty Mississippi was the route followed by Father Marquette, Jolliet and La Salle, who were all Canadians. The French and Canadians extended their empire along the Mississippi by building a chain of forts, much to the annoyance of the English in the Thirteen Colonies.

The physical features of Canada influenced exploration, the conflict between the French and English for North America, the relations with the United States, the creation of the Canadian nation through Confederation and the binding of the country with a transcontinental railway. Geography has caused sectional differences that still exist. Canadian history and geography are intimately related. In one sense, Canadian history is the history of a people building a nation in spite of geography.

C

THE FIRST CANADIANS

When Columbus landed in the New World, he believed that he had reached India, and he called the natives "Indians." This term, although a misnomer, has since been applied to the whole aboriginal population of North, Central and South America, exclusive of the Eskimo. There were more than fifty different Indian tribes in Canada, each with its own dialect, customs and well-defined hunting grounds.

The Indians of the Pacific Coast occupied roughly the coastal area of British Columbia, including the Queen Charlotte Islands and Vancouver Island. In this area were many distinct tribes, foremost among whom were the Haida, Salish, Nootka and Bella Coola.

These Indians, because of their proximity to the sea, were primarily fishermen and sea hunters. They depended, in large measure, on salmon, sea otter and seal for food, tools and clothing. To facilitate fishing and hunting, the Pacific Coast Indians fashioned huge canoes by burning the hearts out of the tall timbers of the coastal area. These seaworthy canoes, which could hold as many as fifty men, enabled the Pacific Coast Indians to travel great distances with relative ease in search of fish and sea otter.

Although these Indians were fishermen and sea hunters, they were, nevertheless, relatively sedentary because they operated from well-established shore bases. This allowed them to build

Nimkish Village at Alert Bay, B.C.

permanent villages and to achieve a high degree of social and tribal organization. Their villages

A Buffalo Surround

usually consisted of a number of houses arranged in a rectangular plan; each house was large enough to accommodate several families. The tribal organizations, ruled by hereditary chiefs, were quite stable.

The famous totem poles were first fashioned on the West Coast by these Indians, although it is quite probable that this art did not develop until the Indians had been introduced to the white man's iron tools. Since European civilization in Canada was originally concentrated in Acadia and in the St. Lawrence Valley, the Pacific Coast Indians had little contact with the early settlers. They did enjoy a great deal of attention from European traders in the late eighteenth century, when the sea otter of the Pacific became more valuable than the beaver of the Canadian Shield.

The Plains Indians consisted largely of the Blackfoot, Sioux, Assiniboine, Plains Cree and Plains Ojibwa tribes. Although they occupied the rich agricultural prairie lands, the Plains Indians were not an agricultural people. They did grow small quantities of tobacco, but they had neither the tools nor the knowledge of agriculture to take advantage of the land's fertility in the short growing season. Moreover, there was no necessity to till the plains. The Indians gathered berries and roots and the region abounded with deer and buffalo. The flesh of these animals provided the Plains Indians with food; the hides, with clothing (tanned deer hides in the summer and buffalo hides in the winter) and covering for their conically shaped tepees; and the bones and horns, with tools.

The dependence on deer and buffalo dictated a nomadic existence for the Plains Indian. Life was a never-ending search for the herds. His survival depended on them; as the herds roamed the plains so did the Indian. At a moment's notice the Indian packed his tepee and few possessions on a *travois** drawn by his dog. The advent of the horse made life easier. When wild herds of horses moved north from Mexico (where they had been brought by the Spaniards), the Plains Indian domesticated them and used them in the hunt. Nevertheless, he continued to be the nomad of the western plains.

The Plains Indians' migratory existence prevented any extensive social or tribal organization. The only time these Indians stayed for any length of time in one place was during the long dreary winter, when they often built low earth hovels to replace the tepee.

In order to feed themselves during the winter and during long summer journeys, the Plains Indians developed a method of preserving buffalo and deer meat. They dried the meat and then pulverized it by means of wooden poles. Then they mixed it with an equal amount of fat from the animal's body. Pemmican, as this food was called, could be kept for over a year without spoiling. It was extremely nutritious; a small quantity provided a man with sufficient energy for a long journey.

* A cloth or hide suspended between two poles. At one end, the poles were attached to each side of a horse or dog; the other end dragged on the ground.

David Thompson's observations:

In questioning them of their origen and from whence they formerly came they appear to have no tradition beyond the time of their great granfathers, that they can depend on. . . . They have no tradition that they ever made use of canoes, yet their old men always point out the North East as the place they came from, and their progress has always been to the south west. . . . Of their origen, they think themselves and all the animals to be indigenus, and from all times existing as at present.

———

The Men are proud of being noticed and praised as good hunters, warriors, or any other masculine accomplishment, and many of the young men as fine dandies as they can make themselves. . . .

The country affords no ornaments for the men, but collars of the claws of the fore paws of the Bear. The Women, as usual with all women are fond of ornaments, but the country produces none, except some of the teeth of the deer, which are pierced, strung together, and form bracelets for the wrists and sometimes a fillet of sweet scented grass round the fore head. . . . Scarce any has ear rings, and never any in the nose.

The Plains Indians, like those of the Pacific Coast, came into later contact with the Europeans. As the fur trade spread westward, the Plains Indians supplied the fur brigades with food in the form of pemmican. So vital did this supply become, that in 1814 it precipitated the "Pemmican War," in which the Selkirk settlement in Manitoba faced extinction.

Linguistically, the Indians of the Eastern Woodlands can be classified into two divisions: those who spoke the Athapascan tongue and those who spoke Algonquian. The Algonquians occupied the Appalachian Highlands and the whole of the Canadian Shield. The Indians of the Athapascan tongue, such as the Chipewyan and the Yellowknife, inhabited the northern and western parts of the Canadian Shield.

The Indians who spoke Algonquian were of great significance. This linguistic group included the Micmac of Nova Scotia, the Malecite of New Brunswick, the Algonquin of the regions of the Ottawa and St. Maurice rivers, the Montagnais, the Cree and the Ojibwa of the Canadian Shield.

As with all other Indians, the Algonquin's existence revolved around the search for food. Like his brother on the plains, the Algonquin was a nomad, traveling the many rivers and streams of the forested Shield and Appalachian Region in pursuit of game and fish. He perfected the construction of the light but durable birchbark canoe and mastered the art of fast travel with heavy loads over long journeys. For winter travel, the ingenious Algonquin developed the snowshoe and became so skilled in its use that he traveled the snowy woodlands with comparative ease.

INDIAN HUNT IN THE WINTER[8]

Champlain described the Indians he met around St. Croix in 1604:

The Indians who live there are few in number. During the winter, when the snow is deepest, they go hunting for moose and other animals, on which they live the greater part of the time. If the snow is not deep, they are scarcely rewarded for their pains, inasmuch as they cannot capture anything except with very great labour, whereby they endure and suffer much. When they do not go hunting, they live on a shellfish called the clam. In winter they clothe themselves with good furs of beaver and moose. The women make all the clothes, but not neatly enough to prevent one seeing the skin under the armpits; for they have not the skill to make them fit better. When they go hunting they make use of certain racquets, twice as large as those of our country, which they attach under their feet, and with these they travel over the snow without sinking, both the women and children as well as the men who hunt for the tracks of animals. Having found these they follow them until they catch sight of the beast, when they shoot at him with their bows, or else kill him with thrusts from swords set in the end of a half-pike. This can be done very easily, because these animals are unable to travel on the snow without sinking in. Then the women and children come up and camp there, and give themselves up to feasting. Afterwards they go back to see whether they can find other animals, and thus they pass the winter. . . . Such is the manner of life of these people in winter, and it seems to me very wretched.

The skill and knowledge these Indians employed in search of food served them in good stead in time of war. They used the speed of the canoe, the mobility of the snowshoe and their familiarity with the forests effectively against their enemies. However, their nomadic existence was not conducive to communal living or organization, and this proved a great weakness in their struggle against the better-organized Iroquois tribes.

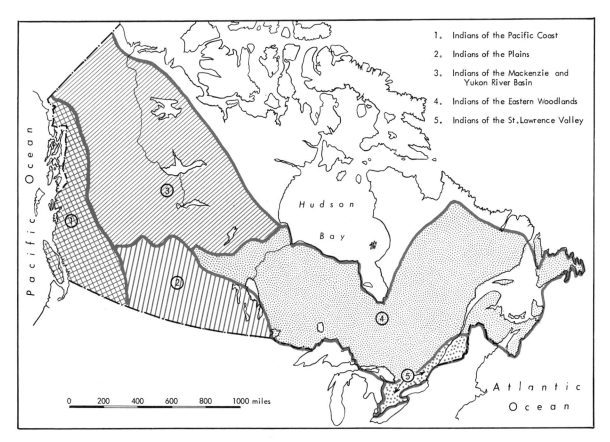

Indians of Canada

The Indian tribes of the St. Lawrence Valley had two things in common: they spoke the Iroquoian tongue and lived in similar environments. The famous tribes of the Five Nations* — Onondaga, Cayuga, Mohawk, Seneca and Oneida — as well as the Huron, the Neutral and the Petun, made their homes in the area that approximates the St. Lawrence Lowlands and the northern portion of New York. This was fertile land with a favourable climate. Sometime in their history these Indians had learned how to grow corn, sunflowers, squash, beans and peas. But with their primitive tools, they could not depend exclusively on agriculture for their existence and therefore were hunters as well as farmers.

HOW THE HURONS PLANTED CORN[9]

Father Gabriel Sagard, who was in Canada in 1623 and 1624, fully described how the Hurons cultivated the land and planted corn:

It is their custom for every family to live on its fishing, hunting, and planting, since they have as much land as they need. . . . Clearing is very troublesome for them, since they have no proper tools. They cut down the trees at the height of two or three feet from the ground, then they strip off all the branches, which they burn at the stump of the same trees in order to kill them, and in course of time they remove the roots. Then the women clean up the ground between the trees thoroughly, and at distances a pace apart dig round holes or pits. In each of these they sow nine or ten grains of maize, which they have first picked out, sorted, and soaked in water for a few days, and so they keep on until they have sown enough to provide food for two or three years, either for fear that some bad season may visit them or else in order to trade it to other nations for furs and other things they need; and every year they sow their corn thus in the same holes and spots, which they freshen with their little wooden spade, shaped like an ear with a handle at the end. . . .

The agricultural basis of their existence caused the Indians of the St. Lawrence Valley to lead relatively sedentary lives, permitting them to develop a social and tribal organization unsurpassed by the other Indian tribes of Canada. Generally, many families of the same clan occupied a long house — a frame building, sided with

* Also referred to as the Iroquois Confederacy.

bark, which quite often extended to lengths of 150 to 200 feet. Since these permanent houses together with the cultivated plots of land were vulnerable to enemy attacks, many of the villages were surrounded with palisades for protection.

AN INDIAN VILLAGE[10]

Marc Lescarbot, a Parisian lawyer who accompanied de Monts to Acadia in 1604, described the Indian village of Hochelaga:

. . . . And amid these fields is situated and placed the said town of Hochelaga, stretching up to a mountain which lies beside it, which is well cultivated and most fertile, and from whose top one can see to a great distance. This mountain we called Mount Royal. The town is built in a circle, and surrounded with a wooden palisade in three tiers, like a pyramid; the top row is crosswise, the centre row upright, and the bottom row is laid lengthwise; the whole compactly joined and lashed together after their manner, rising to about twice the height of a lance. The town has but one gate or entry, closed with bars; on it and at several points along the wall are galleries of a kind, with ladders ascending to them, provided with rocks and stones for its guard and defence. In the town are about fifty houses, each about fifty paces long or more, and twelve to fifteen broad, built all of wood, with roofs and sides made of strips of bark or of wood as broad as a table, well and cunningly knotted together after their fashion; within these are several rooms, large and small; in the midst of each house, on the ground, is a large hall where they light their fire and live in common, afterwards retiring, the men with their women and children, to their said chambers. They also have garners at the top of their houses, where they store their corn. . . .

Of these Indians, the tribes of the Iroquois Confederacy were the most highly developed, politically. Each tribe consisted of smaller units or clans which appointed members (*sachems*) to a general council. Although the tribes and even the clans were fiercely independent, they united in the face of common danger, as they did against the threat from the renegade Hurons and their French allies. The Iroquois, with their skill as warriors and with their political organization, were able to overcome the combined forces of the Huron and Algonquian tribes and bring New France to the verge of extinction.

Geography determined not only the nature of the Indians' existence but also the conflicts in which they became involved. The long-standing struggle between the Hurons and Iroquois increased in intensity with the arrival of the French on the St. Lawrence and the Dutch on the Hudson. The Indians became dependent on European goods, which they could obtain only in exchange for their sole valuable commodity — furs. The St. Lawrence valley supplied few furs; the best furs were found on the Canadian Shield, trapped by the Indians of the Eastern Woodlands. Both the Hurons and Iroquois sought to establish themselves as middlemen between the distant tribes and the European traders.* Geographically, the Iroquois, located south of the St. Lawrence River, were at a disadvantage because the Hurons and the French blocked the path to the great fur-producing region. The Iroquois' solution to this geographic and economic problem was to destroy their rivals. They did destroy the Hurons, and only the efforts of the finest French regiment saved New France from total collapse.

---

* The Hurons acted as middlemen for the French. The Iroquois were the middlemen for the Dutch and English.

D

INDIAN CULTURE

Since the Indian forms the first cornerstone upon which Canadian society rests, it is well to consider his human values. When Europeans first came to Canada, they found a race of people who had come to terms with the harsh environment in which they lived. A man's worth was not judged by European standards such as birth, rank and accumulation of wealth; instead, the perpetual struggle for survival determined that a man be judged by his stamina, agility and skill as a hunter.

HEALTH THROUGH STEAM BATHS[11]

Father Gabriel Sagard wrote about the value of sweating, which the Hurons believed cured many ills:

When anyone wishes to have a sweat, which is the best and most ordinary remedy they use to keep in health and to prevent and forestall diseases, he summons several of his friends to sweat with him, for by himself he could not easily manage it. So they heat a number of stones red-hot in a great fire, then take them out and put them in a pile . . . then all around the pile they arrange sticks planted in the ground, as high as the waist or higher, and bent over at the top, in the shape of a circular table, with a space left between the stones and the sticks sufficient to accommodate the naked men who are to sweat, and who sit on the ground side by side squeezed closely together all round the pile of stones with their knees raised in front of their stomachs. When they are in position the whole sweat-bath is covered above and at the sides with large pieces of bark and a number of skins, so that no warmth nor air can get out of the bath. Then, to heat themselves still more and stimulate sweating, one of them sings, and the rest shout and repeat continually, strongly and violently. . . . When they have sweated enough they go out, and if they are near a river throw themselves into the water; if not, they wash themselves in cold water and then have a feast, for while they are sweating the kettle is on the fire. . . .

The incessant search for food in the rugged wilderness made the Canadian Indian a physically well-developed individual who had remarkably keen senses of sight, hearing and smell. Frequent privation and complete dependence on the forces of nature created in the Indian a stoical outlook. The Indian displayed this attitude of resignation in the face of danger and even when he was tortured by his enemies. His existence revolved around the quest for food, which consumed most of his time and energy and left little time to develop an art or a literature. The Indian concentrated on practical pursuits and he became highly skilled in fishing, hunting and trapping.

The nomadic existence of the Indians hindered elaborate social and tribal organizations. The Indians of the Pacific Coast and of the St. Lawrence Valley did develop some tribal organization, but it was rather limited. Instead, the family was the basic unit of Indian society. The man was the hunter and warrior. The wife cared for the children, prepared the food, made the clothing and tended the crops. Divorce, although easily obtained, seems to have been uncommon. Marriage was usually regarded as a life-long contract by most tribes.

HURONS BAKE BREAD[12]
Father Sagard's account:

In order to eat it [corn] they first boil the grain for a short time in water, then wipe it and dry it a little; after that they crush it and knead it with warm water and bake it, wrapped up in corn-leaves; if no leaves have been put round it they wash it after it is baked. If they have any beans they cook them in a small pot and mix them in the dough without crushing them, or else strawberries, blueberries, raspberries, blackberries, and other small fruits, dried and fresh, to give it taste and improve it; for by itself, without a mixture of these small relishes, it is very insipid . . . they make another kind of bread: they gather a number of ears of corn before it is thoroughly dry and ripe, and then the women, girls, and children bite off the grains, spitting them out of their mouths afterwards into large pots which they keep beside them, and then they finish by pounding it in a large mortar; and since this paste is very soft they must necessarily wrap it in leaves in order to bake it under the ashes in the usual way. This chewed bread is the kind they themselves prize most, but for my part I only ate it of necessity and reluctantly, because the corn had in this way been half chewed, bruised, and kneaded by the teeth of the women, girls, and little children.

The religion of the Indians revolved around the belief in many spirits. All the forces of nature — wind, rain, flood, drought, thunder and lightning — were believed to be spirits. The Indian's religious life was preoccupied with appeasing the spirits with offerings in order that their wrath might not be incurred. Since sickness was believed to be the result of an evil spirit's taking possession of the body, the medicine man, who claimed powers to expel the spirits, had a prominent place in Indian society. The Indians believed in man's dual nature — body and spirit. When a person died, his spirit left the body and continued to exist in a place where the hunt was easy and game always plentiful.

Indian Camp on Lake Huron

Much has been said of the brutality of the Indians. No doubt torture of captured enemies often took place. Captured women and children were usually adopted into the tribe. Depending on the circumstances, the torture of captured warriors served either as an act of vengeance or as a test of bravery. A captured warrior who withstood the ordeals bravely was deemed worthy of adoption into the tribe.

The Indian's values were quite different from those of the European with whom he came in contact. Life in an Indian tribe was characterized by a sense of equality. Little social difference existed between members of the same tribe. Food, even in times of scarcity, was shared by all, and all shared the burden and reward of the hunt. The mistake of judging the Indian by European standards of those days or by present-day standards has contributed much to a misunderstanding of the North American Indian.

It was impossible for the European to transplant his culture to Canada without some modification. It was equally impossible for Indian society to remain unchanged by the advent of the white man. In the inevitable interaction of cultures, it was the Indian way of life that underwent the most change, resulting in a breakdown of Indian society.

The white man introduced the Indian to iron tools and weapons. These items, luxuries at first, soon became necessities and changed the Indian's methods of hunting and fighting. Originally, the Indian hunted, fished and trapped to meet his immediate needs for food and clothing; now, he became a fur trader, motivated by profit. The use of alcohol, unknown to the Indian before the coming of the white man, became the Indian's curse. European civilization brought with it diseases that had been unknown to the Indian. Measles and smallpox took a disastrous toll of Indian lives.

INDIAN DEPENDENCE ON EUROPEAN GOODS[13]

Nicolas Denys, a leading figure in Acadia, wrote in 1672 on the effect of European goods on the Indians:

. . . . They have abandoned all their own utensils, whether because of the trouble they had as well to make as to use them, or because of the facility of obtaining from us, in exchange for skins which cost them almost nothing, the things which seemed to them invaluable, not so much for their novelty as for the convenience they derived therefrom. Above everything the kettle has always seemed to them, and seems still, the most valuable article they can obtain from us. . . .

The musket is used by them more than all other weapons, in their hunting in spring, summer, and autumn, both for animals and birds. . . . With the arrow it was necessary to approach the animal closely: with the gun they kill the animal from a distance with a bullet or two. The axes, the kettles, the knives and everything that is supplied them, is much more convenient and portable than those which they had in former times, when they were obliged to go to camp near their grotesque kettles, in place of which to-day they are free to go camp where they wish. One can say that in those times the immovable kettles were the chief regulators of their lives, since they were able to live only in places where these were.

With respect to the hunting of the Beaver in winter, they do that the same as they did formerly, though they have nevertheless nowadays a greater advantage with their arrows and harpoons armed with iron than with the others which they used in old times, and of which they have totally abandoned the use.

The white man, in turn, learned from the Indian to hunt, to fish, to trap, to use the canoe and snow-shoe, to preserve food and to clothe himself for the harsh climate. The Indian led the French into the interior of the country and showed them how to tap the great fur wealth of the Canadian Shield. The Indian taught the white man how to survive in the harsh environment of North America.

INDIANS AND METIS SPEAK OF CANADA TODAY[14]

[a]*Joe Keeper, executive director of the Manitoba Métis Federation, rejects violence as a means of gaining justice for his people:*

Mr. Keeper said violence should only be "the final step . . . I hope it never has to be taken." He said the problem has been that "the larger society doesn't listen to us" but suggested there are "alternatives to violence in an enlightened society. . . .

"Canadian history is not one of violence. It is one of negotiation, and I hope that this can continue to be the history of Canada."

———

[b]*David Courchene, President of the Manitoba Indian Brotherhood, in an address to a conference of Indians and Métis held in Winnipeg in March 1969, spoke of the Indian in Canadian history:*

. . . . While we would prefer to dismiss the past and the unhappiness, frustration and discouragement, we cannot. The effects of the past live with us today and will effect [sic] our progress tomorrow unless there are substantial changes in prevailing attitudes in both the Indian and the non-Indian community and revolutionary changes in public sector programming.

A hundred years of submission and servitude, of protectionism and paternalism, have created psychological barriers for Indian people that are far more difficult to break down and conquer than are the problems of economic and social poverty. Paternalistic programs of the past, based largely on the idea that we must shelter and protect the ignorant savage have created complex problems to those who want to shelter and protect themselves.

The end result of the whitemen's [sic] misguided interpretation of our needs has been to destroy our society, to tear asunder our self-reliance and to deny us the benefit of human equality and compassionate understanding. . . .

———

Joseph Wapemoose writes of the choice forced on the Indian by the rapid changes of our time:

. . . .Where once the Indian roamed, the factories, farms, and dwellings of a European horde block free passage. We are dispossessed of our ancient ways and faced with life in a city.

———

We know that we can't turn back the clock. We know that we can't live for long in a wilderness that is fast being ransacked of fish and fur to feed and clothe the luxury-minded dwellers of the city. So, we too must enter the confines of the city and try as best we might to make our way.

But, understand, oh white man; understand, lovely lady dressed in fur! It is hard, very hard to know that the land that once was ours will never ever be again our hunting grounds. It is hard to bear the crime-filled streets and the liquor-selling bars where once was only peaceful grass and sobriety. We understand that we must change — and we are changing — but remember; it once was our land, our life, and it is hard.

II

THE FRENCH FOUNDATION

By early in the seventeenth century, the great sea voyages of men such as Cabot, Verrazano, Cartier and Hudson had firmly established the fact that a large land mass obstructed a northwesterly oceanic route from Europe to the Orient. These early voyages made the Atlantic shore line of North America generally well-known. At the same time, these voyages shed little light on two cardinal questions: What was the nature and extent of the new land? Was there a passage through the new land to the Orient?

The fur trade spurred the exploration of the continent. The quest for new sources of fur supplies and new hunters led the French to Hudson Bay in the north, to the Gulf of Mexico in the south, and to the foothills of the Rockies in the west. So essential was the fur trade to the development of New France that it has been referred to as the lifeblood of the colony. The fur trade not only gave birth to French settlement along the shores of the St. Lawrence but also nourished and sustained New France throughout its hundred-and-fifty-year history.

The necessity for regulating the fur trade encouraged the retention of a highly centralized government in New France. In the course of its history, New France had two distinct forms of government: government under the chartered companies and government under the French Crown. Initially, the kings of France pinned their hopes for empire-building on the chartered companies; such companies, with little expenditure of money or effort on the part of the Crown, had given the Netherlands an empire. In exchange for a trade monopoly, the chartered companies of New France undertook the obligation to settle, develop, defend and govern the new land. Although government under company rule underwent some interesting and unique developments, not one of the chartered companies came anywhere near fulfilling its commitments of settlement and defence. The main interest of these companies was the profitable fur trade, and their efforts were largely exerted towards its development.

In 1663, after fifty years of company rule, New France had no more than 2,500 settlers clinging tenuously to the edge of the wilderness for 265 miles along the St. Lawrence River. The chartered companies had failed as instruments of empire-building. Consequently, the French Crown took over the control of New France, giving impetus to settlement, encouraging the development and diversification of the economy, providing for the defence of the colony and instituting a new form of government.

An integral part of French policy in North America was the support of Catholicism as the established Church. Evangelization of the Indians in the wilderness and the spiritual care of the colony itself became the two spheres of activity of the Church in New France. But the fur trade also affected this aspect of life in New France; the Church had to divide its energy between Christianizing the Indians and combatting the evils resulting from the unscrupulous trade with the Indians.

The history of French settlement in North America is a story of resourceful, hardy and stubborn people attempting to establish themselves in spite of great difficulties. Rule of chartered companies, seigneurial land tenure and efforts by government and Church were all employed to advance settlement. But the growth of settlement during the French Régime was slow, due largely to the emphasis on the fur trade. Furthermore, competition for fur and fur routes involved the French in Indian wars, brought them into conflict first with the Dutch and later with the English and, to some extent, contributed to the fall of New France.

3

THE FUR TRADE OF NEW FRANCE

A

FEATURES OF THE FUR TRADE

The fur trade, which affected every aspect of life in New France, rested on *castor canadensis*, the industrious beaver of the North American woodlands. European demands, as well as several characteristics of the beaver itself, caused the fur of this animal to be the principal article of commerce between North America and Europe.

The woodlands of North America contained a plentiful supply of excellent beaver pelts. Trapping beaver required little skill and equipment, since the animal's habit of building houses and damming streams made it easy prey. The beaver pelts suited the demand of European fashion for felt and beaver hats. The barbed nature of the beaver's fur made it ideal for the felting process. The beaver has an outer coat of long guard hair protecting a soft undercoat of fur. Such an unprocessed pelt was called *castor sec*. Pelts that had the guard hair removed were called *castor gras* and were more valuable. Indians produced the *castor gras* by sewing four or five pelts together, scraping and greasing the underside and wearing these robes with the fur next to the body. In fifteen to eighteen months the guard hair would fall out, leaving only the valuable fur undercoat.

Expansion was the key to survival of the fur trade in New France. Although the beaver produces two to five young per year, the demand for pelts was so great and the trapping so intense that fur-bearing regions were quickly depleted. Consequently, there was a constant search for new fur regions and new hunters. As the supply lines extended ever deeper into the interior, it became necessary to set up inland supply bases, which increased the cost of procuring furs. To reduce these rising costs and to make a reasonable profit the fur trade had to become efficient.

Generally, the profits from the trade were high, but so were the attendant risks of a single-staple

Coureurs de Bois Trading with the Indians

economy. The fur market depended on the vicissitudes of fashion in Paris. As a result, the demand for furs was not stable and could fall disastrously overnight. In addition, great risks were involved in shipping furs from the interior of the continent through Montreal and Quebec to Europe, as well as in importing manufactured articles to New France from Europe.

The fur trade, because of increasing costs and great financial risks, could not stand ruinous competition, which would reduce profits considerably by forcing prices in Europe to go down and costs in North America to go up. Competition could be prevented, however, by monopoly control.

The king granted a group of wealthy merchants a monopoly on the fur trade in a charter that gave them exclusive right to control the fur trade in New France and exclusive right to sell the furs in France. In return, the merchants agreed to colonize New France. Thus the king could gain a colony without causing expense or risk to himself. The grant of a monopoly offered the merchants the means of excluding competition and regulating and stabilizing the fur trade. The fur trade was therefore monopolistic and highly centralized.

COMPARISON BETWEEN MONOPOLY CONTROL AND FREE COMPETITION IN THE FUR TRADE[15]

Charles L'Allemant, Superior of the mission of Canada, discussed this subject in a letter to his brother, Father Jerome L'Allemant, in 1626:

. . . . Before the time of the association of those Gentlemen to whom the King gave this trade for a certain time in consideration of certain conditions mentioned in the Articles, the Savages were visited by many people, to such an extent that an Old Man told me he had seen as many as twenty ships in the port of Tadoussac. But now since this business has been granted to the association, which to-day has a monopoly over all others, we see here not more than two ships which belong to it, and that only once a year, about the beginning of the month of June. These two ships bring all the merchandise which these Gentlemen use in trading with the Savages; that is to say, the cloaks, blankets, nightcaps, hats, shirts, sheets, hatchets, iron arrowheads, bodkins, swords, picks to break the ice in Winter, knives, kettles, prunes, raisins, Indian corn, peas, cracker or sea biscuits, and tobacco; and what is necessary for the sustenance of the French in this country besides. In exchange for these they carry back hides of the moose, lynx, fox, otter, black ones being encountered occasionally, martens, badgers, and muskrats; but they deal principally in Beavers, in which they find their greatest profit. I was told that during one year they carried back as many as 22,000. The usual number for one year is 15,000 or 12,000, at one pistole each, which is not doing badly.

"The name 'Sauvages' as used in Canada, is applied to all the aboriginal tribes of America. It is not intended to imply that they are barbarous, ferocious, or savage." Bishop Taché.

B

PHASES OF THE FUR TRADE

Following Cartier's and Roberval's unsuccessful attempts at settlement along the St. Lawrence, France lost interest in settling the northern part of the New World. North America held little promise of gold such as the Spaniards had found in South America. Also, in the latter half of the sixteenth century France was torn apart by a bitter religious struggle that occupied all her interest and energies.

During this period, however, the people of the west coast of France displayed great interest in the cod fisheries of Newfoundland, Nova Scotia and the Gulf of St. Lawrence. French — as well as English, Portuguese and Spanish — vessels sailed regularly to the Grand Banks, as these fishing areas were called, and returned laden with fish to supply the demand of the western European and Mediterranean markets for this dietary staple. But fisheries did not require settlement, even though the fish were dried on shore. European contact with North America in the sixteenth century was restricted to the coastal area and produced no permanent settlement.

Nevertheless, casual contact with the Indians of North America led to the discovery of the real wealth of the New World.

As the European fishermen expressed a desire for some of the luxurious furs worn by the Indians, the Indians, in turn, came to appreciate the trinkets and manufactured goods of the Europeans. The furs had little value in Europe until it was found that beaver pelts made excellent felt.

EARLY FUR TRADE WITH THE INDIANS[16]

Cartier described the contacts he made with the Indians on his voyage of 1534:

The next day [Tuesday, July 7] some of these Indians came in nine canoes to the point at the mouth of the cove, where we lay anchored with our ships. And being informed of their arrival we went with our two long-boats to the point where they were, at the mouth of the cove. As soon as they saw us they began to run away, making signs to us that they had come to barter with us; and held up some furs of small value, with which they clothe themselves. We likewise made signs to them that we wished them no harm, and sent two men on shore to offer them some knives and other iron goods, and a red cap to give to their chief. Seeing this, they sent on shore, part of their people with some of their furs; and the two parties traded together. The savages showed a marvellous great pleasure in possessing and obtaining these iron wares and other commodities, dancing and going through many ceremonies, and throwing salt water over their heads with all hands. They bartered all they had to such an extent that all went back naked without anything on them; and they made signs to us that they would return on the morrow with more furs.

Toward the end of the sixteenth century, two developments occurred that were of great importance to the future development of New France. Fur hats became the fashion, and Henry IV restored peace to France. The religious wars ended with the Edict of Nantes in 1598, which granted a measure of toleration to the Huguenots, the French Protestants. Now France could again turn her attention to the New World. Peace at home and a growing demand for beaver pelts renewed French interest in North America.

The initial phase of the fur trade in New France was a ship-to-shore trade, carried on mainly at the Indian village of Tadoussac, at the mouth of the Saguenay River. Although furs were growing in importance, they were still incidental to fish. However, the infant fur trade of this period created two very important economic demands: the Indians of North America desired European manufactured goods and the Europeans wanted the Indians' furs. North America did possess wealth after all — not the gold of the Incas but the abundant beaver pelts that could be exported to France and sold on the European market at a high profit.

The founding of the first permanent settlement at Quebec in 1608 marked the beginning of a new phase of the fur trade. In this period the fur trade was controlled and developed by monopolists centred at Quebec. The period terminated in 1663, when the French government took over the control of New France and the king revoked the charter of the monopolistic fur company. Throughout this period the French and the Iroquois competed for control of the Ottawa River, which had become the great fur artery into the interior.

CHAMPLAIN'S CHOICE OF QUEBEC[17]

Champlain described the founding of Quebec in 1608:

. . . . I arrived there [Quebec] on the 3rd of July,

when I searched for a place suitable for our settlement, but I could find none more convenient or better situated than the point of Quebec, so called by the savages, which was covered with nut-trees. I at once employed a portion of our workmen in cutting them down, that we might construct our habitation there: . . .

———

I had the work on our quarters continued, which was composed of three buildings of two stories. Each one was three fathoms long, and two and a half wide. The storehouse was six fathoms long and three wide, with a fine cellar six feet deep. I had a gallery made all around our buildings, on the outside, at the second story, which proved very convenient. There were also ditches, fifteen feet wide and six deep. On the outer side of the ditches, I constructed several spurs, which enclosed a part of the dwelling, at the points where we placed our cannons. Before the habitation there is a place four fathoms wide and six or seven long, looking out upon the river-bank. Surrounding the habitation are very good gardens, and a place on the north side some hundred or hundred and twenty paces long and fifty or sixty wide. . . .

———

While the carpenters, sawers of boards, and other workmen were employed on our quarters, I set all the others to work clearing up around our place of abode, in preparation for gardens in which to plant grain and seeds, that we might see how they would flourish, as the soil seemed to be very good.

When Samuel de Champlain planted his little colony at Quebec, he depended on the Indians to bring furs down the rivers of the Shield to Quebec in the same manner that French fishermen had depended on the Indians to bring furs down the Saguenay River to Tadoussac. Quebec soon replaced Tadoussac as the fur centre of New France because the areas surrounding the Saguenay and St. Maurice rivers were quickly trapped out.

The Indians who traded at Tadoussac, the Montagnais and Abenakis, were hunters and trappers. The Iroquois and Hurons of the St. Lawrence Valley, not primarily trappers, sought to establish themselves as middlemen between the Indian tribes of the Shield and the French at Quebec or the Dutch at New Amsterdam, at the mouth of the Hudson River. The Hurons and Iroquois along with the Algonquin tribe became fur wholesalers and engaged in a lucrative exchange of goods between the Europeans and the Indians of the interior.

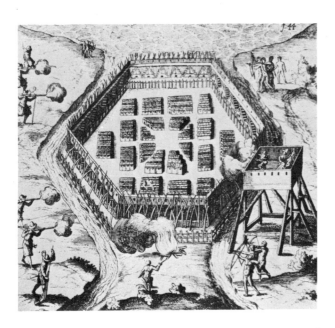

Onondaga Town: Attack by the Hurons, Algonquins and French Auxiliaries, 1615

Geographically, the Hurons and Algonquins were ideally located to act as middlemen because they occupied lands lying across the trade routes between Quebec and the rich fur-bearing Canadian Shield. The Iroquois, just as eager to secure European goods, were situated south of the St. Lawrence away from the main fur routes. Champlain realized the geographic advantage of the Hurons and Algonquins and was therefore easily persuaded to form an alliance with them against their traditional enemies, the Iroquois.

In 1609 Champlain joined his Indian allies in an expedition against the Iroquois. He paddled up the Richelieu River and engaged the Iroquois near the future site of Ticonderoga, at the head of Lake George. The superior French firearms dispersed the bewildered Iroquois. This battle solidified the French-Huron-Algonquin alliance but also heightened Iroquois enmity, which led to the eventual decimation of the Hurons and brought New France to the edge of disaster.

The supply of furs coming to Quebec depended on the Ottawa River route which led to the Huron country around Georgian Bay. The Iroquois sought to control this vital fur highway in order to divert furs to their Dutch allies on the Hudson River. In 1615 Champlain traveled the Ottawa River route to Georgian Bay and once more joined his Huron allies in a war party against the Iroquois. This time, however, the Iroquois, now equipped with Dutch arms, could match the strength of the Huron-French alliance and defeated Champlain and his Indian allies at Lake Oneida.

The Iroquois, motivated by a dependence on European goods and armed with European weapons, now sought complete and exclusive control of the Ottawa River route. This objective could be accomplished only by eliminating the Hurons and the French. The Ottawa River route was, therefore, under constant Iroquois attack. Raiding parties paddled unchecked down the Richelieu River, the back door of New France, and then up the Ottawa River where they waited in ambush to intercept furs destined for Quebec. When Montreal was founded, the Iroquois considered it not as a missionary undertaking but as another French fur outpost. Almost from its beginning, in 1642, Montreal was under continuous Iroquois threat.

New France was too weak at the time to stop the Iroquois harassment of its life line. This weakness stemmed largely from a lack of settlers; the colony was much less populous than New Netherlands. The monopolists considered settlers a necessary evil and a drain on the profits of the fur trade and therefore did not encourage Frenchmen to settle in the North American wilderness. The sparsity of population tended to accentuate the Iroquois scourge.

The Iroquois first annihilated the Neutral and Tobacco Indians. Then, in 1648 and 1649, they dealt the Hurons a death-blow. The Huron villages, along with the Jesuit missions, were razed, and the Hurons were destroyed to the point where they ceased to exist as a nation.

Encouraged by the destruction of Huronia, the Iroquois planned to destroy French settlement along the St. Lawrence. They placed themselves astride the Ottawa River and blocked the route from the interior. The blockade was so effective and Iroquois control so complete, that in 1652 not one fur came to Quebec by way of the Ottawa River.

In 1660, several Iroquois parties came down the Ottawa River, intending to destroy Montreal. At the Long Sault Rapids they encountered Dollard des Ormeaux, a young French fur trader, and sixteen of his youthful companions. A protracted battle ensued in which Dollard and his men were killed. The efforts of this handful of men dissuaded the Iroquois from launching direct attacks on the French settlements.* Nevertheless, French settlements on the St. Lawrence were cut off from the fur supplies of the interior, and New France faced extinction.

---

* Recently, historical controversy has arisen over Dollard. Was he a hero by choice or by accident? Did he go out to meet the Iroquois or was he ambushed?

THE DREAD OF THE IROQUOIS[18]

Lahontan, a member of a French marine detachment, served in New France from 1683 to 1692. He made the following observation of the Iroquois:

The Strength of the *Iroquese* lies in engaging with Fire-Arms in a Forrest; for they shoot very dexterously; besides that they are very well vers'd in making the best advantage of every thing, by covering themselves with Trees, behind which they stand stock still after they have discharg'd, though their Enemies be twice their Number. . . .

———

In the Day time they take all the Precaution in the World to cover their March, by sending out Scouts on all Hands, unless it be that the Party is so strong as to fear nothing; for then, indeed, they March all in a close Body. But they are as Negligent in the Night time, as they are Vigilant in the Day; . . . I was assur'd that the Savages did it by way of Presumption, as reckoning so much upon the Reputation of their Valour, that they imagine their Enemies will not be so bold as to Attack them. . . .

There are a great many Savage Nations in *Canada* that tremble at the very Name of the *Iroquese*, for the latter are a brave sort of People; they are expert Warriors, ready upon all Enterprises, and capable to put them in Execution, with all due Dexterity. . . .

———

France now realized the seriousness of the situation. It was evident that the rule of the monopolists had failed. The flow of furs dwindled to a trickle; New France was only sparsely settled, and the colony lived in constant fear of attack. Only bold and energetic measures on the part of the Crown could save the colony.

Louis XIV, guided by his able Minister Jean-Baptiste Colbert, decided to take a direct hand in the affairs of New France. He revoked the charter that had been given to the Company of One Hundred Associates in 1627. In 1663 New France was made an overseas province of France with a government modeled after a province in the mother country. This form of government, which lasted to the end of the French Régime in Canada, was called Royal Government.

One of the first actions of the new government was to regain control of the Ottawa River route. In 1666 Sieur Prouville de Tracy led the famed Carignan and Salières regiment into the Iroquois country against the Mohawks, the fiercest of the Iroquois tribes. Villages were burned and crops were laid waste. Although the Iroquois Confederacy was not destroyed, the campaign was a success in that the Indians were impressed with French military might. In 1667, the Iroquois came to Quebec to sue for peace. The peaceful twenty-year interlude which followed allowed the colony to grow and the fur trade to expand. New France again controlled the Ottawa route, but new problems developed.

TALON TO COLBERT ON PEACE WITH IROQUOIS[19]

27 October, 1667

As long as all the nations of Iroquois, enjoying the Peace granted to them on behalf of his Majesty, will allow the French Colony to spread itself in this country and labor in profound tranquility at the cultivation of the soil, we consider it inexpedient to wage war against them during the winter; we therefore wait the King's orders, should his Majesty desire for the reasons set forth in your despatch, that a second invasion be made on those of the Lower Nation, notwithstanding the treaty concluded with them.

———

The elimination of the Hurons in 1649 put New France in a difficult position. The colony had lost its most important supplier of furs. With the disappearance of the established middleman, it was necessary for the French traders themselves to go directly to the source of furs — the Indians of the interior.

South of the Great Lakes there was another problem. The English, who had supplanted the Dutch in New Netherlands in 1664, were drawing off some of the St. Lawrence fur trade to their posts at Albany. Aided by their Iroquois allies, they were attracting furs from the Indians around the Great Lakes; the Mohawk-Hudson River route became an important fur artery and a competitor to the St. Lawrence.

English competition from the north posed yet another problem. Ironically, two French fur traders, Pierre Esprit Radisson and his brother-in-law Médard Chouart des Groseilliers, were instrumental in creating this competition. Because they did not share in the control of the fur trade in New France, they had gone over to the English and convinced them to exploit the fur regions around Hudson Bay. In 1670 King Charles II of England granted a charter giving all lands drained by rivers flowing into Hudson Bay* to The

---

* The English claim to these lands was based on Henry Hudson's voyage of 1610.

Piquier, 1665,   Régiment de Carignan-Salières   Mousquetaire, 1666

Governor and Company of Adventurers of England Trading into Hudson's Bay, commonly known as the Hudson's Bay Company. The English now had a direct water route to the rich fur regions of the Canadian Shield. This gave them a decided geographic advantage in the fur trade.

The French were not sitting idly by, but sought solutions to the loss of their Indian middlemen, the challenge from Albany and the competition from Hudson Bay.

The necessity of replacing the Indian middlemen gave rise to the Canadian *coureurs de bois,* who became the vital link in the fur trade. The freedom of the wilderness, the spirit of adventure, as well as remuneration, prompted many independent and energetic French youths to pursue the fur trade, legally or illegally. They traveled to the interior, contacted new tribes, explored new regions, traded with the Indians and brought the furs to the trading posts. The *coureurs de bois* became the new middlemen.

Meeting the challenge from Albany proved to be more difficult. The English enjoyed a decided advantage; their articles of trade — blankets, kettles, knives, tools, guns and rum — were con-

siderably cheaper in price than French goods and superior in quality. To offset this advantage the French resorted to a policy of reaching new Indian tribes ahead of the English. This involved personal contact, friendship, persuasion and diplomacy. The French also obtained trade goods from New York. In addition, they built posts at strategic points, not only to gather furs from the immediate areas and to serve as bases for food supplies but also to prevent the diversion of furs to the Mohawk-Hudson route. Fort Cataraqui guarded the approaches to the St. Lawrence. Fort Michilimackinac, at the junction of Lakes Superior, Michigan and Huron, controlled fur traffic on these important waterways. Fort Niagara, between Lakes Erie and Ontario, interrupted any movement of furs to Albany. Fort Detroit protected the western entrance to Lake Erie. Green Bay intercepted furs coming from the west. The French also built a series of posts along the Mississippi River to tap the furs south and west of the Great Lakes.

The methods employed to meet the challenge from Albany were not applied against English competition at Hudson Bay. Instead, direct military action was undertaken. Between 1686 and 1697, Pierre le Moyne d'Iberville, a brilliant young military leader, led several successful assaults by land and sea against English posts at the Bay. During this period the English managed to recapture the posts, only to lose them again to the persistent d'Iberville. The Treaty of Ryswick in 1697 ended the seesaw struggle and established French supremacy over the Hudson Bay area.

FRENCH DESIGNS ON THE FUR TRADE AROUND HUDSON BAY[20]

Governor Denonville's assessment of the possibility of wresting the fur trade around Hudson Bay from the English is contained in this memoir written on November 12, 1685:

If not expelled thence [from Hudson Bay], they will get all the fat beaver from an infinite number of nations at the North which are being discovered every day; they will attract the greatest portion of the peltries that reach us at Montreal through the Outaouacs and Assinibois, and other neighboring tribes, for these will derive a double advantage from going in search of the English at Port Nelson — they will not have so far to go, and will find goods at a much lower rate than with us. That is evident from the fact that our Frenchmen have seen quite recently at Port Nelson, some Indians who were known to have traded several years ago at Montreal.

By the beginning of the eighteenth century the French had replaced the Indian middlemen, checkmated the English south of the St. Lawrence and driven them from Hudson Bay. However, events in Europe were to determine the future of the fur trade in New France. In 1702, France and England were at war in Europe over the succession to the Spanish throne. The Treaty of Utrecht, which terminated the war in 1713, had important consequences for the fur trade in New France. The Hudson's Bay posts were returned to the English, and France acknowledged English sovereignty over the Hudson Bay area.

Now that the English were firmly entrenched at Hudson Bay, the French fur trade had to compete vigorously for the furs of the Northwest. The Hudson's Bay Company, enjoying handsome profits, sat comfortably at the posts around the Bay and waited for the Indians to bring their furs down the rivers flowing into the Bay.

Between 1731 and 1742, in an effort to outflank the Hudson's Bay Company, Pierre Gaultier de La Vérendrye and his sons established a chain of posts on key rivers and lakes of the Northwest. The purpose of these posts was to intercept Indians on their way to the Bay and to persuade them to trade at the near-by French posts rather than travel the long hazardous journey to the Bay.

The furs collected at these posts had to be transported the long distance to Montreal. So costly was this operation that only the best furs, the *castor gras*, could be shipped to the St. Lawrence and still realize a profit. Increasing costs, available methods of transportation and the organization of the fur trade at the time, set the western limit for the fur trade. The fur trade of New France never extended beyond the posts established by the La Vérendryes.

In the Southwest, particularly in the Ohio Valley, French-English rivalry intensified. Smuggling furs from the West to Albany became a well-organized business. Aided by their cheaper and better-quality goods, the English traders offered effective competition to the French. In an effort to divert furs to the Mohawk-Hudson River route, the English built posts at strategic points, just as the French had done earlier. In 1722 they built Fort Oswego on the south shore of Lake Ontario for this purpose.

In addition to the energetic efforts of the English fur traders, settlers from the Thirteen Colonies began infiltrating into the Ohio Valley, posing yet another threat to French dominance in this area.

ENGLISH DESIGNS ON THE FUR TRADE OF THE OHIO AND MISSISSIPPI RIVER REGIONS[21]

This excerpt is from a letter written by a New York merchant, J. A. Esq., to a Mr. P. C., of London, England, in 1740:

. . . and there have been for many Years past upwards of one hundred young men of this Province, who have gone yearly among the Indians, to supply them with our Goods.

By this means, at a modest Estimate, I am assured that the Indian Trade of this Province is now far above five times as much as when Governor Burnet began to put his Scheme in execution.

And this is not all the Advantages reaped thereby, but a much more considerable one to this, and all other English Colonies is, that not only our own six Nations, but also many far and remote Indian Nations are drawn off from their Dependance on the French, and made, by Trade and Intercourse, dependant on the English; by this means a great Security and Protection is acquired by the English, in case of a War with France; and by this Trade our Settlements in this

Province are extended up to the Onondagues Carrying-place . . . for the more commodious transporting of Goods to trade in the Lakes.

And they are now settling on the Branches of Sasquehanah River; and from the western Branches of this River, there is but a small Land-Carriage to Allegheny, a Branch of that great River Mississippi; which branch extending a thousand Miles from its Mouth, where it enters the said River; and which joins so near to our Settlements, as is above taken notice of, opens as a Trade to that vast Country, called by the French Louisiana, which they possess on the Mississippi.

To meet this two-pronged English advance, the French built military posts along the Ohio River and strengthened the existing posts along the Mississippi in an effort to exclude the English fur traders and settlers from the western lands.

In effect, the Ohio Valley was an armed camp. The inevitable conflict in this area led not only to the loss of the fur trade of New France but also to the loss of New France itself.

C

THE EFFECTS OF THE FUR TRADE

The fur trade had a profound effect on the life of the Indian. He became dependent on European goods, and this dependence led to the breakdown of his old way of life. The fur trade also introduced liquor and European weapons to the Indians, thus creating social problems which also contributed to the breakdown of the traditional Indian society. The struggle for the position of middleman pitted Indian against Indian in a ferocious struggle accentuated by European arms.

The quest for beaver furthered exploration of the continent. The increased demand for furs, the depletion of fur regions and the heightened competition pushed the fur trade ever farther into unexplored areas of the interior. The fur trade and exploration were inseparable; they proceeded hand-in-hand, extending the frontiers of New France.

On the other hand, the incompatibility of the fur trade and settlement was evident throughout the history of New France. New France became merely a fur trading outpost of France; Quebec,

Three Rivers and Montreal were extensions of the commercial houses of Rouen, LaRochelle and Cherbourg. The fur trade discouraged settlement; settlers were expensive to maintain and they were potential competitors. The fur trade attracted young men, and the disappearance of the *coureurs de bois* into the wilderness was a serious drain on the limited population of the colony.

The overwhelming stress on the fur trade prevented effective diversification of the economy of New France. With the predominant emphasis on furs, New France never developed large-scale agriculture or manufacturing, nor exploited other resources.

The fur trade may have limited the development of New France, but it was the fur trade that gave birth to the colony. It was essential to the existence of New France, but it led to an expansion the colony could not sustain, an economy that was vulnerable and a conflict that eventually brought about its downfall.

4

DEVELOPMENT OF AN EMPIRE

A

ADVANTAGE AND MOTIVE FOR EXPLORATION

At the beginning of French settlement in North America, the continent had been discovered but not explored. Yet, by the middle of the eighteenth century, France controlled an empire in North America that extended from the Atlantic to the Prairies, and from the lands surrounding Hudson Bay to the Gulf of Mexico. The building of this vast but tenuous empire was facilitated by geographic advantage.

Cartier had discovered the St. Lawrence River — the key to the North American continent and the pivotal point for French activity. A glance at a map shows that this mighty river provides access to the other major waterways of the continent. The St. Lawrence leads directly to the lower Great Lakes (Lakes Ontario and Erie), and provides easy passage along its tributary — the Ottawa River — to the Upper Great Lakes (Lakes Huron, Superior and Michigan). It is within reach of Hudson Bay by way of either the Saguenay and Rupert Rivers or the Ottawa and Abitibi Rivers. From the Great Lakes it is relatively easy to cross the narrow divide to the Mississippi waterway system leading to the Gulf of Mexico. The Great Lakes also provide an entry to the west over the maze of rivers and lakes from Lake Superior to Lake Winnipeg and its system of rivers leading to either Hudson Bay or the foothills of the Rockies.

The exploration of North America was almost exclusively a French accomplishment, largely because of these geographic advantages, coupled with English disadvantages. While the French had the St. Lawrence as a highway to the heart of the continent, the English had no such comparable access. This disadvantage was accentuated by the Appalachian mountains, which extend the length of the Atlantic seaboard, and which were a natural barrier that, for some time, prevented the west-ward expansion of the Thirteen Colonies. The rivers that did cut through the Appalachian barrier were generally difficult to navigate and they did not link easily with any of the great continental water systems. A significant exception was the Hudson River, cutting through the northern Appalachians. With its tributary, the Mohawk River, the Hudson-Mohawk waterway formed an important link with the Great Lakes.

But geographic advantage alone cannot adequately account for French exploration and empire building in the New World. Other considerations lay behind French exploration — the quest for the Northwest Passage, the demands of the fur trade, the zeal of missionaries, and the lure of the unexplored prompted the French to capitalize upon the geographic advantage of the St. Lawrence.

When the European discoverers failed to find an oceanic route *around* the northern part of the American continent, the search for the Northwest Passage became a search for a passage *through* the New World. The dream and expectation of finding such a passage persisted well into the eighteenth century and lured many explorers deep into the interior of the continent.

French exploration also stemmed from the demands of the fur trade. As older fur regions were exhausted, new fur-bearing regions had to be found. It was desirable and necessary to contact new Indian tribes to meet English competition, and the French delved ever deeper into the unexplored regions of the continent.

The crusading spirit of the missionaries, who came to New France to preach the Gospel to the heathen, urged them on to Indian tribes in remote areas. It was not unusual that fur trader and missionary sailed down the rivers together — the missionary seeking to win the Indian's soul, the fur trader wishing to procure the Indian's furs. This curious combination of missionary and fur trader accounted for much of the exploration of the continent. At times, missionaries blazed the trail to the hinterland and opened a path that was followed by explorers and fur traders.

A motive for exploration that should not be overlooked is the innate curiosity of man — a motive not easily assessed. The desire to search out, to discover, and to know the unknown must have driven many an adventurous young Frenchman to probe the secrets of the continent. Indian tales of the mysterious "lands beyond" and the lure of rivers and lakes were temptations to the venturesome.

B

EXPLORATION OF THE ST. LAWRENCE AND THE GREAT LAKES

After the founding of Quebec in 1608, Champlain, as the effective ruler of the colony, had to attend to the many details of the settlement — law, order, fur trade, survival and evangelization. Despite this, he never lost hope of finding a passage to the Orient. Nor did the numerous demands of the settlement prevent Champlain, the trained geographer, from undertaking journeys of exploration into the unknown vastness of North America.

The 1609 punitive expedition against the Iroquois, in addition to cementing his alliance with the Hurons and Algonquins, also resulted in the exploration of the Richelieu River and Lake Champlain. This hitherto unexplored region — the "back door" to Quebec — became the traditional path for the Iroquois and the English bent upon the conquest or destruction of New France. For the French, the Richelieu-Champlain route put the Hudson river, the life-line of the English fur trade, within striking distance.

Champlain's next important journey was undertaken in 1613. On many occasions, Indians had spoken of a "salt sea" far to the northwest of the Saguenay country. Nicolas Vignau, a young Frenchman whom Champlain had sent to live with the Hurons in 1611, boasted of having reached the Northern Sea (Hudson Bay) and of having seen the wreck of an English ship. Vignau's story and the recent news of Henry Hudson's northern voyage prompted Champlain to undertake a journey to the Northern Sea which might lead to the elusive Northwest Passage.

Exploration of the St. Lawrence and the Great Lakes

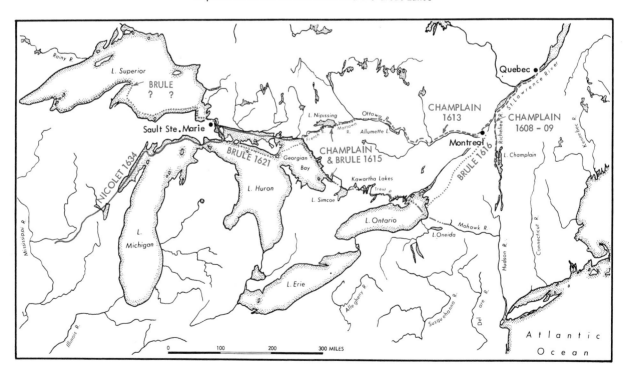

In May, 1613, Champlain with four others, including Vignau, paddled up the Ottawa River. When the party reached Allumette Island, where Vignau had wintered prior to his "journey" to the Northern Sea, Champlain learned from the Indians that Vignau's story was a fabrication. Vignau had never ventured beyond Allumette Island! An angry and disappointed Champlain returned to Quebec. Nevertheless, Champlain had explored a good portion of the Ottawa River and this journey into the region of his Indian allies proved to be the prelude to Champlain's most notable journey of exploration.

VIGNAU, THE LIAR[22]

Champlain's account:

Having related to all those of the pinnace the particulars of my journey and the malice of our liar, at which they were much astonished, I begged them to come together so that in their presence, in that of the savages and of his companions, he might acknowledge his villainy, which they willingly did. Being thus assembled, they had him come, and questioned him as to why he had not shown me the northern sea as he had promised me. He replied to them that he had promised a thing impossible, inasmuch as he had never seen this sea, but that the desire of making the journey had made him say that; also that he did not think I would undertake it. Wherefore he begged them to be so good as to pardon him, as he had begged me, confessing that he had been greatly at fault; but that if I was willing to leave him in the country he would so manage as to make good his error and would visit this sea, and in the following year would bring back definite news in regard to it. For certain reasons I pardoned him, on that condition.

Again in 1615, as in 1609, Champlain agreed to accompany his Huron allies against the Iroquois who were obstructing the flow of furs to Quebec. In July, 1615, Champlain and his party of twelve traveled up the Ottawa River and continued westward up one of its tributaries, the Mattawa River. A short portage brought them to Lake Nipissing, and from here down the French River to Lake Huron — "The Fresh Water Sea."*

On this voyage Champlain had traveled the great Ottawa highway to Lake Huron — the vast lake the Indians had spoken of and which Champlain hoped might lead to the Orient. He had explored the Ottawa River route to the Great Lakes, a route which was more direct and accessible than the St. Lawrence River. This alternate route shortly became the principal artery to the

west and to the north. It was his last and most important exploration in New France. Henceforth, Champlain remained at Quebec and devoted himself to the management of the colony.

The exploration of the continent was continued by Champlain's young protéges. Early in his career at Quebec, Champlain began to send young men to live with the Indians in order to learn their ways, customs and language and to cement friendly relations. These early forerunners of the *coureurs de bois* roamed freely over the wilderness, extended the fur trade, explored unknown regions and acted as interpreters. This practice developed a method of exploration that did not require Champlain's personal participation. Not all of these young men — Vignau, the impostor, for example — were satisfactory or reliable. But trustworthy men like Brulé and Nicolet justified Champlain's faith in his young protéges.

CHAMPLAIN LEAVES BRULE WITH THE ALGONQUINS[23]

I had a young lad, who had already spent two winters at Quebec, and who was desirous of going with the Algonquins to learn their language . . . I concluded that . . . it would be better to send him to this place than elsewhere, that he might ascertain the nature of their country, see the great lake, observe the rivers and tribes there, and also explore the mines and objects of special interest in the localities occupied by these tribes, in order that he might inform us, upon his return, of the facts of the case. . . .

. . . [Chief] Yroquet . . . promised to do so, and treat him as his own son, saying that he was greatly pleased with the idea. He communicated the plan to all the Algonquins, who were not greatly pleased with it, from fear that some accident might happen to the boy, which would cause us to make war upon them. . . . I . . . asked to

* Champlain proceeded to Georgian Bay in the Huron country. Here he was well received and stayed for a time with his Huron allies. After a war-party of over five-hundred men was readied, the expedition went to the Iroquois country by way of the Severn River to Lake Simcoe. From here, the war-party followed the labyrinthine Trent River system to the Bay of Quinte on the large lake which Champlain named Lake of the Iroquois (Ontario). They crossed the northwest extremity of this lake and continued their journey to Lake Oneida where they engaged the Iroquois at present-day Syracuse, in the state of New York. In the ensuing battle Champlain was wounded and his Indian allies were dispersed. He returned to the Georgian Bay area where he spent the winter prior to his return to Quebec in the spring of 1616.

Champlain and Etienne Brulé with Huron warriors on Lake Simcoe, plan an attack on the Iroquois at Oneida, New York, 1615.

speak with the captains . . . and we sat down for a conference. . . . I said that . . . taking the boy would be a means of increasing still more our friendship with them. . . .

———

They said to me: "Since, then, this is your desire, we will take him, and treat him like ourselves. But you shall also take a young man in his place, to go to France. We shall be greatly pleased to have him report the fine things he shall have seen." . . . This presented an additional motive for treating my boy still better than they might otherwise have done. . . .

Etienne Brulé was one of the first young men Champlain sent to live with the Hurons. He is credited with being the first European to have reached Lake Huron. On the 1615 expedition against the Iroquois, Brulé, who had spent five years among the Hurons, accompanied Champlain as his interpreter. Champlain dispatched Brulé as his emissary to the Andastes and Susquehanna Indians, in present-day Pennsylvania, to seek their aid against the Iroquois. He was not heard of

until 1618 when he returned to the St. Lawrence with a group of Indian fur traders. Apparently, during the intervening three years, he had followed the Susquehanna River to Chesapeake Bay and then returned westward. After a thrilling escape from his Iroquois captors, he finally reached Huron territory and then traveled along the north shore of Lake Huron. He may also have reached Lake Superior.

JEAN NICOLET[24]

The Jesuit Relations *of 1642 report the drowning of Nicolet, and give the following account of his life and achievements:*

. . . . He [Nicolet] came to New France in the year sixteen hundred and eighteen: . . . he was sent to winter with the Island Algonquins, in order to learn their language. He tarried with them two years, alone of the French. . . . He accompanied four hundred Algonquins, who went during that time to make peace with the Hyroquois, which he successfully accomplished. . . . After this treaty of peace, he went to live eight or nine years with the Algonquin Nipissiriniens, where he passed for one of that nation, taking part in the very frequent councils of those tribes. . . . He was finally recalled, and appointed Agent and Interpreter. While in the exercise of this office, he was delegated to make a journey to the nation called People of the sea, and arrange peace between them and the Hurons, from whom they are distant about three hundred leagues Westward. . . . When they arrived at their destination, they fastened two sticks in the earth, and hung gifts thereon, so as to relieve these tribes from the notion of mistaking them for enemies to be massacred. . . . He wore a grand robe of China damask, all strewn with flowers and birds of many colors. No sooner did they perceive him than the women and children fled, at the sight of a man who carried thunder in both hands — for thus they called the two pistols that he held. . . . Each of the chief men made a feast for him, and at one of these banquets they served at least sixscore Beavers. The peace was concluded; he returned to the Hurons, and some time later to the three Rivers, where he continued his employment as Agent and Interpreter. . . .

Although Brulé had pushed into areas where no European had preceded him, the extensive exploration of the Great Lakes basin was accomplished by others who followed him. Jean Nicolet, another of Champlain's young men who had lived with Indian tribes, was instructed by Champlain to explore the Great Lakes region. In 1634, he set out to establish contacts with western Indian tribes. It seems that Nicolet, and perhaps Champlain, had hopes that the western lakes might lead to a passage to China. Nicolet readied himself for such an eventuality. He took with him Chinese robes to wear when and if he should be presented in the court of the Sovereign of China!

He followed Lake Huron, through the Strait of Mackinac, and took a southerly route across Lake Michigan into Green Bay. From here he went up the Fox River and reached the Winnebagoes, Illinois, and Assiniboian tribes — Indians who had remained untouched by the impact of fur traders. Nicolet may not have put his Chinese robes to the use intended, but he managed to persuade the newly contacted tribes to take their furs to Three Rivers. His journey inaugurated an active trade and also charted the route for fur flotillas to the French trading posts on the St. Lawrence. Furthermore, Nicolet's activities in the Green Bay region led to the later discovery of the Mississippi River which in succeeding years carried fur traders, explorers and missionaries south to the Gulf of Mexico.

Additional knowledge of the Great Lakes region was obtained by the travels of fur traders and missionaries. In 1640, Father Brébeuf, in the course of his missionary work in Huronia, reached Lake Erie — the last of the Great Lakes to be discovered. A year later, Father Jogues, the heroic Jesuit who preached to the Iroquois, traveled in the vicinity of Sault Ste. Marie. Through their search for souls to be saved, the bearers of the cross probed the hinterland and unknown lands beyond.

Radisson and his brother-in-law Groseilliers, two experienced *coureurs de bois*, made important contributions to the exploration of the Great Lakes area. Their exploits have been pieced together from Radisson's rather vague written accounts. The search for furs prompted their explorations. Their aim was to trade directly with interior Indians to reap greater profits from furs in by-passing the Indian middleman. It appears that in 1654 they set out from Three Rivers for the Great Lakes. They followed Nicolet's route by way of the Ottawa River to Georgian Bay, past Mackinac Strait and south on Lake Michigan to Green Bay. They traveled extensively west of Green Bay, and it is possible that they reached the upper Mississippi River. On their return to Montreal they came upon the tragic remains of Dollard's party at the Long Sault. In Montreal, the arrival of the two *coureurs de bois* with large supplies of furs evoked great jubilation. Radisson and Groseilliers were welcomed as heroes because they had run the Iroquois blockade of the Ottawa route, a blockade that was paralyzing the economic life and the very existence of the beleaguered colony. Their arrival at Montreal did not terminate their activities. Later, they figured prominently in exploration north of the St. Lawrence-Great Lakes system.

With the stability that resulted from the intervention of King Louis XIV in the affairs of New France, further impetus was given to exploration. Talon, a royal official of New France, sent Louis Jolliet to investigate a reported copper deposit on the northern shores of Lake Superior in 1669. On his return to Quebec, Jolliet followed a rather circuitous route. From Lake Superior he traveled south on Lake Huron, crossed into Lake Erie, portaged around Niagara to Lake Ontario and then down the St. Lawrence River to Quebec.

Although by now the Great Lakes were well-known and well traveled, it was only in 1671 that Talon sent Saint-Lusson to Sault Ste. Marie to make formal claim to the western lands. In an impressive ceremony, a cross was planted and all western lands were claimed in the name of Louis XIV. The frontier of New France was pushed to the western edge of the Great Lakes.

On November 2, 1671, Talon, in a letter to the King, reported on Saint-Lusson's explorations:

. . . . Sieur de Lusson is returned, after having advanced as far as five hundred leagues from here, [at the Falls of St. Mary] and planted the cross and set up the King's arms in presence of seventeen Indian nations, assembled, on this occasion, from all parts; all of whom voluntarily submitted themselves to the dominion of his Majesty, whom alone they regard as their sovereign protector. This was effected, according to the account of the Jesuit Fathers who assisted at the Ceremony, with all the pomp and eclat the country could afford. . . .

The place to which the said Sieur de Saint Lusson has penetrated is supposed to be no more than three hundred leagues from the extremities of the Countries bordering on the Vermilion or South Sea. Those bordering on the West Sea appear to be no farther from those discovered by the French. According to the calculation made from the reports of the Indians and from Maps, there seems to remain not more than fifteen hundred leagues of navigation to Tartary, China and Japan. . . .

Sieur de Lusson's voyage to discover the South Sea and the Copper Mine will not cost the King anything. I make no account of it in my statements, because having made presents to the Savages of the Countries of which he took possession, he has reciprocally received from them in Beaver what can balance his expense.

In 1679-80, Daniel Greysolon, Sieur du Lhut,* a successful *coureur de bois* and fur trader, who had operated around Lake Superior, established posts at Kaministiquia (Fort William) and near Lake Nipigon. Thus exploration entered a new phase. Efforts were begun to consolidate what had been explored by the building of permanent fur posts at strategic points. This pattern of exploration, followed by the establishing of key outposts, became the cornerstone for French expansion to the South and to the West.

* The city of Duluth, Minnesota, is named after him.

C

EXPLORATION NORTH OF THE GREAT LAKES

Before the exploration and consolidation of the Great Lakes region were completed, exploration north of the Great Lakes was undertaken by Radisson and Groseilliers. Ironically, these two were directly responsible for the entry of the English into the fur trade around Hudson Bay.

In 1661, having been denied a fur trading permit by Governor d'Avaugour, Radisson and Groseilliers defied the Governor's order and illegally left Three Rivers for the Lake Superior country. Their movements are shrouded in uncertainties, but they may have reached Hudson Bay. In any event, they traded in the rich fur bearing areas of the Canadian Shield, north of the Great Lakes, in the vicinity of the Bay. They returned to Montreal in 1663, with large quantities of furs — the only furs, in that year, to reach the St. Lawrence by way of the Ottawa route. Little did Radisson and Groseilliers suspect the financial disaster that was awaiting them. Heavy fines and confiscation by the Governor for their violation of the law left Radisson and Groseilliers little to show for their two arduous years in the wilderness. All their appeals to the authorities both in New France and in France went unheeded.

RADISSON AND GROSEILLIERS HAVE TROUBLE WITH THE GOVERNOR[26]

This is Radisson's own account of the treatment he and Groseilliers received from the Governor upon their return to Quebec:

. . . . The governor, seeing us come back with a considerable sum of our own particular, and seeing that his time was expired and that he was to go away, made use of that excuse to do us wrong and to enrich himself with the goods that we had so dearly bought. . . . He made also my brother [in-law] prisoner for not having observed his order and to be gone without his leave. One of his letters made him blush for shame, not knowing what to say but that he would have some of them [beaver pelts] at what price soever, that he might the better maintain his coach and horses at Paris. He fined us four thousand pounds to make a fort at Three Rivers, telling us for all manner of satisfaction that he would give us leave to put our coat of arms upon it, and, moreover, six thousand pounds for the country, saying that we should not take it so strangely and so bad, being we were inhabitants and did not intend to finish

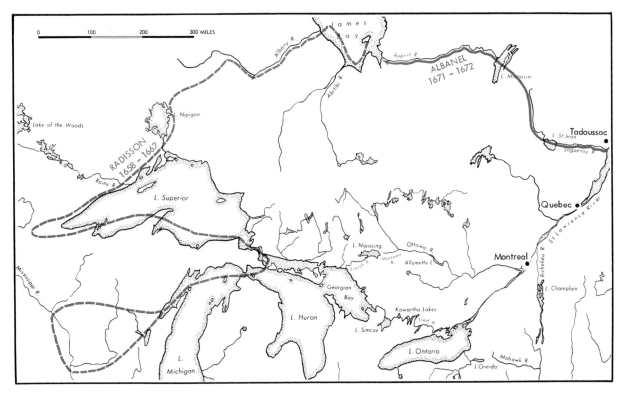

Exploration North of the Great Lakes

our days in the same country with our relations and friends . . . made us pay a custom which was the 4th part, which came to fourteen thousand pounds, so that we had left but 46 thousand pounds, and took away 24,000 [livres]. Was not he a tyrant to deal so with us, after we had so hazarded our lives and brought in less than 2 years by that voyage, as the factors of the said country said, between 40 and 50 thousand pistoles?

Thoroughly disillusioned and disappointed, the two embittered *coureurs de bois* went to England where they offered their services. Their account of the rich fur bearing area south of the Bay and the advantages of reaching this territory by sea, easily secured them financial backing by English investors. In 1668, an expedition was undertaken in two ships, the *Eaglet* commanded by Radisson and the *Nonsuch* by Groseilliers. Stormy seas forced the *Eaglet* to return to England, but the *Nonsuch* crossed the North Atlantic and sailed into James Bay. The return of the *Nonsuch*, heavily laden with furs, convinced English investors of the enormous profits that could be derived from the Hudson Bay trade route.

Little time was lost in securing a monopoly. On May 2, 1670, King Charles II of England granted a charter incorporating the Hudson's Bay Company. With a stroke of the pen, the King granted over one million square miles of territory, the rights of sole trade and commerce, the mineral resources of this territory and the control of law and order over all existing and future inhabitants to "The Governor and Company of Adventurers Trading into Hudson's Bay." Shortly after, posts were established at the mouths of the Hayes, Albany, Moose, Nelson and Severn Rivers. Thus the activities of Radisson and Groseilliers led to the establishment of the English at the Bay and opened up a vast area for competition and conflict.

Rumors of an English fur trade at the Bay were disconcerting to the French. To ascertain the extent of such English activity, Father Albanel undertook a journey to the Bay in 1671. He travelled up the Saguenay River, across numerous and treacherous portages to the Rupert River, and down the Rupert to James Bay. Here he discovered a thriving English-Indian fur trade. Albanel's voyage was also significant in that a link had been discovered betwen the St. Lawrence and the Bay. Later, other connections between these two were found, the most notable of which was the route along the Ottawa and Moose Rivers to James Bay, followed by the military expedition of Chevalier de Troyes, 1686.

EXPLORATION SOUTH OF THE GREAT LAKES

French exploration north of the Great Lakes was prompted, to some extent, by English incursion at the Bay, but French exploration south of the Great Lakes was motivated by the search for a passage to the Pacific. The French were convinced, from the many stories told by the Indians who traded at Green Bay, of the existence of the Mississippi River. However, the French had no knowledge of the exact extent and direction of this great waterway. Louis Jolliet, the first Canadian-born explorer, who had extensive trading experience around Green Bay, and Father Jacques Marquette, who had worked as a missionary in the Lake Michigan region, were commissioned by Frontenac and Talon to explore the fabled Mississippi River.

In 1673, the small party, headed by Jolliet and Marquette, travelled southward along Lake Michigan to Green Bay, up the Fox River, and over a short portage to the Wisconsin River — a tributary of the Mississippi River. A short journey down the Wisconsin River brought them onto the swift-flowing waters of the mighty Mississippi. They followed a southward course down the Mississippi as far as the Arkansas River. Having travelled the Mississippi for over six-hundred miles in a southerly direction, they felt certain that this river continued southward into the Gulf of Mexico. Fearing the consequences of trespassing on Spanish territory, Jolliet and Marquette returned to Quebec.

Jolliet and Marquette had found a bridge between the Great Lakes and the Mississippi River — a connection less difficult than that between the Great Lakes and Hudson Bay. It is understandable that French expansion southward followed the Mississippi River.

Robert Cavelier de la Salle, a daring and

La Salle at the Mouth of the Mississippi, 1682

fascinating French fur trader, dreamt of an elaborate fur trade and a French empire extending from the St. Lawrence to the Gulf of Mexico. In 1682, starting from the foot of Lake Michigan, La Salle reached the Illinois River and followed it to the Mississippi River, and sailed all the way south to its mouth at the Gulf of Mexico. He claimed all the land drained by the Mississippi River and its tributaries for King Louis XIV of France.

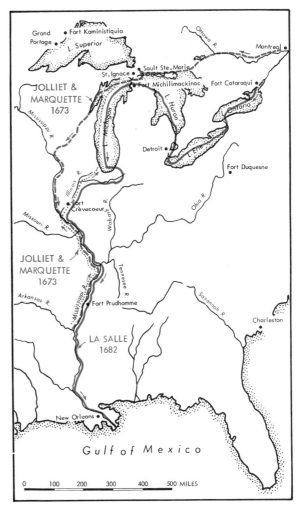

Exploration South of the Great Lakes

LA SALLE REACHES THE MOUTH OF THE MISSISSIPPI[27]

An associate of La Salle's describes their reaching the mouth of the Mississippi River on April 9th, 1682:

. . . .Here we prepared a column and a cross, and to the said column were affixed the arms of France, with this inscription:

'LOIS LE GRAND, ROI DE FRANCE ET DE NAVARRE, REGNE: LE NEUVIEME AVRIL, 1682.'

The whole party, under arms, chanted the *Te Deum*, the *Exaudiat*, the *Domine salvum fac Regem*; and then, after a salute of firearms and cries of *Vive le Roi*, the column was erected by M. de la Salle, who, standing near it, said, with a loud voice, in French: 'In the name of the most high, mighty, invincible and victorious Prince, Louis the Great, by the Grace of God King of France and of Navarre, Fourteenth of that name, this ninth day of April, one thousand six hundred and eighty-two, I, in virtue of the commission of his Majesty which I hold in my hand, and which may be seen by all whom it may concern, have taken, and do now take, in the name of his Majesty and of his successors to the crown, possession of this country of Louisiana, the seas, harbors, ports, bays, adjacent straits, and all the nations, people, provinces, cities, towns, villages, mines, minerals, fisheries, streams and rivers comprised in the extent of said Louisiana, from the mouth of the great River St. Louis, on the eastern side, otherwise called Ohio . . . as far as its mouth at the sea, or Gulf of Mexico . . . upon the assurance which we have received from all these nations that we are the first Europeans who have descended or ascended the said River Colbert. . . .

It was evident to La Salle that if France could control the outlet of the Mississippi, she would, in fact, control the whole Mississippi River. With the blessing and support of Louis XIV, La Salle attempted to found a colony at the mouth of the Mississippi, on the Gulf of Mexico. With the establishment of this colony in Louisiana — the newly claimed territory — French possession in North America would extend, in a broad arc, from New France to the Gulf of Mexico, linked by the great continental water systems of the St. Lawrence, the Great Lakes, and the Mississippi. This extended empire would not only confine the English Thirteen Colonies to the Atlantic seaboard, but would also assure French control of the fur trade west of the Mississippi River.

La Salle's plan for a French empire in North America became a blueprint for future French development south of the Great Lakes. The shiploads of settlers that had sailed from France, in 1684, to the Gulf of Mexico, missed the mouth of the Mississippi River and landed on the barren shores of present-day Texas. The planned colony at the mouth of the Mississippi River did not materialize. It was not until 1699 that d'Iberville established a colony in Louisiana near the mouth of the Mississippi River.

Jolliet and Marquette had bridged the gap between the Great Lakes and the Mississippi River; La Salle had followed the Mississippi River to its mouth and extended the frontier of New France to the Gulf of Mexico. Once the link between the St. Lawrence and the Gulf of Mexico had been established, the French systematically built a series of strategic outposts and forts along the Ohio and Mississippi Rivers to consolidate and secure what had been explored and claimed.

E

EXPLORATION WEST OF THE GREAT LAKES

After the Treaty of Utrecht, in 1713, when France gave up all claims to the lands around Hudson Bay, the French attempted to establish a fur trade west of Lake Superior, and thus outflank the English at the Bay. At the same time, finding a westward passage to the Pacific was still considered quite probable.

By the early 1720's an active fur trade centered about Kaministiquia and Lake Nipigon. Also, the Grand Portage — the route from Lake Superior by way of the Pigeon River and along the present Canadian–United States boundary to the Lake of the Woods — was well-known. But it was not until the 1730's that any extensive exploration west of Lake Superior was carried out. The dominant figure in this exploration was Pierre Gaultier de la Vérendrye, assisted by his nephew De la Jemeraye, and by his sons Jean, Pierre, Francois and Louis-Joseph.

La Vérendrye, a native of Three Rivers and a former officer in the Troupes de la Marine, was in charge of the fur trading post on Lake Nipigon. Here he came in contact with Indians who frequently spoke of a Western Sea, not far beyond Lake Superior. La Vérendrye was determined to search for the long-sought-after passage to the Pacific.

In 1730, La Vérendrye managed to obtain a monopoly of the fur trade west of Lake Superior and to gain financial support from a group of wealthy Montreal merchants. As he advanced westward, he would build a chain of posts to serve as supply depots and fur trading centres, closer and more accessible for the Indians than the remote posts at the Bay. The government saw in La Vérendrye's scheme a means of extending the French empire westward; the merchants saw large profits from the increased fur trade.

Exploration West of the Great Lakes

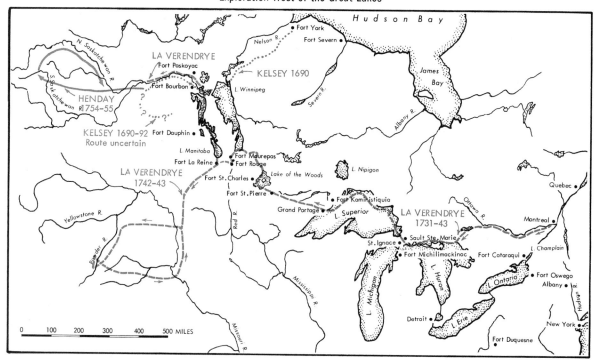

Having in mind his obligations to his financial backers, La Vérendrye set out, in 1731, in search of the western passage. In the following seventeen years, dogged by financial setbacks and personal misfortunes, La Vérendrye and his sons established strategically located posts which formed the backbone of the western French empire.

In 1731, by way of the Pigeon River and many portages, the party reached Rainy Lake where Fort St. Pierre was built. From here, following Rainy River, they came to Lake of the Woods where they constructed Fort St. Charles. Three years later, they followed the Winnipeg River to Lake Winnipeg and built Fort Maurepas where the Red River empties into this lake. Traveling south on the Red River, they came to "The Forks" of the Red and Assiniboine Rivers where they established Fort Rouge (Winnipeg), in 1738, and then proceeded westward on the Assiniboine. At the present site of Portage la Prairie, they erected Fort la Reine.

From Fort la Reine, the activities of the La Vérendryes branched out to the southwest to search for the Western Sea, and to the north to establish posts closer to the waterways flowing into Hudson Bay. In two voyages to the southwest, it is certain that the La Vérendryes reached the Black Hills of South Dakota and it is possible that they may have reached the Rockies. These two expeditions, however, brought them no nearer to the discovery of a western passage to the Pacific. In their activities north of Fort la Reine, the La Vérendryes were more successful. By establishing Fort Dauphin on Lake Dauphin, Fort Bourbon on Cedar Lake, and Fort Paskoyac near the Saskatchewan River, they extended the French fur trade northward, offering effective competition to the Hudson's Bay Company.

LA VERENDRYE DEFENDS HIS REPUTATION[28]

There was much difference of opinion as to La Vérendrye's actions and motives. He returned to Montreal to defend himself:

Finally I arrived at Montreal on the twenty-fifth of August [1740], and found there that a suit was being brought against me, who have a horror of such things, never having had anything in my life to do with them, in regard to the posts I had established. I settled the matter to my great loss, though I was far from having done anyone any wrong.

I went down to Quebec, where I had the honour of giving an account of my travels to the General [Beauharnois], who had the kindness to offer me the hospitality of his house. I remained there and next spring followed him to Montreal, and again

La Vérendrye at Lake of the Woods

he did me the favour of honouring me with his orders to return and pursue my discovery. . . .

If debts that I have on my shoulders to the amount of more than forty thousand livres are an advantage, I can flatter myself that I am very rich, and if I had gone on I should have become richer still. People do not know me: money has never been my object; I have sacrificed myself and my sons for the service of His Majesty and the good of the colony; what advantages shall result from my toils the future may tell.

Besides, should no account be taken of the great number of persons to whom this enterprise means a living . . . and the furs of which formerly the English got the benefit?

In all my misfortunes I have the consolation of seeing that the General enters into my views, recognizes the uprightness of my intentions, and continues to do me justice in spite of the opposition of certain parties.

In 1751, Boucher de Niverville traveled west on the Saskatchewan River and built Fort Jonquière, near the present site of Calgary. This was the farthest western penetration of the French in search of the Western Sea.

The La Vérendryes opened the route from Lake Superior to Lake Winnipeg and the Saskatchewan River. They explored a vast territory and extended the fur trade and the frontier of New France beyond Lake Winnipeg.* With de Niverville's thrust to the West, the French empire in North America had reached its territorial limits — from the Atlantic to the foothills of the Rockies, and from the Great Lakes to the Gulf of Mexico. The building of this empire was a remarkable achievement. It was not an empire won at pistol point in the European tradition. Instead, a handful of resolute and adventurous men had hacked an empire out of the North American wilderness. The fur trader, explorer and mission-ary had created this extraordinary empire, whose ultimate fate, after the Seven Years' War, was to be decided at the council tables in Europe.

* In the main, the Hudson's Bay Company lacked initiative in exploration, and was content "to sleep by the Bay." But, as early as 1690, Henry Kelsey, one of their employees, traveled as far south as the Prairie. In 1754, Anthony Henday, another employee, traveled almost 2,000 miles from Fort York to the foothills of the Rockies. He suggested that the Hudson's Bay Company meet French competition by building inland trading posts.

5

THE GOVERNMENT OF NEW FRANCE

A

GOVERNMENT UNDER CHARTERED COMPANIES

Invariably, part of the charter granted to the early companies stipulated that a company had the authority and obligation to govern a colony. Because the monopolists, without exception, failed to live up to their obligation regarding colonization, there were very few settlers in Quebec in the early days of New France. Such a small community required no elaborate system of government.

A governor, appointed by the holders of the charter, was vested with the authority to act as their agent, to regulate the fur trade, to defend the colony, to dispense justice and to legislate for the colony. All the powers of government rested with the governor — the governor was the government. This all-embracing role is illustrated by Champlain's wide-ranging activities. As the governor of the colony, Champlain had to deal with the Indians, stamp out illegal fur trade, wage war against the Iroquois, undertake exploration, bring out settlers, make and enforce laws, act as judge and provide for the spiritual needs of the Indians and colonists.

So poor were the early chartered companies as instruments of colonization that by 1627, after almost twenty years of "growth," there were only sixty-five colonists in New France. Champlain brought this sorry state of affairs to the attention of Cardinal de Richelieu, the chief Minister of France. Under Richelieu's influence, in 1627, the De Caen brothers, the holders of the charter, were induced to surrender their monopoly. A new, broadly-based chartered company — the Company of One Hundred Associates — was formed. Most of the shareholders of this company (also known as the Company of New France) were wealthy merchants, members of the nobility and influential government officials.

The Sovereign Council, 1663

ESTABLISHMENT OF THE COMPANY OF ONE HUNDRED ASSOCIATES, 1627[29]

Several of the terms embodied in the charter of the Company of One Hundred Associates:

. . . . Those to whom we had entrusted the care of the colony were so little interested that, to date, there is but one settlement . . . in which are maintained forty or fifty Frenchmen favouring the interests of the merchants rather than the . . . interests of the King; so badly maintained have they been . . . and so neglected has been the development of agriculture that if yearly provisions had been delayed . . . the small group of inhabitants would have starved to death, having but one month's supplies in store. . . .

51

1–. . . The Hundred Associates promise to transport two or three hundred settlers of all trades by 1628 and in the following fifteen years, until a total of four thousand is reached . . . and to shelter, nourish and maintain them . . . for three years. . . .

2–. . . It will not be permitted, however, to transport aliens . . . but rather the colony must be settled by French Catholic citizens. . . .

7–. . . Further, His Majesty grants . . . forever all traffic in pelts and furs . . .; and for fifteen years . . . all other commerce . . . except . . . cod fishing and whaling which His Majesty wishes to be free to all his subjects. . . .

8–. . . French inhabitants and their families settled in the country and not maintained by the . . . Company . . . may engage in the fur trade . . . as long as the pelts are sold to the Company. . . .

17–. . . The descendants of Frenchmen, as well as any converted natives . . . will be considered . . . as . . . French citizens and as such may live in France . . . without any further declaration of naturalization. . . .

Armand, Cardinal de Richelieu

This ambitious enterprise was plagued with difficulties from the very beginning. France and England were at war in Europe at the time, and the first fleet of the Company of One Hundred Associates carrying supplies and settlers to New France was captured by the Kirke brothers marauders from England. Moreover, in 1629, Quebec itself was captured by the Kirke brothers, and the colony was not returned to French control until the Treaty of St. Germain-en-Laye in 1632. Added to these troubles, the Company was embroiled in costly lawsuits with the de Caen brothers over the cancellation of the de Caen charter. Worst of all, the Company realized no profits from its operations; so far, the venture had, by force of circumstances, been one large expenditure. It is understandable why, in 1645, the Company of One Hundred Associates handed over its monopoly of the fur trade to a group in Quebec known as the Company of Habitants.* The Company of One Hundred Associates, however, retained the rights of government in the colony and the right to grant land.

The Company of Habitants gave prominence to a class that had been steadily emerging as a result of the fur trade. This "beaver aristocracy" — wealthy merchants, army officers and large landholders — became the controlling shareholders in the company. Their activities evoked resentment, and the settlers of the colony complained bitterly about the power wielded by this small privileged group. In response to the numerous complaints of the colonists, the king issued an edict creating the Council of Quebec in 1647.

THE ELECTIVE COUNCIL OF QUEBEC[30]

Gustave Lanctot, the eminent French-Canadian historian, expresses his views on the Council of Quebec:

. . . the extraordinary complexity of the government of New France. . . . At the top stood the king, royal suzerain and absolute legislator. Under him came the Company of New France, feudal owner of the country, granting seignories and collecting fees, appointing officials of justice and paying their salaries. Next stood the governor who, nominated by the company, but appointed by the king, was the colony's highest court of appeal, wielded absolute authority in military and civil regulations, and even in trade and financial matters, in any case of emergency. Under him the *Communauté* of the Inhabitants possessed the monopoly of the fur-trade, while the Quebec council, composed of members elected from the colony at large, regulated the commercial policy and public expenditure of the country. . . .

But even with its limitation to trade and financial matters and its subjection to the governor's possible overruling, . . . it is an extraordinary fact to find that at a time of complete royal autocracy in France the two thousand colonists of Canada were enjoying a sort of system of popular representation, and were electing representatives empowered to regulate and administer the most important activities of government in the fields of trade and public finance. Thus, to a certain extent, the Quebec Council may be said to have been in an embryonic way the first Canadian parliament.

The Council of Quebec represented a novel development in the government of New France. It was a representative body composed of the Governor of New France, the Governor of Montreal, the Superior of the Jesuit Order and a number of *syndics* from Quebec, Three Rivers and Montreal. These *syndics*, the elected representatives of the inhabitants, had the right to attend meetings of the Council and to express points of view. Unlike the other members of the Council, they had no voting rights. The Council of Quebec,

* The company had the following obligations: to pay an annual tribute of 1000 beaver pelts and to bring out and maintain twenty settlers yearly.

from time to time, underwent minor modifications but during its existence (1647-1663) it never lost its representative character. It is remarkable that in an age when kings ruled by Divine Right and when the authority of the monarch was absolute, the people of New France had representation in the government.

B

GOVERNMENT UNDER THE CROWN

The creation of a French empire in North America, entrusted to the chartered company, had been a complete failure. By 1663, the population of New France was no more than 2,500. Agriculture had developed so slowly that New France could not even feed itself and had to depend on supplies from France. The supply of furs, the economic life-blood of the colony, had been reduced to a trickle by constant Iroquois raids. New France was so pitifully weak that it could not defend itself, and the inhabitants lived in daily fear of attack. Internal dissensions between the governor and the clergy and between the citizenry and the Council further weakened the colony. Acadia was in the hands of the English. New France was on the brink of disaster. Only the expenditure of large sums of money, military support on a large scale and bold, far-reaching policies and programs could infuse new life into the dying colony.

It was fortunate, however, that when the situation in New France was so desperate, France had just emerged as the dominant power in Europe. Two great and ambitious men — Louis XIV and Jean-Baptiste Colbert — guided the destiny of France, and mercantilist economic thought attached very great importance to colonies.

As a result of the Thirty Years' War in Europe, France's frontiers were extended and secured. France had little to fear from her traditional enemies. The power of Spain was broken. Germany was splintered into thirty different states. England, after the restoration of Charles II, was busy healing the wounds of internal dissension. Internally, France had been enjoying a period of stability ever since Richelieu and his successor, Cardinal Mazarin, broke the power of the French nobility.

When Louis XIV became king of France, the throne of France was supreme and unchallenged. He was young, strong, wise and ambitious, and determined to extend French power and construct a mighty empire. He was also fortunate in having the talented Colbert as his principal architect for these imperial designs.

Colbert, Louis' chief Minister, was imbued with the seventeenth century ideas of mercantilism and vigorously implemented its principles as the basis for the French empire. Mercantilism held that a country gained strength and greatness by achieving self-sufficiency. To accomplish this, a country must surround herself with colonies which would serve the mother country as a source of raw materials and a market for finished products. Not only would this trading system, closed to other nations, stimulate trade and shipping between the mother country and her colonies; it would also free the mother country from her dependence on other nations.

Colbert envisaged a revitalized New France as an essential link in the mercantilist chain. The master plan for New France, designed by Colbert and sanctioned by Louis XIV, required that New France be defended, her land settled, her resources developed and her economy diversified. Above all, the growth of the colony must be orderly. New France must centre her efforts upon building a strong, compact colony concentrated in the St. Lawrence Valley, rather than a weak one spread over the continent. The machinery for the realization of these aims must be a strong centralized government, closely controlled from France.

Building on the institutions that had already developed in New France, and modelling the new government along the lines of the administration of a French province, an edict of Louis XIV, dated April 28, 1663, established Royal Government in New France. The charter of the Company of One Hundred Associates had previously been cancelled, paving the way for the new government. The Council of Quebec was replaced by a Sovereign Council consisting of three major officials — a Governor-General, an Intendant and a Bishop, and a number of minor officials — five councillors, an attorney-general and a clerk. This Sovereign Council was to be the sole governing authority in the colony and the intermediary between the king in France and his overseas subjects in New France.

The Sovereign Council acted as a legislative, administrative and judicial body. As a legislative or law-making body, the Sovereign Council was given authority to make laws for the colony concerning finance, order and trade — subject, of course, to amendment and veto by the king. However, major decisions were made in France, and the Sovereign Council, as an administrative body, registered, proclaimed and enforced the king's edicts. As a judicial body, the Sovereign Council exercised the authority to set up lower courts and to act as a court of appeal.

EDICT FOR THE CREATING OF THE SOVEREIGN COUNCIL OF QUEBEC, MARCH, 1663[31]

Louis, by the Grace of God King of France and Navarre . . . in order to promote the interests of . . . those who inhabit them to experience the same repose and happiness Our other subjects enjoy . . . and being well informed that the distance of places is too great to admit of a remedy from hence in all matters with the requisite diligence, the circumstances of said affairs being ordinarily changed when Our orders arrive on the spot, and that the conjuncture and evils require prompter remedies than those We can apply to them from so great a distance; We have considered that we could not adopt a better resolution than to establish a regulated Justice and a Sovereign Council in said Country for the encouragement of law, the maintenance and support of the good, the chastisement of the wicked, and the keeping each within his duty, causing the observance as much as possible there, of the same form of justice as obtains in Our Kingdom, and the said Sovereign Council to be composed of a number of officers suitable for its functions. . . . We have also given and granted, give and grant to the said Sovereign Council, the power to try all civil and criminal cases, to judge sovereignly and in last resort, according to the laws and ordinances of Our Kingdom . . . reserving to ourselves, however, to change, reform and amplify, according to our Sovereign Power the said Laws and ordinances, to derogate from and abolish them. . . .

The offices of the three major officials in the Sovereign Council also entailed specific duties. The Governor-General, appointed by the king, was the senior official in the colony. As such, he could veto the actions of the other officials, but the Governor seldom used this power because he had to account for his actions to the king. The Governor was responsible for the defence of the colony and for relations with the Indians and with the English colonies to the south.

Next in rank to the king's representative in New France was the Bishop. His office was charged with providing for the spiritual needs of the colony and for the evangelization of the Indians. For two years the Bishop shared with the Governor the right to appoint councillors to the Sovereign Council.

Although of lesser rank than that of the Governor and the Bishop, the office of Intendant became the most important in the Sovereign Council. Gradually, the legislative and administrative functions of the Sovereign Council were absorbed by the Intendant, and the Sovereign Council concerned itself primarily with the dispensing of justice. So important did the Intendant become that after 1674 he replaced the Governor as the presiding officer of the Sovereign Council. The wide-ranging activities of the Intendant can be gathered from his title — "Intendant of Justice, Police, and Finance." There was hardly an aspect of life and activity in the colony that escaped his attention. He was responsible for such matters as law and order, the raising of revenue, expenditures, grants to institutions, regulation of the fur trade, settlement, the land-holding system, public works, supplies for the military and the incoming and outgoing trade. In carrying out this multiplicity of duties, the Governor created the important position of Captain of Militia, in each locality, to serve as the liaison between the Intendant and the habitants. As the "business manager" of New France, the Intendant also sent frequent dispatches to the king reporting on all the affairs of the colony.

COMMISSION OF TALON TO BE INTENDANT OF NEW FRANCE[32]

Louis, by the Grace of God, King of France and Navarre, to our trusty and beloved Councillor in our Councils, Sieur Talon, Greeting. Considering it expedient for the good of Our people, and the regulation of Justice, Police and Finance in Our Country of Canada, to establish in the office of Intendant on the spot, a person capable of worthily serving Us, We have to this end laid eyes on you by reason of the special confidence We repose in your experience, good conduct and integrity, qualities of which you have given proofs on all occasions. . . . For these and other reasons . . . We have commissioned, ordered and deputed, and by these presents signed by Our hand, commission, order and depute you Intendant of Justice, Police and Finance . . . to hear the complaints which shall be made to you by Our people of said Country . . . of excesses, wrongs and violences: render them good and quick justice; take information touching all enterprises, practices and intrigues committed against Our Service; proceed against those guilty of any crime of what quality or condition soever they may be; pro-

Talon Visiting Settlers

secute and perfect the trial unto definitive Judgment and execution thereon inclusive . . . to preside in the Sovereign Council in the absence of . . . Governor . . . to judge sovereignty alone in Civil matters and to order every thing as you shall see just and fit. . . . We will likewise that you superintend the direction, management and distribution of Our funds destined, and hereafter intended for the support of the military; also of the provisions, ammunition, repairs, fortifications, contingencies, loans and contributions . . . which will be made there for our service. . . . Given at Paris, the 23ᵈ day of March in the year of Grace 1665, and of our Reign the 22ᵈ.

Signed　　　　　Louis.

A fundamental feature of Royal Government was the centralization and concentration of authority in the hands of the king. This was in accord with the absolutism that had evolved in France and England in the first half of the seventeenth century. In theory, the king was the state. The authority of the king was so absolute that the affairs of state were conducted without consulting the national assembly. This parliament or Estates-General composed of the clergy, nobles and middle-class was not convened from 1618 to 1789.

It was natural that Louis XIV viewed anything resembling representative institutions in his overseas province with disfavour and suspicion. When Governor Frontenac, upon his arrival in 1672, called together the representatives of the four classes of society to swear allegiance to the king's new representative, he was soundly rebuked by Colbert who insisted that not only should an Estates-General never be convened but the office of *syndic* should be suppressed. In a society where a king ruled by Divine Right there was no room for representative institutions. Colbert's instruction to Frontenac, in 1673, clearly stated this principle: "It is well that each speak for himself and none for all."

Although the system was highly authoritarian and centralized, it was neither despotic nor tyrannical. In form, New France had no semblance of representative government such as an assembly of elected members. But in fact, government was conducted to a large extent with the interests and views of the people in mind.

When Frontenac was the Governor and Laval the Bishop, the brandy question flared up once more. Louis XIV, beleaguered by petitions and appeals, sanctioned the appointment of prominent citizens to meet and recommend a policy on the sale of brandy to the Indians. The consensus of this "Brandy Parliament" of 1678 was that the sale of brandy was essential to the successful operation of the fur trade. A prohibition of the brandy traffic would channel more furs to the English, who imposed no restrictions on the barter of furs for rum. Subsequently, an edict of the king embodied some of the wishes of the "Brandy Parliament" into law.

THE BRANDY PARLIAMENT OF 1678[33]

An account of some of the opinions expressed:

The most elaborate statement was that made by the explorer La Salle. There was no mistaking his attitude on the subject. He was for trade and transportation without restraint, such action "being necessary to preserve peace and commerce." If the transportation of liquor to the wilderness were not permitted, the right to sell it at the French settlements would be of little value because many of the Indians buy it to sell among their own people. It was for laymen, La Salle urged, and not for the clergy to decide what was the best policy in matters of commerce.

Thus far, opinions had run in the same groove. There were five dissenters, . . . Nicholas Duplessis-Gâtineau was opposed to the continuance of the trade, believing that it spelt the ruin of religion. The Indians got drunk continually, neglected the sacraments and their prayers, and lived like unbelievers. . . . The Indian went into debt to get liquor; in two months he would spend more on drink than would suffice to maintain his family for two years. . . . Louis Jolliet was of the same opinion. The transportation of brandy into the Indian country should be forbidden "under penalty of death". But letting the Indians have a little liquor at the homes of the French inhabitants was another thing, . . . provided due care be taken "not to make them drunk. . . ."

On matters directly affecting the welfare of the people of New France, it became the custom for the Governor and Intendant to call a general meeting of the populace in order to ascertain its views and wishes as a guide for government policy. In 1695, such an assembly proposed that meat prices in the colony be fixed. Jean Bochart de Champigny, the Intendant, disagreed with this view. Nevertheless, he bowed to the wishes of the citizenry and meat prices were regulated.

Centralization and concentration of authority in the monarch, three-thousand miles removed from New France, tended to break down somewhat because of the slowness of communication. Government was carried on by correspondence, and in the absence of instructions from France, colonial officials were expected to act on their own initiative. Thus the Intendant Jacques de Meulles, in 1685, hard-pressed to pay his soldiers because of the lack of French currency, issued the famous card-money of New France. Playing-cards, stamped with the seal of the Governor became legal currency in New France. The French government was shocked by this measure, but learned of it only after it had been in use for some time.

INTRODUCTION OF CARD MONEY[34]

Because of a scarcity of coins, Intendant Jacques de Meulles issued the following order on June 8, 1685:

Duly considering His Majesty's lack of funds and the need we have experienced of money for maintaining and subsisting the troops, . . . We, after having subsisted the said troops from our own resources and through our credit for the period of four or five months, and considering the scarcity of money in the country, and the inability of the shop-keepers and others to lend any at present, . . . Have Judged [it] suitable to have notes issued signed by us with the seal of our arms and our paraph on the back of them, . . . Declaring that all the said notes shall serve them as ready money, and that we shall hold them good alike for the soldiers and the people of the colony, when they fall into their hands, assuring them that they shall be paid from the first funds, which His Majesty will surely send us by the vessels of the present year. . . .

Taking advantage of the distance from the mother country and the slowness of communication, Talon and Frontenac were able to commission La Salle and other *coureurs de bois* to build inland fur posts — an action contrary to Colbert's compact colony plan. Thus, government by correspondence contributed to the frustration of Colbert's mercantilist designs for New France.

COLBERT'S COLONIAL PLAN[35]

In a letter to Frontenac, May 17, 1674, Colbert stresses the need for a compact colony:

. . . his Majesty's intention is not that you undertake great voyages nor that the inhabitants spread themselves, for the future, further than they have

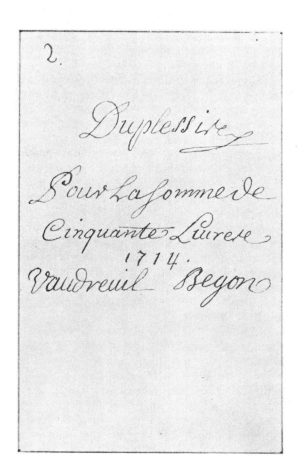

Verso   Recto

Playing Card Money

already done. On the contrary, he desires that you labor incessantly and during the whole time you are in that country to consolidate, collect and form them into Towns and Villages, that they may be placed in a position the more easily to defend themselves successfully . . . he deems it much more agreeable to the good of this service that you apply yourself to the clearing and settlement of those tracts which are most fertile and nearest the sea coasts and the communication with France, than to think of distant discoveries in the interior of the Country, so far off that they can never be settled nor possessed by Frenchmen.

Paternalism was another outstanding feature of Royal Government. Every detail of life was regulated. Talon issued edicts fining unmarried men, fixing the number of bakeries and the cost of bread, offering pensions to fathers of ten or more children and even forbidding individuals from going into the woods for more than twenty-four hours without a permit. The police regulations for the town of Quebec of 1676 dealt with such speci-

fics as weights and measures, plumbing, garbage disposal, fire regulations, butchers, bakers, inn-keepers, millers, blasphemy, boat thefts, transportation of goods in boats, vagabonds, weed control and wandering animals. The Intendant Raudot issued an edict in 1706 prohibiting people from leaving church during the sermon and smoking at the door of the church.

Paternalism by the government did not necessarily mean submissiveness by the inhabitants of New France. When Bishop Laval ordered that all persons pay one-thirteenth of their produce as a tithe for the support of the Church, the people of New France refused to comply. Eventually, the tithe had to be lowered to one-twenty-sixth, and this applied only to grain. Threats and edicts failed to stop the flow of *coureurs de bois* into the forests just as fines and penalties failed to stop the sale of brandy to the Indians. Gilles Hocquart, the Intendant who held office from 1731 to 1748 described the people of New France: "They are commonly pliant enough when one appeals to their honour and governs them justly, but they are naturally intractable."

The numerous decrees probably resulted from the independence and intractability of the people of New France. But edicts and regulations could not suppress the spirit of independence and initiative of a people living in such close proximity to an untamed and beckoning wilderness.

A discrediting aspect of Royal Government, particularly in its early years, arose from the conflicts among the Governor, Bishop and Intendant. Most of the quarrels stemmed, in large measure, from the personalities of the major officials involved as well as from the overlapping nature of their duties.

As early as 1665, Francois de Laval de Montigny, the first Bishop, fought with De Mézy, the first governor, over the appointment of councillors to the Sovereign Council. This conflict resulted in the Bishop's losing his authority to share with the Governor the right of appointment of councillors.

A burning issue of the early years that produced acrimonious debates, charges and counter-charges, divisions within the colony and appeals and petitions to the king was the contentious question of selling brandy to the Indians. The Bishop insisted that it was a spiritual matter — his responsibility. The Governor countered that it involved relations with the Indians — his responsibility. The Intendant maintained that it concerned trade and commerce — his responsibility.

FRICTION BETWEEN INTENDANT AND GOVERNOR[36]

Intendant Du Chesneau, in a lengthy letter to de Seignelay on November 13, 1681, lists complaints against Governor Frontenac:

Matters have at length arrived at the extremity I always anticipated. Disorder is introduced every where; universal confusion prevails throughout every department of business; the King's pleasure, the orders of the Sovereign Council, and my Ordinances continue unexecuted; justice is openly violated, and trade is entirely destroyed.

Violence, upheld by authority, decides everything; and nought could console the people, who groan without daring to complain through fear of destroying themselves irreparably, but the hope, My Lord, that you will have the goodness to deign to be moved by their misfortunes, in spite of all the precautions the authors take to conceal them from you.

I now repeat it, My Lord, since the animosity of which I am accused has no part in what I have written on the subject of the Count de Frontenac. . . .

. . . My Lord, in consequence of the insults, reproaches and rudeness the Governor is daily guilty of towards me in the Council, where he charges me with rashness and insolence; of the prison with which he frequently threatens me; and of the defamatory libels against me by his authority. . . . But all this has not affected me; I regarded it with indifference, and have not failed to cooperate [with him] in the King's affairs, and to visit him as usual, and shall continue so to do. . . .

Another area of conflict among the officials of Royal Government involved the control of the fur trade. In 1672, Louis de Buade, Comte de Frontenac, the best-known governor of New France, had built Fort Cataraqui (Fort Frontenac, present-day Kingston) where the St. Lawrence River flows out of Lake Ontario. Frontenac justified the construction of this fort on the grounds that it was a necessary military outpost against the Iroquois. Montreal fur interests, however, openly accused Frontenac of being actively engaged in the fur trade and of using Cataraqui to intercept furs that would normally go to Montreal. Jacques Duchesneau, the Intendant at the time, sided with the Montreal interests. The competition between Montreal and Cataraqui found expression in a number of infamous disputes between the Intendant and the Governor. The spectacle of major royal officials quarrelling in public was most embarrassing to the Crown. In 1682, King Louis XIV recalled both Frontenac and Duchesneau.

It is unlikely that the confusion of authority that existed in Royal Government was planned deliberately. The concept of having one official check and balance the authority and actions of another so that no one official became too powerful was foreign to seventeenth century European political thought. It is more likely that personalities, vital interests and the lack of clearly defined areas of authority caused the disputes that discredited Royal Government in its early years.

Royal Government had endowed New France with an efficient, capably administered form of government that lasted until the Conquest. In spite of the shortcomings of Royal Government, the small colony grew and prospered; its frontiers were secured and its economy was set on a reasonably firm footing. Any weakness it exhibited rose more out of French neglect, the nature of the North American continent and the strains of colonial wars than out of any defects in the government of the colony or the quality of the inhabitants of New France.

6

THE CHURCH IN NEW FRANCE

A

THE CHURCH IN THE WILDERNESS

The founding of New France coincided with a great Catholic revival in Europe in the early seventeenth century. France, in particular, had just emerged from bitter religious civil wars. The great religious zeal which the wars generated reflected itself in missionary activity in New France.

The task of converting the Indians to Christianity was arduous indeed. The missionaries found physical survival in the wilderness no less a task than conversion. Disease, filth, vermin and the hardships of travel with the Indians in their never-ending quest for food tried the missionaries' human endurance. Life with the nomadic tribes was so difficult that evangelization was almost impossible, and the missionaries soon decided to devote their major efforts to the more sedentary Indian tribes.

FATHER LE JEUNE'S ADVICE[37]

In the Jesuit Relations *of 1636, Father le Jeune tells of the conditions in the wilderness that missionaries, coming from France, may expect:*

. . . . Be with whom you like, you must expect to be, at least, three or four weeks on the way, to have as companions persons you have never seen before; to be cramped in a bark canoe in an uncomfortable position . . . in danger fifty times a day of being upset or of being dashed upon the rocks. During the day, the Sun burns you; during the night you run the risks of being a prey to Mosquitoes. You sometimes ascend five or six rapids in a day; and in the evening the only refreshment is a little corn crushed between two stones and cooked in fine clear water; the only bed is the earth, sometimes only the rough, uneven rocks, and usually no roof but the stars; and all this in perpetual silence. If you are accidentally

hurt, if you fall sick, do not expect from these Barbarians any assistance, for whence could they obtain it? . . .

Instead of being a great master and great Theologian as in France, you must reckon on being here a humble Scholar, and then, good God! with what masters! — women, little children, and all the Savages, — and exposed to their laughter. The Huron language will be your saint Thomas and your Aristotle; and, clever man as you are, and speaking glibly among learned and capable persons, you must make up your mind to be for a long time mute among the Barbarians. You will have accomplished much, if, at the end of a considerable time, you begin to stammer a little.

And then how do you think you would pass the Winter with us? . . . I say it without exaggeration, the five or six months of Winter are spent in almost continual discomforts — excessive cold, smoke, and the annoyance of the Savages. We have a Cabin built of simple bark, but so well jointed that we have to send someone outside to learn what kind of weather it is; the smoke is very often so thick . . . it is all you can do to make out a few lines in your Breviary. . . . As regards the food, it is not so bad, although we usually content ourselves with a little corn, or a morsel of dry smoked fish, or some fruits. . . .

. . . Add to all this, that our lives depend upon a single thread; and if, wherever we are in the world we are to expect death every hour and to be prepared for it, this is particularly the case here. . . .

. . . But enough of this; the rest can only be known by experience.

The Jesuit Missionary

The Indian medicine-man, who saw his position threatened, hindered and frustrated the work of the missionaries. His task of preserving the rooted Indian beliefs was much easier than the missionaries' work of preaching the new faith. It was simple for the medicine-man to blame the "black-robes" for every misfortune — disease, famine, natural catastrophes — that befell the individual and the tribe. The misdeeds and misconduct of some *coureurs de bois* and traders helped the medicine-man in his struggle against the missionaries: the Christian virtues so eloquently extolled by them obviously were not practiced.

Perhaps the greatest difficulty the missionaries faced in their work was the Indian's natural reluctance to accept a foreign faith. It was not easy to persuade the Indian to give up the comforts of his own beliefs for a new religion with its many strange ethical concepts. The Christian heaven was not as appealing as the Indian paradise. Native beliefs were much simpler and less restrictive than the complex, sophisticated religion of the French. The missionaries found that the rudimentary Indian dialects did not lend themselves to a satisfactory expression of the essential Christian teachings.

INDIANS RESIST CHRISTIANIZATION[38]

Lahontan's observations:

. . . . But the poor Wretches are such obstinate Infidels, that all the Characters of Truth, Sincerity and Divinity that shine throughout the Scriptures, have no impression upon them. . . .

. . . They plead, That a Man must be a Fool who believes that . . . God Created *Adam* on purpose to have him tempted by an evil Spirit to eat of an Apple, and that he occasion'd all the Misery of his Posterity by the pretended transmission of his Sin. They ridicule the Dialogue between *Eve* and the Serpent, alledging that we affront God in supposing that he wrought the Miracle of giving this Animal the use of Speech, with intent to destroy all the Humane Race.

. . . They argue, 'That . . . the Christians build a Religion without a Foundation, which is subject to the Changes and Vicissitudes of Humane Affairs. That this Religion being divided and subdivided into so many Sects, as those of the *French*, the *English*, etc. it can be no other than an Human Artifice: For had God been the Author of it, his Providence had prevented such diversity of Sentiments. . . . That if the Evangelical Law had descended from Heaven . . . God . . . would have deliver'd his Precepts in such clear and precise terms as would leave no room for Disputes.'

While the task of evangelization may have seemed insurmountable, the missionaries who came to the North American wilderness were men of fervent faith, ardent zeal and stubborn determination, dauntlessly devoted to the task of conversion. Many toiled for years in the unfriendly environment, winning but few converts, and in the end suffering a martyr's death. The success of the Church in the wilderness cannot be measured in the number of converts; there never was a wholesale conversion of Indians to Christianity. Yet, before the colony was fifty years old, the missionaries had written a bold and heroic chapter in the history of New France.

In 1615, upon the request of Champlain, the Recollets, the first missionaries of New France, came to Quebec. Father le Caron and his two associates attended to the spiritual needs of the tiny colony and attempted missionary work among the Indians. In the same year, he preceded Champlain to the Huron country around Georgian Bay. Father le Caron compiled the first dictionary of the Algonquin language, and he is believed to have performed the first Christian marriage in New France. However, the Recollets, a branch of the Franciscan Friars, found the financing of their missionary activity beyond their meagre resources. In time, the Recollets turned over this fertile missionary field to the Jesuits, primarily a missionary order with greater manpower and resources.

LE CARON'S JOURNEY[39]

Father Joseph le Caron describes his journey up the Ottawa River in July, 1615:

It would be hard to tell you . . . how tired I was with paddling all day, with all my strength, among the Indians; wading the rivers a hundred times and more, through the mud and over the sharp rocks that cut my feet; carrying the canoe and luggage through the woods to avoid the rapids and frightful cataracts; and half starved all the while, for we had nothing to eat but a little *sagamite*, a sort of porridge of water and pounded maize, of which they gave us a very small allowance every morning and night. But I must needs tell you what abundant consolation I found under all my troubles; for when one sees so many infidels needing nothing but a drop of water to make them children of God, one feels an inexpressible ardor to labor for their conversion, and sacrifice to it one's repose and life.

The Jesuit Order, founded in 1534 by a Spanish soldier, Ignatius Loyola, was organized along military lines and was the most militant arm of the Catholic Church. The Order was made up of a select group of highly educated, rigorously trained, well-disciplined men intensely loyal to the Papacy. The Jesuit fathers had engaged in extensive missionary work from Paraguay to Japan and they were not strangers to North America. Jesuit fathers had accompanied early settlers to Acadia.

When Cardinal Richelieu came to power in France, he was instrumental in sending the Jesuits to New France. In 1625, a small group of Jesuit missionaries arrived in Quebec. One of these, Father Jean de Brébeuf, attempted a mission among the nomadic Algonquin and Montagnais tribes. His efforts, like those of the Recollets' before him, were unsuccessful. This prompted the Jesuits to direct their missionary work toward the more settled Hurons around Georgian Bay. This work was interrupted in 1629 when the Kirke brothers captured Quebec. With the restoration of the colony to France in 1632, the Jesuits pursued their missionary work with increased zeal.

When the Jesuits returned to New France, they reached out to many Indian tribes but their efforts were concentrated mainly in Huronia. In 1632, Father Le Jeune, the Superior of the Order in New France, undertook the almost impossible task of ministering to the migratory Algonquin and Montagnais tribes. In 1642, Father Isaac Jogues, on his way to Huronia, was captured by the Iroquois. He was tortured and mutilated, but he managed, with the help of some Dutch traders, to escape to France. Four years later, undismayed by his previous experience, he returned to the Iroquois country on a peace mission. The hostile Mohawks were in no mood to accept an emissary of New France. Father Jogues was captured and he died a martyr's death.

The most successful Jesuit missionary work was accomplished in Huronia — the territory of the Hurons around Georgian Bay. Recollets and Jesuits had visited there before, but it was not until 1634 that a permanent mission was established. In that year, Fathers Brébeuf, Antoine Daniel and Jérôme Lalemant set out for Huronia and began the struggle for the Indian's soul. Eventually, Ste. Marie (near present-day Midland, Ontario) was established as the headquarters for eleven other mission stations scattered throughout the area. By 1648, eighteen Jesuit priests and four Jesuit brothers were ministering to their Huron flocks.

The most successful Jesuit missionary work in New France were not unknown to the people of France. Each Jesuit was required to keep a detailed account of his work and life in the North American wilderness. These annual reports, known as the *Jesuit Relations*, fully described the life and habits of the Indians, the climate and geography of the country and the progress and difficulties of the missionary work. The *Relations*, published in France and avidly read, aroused considerable interest. These publications also succeeded in gaining financial support from wealthy benefactors in France as well as new recruits for the missionary work. The founding of Montreal

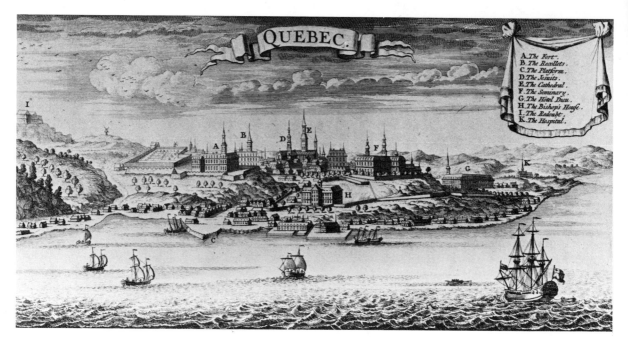

View of Quebec, c. 1730

in 1642 may be directly attributed to the missionary zeal that the *Jesuit Relations* engendered among some wealthy and dedicated French Catholics.

THE FOUNDING OF MONTREAL[40]

Montreal was founded as a mission by the Société de Notre-Dame de Montréal, under Maisonneuve, in 1642. This description is based on Dollier de Gasson's narrative:

On the seventeenth of May 1642, Maisonneuve's little flotilla — a pinnace, a flat-bottomed craft moved by sails, and two row-boats — approached Montreal; and all on board raised in unison a hymn of praise. . . .

Maisonneuve sprang ashore, and fell on his knees. His followers imitated his example; and all joined their voices in enthusiastic songs of thanksgiving. Tents, baggage, arms, and stores were landed. An altar was raised on a pleasant spot near at hand; and Mademoiselle Mance, with Madame de la Peltrie, aided by her servant, Charlotte Barré, decorated it with taste which was the admiration of the beholders. Now all the company gathered before the shrine. Here stood Vimont, in the rich vestments of his office. Here were the two ladies, with their servant; Montmagny, no very willing spectator; and Maisonneuve, a warlike figure, erect and tall, his men clustering around him, — soldiers, sailors, artisans, and laborers, — all alike soldiers at need. They kneeled in reverent silence as the Host was raised aloft; and when the rite was over, the priest turned and addressed them:

"You are a grain of mustard-seed, that shall rise and grow till its branches overshadow the earth. You are few, but your work is the work of God. His smile is on you, and your children shall fill the land."

The afternoon waned; the sun sank behind the western forest, and twilight came on. Fire flies were twinkling over the darkened meadow. They caught them, tied them with threads into shining festoons, and hung them before the altar, where the Host remained exposed. Then they pitched their tents, lighted their bivouac fires, stationed their guards, and lay down to rest. Such was the birth-night of Montreal.

Unfortunately, the fur trade was responsible for bringing the years of struggle and heroic efforts in Huronia to a tragic end. In a concerted effort to control the vital Ottawa River fur route, the Iroquois set out to destroy the Hurons — their chief rivals in the fur trade. In 1648 and 1649, the Iroquois unleashed their fury, obliterating Huronia and sweeping aside the many years of Jesuit missionary endeavours.

The martyrdom of Fathers Daniel, Brébeuf, Gabriel Lalemant, Charles Garnier and Noel Chabanel did not end the work of the missionaries. Men of lesser courage might have abandoned all efforts, but the Jesuits persisted in their evangelization of the Indians. Missionaries like Father Albanel and Marquette, in doing the work of God, also aided exploration, expanded the fur trade and extended the frontier of New France.

B

THE CHURCH IN THE SETTLEMENT

The Church in the settlement faced problems different from those encountered in the wilderness. Essentially, these problems stemmed from two opposing views of the power and authority of the Catholic Church. The concept of Gallicanism maintained that the Church was subject to the will and pleasure of the Crown since the monarch ruled by Divine Right. The opposing view, ultramontanism, insisted that the Pope reigned supreme in the affairs of the Church and that the Church was not subject to control by the Crown. Gallicanism in New France meant that the Church was to be used as an instrument in achieving Colbert's mercantilist designs. If necessary, the interests of the Church were to be subordinated to the needs of the Crown. Arrayed against these Gallican tendencies in New France were the powerful Jesuits and their choice for Bishop, the strong-willed and ultramontane Laval.

CHARACTER OF BISHOP LAVAL[41]

The historian Francis Parkman gives this character sketch of Bishop Laval:

On his [Laval's] first arrival in Canada Mother Marie de l'Incarnation, Superior of the Ursulines, wrote to her son that the choice of such a prelate was not of man but of God. "I will not," she adds, "say that he is a saint, but I may say with truth that he lives like a saint and an apostle." And she describes his austerity of life; how he had but two servants, a gardener — whom he lent on occasion to his needy neighbors — and a valet; how he lived in a small hired house, saying that he would not have one of his own if he could build it for only five sous; and how, in his table, furniture, and bed, he showed the spirit of poverty, even, as she thinks, to excess. His servant, a lay brother named Houssart, testified after his death, that he slept on a hard bed, and would not suffer it to be changed even when it became full of fleas. . . . Houssart also gives the following specimen of his austerities: "I have seen him keep cooked meat five, six, seven or eight days in the heat of the summer, and when it was all mouldy and wormy he washed it in warm water and ate it, and told me that it was very good."

He is one of those concerning whom Protestants and Catholics, at least ultramontane Catholics, will never agree in judgment. . . . He believed firmly that the princes and rulers of this world ought to be subject to guidance and control at the hands of the Pope, the vicar of Christ on earth. But he himself was the Pope's vicar, and so far as the bounds of Canada extended, the Holy Father had clothed him with his own authority. The glory of God demanded that this authority should suffer no abatement, and he, Laval, would be guilty before Heaven if he did not uphold the supremacy of the church over the powers both of earth and of hell.

The work of the Church in the settlement required and received little attention until the arrival of Laval in 1659. With the establishment of Royal Government, the Church was assigned an important role in the colony. Its authority extended over the spiritual life, missionary work, charitable institutions, hospitals and the education of the young.

There is no doubt that the Church in New France owed its ultramontane character to Laval. He jealously guarded against incursions by the state into spheres that concerned only the Church. Laval insisted that the Church exercise its authority free of state interference. This principle (unequivocally insisted upon in the brandy question) brought him into constant conflict with the other royal officials. Talon sought to offset the power of Laval and the Jesuits by bringing the Recollets back to New France in 1669. The Sulpician Order at Montreal served the same purpose for Frontenac. In time, such rigidly held views on Church authority, often made more acute by the personalities involved, tended to moderate. By the eighteenth century, the more contentious issues had been settled and a mutual understanding of the limits of their respective authorities was tacitly agreed upon by state and church.

RELATIONS BETWEEN CHURCH AND STATE[42]

ᵃ*Colbert to de Courcelles, May 15, 1669:*

Regarding the too great authority assumed, as you experience, by the Bishop of Petrée [Laval] and the Jesuits, or, to speak more correctly by the latter in the name of the former, I must inform you that you will have to act with great prudence and circumspection in that matter, especially as it is of such a nature that, when the country will increase in population, assuredly the Royal will predominate over the Ecclesiastical authority, and resume its true extent. Meanwhile, without either any rupture between you, or partiality on your part being perceptible, you will be always able adroitly to prevent the too vast undertaking they may attempt; whereupon you can always consult M. Talon and act in concert with him.

ᵇColbert to Frontenac, May 17, 1674:

As to the request the Jesuits made to continue their Missions in the far countries, his Majesty thinks 'twould be more advantageous for the Religion and his service if they attend to those more near. . . . His Majesty, however, does not pretend that these good Fathers be in any wise circumscribed in their functions. He merely desires that you would communicate to them, and gently encourage them to second, His Majesty's views.

Frontenac to Colbert, November 14, 1674:

. . . they [Jesuits] . . . declared to me they were here only to endeavor to instruct the Indians, or rather, *to get Beavers*, and not to be Parish priests to the French.

They . . . withdrew two Fathers whom they always kept at their settlement at Cape de la Madelaine, one of the most populous in this country, because a sufficient number of Indians do not resort there at this moment. . . .

If the Recollet Fathers were more numerous, and were employed, they would assuredly do wonders in the missions; but the two whom you did me the honor to inform me that you demanded last year did not come, nor the four this year. I presume they were retarded by some mysterious means, as there begins to be great jealousy of them, however fair a face be shown them.

As France's interest in New France waned, it became necessary to develop a *Canadien* clergy. As early as 1663, at Quebec, Laval founded a seminary, the forerunner of the Séminaire de Québec, not only to train men for the priesthood but also to house itinerant parish priests. The state wanted permanently appointed priests to live in the parishes, but Laval argued that this was not possible since priests were too few in number and the clergy could not be supported from tithes alone. With priests operating from the seminary, Laval exercised the right of appointment and removal and thus ensured his control over the clergy. His successor, Bishop Saint-Vallier, eventually gave in to the pressures of the state for appointment of priests to the parishes, but the Bishop retained the right of appointment and removal.

The Church was the sole educational agency in New France. The earliest educational efforts were made by the missionaries. It is remarkable that as early as 1635, when the colony numbered only three-hundred, a college, supported by religious societies in France, was founded in Quebec. The Ursuline nuns had established a school for girls at Quebec in 1639; at Montreal Mme. de la Peltrie started a similar school for Indian girls and the Sulpicians maintained a seminary and a school for Indian children. The Recollets operated their seminary at Three Rivers. At Quebec, Laval, in addition to the seminary already established, had founded a junior boys' seminary and, at St. Joachim, a trade school.

INSTRUCTIONS TO URSULINE TEACHERS[43]

A mistress must give her pupils high ideas of the majesty of God and speak often to them of His adorable perfection; she must accustom them often to make acts of faith, hope, and charity, and inspire them with a deep love for Jesus Christ. . . . She will make them fear and avoid any occasion of sin — bad companions, dances, staying up late at night, vanity in dress, etc. She will encourage them to love chastity, modesty, reserve, simplicity in dress, obedience to superiors, respect for those who are consecrated to God. She will forbid them to be curious or to pry into their neighbors' affairs, and will make them love silence. She will inspire them with a horror of scandal and accustom them to speak well of everybody and evil of nobody, to avoid idleness, and to love work. She will forbid them ever to show themselves to anybody — even to their family — without being completely and modestly dressed.

After the establishment of Royal Government, royal subsidies constituted a substantial part of the revenues for education. Although education in New France was religiously oriented, it was patterned after the classical schools of France. The state saw in a classical education a means for the assimilation of the Indians.

INSTITUTIONS OF FORMAL EDUCATION[44]

1635 *Petite Ecole of the Jesuits, Quebec.* It began as an elementary school with an enrolment of twenty boys. But Latin was introduced in 1636 and the school developed into a college for secondary education by 1655. The elementary school continued in operation.

1642 *School of the Ursulines, Quebec.* This was a boarding and day school for girls. In time it also offered more advanced education.

1659 *School of Marguerite Bourgeoys, Montreal.* At first this was an elementary school for young boys and girls, but from about 1666 it was for girls only.

1663 *Grand Séminaire, Quebec.* This was a seminary for the training of priests.

1666 *School of the Sulpicians, Montreal.* At first an elementary school for boys. It was expanded to include also a seminary for the preparation of priests.

1668 *Petit Séminaire, Quebec.* This was a seminary for boys destined for the priesthood.

1668 *School of St. Joachim.* This school for boys offered training in practical arts and trades.

1694 *School of Brothers Hospitalers, Montreal.* This was a school for boys.

Among the many concerns of the Church in New France were hospitals and charitable institutions. At Quebec, in 1639, three Augustinian nuns started the Hôtel Dieu, Canada's first hospital. When Montreal was founded in 1642, Jeanne Mance, a French nurse, organized a hospital for the sick and wounded in that area. Most religious orders also undertook the work of charity and cared for orphans, the aged, widows and the needy. Aside from its spiritual work, the Church shouldered responsibility for many of the social services of the community.

The Church in New France made a significant contribution to the material progress of the colony. By the time of the Conquest, the Church held two-sevenths of all the land of New France, and exercised its seigneurial obligations with thoroughness and diligence. Some of the best and wealthiest seigneuries belonged to the Church and these became the experimental farms of New France, where livestock was bred, new farming methods were tried and new varieties of crops suitable for the Canadian climate were developed. While other seigneuries lay idle and undeveloped, those of the Church prospered and flourished. While most of the energy of New France was expended in the pursuit of furs, the Church seigneuries fostered agriculture as a basis for life in New France.

The work of the Church in the settled areas of New France was not as spectacular as its work in the wilderness, but it was no less important. The spiritual and temporal activities of the Church pervaded the life of the people of New France. The arguments between the Church and its flock were not on questions of doctrine but rather on the extent to which the Church could control the life of the colony. The pious habitant or the avidly Catholic royal official saw no inconsistency or incompatibility in his resistance to Church pressure when it concerned his personal or economic life. Nevertheless, the Church — the bearer of Christianity to the Indians, the spiritual mentor in the parishes, the educator of the young, the healer of the sick, the benefactor to the poor and the tiller of the soil — gained an honoured and revered place in the hearts of the people of New France.

7

SETTLEMENT AND LIFE IN NEW FRANCE

A

SETTLEMENT IN ACADIA

France displayed a consistent disinterest in Acadia and, except for the coastal fisheries, this neglect bordered on abandonment. The limited settlement that did develop was further weakened by bitter intervals of strife which, at times, amounted to civil war. To add to these difficulties, repeated and successful attacks from New England destroyed the principal settlements along the shores of the Bay of Fundy.

Settlement in Acadia began in 1604, when Pierre du Guast, Sieur de Monts, a Protestant gentleman and holder of the monopoly for Acadia, brought settlers to the island of St. Croix, where the St. Croix River empties into the Bay of Fundy. St. Croix proved to be a poor location; in the spring of 1605 the settlement was moved across the Bay of Fundy to Port Royal (Annapolis Royal). The new settlement was left to the guidance of Champlain and Pontgravé when de Monts returned to France in 1605. Here the settlement fared much better — the settlers had learned much from their earlier experiences and errors at St. Croix. At Port Royal, Champlain organized the famous Order of Good Cheer, which provided a variety of wholesome food to prevent scurvy and entertainment to avert boredom during the long winter months. Just when the colony began to prosper, intrigues in the French court brought an end to de Monts' charter, and in the summer of 1607 the colony was abandoned.

THE ORDER OF GOOD CHEER[45]

Lescarbot relates his experience in the winter of 1605-1606 at Port Royal:

. . . I shall relate how, in order to keep our table joyous and well provided, an Order was established . . . which was called the Order of Good Cheer, originally proposed by Champlain. To this Order each man of the said table was appointed Chief Steward in his turn, which came round once a fortnight. Now this person had the duty of taking care that we were all well and honourably provided for. This was so well carried out. . . . For there was no one who, two days before his turn came, failed to go hunting or fishing, and to bring back some delicacy in addition to our ordinary fare. So well was this carried out that never at breakfast did we lack some savoury meat of flesh or fish, and still less at our midday or evening meals; for that was our chief banquet, at which the ruler of the feast or chief butler . . . having had everything prepared by the cook, marched in, napkin on shoulder, wand of office in hand, and around his neck the collar of the Order, which was worth more than four crowns; after him all the members of the Order, carrying each a dish. The same was repeated at dessert, though not always with so much pomp. And at night, before giving thanks to God, he handed over to his successor in the charge the collar of the Order, with a cup of wine, and they drank to each other. I have already said that we had abundance of game, such as ducks, bustards, grey and white geese, partridges, larks, and other birds: moreover, moose, caribou, beaver, otter, bear, rabbits, wild-cats (or leopards), nibaches, and other animals . . . of all our meats none is so tender as moose-meat . . . and nothing so delicate as beaver's tail. Yea, sometimes we had half-a-dozen sturgeon at once, which the savages brought us, part of which we bought, and allowed them to sell the remainder publicly to barter it for bread, of which our men had abundance.

The abandonment of Port Royal did not end French colonization in Acadia. In 1610, Baron de Poutrincourt and his son Biencourt, who had been

The Habitant's Cottage

in the settlement at Port Royal, returned with a group of settlers. The revived colony struggled along until 1613, when it was destroyed by an expedition headed by Samuel Argall from the English colony of Virginia. Nevertheless, a handful of tenacious French settlers stayed on at Port Royal.

In the meantime, England displayed interest in this area because of its fisheries and its strategic approach to the St. Lawrence. In 1621, King James I of England granted all of Acadia as a feudal realm to Sir William Alexander. He renamed it Nova Scotia. In 1628, his son attempted to establish the first English colony in Nova Scotia, but the settlement lasted only a short while. In 1632, by the Treaty of St. Germaine-en-Laye, the whole of Acadia was restored to France.

The period from 1604 to 1632 had not only witnessed the shaky beginnings of French settlement of Acadia but had also initiated a French-English contest for the control of this Maritime region. Loss and restoration became the pattern for the future of Acadia.

After the restoration of 1632, Isaac de Razilly, a cousin of Cardinal Richelieu, was sent to Acadia as Lieutenant-General, the representative of the King of France and of the Company of One Hundred Associates. He, with his cousin Charles de Menou, Sieur d'Aulnay and de Charnisay, and their settlers established a moderately prosperous colony around Port Royal. In 1635, upon the death of Razilly, d'Aulnay succeeded to the Lieutenant-Generalcy of Acadia.

Another French settlement across the Bay of Fundy at the mouth of the St. John River, under the leadership of Charles de St. Etienne de la Tour, was enjoying some success. When Biencourt had returned to France, la Tour had been left in charge of the colony in Acadia and had taken full possession of it upon the death of Biencourt in 1623. The settlement under la Tour had managed to operate even during the period of English control of Acadia.

The accession of d'Aulnay ushered in a period of bitter strife and rivalry between his colony at Port Royal and la Tour's at the mouth of the St. John River. This was essentially a conflict over the fur trade in Acadia. Both d'Aulnay and la Tour had been given authority by the Company of One Hundred Associates to participate jointly in the Acadian fur trade. This arrangement led to such bitter conflict that la Tour even intrigued with the English of Massachusetts and enlisted their help against d'Aulnay. In 1645 d'Aulnay finally established himself as the sole authority in Acadia; he successfully attacked his competitor's headquarters when la Tour was in Boston.

THE CAPTURE OF LA TOUR'S FORT[46]

This incident is related by Charlevoix, an eighteenth-century French historian who was in New France between 1705 and 1709:

. . . Charnisé learning that de la Tour had left his Fort St. Jean with the best part of his garrison, thinking it a favorable opportunity for seizing it, marched thither with all his troops.

Madame de la Tour had remained there, and although surprised with a small number of soldiers, she resolved to defend the place to the last: which she did so courageously for three days, that she compelled the besiegers to draw off; but on the fourth day, which was Easter Sunday, she was betrayed by a Swiss, who was on guard, and whom Mr. de Charnisé succeeded in corrupting. Yet she did not deem her case hopeless: when she learned that the enemy were scaling the wall, she reached forward at the head of her little garrison to defend it.

Charnisé thinking this garrison stronger than he had at first supposed, and who feared a repulse, proposed to the lady to give her terms; and she consented, in order to save the lives of the few brave men who had so well supported her; but Charnisé had no sooner entered the fort then, ashamed of having made terms with a woman who had met him only with her courage and a handful of men picked up, he complained of having been deceived, and deeming himself absolved from the articles of capitulation, hung all Madame de la Tour's men except one, whose life he spared on condition of his acting as hangman to the rest; and he forced his prisoner, Madame de la Tour, to witness the execution with a rope around her neck.

For the next five years d'Aulnay ruled unchallenged in Acadia and contributed much to its progress. More settlers were brought in, schools and churches were built and an improved government administration was established.

In 1650, however, d'Aulnay drowned, and the way was opened for la Tour's return. But the earlier conflict was not renewed. Instead, the long-standing d'Aulnay–la Tour feud resolved itself in the traditional European fashion — in 1653 la Tour married d'Aulnay's widow. Just when it seemed that internal strife had ended, an expedition from Massachusetts under the command of Francis Nicholson captured Acadia, and in 1654 France once again lost the colony. The capture of Acadia was not followed by a French exodus or by an English immigration. The Acadian population continued to grow under English control until Acadia was again restored to France by the Treaty of Breda in 1668.

Upon its restoration, Acadia technically came under the jurisdiction of the Royal Officers at Quebec. However, the distance from Quebec and poor communications allowed the Acadians to continue their way of life without excessive interference. Royal intervention, which had given New France a new lease on life, hardly touched Acadia. This neglected step–child of France was left largely to fend for itself. Nevertheless, for the next twenty years Acadia prospered. Its population, which had been less than 400 at the time of restoration, was almost 900 by 1686. During this time more land was brought under cultivation, extending the settlement along the Annapolis and St. John valleys. But once again, conquest by the English interrupted the progress of the colony. Port Royal was captured and destroyed in 1690 by William Phips; it was restored again to France by the Treaty of Ryswick in 1697.

Acadia, in spite of continuous neglect by the mother country, enjoyed its greatest growth and prosperity from 1668 to 1697. Once again, however, the accomplishments of the hard-working Acadians were devastated by English attack.

After 1697 English raids, part of the larger French-English conflict in North America and Europe, became more frequent. In 1710 a combined British and colonial force captured Port Royal; by the Treaty of Utrecht of 1713, France gave up all claims to Acadia. The Fleur-de-Lis came down for the last time. The Acadians, conditioned by French neglect and by exposure to periods of English control, now sought to preserve and maintain their distinctive way of life under the Union Jack.

B

SETTLEMENT IN QUEBEC

French policy for establishing a North American empire emphasized the exploitation of the St. Lawrence valley. These plans could be fulfilled only if there were a sufficient population to settle the land. Settlement was to be accomplished through the seigneurial system. In 1541, Francis I gave Roberval full feudal authority to distribute land to gentlemen who would, in turn, grant land to tenants and collect annual rents. The king hoped that this system of land distribution would encourage lesser nobility in France to acquire the position of lord in the new land; that it would offer poor Frenchmen the opportunity of owning land, and of making a new start in the new land; and that it would promote colonization — the essential basis for an empire in North America — at little or no cost to the Crown.

This desire for colonization prompted the Crown to impose the obligation of bringing out settlers as one of the conditions of obtaining a monopoly. Thus, in 1597 de la Roche brought colonists to Sable Island, and in 1600 Chauvin landed fifty settlers at Tadoussac, as did de Chastes, his successor to the monopoly, in 1603. In 1604, in return for the monopoly in Acadia, de Monts agreed to settle one hundred colonists a year for ten years. These early attempts at permanent settlement failed; the settlers who survived returned to France. When Champlain founded the colony at Quebec, he planned to bring out settlers with the profits from the fur trade which he controlled. But even the dedicated Champlain had difficulty in finding willing settlers for New France.

It soon became obvious that furs were uppermost in the minds of the monopolists. Obligations for settlement were never met, and the Crown often overlooked, adjusted or rescinded these obligations. In 1627 the population of New France was only sixty-five.

In 1627 New France was given as a seigneurie — a feudal holding — to the Company of One Hundred Associates. The Company was to bring out 300 settlers a year for three years, and a total of 4,000 colonists within fifteen years. Yet in 1645, when the Company of One Hundred Associates leased part of its monopoly to the Company of Habitants, the population of New France was only 400. Obviously, the Company of One Hundred Associates had failed to live up to its responsibility. The Company of Habitants, which had agreed to bring out twenty settlers annually, likewise defaulted on this small commitment.

Since over half a century of apathetic efforts by the chartered companies had failed to provide New France with an adequate population, Royal Government was established in an effort to supply the colony with people. Colbert had envisaged a large population on the St. Lawrence, tilling the soil and developing the resources, making New France an important unit within the overall French mercantilist system. In 1665, Jean Talon was commissioned Intendant of New France to carry out Colbert's carefully prepared plans for the colony.

Abstract of the Roll of Families in the Colony of New France.

QUEBEC	
Five hundred and fifty-five	555
BEAUPRE	
Six hundred and seventy-eight	678
BEAUPORT	
One hundred and seventy-two	172
ISLAND OF ORLEANS	
Four hundred and seventy-one	471
ST. JEAN, ST. FRANCOIS AND ST. MICHAEL	
One hundred and fifty-six	156
SILLERY	
Two hundred and seventeen	217
NOTRE DAME DES ANGES AND RIVER ST. CHARLES	
One hundred and eighteen	118
COTE DE LAUZON	
Six	6
MONTREAL	
Five hundred and eighty-four	584
THREE RIVERS	
Four hundred and sixty-one	461
Total	3,418

Return of the number of men capable of bearing arms from 16 to 50 years of age, ... 1,344

There are, no doubt, some omissions in the Roll of families, which will be corrected during the winter of the present year, 1666.

(signed)   TALON

Talon's census of 1666 showed a population of 3,215 (excluding the military and the clergy) of which only 1,181 were females. This census not only confirmed the need for more settlers but also revealed a lack of women in the colony. Because of this imbalance between the number of males and females, in the 1660's and 1670's the government of France sent a number of carefully selected young women of marriageable age for the eligible bachelors of New France. However, Talon's entreaties for large-scale immigration went unheeded; Louis XIV was not prepared "to depopulate his Kingdom . . . to people Canada."

GIRLS FOR THE BACHELORS OF NEW FRANCE[48]

Talon to Colbert, November 10, 1670:

. . . it will be well to recommend strongly that those destined for this country be in no wise naturally deformed; that they have nothing exteriorly repulsive; that they be hale and strong for country work, or at least that they have some aptness for hand-labor. . . . Three or four young women of good family and distinguished for their accomplishments, would tend, perhaps, usefully to attach by marriage some officers who are interested in the Country only by their allowances and the profit of their lands, and who do not become further attached in consequence of disproportion of rank.

The girls sent last year are married, and almost all pregnant or mothers; a proof of the fecundity of this country.

Talon, therefore, pursued a policy that tended to increase the population of New France through natural growth. He encouraged early marriages, gave baby bonuses, offered pensions to fathers of large families and fined bachelors who hestitated to take the path of matrimony. Also, through the offer of free land, Talon induced many disbanded soldiers from de Tracy's forces to settle along the Richelieu River — the main avenue of Iroquois attack on New France. This was a masterful stroke that extended the settlement and strengthened its defences. By the time Talon left New France in 1672, the population of the colony had grown to more than 7,000.

"FAMILY ALLOWANCE" IN NEW FRANCE[49]

In order to encourage the natural growth of the population of New France, the following decree was issued, in 1660:

Order of the Council of State of the King to Encourage the Marriage of Boys and Girls in Canada.

. . . In order to multiply the number of children and encourage marriage, His said Majesty, in Council, has ordered and orders that in future all the inhabitants of the said country (of New France) who have up to ten children born in legitimate marriage and not priests or religious will be paid from the funds that His Majesty will send to the said country, a pension of three hundred livres for each one, and to those who will have twelve of them, four hundred livres; for this purpose, they are to represent to the Intendant of justice, police and finance, who will be established in the said country, the number of their children in the month of June or July each year, who after having verified it will order the payment of the said pension to them, one half immediately and the other half at the end of each year. His said Majesty wishes further that there be paid by the said Intendant to each boy of the age of twenty

Girls Sent Out as Brides Land at Quebec

or younger and to each girl of sixteen or younger who marries twenty livres on the day of their wedding, which will be called a present from the King; that the Sovereign Council established at Quebec for the said country make a general division of all the inhabitants into parishes and market towns, that honours be given to the principal inhabitants who will take care of the affairs of each town and community either according to their rank in the church or elsewhere, and that those inhabitants who have the greater number of children be always preferred to the others, if no reason prevents it; and that there be established some small financial levy, the proceeds to go to the local hospitals, upon fathers who have not their boys married at the age of twenty and girls at the age of sixteen. . . .

Made at the Council of State of the King, His Majesty being present, held at Paris the twelve day of April, 1660.

Signed:

Colbert

After 1678 immigration from France virtually ceased, and the problem of populating the colony was left to the people of New France. By the time of the Conquest, the population of New France had grown to almost 60,000. It was almost wholly a native-born population and distinctively *Canadien*.

LAND TENURE IN NEW FRANCE

Seigneurialism, the system of land distribution and land holding in New France, was an imitation of the feudal system of France, modified to meet North American conditions. In instituting seigneurialism, France sought to distribute, settle and cultivate the land by means of a system of land tenure familiar to the people of New France. But the feudal system of France, which had created a wealthy land-owning class thriving on a depressed peasantry, could not be transplanted without modification to the frontier conditions of New France.

The method of land distribution was relatively simple. The Crown granted a large tract of land to a *seigneur*. He subdivided the land into smaller parcels, which he distributed to *censitaires* (tenant farmers) in exchange for yearly rents and services. Each grant of land, whether a seigneurie to a seigneur or a farm to a censitaire, involved the recipient in a number of rights and obligations closely supervised by the Crown.

A seigneur was granted a seigneurie in a ceremony that took place at the Castle St. Louis in Quebec. The seigneur paid homage and swore *fealty* (loyalty) to his King, in the person of the Governor. Within forty days of taking possession of the seigneurie, the seigneur had to supply a map of his property, a census of population and an inventory of livestock, produce and the number of arpents under cultivation. In return for the seigneurie, the seigneur accepted certain obligations to the Crown. His primary responsibility was to settle habitants on the land and bring it under cultivation. He also accepted the responsibility to defend the seigneurie in time of attack. The Crown reserved the right to build forts on and roads through the seigneurie as well as the right to the oak timber for naval construction. The Crown, desiring orderly and permanent settlement, granted the seigneurie in perpetuity to the seigneur and his descendants, provided the obligations were fulfilled. If the seigneur chose to sell his holding, the purchaser had to pay the *quint* (one-fifth of the selling price) to the Crown.

Although the seigneur had the right to receive annual rents and services from his censitaires, he had certain obligations toward them. He could not refuse a land grant to an applicant. He had to build a manor house as an administrative centre for the seigneurie as well as a flour mill for the use of the censitaires. He had to provide a seigneurial court for lower justice where minor disputes between his tenants could be settled; the expense of this court had to be borne by the seigneur.

The censitaire, the essential element in the seigneurial system, owed certain fixed rents and services to the Crown and to his seigneur in exchange for his land. Like the seigneur, the censitaire was responsible for the defence of the settlement and had to give military service when called upon. The Crown also required that the censitaire clear and cultivate the land and maintain a permanent dwelling on it. Occasionally the Crown demanded several days' work on the construction of roads, bridges and fortifications.

However, most of the censitaire's seigneurial obligations were rendered to his seigneur. The censitaire had to pay *cens et rentes* (annual rent) partly in money and partly in produce, to the seigneur for the use of the land. The *banalité*, another seigneurial payment the habitant was required to pay was one-fourteenth of the flour ground at the grist mill, a small payment of bread for the use of the bake oven (if one were provided) and one of every eleven fish caught in the seigneur's streams. The censitaire also had to work on the seigneur's land several days a year at seeding and harvest time. This obligation was known as the *corvée*. The censitaire's holding passed on to his sons through inheritance; if he wished to sell it, the purchaser had to pay the *lods et ventes* (one-twelfth of the selling price) to the seigneur.

The seigneurial contracts were specific as to the mutual rights and obligations of the participants within the seigneurial system. The Crown, through the Intendant, watched over both seigneurs and habitants,* making sure they exercised no more than their lawful rights and fulfilled their legitimate obligations.

The rivers of New France determined the pattern of land grants, which were rectangular parcels of land with the width forming the river frontage. Talon did attempt to establish circular seigneuries with the manor house and church at the centre and the farms radiating from the hub of the seigneurie. The people of New France, however, favoured the rectangular strip arrangement; the frontage on the river supplied them with fish and transportation.

---

* Because of the favourable position of the censitaire in the colony, it became increasingly common to refer to the tenant as an *habitant*.

THE GROWTH OF VILLAGES[50]

Talon reports to Colbert, October 27, 1667:

Agreeably to your idea, I render the fee of the three villages which I caused to be formed in this vicinity, to strengthen this principal post by a greater number of Colonists . . . the Company, will remain the Lord proprietor thereof, holding *domaine utile* and the rights which I stipulated in the contracts of settlement distributed to the soldiers, to the recently arrived families and to the volunteers of the country who have married the young women you sent me. . . . My principal object is hereby to people the neighborhood of Quebec with a good number of inhabitants capable of contributing to its defence, without the King having any of them in his pay. I shall, as much as possible, practice the same economy in all the places at which I shall form towns, villages and hamlets, mingling, thus, soldiers and farmers, so that they may mutually instruct one another in the cultivation of the soil and be aiding to each other when necessary.

Government Map of Quebec and Environs, 1709

The seigneuries varied in size from one square mile to one thousand square miles, but the average seigneurie was twelve square miles. The size of the grant varied with the rank of the seigneur, the type of land and the location of the seigneurie. Up to 1663, most of the seigneuries were located along the north shore of the St. Lawrence River. Afterwards, some were established along the south bank of the St. Lawrence River as well as along the Richelieu River. Seigneuries along the Richelieu River were granted to disbanded soldiers, seasoned veterans of the Carignan-Salières regiment. In addition to settling the land, this move protected New France, since the seigneuries lay astride the traditional Iroquois invasion route.

The importance attached to seigneurialism as a means of colonization was reflected in the number of seigneuries granted at various times. During the rule of the Company of One Hundred Associates, between 1627 and 1663, about 50 seigneuries were granted. With the advent of Royal Government, settlement and the granting of seigneuries took on greater significance. In the single year of 1672, 46 seigneuries were awarded. Thereafter, until the Conquest, only 110 additional seigneuries were assigned. By the end of the French Régime, seigneurial holdings in New France sprawled along the major waterways. Seigneuries surrounded almost the whole Lake Champlain and Richelieu River area and extended for over 70 miles west of Montreal along the Ottawa River. The greatest number of seigneuries

was along the St. Lawrence River, in varying depths, reaching along the north shore almost as far as the Saguenay River and extending along the south side to the Gaspé Peninsula.

The tendency of feudalism in France was to create well-defined social classes. A wide social and economic gap existed between the lord and his tenants. The seigneur in New France, unlike his counterpart in France, seldom became a lord or member of a privileged aristocratic class. The habitant, unlike his counterpart in France, never became a downtrodden serf of an impoverished peasant class.

The emergence of an extensive aristocratic landowning class in New France came about slowly because the accumulation of wealth through the ownership of land was difficult. Before 1663, most seigneurs waited for population growth to raise the value of their land; that is, they held the land for speculation. But, as few settlers came, there was little demand for land and land values remained low. With the coming of Royal Government, immigration increased and the demand for land grew. However, the whole seigneurial system came under the close supervision of the Intendant. Detailed regulations specified that land be settled and cultivated, and that idle seigneuries revert to the Crown; this move was intended to prevent land speculation.

Furs were the real wealth of New France. However, in the first decade of the eighteenth century, decreasing demand for furs in Europe and declining prices adversely affected the fur trade. Many settlers turned to the more secure agricultural life. The demand for farm land grew, and land values rose. At this time, when it might have been possible for seigneurs to become a wealthy land-owning class, the state intervened and issued the Edicts of Marly in 1711. These stipulated that land was to be granted without initial payments, that the land was to be cultivated and that seigneuries which were not developed were subject to forfeiture.*

Thus, throughout the history of New France, either the absence of a demand for land or the close state surveillance of the seigneurial system prevented the development of a seigneurial class with a status similar to that of the land-owning nobility of France. At the same time, state surveillance, which demanded the settling and cultivating of the seigneuries, gave the habitant a status well above the peasant of France.

The habitant became the most essential element in the seigneurial system of New France. Seigneurialism could fulfill its purpose of colonization only if there were a sufficient number of habitants willing to settle and cultivate the land. State intervention assured that the habitant's rights and privileges were well protected; when disputes arose between seigneur and habitant, the Intendant almost invariably sided with the habitant. Furthermore, the habitant's occupancy of the seigneurie secured for the seigneur the right of tenure. Both seigneur and habitant were aware of this; the seigneur readily overlooked lapses in obligations and delinquencies in payments of seigneurial dues. Unlike the peasant in France, the habitant had an alternative. In the event that life on the seigneurie became unbearable, the wilderness with its riches and opportunities lay beckoning near-by.

To what extent was the seigneurial system of New France successful in fulfilling the purpose for which it was instituted? Seigneurialism was only moderately successful as an instrument of colonization, but it did build a framework which made possible the acceptance of a large-scale immigration to New France. The fact that immigration on a scale comparable to that of the Thirteen Colonies never materialized was not the fault of the seigneurial system. The compelling reasons that drove Englishmen to North America — unemployment in the cities, scarcity of farm land and the desire for religious freedom — were, for the most part, absent in France.†

The seigneurial system provided for a gradual but orderly growth of agricultural settlement along the rivers of New France; the seigneuries became self-sufficient rural communities. Since the seigneurie was essentially an agricultural unit, and since most of the people of New France lived on seigneuries, the seigneurial system imparted an agricultural character that the province of Quebec has retained well into the twentieth century.

VIEWS ON SEIGNEURIAL SYSTEM[51]

[a]*Lahontan saw the seigneurial system giving poor immigrants the chance to own land:*

Most of the Inhabitants are a free sort of People that remov'd hither from *France,* and brought with 'em but little Money to set up withal: The rest are those who were Soldiers . . . [when] the Regiment of *Carignan* was broke, and they exchang'd a Military Post, for the Trade of *Agriculture.* Neither the one nor the other pay'd any thing for the grounds they possess. . . .

––––––––

[b]*The Canadian historian Arthur R. M. Lower sees the seigneurial system as a deterrent to initiative:*
. . . this method of settlement encouraged the excessively paternalistic tone of French colonial life, leaving the habitant with too little self-reliance . . . the seigneurial system of settlement was only a reflection of the French system of society, which was authoritarian and paternalistic throughout. . . .

Seigneurialism was so firmly entrenched that it survived the calamitous Conquest. The English realized the chaos that would result from the destruction of such a deeply rooted way of life. They found it expedient to perpetuate and protect seigneurialism, and it was not until 1854 that circumstances in Canada permitted the abolition of the seigneurial system. Even then, some vestiges of seigneurialism lingered on, and these were finally cleared up in 1940.

* In the year 1741, twenty seigneuries reverted to the Crown.
† While a few Huguenots may have wished to emigrate to New France, French policy after 1627 discouraged their entry.

D

LIFE IN NEW FRANCE

By the middle of the eighteenth century New France had grown from a frontier fur-trading outpost of France into a vigorous colony with a distinctively *Canadien* society. Throughout its period of growth, it was motivated economically by the fur trade, governed paternalistically by representatives of the Crown, guided spiritually by Catholicism, and rooted agriculturally by seigneurialism.

Life in New France became more and more rural and centred around the seigneurie. The seigneur who owned the land (at the pleasure of the Crown), although economically not too far removed from his habitants, enjoyed considerable prestige and respect. Seigneurial dues and the ownership of land did not bring with them independent wealth for the seigneur. In many cases he had to work just as hard on his land as did the habitants on theirs, and it was not unusual for the seigneur to turn to fur trading or government service to augment his income.

What then prompted individuals to assume the position of seigneur? It offered the opportunity for lesser nobility in France, wealthy merchants, retired officers of the military and a few thrifty habitants to establish a family tradition in a new land. Although the ownership of a seigneurie did not bestow a title of nobility, the seigneur's position carried with it social prestige.

Because he was the land owner, the seigneur was a natural leader who commanded respect from the community. The habitant regarded his seigneur as a leader and adviser and recognized him as a man of rank. The government attached esteem to the position of seigneur because seigneurs were so essential to the colonization of New France. The Church also honoured the seigneur with special privileges in religious processions, festivals and other observances.

However important the seigneur may have been, it was the life of the habitant that gave rural New France its distinctive character. Although the habitant has often been depicted as a docile individual, lacking self-reliance, oppressed by a bureaucratic government, badgered by an authoritarian church and saddled with burdensome seigneurial dues, scrutiny of the habitant's life seems to dispel this impression.

It has been estimated that the annual payment of all dues came to approximately $65, for which the habitant received approximately one hundred acres of land, the use of the facilities and the protection of the seigneurie. The Intendant, Champigny, remarked that those "who really laboured on their land were well off, or at least

THE CHARACTER OF THE PEOPLE OF
NEW FRANCE[52]

Hocquart, the Intendant of New France between 1731 and 1748, gave his views on the people of New France:

The colony of New France is comprised of about 40,000 persons of all ages and sex, of which there are ten thousand men capable of bearing arms. The Canadians are naturally tall, hardy, and of vigorous temperament. As the trades are not too accomplished, and since at the establishment of the colony tradesmen were rare, necessity has made them more skillful from generation to generation. The rural inhabitants handle the axe very adroitly. They make most of their own tools for constructing their houses and barns. Several are weavers who make large cloths and fabrics which they call *droguet* which they use to clothe themselves and their families.

They like honours and praise, take pride in bravery, are extremely sensitive to scorn and the least reproof; they are selfish, vindictive, subject to drunkenness, make extensive use of alcohol, and have a reputation for not being truthful.

This portrait applies to the majority, particularly to the country folk. Those in the cities are less vice-ridden. All are attached to religion. There are very few scoundrels. They are fickle, and their conceit prevents them from succeeding as they should in the trades, agriculture, and commerce. This is linked with laziness occasioned by the length and harshness of the winter. They like hunting, sailing, and travelling and are not as gross and rustic as our peasants in France. They are all rather amenable when they are treated respectfully and when they are justly governed, but they are naturally indocile. . . .

lived very comfortably, having their fields, a goodly number of cattle and good fishing close to their home." Another Intendant referred to the independent nature of the habitants when he said that they were "naturally intractable." In 1749 Peter Kalm, a Swedish traveler, observed that the habitants were "quick, happy, and cheerful."

The habitant lived in a frame house with a straw-thatched, peaked, wooden roof. Nearby was his barn, larger than his house. Besides the grain he milled in the seigneurie's grist mill, his farm produced beans, pumpkin and squash. The maple trees yielded syrup, some of which he dried in pans to extract sugar for sweetening purposes.

The nearby forest supplied him with game. Most government officials and travelers in New France agreed that the habitants lived a much better and more comfortable life than did the peasants in France.

HOMES IN NEW FRANCE[53]

. . . their dwellings were simple and unadorned. . . . Few had any upper storey. Most contained a stable partitioned from the living quarters and located in a northern corner. Fireplaces were, of course, the only means of heating or cooking. Chimneys were of clay and this fact together with the extreme cold of the winters and the inflammable nature of the thatch or shingle roof caused many fires. Window glass may have been used by the wealthy but apparently oiled paper or thin parchment was sometimes employed as a window covering. Floors and interior walls were made of boards as were the partitions separating the living and sleeping quarters . . . the colonists used built-in bunks along the walls . . . the wealthier families had beds and other fine furniture brought from France. Chairs seem to have been very rare. Evidently long backless benches served instead. Chests of all sizes were used for a variety of storage purposes, as indeed was the case in Europe at this time. Utensils were almost all of metal. Cooking pots were of iron or copper as were the big spoons and ladles. . . . There was almost no earthenware. Practically everything for the table was made of pewter: forks, spoons, cups, plates, porringers, as well as the measuring cups used in cooking. . . .

The communal life of the habitant centred around the manor house and the church. The time to pay the seigneurial dues and religious feast days became occasions for joyous festivities. The educational needs of the children were attended to by the traveling curé, who provided them with a rudimentary education suited to the rural agricultural life of the pious, church-going habitant.

The habitant's link with the government at Quebec was the captain of militia — an official chosen from the ranks of the habitants. This unique position was created by Talon so that royal edicts could be transmitted to the habitant and the habitants' complaints could be channelled to the Intendant. This position carried with it not only prestige but also authority. When the Intendant called for a royal corvée, even the seigneur was under the command of the captain of militia. As the name implies, he was also responsible for the organization and training of the local militia.

THE CAPTAINS OF MILITIA[54]

. . . Every one of them was an *habitant* — the foremost in his locality for intelligence, activity, and good character. He was a true representative of the people, and at the same time he was an agent of the central power. . . . He dealt direct with the governor-general; with the lieutenant-governor, the judges, the curé, the seignior, and with every family. He served without pay, but the honour was great. . . .

. . . the captain of militia was not only a military personage; he was five or six other personages, all in the same man. He was recorder, and he was superintendent of roads. No government case before a tribunal was examined without his being present, notwithstanding that the official attorney was there also. Any dealings between the seignior or the curé and the civil authorities passed through him. If an accident happened somewhere, it was the captain of the place who wrote the report, and any action taken subsequently was under his management. If a farmer wished to approach the government or the judge, the captain took the affair into his hand. When a seignior trespassed on the land of a farmer, the captain came between the two, and his report was considered first of all. When the high functionaries, such as the governor, the intendant, or the judge, travelled, they were invariably the guests of the captain. He had even an eye on the mail bags and the transport of packages. He was of more importance in the community than is one of our members of parliament to-day.

It would seem that the habitant's struggle was not with his seigneur, government or church, but with the stubborn soil and difficult climate of New France. His value within the seigneurial system gave him a sense of dignity and worth, and the freedom of the frontier bred in him a spirit of self-reliance.

By the middle of the eighteenth century, approximately one-quarter of the population of New France lived in the three major centres of Quebec, Three Rivers, and Montreal and their environs. This urban population included government officials, merchants, fur traders, skilled artisans and military personnel.

As the population grew, the number of government officials increased and formed a discernible social group. It was acceptable for government officials to build fortunes through the fur trade, and most did. Favouritism played a large role in the appointment of minor officials; loyalty and service were rewarded with appointments and promotions. Thus, a firmly entrenched bureaucracy was established and perpetuated.

Dance at the Chateau St. Louis, the Governor's Residence, 1801

Another powerful group, which often included higher government officials, was the beaver aristocracy whose common interest was the wealth and control of the fur trade. The beaver aristocracy — senior government officials, company officials, wealthy merchants and high army officers — formed a small, powerful ruling clique. Some of its members sat on the Sovereign Council, others grouped themselves around the Intendant or Governor and thus wielded considerable influence and power. The beaver aristocracy lived in comparative luxury and imitated Parisian life.

THE BEAVER ARISTOCRACY[55]

Lahontan relates the state of the wealthy merchants, October 2, 1685:

Almost all the Merchants of [Montreal] act only on the behalf of the *Quebec* Merchants, whose Factors they are. The Barques which carry thither dry Commodities, as well as Wine and Brandy, are but few in number; but then they make several Voyages in one Year from the one City to the other. The Inhabitants of the Island of *Monreal*, and the adjacent Cantons, repair twice a Year to the City of *Monreal*, where they buy Commodities fifty *per Cent.* dearer than at *Quebec*. The Savages of the neighbouring Countries, whether settled or erratick, carry thither the Skins of Beavers, Elks, Caribous, Foxes, and wild Cats; all which, they truck for Fuses, Powder, Lead, and other Necessaries. There every one is allow'd to trade; and indeed 'tis the best place for the getting of an Estate in a short time. All the Merchants have such a perfect good understanding one with another, that they all sell at the same price. . . . The Gentlemen that have a Charge of Children, especially Daughters, are oblig'd to be good Husbands, in order to bear the Expence of the magnificent Cloaths with which they are set off; for Pride, Vanity, and Luxury, reign as much in *New France* as in *Old France.* . . .

Social stratification in New France seems to have been more pronounced in the towns than on the seigneuries. At the bottom of urban society were skilled artisans, shopkeepers and day labourers. These usually lived in the less favourable districts of town. It is interesting to note that the demand for skilled labourers, such as carpenters and bricklayers, was so high that these artisans could command high wages.

The most distinctive segment of New France's population was the *coureur de bois*. Few in number, free in spirit and adventurous at heart, they were in love with the Canadian wilderness. They adapted readily to the *pays des sauvages* — the ways of the Indians. Skilled in the life of the wilderness, the *coureurs de bois* were the backbone of the fur trade. They were also the explorers who pushed the frontier of New France into the interior. However, they were lost to the settlement and to the Church. Royal threats and edicts did not change their life of roaming in the forest. The Church frowned on their activities both in the settlements and in the wilderness. The clergy did not approve of their carousing and freebooting in the towns. They argued that the *coureurs de bois*, by selling brandy, undid the church's missionary work among the Indians. Nevertheless, the *coureurs de bois* cemented friendly relations with the Indians; through intermarriage they produced the mixed-blood nationality — the *Métis*.

In New France, a fur trading outpost of France, the habitant struck roots in the stubborn soil. Up sprang the *coureur de bois* to enrich the fur trade.

COUREUR DE BOIS[56]

. . . . The problem of the *coureur de bois* for both government and church in New France lay in the fact that this group of men, with the manner of life and the attitude of mind which they exhibited, constituted the most imposing, the most adamantine obstacle in the path of those who desired to establish a strong, secure, and religious colony on a lasting foundation . . . they deserted the settlements . . . by this abandonment they retarded agriculture, cripped industry, played havoc with the labours of the missionaries, undermined commercial development, diminished religious feeling, threatened the defence of the colony, insulted the traditions and conventions, and menaced the continuance of French control in the region. . . .

When the time was ripe, artisans were brought in to create more wealth. With the increase of wealth, the close relationship between habitant, *coureur de bois* and trader began to widen. Eventually, the disparity between traders and habitants resulted in a multitude of vague, undefined groups based on economic status.

8

THE FALL OF NEW FRANCE

During the early part of the seventeenth century, France and England staked claims to their respective areas of control in North America. French settlements were founded in the northern part of the North American continent and, at the same time, English colonies were established to the south, along the Atlantic seaboard. In their colonies, France and England not only transplanted their respective cultures but also sowed the seeds of their traditional rivalry.

Throughout this century, both the French and English struggled to control the extensive North Atlantic fisheries and the lucrative fur trade. In the eighteenth century, although the control of the fur trade remained a focal point for conflict, imperial considerations began to assume larger significance. The Thirteen Colonies, emerging from their confined area along the Atlantic seaboard, came into head-on conflict with the French who were determined to preserve the lands west of the Alleghenies for the fur trade and for future French settlement.

Wars between France and England in Europe had repercussions in North America and served as excuses to bring the existing rivalries into open warfare. By the middle of the eighteenth century, Indian-supported hit-and-run border raids had grown into large-scale military campaigns. In the eighteenth century, British and French regular troops transformed the punitive raids of the seventeenth century into wars that aimed at the compete elimination of the adversary from the North American continent. The struggle for imperial supremacy in North America terminated in 1760, when the French surrendered New France to Britain.

French-English rivalry in North America dates back to the early days of the seventeenth century when the contest was to control the fisheries of Newfoundland and Acadia. The history of Acadia is a recital of numerous raids by sea and land against French settlements. Wars between France and England in Europe often provided the occasion for English privateers or naval expeditions from the newly-established English colonies to raid and pillage Acadian settlements and the French fishing villages at Placentia, in the southern part of Newfoundland. Occasionally, these sorties attempted to capture and destroy Quebec as well. Such was the case when the marauding Kirke brothers destroyed Port Royal and captured Quebec in 1629. The repeated capture and destruction of French settlements in Acadia hindered the orderly and continual growth of the colony. Perhaps, because of this, Acadia never did develop to its full potential.

As furs became the important commodity of trade on the St. Lawrence, a long and bitter struggle took place between French and Dutch traders and between the French and English (who replaced the Dutch) for the control of the fur trade. Both sides enlisted Indian allies, supported them and armed them with European weapons. New France was subjected to disastrous raids and the settlement felt the "Iroquois scourge," which threatened the very existence of the colony. In retaliation, de Tracy's regular French troops, supported by colonial militia and Indian allies, carried out punitive expeditions against the Iroquois and succeeded in securing a twenty-year period of uneasy peace.

By the 1680's the Iroquois, encouraged and supported by their English backers, were making renewed incursions into the fur trade of the Great Lakes regions. Governor Jacques René de Brisay, Marquis de Denonville, won the support of the Crown for a preventative war against the Iroquois to protect the fur trade and to exclude competition from the English-Iroquois alliance. In 1687, Denonville headed a French force and struck at the Iroquois; as a result, border raids flared anew.

The War of the League of Augsburg* which broke out in Europe in 1688 intensified the existing conflict in North America. In 1689, the Iro-

A View of the Taking of Quebec, September 13, 1759

DENONVILLE'S EXPEDITION AGAINST THE IROQUOIS[57]

In a letter of June 8, 1687, Lahontan expresses doubts about the success of this expedition:

. . . The day after to morrow, Mr. *de Denonville* means to march at the Head of his little Army . . . Every body is apprehensive that this Expedition will prove as successless as that of Mr. *de la Barre*: And if their Apprehensions are not disappointed, the King lays out his Money to no purpose. For my own part, when I reflect upon the Attempt we made three Years ago, I can't but think it impossible for us to succeed. Time will discover the Consequences of this Expedition; and perhaps we may come to repent, tho' too late, of our complying with the Advice of some Disturbers of the Publick Peace, who project to enlarge their private Fortunes in a general Commotion. I lay this down for an uncontested Truth, that we are not able to destroy the *Iroquese* by our selves: besides, what occasion have we to trouble 'em, since they give us no Provocation? . . .

quois descended on the French settlement at Lachine, killed twenty-four inhabitants and captured fifty prisoners, forty-two of whom were subsequently put to death. This raid terrified the French settlements and aroused the ire of the populace. Frontenac, who in 1689 returned as Governor of New France for a second term, started a series of retaliatory measures against the real enemy — the English, whom he held responsible for the massacre at Lachine. The French, with their Indian allies, swooped down on outlaying New York and New England settlements, slaughtering the inhabitants and pillaging and devastating the countryside.

FRONTENAC'S RETURN[58]

Lahontan gives an account of Frontenac's return in 1689:

This new Governour arriv'd at *Quebec* the 15th of *October*. He came on shoar at eight a Clock

* King Henry IV, the first Bourbon King of France, issued the Edict of Nantes in 1598. This gave the Huguenots the right of private worship and of public worship in certain designated areas, equal political rights with the Catholics, the right to hold government offices, possession of some 200 fortified towns and the promise of government support to Protestant schools. In 1685, Louis XIV revoked the Edict of Nantes. William of Orange, the King of the Netherlands, was able to enlist Sweden, Spain and the Electors of Bavaria, Saxony and the Palatine against France. When William came to the English throne in 1688, he brought Protestant England into this alliance against Louis, who gave refuge to James II, the exiled King of England. The war started when France invaded the Palatinate, and the main battles took place in the Netherlands. The war against Louis XIV in North America is known as King William's War.

at Night, and was receiv'd by the Supreme Council, and all the Inhabitants in Arms, with Flambeau's both in the City, and upon the Harbour, with a triple Discharge of the great and small Guns, and Illuminations in all the Windows of the City. That same Night he was complimented by all the Companies of the Town, and above all, by the Jesuits, who upon that occasion made a very pathetick Speech, though the Heart had less hand in it, than the Mouth. . . . Several Persons made Fireworks, while the Governour and his Retinue sung *Te Deum* in the great Church. These solemn Demonstrations of Joy, increas'd from day to day, till the new Governour set out for *Monreal*; and the Conduct of the People upon this Head, afforded signal proofs of the satisfaction they had in his return, and of their resting assur'd, that his wise Conduct, and noble Spirit, would preserve the Repose and Tranquility that he always kept up, during his first ten years Government.

Resentment and vengeance resulted in further reprisals by both sides. In 1690 a New England naval expedition under Sir William Phips captured and destroyed Port Royal and seized Placentia. Later that year, Phips sailed to Quebec but was unable to obtain a surrender from the indomitable Frontenac. An English colonial army under Colonel Peter Schuyler, advancing along the Lake Champlain-Richelieu River route, failed to carry out a planned attack on Montreal.

PHIPS AT QUEBEC[59]

Phips' demand for the surrender of Quebec, October 6, 1690:

. . . I, the aforesaid William Phips, Knight, do hereby, in the name of their Excellent Majesties William and Mary, King and Queen of England, Scotland, France and Ireland, and by order of their aforesaid Majesties' government of Machazuzet Colony in New England, demand that you surrender your forts and castles undemolished with your stores; also promptly deliver your prisoners, your persons and estates to my disposal. Upon doing whereof you may expect mercy from me as a Christian according to what shall be found for their Majesties' service and their subjects' security. Should you refuse the terms I propose, I am wholly resolved, by the help of God in whom I trust, to revenge, by force of arms all wrongs and injuries offered us and bring you under subjection to the Crown of England, which if you wish, you will regret, when too late, not to have accepted the favor I offer you.

Your answer positive will be returned in an

hour by your trumpet with the return of mine. This is what I require of you upon the peril that will ensue.

Signed,   William Phips

Likewise, Frontenac's attempt to capture Albany in 1692 also failed. But his expeditions against the Mohawks. Onondagas and Oneidas were successful in that these raids brought about the final defeat of the Iroquois in 1696 and restored the wavering allegiance of New France's western Indian allies. The French also enjoyed success in Newfoundland and in the Hudson Bay region. The brilliant d'Iberville, in spectacular fashion, succeeded in destroying English coastal fishing hamlets in Newfoundland. In spite of English naval superiority, d'Iberville captured all the fur posts of the Hudson's Bay Company, except Fort Albany.

D'IBERVILLE'S EXPLOITS AT HUDSON BAY, 1697[60]

A first-hand description of the expedition against Fort Nelson:

On September 3, 1697, we arrived within sight of Fort Nelson (or Bourbon), from which the English fired some cannon-shots, which were apparently signals for the ships they were expecting from England. . . .

At day-break on the 5th, we perceived three vessels . . . being the *Hampshire* of fifty-six guns and two hundred and fifty men, the *Dering* of thirty-six guns, and the *Hudson's Bay* of thirty-two.

The combat was not at all an equal one. Nevertheless, we made the English recognize in the sequel that the King's arms could be immortalized with as much honour and glory in the seas of ice as in the other remotest parts of the earth. . . .

The enemy drew up in line. The *Hampshire* was at the head, the *Dering* followed, and the *Hudson's Bay* came behind, all three close together. The fight began at half past nine in the morning. We made straight for the *Hampshire*, which, thinking we were going to board her let fall her mainsail and shook out her topsails. After this refusal, we went to the *Dering* and out the tackle of her mainsail, and, the *Hudson's Bay* coming in front, we sent her the rest of our broadside. The *Hampshire* . . . fired a volley of musketry on our forecastle. . . . The fight grew stubborn, the three vessels keeping up a continual fire on us, with the object of dismasting our ship. . . . As they ran along by our ship, we fired our batteries which were so well aimed that they proved most effective, for we were no sooner separated from one another than the *Hampshire* immediately foundered under sail. The *Dering* which was close to us, sent us her broadside, but the encounter was a cruel catastrophe for the English, because the *Hudson's Bay* lowered her flag, and the *Dering* took flight.

The Treaty of Ryswick in 1697 ended the war in Europe and hostilities in North America came to a halt. The Treaty restored to the belligerents the territories in North America they held before the war, but France was given all English posts around Hudson Bay except Fort Albany. The restoration of Acadia and the recognition of French control of Hudson Bay greatly strengthened and enhanced French power and prestige in North America. By the end of the seventeenth century, France predominated in North America.

However, the peace ushered in by the Treaty of Ryswick was short-lived, and the events of the early eighteenth century proved this treaty to be only a temporary truce. Events in Europe again shaped the course of history in North America. The outbreak of the War of the Spanish Succession,* in 1702 offered yet another occasion for the resumption of hostilities in North America. Acadia — the guardian of the fisheries and the sentinel of the St. Lawrence — was the chief area of operations in this war; old feuds between Acadia and New England were once more renewed.

The war in Europe might have left North America untouched were it not for the advance of New Englanders northward into the territory of the Abenaki Indians. These Indians, fearful of being displaced from their lands, made an alliance with the French in Acadia. To stop the northward movement of the New Englanders, the French-Abenaki alliance employed guerilla warfare against New England settlements. The incensed New England colonists were determined to remove the threat from Acadia and possibly expel the French from the whole of North America.

The immediate objective of New England's retaliation was to eliminate the headquarters of French sea raids against New England shipping by capturing Port Royal. Several expeditions against Acadia by sea and land proved unsuccessful both in capturing Port Royal and in splitting the French-Abenaki alliance. In 1710 a naval force of 3,400 men, under the command of Colonel Francis Nicholson, was able to effect the capture of Port Royal, which he renamed Annapolis Royal in honour of Queen Anne of England. Apart from some isolated but unsuccessful raids by the French from the unoccupied areas of Acadia, the Acadians settled down to life under English rule.

The Treaty of Utrecht in 1713 brought the War of the Spanish Succession to an end. By the terms of the Treaty, as they affected North America, France gave up all claims to Acadia, Newfoundland and the Hudson Bay region. France retained Isle St. Jean (Prince Edward Island), Isle Royale (Cape Breton Island) and the St. Lawrence Valley.

The Treaty of Utrecht was a serious blow to French power in North America. The loss of Acadia and Newfoundland put the sea lanes leading to the St. Lawrence under English control. The re-establishment of English competition at Hudson Bay had serious implications for the fur trade of New France. But the Treaty did not define the rights west of the Alleghenies. The French could still realize La Salle's dream of an empire from the St. Lawrence to the Gulf of Mexico.

France recognized the precarious nature of her supply lines with New France resulting from the loss of Acadia and Newfoundland. To compensate for this strategic loss and to regain some measure of control over the approaches to the St. Lawrence, in the 1720's France started to build Louisbourg on the northeastern tip of Isle Royale. This fortified bastion was also to protect the fisheries, to provide a nucleus for future French settlement and to engage in trade with the West Indies. Designed and built by the ablest military engineers of that time, Louisbourg was to be an impregnable fortress — the Gibraltar of North America.

The English colonists were alarmed at the potential threat to their safety and trade from the mighty naval base of Louisbourg. Also, France retained present-day New Brunswick; the French insisted this region was not part of Acadia and, therefore, not ceded by the Treaty of Utrecht.

---

* Charles II of Spain died in 1700. He had willed Spain and its overseas possessions, in total, to Philip of Anjou, the grandson of Louis XIV of France. This opened the prospect of a powerful union of the crowns of France and Spain that could dominate all of Europe, indeed the world. King William III of England forged an alliance of European powers, which included Holland, Austria and later Portugal, against France. Shortly after the war started in 1702, King William died, but Queen Anne of England carried on with the war against France. It was during this war that the great English general, the Duke of Marlborough, the former John Churchill, scored his famous victories. The American phase of the War of the Spanish Succession is referred to as Queen Anne's War.

The outbreak of the War of the Austrian Succession* in 1740 provided New England with an excuse to eliminate the threat from Louisbourg.

The most outstanding event of the war in North America was the capture of Louisbourg. Governor William Shirley of Massachusetts organized a force of 4,000 militiamen which sailed for Louisbourg in 1745 under the command of William Pepperell. The British navy supplied a squadron of fighting ships, under the command of Commodore Peter Warren, to support Pepperell's force. The British navy successfully prevented reinforcements and supplies from France from reaching the beleaguered fortress. After six weeks of resistance, the bombarded and blockaded garrison surrendered. A subsequent attempted recovery of Louisbourg in 1746 proved hopelessly inadequate and ended in disaster.

THE CAPTURE OF LOUISBOURG[61]

A letter from Benjamin Franklin to his brother John:

Philadelphia [May ?], 1745
Our people are extremely impatient to hear of your success at Cape Breton. My shop is filled with thirty inquiries at the coming in of every post. Some wonder the place is not yet taken. I tell them I shall be glad to hear that news three months hence. Fortified towns are hard nuts to crack; and your teeth have not been accustomed to it. Taking strong places is a particular trade, which you have taken up without serving an apprenticeship to it. Armies and veterans need

The Expedition Against Cape Breton in Nova Scotia, 1759

skilful engineers to direct them in their attack. Have you any? But some seem to think forts are as easy taken as snuff. Father Moody's [Rev. Samuel Moody who accompanied the expedition] prayers look tolerably modest. . . .

If you do not succeed, I fear I shall have but an indifferent opinion of Presbyterian prayers in such cases, as long as I live. Indeed, in attacking strong towns I should have more dependence on *works,* than on *faith,* for, like the kingdom of heaven, they are to be taken by force and violence; and

* Charles VI, the Emperor of Austria, had no male offspring; throughout his reign (1711-1740) he made provisions to secure the lands of the Austrian Empire. In his "Pragmatic Sanctions" he decreed the terms of the succession to his throne: the lands of the Austrian Empire were to be indivisible; his eldest daughter, Maria Theresa, was to succeed him to the throne. In numerous negotiations Charles VI secured guarantees from other European rulers that they would respect the terms of the "Pragmatic Sanctions."

When Charles VI died in 1740, Maria Theresa became the ruler of the Austrian territories. Ambitious Frederick II, the Great, who came to the throne of Prussia in 1740, coveted the rich and fertile Austrian province of Silesia. He marched his well-disciplined army into Silesia, and without a formal declaration of war annexed the province to Prussia. France and Bavaria joined the attack on Austria, but England and Holland entered the war in support of Austria in a move to prevent France from seizing the Austrian (Belgian) Netherlands. The war between Britain and France in North America is known as King George's War.

in a French garrison I suppose there are devils of that kind, that they are not to be cast out by prayers and fasting, unless it be by their own fasting for want of provisions. . . .

The War of the Austrian Succession ended with the Treaty of Aix-la-Chappelle in 1748. The war in Europe was indecisive; at the conference table France successfully negotiated the restoration of Louisbourg to French control.

The return of Louisbourg to the French was a shattering blow to the New Englanders who had put so much effort into capturing it. In their disillusionment, many Anglo-Americans became convinced that England sacrificed the interests of the colonies for imperial considerations. The spectre of a reactivated Louisbourg haunted the New Englanders who feared that it might again become the base for French privateers and a threat to the safety of New England.

Britain, aware of the resentment and fears of her American colonists, founded Halifax in 1749. Situated on the shores of the fine natural harbour of Chebucto Bay, Halifax was to be a fortified naval base to counteract the effectiveness of Louisbourg. As it became apparent that the peace of Aix-la-Chappelle was only a temporary truce and a renewal of hostilities was a certainty, Britain took steps to make Nova Scotia secure for the coming struggle. Halifax, manned by British regular troops, was to be the base of operations against Louisbourg, which held the key to the St. Lawrence. Also, in an attempt to bolster the defences of Nova Scotia, Fort Lawrence was established in 1750 on the Isthmus of Chignecto to check the French who had previously built Fort Beausejour in that area.

THE FOUNDING OF HALIFAX[62]

Advertisement from the London Gazette:

Whitehall, March 7, 1748-9

A proposal having been presented unto his Majesty, for establishing a civil government in the province of Nova Scotia, in North America, as also for the better peopling and settling the said Province, and extending and improving the fishery thereof, by granting lands within the same, and giving other encouragement to such of the officers and private men lately dismissed his Majesty's land and sea service, as shall be willing to settle in the said province; and his Majesty having signified his Royal approbation of the purport of the said proposals, the Right Hon. the Lords Commissioners for Trade and Plantations, by his Majesty's command, give notice, that proper encouragement will be given to such of the officers

and private men lately dismissed his Majesty's land and sea service, and to artificers necessary in building or husbandry, as are willing to accept of grants of land, and to settle with or without families in the province of Nova Scotia.

Britain also encouraged Protestant colonization in Nova Scotia to minimize the overwhelming Catholic Acadian majority. Under Lieutenant-Governor Edward Cornwallis, some 3,000 colonists, mostly British and German Protestants, were settled at Halifax and Lunenburg along the eastern coast of Nova Scotia, away from the concentration of Acadians on the western shores of the peninsula.

To strengthen further the security of Nova Scotia, Governor Charles Lawrence took drastic precautionary measures against the Acadians in order to eliminate them as a possible threat in case of war with France. The Treaty of Utrecht of 1713 made explicit provision for the Acadians to leave Nova Scotia within a year or else remain and take an oath of allegiance to Britain. As British subjects, the Acadians would have the right to practise their religion "according to its usage of the Church of Rome, as far as the laws of Great Britain do allow the same." The Acadians refused to take this oath which, in effect, would have given them very limited religious freedom. Furthermore, the oath implied the possibility of having to bear arms on the side of the British against the French in the event of war. Some Acadians did migrate to Isle Royale and Isle St. Jean. For those who remained in Nova Scotia, the British authorities did not press the matter of the oath too seriously since they were not anxious to see a mass exodus of Acadians.

However, after the War of the Austrian Succession, the Acadians were encouraged by the French authorities at Quebec and by Abbé le Loutre, an adventurous priest, to resist the oath and to maintain their loyalty to France. Operating from Fort Beausejour, le Loutre organized resistance among the Indians and some Acadians against British authority.

THE ABBÉ LE LOUTRE[63]

[a]*Francis Parkman appraised the character of this controversial priest:*

Louis Joseph Le Loutre, vicar-general of Acadia and missionary to the Micmacs, was the most conspicuous person in the province. . . . He fed their traditional dislike of the English, and fanned their fanaticism. . . . Thus he contrived to use them on the one hand to murder the English, and on the other to terrify the Acadians. . . . Le Loutre was a man of boundless egotism, a violent spirit of domination, an intense hatred of the English, and a fanaticism that stopped at nothing. Towards the Acadians he was a despot; and this simple and superstitious people, extremely susceptible to the influence of their priests, trembled before him. He was scarcely less masterful in his dealings with the Acadian clergy; and, aided by his quality of the Bishop's vicar-general, he dragooned even the unwilling into aiding his schemes. Three successive governors of New France thought him invaluable, yet feared the impetuosity of his zeal, and vainly tried to restrain it within safe bounds. . . .

———

[b]Another appraisal of le Loutre:

It is not easy at this distance of time to appraise the character of Abbé le Loutre. Accounts of his activities have come down to us from a period when national prejudices were intensified by the bitterness of the desperate struggle for the mastery of the North American continent. It was not strange that Cornwallis thought him a scoundrel. Nor was it surprising that the French authorities esteemed him a single-minded patriot. Parkman calls him the evil genius of the Acadians. . . . That he used his influence over the Micmacs to oppose the power of Great Britain is indisputable; that he incited his Indians to acts of barbarity is probable. But, even when this is established beyond reasonable doubt, it remains true that he used a weapon which was employed by both British and French without scruple during the several phases of the American conflict. It is noteworthy that when he became a priest he did not cease to be a Frenchman. As a Frenchman he caught a vision of a new Acadia, secure in its allegiance to his king and firm in its fidelity to his church. Had he succeeded . . . his claim to eminence would not be unacknowledged. . . .

With the mounting possibility of war between France and Britain, Governor Lawrence was anxious to assure the loyalty of the Acadian population of Nova Scotia and he insisted that they take the oath of allegiance. The oath was even modified in such a way that would exempt the Acadians from military service against the French. It was thought that this concession would at least assure the neutrality of the Acadians. But the Acadians still refused to take the oath on the grounds that it would circumscribe their religious freedom. Lawrence was in a precarious situation. A large, unreliable Acadian population in Nova Scotia was a potential enemy and could be the decisive factor in time of war. The disconcerting activities of le Loutre, emanating from Fort Beausejour, reinforced the desirability of insuring

a loyal population in Nova Scotia. Also, Lawrence was under pressure from the New Englanders, who were clamouring for the fertile cultivated farms of Acadia.

After repeated attempts to have the Acadians take the oath of allegiance and with a British-French conflict imminent, Lawrence decided to meet Acadian intransigence with forcible expulsion from Nova Scotia, and deliberate dispersal of Acadians to the other British North American colonies. In 1755 the expulsion of the Acadians began. In all, between 6,000 and 10,000 Acadians were forced from their homes and transported to the English colonies. The deportation was a nightmare of hardship and suffering for the unfortunate Acadians, uprooted from their homeland and uncertain of their future. Many families were split up and some never reunited. Longfellow's poetic narrative *Evangeline*, vividly describes the tragic plight of the Acadians. The real tragedy of the expulsion of the Acadians was the utter helplessness of the hard-working people pursuing their everyday tasks, caught between the imperial ambitions of two powerful European empires.

EXPULSION OF THE ACADIANS[64]

Governor Charles Lawrence, in a letter to Col. Monckton, states why he favoured expulsion:

Halifax, 31 July, 1755

The Deputies of the French inhabitants of the districts of Annapolis, Mines and Piziquid, have been called before the Council, and have refused to take the oath of allegiance to His Majesty, and have also declared this to be the sentiments of the whole people, whereupon the Council advised and it is accordingly determined that they shall be removed out of the Country as soon as possible, and as to those about the Isthmus who were in arms and therefore entitled to no favour from the government it is determined to begin with them first; and for this purpose orders are given for a sufficient number of Transports to be sent up the Bay with all possible dispatch for taking them on board. . . .

Governor Lawrence to Board of Trade:

Halifax, 18 October, 1755

The only safe means that appeared to us, of preventing their return of their collecting themselves again into a large Body, was distributing them among the Colonies from Georgia to New England. . . .

As soon as the French are gone, I shall use my best endeavours to encourage People to come from the continent to settle their lands, and if I succeed in this point we shall soon be in a condition of supplying ourselves with provisions, and

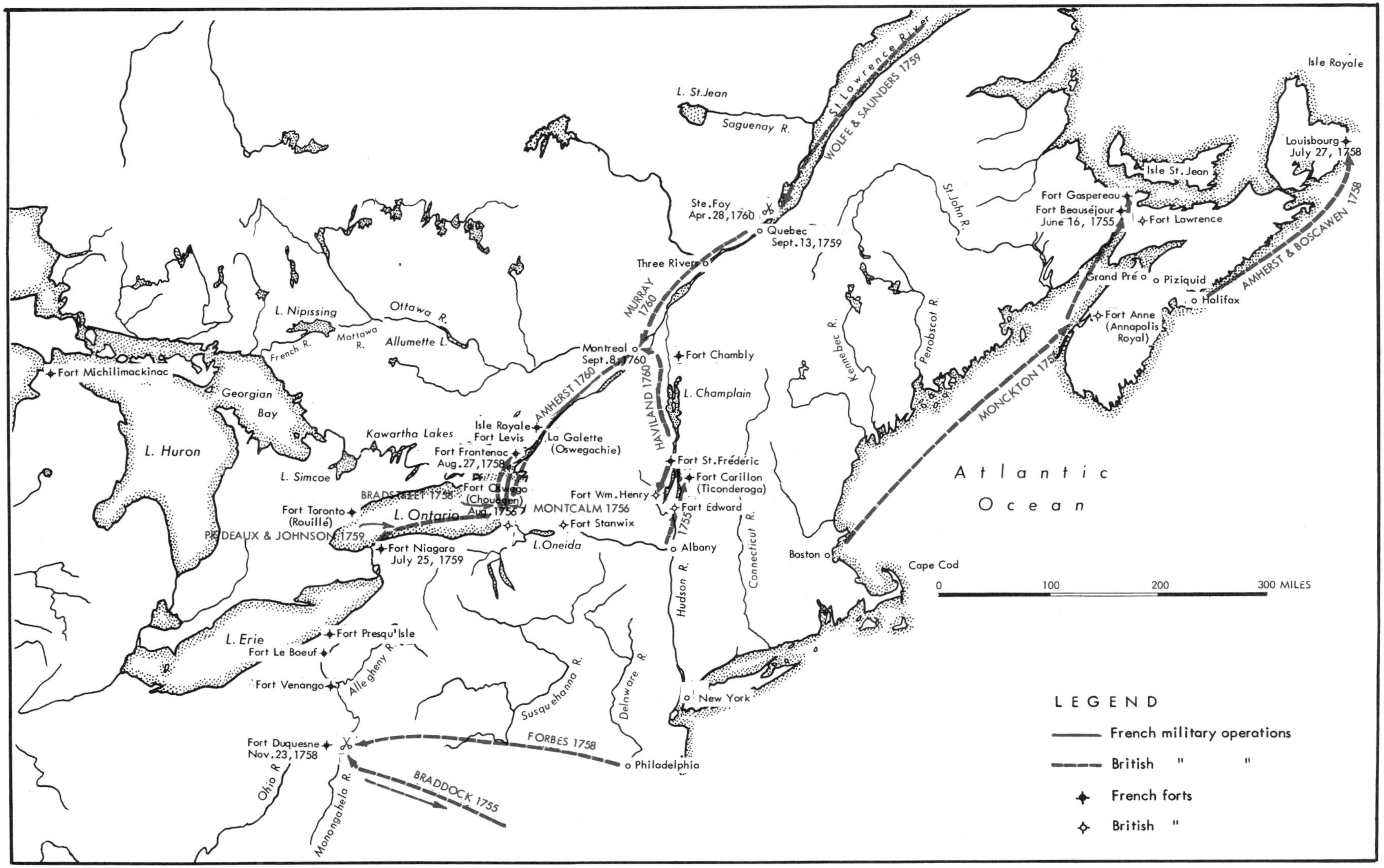

The Seven Years' War

L E G E N D

French military operations ———
British " " – – –
French forts ✦
British " ✧

300 MILES
0   100   200

Atlantic Ocean

Isle Royale

Louisbourg July 27, 1758
AMHERST & BOSCAWEN 1758

Isle St. Jean
o Halifax
✦ Fort Lawrence
Grand Pré o   o Piziquid
Fort Gaspereau
Fort Beauséjour June 16, 1755
✧ Fort Anne (Annapolis Royal)

MONCKTON 1755

St. John R.

Penobscot R.

Kennebec R.

Cape Cod
o Boston

WOLFE & SAUNDERS 1759
St. Lawrence River

Saguenay R.

L. St. Jean

o Quebec Sept. 13, 1759
Ste. Foy Apr. 28, 1760
Three Rivers o
MURRAY 1760

✦ Fort Chambly
L. Champlain
Fort St. Frédéric
Fort Carillon (Ticonderoga)
Fort Edward
1755
1755

o Albany
Hudson R.

Connecticut R.

o New York

Delaware R.

o Philadelphia

FORBES 1758

Susquehanna R.

Montreal Sept. 8, 1760
HAVILAND 1760
AMHERST 1760
La Galette (Oswegachie)
Isle Royale
Fort Lévis
Fort Frontenac Aug. 27, 1758
Fort Oswego (Chouagen)
Fort Wm. Henry 1756
MONTCALM 1756
Fort Stanwix
L. Oneida

Ottawa R.
Allumette L.
Mattawa R.

L. Nipissing
French R.

Georgian Bay

L. Huron

Fort Michillimackinac

Kawartha Lakes
L. Simcoe
Fort Toronto (Rouillé)
PRIDEAUX & JOHNSON 1759
BRADSTREET 1758
L. Ontario
Fort Niagara July 25, 1759
Fort Presqu'Isle
L. Erie
Fort Le Boeuf
Fort Venango
Allegheny R.

Fort Duquesne Nov. 23, 1758
Ohio R.
Monongahela R.
BRADDOCK 1755
BRADDOCK 1755

I hope in time to be able to strike off the great Expense of the Victualling the Troops; This . . . driving the French off the Isthmus . . . furnishes us with a large quantity of good land ready for immediate cultivation, renders it difficult for the Indians . . . to make incursions upon our settlers, and I believe the French will not now be so sanguine in their Hopes of possessing a province that they have hitherto looked upon as ready peopled for them the moment they could get the better of the English.

Although Acadia had borne the brunt of French-English conflict since the end of the seventeenth century, it was the possession of the Ohio Valley that locked the French and English in mortal combat in North America. By the middle of the eighteenth century, English fur traders were successfully encroaching upon the fur trade of the Ohio Valley. New France was even more alarmed at the formation, in 1748, of the Ohio Land Company, which contemplated bringing English settlers into this region. New France was determined to check English fur traders, to block projected English settlement of the Ohio Valley and to protect the lines of communication between New France and Louisiana.

In 1749 France laid formal claim to the Ohio Valley; an expedition led by Céloron de Blainville planted lead plates bearing the coat-of-arms of France throughout the region to signify French possession. This was followed by the construction of a chain of forts between Lake Erie and the Ohio River to bar English advances into the area. Angered by Canadian audacity, some leading Virginians who had financial interest in the Ohio Land Company raised a force of 300 men under a young officer, George Washington, to dislodge the intruders from the Ohio Valley. In 1754 Washington's force proceeded to Fort Le Boeuf where it was decisively defeated. The Canadians continued their fortification of the water routes of the Ohio Valley and built Fort Duquesne at the fork of the Ohio and Allegheny rivers. The first English colonial attempt to gain possession of the Ohio Valley had failed.

FRANCE TAKES POSSESSION OF THE OHIO VALLEY[65]

Copy of the record of the deposition of the leaden plate and the King's arms, buried at the mouth of the Ohio River, and of the inscription:

In the year one thousand seven hundred and forty-nine, we, Céloron . . . captain commanding a detachment sent by order of the Marquis de la Galissonnière, Captain-General in Canada, and the Beautiful River, otherwise called the Ohio. . . . have buried, at the foot of a red oak tree, on the South bank of the River Ohio, and opposite the point of a little island, where the two rivers, Ohio and Kanaougon, unite, . . . a leaden plate, with the following inscription engraved thereon:

Inscription

In the year one thousand seven hundred and forty-nine, in the reign of Louis XV, King of France.

We, Céloron, commanding officer of a detachment sent by the Marquis de la Galissonnière, Captain-General of New France, to reëstablish peace in some Indian villages of these Cantons, have buried this plate at the confluence of the Rivers Ohio and Kanaouagan, this twenty-ninth day of July, as a monument of the renewal of the possession which we have taken of the said River Ohio, and of all the lands on both sides, up to the source of the said rivers, as the preceding Kings of France have enjoyed, or ought to enjoy, the same, and have maintained themselves there by arms and treaties, and especially by those of Riswick, Utrecht and Aix-la-Chappelle. We have, moreover, affixed the King's arms at the same place to a tree. In testimony whereof, we have signed and drawn up this present procés verbal.

Done, at the mouth of the Beautiful river, this twenty-ninth July, one thousand seven hundred and forty-nine.

Signed by all the officers.

     Signed   Céloron

The incessant requests for help by Governor Robert Dinwiddie of Virginia convinced Britain that she could not depend on the colonial militia to wrest control of the Ohio Valley from the French and Canadians. Therefore, in 1755 Major General Edward Braddock, with two regiments of British troops was dispatched to the Thirteen Colonies. In the same year France sent Baron Dieskau with 3,000 French regulars to bolster

Louisbourg, near the Light House, 1758

New France's defences. The North American situation was rapidly deteriorating. In 1755, even before the Seven Years' War had broken out in Europe, the North American combatants had engaged each other.

In 1755, the British undertook a four-pronged attack on the circumference of New France's defences. Massachusetts' Governor William Shirley's planned attack on Fort Niagara was abandoned. Sir William Johnson's offensive against Crown Point was effectively checked by Dieskau. General Braddock's forces suffered a stunning defeat in their attempt to capture Fort Duquesne. Only Lawrence's action against Fort Beausejour was successful.

BRADDOCK'S DEFEAT AT FORT DUQUESNE, 1755[66]

In a letter to his mother, George Washington gives his view of the attack on Fort Duquesne:

Fort Cumberland, 18 July, 1755

Honored Madam,

As I doubt not but you have heard of our defeat, and, perhaps, had it represented in a worse light, if possible, than it deserves, I have taken this earliest opportunity to give you some account of the engagement as it happened, within ten miles of the French fort, on Wednesday the 9th instant.

We marched to that place, without any considerable loss, having only now and then a straggler picked up by the French and scouting Indians. When we came there, we were attacked by a party of French and Indians, whose number, I am persuaded, did not exceed three hundred men; while ours consisted of about one thousand three hundred well-armed troops, chiefly regular soldiers, who were struck with such panic, that they behaved with more cowardice than it is possible to conceive. The officers behaved gallantly, in order to encourage their men, for which they suffered greatly, there being near sixty killed and wounded; a large proportion of the number we had.

The Virginia troops showed a good deal of bravery, and were nearly all killed; for I believe, out of three companies that were there, scarcely thirty men are left alive. . . . In short, the dastardly behaviour of those they call regulars exposed all others, that were inclined to do their duty, to almost certain death; and, at last, in despite of all the efforts of the officers to the contrary, they ran, as sheep pursued by dogs, and it was impossible to rally them. . . .

The campaigns of 1755 in North America took place while France and Britain were technically at peace in Europe; it was only in 1756 that the Seven Years' War between the empires of Britain and France broke out around the world. Basic strategy for this global conflict shaped the course of the war in North America. France hoped to secure victories in continental Europe while New France was fighting a defensive war in North America. France expected to win major colonial concessions at the conference table. Britain, on the other hand, planned to cripple France by cutting her off from her overseas possessions and to fight the war in Europe to a stalemate. In North America, Britain was going to wage an all-out offensive war against New France.

General Louis Joseph Marquis de Montcalm, who had replaced Dieskau in 1756 as the commander of the French and Canadian forces in North America, promptly took to the field to secure the approaches to the St. Lawrence. In 1756 he captured Fort Oswego, the key to English entry to the Great Lakes and thus he added to the protection of the upper St. Lawrence River. The following year, in an effort to safeguard the Lake Champlain–Richelieu River approach to New France, Montcalm struck from Fort Ticonderoga and captured Fort William Henry. In the long run, these initial victories proved to be only delaying actions. In 1758, the tide of war in North America turned.

In 1757 William Pitt had risen to power in Britain, and the conduct of the war took on a new character. Pitt staffed the army with competent officers and dictated a grand strategy whereby the superior British navy was to assume the major role in the war. In 1758, a massive British offensive was hurled at the three French strongpoints — Ticonderoga, Duquesne and Louisbourg. Montcalm decided to concentrate his limited forces at Ticonderoga in the path of the most direct route to New France. Here he withstood repeated assaults by a British force three times as large as his own, under the command of Sir James Abercrombie. In the meantime, a smaller British detachment under Colonel John Bradstreet captured and destroyed Fort Frontenac. This British victory left the French forces at Fort Duquesne cut off from New France, and the fort was promptly abandoned. The Ohio Valley had fallen to the British.

The attack on Louisbourg was also successful. The British fleet effectively blockaded Louisbourg, and the mighty fortress, the "Gibraltar of North America," crumbled from broadsides of British warships. The army, under General Jeffrey Amherst, captured Louisbourg. Now, the sea lanes to Quebec were wide open to the British navy.

With the fall of Louisbourg and Fort Frontenac, Montcalm had no alternative but to retreat to

Quebec where he could deploy his limited forces in a last-ditch defence of New France. In 1759, as he withdrew to Quebec, Montcalm left a small force at Ticonderoga to fight a delaying action against the advancing British troops. General Amherst, fresh from victory at Louisbourg, proceeded cautiously down the Lake Champlain-Richelieu River route. This caution and the tenacious stand of Montcalm's rear-guard force saved Montreal from attack that year. But at the same time, the British fleet, commanded by Admiral Saunders, was transporting General James Wolfe's 9,000 troops up the St. Lawrence River towards Quebec.

The decisive battle in the North American phase of the Seven Years' War was about to begin. With little success, Saunders' ships bombarded the natural fortress of Quebec. A landing attempt by British troops at Beauport proved unsuccessful; the French defences held. As winter was approaching, Wolfe was faced with the possibility of having to withdraw from Quebec. In a desperate move to land his army, Wolfe was fortunate in discovering the poorly guarded Anse au Foulon, and through this cove his troops effected a surprise landing on the night of September 12, 1759. Montcalm chose to engage Wolfe's forces on the open fields of the Plains of Abraham, and after a short but bitter struggle, in which both Montcalm and Wolfe were killed, Quebec fell to the British.

THE DEATHS OF MONTCALM AND WOLFE[67]

John Knox, one of Wolfe's officers on the Plains of Abraham, offers this account:

The Sieur de Montcalm died late last night; when his wound was dressed and he settled in bed, the Surgeons who attended him were desired to acquaint him ingenuously with their sentiments of him, and, being answered that his wound was mortal, he calmly replied, 'he was glad of it:' his Excellency then demanded, 'whether he could survive it long, and how long?' He was told, 'about a dozen hours, perhaps more, peradventure less.' 'So much the better,' rejoined this eminent warrior; 'I am happy I shall not live to see the surrender of Quebec.' . . .

After our late worthy General Wolfe, of renowned memory, was carried off wounded, to the rear of the front line, he desired those who were about him to lay him down; being asked if he would have a Surgeon? he replied, 'it is needless; it is all over with me.' One of them then cried out, 'they run, see how they run.' 'Who runs?' demanded our hero, with great earnestness, like a person roused from sleep. The Officer

answered, 'The enemy, Sir: Egad they give way every-where.' Thereupon the General rejoined, *'Go one of you, my lads, to Colonel Burton—; tell him to march Webb's regiment with all speed down to Charles's river, to cut off the retreat of the fugitives from the bridge.'* Then, turning on his side, he added, *'Now, God be praised, I will die in peace:'* and thus expired.

In the spring of 1760, a French force from Montreal, under Chevalier de Lévis, made a gallant attempt to liberate New France. General James Murray, the new commander of the British forces, met this French army near Ste. Foy, where he suffered a severe defeat. But Quebec's fate was sealed when, on May 9, the British fleet appeared. The British forces from Lake Champlain, Fort Frontenac and Quebec then converged on Montreal to eliminate the last French stronghold. On September 8, Governor Pierre de Vaudreuil Cavagnal surrendered the whole of New France to General Amherst; 150 years of French rule came to an end.

New France suffered from a basic weakness which inevitably led to her defeat. It could hardly be expected that 60,000 Canadians could defend New France's far-flung frontiers against the overwhelming pressure of the million and a half Englishmen of the Thirteen Colonies in a prolonged war. The British forces engaged in the North American phase of the war were about equal in number to the entire population of New France. The sheer weight of numbers alone assured English victory.

In the unequal struggle in North America, New France was also handicapped by dependence on the mother country for supplies and reinforcements. Manufacturing hardly existed in New France; her farms produced little more than sufficient food for home consumption in time of peace. France was too preoccupied with the war in Europe to lend much assistance to her beleaguered colony. Moreover, the British navy reigned supreme on the high seas and was effectively able to blockade New France from the few supplies and reinforcements that France did send. The British forces, on the other hand, could draw on the more ample manpower and supplies of the Thirteen Colonies, on the resources of Britain if need be and on the support of the British navy.

A centralized New France could more than hold her own against the divided Thirteen Colonies in a hit-and-run warfare of short duration, but lack of men and resources made her especially vulnerable in the face of concerted action on the part of the British and Anglo-Americans in a large scale, protracted war.

III

THE BRITISH FOUNDATION

Under British colonial rule, the French Canadians, a defeated people, lived in uncertainty as to their future. Britain had the problem of governing a people of different religion, customs and culture. Both victor and vanquished faced the problem of adjustment.

For four years, pending the conclusion of the Seven Years' War in Europe and of a treaty of peace, a military regime carried on the administration of New France. During this time, Britain pursued a policy of leniency to gain the goodwill of the new subjects. The Treaty of Paris in 1763 settled the final disposition of what had been French possession in North America; New France became part of the British Empire.

The Proclamation of 1763 replaced military rule with a civilian government. The Proclamation also outlined the shrunken boundaries of Quebec, its form of government, the laws to be used and the status of the Roman Catholic Church. However, the terms of the Proclamation were so vague that the French Canadians were apprehensive about their status within the Empire and the newly arrived British commercial class in Quebec was incensed by what it claimed was the denial of the rights of Englishmen. Obviously, the Proclamation failed to meet the needs of both the old and new subjects.

The Quebec Act of 1774, passed by the British Parliament, was to provide a clear-cut and realistic approach to replace the ill-conceived Proclamation. It was an act of expediency prompted by British imperial self-interest and by the recognition that Quebec was to remain French and Catholic. On the whole, it was a lenient and generous Act for a defeated people. The Quebec Act was built on Guy Carleton's premise that in order to assure British possession of Quebec and to thwart the ambitions of the Thirteen Colonies, it was necessary to secure the unwavering loyalty and collaboration of the seigneurs and clergy. These "natural" leaders of the Canadians, Carleton believed, would generate the loyalty of the inhabitants. The magnanimous measures embodied in the Quebec Act and the disregard for the British minority in Quebec inevitably brought forth reactions and repercussions.

The imperial policy for North America, as unveiled in the Royal Proclamation of 1763, caused great resentment in the Thirteen Colonies. The implementation of the Quebec Act — which withheld representative government — was regarded by the Americans as yet another example of Britain's tyrannical intentions. Within two years, the American Revolution had begun. The unity of the North American continent imposed by the British military successes during the Seven Years' War was shattered. The revolt of the Thirteen Colonies ended with the division of British North America and the withdrawal of the Thirteen Colonies from the Empire. An ill-defined boundary separated the recently victorious republican United States from the loyal monarchical colonies of British North America.

The American Revolution affected British North America no less than it did the Thirteen Colonies. The Revolution drove 50,000 loyal British Americans into Nova Scotia and Quebec. The sudden and unprecedented population increase with the coming of the United Empire Loyalists, as the immigrants were called, created problems for the northern colonies. But they also gave British North America new directions, new institutions, new vitality and a strong tradition of loyalty to the British Crown.

The influx of Loyalists posed new problems for Great Britain — how to meet the demands of the newly arrived loyal British subjects without alienating the French-Canadian majority. The Constitutional Act of 1791, by dividing Quebec into Upper and Lower Canada, would allow the French and English to live unhindered in their separate environments. The two provinces were given representative governments which had been denied the British minority in both the Proclamation and in the Quebec Act. The Constitutional Act contained the seeds of future discord but, for the time being, it solved the complicated problem of the Loyalists in a predominantly French-speaking and Catholic Canada.

It was not loo long before Canada was to face, once again, invading American armies. The Treaty of Versailles of 1783 did not create an enduring peace between the newly established United States and the British North American colonies. Friction soon arose over the ambiguous wording of the treaty itself as well as Britain's delay in implementing certain provisions of the treaty. Peaceful negotiations and conciliation did bring about mutual agreement on most issues. But the Napoleonic Wars in Europe created strained relations between Britain and the United States, a fact which led to an America invasion of British North America. The war of 1812 was another "war of independence" — Canadian independence. The conclusion of the war affirmed and assured the right of the British North American colonies to a separate existence on the North American continent.

In the meantime, while the Maritime colonies and the Canadas were being reshaped and refitted into the Second British Empire, a vast and exclusive fur trading empire west of the Great Lakes was rapidly developing. By the end of the eighteenth century, the relentless search for new fur-bearing areas and the keen competition between the rival fur companies had driven explorers and fur traders to the Arctic and Pacific Oceans. The continent had been spanned and the fur frontier pushed to its geographic limit. Meanwhile, the frontier of settlement was also moved a step farther west as the tiny Selkirk Settlement took hold in the rich prairie soil of the fertile Red River Valley.

9

THE PROBLEMS OF CONQUEST: 1760-1763

The Seven Years' War in North America ceased on September 8, 1760, with the surrender of Montreal. Governor Vaudreuil, the representative of the King of France, conferred with General Amherst, the Commander-in-Chief of all British forces in North America, to negotiate the surrender. It was not an unconditional surrender. Discussion took place and Vaudreuil laid down certain conditions for the capitulation. Not all were accepted. Nor were all rejected; some were left for future decision by the English Crown. The final document resulting from the negotiations between Amherst and Vaudreuil — the Articles of Capitulation — outlined the terms under which the French and Canadians surrendered to the British in North America. The Articles were binding until a formal peace was concluded between France and Britain, who were still at war in Europe. The final disposition of New France had to await the conclusion of the Seven Years' War.

REASONS FOR RESTORING CANADA TO THE FRENCH[68]

After the fall of Quebec, while Montreal was still holding out and the Seven Years' War was still going on, articles appeared in the British press about the terms of peace. Some even suggested the restoration of Canada to France. The following excerpt is from a humorous letter, attributed to Benjamin Franklin, which appeared in The London Chronicle *of December 27, 1759:*

2. We should restore it [Canada], lest, thro' a greater plenty of beaver, broad-brimmed hats become cheaper to that unmannerly sect, the Quakers.
3. We should restore Canada, that we may *soon* have a new war, and another opportunity of spending two or three millions a year in America; there being great danger of our growing too rich,

our European expences not being sufficient to drain our immense treasures.
4. We should restore it, that we may have occasion constantly to employ, in time of war, a fleet and army in those parts; for otherwise we might be too strong at home.
5. We should restore it, that the French may, by means of their Indians, carry on . . . a constant scalping war against our colonies, and thereby stint their growth; for otherwise, the children might in time be as tall as their mother.
. . . Only permit me to suggest, that there is one method of avoiding fairly all future dispute about the propriety of *keeping* or *restoring* Canada; and that is, *let us never take it.* The French still hold out at Montreal and Trois Rivières, in hopes of succour from France. Let us be but *a little too late* with our ships in the river St. Laurence so that the enemy may get their supplies up next spring, as they did last, with reinforcements sufficient to enable them to recover Quebec, and there is an end of the question. . . .

The Capitulation stated that those who fought for France in North America had to lay down their arms. British military forces now took possession of all of New France, a territory that stretched from the Atlantic to the Prairies, and from Hudson Bay to the Gulf of Mexico. Provision was made for those who wished to leave Quebec to be transported to France. Senior government officials, higher army officers and some merchants and businessmen took advantage of this offer. The Canadians, as a rule, chose to remain in the land of their birth. They had neither the desire nor the motive to go to unfamiliar France. Most of them had never been to France, and many were third generation Canadians. Those who remained were assured that their property would be left undisturbed. The people of New France were allowed the freedom to practice their Roman

Rue des Récollets, Quebec City, c. 1760

Catholic faith. While the orders of nuns were allowed to carry on their work undisturbed, the Jesuits, Recollets and Sulpicians were not so privileged. The question of the use of French laws was left for later consideration. The terms of the capitulation were, perhaps, more generous than the Canadians had expected.

THE CAPITULATION[69]

Arthur Maheux attempts to give an account of the impact of capitulation on the French Canadians:

Fear of deportation was very strong. . . . Scarcely four years had passed since the deportation of the Acadians, an event which the people of Quebec could not forget as they had welcomed some of these Acadians to their city and received them into their homes. . . . But what would be the fate of the Canadians? Born in America . . . indeed the greater number established for three, four, five or more generations, they had no connections in France, not even relatives able to receive and harbor them. Their country, their only country, was America . . . [they] would not want to leave for France, but would prefer some corner of America. . . .

But would the English accord these privileges? Or would they repeat the cruel stroke of 1755? . . .

When . . . the terms of the surrender had been granted . . . there was unquestionably tremendous relief. . . . The majority were doubtless grateful for the enemy's generosity and began to think that it would be possible to get along with these English Protestants.

For the first time since 1632, when the Kirkes restored Quebec to the French, the Canadians no longer had any relations with France. Now they had English rulers and military rulers at that. . . .

The Canadians slowly awakened from their sense of disbelief in the Conquest to the reality of the Capitulation. Although many hoped that New France might be restored to France either by conquest or by negotiations at the conference tables in Europe, they nevertheless felt that they had been abandoned by France during the war. They blamed, with justification, the rapacious Bigot, Vaudreuil and other French officials for the defeat. France had lent very little military aid to New France during the war. The people in France were generally indifferent to the fall of New France; only in commercial circles which had business connections with New France was there any concern. Perhaps Voltaire expressed a widely held view when he said that "France could be quite happy without Quebec," and that it was not worth worrying over the loss of those "few acres of snow." The Canadians had to face the reality of the conquest and, under a foreign rule, to conserve their distinctive *Canadien* way of life which had been born and nurtured on the shores of the St. Lawrence.

THE IMPACT OF THE CONQUEST[70]

Michel Brunet, a French-Canadian historian, assesses the impact of the conquest on French-Canadian society:

The judicious conduct of the British authorities greatly helped to reconcile Canadians to the new regime. Amherst, Murray, Gage, Burton and Haldimand were prudent administrators, careful to reassure a population which had expected the worst. Official French propaganda had repeatedly stated that defeat would mean terror. But the measures taken by the military commanders aided a rapid return to normal daily life. . . .

. . . The victors had before them an exhausted populace, ready to be governed. All circumstances and factors helped to render the establishment of British rule easy.

The *elite* of Canadian society showed a spirit of open collaboration with the victors. . . .

Canadians of the upper class, who refused to submit to the victors, emigrated. . . . The most powerful businessmen understood that their enterprises would not prosper without the British commercial system.

. . . Deprived of the indispensable backing of its mother country, left to its own resources, submitting to the rule of a foreign upper class, French Canada lived in a state of subordination.

For the majority of the population there was no question of emigration. . . . The clergy . . . were ready to . . . do homage to "the legitimate authority". . . .

The Canadian business men . . . hoped to improve their lot quickly. . . .

As to the lowest strata . . . the immense majority . . . there was a strong impression of having been betrayed by those in authority . . . they took refuge in a state of passive resistance. . . . Sooner or later, they thought, the "Londoners", the English, would be forced to quit the country.

The Seven Years' War and the aftermath of defeat created problems for both the Canadians and the British government. The war left a trail of devastation and an impoverished economy. During the war, the fur trade — the life-blood of New France — had been ruined and agriculture neglected. After the war, under British rule, French paper money in circulation was worthless and many Canadians were financially ruined. Also, New France's economic ties with France were severed. With the exodus from New France of higher administrative and commercial officials, the upper layer of French governmental and economic life disappeared. What was left in Quebec was a largely rural agricultural population. Thus the balance between the progressive commercial element and the conservative agricultural group in Canadian society had been upset. To fill the commercial void which the Conquest had created, British merchants (mostly from the American colonies), anxious to provision the British forces and to inherit and revive the once lucrative Canadian fur trade, came to Quebec.

An immediate problem for the British government was the establishment of an interim government to rule until the conclusion of the war in Europe. This temporary government took the form of rule by the occupying British forces — Military Rule. To facilitate the administration of the country, the traditional division of Quebec into the three districts of Quebec, Three Rivers and Montreal, each headed by a military governor, was retained. The Governors — General James Murray of Quebec, Colonel Ralph Burton of Three Rivers and General Thomas Gage of Montreal — were responsible to General Jeffrey Amherst, the Commander-in-Chief of all British forces in North America, with headquarters in New York.

VIEWS ON MILITARY RULE[71]

Conflicting views, ranging from "tyranny" to "highly laudable," of the Military Regime have been expressed by French-Canadian historians. Two views are presented below:

[a]*Francis-Xavier Garneau writing at mid-nineteenth century:*

The victors, on their part, took fit measures for making sure of their precious conquest. Amherst . . . divided Canada into three departments, corresponding to the old divisions, and put them under martial law. . . .

This martial system was adopted in violation of the capitulations, which guaranteed to the Canadians the right of British subjects . . . they [Canadians] saw their . . . whole social organization upset, to make room for the most insupportable of all tyranny, that of court martial. . . .

The military organization adopted, attested the fear Canadian resistance to alien domination had

British Soldiers Drawing Wood from Ste. Foy to Quebec, 1760

inspired, and its existence was approbated in Britain. . . . Yet the colony remained four years under martial law. This epoch in our annals is designated as the "Reign of the Soldiery" (*le règne militaire*).

bMarcel Trudel writing at mid-century:

But because this regime bears the name of military regime, one might be tempted to consider it a regime of oppression . . . minute examination . . . does not warrant us to cry out against oppression. . . .

. . . the military regime . . . presents itself to us as a very commendable regime and it seems to deserve still more praise. . . .

This military regime, however, is not perfect . . . one can be certain that he [the habitant] has badly endured the immediate presence of the conqueror.

The historian Garneau . . . does not seem to have understood that England absolutely could not give the Canadians the privileges accorded English subjects because the Canadians were to be considered subjects of France as long as a final treaty has not decided their fate. . . .

cThe historian A. L. Burt expressed an Anglo-Saxon view of the Military Regime:

The military heel has ground out-groans from conquered people, in many lands. But the rule of the soldier, though proverbially heavy, was particularly light in Canada during the first few years of British rule. These years are known as the military régime or *règne militaire*. . . .

On looking back over all the enactments of the military regime, one is struck by the fact that the governors did more than follow the forms of the old regime. They caught its best spirit. They speak not as conquerors to a subject race, but as fathers to their children; their words are less stern commands than paternal admonitions. . . .

dThe Captains Of Militia Under British Rule:

. . . At the time of the conquest, the captain of militia was still in all the glories of his situation. The first step taken by General Amherst was to put the militia officers at the head of their parishes, and they continued to be for many years under British rule the intermediaries between all classes and the central power. Indeed, as late as the beginning of the nineteenth century, after representative institutions had been established, they retained their position; and it was not until 1868 that they finally disappeared. After 1760 there was no more drill, but the captain of militia remained because of his other functions and his recognized usefulness. The Militia Act of 1868 abolished the militia on paper, and thereby all that had been kept of the old system.

Military rule was to pursue a policy of leniency, conciliation and justice in order to gain the confidence, and possibly the friendship, of the Canadians and to avoid major dislocations in the life of the country. The governors were provided with

French-speaking secretaries. The Canadian captains of militia became Justices of the Peace and local magistrates to settle minor disputes among the inhabitants. The seigneurial system was left untouched. The practice of Catholicism was allowed and the priests were permitted to collect tithes, but the government authorities took no part in the enforcement of such payments. British troops, with few exceptions, orderly and well behaved, quickly won the respect of the Canadians. The British forces, by paying hard cash for local products and services, aided the failing economy of the country.

British Military Rule left the fundamental structure of New France undisturbed. It did not interfere with the laws, religion and language; and it retained government by council, the seigneurial system and the captains of militia.

Although the Seven Years' War in North America ended with the surrender of Montreal in 1760, the guns in Europe were not silenced until 1762, and it was not until February 1763 that the Treaty of Paris formally ended the war. Many British statesmen argued that Britain ought to take the sugar island of Guadeloupe and return Canada to France. Many French statesmen were just as eager to retain Guadeloupe and cede Canada to Britain. Pressure from influential British commercial interests, who did not want Guadeloupe in the British Empire, and consideration for the security of her American colonies prompted Britain to keep Canada.

CANADA OR GUADELOUPE[72]

. . . 'Some,' said Pitt in the House of Commons, 'are for keeping Canada, some Guadeloupe; who will tell me which I shall be hanged for not keeping?' . . . The West Indies, it was said, supplied England with more of the goods she needed; the American continent already, it was answered, provided a better market for English manufactures,

and . . . this market was likely to improve. One foreseeing writer urged that it would be better to retain the West Indian conquests than North America, 'which cannot be prevented from rising to independency and Empire'. . . . But the weight of authority was in favour of retaining Canada . . . that Senegal, Goree and Guadeloupe should all, if necessary, be sacrificed to the paramount need of giving security to the continental colonies by removing the French from Canada. . . . On the same side, too, was Pitt's friend Beckford, representing the powerful interests of the sugar-planters, who were afraid that the acquisition of the French sugar islands might infringe upon their monopoly. . . . 'I state to you the importance of America,' he Pitt said in one of his later speeches; 'it is a double market, the market of consumption and the market of supply'; and in another he called America 'the fountain of our wealth, the nerve of our strength, the nursery and basis of our naval power.' This care for our naval power made him attach even greater importance to the Canadian fisheries than to Canada itself. While determined to take enough of Canada to give secure boundaries to the American colonists, he was indifferent whether the rest of Canada or Guadeloupe and Goree were given up so long as the fisheries remained British.

By the terms of the Treaty of Paris relevant to North America, France gave up all claims to Canada, Cape Breton and Acadia. France transferred the possession of Louisiana to Spain; Britain gained Florida. France was given the islands of St. Pierre and Miquelon which were to be unfortified fishing stations, and fishing rights off the shores of Newfoundland. The Canadians were granted the right to practice their Catholic religion and freedom of worship "according to the rites of the Romish Church, as far as the laws of Great Britain permit."

10

THE PROBLEMS OF SOVEREIGNTY

A

ROYAL PROCLAMATION, 1763

After the Treaty of Paris had finalized the status of New France, it was necessary to replace military rule with civilian government. But before Britain could announce governmental changes in an official proclamation, Pontiac's uprising, erupting in the summer of 1763, profoundly influenced the formulation of British policy for North America.

The end of the Seven Years' War in North America eliminated the English-French competition in the fur trade, a fact which resulted in the Indians receiving lower prices for their furs. More disturbing to the western Indians was the influx of settlers from the colonies into the Ohio Valley. In the past, the French had come into the area as traders and had depended on the Indians for furs; now, the English colonists came as settlers and displaced the Indians. Pontiac, the chief of the Ottawas, was successful in welding a coalition of many Indian tribes south of the Great Lakes and east of the Mississippi in a united resistance against the encroaching English settlers. The uprising, an almost simultaneous attack against the British western posts, was so successful that most of them fell under the devastating onslaught. The enormous property damage and loss of life indicated the magnitude and intensity of the revolt. Many tribes deplored the loss of the French traders, and spoke of the new French-Indian alliance which would drive the English intruders back across the Alleghenies.

Although the uprising was eventually crushed, the British government was disturbed by the prospect of a renewal of Indian wars in North America. The Royal Proclamation, which the British Crown enacted on October 7, 1763, initiated a policy of pacification of the western Indian tribes, and also proclaimed the form of government which was to replace military rule.

The Proclamation established a new boundary which confined the colony of Quebec — the new name given New France — to a small territory approximating the seigneurial holdings on the St. Lawrence. The boundary of Quebec ran from the mouth of the St. John River to its source, then in a straight line southwest through Lake St. John and continued to the southeast tip of Lake Nipissing. From there the boundary ran southeast to the forty-fifth parallel and along this latitude across the St. Lawrence River and Lake Champlain to the "High Lands which divided the Rivers that empty themselves into the said River St. Lawrence from those which fall into the Sea." Then it followed northward to the Bay of Chaleur, and across the Gulf of St. Lawrence to the mouth of the St. John River.

South of the colony of Quebec, a Proclamation Line, following the western extremities of rivers flowing to the Atlantic, set the limits for Anglo-American expansion. The lands west of this line and west of the boundaries of Quebec were reserved for the Indians. Settlement west of these limits was expressly prohibited; trade in this area could be carried on only by licence. Thus the Ohio Valley, which had precipitated the Seven Years' War in North America, was, by British proclamation, denied to both Quebec and the British-American colonies. The territory of Rupertsland, the chartered land of the Hudson's Bay Company, remained intact. The land east of the St. John River, present-day Labrador, was joined to Newfoundland for the more effective British control of the fisheries. Nova Scotia included Cape Breton, Prince Edward Island and present-day New Brunswick.

By arresting the westward expansion of the Thirteen Colonies, Britain hoped to secure peace

Pontiac in Council

with the Indians and to encourage a northward movement of British-American colonists to Quebec. Such a migration did not materialize — only a handful of merchants came to Quebec. Unlike Acadia in 1755, there was no forced (or voluntary) exodus of Canadians leaving large stretches of fertile, cultivated lands to be occupied.

The new civil government for Quebec was to be a conciliar government consisting of an appointed Governor and an appointed Council. In 1764, James Murray was appointed Governor-General of the whole colony with headquarters at Quebec; he appointed a Council consisting of the Lieutenant-Governors of Three Rivers and Montreal, a Chief Justice, a Surveyor-General of Customs and eight people chosen "from amongst the most considerable of the Inhabitants of, or Persons of Property in Our said Province." The laws of England, which applied to Quebec, specifically prohibited Roman Catholics from holding office; thus the Council which was to guide the destiny of the overwhelming Canadian majority was selected from the few hundred Protestants. The Council was to advise the Governor-General, act as a court of appeal and pass laws and regulations for the colony. It was understood that this was an interim government, and that an elected legislative assembly — a well-established British institution — would be instituted "as soon as the state and circumstances of the said Colony will admit thereof."

It seems that the Proclamation intended to replace French laws with the laws of England, but Murray soon found this to be impractical. It was necessary to retain certain laws and regulations from the French regime. In 1764, Murray created two courts of law. A Superior Court, or Court of King's Bench, would deal with more serious cases, and would judge according to the laws of England and existing regulations of the colony. A lesser court, or Court of Common Pleas, would hear minor cases; here the old French laws were largely retained; Canadian lawyers could practice, and Canadians could serve on juries. That is, the Court of Common Pleas would dispense with the services of the captains of militia who, in the past, settled minor disputes. The duality in the legal system, which was to satisfy the old (British) and new (Canadian) subjects, inevitably led to confusion and dissatisfaction.

The Proclamation was neither clear nor specific about the extent of religious rights in the colony. Freedom of worship was continued, but further instructions to Murray seemed to indicate the intention of establishing the Protestant Church and the setting up of Protestant schools as a means of assimilating the new subjects. Although Murray mistrusted the *curés* who were in close touch with the inhabitants, he pursued a policy of obtaining the co-operation and goodwill of the higher clergy.

MURRAY INSTRUCTED TO ANGLICIZE FRENCH CANADIANS[73]

December 7, 1763

And to the End that the Church of England may be established both in Principles and Practice, and that the said Inhabitants may by Degrees be induced to embrace the Protestant Religion, and their Children be brought up in the Principles of it; We do hereby declare it to be Our Intention, when the said Province shall have been accurately surveyed, and divided into Townships, Districts, Precincts or Parishes, in such manner as shall be hereinafter directed, all possible Encouragement shall be given to the erecting Protestant Schools in the said Districts, Townships and Precincts, by settling, appointing and allotting proper Quantities of Land for that Purpose, and also for a Glebe and Maintenance for a Protestant Minister and Protestant School-Masters; and you are to consider and report to Us, by Our Commissioners for Trade and Plantations, by what other Means the Protestant Religion may be promoted, established and encouraged in Our Province under your Government.

The Proclamation boundary aroused universal dissatisfaction in the Thirteen Colonies. The Ohio Valley, for which they had fought during the Seven Years' War, was again denied them. Again, the Alleghenies marked the western limit of colonial expansion.

PETITION OF MERCHANTS OF ALBANY TO THE LORDS OF TRADE[74]

To the Right honourable the Lords Commissioners for Trade & Plantations.
The petition of us the Subscribers being Indian Traders & Mercts residing in the City and County of Albany in America.

March, 1764

Humbly Sheweth

That your Petitioners as well as their Ancestors have for near a Century and a half carried on a free trade with the Indians living Westward of Albany . . . the trade whilst centured at Oswego, flourished . . . without being subject to any

Prohibition of Rum or other spiritous liquors, till the commencement of hostilities by the French and Indians on the Ohio . . . subsequent Armies in the reduction of Niagara and afterwards Canada with its dependencies, encouraged your Petitioners to use their endeavours in carrying on this valuable branch of Trade in a more extensive manner than had hitherto been practized, tho in pursuit of this plan your Petitioners by some new invented regulations were totally prohibited from carrying rum and other spiritous liquors, the enforcement of which regulations your Petitioners conceive was founded on a mistaken notion, if not on some lucrative views. . . .

———

Your Lordships Petitioners beg leave farther to observe that unless some salutary remedy be put in practice your Petitioners conceive it may occasion a Stagnation in said Trade . . . the Indians . . . having a safe retreat to the Mississippi, where it is the interest of the French not only to protect but also to encourage them. . . .

The Proclamation evoked bitter outcries from the British merchants who had come into Quebec in the wake of the French defeat. These merchants had looked forward to an elected legislative assembly such as they were accustomed to in the Thirteen Colonies and which had been granted to Nova Scotia in 1758. But the Proclamation held forth only the promise of an assembly. To the merchants, a legislative assembly was a means of gaining political power and control of Quebec. By controlling an assembly, they could govern the colony for the benefit of the British commercial community and limit the rights of the Canadian majority. They felt that British subjects ought not to be denied British institutions. Murray, on the other hand, held that it was neither just nor advisable to hand over such wide law-making powers to the less than 500 British Protestants who would dominate 80,000 Canadian Catholics. The granting of an assembly to 450 "contemptible sutlers" would nullify the goodwill he had created by his lenient, conciliatory and just treatment of the new subjects.

PETITION OF THE QUEBEC TRADERS FOR A LEGISLATIVE ASSEMBLY: OCTOBER 29, 1764[75]

Your Petitioners . . . beg leave also most humbly to petition that it may please your Majesty to order a House of Representatives to be chosen in this as in other your Majesty's Provinces; there being a number more than Sufficient of Loyal and well affected Protestants, exclusive of military Officers, to form a competent and respectable

James Murray

House of Assembly; and your Majesty's new Subjects, if your Majesty shall think fit, may be allowed to elect Protestants without burdening them with such Oaths as in their present mode of thinking they cannot conscientiously take.

We doubt not but the good Effects of these measures will soon appear, by the Province becoming flourishing and your Majesty's People in it happy. . . .

The British merchants found other clauses of the Proclamation equally objectionable. The restrictions on the fur trade in the newly created Indian reserve and the necessity of carrying on some commercial transactions according to French laws were viewed by the merchants as a betrayal of loyal British subjects.

The Canadians were fearful of the changes that the Proclamation brought, and suspicious of the innovations that the Proclamation promised. Like the British merchants and the British Americans, they disliked the new boundary. The promise of an elected assembly alarmed them. Such an assembly might pass restrictive laws and levy taxes — obligations which had rarely been imposed on the Canadians during the French regime. They were uneasy about the lack of clear guarantees for the Roman Catholic religion and resented veiled British attempts at assimilation.

The Canadians found an unexpected champion of their cause in Governor Murray. He had a soldier's contempt for the ambitious and obstre-

perous merchants. His dislike of these "Licentious Fanaticks" only heightened his admiration for the law-abiding and obedient habitants. The British merchants were vociferous in their protests to the British government. Their target was Murray, and through their influential intermediaries in London, they brought about Murray's recall in 1766.

MURRAY AND THE BRITISH-AMERICAN
MERCHANTS[76]

Governor Murray to the Lords of Trade:

Quebec, 29th Oct'r 1764

Little, very little will content the New Subjects but nothing will satisfy the Licentious Fanaticks Trading here, but the expulsion of the Canadians who are perhaps the bravest and the best race upon the Globe, a Race, who cou'd they be indulged with a few priveledges which the Laws of England deny to Roman Catholicks at home, wou'd soon get the better of every National Antipathy to their Conquerors and become the most faithful and most useful set of Men in this American Empire.

. . . unless the Canadians are admitted on Jurys and are allowed Judges and Lawyers who understand their Language his Majesty will lose the greatest part of this Valuable people.

Petition of the Quebec Traders:

The Governor instead of acting agreeable . . . in giving a favourable Reception to those of your Majesty's Subjects, who petition and apply to him . . . doth frequently treat them with a Rage and Rudeness of Language and Demeanour, as dishonorable to the Trust he holds of your Majesty as painful to those who suffer from it.

His . . . most flagrant Partialities, by fomenting Parties and taking measures to keep your Majesty's old and new Subjects divided from one another, by encouraging the latter to apply for Judges of their own National Language.

We could enumerate many more Sufferings which render the Lives of your Majesty's Subjects, especially your Majesty's loyal British Subjects, in the Province so very unhappy that we must be under the Necessity of removing from it, unless timely prevented by a Removal of the present Governor.

The initial British attempt at governing a large French-speaking Roman Catholic population in close proximity to the English-speaking Protestant population of the Thirteen Colonies seemed to have lacked clear-cut policies. Moreover, the period had focussed attention on a number of crucial problems that stemmed from the Conquest.

In the new colony of Quebec, two irreconcilable ways of life were evident. On the one hand was the small minority of British Protestant merchants dedicated to the creation of a commercial state on the St. Lawrence. On the other hand was the large majority of Canadian Roman Catholic subjects devoted to the preservation of a rural agricultural way of life. For Britain, the practical problem of the Conquest was how to give the old British subjects in Quebec the traditional British institutions and rights of Englishmen and at the same time to reconcile an alien population to British rule. The first attempted solution — the Royal Proclamation of 1763 — failed to define the status of the Canadians within the British Empire. The Quebec Act of 1774 took a more realistic approach to the problem.

B

QUEBEC ACT

In 1766 the British government sent Sir Guy Carleton to replace Murray. Like his predecessor, Carleton was a military man, but he seemed to have great political talent. He came to Quebec with set ideas about how the conquered Canadians ought to be treated, and with a measure of hostility toward Murray's appointees on the Council. Shortly after his arrival, he dismissed some of Murray's closest associates from the Council, an act which clearly indicated his sympathy towards the British merchants, who saw in Carleton a supporter of their cause — a welcome change from the unfriendly Murray.

Within a year, Carleton had come around to Murray's views on the Canadians and the British merchants. In his disgust with the defiant and vociferous merchants he began to admire the obedient and law-abiding Canadians and their orderly, feudal way of life. He began to see the Canadians not as enemies to be suspected but as potentially loyal British subjects to be treated with dignity. The British merchants with their ambitious pretensions for sharing political power in an elected legislative assembly, aroused in Carleton a soldier's and aristocrat's disdain. He suspected them of being imbued with American democratic tendencies. Carleton came to the firm conclusion that British policy in Quebec should be based on conciliation of the Canadian majority even if it meant disregarding the demanding British minority. Reasons other than mere admiration of the Canadians, however, shaped Carleton's views.

Carleton was fully convinced that Quebec would "to the end of Time, be peopled by the Canadian Race." He was certain that English settlers would not be attracted to the inhospitable climate and hardships of Quebec. If Quebec was to be a French province within the British Empire, then Britain ought to do everything possible to conciliate this majority and secure the loyalty of the Canadians to the British Crown.

CARLETON ON THE RELATION OF THE OLD SUBJECTS AND THE NEW[77]

Quebec, 25th Nov., 1767

The King's Forces in this Province . . . would amount to sixteen hundred and twenty seven Men, the King's old subjects in this Province . . . might furnish about five hundred Men. . . .

The new Subjects could send into the Field about eighteen thousand Men, well able to carry Arms; of which Number, above one half have already served, with as much Valor, with more Zeal, and more military Knowledge for America, than the regular Troops of France, that were joined with them.

Having arrayed the Strength of His Majesty's old and new Subjects, and shewn the great Superiority of the Latter, it may not be amiss to observe, that there is not the least Probability, this present Superiority should ever diminish, on the Contrary 'tis more than probable it will increase and strengthen daily: The Europeans, who migrate never will prefer the long unhospitable Winters of Canada, to the more cheerful Climates, and more fruitful Soil of His Majesty's Southern Provinces; The few old Subjects at present in this Province, have been mostly left here by Accident, and are either disbanded Officers, Soldiers, or Followers of the Army . . . or else they are Adventures in Trade . . . barring Catastrophe shocking to think of, this Country must, to the end of Time, be peopled by the Canadian Race. . . .

Carleton was becoming more alarmed by the events in the Thirteen Colonies. Friction between the colonies and the mother country was steadily increasing and he feared that it might lead to an open break — a revolt in the British-American colonies. In such an eventuality, it was absolutely imperative to have loyal subjects in Quebec. Carleton felt that the policies of the Proclamation had failed to reconcile the Canadians to British rule; instead, they had left a sullen and resentful majority whose loyalty was questionable. Circumstances demanded that Britain ought to do everything possible to gain the goodwill and loyalty of the Canadians. A loyal Canadian population would not respond to French appeals for help in the event of a future Anglo-French conflict. Furthermore, a loyal Quebec could be used as a secure base for military operation against the Thirteen Colonies. In 1770, Carleton returned to London, and in the following four years used his influence to persuade the British government to adopt a benevolent policy of conciliation towards the Canadians.

Carleton argued that Britain had to accept the reality of the North American situation; Quebec had to retain its French character if she were to remain within the British Empire. All thoughts of assimilation had to be discarded; French laws, customs, language and the Roman Catholic religion had to be guaranteed by British statute. Carleton was convinced that the docile habitants could be influenced to aid Britain against its recalcitrant Thirteen Colonies by gaining the collaboration of Quebec's natural leaders — the seigneurs and clergy. So confident was Carleton in the wisdom of his proposals that he counted upon Quebec putting 18,000 men, capable of bearing arms, into the field on the side of Britain.

Carleton was so persistent and his assessment of the North American situation was so convincing that, in 1774, the British Parliament embodied many of his proposals in the Quebec Act — a statute that defined a new status for the French Canadians within the British Empire.

The Quebec Act enlarged the territory of Quebec beyond the boundaries created by the Proclamation of 1763; the Indian reserve on the western lands, including the Ohio Valley, was attached to Quebec. Ostensibly, this expansion would establish better law and order and more effective protection of Indian interests in the western lands. Perhaps more pressing reasons prompted this extension of Quebec. Carleton fully realized the military significance of the control of the Ohio Valley. Inclusion of the Ohio Valley within the boundaries of Quebec would thwart the westward expansion of the British-American colonies which were becoming troublesome and were speaking of independence. Restoration of the Ohio Valley to Quebec would remove the restrictions on the fur trade, appease the British merchants on the St. Lawrence and give them a considerable advantage over their competitors on the

Guy Carleton

Mohawk-Hudson route. The boundary of Rupertsland remained the northern limit of Quebec, but on the east Labrador was added, giving Quebec control over seal-hunting and coastal fishing.

The Quebec Act altered the basic form of government very little. An elected legislative assembly was specifically denied; Quebec would still be governed by an appointed Governor and Council. The Council, composed of no less than seventeen and no more than twenty-three appointed members, was open to Roman Catholic office holders, thus allowing the seigneurial class to participate in government. The Council was given the power to make laws for the colony subject to the approval of the Crown. In the British tradition, the Council — an appointed body — was not empowered to levy taxes, but it had the right to impose periodic charges for public roads and buildings. To supply regular revenue for the maintenance of government and for the administration of the judicial system, the British Parliament passed the Quebec Revenue Act in 1774 which authorized the imposition of duties on imported goods.

THE QUEBEC ACT PROVIDES FOR CONCILIAR GOVERNMENT[78]

. . . . And whereas it is at present inexpedient to call an Assembly; be it therefore enacted . . . That it shall and may be lawful for His Majesty . . . to constitute and appoint a Council for the Affairs of the Province of *Quebec* . . . not exceeding Twenty-three, nor less than Seventeen, as His

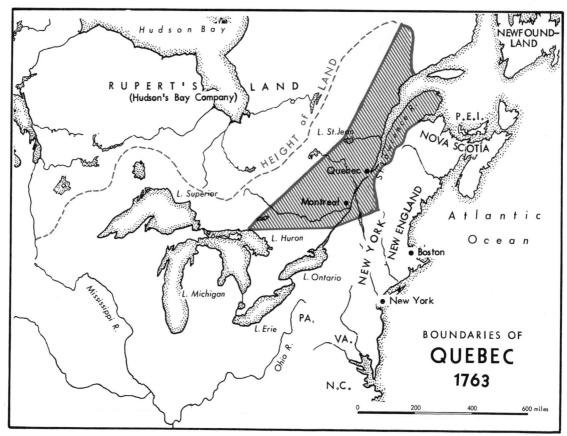

BOUNDARIES OF QUEBEC 1763

Majesty . . . shall be pleased to appoint . . . which Council, so appointed and nominated . . . shall have Power and Authority to make Ordinances for the Peace, Welfare, and good Government, of the said Province, with the Consent of His Majesty's Governor. . . .

Provided always, That nothing in this Act contained shall extend to authorise or impower the said legislative Council to lay any Taxes or Duties within the said Province. . . .

The official reason for the denial of an elected legislative assembly was the inability of the French Canadians to use and operate an elected representative form of government. In truth, the granting of an assembly would create an inextricable dilemma for Britain. If Catholics were denied the vote (as in Britain), then the assembly, dominated by the small English minority, would be unfair. If Catholics were permitted the vote, then the assembly, dominated by the large French-Canadian majority, might prove dangerous and even more troublesome than the assemblies in the Thirteen Colonies. Obviously, the British government agreed with Carleton and ignored the English minority.

In the religious provisions of the Quebec Act, the British government accorded freedoms to Roman Catholics in Quebec which far surpassed those enjoyed by Roman Catholics in Great Britain.* Although Jesuit property, confiscated in 1763, was not restored, Catholics were to have full freedom of worship without the restrictions imposed by either the Treaty of Paris or the Proclamation. The right to collect tithes was restored to the clergy and payment was enforced by the government. Roman Catholics were allowed to hold public office, and in order to facilitate this a special oath of allegiance, compatible with their religious beliefs, was designed. The Protestant religion was not overlooked — the King could make provisions for the maintenance of the Protestant clergy, if he so desired.

SPECIAL OATH FOR CATHOLIC OFFICE HOLDERS[79]

I A. B. do sincerely promise and swear, That I will be faithful, and bear true Allegiance to His Majesty King GEORGE, and him will defend to the utmost of my Power, against all traiterous Conspiracies, and Attempts whatsoever, which

---

* In 1829, the British Parliament passed the Catholic Emancipation Act which granted the Catholics the right of suffrage, the right to sit in Parliament and eligibility for public office.

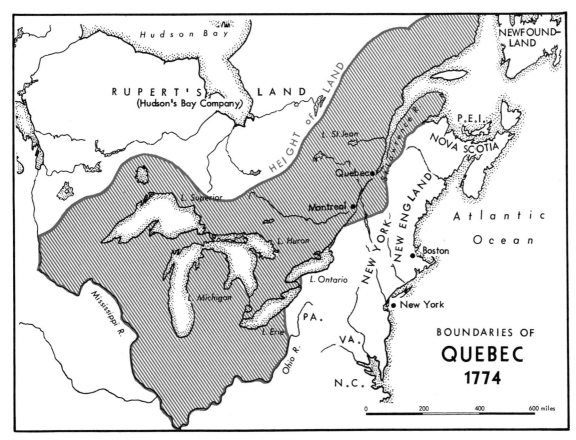

BOUNDARIES OF
QUEBEC
1774

shall be made against His Person, Crown, and Dignity; and I will do my utmost Endeavour to disclose and make known to His Majesty, His Heirs and Successors, all Treasons, and traiterous Conspiracies, and Attempts, which I shall know to be against Him, or any of Them; and all this I do swear without any Equivocation, mental Evasion, or secret Reservation, and renouncing all Pardons and Dispensations from any Power or Person whomsoever to the Contrary.

SO HELP ME GOD.

It was evident that the British government, in line with Carleton's thinking, made magnanimous religious provisions in an attempt to win the goodwill and loyalty of the Roman Catholic clergy in particular and of the French Canadians in general.

RELIGIOUS PROVISIONS IN THE QUEBEC ACT[80]

And, for the more perfect Security and Ease of the Minds of the Inhabitants of the said Province, it is hereby declared, That His Majesty's Subjects, professing the Religion of the Church of *Rome* of and in the said Province of *Quebec*, may have, hold, and enjoy, the free Exercise of the Religion of the Church of *Rome* . . . and that the Clergy of

the said Church may hold, receive, and enjoy, their accustomed Dues and Rights, with respect to such Persons only as shall profess the said Religion.

Provided nevertheless, That it shall be lawful for His Majesty . . . to make such Provision out of the rest of the said accustomed Dues and Rights, for the Encouragement of the Protestant Religion, and for the Maintenance and Support of a Protestant Clergy within the said Province, as he . . . from Time to Time, think necessary and expedient.

The Quebec Act attempted to resolve the confusion in the legal system resulting from the Proclamation. French civil laws, the *Custom of Paris* — those that were in force at the time of the Conquest — were to be used. English criminal law, instituted by the Proclamation, was to continue in use. The seigneurial system was retained, but provisions were also made for freehold tenure* for those British subjects who might contemplate immigration to Quebec.

The retention of the seigneurial system was a calculated attempt to win the support, loyalty and collaboration of the seigneurial class. French civil

* The whole right and title of the land rests with the owner, subject to the laws of the state. The owner owes no services or fees to a feudal lord or seigneur.

laws, which affected the every-day life of the people, were retained in order to gain the goodwill of the French-Canadian population in general. It was thought that the continuance of British criminal law, which was assumed to be more lenient than French criminal law, would also serve to placate the general populace.

PROVISIONS FOR LAWS IN THE QUEBEC ACT[81]

. . . and that in all Matters of Controversy, relative to Property and Civil Rights, Resort shall be had to the laws of *Canada*, as the Rule for the Decision of the same. . . .

———

And whereas the Certainty and Lenity of the Criminal Law of *England*, and the Benefits and Advantages resulting from the Use of it, have been sensibly felt by the Inhabitants, from an Experience of more than Nine Years . . . be it therefore further enacted . . . That the same shall continue to be administered, and shall be observed as Law in the Province of *Quebec*. . . .

Carleton was also instructed to provide for the welfare of the English minority — the Quebec Act empowered the governor to introduce such basic British legal rights as *habeas corpus* and trial by jury. But Carleton chose not to do so. He disregarded the English minority in order to win the loyalty of the French Canadians.

The Quebec Act inflamed political, economic, racial and religious sensitivities of two widely divergent ways of life and aroused varied reactions. Whereas the French Canadians hailed the Quebec Act as a "Magna Carta" enunciating their rights, the British Americans damned it as an "Intolerable Act" fettering their liberties.

The English mercantile group in Quebec and the French Canadians responded favourably to the revised boundaries of Quebec. Both were gratified that the Ohio Valley, once again, became the exclusive domain of the St. Lawrence–centred fur trade, and both welcomed the annexation of the coastal fisheries off Labrador to Quebec. The British-American colonies, however, regarded the inclusion of the Ohio Valley in a greater Quebec as further proof of British intentions to restrict their westward expansion. The Proclamation was bad enough in excluding the British Americans from the Ohio Valley. But a proclamation line might be modified or removed. However, the Quebec Act, by attaching the Ohio Valley to Quebec, removed all possibility of territorial acquisition of this area by the Thirteen Colonies.

In the British-American view, Britain simply continued France's earlier policy of confining the colonies east of the Alleghenies.

THE QUEBEC ACT AND THE BRITISH-AMERICAN FUR TRADE[82]

Simon McTavish, in a letter to a Detroit merchant, gives some indication of the turmoil in the western fur trade caused by the Quebec Act:

New York, December 24th, 1774
Your friend Isaac Todd has his hands full of the publick business, being one of those delegated by the Merchants of Montreal to prepare two Petitions, One to His Majesty, & the other to the Common Council of London, begging the repeal of the Canada Bill [Quebec Act], which is so justly looked on by them with horror — Their present Governor [Guy Carleton], (the first contriver & great promoter of this Evil) is universally detested. I apprehend this Bill will be of infinite hurt to our Trade, for shou'd it be repealed in the first Session of the New Parliament we will not have the News before July or Augᵗ, & in the mean time, what are we to do for Rum? As we will not be allowed to bring up any from Schenectady — But in case it shou'd not be repealed at all, we must inevitably break off our Connexion with this Province [New York] & have our Supplies from Canada. . . . I am afraid Indian Trade will be at a stand Next Year for want of Ammunition, as His Majesty (who is certainly damnably frightened) has Issued a proclamation prohibiting the exportation of firearms or any kind of Ammunition from Great Britain for 6 Months. . . .

The government instituted by the Quebec Act only continued the form of government to which the French Canadians had long been accustomed. The French Canadians welcomed this status quo: the denial of a legislative assembly assured them that they would not be dominated by a British commercial minority. But the British merchants were incensed that they had been denied a basic right of Englishmen — an elected legislative assembly — long enjoyed by Anglo-Saxons in the Thirteen Colonies and, since 1758, in Nova Scotia. The British-American colonies were astounded by Britain's disregard for the loyal British Canadians. To the British Americans, the establishment of an authoritarian government in Quebec was evidence of British intention to suppress popularly elected assemblies in North America.

PETITION FOR THE REPEAL OF THE QUEBEC ACT[83]

TO THE KING'S MOST EXCELLENT MAJESTY:

THE PETITION of your Majesty's most loyal and dutiful your ancient Subjects in the Province of Quebec,

MOST HUMBLY SHEWETH

. . . . We humbly crave leave to say that we have paid a ready and dutiful Obedience to Government and have lived in Peace and Amity with your Majesty's new Subjects. Nevertheless we find and with unutterable Grief presume to say that by a late Act of Parliament intitled "An Act for the making more effectual Provision for the Government of the Province of QUEBEC in North America" We are deprived of the Franchises granted by Your Majesty's Royal Predecessors and by us inherited from our Forefathers THAT We have lost the Protection of the English Laws . . . and in their Stead the Laws of CANADA are to be introduced to which we are utter Strangers disgraceful to us as Britons and . . . ruinous to our Properties as we thereby lose the invaluable Privilege of TRIAL by JURIES . . . the HABEAS CORPUS ACT is dissolved and we are Subjected to arbitrary Fines and Imprisonment at the Will of the Governor and Council . . . .

We therefore MOST HUMBLY IMPLORE your Majesty to take our unhappy state into your Royal Consideration and grant us such Relief as your Majesty in your Royal Wisdom shall think meet.

Quebec 12th November 1774.

The generous religious liberties of the Quebec Act met universal acceptance by the French Canadians. The restoration of payment of tithes won the enthusiastic approval of the clergy, but the habitants, naturally, disliked this imposition, which had not been officially enforced since the Con-quest. The merchants in Quebec and the British-American colonists shared a common resentment over the religious provisions of the Quebec Act. To them it was inconceivable that the British Parliament should establish the Catholic Church within the boundaries of the Empire and allow Roman Catholics in Quebec rights and privileges which the King of England denied Catholics in his own country.

The French Canadians were pleased with the retention of French civil laws and had no serious objections to the use of British criminal law. The restoration of the seigneurial system with its seigneurial dues found favour with the seigneurs but the habitants resented it. The institution of French civil laws and the seigneurial system added to the British minority's resentment. This commercial community saw no reason why loyal British subjects, living in a British possession, should have to conduct business transactions according to foreign laws. The British Canadians, although they were provided with freehold tenure, objected to the maintenance of a seigneurial land holding system, which they considered an antiquated and backward feudal system.

The Quebec Act was an act of faith in Carleton's convictions regarding the influence of the seigneurs and clergy and the docility of the habitants. Subsequent events proved that Carleton erred in his judgment; the powerful seigneurs and clergy were not so influential, and the docile habitants were not so submissive. Whatever the immediate consequences, the Quebec Act, a statute of the British Parliament, gave legal recognition to the Catholic Church, French law, and customs in Quebec; these fostered and strengthened the French-Canadian identity which has endured to the present. The disregard of the British merchants in Quebec, the establishment of the Roman Catholic Church, the denial of an elected legislative assembly, and the new boundary of Quebec provided more fuel for the fires of rebellion in the British-American colonies.

11

BRITISH NORTH AMERICA AND THE AMERICAN REVOLUTION

A

AMERICAN REVOLUTION

The British victory in the Seven Years' War removed the French threat to the security of the Thirteen Colonies. In a British North America, the Colonies looked toward the realization of a cherished dream — westward expansion. The war had been a big drain on the British treasury, and Pontiac's uprising revealed both the incapability of the colonies to defend themselves and the need for a standing British army in North America. The British government was determined that the colonies should pay part of the cost of colonial defence, and set about reorganizing the Empire and instituting tighter controls and efficiency in the colonial administration.

Britain was dissatisfied with the colonial militia's performance during the Seven Years' War. Although the colonies provided some forces, the British regular troops did most of the fighting. Britain was also irritated with the British Americans, many of whom had profiteered by illegal trading with the French throughout the war. After the war, in order to stop the wide-spread smuggling that had developed and to realize more revenue from the customs duties for the maintenance of a British army in North America, the British government enforced the terms of the Navigation Acts more rigidly. The "incorruptible" British navy was entrusted with the task of curbing smuggling. Smugglers were tried in the Admiralty Court where there was no trial by jury; previously, colonial juries seldom convicted fellow-merchants and smugglers. The British Americans raised the cry that they were being deprived of trial by jury — an inalienable right of Englishmen. Customs regulations were tightened to eliminate the evasion of payment of duties, and corrupt customs officials were replaced. The colonies accused Britain of deliberately stifling the economic life of the colonist by restricting colonial trade. In truth, efficient enforcement of the Navigation Acts did cause hardships and even bankruptcy for some shipowners and merchants.

To raise additional revenue, the British Parliament passed the Stamp Act in 1765, which made it obligatory to have stamps affixed to newspapers and legal documents. The income from this imposition was to contribute, in part, to the cost of colonial defence — a burden hitherto shouldered by the tax payers in Britain. This was the first time in the history of the colonies that the British Parliament had levied a direct tax on the colonies.

When the stamps and stamp officers arrived from Britain, mobs rioted in several cities including Boston, and threatened and harassed the stamp officers. British Americans feared that this tax was only a prelude to a series of similar taxes. The Stamp Act Congress — a meeting of representatives from the Thirteen Colonies convened at New York — decided to boycott British goods and thus put pressure on the merchants and Parliament in Britain. The Congress also coined the slogan "no taxation without representation" and urged the population to disregard the Stamp Act. This course of action hampered the conduct of business since commercial transactions could not be legalized without the affixing of stamps. The turmoil created by the unpopular Stamp Act brought about its repeal in 1766. However, the British government issued the Declaratory Act which asserted the King's right and authority, subject to Parliament's consent, to make laws for the colonies. The Declaratory Act made it clear that Britain was neither adopting a general policy of retreat nor abrogating its colonial rights.

The British Americans found another cause for grievance in the Quartering Act of 1765, which authorized the housing of British troops in private homes. This practice, to which Europeans and the British had long been accustomed, was vehemently resented by the British Americans. They viewed it as an infringement of their personal liberties. The Legislative Assembly of New York refused to make provision for the quartering of General Gage's troops.

In a further attempt to raise revenue to defray the costs of defence, the British Parliament passed the Townshend Acts in 1767. These acts, which imposed duties on imported glass, paints, paper and tea, aroused bitter protestations. A town meeting in Boston adopted a non-importation resolution which called for a complete boycott of British goods. But it was the Boston Massacre of 1770 — a clash between citizens and British troops, which resulted in some loss of life — that led the British government to repeal all the duties imposed by the Townshend Acts except a small tax on imported tea.

The apparent retreat by the British Parliament —the repeal of the Stamp Act and the withdrawal of the duties of the Townshend Acts — was interpreted by many radical British Americans as a sign of weakness on the part of the British government. The radical elements were encouraged to press the cause of colonial freedom with increased vigour. To protest the "tea tax," a group of Boston citizens, some disguised as Indians, boarded British ships and dumped their cargo of tea into the harbour. Provoked by this lawlessness, the British government sent additional troops to Boston and Parliament passed a series of punitive laws — the Coercive Acts.

These Acts were intended to make an example of Boston. The Boston Port Act closed the port of Boston causing a halt to commercial activities. The Massachusetts Government Act revoked the charter of Massachusetts, suspended the Assembly, prohibited township meetings and circumscribed the rights of the people. The Administration of Justice Act provided that British soldiers accused of crimes committed in the course of their duties in the colonies could be tried in the calm of a London court rather than in the hostile atmosphere of the colony itself. The Quartering Act was diligently enforced and British troops were moved into the city. The British Americans saw in these "Intolerable Acts" a British plot to destroy the Massachusetts colony. But it was the passage of the Quebec Act — the fifth "Intolerable Act" — which fully convinced the British Americans that Britain was intent upon suppressing the political institutions and stifling the economic life of all the British-American colonies. Under these circumstances the other colonies rallied around Massachusetts in its struggle against Britain.

But the British Americans, as a whole, were not talking rebellion. The first Continental Congress, meeting in Philadelphia in 1774, declared a boycott on British goods — the retaliatory weapon that had been so successful in the past. The assembled delegates were confident that a boycott would force the British government to repeal the Coercive Acts just as it had forced the repeal of the Stamp and Townshend Acts.

NEITHER WHIGS NOR TORIES SPOKE OF REVOLUTION[84]

The view of an American historian in 1864:

. . . do the men who were born under it [the Colonial system of government], and were reconciled to it, justice — simple justice; and if, as Mr. Jefferson says, a *"possibility"* of the necessity of a separation of the two countries, "was contemplated with *affliction by all*," and if the statements made by Franklin, Adams, Jay, Madison, and Washington, are to be considered as true and as decisive . . . what other line of difference existed between the Whigs and Tories, than the *terms on which the connection of the Colonies with England should be continued.*

. . . [it is necessary] to remove the erroneous impression which seems to prevail, that the Whigs *proposed*, and the Tories *opposed* independence, at the very beginning of the controversy. Instead of this, we have seen, that quite fourteen years have elapsed before the question was made a party issue, and that, even then, "necessity," and not "choice," caused a dismemberment of the empire. Since it has appeared, therefore, from the highest sources, that the Whigs resolved finally upon revolution because they were denied the rights of Englishmen, and not because they disliked monarchical institutions, the Tories may be relieved from the imputation of being the only "monarchy-men" of the time.

However, tensions between Britain and her Thirteen Colonies were intensified by the presence of British troops in Boston in the midst of a hostile citizenry. In this potentially explosive situation, a relatively minor incident plunged the colonies into open rebellion and war against the mother country. In April, 1775, General Thomas Gage, the Commander-in-Chief of the British forces, detailed some troops from Boston to seize a cache of arms at neighbouring Concord. On their way, at Lexington, the troops clashed with colonial militiamen. Shots were fired, a skirmish followed, and the alarm spread that British troops were shooting innocent citizens. The revolution had begun. The Second Congress, in session in Philadelphia, authorized the recruitment of an army and appointed

George Washington as commander-in-chief of the forces.

The British North American colonies, especially Quebec, were considered important objectives for the success of the revolution. Some radical British-American patriots, shortly after the passage of the Quebec Act, advocated setting aside the provisions of this Act, especially the boundary, by aligning Quebec with the Thirteen Colonies. The Congress, in session at the time, was quite certain that an appeal to Quebec to join in the cause against British tyranny would find sympathetic acceptance. The British Americans counted upon widespread support from the merchants of Quebec, most of whom had emigrated from the Thirteen Colonies. It was also hoped that the French Canadians, whose loyalty to their British conquerors was uncertain, could be induced to join the cause of the colonies. In 1774, an appeal, the "Address to the Inhabitants of the Province of Quebec," urged French Canadians to send delegates to the Congress and to join in the struggle for liberty. Quebec was invited to become the fourteenth colony.

ADDRESS OF THE GENERAL CONGRESS TO THE INHABITANTS OF THE PROVINCE OF QUEBEC[85]

October 26th, 1774

.... Seize the opportunity presented to you by Providence itself .... You are a small people, compared to those who with open arms invite you into fellowship . . . to have all the rest of North America your unalterable friends or your inveterate enemies . . . The value and extent of the advantages tendered you are immense . . . .

We are too well acquainted with the liberality of sentiment distinguishing your nation, to imagine, that difference of religion will prejudice you against a hearty enmity with us . . . Swiss Cantons . . . composed of Catholic and Protestant states, living in the utmost concord and peace with one another. . . .

We do not ask you, by this address, to commence hostilities against the government of our common sovereign. We only invite you . . . not to suffer yourselves to be inveigled . . . to become the instrument of their cruelty and despotism, but to unite with us in one social compact, formed on the generous principles of equal liberty. . . . In order to complete this highly desirable union, we submit it to your consideration, whether it may not be expedient for you to . . . elect deputies who after meeting in a provincial congress, may chuse delegates, to represent your province in the continental congress, to be held at Philadelphia, on the tenth day of May, 1775.

Signed,

Henry Middleton, President

The appeal failed to arouse the wide sympathy which the Congress had anticipated. The British merchants, although resentful over the Quebec Act, had close economic ties with Britain; the British regulations for the colonies and the "Intolerable Acts" that the British Americans so vehemently opposed disturbed the merchants of Quebec only slightly, if at all.

THE QUEBEC MERCHANTS AND THE AMERICAN REVOLUTION[86]

Donald Creighton, the Canadian historian, maintains that the English-speaking merchants in Quebec, mainly because of their interests in the commercial prosperity on the St. Lawrence, refused to support the Revolution:

. . . . Union with the Americans would at once submerge the identity of Quebec in a general American federation and cut the vitally necessary economic relations with England; and these consequences were inimical to every interest of the northern commercial state. . . . . They had no desire to endanger their own commercial system. . . . They wished to dominate in Quebec; but they were unwilling to cut the connection with London or to abandon their competition in North America.

The link between Canada and the Thirteen Colonies was . . . a personal connection, maintained by a few American colonists in Quebec. . . . It was the new constitution [Quebec Act] which gave the Canadian merchants a momentary interest in the miseries and the new religions of the people to the south. . . .

. . . . To send delegates to the continental congress would involve Canada's acceptance of the non-importation agreement; and to cut the simple and essential tie with London would ruin the merchants and destroy their commercial state. . . .

But there were pro-Americans at Montreal. . . . The large majority of them were natives of the Thirteen Colonies . . . and with the possible exception of Thomas Walker, there was not a single important fur-trading name in the whole group . . . it was the men whose business activities were least attuned to the distinctive commercial system of the north, who went over to the enemy.

. . . . Those who were most completely committed to the really Canadian commercial system which was based upon the fur trade could not assist an American invasion. . . .

Although dissatisfied with certain provisions of the Quebec Act, the French Canadians were not

Carleton reviews his troops on Place d'Armes before attacking Ethen Allan at Longue Pointe, 1775.

volved in the revolution. The Americans launched a series of raids along the border of Nova Scotia and a two-pronged attack against Quebec.

In 1775, General Richard Montgomery, who had served with Amherst at Quebec in 1759, led an American force along the traditional Lake Champlain-Richelieu River invasion route. At the outset of the revolution, Carleton, who had expected a large enlistment of French-Canadian volunteers, had dispatched a considerable part of his forces to aid General Gage at Boston. Carleton's expectations of the French Canadians did not come to pass, and the depleted British forces suffered some early reverses. The British troops at St. John surrendered, Montreal fell to Montgomery and Carleton retreated with his forces to Quebec. At the same time, an American army under Benedict Arnold was marching from Maine toward Quebec — a rigorous and arduous march across New Brunswick in the middle of the winter. Montgomery's and Arnold's forces joined in a concerted assault on Quebec on December 31, 1775. Carleton's troops fought well and the defences held. Montgomery was killed, Arnold was wounded and the Americans maintained a seige on Quebec throughout the winter.

moved by British-American expressions of friendship and goodwill; they were aware of British-American hostility toward the privileges which the Quebec Act gave the French-Canadian Catholic population in Quebec. It would have been foolhardy for the French Canadians to give up the assurance of the Quebec Act for the nebulous promises of the Congress, or to give up majority status in Quebec for submergence in a hostile English-speaking environment. Moreover, the "Address" came only a few days after an earlier appeal by the Congress, an "Address to the People of Great Britain," which was a virulent anti-Catholic outburst against the Quebec Act. It is not surprising that the appeal made little impression on the French Canadians.

In Nova Scotia, as in Quebec, there was little support for the British-American cause. In spite of the fact that a large number of New Englanders lived there, Nova Scotians displayed little interest in joining the British Americans against Britain. Economic links with and patriotic attachments to Great Britain were too vital to throw overboard for the risky venture of the British-American colonies. Also, as was the case in Quebec, the duties, acts and regulations imposed by Britain on her American colonies were not considered burdensome or oppressive by the Nova Scotians. Furthermore, the large British naval base at Halifax engendered a healthy respect for British authority. Nova Scotia's attachment to Britain surpassed its concern for the neighbouring British-American colonies. When the revolution broke out, it became evident that persuasion had failed to move Quebec to the British-American cause. The Americans planned to capture Quebec and, thereby, deny Britain a base of military operation against the colonies. Thus Canada became in-

NOVA SCOTIA AND THE AMERICAN REVOLUTION[87]

What was it that moulded Nova Scotia's attitude towards the American Revolution? Some observations on this:

. . . it is difficult to understand why Nova Scotia did not follow the lead of New England. The character of the population did not promise any high degree of loyalty. It was composed largely of emigrants from New England, who had only recently, at the time of the Stamp Act agitation, left their old homes; and there was another element of danger to the British connection in the presence of a number of Acadians who had escaped the intended doom of exile or had contrived to return to the province. . . .

———

The interests of Halifax itself were indeed all on the side of the established order of things . . . it was the chief seaport, the seat of government for the province, and a British naval and military station, and in those days its prosperity, its importance, its very existence, depended on these conditions. Such specie as circulated was introduced into the country by the army and navy.

During the seige, American emissaries came to Montreal to convince French Canadians to join

in the fight against Britain. The habitants displayed no more enthusiasm for these entreaties than they did for Carleton's earlier call to arms. Even the Bishop of Quebec's exhortations to aid benevolent Britain failed to stir the habitants. The Americans, too, found the habitants unresponsive.

French-Canadian indifference to the American invasion baffled British officials. Apparently, Carleton under-estimated the habitants. Chief Justice of Quebec William Hey is critical of Carleton's expectations:

Quebec, August 28, 1775

. . . . Your Lordship will remember how much has been said by us all of their [French Canadians'] Loyalty, obedience & Gratitude, of their habitual submission to Government, & their decent civil & respectfull demeanour to those who had the conduct of it, but time and accident have evinced that they were obedient only because they were afraid to be otherwise & with that fear lost (by withdrawing the troops) is gone all the good disposition that we have so often and steadily avowed in their names & promised for them in ages to come.

. . . it may be truly said that Gen. Carleton had taken an ill measure of the influence of the seigneurs & Clergy over the lower order of people whose Principle of conduct founded in fear & the sharpness of authority over them now no longer exercised, is unrestrained, & breaks out in every shape of contempt or detestation of those whom they used to behold with terror & who gave them I believe too many occasions to express it. . . .

The French Canadians showed little interest in the American cause; they kept to themselves and were indifferent to the struggle between Britain and her colonists. Appeals and promises of both Britain and the Colonies failed to involve them — they refused to become embroiled in an Anglo-Saxon family squabble and sat back uncommitted to await the outcome of the struggle.

BISHOP BRIAND'S APPEAL TO THE
FRENCH CANADIANS[89]

May 22, 1775

A troop of subjects in revolt against their lawful Sovereign, who is at the same time ours, have just made an irruption into this province, less in the hope of maintaining themselves here than with a view of dragging you into their revolt or at least preventing you from opposing their pernicious design. The remarkable goodness and gentleness with which we have been governed by his very gracious Majesty, King George the Third, since the fortune of war subjected us to his rule; the recent favours with which he has loaded us, in restoring to us the use of our laws and the free exercise of our religion; and in letting us participate in all the privileges and advantages of British subjects, would no doubt be enough to excite your gratitude and zeal in support of the interests of the British Crown. But motives even more urgent must speak to your heart at the present moment. Your oaths, your religion, lay upon you the unavoidable duty of defending your country and your King with all the strength you possess.

In May, 1776, British ships were approaching Quebec with reinforcements and supplies. The Americans, badly hurt and disease-ridden, lacking ammunition and provisions, began to retreat southward to the safety of prepared positions along the Lake Champlain route. Carleton pursued the retreating Americans, who made a stand at Crown Point and Ticonderoga, but he failed to take full advantage of the precarious position of the revolutionary army. The British government replaced Carleton with Major-General John Burgoyne who was to dislodge the Americans from the Lake Champlain region.

Burgoyne, with his regular troops aided by loyalist groups, such as Butler's Rangers of New York, engaged a reinforced American army at Saratoga where he suffered a crushing defeat. The surrender of the British troops at Saratoga marked a turning point in the revolution. France, who had given some help to the revolution, now became convinced of the possibility of victory for the colonies and formed an alliance with the revolutionists. France envisioned the recapture of Quebec and urged a concerted effort to seize Quebec. The Americans mistrusted French intentions and had no desire to re-establish French power on the northern frontier. The capture of Quebec, at one time a strong possibility, was eliminated from the revolutionary strategy. Henceforth, the main battles in the revolutionary war were fought farther south. The British were defeated at Yorktown, where Cornwallis surrendered his forces in 1781.

American attempts in Nova Scotia were no more successful than those in Quebec. The former New Englanders living in Nova Scotia were expected to be sympathetic to the American cause. However, aside from nuisance raids along the border and some privateering by sea, only an insignificant attempted uprising in Cumberland

The British Fleet Ready to leave New York, 1783

County in 1776 disturbed the calm that permeated the Maritimes during the war. Nova Scotian attachment to Britain was stronger than the appeal from the Thirteen Colonies.

In 1783, Great Britain, France and the newly formed United States of America negotiated the peace treaty. France, who had lent large scale support to the Americans, was intent upon an independent but weak United States which would have to lean heavily on French support. Thus France could foresee the possibility of her re-entry into North America. Both Britain and the United States saw through these French designs and were anxious to prevent any re-establishment of French influence in North America. Britain, who had fought two costly wars within twenty years in North America, adopted a conciliatory attitude towards the United States in the hope of winning a lasting peace, assuring the safety of her northern colonies and detaching the United States from France. The United States, flushed with victory, wished to exclude France from North America entirely, confine British influence to the northern part of the continent and thus gain possession of the long-disputed western lands.

The Treaty of Versailles, above all, recognized by treaty what had been accomplished on the battlefields — the independence of the United States of America.

Britain was determined to settle the boundary negotiations in a manner that would not cause future friction with the United States. To a large extent, the possession of the Ohio Valley had precipitated the revolution; it was imperative that this long-disputed territory be included within the United States. The boundary, as delineated by the treaty, ran from the mouth of the St. Croix River to its source and to the Highlands that form the watershed between the St. Lawrence and the Atlantic, along the Highlands to the northwesternmost head of the Connecticut River, down this river to the forty-fifth parallel, westward along this latitude to the St. Lawrence River and along the middle of this and other rivers and lakes to Lake Superior. From here the boundary followed Rainy Lake and River across the Lake of the Woods to its northwestern point; from there it ran due west along the forty-ninth parallel, to the headwaters of the Mississippi River, which was erroneously believed to originate north of its actual source. In spite of the apparent exactness of the boundary, it was ambiguous and later proved to be a source of friction.

The Americans were insistent upon retaining their fishing rights off the shores of the British North American colonies. Theoretically, these rights had lapsed with the withdrawal of the Thirteen Colonies from the Empire. Britain granted the United States the right to fish off the coasts of Newfoundland and Nova Scotia and in the Gulf of St. Lawrence. Americans could also dry fish on uninhabited coastal areas. Britain hoped that these concessions would avoid a possible source of future friction.

At the peace conference, Britain interceded on behalf of the loyalists — those British Americans who had remained loyal to the British Crown during the revolution. These Loyalists had been badly treated during the revolution, and Britain requested that the United States consider loyalist claims, pay compensation for damage suffered, make restitution of confiscated property and pay debts owed by Americans to Loyalists. The American delegates promised to use the good offices of the Congress and recommend to the individual states involved that the loyalist claims be considered justly. Since the Congress had no jurisdiction over the individual states, the promises of the American delegates proved hollow indeed, and in fact, very little or no compensation or restitution was made to the Loyalists.

COMPENSATION FOR LOYALISTS IN TREATY OF PARIS, 1783[90]

It is agreed that the Congress shall earnestly recommend it to the Legislatures of the respective States, to provide for the restitution of all estates, rights, and properties which have been confiscated, belonging to real British subjects: and also of the estates, rights, and properties of Persons resident in Districts in the possession of His Majesty's arms, and who have not borne arms against the United States: and that Persons of any other description shall have free liberty to go to any part or parts of the 13 United States, and therein to remain 12 months unmolested in their estates, rights and properties as may have been confiscated; and that Congress shall also earnestly recommend to the several States, a reconsideration and revision of all Acts or Laws regarding the premises, so as to render the said Laws or Acts perfectly consistent, not only with justice and equity, but with that spirit of conciliation which on the return of the blessing of Peace, should universally prevail. And that Congress shall also earnestly recommend to the several States, that the estates, rights, and properties of such last-mentioned Persons shall be restored to them, they refunding to any Persons who may be now in possession the *bonâ fide* price (where any has been given) which such Persons may have paid on purchasing any of the said lands, rights or properties since the confiscation. . . .

Some interpret the events of the American Revolution as a vindication of the Quebec Act. They argue that although the French Canadians did not fight for Britain, they did not rebel against her. Therefore, they claim, the Quebec Act was successful: it assured the neutrality of the French Canadians. It is questionable whether the French Canadians, even without the Quebec Act, would have thrown in their lot with the hostile anti-Catholic Americans. But the Quebec Act was designed to gain the active loyalty, not the passive neutrality, of the habitants.

THE QUEBEC ACT AND THE AMERICAN REVOLUTION[91]

In a letter to Germain, from Quebec, October 25, 1780, Haldimand maintains that the Quebec Act kept Quebec from joining the Revolution. He advises to keep the Act unaltered:

. . . in Considering the Canadians as the People of the Country . . . Regard is to be paid to the Sentiments and Manner of thinking of 60,000 rather than of 2,000 — three fourths of whom are Traders & Cannot with propriety be Considered as Residents of the Province. — In this point of view the Quebec Act, was both just and Politic, tho' unfortunately for the British Empire, it was enacted Ten Years too late — It Requires but Little Penetration to Discover that had the System of Government Solicited by the Old Subjects been adopted in Canada, this Colony would in 1775 have become one of the United States of America.

On the other hand the Quebec Act alone has prevented or Can in any Degree prevent the Emissaries of France and the Rebellious Colonies from Succeeding in their Efforts to withdraw the Canadian Clergy & Noblesse from their Allegiance to the Crown of Great Britain. For this Reason amongst many others, this is not the time for Innovations and it Cannot be Sufficiently inculcated on the part of Government that the Quebec Act is a Sacred Charter, granted by the King in Parliament to the Canadians as a Security for their Religion, Laws, and Property.

The events of the revolution confirmed the fact that Carleton had won the support of the seigneurs and clergy but had failed to enlist the active participation of the habitants. Furthermore, the revolution revealed a widening gap in French-Canadian society; the habitants regarded those who had collaborated with Britain as *vendus* — sell-outs to the conquerors. The refusal of the French Canadians to become involved in the revolution clearly demonstrated the unique status of Quebec within the Empire. It was apparent that the French Canadians would continue to remain unconcerned with British imperial affairs. They were interested only in maintaining the culture and identity bred by the Canadian wilderness and guaranteed by the Quebec Act.

HOW EFFECTIVE WAS THE QUEBEC ACT[92]

The twentieth century French-Canadian historian, F. Ouellet, claims that support of Britain or neutrality did not necessarily result from the Quebec Act. Other considerations determined the attitude of French Canadians towards the American Revolution:

In 1774, everything united the clergy and the seigneurs to the government. . . . Having the origin in the religious convictions of these two social groups, loyalty to the king remained the strongest sentiment. There could be no longer a question, simply because of the basic adherence of the élite, of its rising up against England. The principle of the union of Church and State was another incontestable credo which linked the clergy to the political power. As for the nobility, it had always considered military activity as one of its essential social functions. To it fell, more than to any other class, the duty of defending the country. Moreover, were the values proposed by the rebels acceptable? Condemnable in principle, the revolution strove to disrupt the traditional political ties. They invoked the theme of liberty, whereas the French-Canadian élite believed in authority, in obedience, and in the aristocratic values.

———

In their part, the peasants chose neutrality to the outrage of the governor and the élite . . . .
. . . . It is certain that the weakness and the lack of military preparation of the government had removed all feelings of security from the habitant, engendering a reflex of fear.

———

. . . . Voluntary service gave way . . . to the option of neutrality. . . . By remaining on his farm, the tiller of the soil felt he would be able to collect some hard cash for his wheat . . . in the main, rural French-Canadian society remained loyal to the British regime. . . .

After the revolution, the British North American colonies found themselves living in close proximity to a large, populous and somewhat hostile neighbour. Although the Treaty of Versailles had been very advantageous to the United States, the anti-British feeling that pervaded the revolution was now also directed towards the British North American colonies. It was in this uneasy atmosphere that British North America had to adapt itself to sharing the continent with its republican neighbour. Inevitably, relations between Britain and the United States would have a profound effect on British North America. No sooner had the Treaty of Versailles been concluded, than the British merchants in Quebec accused Britain of sacrificing the interests of her North American colonies in order to gain the friendship and goodwill of the United States.

B

LOYALIST MIGRATION

Not all the people of the Thirteen Colonies rose in rebellion against Great Britain. There were loyal British subjects who wished to maintain the British connection and to live in a United Empire. Many such Loyalists, voluntarily or by force of circumstances, left the United States. Some came to live in the British North American colonies. This large influx of Loyalists was bound to affect the economic, political and social life in Nova Scotia and Quebec. Beyond the immediate problems created by the coming of the Loyalists, their presence in large numbers produced significant constitutional changes and altered the very character of British North America.

Sam Adams, a prominent leader of the American Revolution, estimated that only one third of the people in the Thirteen Colonies actively supported the revolutionary cause, one third remained neutral and the remainder actively supported Great Britain. That is, many British Americans, from many motives, chose to remain loyal to Britain. It is safe to state that most of the Loyalists shared a deep allegiance to the British monarchy. Loyalty to the Crown was a deep-rooted tradition, not confined to any particular social class or occupation, and among the Loyalists were professional men, office holders, merchants with British connections and farmers and artisans of modest means. Many of the Loyalists either aided the British forces or fought in Loyalist units alongside British regular troops.

WHO WERE THE LOYALISTS?[93]

[a]*This tribute was written by a contemporary, an Englishman who witnessed the Revolution and came to know many of the Loyalists:*

How sad has been the fate of all those truly meritorious but unhappy men, the *American Loyalists* of every denomination! True to their king, faithful to their country, attached to the laws and constitution, they have continued firm and inflexible in the midst of persecutions, torments, and death. Many of them have abandoned their homes, their friends, their nearest and most tender connections, and encountered all the toils of war, want, and misery, solely actuated by motives the most disinterested and virtuous.

In short they have undergone trials and suffering, with a determined resolution and fortitude, unparalleled in history; and have submitted even to death sooner than stain their integrity, honour, and principled loyalty with the odious guilt of rebellion against their king. . . .

No compensation whatever can be adequate to

the loss sustained by these deserving men, not only of their possessions, and the society of their friends and relations, but of that apparently established felicity and affluence, which they themselves, and their posterity after them, had the prospect of enjoying for ages to come.

―――――

b Arthur R. M. Lower, the Canadian historian, tends to destroy a widely-held glorification of all Loyalists:

It is therefore wrong to believe that the Loyalists could have been chosen spirits, resolved to die rather than submit to a political philosophy of which they disapproved. There were relatively few such men; there were far more whose place in society had singled them out as "Tories" and who were repudiated as such by the new society. But the majority of them must have been plain, bewildered people who found themselves on the losing side for obscure reasons. They had just happened to put their money on the wrong horse. Allegiance is not readily changed and it is now generally agreed that the American revolution, like other revolutions, was made by one minority of active spirits, that the masses were in varying degrees passive and that another minority was actively 'loyal'. The passive many would take their allegiance to the crown for granted but that in itself would not be a cause of exile. . . . Suspicion would fall at once on the people of communities in which active Loyalism was dominant . . . Persons who from whatever reason openly espoused the king's side would be driven out. . . . Whatever their reasons for enlisting (and men enlist for dozens of reasons, among which the pure fire of faith in the cause is usually secondary) the King's soldiers could not stay in the rebels' territories. A large proportion of the Loyalists, especially among those going to Nova Scotia, were soldiers, members of the various Loyalist corps that had been raised during the war.

Not all who remained loyal left the United States; many assessed the new situation and realistically faced the new conditions. In some places, Loyalists or suspected Loyalists were severely mistreated. Wherever loyalist sympathy ran high, as in New York and Pennsylvania, the reaction against the Loyalists was particularly bitter. But in all colonies, many people classified as Loyalists if only because of their sentimental feeling for Britain, lived in an unfriendly atmosphere.

During the revolution, gross injustices were perpetrated against Loyalists and suspected Loyalists in the name of the noble revolutionary ideal. The mere denunciation of the Loyalists as traitors

MISTREATMENT OF LOYALISTS DURING THE REVOLUTION[94]

Ryerson's view, 1880:

In the position of that considerable class of persons who had remained in doubt, the Declaration of Independence and the assumption of State government made a decided change. It was now necessary to choose one side or the other.

Very serious, too, was the change in the legal position of the class known as Tories. . . . Of those thus stigmatized, some were inclined to favour the utmost claims of the mother country; *but the greater part, though determined to adhere to the British connection, yet deprecated the policy which had brought on so fatal a quarrel.* This loyal minority, especially its more conspicuous members . . . had been exposed to the violence of mobs, and to all sorts of personal indignities, in which private malice or a wanton and insolent spirit of mischief had been too often gratified under the disguise of patriotism. The barbarous and disgraceful practice of tarring and feathering and carting Tories, placing them in a cart and carrying them about as a sort of spectacle, had become in some places a favourite amusement. . . .

By the recent political changes, Tories and suspected persons became exposed to dangers from the law as well as from mobs . . . the new State authorities claimed the allegiance of all residents within their limits, and under the lead and recommendation of Congress, those who refused to acknowledge their authority, or who adhered to their enemies, were exposed to severe penalties, confiscation of property, imprisonment, banishment, and finally death.

to the revolution brought them untold suffering. Vigilante committees, acting as defenders of the revolution, took the law into their own hands. Suspected Loyalists suffered indignities, persecution, loss of livelihood and even personal harm. Persons in office, unsympathetic to the revolution, were subjected to political persecution and were ousted from their positions. Those who fought on the side of Britain or who were suspected of aiding Britain often had their property and possessions confiscated. Unruly mobs pillaged and looted the homes of the Loyalists, who had no protection from the law. Many were condemned without judge or jury; some were imprisoned or banished. In areas where the forces of the revolution suffered setbacks, feelings ran high and mobs vented their anger against suspected British sympathizers. The feeling of hostility and resentment against the Loyalists did not abate with the success of the revolution. Victory only increased the hatred against those who had failed to display enthusiasm for the revolutionary cause. In this antagonistic environment, Loyalists found life unbearable, and approximately 50,000 left the United States and took refuge within the Empire. Many went to England, some found their way to Bermuda, others emigrated to Nova Scotia. The conquest of Canada by Britain had provided a new homeland for the colonists who no longer felt at home in the Thirteen Colonies.

At the end of the revolutionary war, New York became the assembling point for Loyalists from the Atlantic coastal colonies. At New York, Carleton made preparations for the evacuation of the thousands who wished to leave the United States. The Atlantic colonists, in the past, had found a kinship with the British colony of Nova Scotia. Now, in this time of need, these refugees were transported in British ships to Nova Scotia where land was plentiful and the British political and social climate was to their liking. Among the arrivals were many Acadians, who returned to their former homeland, and several thousand Negroes. By the end of 1783, more than 30,000 had reached Nova Scotia and had swamped the Nova Scotia population of 17,000.

Of those who came, about 600 went to Prince Edward Island, 3,000 to Cape Breton Island and almost 10,000 disbanded members of loyalist regiments settled along the St. John River, in the fertile St. John Valley, far removed from the seat of government at Halifax. On the southeastern coast near Port Roseway, renamed Shelburne, 10,000 Loyalists set to work to build a port city that would rival Halifax in size and importance.

INDUCEMENTS TO LOYALISTS TO SETTLE IN CAPE BRETON[95]

BY HIS EXCELLENCY JOSEPH FREDERICK WALLET DES BARRES Esq[r]. Governor of the Island of Cape Breton and Dependencies, Commanding His Majesty's Forces therein &c, &c.

A PROCLAMATION

. . . . I have thought fit to inform them [Loyalists]; that a large Body of Land . . . on the Eastern Shore of Sydney Harbor . . . is laid out upon a Plan, calculated to become an opulent Fishing Town surrounded by a fine Farming Country, for the Reception and accommodation of Families who intend to carry on Navigation, Trade, Fishing and Farming, and peculiarly adapted for establishing the Whale Fishery on the largest Scale.

. . . every Settler will have the Choice of as much land, as he can undertake to cultivate, in an Eligible situation either abutting upon some Navigable Water, or upon some principal great Road,

which are opening to form an easy intercourse of Commerce with all parts of the Island.

Provisions will be allowed at the same Rate, and for the same Time as has been allowed to Loyalists in Nova Scotia . . . they will also have a Supply of Implements and Material for Building. . . . Every reasonable assistance to those who may stand in need thereof for their removal will be afforded.

. . . . I have also set apart the Harbour and District around Louisbourg, as appearing to me peculiarly advantageous for the Reception and accommodation of Families who intend to follow the Fishery and principally the Whaling Business.

Dated at Sydney the 1st of September 1785

GOD SAVE THE KING

The British government undertook to settle and assist these refugees as compensation for their loyalty to the Crown. The government of Nova Scotia was instructed to grant one hundred acres of land to the head of a family and fifty acres for each member. Former members of the British forces were given larger grants of up to one thousand acres for a field officer. The newcomers were also provided with tools and provisions to tide them over until they gathered their first harvest.

This large and sudden influx of immigrants was bound to cause difficulties and dislocations. Surveying the land grants was an enormous task, and the shortage of surveyors caused delays in the issuing of land titles. Most of the Loyalists came from the larger towns and cities, and these city dwellers, unaccustomed to the hardships of pioneer life in frontier Nova Scotia, found it extremely difficult to adapt to the new environment. Poor crops and shortages of supplies disheartened many. The Loyalist settlers at Shelburne met financial disaster. Many of them had invested their life savings in expectation of great developments. But Shelburne was poorly located. It was not a year round port and the soil around it was very poor for farming. Shelburne remained only a small fishing village and the newcomers lost their meagre savings. Some Loyalists, unable to face the heartbreaking challenges of the frontier, drifted back to the United States and some who were financially able went to England.

Other difficulties soon became apparent. The Loyalists resented, to some extent, the older established residents of Nova Scotia who had not flocked to the side of Britain during the Revolutionary War. Friction soon developed between the farm element and the urban Loyalists, between civilians and former Loyalist soldiers and between former Loyalist officers and enlisted men. Some of the Loyalists made pretentious demands and exaggerated claims — they felt that they were entitled to many privileges as a reward for their loyalty. All in all, it was a difficult task to adapt to the new and trying conditions; the resulting frustrations bred rivalry, resentment and ill-feeling. Nevertheless, most of the Loyalists remained, settled, built a new life for themselves and their children and contributed greatly to the development of the Maritimes.

South View of Halifax, Nova Scotia, in 1780

THE LOYALISTS IN NOVA SCOTIA[96]

Governor Parr's dispatch on the loyalists, Jan. 24, 1784, seems to indicate some dissatisfaction:

. . . with about 30,000 Souls added to this Province, all of which, except a few lately arriv'd, have got under tolerable Shelter for the Winter, and are accomodated as well as the nature of their situation would admit yet, notwithstanding that I have used every exertion, have done every thing in my power for them, some few discontented Rascals, at the most distant Settlements, begin to be clamorous and seditious, expecting more than possibly can be done in so short a time . . . and I am told have wrote complaints home against me, without having them made known here. . . . Tho they plague me with complaints, and quarrel among themselves &c, I shall continue to render them every good office in my power, and may venture to assert with great confidence, that a *very great* Majority indeed, approve of my Conduct, but there are some not to be pleased or satisfied.

COMPLAINTS ABOUT LAND GRANTS[97]

Mr Stewart's memorandum

March 1802

Nothing has contributed so much to prevent the Settlement of these two Colonies [New Brunswick and Nova Scotia], as the mode in which the granting Land has hitherto been conducted; immense tracts being granted to Individuals, who . . . keep them in an unsettled state on Speculation. . . . In this way large Tracts of Land in both Provinces particularly in Nova Scotia is locked up in the hands of Individuals to the manifest Injury to the Publick.

It is true that many large grants in both Provinces have been escheated for non-performance of the terms of settlement, but . . . these escheated Lands, instead of being parcelled out in small Tracts to actual Settlers, or kept in the hands of Government for that purpose, have been immediately regranted in whole, or in part, to Persons of Consequence in the Province, who by making a

shew of complying with the terms, are by their Influence enabled to keep them in a State of very little more value to the General Prosperity of the Country, than if they had been left in the hands of the Original Grantees.

. . . above one half the extent of both Provinces is totally unfit for Cultivation, being either covered with Rocks or barren Swamps. And it may easily be conceived that it has been the best Lands that have become the Objects of these Speculations. . . . The effect of which has been the driving away of many thousand People who, disgusted at seeing so much of the best Land and most convenient situations in the Province taken up in this manner and not to be obtained but by Purchase, have emigrated to the American states.

No less discouraging than the experiences in Nova Scotia were the trials of the Loyalists who settled in Prince Edward Island. After they had settled and cultivated the land, they discovered that their titles to the land were not valid — they were squatters on land owned by absentee landlords. Many of the Loyalists left Prince Edward Island and those who remained did so as tenant farmers. Not until 1873, when Prince Edward Island joined Confederation, was the whole question of the absentee landowners cleared up.

THE LOYALISTS IN NEW BRUNSWICK[98]

Co. Thomas Dundas to Earl Cornwallis
City of St. John, Province of New Brunswick,
December 28, 1786.

. . . . The new settlements made by the Loyalists are in a thriving way, although rum and idle habits contracted during the war are much against them. They have experienced every possible injury from the old inhabitants of Nova Scotia, who are even more disaffected towards the British Government than any of the new dependent.

To all appearances the country will be able to furnish corn, vegetables and cattle to the West Indies. . . . I cannot say much for the industry of the disbanded soldiers. . . . All the tradesmen who would be valuable at home are starving here or gone to the States.

Edward Winslow to Gregory Townsend,
Kingsclear, 17th January, 1793.

Our province goes on in the old way slowly but tolerably sure. The inhabitants gradually extend their cultivation and we begin to feel the benefit of our exertions. We have good markets in the towns, and the Farmers live comfortably. One arrangement, however, I think we shall have cause to regret — our Gentlemen have all become potato planters and our shoemakers are preparing to legislate. If the operations of the latter do not turn out more profitably than those of the former we shall certainly have a damn'd bad system.

LOYALISTS IN PRINCE EDWARD ISLAND

Lord Selkirk, in his diary, tells of the difficulties a Loyalist settler, Jo Laird in Vernon River, encountered:

. . . part of what Laird told me of his situation — he began here quite bare 8 years ago — has now 50 acres cleared, much upland hay, and a good stock of sheep & cattle, an orchard, a comfortable house & plenty of everything . . . he has 200 acres assigned him as a Loyalist — under a bargain which was made between the Govt & the Grantees of this island several of whom agreed to give up one fourth of their lots to be divided among the Refugees, gratuitously — this they did with a view of peopling their neighbourhood so as to improve the value of the rest of the lot. Laird has been formerly settled on another lot, but after 9 years, it was discovered that by a mistake of the Surveyor he was set down on a lot that was not his own, & he was obliged to remove without receiving any compensation for his improvements. — He does not seem at an end of his troubles — for last year the Govt (now proprietor of this general lot) brought an action of Ejectment on an allegation of a similar error tho' Ld says he holds a patent signed by the Gov. himself. . . .

The Loyalists who came to Quebec were mostly from New York, Pennsylvania and western New England. Unlike those who went to the Maritimes, most of the Loyalists who came to Quebec were backwoods farmers, better suited to the hardships of pioneer life. Even during the war (especially after the defeat of the British forces at Saratoga) Loyalist refugees began drifting into Montreal. At the end of the war, following the well-traveled

Lake Champlain-Richelieu River highway, about 10,000 Loyalists came to Quebec and settled in the untouched stretches of this British colony. Many had been members of Loyalist militia units — such as Butler's Rangers and Johnson's Rangers — which had fought alongside the British against the Americans. There were also many disbanded German, Swiss and Dutch mercenaries who had served in the British army; and some Indian Loyalists, notably those led by the brilliant Chief Brant of the Six Nation Confederacy. There were also a few Quakers and Mennonites who, because of their deep religious convictions, had refused to bear arms in the cause of the revolution. A number came because land grants were given to all who sought haven in this British colony; free land rather than loyalism attracted these "land loyalists."

Understandably, the Loyalists had no desire to live under the French seigneurial system with its alien language, customs, laws and religion. Therefore, Loyalist land grants tended to skirt the settled areas of Quebec. From the principal assembly point at Sorel (Fort William Henry), some Loyalists took up grants of land along the sparsely populated southern shore of the St. Lawrence. These settlements, later to be known as the Eastern Townships, laid the foundation for the English-speaking tradition in the present province of Quebec. The majority of the Loyalists, however, moved west of the settled areas of Quebec to the upper St. Lawrence and the Niagara Peninsula where, together with those who came directly from the American colonies, they laid the foundation for a new English-speaking colony.

Four areas were discernible in the pattern of Loyalist settlement in Quebec. These were the lands on either side of the Grand River, the Upper St. Lawrence between Montreal and Lake Ontario, the Niagara Peninsula and the lands surrounding the Bay of Quinte. As much as possible, Governor Haldimand attempted to keep members of the same military units together. Thus Brant's Indian followers were settled on a reserve along the Grand River; the King's Royal Regiment of New York located along the Upper St. Lawrence; Butler's Rangers took up land along the Niagara River; and the Glengarry Highlanders settled around the Bay of Quinte.

GRANT OF LAND TO THE SIX NATION INDIANS[99]

Haldimand's Proclamation of October 25, 1784:

Whereas His Majesty having been pleased to direct that in Consideration of the early Attachment to His Cause manifested by the Mohawk Indians, & of the Loss of their Settlement they thereby sustained . . . I do hereby in His Majesty's name authorize and permit the said Mohawk Nation, and such other of the Six Nation Indians as wish to settle in that Quarter to take Possession of, & Settle upon the Banks of the River commonly *called Ours* [Ouse] or Grand River, running into Lake Erie, alloting to them for that Purpose Six Miles deep from each Side of the River beginning at Lake Erie, & extending in that Proportion to the Head of the said River, which them & their Posterity are to enjoy for ever.

Land grants and assistance given the Loyalists in Quebec were similar to those given in Nova Scotia. The difficulties of Quebec Loyalists were also similar to those of the Nova Scotia Loyalists and no less trying or rigorous. There were the usual delays in obtaining land grants. Clearing the

A View of Cataraqui, July 16, 1784

LAND GRANTS TO LOYALISTS IN QUEBEC[100]

Additional Instructions to Haldimand, July 16th, 1783.

. . . . It is Our Will and pleasure, that immediately after you shall receive this Our Instruction, you do direct our Surveyor General of Lands for our said Province of Quebec, to admeasure & lay out such a Quantity of Land as you with the advice of our Council shall deem necessary & convenient for the Settlement of our said Loyal Subjects. . . .

To every Master of a Family, One Hundred Acres, and Fifty Acres for each person, of which his Family shall consist.

To every single Man Fifty Acres.

To every Non-Commissioned Officer of our Forces reduced in Quebec Two Hundred Acres.

To every private Man reduced as aforesaid One Hundred Acres.

And for every Person in their Family Fifty Acres.

virgin forests presented difficulties on the western frontier similar to those encountered in Nova Scotia. Furthermore, in 1786, when British aid ceased, the precarious conditions of the Loyalist settlements worsened. In 1788, "The Hungry Year," the settlers were faced with crop failures, shortage of food and a severe winter.

THE "HUNGRY YEAR"[101]

A description:

. . . many are the touching stories . . . of this sad first page in the history of Upper Canada when from Lower Canada to the outskirts of the settlement was heard the cry for *bread! bread! bread!*

The year of the famine is spoken of sometimes as the "scarce", sometimes as the "hungry year," or the "hard summer." The extreme distress seems to have commenced in the year 1787. With some, it lasted a part of a year, with others a year, and with others upwards of a year. The height of the distress was during the spring and early summer of 1788. . . .

. . . . One individual has left the record that she used to allay pangs of hunger by eating a little salt. But the majority of the settlers had no salt, and game and fish, when it could be caught, was eaten without that condiment. . . . Often when fish or game was caught, it was forthwith roasted, without waiting to go home to have it dressed. As spring advanced, and the buds of the trees began to swell, they were gathered and eaten. Roots were digged out of the ground; the bark of certain trees were stripped off and consumed as food. One family lived for a fortnight on beech leaves. Everything that was supposed to be capable of alleviating the pangs of hunger, whether it yielded nutriment or not, was unhesitatingly used; and . . . some were killed by eating poisonous roots. Beef bones were, in one neighbourhood, not only boiled again and again, but actually carried from house to house, to give a little taste to boiled bran, until there remained no taste in the boiling water. . . .

The summer of 1789 brought relief to most of the settlers, — the heaviest of the weight of woe was removed. But, for nearly a decade, they enjoyed but few comforts, and were often without the necessities of life. . . .

But in spite of the hardships, the Loyalists in Quebec generally adjusted much better than those in Nova Scotia. The rigors of frontier life were not new to the farmers who had come to Quebec from

A Winter Scene in Fredericton, 1833

hand . . . in later years, occasionally spinning wheels and looms were brought in. . . .

When the skins of sheep, and of calves, and beef became available, every farmer became his own tanner . . . and then his own shoemaker. . . .

It was not until the close of the last [18th] century, that wearing articles, other than those made out of flax and wool, were to be obtained. A calico dress was a decided luxury. The petticoat and short gown of linen, was more common. A long chintz dress to go to a meeting was the height of many a damsel's ambition, or a grogram dress and short petticoat. . . .

the American colonies. These hewers of the forests and tillers of the soil laid a British foundation in a colony which, twenty years earlier, Carleton had asserted was to be French "to the end of Time."

LOYALISTS CLOTHE THEMSELVES[102]

. . . . Tight knee-breeches and silver buckles would decorate the bodies of some, who had in other days mixed in the fashionable throng, perhaps luxuriated in the gay city of New York. . . . Those who left their homes hurriedly during the course of the war . . . brought only what was upon their backs. . . . The disbanded soldiers had no more than what belongs to a soldier's kit. . . . A few year's of exposure to the wear and tear of pioneer life would quite destroy the best supplied wardrobe, however carefully husbanded, or ingeniously mended by the anxious wife . . . the supply of clothing was scant and dear . . . the vast majority of the inhabitants had to look to the production of their lands wherewith to cover the nakedness of their families. . . .

The Indians . . . gave to the settlers the idea of manufacturing garments out of deer skin. . . . Trowsers made of this material were not only comfortable for winter, but very durable. . . . Petticoats for women were often made of the same material . . . moccasins were procured from the buck-skin, and some had enough deer-skin to make covering for beds . . . the settlers commenced at an early period to cultivate flax, and as soon as possible to procure sheep. For many years almost every family made their various garments, for both sexes, of the coarse linen made from flax, and cloth wool raised at home and carded by

The Loyalist migration represented the first substantial increase in the population of Canada since the efforts of Colbert had enticed some Frenchmen to settle in the Canadian wilderness. However, the Loyalist influx was not to be the last large migration to Canada. On two later occasions — the Great Migration of 1815-1850 and the Laurier-Sifton migration of 1897-1914 — Canada was again to experience the dislocation and exhilaration resulting from large scale immigration. Each of these four migrations altered the character of Canada. However, the most profound economic, social and political changes were brought about by the coming of the Loyalists. It is difficult to understate the effects of the Loyalist migration on British North America. The addition of 50,000 Loyalists to the population of British North America injected new vitality into the economic life of the colonies, extended the frontier of settlement westward, endowed the colonies with long-lasting traditions of loyalty to the British Crown and initiated far-reaching political and constitutional changes.

Generally, the Loyalists had enjoyed a vigorous economic existence in the Thirteen Colonies. Their coming gave British North America a semblance of a middle class. Doctor and lawyer, politician and shopkeeper, farmer and pioneer, tradesman and businessman had come and immediately had begun practicing his profession, trade or skill. With the growth of towns, public works were undertaken, schools built, more newspapers founded. Small shops tendered to the needs of the townspeople, while giant enterprises in fishing, lumbering and shipbuilding catered to the demands of the Empire. A brisk carrying trade with the West Indies also developed. At last, the Canadian economy was becoming diversified. Diversification, however, did not mean the end of the fur trade. Furs and the revenue derived from them continued to be a prime factor in the economic life of

British North America. Fur traders continued their frantic search for new fur areas to meet the challenge of American competition.

While the fur frontier was moving systematically westward across the continent, the farm frontier was also moving, though at a slower pace, and reached only as far as Lake Erie. With the coming of the Loyalists, new farms sprang into existence in the hitherto untilled fertile land of the Upper St. Lawrence and in the Niagara Peninsula. From the Maritimes to the Great Lakes Loyalist towns such as Shelburne, Saint John, Niagara, Kingston and York dotted the map of British North America.

The Loyalists had a profound effect on the economic life and the movement of the frontier. But they had no less an effect on the attitudes and character of British North America. Many of the Loyalists had come because they cherished the British connection; the Empire, the King, the aristocracy, the rule of law, parliament and the rights of Englishmen were sacred to them. The Loyalists could not conceive of an existence outside the British Empire, divorced from the heritage they treasured. They despised the radical republicanism of the United States whose adherents had dared to rise in rebellion against King and Parliament. To the Loyalists, life in British North America within the confines of the Empire was preferable to the untried and risky path of republicanism with its "rule by the rabble."

Not only had the Loyalists brought with them useful trades and professions; they had also transplanted their ideals and attitudes to British North America. Sheer weight of numbers allowed the Loyalists to impress upon the somewhat unenthusiastic British North American colonies the value of British institutions and the necessity of the British connection. As a result of the coming of the Loyalists, the organization and political institutions of British North America, particularly in Quebec, underwent fundamental changes. The presence of large numbers of Loyalists on the north shore of the Bay of Fundy — far removed from the capital in Halifax — resulted in the creation of the new colony of New Brunswick.

POLITICAL INFLUENCE OF THE LOYALISTS[103]

Loyalists who settled at the St. John River came into conflict with Governor Parr. They wanted additional representation in the Nova Scotia Assembly. Soon they demanded separation from Nova Scotia:

The Loyalists then began to agitate for a divi-sion of the province — a policy which was strongly opposed by the Governor. Parr went as far as to remove some of the Loyalists to the other side of the Bay of Fundy, in the hope that that would settle the agitation; but it only increased it, and the Loyalists, who had many warm and influential friends at court, urged a division so earnestly that the Ministry yielded to their wishes, and the Province of New Brunswick was created (in 1784), so called out of compliment to the reigning family of England. . . .

Like Nova Scotia and Prince Edward Island (which had been established as a separate colony in 1769), New Brunswick was to have a representative government — that is, an elected assembly. But the creation of a new province in the Maritimes was a relatively simple solution to a relatively simple problem.

The problem of the Loyalists in Quebec could not be resolved so easily. In Quebec, the very presence of 10,000 English-speaking, largely Protestant Loyalists rendered the Quebec Act of 1774 obsolete. The Quebec Act had been formulated to govern a French, Roman Catholic population and to protect and guarantee a culture that was foreign to the Loyalists. It was unrealistic to expect that British subjects, who had sacrificed their homes and possessions in order to perpetuate their British heritage, would live under French customs and laws. It was also unjust to deny (as the Quebec Act had done) an elected assembly to the Quebec Loyalists while those in the Maritimes enjoyed representative government. The whole problem of Quebec — an English-speaking minority in a British colony, governed by a constitution geared to a French-speaking majority — occupied the attentions of many British and colonial statesmen. The Constitutional or Canada Act of 1791 was devised as the solution.

REQUEST FOR CHANGE IN THE LAND TENURE SYSTEM[104]

Dorchester to Sydney:

Quebec 13 June 1787.
. . . . The English party has gained considerable strength of late years by the Loyalists . . . so that it is more than probable the desire for an Assembly will annually increase; yet common prudence seems to require . . . in a country composed of different languages, manners, and religions (where

nine tenths of the people are ignorant of the nature and importance of an Assembly) that the whole plan should be minutely unfolded, and its effects upon the Legislature and the provincial economy clearly discerned ... I confess myself as yet at a loss for any plan likely to give satisfaction. ...

But what urges more immediately is an alteration in the tenure of lands to be granted by the Crown. The Instructions [July 2nd, 1771, which Carleton had recommended] direct that these lands be granted in a manner similar to the tenure under the French Government ... so great have been the changes of late years on this Continent, that a new line of policy, adapted to the present relative condition of the Neighbouring States, and suited to the minds and temper of the King's subjects, is become indispensably necessary for Great Britain. I therefore humbly recommend that His Majesty would be graciously pleased to allow His Governor and Council to grant His lands in free and common soccage, unincumbered with any crown rent whatever. ...

C

THE CONSTITUTIONAL ACT

Even before the American Revolution had broken out, some politicians and statesmen in Great Britain began to doubt the wisdom of the whole imperial concept. They argued that colonies were expensive to maintain, difficult to defend and impossible to manage. In their judgment, the disadvantages of colonies far outweighed the advantages that Britain obtained by controlling colonial trade and commerce. Moreover, the American Revolution had pointed out to them the inevitability of colonial independence. Their opinion was that Britain should dissolve the ties binding her to the colonies before she was faced with another great colonial tragedy.

However, the opinion that prevailed in Britain was that the mercantilist concepts of empire were still valid and that colonies were absolutely essential to Britain's well-being. It was argued that the American Revolution, although unfortunate, had taught a very valuable lesson in colonial management. Neither Britain's efforts to tax the colonies nor her control of colonial trade was the real cause of the revolution. The revolution had been caused by the all too active colonial assemblies. The imbalance between the prerogatives of the Crown and the democratic assemblies had thrown the whole imperial system out of kilter. The colonial assemblies had grown far too powerful. Their control of the purse-strings had hamstrung the Governor — the representative of the Crown. Finally, with no established church and no hereditary aristocracy to counterbalance the democratic element, the assemblies had grown to the point where they challenged imperial authority itself.

Therefore, in reorganizing the Empire, certain precautions had to be taken. Colonies were to be kept small, separate and dependent — the principle of divide and rule was to apply. Elected assemblies were to be tolerated because they would enable the imperial government to raise taxes in the colony without risking the old charge of taxation without representation. But the assemblies were to be restrained, lest they become too powerful. Traditions of loyalty and respect for imperial authority were to be inculcated by structuring colonial society, as far as possible, along the lines of British society. Dangerous democratic tendencies were to be checked by the leadership of a colonial aristocracy and the moderating influence of an established church. Colonial political systems were to become carbon copies of Great Britain's. Governor, Executive Council, Legislative Council and Legislative Assembly would become the colonial counterparts of the Crown, Cabinet, House of Lords and House of Commons.

William Smith, a prominent Loyalist and the first Chief Justice of Canada, argued that such organization of the colonies was the surest guarantee of loyalty. He was convinced that some of the rebellious American colonies might willingly rejoin the Empire were they to see the advantages accruing to British North America from the exercise of British institutions.

The Constitutional Act assumed the division of Quebec roughly along the Ottawa River into Lower Canada to the east and Upper Canada to the west. This would allow the French (and a small English minority) in Lower Canada and the Loyalists in Upper Canada to work out their separate destinies. It recognized the fact that there were two races, two languages, two cultures and two sets of institutions in Canada.

"A Bill for the better government of Canada was brought forward by Mr. Pitt. It was proposed to divide province into two parts." Pitt gives the reason in a speech to the House of Commons:

This division could, I hope, be made in such a manner as to give each a great majority in their own particular share, although it cannot be expected to draw a line of complete separation. Any inconveniences to be apprehended from ancient Canadians being included in the one, or British settlers in the other, would be remedied by the double legislature which I seek to establish, by appointing in each a House of Assembly, and a Council, so as to give them the full advantages of the British Constitution. . . . If the province were not to be divided, there would be only one House of Assembly; and there being two parties, if these parties had been equal, or nearly equal, in the Assembly, it would have been the source of perpetual faction; while if one party had been much stronger than the other, the minority might not without some justice call itself oppressed.

The Constitutional Act created new governments in both Canadas. There was to be a Governor-General, appointed by the Crown, over both colonies, with nominal authority over all British North America. Under him, each of the Canadas was to have an appointed Lieutenant-Governor. In practice, however, the Lieutenant-Governor of Upper Canada usually acted quite independently of the Governor-General. Also, the Governor-General, who resided in Quebec, handled the office of Lieutenant-Governor of Lower Canada. In actuality, there was a Governor in Upper Canada and a Governor in Lower Canada.

In each colony there was to be an Executive Council whose members were appointed for life. This Council was to advise the Governor and its members were to be the managers of the public business. Although there are some very fundamental differences, Executive Councillors of Upper and Lower Canada performed functions similar to present day Cabinet ministers when they act as leaders of government departments.

The Constitutional Act also provided for a second council — a Legislative Council in both Upper and Lower Canada. The members of these Councils were also to be appointed for life and were, thus, beyond the control of the people or the elected assembly. This Council would share legislative (law-making) authority with the Assembly. No measure proposed by the Assembly could become law without the consent of the Legislative Council. The Legislative Councils were to be a further check on any radicalism that might develop within the Assemblies.

Provision was also made for elected Assemblies in both Upper and Lower Canada. Nova Scotia had had such an Assembly since 1758; the newer Maritime colonies of New Brunswick and Prince Edward Island also elected Legislative Assemblies. In view of the circumstances in the Maritimes, it was felt that Assemblies could not be withheld from the Canadas. Moreover, Upper Canadian Loyalists, accustomed to a Legislative Assembly in the Thirteen Colonies, expected to be granted this basic British institution. In the light of her American experience, Britain was reluctant to impose taxes on her colonies. Legislative Assemblies in the Canadas would be empowered to levy taxes for local purposes. Thus, Britain would be absolved from the necessity of levying direct taxes on the people of her North American colonies.

Members were elected to the Legislative Assemblies by voters who either possessed property or paid a specific minimum yearly rental. The Assemblies were to be called into session at least once every twelve months, and an election of a new Assembly would have to take place at least once every four years. While the grant of Assemblies conceded representative government to the Canadas, the authority of these Assemblies was severely limited. A measure passed by the Assembly had to receive the consent of the Legislative Council and the Governor before it became law. Even then, the British government could rescind a law any time within two years of its passage.

To avoid the situation that had developed in the American colonies, where the Governor had to depend on the Assembly for funds to run the government, the Constitutional Act gave the Governor a source of revenue free of Assembly control. An amount equal to one-seventh of all public lands granted was reserved for the expenses of the government. It was hoped that the money earned from the sale of these Crown Reserves would enable the Governor and his Executive Council to finance the operations of government independently of the Assembly.

The Constitutional Act envisaged the creation of a colonial aristocracy and an established church. The provision for granting titles was never introduced into the Canadas. It is difficult to imagine a titled nobility in the frontier environs of North America. However, one-seventh of all the lands granted were set aside for the maintenance of a "Protestant Clergy" in both Upper and Lower Canada. The Governor of each colony was also empowered to erect and endow parsonages as he saw fit.

Ontario's First Parliament Buildings, 1796

THE CONSTITUTIONAL ACT PROVIDES FOR CLERGY RESERVES[106]

XXXVI. And whereas his Majesty has been graciously pleased, by Message to both Houses of Parliament, to express His Royal Desire to be enabled to make a permanent Appropriation of Lands in the said Provinces for the Support and Maintenance of a Protestant Clergy within the same . . . be it enacted . . . to authorize the Governor or Lieutenant Governor of each of the said Provinces . . . to make, from and out of the Lands of the Crown within such Allotment and Appropriation of Lands, for the Support and Maintenance of a Protestant Clergy . . . as may bear a due Proportion to the Amount of such Lands within the same as have at any Time been granted by or under the Authority of His Majesty . . . and that such Lands, so allotted and appropriated, shall be, as nearly as the Circumstances and Nature of the Case will admit, of the like Quality as the Lands in respect of which the same are so allotted and Appropriated, and shall be, as nearly as the same can be estimated at the Time of making such Grant, equal in Value to the Seventh Part of the Lands so granted.

Although the Constitutional Act was prompted by the necessity of satisfying Loyalist demands, the British government had no intention of accomplishing this at the expense of the French-Canadian population. France was in the throes of revolution, and there was a danger that an alienated and discontented French-Canadian population might embrace the spirit of the French Revolution. Therefore, the provisions of the Quebec Act dealing with freedom of religion, French civil law and seigneurial tenure were retained in Lower Canada, although, if desired, the Governor could grant lands according to British freehold tenure. In Upper Canada, of course, freehold tenure was instituted and the British legal system came into use through legislative enactment.

The social and political climate of the times ensured the smooth operation of the Constitutional Act, and for the time being gave a measure of stability to British North America. The Loyalists were satisfied with the Act and were not seriously concerned with the restrictions placed on the Assembly. They were quite contented with oligarchic rule. The French Canadians were not unduly disturbed over the addition of an Assembly which they controlled. For the time being they had only quiet reservations about the English-dominated Legislative Council. After all, the guarantees of the Quebec Act were further assured by the new Act. Only the perennially discontented English-speaking merchants in Lower Canada raised serious objections. At long last they had been granted an Assembly, but it was an Assembly they could not control.

Just as a migration of people had given birth to the Constitutional Act so also did a later migration of people herald its death. Serious difficulties were to arise over the limitations placed upon the Assembly. The Crown and Clergy Reserves were to arouse bitter discord. The very division of Quebec was later to be questioned. The new immigrants, who began pouring into British North

Quebec from Point Lévis, 1818

America after 1815, were to challenge the economic and political ascendency of the Loyalists and the Act which made this ascendency possible.

PRAISE OF THE CONSTITUTIONAL ACT[107]

[a]*Lieutenant-Governor John Graves Simcoe, when closing the session of the Legislative Assembly of Upper Canada on October 15, 1792, praised the Constitutional Act as follows:*

. . . at this juncture I particularly recommend you to explain that this province is singally blessed, not with a mutilated Constitution, but with a Constitution which has stood the test of experience, and is the very image and transcript of that of Great Britain, by which she has long established and secured to her subjects as much freedom and happiness as is possible to be enjoyed under the subordination necessary to civilized society.

CRITICISM OF THE CONSTITUTIONAL ACT

[b]*Goldwin Smith, the nineteenth century Canadian historian and economist, commented on Simcoe's praise of the Constitutional Act:*

Though it might be the express image in form, it was far from being the express image in reality of Parliamentary Government as it exists in Great Britain, or even as it existed in Great Britain at the time. . . . Thus the imitation was somewhat like the Chinese imitation of the steam-vessel, exact in everything except the steam. . . .

In spite of the inherent weakness within the Constitutional Act, it did provide a stable political framework within which the colonies could grow and prosper. This political stability proved to be their strength in 1812, when the second war with the Americans threatened the very existence of the colonies.

12

BRITISH NORTH AMERICA SURVIVES AND EXPANDS

A

THE WAR OF 1812

After 1783, Britain, in the hope of recovering the Ohio Valley ceded to the United States in the Treaty of Versailles, delayed the transfer of the western posts she held on American soil. Although Britain used American failure to compensate Loyalist claims as a pretense for holding on to the western posts, there were more important reasons. The retention of the posts gave the disgruntled Montreal fur interests continued access to the fur lands from which they were technically barred by the Treaty of Versailles. Perhaps of greatest importance to Britain was the Indian problem; the retention of the western posts was to signify that Britain had no intention of abandoning her Indian allies for whom the Versailles Treaty made no provision.

The Indians, alarmed by the relentless move of American settlers westward, carried out successful raids and between 1786 and 1791 recovered some territory south of the Ohio River. Lord Dorchester (Sir Guy Carleton), the Governor of Quebec, feared a renewed war between Britain and the United States, and he believed that it was necessary to retain the western posts. Such a course would regain Indian confidence and eliminate the possibility of Indian attacks on Quebec. Also, in the event of war with the United States, the Indian territory could serve as a buffer zone between the United States and Quebec.

Britain's retention of the western posts offended American national pride. The renewed Indian warfare confirmed American suspicion that Britain was inciting Indian hostility against the United States. The Americans took a determined stand; in 1794 they decisively defeated the Indians at Fallen Timbers. But since Britain was already at war with revolutionary France, it was essential to avert a possible war with the United States; Britain readily concluded Jay's Treaty with the United

States in 1794 in order to settle outstanding differences over the boundary, the western posts, and the Indian frontier.

Jay's Treaty specified that Britain was to surrender the western posts by 1796. The United States also promised to review the long delayed and unsettled Loyalist claims. As a result of the wording of the Treaty of Versailles, friction had arisen between Maine and New Brunswick over which was the "St. Croix River" and what constituted the "Highlands." The dispute was referred to a joint Anglo-American commission which, in 1798, concluded a temporary agreement. However, the Maine-New Brunswick boundary was not fully defined until the Webster-Ashburton Treaty of 1842.

Although Jay's Treaty ushered in a period of cordial relations between Britain and the United States, the war in Europe cast ominous shadows on Anglo-American friendship. The United States, neutral in the conflict, carried on a brisk and thriving trade with both belligerents. Britain viewed with some misgivings the aid France was deriving from this neutral trade. Britain managed to tighten her naval blockade of Europe, and in so doing infringed upon the rights of neutral traders, particularly the Americans. She exercised her traditional right to search neutral ships for deserters from the British navy. Also, she began to seize neutral cargoes destined for the Continent. Americans suffered no financial loss since the shippers were compensated by the British government. The restriction of trade, the seizure of cargoes and the removal from American vessels of suspected deserters aroused some objection in the United States, but not enough to create extensive anti-British sentiments.

After a short peace, the war in Europe resumed in 1803. Britain, intent upon checking Napoleon's

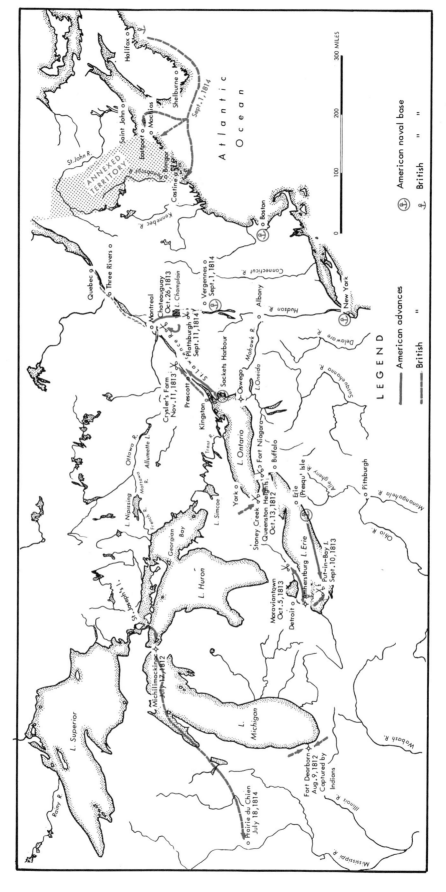

The War of 1812

Action Between H.M.S. **Shannon** and U.S. Frigate **Chesapeake**, off Boston Light House, June 1, 1813

imperial ambitions, relied even more on her sea power and she renewed her right of search of neutral American vessels on the high seas. Flushed with her maritime victory at Trafalgar, she declared the coast of western Europe blockaded. In answer to this British action, Napoleon issued his Berlin Decree in 1806 which ordered the blockade of the British Isles and prohibited neutral vessels from trading with Britain. This "Continental System" aimed to close the European continent to British trade. Britain, in 1807, retaliated with her Orders-in-Council which further tightened her blockade of the coast of Europe from Copenhagen to Trieste. Neutral vessels had to be cleared in a British port and had to pay duties there before they were allowed to proceed to a European port. In the same year, Napoleon countered with his Milan Decree which declared that ships which obeyed the British Orders-in-Council lost their status of neutrality.

The war in Europe had become a series of blockades and counter-blockades in which the freedom of the seas was denied to neutrals. Since France was in no position to enforce any effective naval blockade, Napoleon's decrees scarcely impeded American trade with Britain. On the other hand, Britain's Orders-in-Council effectively cut off trade between the United States and the Continent. The United States resented British interference with the American trade.

In addition, Britain insisted on the right of searching American vessels for deserters from the British navy. At this time, conditions in the British navy were severe and desertions were common. Many of the deserters served on American ships. British warships forcibly stopped American merchant ships on the high seas and removed suspected deserters. Frequently, American sailors were seized and forced to serve on British ships. The

United States justifiably considered the right of search as a violation of the freedom of the high seas and also as an interference with American sovereignty.

The searching of American vessels inevitably led to a number of incidents, the most famous of which was the *Chesapeake* affair. In June, 1807, the *Leopard,* a British warship, fired on the *Chesapeake* in the coastal waters of Virginia and removed four supposed British deserters from the American ship. Britain readily admitted that the action of the *Leopard* in American waters was illegal. Nonetheless, Americans were deeply indignant over the incident and antagonism towards Britain mounted. It was only President Jefferson's calmness which prevented the *Chesapeake* affair from developing into an open conflict between the United States and Britain.

President Jefferson took steps to avert war. In 1807, the Embargo Act was passed. It forbade both the departure of ships for foreign ports and trade with any foreign country. In 1809, the Non-Intercourse Law forbade commerce and trade with the belligerents only. Jefferson earnestly expected that his actions would force France and Britain to withdraw their restrictions on American trade. The Americans, however, interpreted Jefferson's efforts as a sign of weakness. In truth, America's neutral role had little, if any, impact on the events in Europe; neutrality hurt only American merchant shipping which lay idle in the home ports. American neutrality benefited only the British North American colonies. The ports of Nova Scotia became important naval bases and shipping centres. British North America became a source of supply for many goods that Britain had previously purchased in the United States and Europe. The curtailment of American maritime trade began to affect the American economy and became the major grievance against Britain. The Americans were in no mood for Jefferson, the man of peace. When James Madison was elected president in 1809, Americans looked upon the new president to take effective action against Britain.

A WAR HAWK DEMANDS WAR[108]

Representative Felix Grundy of Tennessee, in an eloquent speech in Congress on December 9, 1811, expressed Western thinking:

. . . . The rapid growth of our commercial importance has not only awakened the jealousy of the commercial interests of Great Britain, but her statesmen, no doubt, anticipate with deep concern the maritime greatness of this republic. . . .

What . . . are we now called on to decide? It is whether we will resist by force the attempt, made by the [British] government, to subject our maritime rights to the arbitrary and capricious rule of her will. For my part I am not prepared to say that this country shall submit to have our commerce interdicted, or regulated, by any foreign nation . . . I prefer war to submission.

My mind is irresistibly drawn to the West. . . . It cannot be believed . . . that the savage tribes, uninfluenced by other powers, would think of making war on the United States. They understand too well their own weakness and our strength. . . . How, then . . . are we to account for their late conduct? In one way only . . . . Great Britain alone has intercourse with those Northern tribes. I therefore infer that if British gold has not been employed, their baubles and trinkets, and the promise of support and a place of refuge, if necessary, have had their effect.

Ask the Northern man, and he will tell you that any state of things is better than the present. Inquire of the Western people why their crops are not equal to what they were in former years; they will answer that industry has no stimulus left, since their surplus products have no markets. . . .

This war, if carried on successfully, will have its advantages. We shall drive the British from our continent. They will no longer have an opportunity of intriguing with our Indian neighbors and setting on the ruthless savage to tomahawk our women and children. That nation will lose her Canadian trade, and, by having no resting place in this country, her means of annoying us will be diminished.

Madison's ascendency to the presidency encouraged the War Hawks — western members of Congress who advocated war with Britain and an invasion of British North America. They were supported by southern Congressmen who wanted to annex Florida in order to remove any Spanish threat from the south. But the United States was a divided nation on the question of war with Great Britain, with whom the coastal states, especially New England and New York, enjoyed a vigorous trade. But in the event of a war they would be vulnerable to British naval attacks. It was the outbreak of Indian wars that fanned the war spirit and played into the hands of the War Hawks.

OPPOSITION TO THE WAR HAWKS[109]

Congressman John Randolph of Virginia rejects Grundy's contentions:

. . . Advantage had been taken of the spirit of the Indians, broken by the war . . . they had been pent up by subsequent treaties into nooks, straightened in their quarters by a blind cupidity seeking to extinguish their title to immense wildernesses, for which (possessing, as we do already, more land than we can sell or use) we shall not have occasion for half a century to come. It was our own thirst for territory, our own want of moderation, that had driven these sons of nature to desperation, of which we felt the effects. . . .

Our people will not submit to be taxed for this war of conquest and dominion. The government of the United States was not calculated to wage offensive foreign war — it was instituted for the common defense and general welfare.

. . . Sir, if you go to war it will not be for the protection of, or defense of, your maritime rights. Gentlemen from the North have been taken up to some high mountain and shown all the kingdoms of the earth; and Canada seems tempting in their sight. . . .

Agrarian cupidity, not maritime right, urges the war . . . we have heard but one word — like the ship-poor-will, but one eternal monotonous tone — Canada! Canada! Canada! Not a syllable about Halifax, which unquestionably should be our great object in a war for maritime security.

It is to acquire a prepondering Northern influence that you are to launch into war. For purposes of maritime safety, the barren rocks of Bermuda were worth more to us than all the deserts [of Canada] through which Hearne and McKenzie had pushed their adventurous researches.

Tecumseh, the chief of the Shawnee Indians, like Pontiac before him, attempted to form a confederacy of all tribes to halt American penetration into Indian lands. The United States viewed this development seriously and took decisive action against Tecumseh. In 1811, the battle of Tippecanoe, the Indians were defeated and Tecumseh's coalition was destroyed. The War Hawks argued that Britain was behind the Indian unrest and that British North America had provided the Indians with guns and ammunition. In 1812, Indian wars in the west broke out again, and the War Hawks intensified their clamour for war against Britain.

TECUMSEH CHALLENGES AMERICAN LAND PURCHASE[110]

William Henry Harrison, the aggressive governor of Indiana Territory, had negotiated a series of land-grabbing agreements with the Indians. Two Indian tribes, ignoring the rights of all others and succumbing to firewater, sold 3,000,000 acres for a pittance. The gifted Shawnee chief Tecumseh, confronted Harrison and threatened to resist white occupancy of the ceded land:

. . . [the Indians] once a happy race, since made miserable by the people, who are never contented, but always encroaching . . . to check and stop this evil is for all the red men to unite in claiming a common equal right in the land, as it was at first, and should be yet. For it never was divided, but belongs to all for the use of each. That no part has a right to sell, even to each other, much less to strangers; those who want all, and will not do with less.

The white people have no right to take the land from the Indians, because they had it first. It is theirs. They may sell, but all must join. Any sale not made by all is not valid. The late sale is bad. It was made by a part only. Part do not know how to sell. It requires all to make a bargain for all. All red men have equal rights to the unoccupied land. The right of occupancy is as good in one place as in another. There cannot be two occupations in the same place. The first excludes the others. It is not so in hunting or traveling; for there the same ground will serve many, as they may follow each other all day. But the camp is stationary, and that is occupancy. It belongs to the first who sits down and on his blanket or skins which he has thrown upon the ground; and till he leaves it no other has a right. . . .

The War Hawks became more brazen in their insistence upon the conquest of British North America in order to remove the cause of Indian unrest. To whet American appetite for war, the War Hawks spoke of an easy victory. While Britain was occupied with the intensified war in Europe, she could offer only limited help to her colonies in North America. The half million population of British North America was hardly a match for the eight million Americans. The long, poorly defended border could be crossed at will by an American army. Also, an invading American army could count upon the many Americans who had settled in both Upper and Lower Canada to welcome it as a liberator who would throw off "the yoke of British oppression." An easy conquest would open the rich fertile land of Upper Canada for American occupancy; and the annexation of British North America would give the United States control of the St. Lawrence as a seaway to Europe.

NEWSPAPER EDITOR URGES WAR[111]

This editorial in the DAILY NATIONAL INTELLI-GENCE, *a Washington newspaper, of April 14, 1812, urges to stab Britain in the back while she is engaged in war against Napoleon:*

. . . . It is said that we are not prepared for war. . . . This is an idle objection. . . . The fact is otherwise. . . .

Do we apprehend danger to ourselves? From what quarter will it assail us? From England, and by invasion? The idea is too absurd to merit a moment's consideration. Where are her troops? But lately she dreaded an invasion of her own dominions from her powerful and menacing neighbor [France]. That danger, it is true, has diminished, but it has not entirely and forever disappeared. . . .

The war in the [Spanish] Peninsula, which lingers, requires strong armies to support it. She [England] maintains an army in Sicily; another in India; and a strong force in Ireland, and along her own coast, and in the West Indies. Can anyone believe that, under such circumstances, the British government could be so infatuated, or rather mad, as to send troops here for the purpose of invasion?

Have we cause to dread an attack from her neighboring provinces [Canada]? That apprehension is still more groundless. Seven or eight millions of people have nothing to dread from 300,000. From the moment that war is declared, the British colonies will be put on the defensive, and soon after we get in motion must sink under the pressure.

The advantages of a retaliatory war on British North America seemed most appealing. The prospects of an easy victory held promise for the successful solution of all problems and grievances. Many American newspapers began to beat the drums of war and championed war on British North America as a punitive measure against Britain. A successful war would rescue American national honour and affirm America's sovereignty. A successful war would end the economic depression which resulted from the strangulation of trade caused by the British blockade and would eliminate Britain, the instigator of the Indian troubles, from the North American continent.

NEWSPAPER EDITOR REJECTS WAR[112]

Editor William Coleman of the NEW YORK EVEN-ING POST, *in an editorial of April 21, 1812, opposes a war against Britain:*

Citizens, if pecuniary redress is your object in going to war with England, the measure is perfect madness. You will lose millions when you will gain a cent. The expense will be enormous. It will ruin our country. Direct taxes must be resorted to. . . .
. . . Our territories are already too large. The desire to annex Canada to the United States is as base an ambition as ever burned in the bosom of Alexander. . . . Canada, if annexed to the United States, will furnish offices to a set of hungry villains, grown quite too numerous for our present wide limits. And that is all the benefit we ever shall derive from it.

. . . Their [Britain's] fleets will hover on our coasts, and can trace our line from Maine to New Orleans in a few weeks. Gunboats cannot repel them, nor is there a fort on all our shores in which confidence can be placed. The ruin of our seaports and loss of all vessels will form an item in the list of expenses. . . .

As to the main points of attack or defense, I shall only say that an efficient force will be necessary. A handful of men cannot run up and take Canada, in a few weeks, for mere diversion.

The conflict will be long and severe, resistance formidable, and the final result doubtful. A nation that can debar the conqueror of Europe [Napoleon] from the sea, and resist his armies in Spain, will not surrender its provinces without a struggle. Those who advocate a British war must be perfectly aware that the whole revenue arising from all British America for the ensuing century would not repay the expenses of that war.

President Madison was under pressure from the western and southern representatives in Congress. On June 1, 1812, he delivered his War Message to Congress. In it, he outlined American grievances against Britain as follows: impressment, violation of American territorial waters, interference with American trade, the blockade and Indian attacks instigated by Britain.

CONGRESSIONAL VOTING ON THE DECLARATION
OF WAR, BY STATES[113]

| | HOUSE OF REPRESENTATIVES | | SENATE | |
	For	Against	For	Against
New Hampshire	3	2	1	1
Vermont	3	1	1	0
Massachusetts (Including Maine)	6	8	1	1
Rhode Island	0	2	0	2
Connecticut	0	7	0	2
New York	3	11	1	1
New Jersey	2	4	1	1
Delaware	0	1	0	2
Pennsylvania	16	2	2	0
Maryland	6	3	1	1
Virginia	14	5	2	0
North Carolina	6	3	2	0
South Carolina	6	0	2	0
Georgia	3	0	2	0
Ohio	1	0	0	1
Kentucky	5	0	1	1
Tennessee	3	0	2	0
	79	49	19	13

Britain too was under pressure. The commercial interests in Britain pressed for the removal of the Orders-in-Council. The British government decided to abandon the Orders-in-Council on June 17 — the same day the American Senate voted for war. The slowness of communication must bear some responsibility for the declaration of a war which might have been averted had the American Congress been aware of the suspension of the Orders-in-Council. On June 18, 1812, the United States declared war on Britain.

PROCLAMATION OF BRIG.-GENERAL HULL[114]

A Proclamation

[July 12, 1812]

INHABITANTS OF CANADA! . . . The army under my Command has invaded your Country. . . . I come to *find* enemies not to *make* them, I come to *protect* not to *injure* you.

. . . You have felt her [Great Britain's] Tyranny, you have seen her injustice, but I do not ask *you* to avenge the one or to redress the other. . . . I tender you the invaluable blessings of Civil, Political, & Religious Liberty. . . . That liberty which gave decision to our counsels and energy to our conduct in our struggle for INDEPENDENCE. . . .

That Liberty which has raised us to our elevated rank among the Nations of the world. . . .

. . . Had I any doubt of eventual success I might ask your assistance but I do not. I come prepared for every contingency. I have a force which will look down all opposition and that force is but the vanguard of a much greater. If contrary to your own interest & the just expectation of my country, you should take part in the approaching contest, you will be considered and treated as enemies and the horrors, and calamities of war will Stalk before you.

If the barbarous and Savage policy of Great Britain be pursued, and the savages are let loose to murder our Citizens and butcher our women and children, this war will be a war of extermination.

. . . *No white man found fighting by the Side of an Indian will be taken prisoner.* Instant destruction will be his Lot. . . .

The United States offer you *Peace, Liberty,* and *Security.* Your choice lies between these, & War, *Slavery, and destruction.* . . .

While an American army was preparing to launch the invasion of Upper Canada from Detroit, Brigadier General William Hull issued a proclamation in which he asked Canadians to welcome his troops as an army of liberation. The

THE MORALE OF THE PEOPLE IN UPPER CANADA[115]

From Brock at Fort George to Prevost at - - - - -.

Fort George, U.C.
July 12th 1812

The Militia which assembled here immediately on the account being received of war being declared by the United States have been improving daily in discipline, but the men evince a degree of impatience under their present restraint that is far from inspiring confidence — So great was the clamour to return and attend to their farms, that I found myself, in some measure, compelled to sanction the departure of a large proportion, and I am not without my apprehension that the reminder will, in defiance of the law, which can only impose a fine of twenty pounds, leave the service the moment the harvest commences — There can be no doubt that a large portion of the population in this neighbourhood are sincere in their professions to defend the country, but it appears likewise evident to me that the greater part are either indifferent to what is passing, or so completely American as to rejoice in the prospects of a change of Governments — Many who now consider our means inadequate would readily take an active part were the regular troops encreased — these cool calculators are numerous in all societies.

situation in Canada worried Major General Isaac Brock, the Lieutenant-Governor of Upper Canada and commander of the British forces. He detected a feeling of despair—the people of Upper Canada felt that it was a hopeless struggle and that a surrender to the superior American forces was inevitable. He also realized the danger in the presence of so many American settlers in Upper Canada who might, with open arms, welcome an invading American force. In addition, Brock was uncertain of the support of the wavering Indian allies, and he was doubtful of the loyalty of the French Canadians in Lower Canada.

BROCK'S PROCLAMATION[116]

(22nd July, 1812.)

An excerpt:

The unprovoked declaration of War, by the United States of America, against the United Kingdom . . . has been followed by the actual invasion of this Province . . . [Hull] has thought proper to invite His Majesty's subjects, not merely to a quiet unresisting submission, but insults them with a call to seek voluntarily the protection of his Government . . . where is the Canadian Subject who can truly affirm to himself that he has been injured by the Government in his person, his

liberty, or his property? Where is to be found in any part of the world, a growth so rapid in wealth and prosperity, as this colony exhibits. . . . This unequalled prosperity could not have been attained . . . had not the maritime power of the mother country secured to its Colonists a safe access to every market where the produce of their labor was in demand.

The unavoidable and immediate consequence of a separation from Great Britain must be the loss of this inestimable advantage; and what is offered you in exchange? to become a territory of the United States . . . and it is but too obvious that once exchanged [estranged] from the powerful protection of the United Kingdom you must be reannexed to the dominion of France, from which the Provinces of Canada were wrested by the Arms of Great Britain, at a vast expense of blood and treasure . . . this restitution of Canada to the Empire of France was the stipulated reward for the aid afforded to the revolted colonies, now the United States; the debt is still due, and there can be no doubt but the pledge has been renewed. . . . Are you prepared, Inhabitants of Upper Canada, to become willing subjects or rather slaves to the Despot who rules the Nations of Europe with a rod of Iron? If not, arise in a Body, exert your energies, co-operate cordially with the King's regular Forces, to repel the invader, and to not give cause to your children when groaning under the oppression of a foreign Master to reproach you with having too easily parted with the richest Inheritance on Earth — a participation in the name, character and freedom of Britons.

This precarious situation did not deter Brock from launching an attack at Michilimackinac. With a small force of British regulars, Canadian militia and Indian allies, he captured Michilimackinac in a surprise attack. This victory was of strategic importance. The capture of this key western post not only bolstered the allegiance of the wavering western Indians, but also posed a threat to Detroit. This unexpected victory heartened the Upper Canadians.

Brock then assembled a force of British regulars, militia and Indians under Tecumseh to engage Hull's American army. On August 16, 1812, Hull surrendered his large army to the much smaller British force. This ignominious defeat for the Americans, and also the capture of Detroit, gave the Canadians hope and confidence. The setbacks in the west prompted the Americans to strike at Queenston Heights in an attempted invasion of Canada through the Niagara Peninsula. In the decisive battle of Queenston Heights on October 13, 1812, the superior American forces were again thrown back. However, Queenston Heights was a costly victory for the Canadians. General Brock, who had so far kept Upper Canada free of American invaders, lost his life.

THE CAPTURE OF DETROIT[117]

ᵃ*Major-General Brock to Sir George Prevost:*

Head Quarters Detroit
August 16th 1812

Sir:

I hasten to apprize Your Excellency of the Capture of this very important Post: 2,500 troops have this day surrendered Prisoners of War, and about 25 Pieces of Ordnance have been taken, without the Sacrifice of a drop of British blood; I had not more than 700 troops including Militia, and about 400 Indians to accomplish this Service. When I detail my good fortune Your Excellency will be astonished. I have been supported admirably by Colonel Procter, the whole of my Staff and I may justly say every individual under my command.

ᵇ*General Isaac Brock and Tecumseh*

Soon after Detroit was surrendered, General Brock took off his sash, and publicly placed it around the body of the chief Tecumseh, who received the honour conferred on him with evident gratification; but was seen the next day without his sash. The British general, fearing that something had displeased the Indian chief, sent his interpreter for an explanation. Tecumseh told him that he did not wish to wear the sash as a mark of distinction, when an older warrior than himself was present; he had transferred the sash to the Wyandot chief, Roundhead.

On congratulating General Brock, after the capture of Detroit, Tecumseh said to the General, 'We observed you from a distance standing the whole time in an erect position, and when the boats reached the shore, you were the first man on the land; your bold and sudden movements frightened the enemy, and so compelled them to surrender to half their number.'

General Brock engaged the Indians to throw away the scalping knife — implanting in their hearts the virtue of clemency, and teaching them to feel the pleasure and pride in compassion extended to a vanquished enemy. In return, they revered him as their common Father, and whilst under his control, were guilty of no excesses; and thereby the noble Tecumseh was humane as well as brave.

Tecumseh

ᶜ*Extract from a letter by A. W. Cochran to his father:*

[Montreal, Octʳ. 10 1812]

The man who came in from the American Camp brought a Plattsburgh paper of the 3rd instant and an Albany paper of the 22nd ulto. In the Plattsburgh paper was General Hull's official letter to his Govt. in which he makes out a good story for himself, by underrating his own force at *600* effective men and overrating our's at *2000* of whom he says *800* were regulars so that what with one lie and another he makes it out as clear as noonday that Alexander the Great himself cd. have done no more than he did, — In one place he says that his officers & men wd have fought until their last cartridge was expended and their bayonets worn to the sockets! The Americans I think bid fair to rival & surpass the French in gasconading [boasting] as well as in every thing that is dishonourable base & contemptible. . . . In the Albany paper was contained the official report of Colonel Cass to the Secy. at War in which he delivers (he says) the opinions of all the Colonels, who were with Hull; And Cass denies positively and roundly every fact stated by Hull as a reason for the surrender; His letter gives the lie point blank to Hull's whom he calls a coward or traitor . . . for he says that the Surrender was the effect of the General's *personal feelings* alone, — now those feelings must have been such as will stamp

[him] either for a coward or a traitor; Colonel Cass letter is so far good that the material facts are truly stated, but these Yankees can not tell a plain story like other folks . . . Cass's high prancing words fall very little short of General Hull's . . . gasconades in point of vanity and absurdity.

The initial British victories shocked the Americans. The expected easy conquest of British North America eluded their grasp. The United States was a house divided — New England derisively referred to the war as "Mr. Madison's War," and a virtual state of neutrality existed along its boundary with New Brunswick and Nova Scotia. New York, likewise, showed little enthusiasm for the war, and its frontier with Lower Canada remained quiet. In Upper Canada, the invading American troops were not looked upon as liberators to be embraced but as conquerors to be repulsed — there was to be no easy conquest.

A SOLDIER'S OBSERVATIONS ABOUT THE WAR[118]

[Fort Erie, October 13, 1812]
How strange and unaccountable are the feelings induced by war! Here were men of two nations, but of a common origin, speaking the same language, of the same creed, intent on mutual destruction, rejoicing with fiendish pleasure at their address in perpetrating murder by wholesale, shouting for joy as disasters propagated by the chances of war hurled death and agonizing wounds into the ranks of their opponents! And yet the very same men, when chance gave them the opportunity, would readily exchange, in their own peculiar way, all the amenities of social life, extending to one another a draw of the pipe, and quid, or glass; obtaining and exchanging information from one and the other of their respective services, as to pay, rations, and so on — the victors, with delicacy, abstaining from any allusions to the victorious day. Though the vanquished would allude to their disaster, the victors never named their triumphs.

Such is the character of acts and words between British and American soldiers which I have witnessed, as officer commanding a guard over American prisoners.

J. Driscol [Lieutenant] of the 100th Regiment.

After their humiliating defeat at Queenston Heights, the Americans, shifted their efforts to naval warfare on Lake Erie in 1813. Control of Lake Erie would prevent reinforcements and supplies from reaching the British forces around Detroit. On April 27, 1813, an American fleet bombarded and razed York. The Americans gained supremacy on Lake Erie on September 10,

Battle of Queenston, October 13, 1812

1813, in their important naval victory at Put-in-Bay, where most of the British warships were sunk. Cut off from the rest of Upper Canada, the British forces at Detroit were now forced to retreat. On October 5, 1813, American forces scored a major victory over the retreating British army at Moraviantown.

THE RAVAGES OF WAR[119]
The Burning of York:

In 1813—April—the public buildings of York, the capital of Upper Canada, were burnt by the troops of the United States, contrary to the article of capitulation. These public buildings consisted of two elegant halls, with convenient offices for the accommodation of the Legislature and the Courts of Justice. The library and all the papers and records belonging to these institutions were consumed at the same time. The Church was robbed, and the town library perfectly pillaged. Commodore Chauncey, who has generally behaved honourably, was so ashamed of this last transaction, that he endeavoured to collect the books belonging to the town and legislative library, and actually sent back two boxes filled with them; but hardly any were complete. Much private property was plundered, and several houses left in a state of ruin.

The Americans Burn Newark:

Two churches were burnt to the ground. . . . Many farmhouses were burnt during the summer; and, at length, to fill up the measure of iniquity, the whole beautiful town of Newark, with a short previous intimation — so short as to amount to none, and in an intense cold day of the 10th of December — was consigned to the flames.

. . . . More than 400 women and children were exposed without shelter, on the night of December 10th, to the inclement cold of a Canadian winter. A great number must have perished, had not the flight of the American troops, after perpetrating their unfeeling act, enabled the inhabitants of the country to come to their relief.

President Madison has attempted to justify this cruel act as necessary for the defence of Fort George. Nothing can be more false. The town was some distance from the fort; and instead of thinking to defend it, General McClure was actually retreating to his own shore when he caused Newark (Niagara) to be burnt. This officer says that he acted in conformity with the orders of his Government.

. . . He not only complied with his instructions; but he refined upon them, by choosing a day of intense severity, giving the inhabitants almost no warning until the fire began, and the conflagration in the night.

However, the Americans failed to follow up their success at Moraviantown, and the war deteriorated to border raids, reminiscent of the old Indian warfare. The Americans burned and pillaged Newark, and in retaliation the British captured Fort Niagara and burned and pillaged Buffalo.

Late in 1813, the United States shifted the offensive towards Lower Canada which had hitherto been spared. A two-pronged attack was launched against Montreal. One column headed north from Lake Champlain. At Chateauguay, on October 26, 1813, a combined force of British troops and French-Canadian militia under Colonel Charles de Salaberry turned back the American advance on Montreal. The other American column, from Lake Ontario, by-passed Kingston (which the Americans considered too difficult to take) and proceeded towards Montreal. By taking Montreal, the Americans hoped to drive a wedge between the Canadas. At Crysler's Farm on November 11, 1813, the Americans were defeated by an inferior British force. The attempted invasion of Lower Canada by the United States had failed.

In 1814, the main fighting centred on the Niagara frontier. The Americans captured Fort Erie on July 3 and two days later followed it up with a victory at Chippawa Plains. They advanced again on Queenston but once again fell back. At Lundy's Lane on July 25 a major battle took place. Both sides suffered heavy casualties and the Americans were forced to withdraw. Another attempt was made against Montreal. The Ameri-

cans were defeated at La Colle Mill and were forced to retreat to Plattsburg, New York.

In the meantime, Napoleon's defeat and abdication brought an end to the war in Europe. Britain turned her attention to North America. Sixteen thousand British regulars were dispatched to Canada, and an invasion was begun by way of Lake Champlain under the command of Sir George Prevost. He led a strong British force in an attempt to secure Lake Champlain. Prevost's efforts were unsuccessful and the Americans scored a decisive naval victory at Plattsburg. But Lake Ontario, which neither side controlled throughout the war, was now secured by superior British naval forces.

In 1814, Britain changed her tactics and employed her superior sea power to bring the war in North America to a successful conclusion. A British fleet sailed against Washington, the American capital, and bombarded it as a reprisal for the earlier destruction of York. The British navy invaded Maine and annexed all the territory east of the Penobscot River to New Brunswick. Furthermore, the British navy enforced a strict blockade and virtually paralyzed the trade of the Atlantic coastal states. In the west, British troops advanced from Michilimackinac to Prairie du Chien, deep in Wisconsin territory. The British offensive showed itself as far as the Oregon Territory, far to the West, where British traders captured the important fur trading post of Astoria. The fortunes of war were turning against the Americans. The British seemed to have gained the initiative in the war and were pushing their advantage effectively.

BURNING OF WASHINGTON[120]

To [Major-General Robert] Ross . . . the Navy Yard [put to torch by the Americans] flames may have suggested his next actions. With [Rear-Admiral George] Cockburn he talked over Admiralty instructions to put all American military and public property to the torch in order to prevent "a repetition of the uncivilized proceedings of the troops of the United States." Cockburn urged burning the entire city; Ross consented to burning public buildings.

They began with the Capitol and, as Midshipman Lovell commented, "the blaze that burnt York reached Washington."

British soldiers fired a volley through the windows of Congress House and broke into the Hall of Representatives. . . .

American congressmen later related that Cockburn began this pyromaniacal night by mounting the Speaker's chair and putting the question to assembled redcoats: "Shall this harbor of Yankee democracy be burned? All for it will say, Aye."

. . . [Benjamin H. Latrobe reports] "they made a great pile in the centre of the room of furniture . . . set fire to a quantity of rocket stuff in the middle. The whole was soon in a blaze." . . .
  The Senate wing blazed similarly. . . . Nearby homes, including one owned by George Washington, went up in the inferno that consumed the Library of Congress. . . .

[Congressman Charles Jared Ingersoll reports] "The Capitol wrapped in its winding sheet of fire, the troops slightly refreshed after that first perpetration were led by the General and Admiral along . . . the eternal Pennsylvania Avenue — without beat of drum or other martial sound than their ponderous tramp, a mile and a quarter towards the President's House, the Treasury and War Offices, to burn them."

The War Hawks became disenchanted with the war. The New England merchant class and shipping interests saw their trade crippled by the British naval blockade. New England threatened secession from the Union. The Americans were tired of the war and desired an honourable peace. Although Britain was on the offensive and the war was going in her favour, she too wished an end to the war. Both countries began negotiations to end the war.

The Treaty of Ghent, December 24, 1814, was an armistice that ended the War of 1812. At the war's end, Britain held territory in Maine and in the west, and on the strength of this sought to revise the boundary of 1783. The United States was determined not to relinquish any of her territory, even if it meant the resumption of hostilities. Britain agreed upon a mutual restoration of territory and the establishment of a commission to settle oustanding boundary disputes. The Canadas had hoped that Britain would retain the fur trading territories she had captured during the war and that the boundary would be revised to include these areas within British North America. The restoration of captured American territory left Canadians with the impression that Britain had sacrificed Canadian interests for the sake of American friendship.

Whereas the Treaty of Ghent was only an armistice, the Rush-Bagot Agreement, on April 28, 1817, was the peace that concluded the war. The United States and Great Britain agreed to limit their armed vessels on the Lakes in order to avoid a naval arms race. Both countries were allowed one armed vessel on each of Lake Champlain and Lake Ontario and two on the Upper Lakes. This agreement was somewhat advantageous to Britain since the United States was in a more favourable position to build and maintain naval forces on the Lakes.

The final agreement between Britain and the United States on issues arising from the War of 1812 was embodied in the Convention of 1818. The boundary between the United States and British North America was further clarified. The western boundary was agreed upon, although the Maine-New Brunswick boundary was not settled. Beyond the Lake of the Woods, the boundary followed the forty-ninth parallel west to the Rocky Mountains, and left the disputed Oregon Territory to be shared jointly by Britain and the United States pending final agreement. Thus Britain was able to protect the fur trade that the North West Company had established and developed in this region. Agreement was also reached on fishing rights for America off the coastal waters of British North America. Americans would henceforth be allowed to fish in the Atlantic coastal waters and to dry fish on uninhabited shores.

The outcome of the war was aptly summarized by the Canadian historian A. R. M. Lower:

The War itself was satisfactory to all parties in that both sides won it: the American tradition is one of glorious victories and so is the Canadian. The British, who did most of the fighting and whose navy was the major instrument in ending the war, have no tradition at all and there are few English people who have ever heard of it.

Americans regarded the war as their Second War of Independence against Britain, whose sea power, as in colonial days, threatened to restrict American trade and commerce. The United States demonstrated that she would not tolerate interference with her sovereignty or with her neutrality on the high seas. The Americans felt that the war confirmed these rights and also abated Indian hostility. But the Americans had failed to gain the objective for which they went to war — the conquest of British North America.

Britain's conduct during the war made it abundantly clear that she was intent upon the preservation of British North America as an integral part of the British Empire. In the treaties and agreements with the United States following the conclusion of the war, Britain confirmed the 1783 boundary. Although she negotiated from a position of strength, the restoration of conquered American territory unmistakably underlined British policy regarding the United States — Britain was not interested in conquering her former American colonies but instead desired the goodwill and friendship of the United States, even at the expense of British North American interests.

For British North America it was the second time that it had to repulse an American invasion. Canadians were not anxious to "throw off the British yoke," and fought side by side with British troops against the American "liberators." French Canadians, in contrast to their indifference during the Revolutionary War, rallied to the defence of their homeland. The American invasion and the burning and pillaging of the countryside released a surge of anti-American feeling, which led to suspicion and the mistreatment of many Americans even though many had served in the Canadian militia. They were persecuted because of their suspected loyalty to the United States, and their plight, in many instances, was not unlike that of the British Loyalists in the Thirteen Colonies during the Revolution.

Britain's defence of her North American colonies and her generous trade benefits during the war strengthened the ties with the mother country. French Canadians, in their defence of their homeland, were also fighting to preserve the rights and privileges they obtained from Britain in the Quebec Act. The preservation of the French-Canadian heritage in North America was tied to the British Empire. The war aroused a great pride in the people of British North America; they had foiled the American plan of conquest. At the same time, British North America was aware that it had to adjust itself to living in close proximity to a large and powerful neighbour with whose fortunes the future of British North America was to be intimately linked.

RESULTS OF THE WAR OF 1812[121]

Arthur Lower assesses the results of the war:

. . . the struggle left Upper Canada and the uneasy heritage of the alien question. . . . All who could not prove themselves British subjects could be presumed to be aliens. As such they could be (and for a time, were) declared incapable of owning land . . . . Many a quiet settler . . . had to think out his problem of allegiance and . . . it must have meant cutting of all ties with the old homeland. In this way, the war and its aftermath turned Upper Canada from an American province into a British colony peopled by Americans.

The effects were not so sharp in the other colonies. French-Canadians had fought valiantly in the war and inserted an additional martial leaf in their French tradition which they have never forgotten. To the Maritime provinces the economic aspects had been the most significant; the war of 1812 is not a very formative tradition in Maritime life, not the basis of community, as it is in Upper Canada.

––––––

. . . . The sense of Canadian nationality, which has radiated out from Upper Canada . . . through all the west and to some degree into the Maritime provinces, dates from the war of 1812. It gave to Upper Canada an official tradition of military glory. It did not matter that this was rather insecurely based; people believed in it and it influenced their loyalties. It accentuated Upper Canada's dominant hatred, whose incidence it changed slightly, from hatred of "republicanism" to hatred of "the Americans" or "the damn Yankees". . . . Upper Canada emerged from the War of 1812 a community, its people no longer Americans or merely British subjects, but Upper Canadians. The essence of the War of 1812 is that it built the first story of the Canadian national edifice.

B

WESTWARD TRADE AND EXPLORATION

Once the Seven Years' War had established Britain's supremacy in North America, many enterprising British Americans from the Thirteen Colonies moved into Quebec and gained control of the fur empire that New France had created. The French fur traders, whose skills and knowledge of the wilderness were essential to any fur trading venture, very often became employees of the numerous small enterprises that sprang up at Montreal. Competition in the fur trade became so keen that often violence was used against competitors.

Although the control of the fur trade had changed hands, most of the furs from the regions south and west of the Great Lakes continued to flow into the St. Lawrence trading system. Montreal continued to outrank New York as the fur trading capital of North America, and the St. Lawrence-Great Lakes trading route continued to overshadow the Hudson-Mohawk route. However, as a result of the American Revolution, the St. Lawrence fur merchants were soon to be deprived of the well-established southwest fur trade.

According to the Treaty of Versailles of 1783, Britain ceded the Ohio Valley to the United States. Although Britain did not vacate the western posts of the Ohio Valley until 1796, the Treaty of Versailles foreshadowed the end of the southwest fur trade. It was evident that Britain could not hold these posts on American soil indefinitely. In accordance with Jay's Treaty,

Canoe Manned by Voyageurs

Britain finally vacated the western posts and the southwest fur trade was lost to the St. Lawrence. The Montreal fur interests turned their energy and resources to the already active and competitive northwest trade.

Although the Conquest had established British supremacy on the North American continent, the contest between the trading systems of Hudson Bay and the St. Lawrence continued unabated. The relatively small enterprises centred in Montreal reconstructed the old French northwest fur trade which the La Vérendryes had pushed as far as Lake Winnipeg.

JAY'S TREATY AND THE FUR TRADE[122]

In 1797, after the surrender of the forts under the terms of Jay's Treaty, there was an optimism about the future of the St. Lawrence-based fur trade:

. . . . Several traders, citizens of the States, have established themselves at Michillimakinac; but as the British traders have fixed their new post so close to the old one, it is nearly certain that the Indians will continue to trade with their old friends in preference. . . . From this statement it appears evident, that the people of the States can only acquire by their new possession a small part of one branch of the fur trade, namely, of that which is carried on on one of the nearer lakes. The furs brought down from the distant regions in the north-west to the grand portage, and from thence

in canoes to Montreal along the Utawa River, are what constitute by far the principal part, both as to quantity and value, of those exported from Montreal; to talk, therefore, of their acquiring possession of three-fourths of the fur trade by the surrender of the posts on the lakes, is absurd in the extreme; neither is it likely that they will acquire any considerable share of the lake trade in general, which, as I have already pointed out, can be carried on by the British merchants from Montreal and Quebec, by means of the St. Lawrence, with such superior advantage.

In this renewed competition, the Hudson's Bay Company no longer had the advantage of superior trade goods — the St. Lawrence interests also offered the same high quality English manufactured goods. But the Hudson's Bay Company continued to enjoy the geographic advantage of a direct water route to the heart of the continent. To offset this advantage, the St. Lawrence traders pushed the fur trade further westward in an effort to reach new Indian tribes and new fur areas. The fur trade was carried to the Indians' tepees in order to divert the flow of furs from the Hudson Bay trading system to the St. Lawrence system. In essence, the Montrealers were resorting to the same strategy that the French had employed in the past. However, increasing competition and rising costs became too burdensome for the small temporary partnerships that centred in Montreal, and eventually this led to consolidation.

John McDonell, a brother of the first governor of the Red River Colony, became a partner in the North West Company in 1796. In 1797, he remarked on the geographic advantage enjoyed by the Hudson's Bay Company:

River *Tremblante* is next to River *La Coquille* and distant from it a little further than it is from *Rivière qui appelle*. This, and the temporary posts established above it furnish most of the beaver and otter in the Red River returns, but this trade has been almost ruined since the Hudson Bay Company entered the Assiniboil River by way of Swan River, carrying their merchandise from one river to the other on horseback — three days' journey — who by that means and the short distance between Swan River and their factory at York Fort, from whence they are equipped, can arrive . . . in the Assiniboil River a month sooner than we can return from the Grand Portage, secure the fall trade, give credits to the Indians and send them to hunt before our arrival; so that we see but very few in that quarter upon our arrival. River *Tremblante* has been Mr. Cuthbert Grant's [of the North West Company] favourite residence since he came to Red River.

The St. Lawrence-centred fur trade suffered from a serious handicap. The fur merchants competed not only against the Hudson's Bay Company but also amongst themselves. Moreover, as it became apparent that the southwest trade was coming to an end, merchants who had previously been active in this area entered the northwest trade. This further intensified the rivalry for furs in the northwest. Competition between the numerous St. Lawrence enterprises was becoming ruinous to many and was working to the disadvantage of all.

RIVALRY IN THE FUR TRADE[124]

From Harmon's Journal. Fort Alexandria, on the upper Assiniboine, August 22, 1803:

. . . . It is now several Days since the X. Y. People arrived from the Grand Portage, but give us no news . . . neither Company will convey the other in the least news that can in any way concern their affairs in this Country. In a word the North West Co. look upon their opponents the X. Y. Co. as encroachers of *their* territories, while the latter people consider that the former have no better right to commerce in this part of the World than they themselves have, but if the truth be told, as they are weaker, that is have not been in this country long enough to gain much footing, *we*

would wish to crush them at once, before they have too much strength, when it will be more difficult if not impossible. And this jarring of interests keep up continual misunderstandings and occasions frequent broils between the two contending parties, and some times the enmity that exists between them rises to such an unbecoming height as to cause bloodshed, and in several instance's even lives have been sacrificed!

Competition brought about expansion, and expansion led to ever-rising costs. With the extension of the fur trade westward beyond Lake Winnipeg, costs inevitably increased. It was becoming impossible for a trading party to leave Montreal, purchase furs and return in the same year. As the supply lines lengthened, the cost of outfitting a trading party with food supplies and trade goods correspondingly rose. As the competition became keener, the Indians began demanding more trade goods in exchange for their furs. The everlengthening distance between the fur supplies and Montreal made it increasingly necessary to build inland posts in which trade goods and furs could be stored. Larger amounts of capital were becoming necessary to sustain a successful fur trading venture. Quite often, two or three years elapsed before a Montreal group would receive any return on its investment. Ruinous competition and rising costs, as well as the need for large capital investment, led to a reorganization of the St. Lawrence-centred fur trade.

In 1787, the North West Company, a loosely united but permanent organization of the Montreal fur interests, was formed through the consolidation of their capital and resources. Instead of competing with each other as they had done in the past, the Montreal fur traders could now concentrate upon wresting the lucrative fur trade from the Hudson's Bay Company. Many French Canadians joined the new company as employees and brought their wide experience in canoe travel and Indian trade into the North West Company. Moreover, the North West Company now had larger amounts of capital available with which to build and maintain inland posts. It could afford to invest in exploration, push westward and outreach the Hudson's Bay Company. Nevertheless, the Hudson's Bay Company still enjoyed the geographic advantage. To become successful, the North West Company had to be efficient and progressive.

To overcome the problem of distance, the North West Company in effect split its supply line into two parts. Fort William became the hinge around which the North West Company trade revolved. The "wintering" partners collected furs and brought them to Fort William. The "Montreal" partners then transported these furs to Montreal, from which point they were exported. Conversely, trade goods were purchased and transported to Fort William by the Montreal partners. These goods were then carried by the wintering partners to the West where they were exchanged for furs.

PRAISE OF FRENCH-CANADIAN VOYAGEURS[125]

Colin Robertson, who was dismissed from the North West Company, was hired by the Hudson's Bay Company to advise on ways for improving its operation. In 1812, he suggested the use of Canadian voyageurs rather than newcomers from Scotland:

One great obstacle to your inland commerce, is a want of men, and even those you employ are but ill calculated for the country. When an Orkney man engages in your service it is more from necessity than inclination; he can find employment nowhere else . . . [after] gathering a few pounds, he bids farewell to a country that affords him no pleasure. . . . Another thing Orkney men are unacquainted with the manner of voyaging in Canoes, by which the Northern business is conducted. . . .

I would warmly recommend to your notice the Canadians. — It is from these active, subordinate men that the North West Company derives their greatest profit.

. . . these poor people, notwithstanding the extravagant price they pay for their necessaries [bought from the Company], are so much attached to the country that they seldom or ever complain. . . .

Every spring, the partners of the North West Company converged upon Fort William. Out of the wilderness, in their small canoes laden with furs, came the wintering partners. Across the Great Lakes, in their large freight-canoes laden with trade goods and supplies, came the Montreal partners. Furs and trade goods were exchanged, dividends were paid and plans were drawn up for further extension of trade and exploration.

ACTIVITY AT GRANDE PORTAGE[126]

Mackenzie's Description:

. . . the North men begin to arrive from their winter quarters . . . early in July. At this period, it is necessary to select from the pork-eaters, a number of men, among whom are the recruits, or winterers, sufficient to man the North canoes necessary to carry, to the river of the rainy lake, the goods and provision requisite for the Athabasca country; as the people of that country (owing to the shortness of the season and length of the road, can come no further), are equipped there, and exchange ladings. . . .

The North men being arrived at the Grande Portage, are regaled with bread, pork, butter, liquor, and tobacco, and such as have not entered into agreements during the winter, which is customary, are contracted with, to return and perform the voyage for one, two, or three years; their accounts are also settled, and such as choose to send any of their earnings to Canada, receive drafts to transmit to their relations or friends; and as soon as they can be got ready, which requires no more than a fortnight, they are again despatched to their respective departments. . . .

The North West Company not only adapted its trade to the necessities of the extended supply line but also discovered a new source of food for its fur brigades. Fur traders required nutritious food to furnish the body with energy for the long canoe journeys and the arduous portages. This food could not be bulky and had to keep for long periods without spoiling. The French-Canadian fur traders had used dried peas and corn as their dietary staple. But as the fur trade moved farther westward, dried peas and corn had to be transported from the farms on the St. Lawrence to Fort William and then, with the fur traders, to the farthest reaches of the West. The Nor'Westers found a substitute in pemmican which could be purchased in the West. The Indians and Métis of the prairies developed a way of life based on supplying the Nor'Westers with pemmican. The

THE VALUE OF THE INDIAN IN THE FUR TRADE[127]

The following is an extract from a statement regarding "an Enquiry into a bill for prohibiting the use of aspirituous liquors among the savages of North America" — a bill sponsored in the British House of Commons. The statement was prepared by the North West Company and by McTavish, McGillivray & Company, dated Montreal, October 3, 1808:

. . . although . . . these Indians, as well as their neighbours within our territory, have no valuable furs, their friendship and co-operation, is necessary to the support of the trade carried with the others. *They alone supply all the food on which the company's servants subsist*; without which they could be compelled to abandon three fourths of the country, and all the valuable part of the trade.

The sole employment of these Indians, is to kill the large animals with which their country abounds; to select particular parts of their flesh and tallow; and prepare it in the usual manner and deposit it at the posts where the Company's servants will find it, as they progress from and return to the general rendezvous . . . their principal inducement to perform the services we have enumerated in the *present of rum,* which they receive at stated periods. These are the most independent, warlike and restless, of all the Indian tribes; and require to be managed with the greatest delicacy; more particularly as they form the link which binds in a common interest with the North West Company the whole Indian population of the interior country.

pemmican trade soon became essential to the fur trade and the Nor'Westers came to depend on the supply of pemmican as the food-fuel for the fur brigades. The Indians and Métis who lived around the Nor'Westers' posts relied upon the pemmican trade as a means of securing manufactured goods. Pemmican became the life-blood of the Nor' Westers' fur trade.

SUGGESTION FOR DIVIDENDS TO HUDSON'S BAY CO. EMPLOYEES[128]

In 1812, Colin Robertson suggested payment of dividends as done by the North West Company:

. . . the only substitute for the shares which are held up by the North West Company, to their young men, is allowing the clerks in your [Hudson's Bay Co.] service a commission on the profits arising from their exertions. This in my opinion with a salary would have the desired effect. . . .

———

It is evident that the posts against which our adversaries direct their peculiar hostility, cannot be expected to carry on a very advantageous trade, yet they must be maintained as a barrier to defend the rest of our establishments; and it is of essential consequence, that the very best of our officers should be selected to command these advanced guards. But according to the arrangements which now subsist, the Factors and Traders who manage these frontier posts, will have the smallest emoluments. . . .

. . . the most feasible plan appears to be, that the profit of all the Factories should be thrown into our aggregate fund, out of which shares should be distributed among the officers of our whole establishment in various proportions according to the importance and difficulty of the station assigned to each individual.

The North West Company had reorganized the St. Lawrence fur trade and developed new techniques that allowed it to gather furs from the farthest points of the Canadian West. However, it was the aggressiveness of the North West Company as much as its organization and technique that enabled it to compete successfully with the Hudson's Bay Company. The profit-sharing partners of the North West Company were naturally more concerned with their trade than the salaried employees of the Hudson's Bay Company. The Nor'Westers always displayed the initiative and were more progressive than the conservative factors of the Hudson's Bay Company. It was the Nor'Westers who usually discovered new fur areas and new Indian tribes with which to trade. Although the Hudson's Bay Company enjoyed the geographic advantage, the North West Company made up for this by its organization, efficiency and aggressiveness. Nowhere were these features of the North West Company better exhibited than in the exploration of the Far West. Although men like Henday and Hearne of the Hudson's Bay Company won an honoured place in Canadian history by their exploration, the penetration of the Far West was largely the work of adventurous men like Mackenzie, Fraser and Thompson of the North West Company.

THE HUDSON'S BAY COMPANY AND EXPLORATION[129]

David Thompson remarks about the Hudson's Bay Company's niggardly attitude towards exploration:

How very different the liberal and public spirit of this North West Company of Merchants of Canada; from the mean selfish policy of the Hudson's Bay Company styled Honorable; and whom, at little expense, might have had the northern part of this Continent surveyed to the Pacific Ocean, and greatly extended their Trading Posts; whatever they have done, the British Government has obliged them to do. . . .

As in the days of New France, the fur trade proved to be the greatest single motivating force in exploration. Expansion was still the key to the success of the fur trade. The North West Company, in its bid to outreach the Hudson's Bay Company, pushed westward in an attempt to intercept furs destined for the Bay and to open up rich new fur areas. Gradually, through the necessity of meeting the competition of the "Pedlars," as the employees of the Bay called the Nor'Westers, the Hudson's Bay Company abandoned its policy of "sleeping by the Bay." Thus the Hudson's Bay Company began building inland posts to meet the competition. Frequently, the Nor'Westers and Hudson's Bay Company posts were within sight of each other and violence often erupted. To meet the competition from the Hudson's Bay Company, the Nor'Westers would move farther westward to be followed by the Hudson's Bay Company. Like a giant game of hop-scotch, the fur frontier was rapidly pushed toward the Pacific Coast.

As early as 1754, Anthony Henday, an employee of the Hudson's Bay Company, had traveled from Fort York to the foothills of the Rockies in an attempt to convince the Indians of the West to bring their furs to the Bay. Another employee of the Hudson's Bay Company, Samuel Hearne, had heard Indian tales of a great river where rich deposits of copper were to be found. Hearne left Fort Prince of Wales in 1771 in search of the fabled river. Eventually, he found the Coppermine River and followed it to its mouth but failed to find any appreciable quantity of copper. On his return journey, Hearne headed west and discovered the hitherto unknown Great Slave Lake. After an eventful journey, fraught with difficulties, he returned to Fort Prince of Wales — two years and seven months after his departure.

Samuel Hearne

THE MURDER OF ESKIMOS ON THE COPPERMINE RIVER BY CHIPEWYAN INDIANS, 1771[130]

July 17, 1771.

. . . it was near one o'clock in the morning . . . when finding all the Esquimaux quiet in their tents, they [the Indians] rushed forth from their ambuscade, and fell on the poor unsuspecting creatures, unperceived till close at the very eyes of their tents, when they soon began the bloody massacre, while I stood neuter in the rear.

In a few seconds the horrible scene commenced; it was shocking beyond description; the poor unhappy victims were surprised in the midst of their sleep, and had neither time nor power to make any resistance; men, women, and children, in all upward of twenty, ran out of their tents stark naked. . . .

The shrieks and groans of the poor expiring wretches were truly dreadful; and my horror was much increased at seeing a young girl, seemingly about eighteen years of age, killed so near me, that when the first spear was stuck into her side she fell down at my feet, and twisted round my legs. . . . As two Indian men pursued this unfortunate victim, I solicited very hard for her life; but the murderers made no reply till they had stuck both their spears through her body and transfixed her to the ground . . . [the Indians]

Simon Fraser

Alexander Mackenzie

paid not the smallest regard to the shrieks and agony of the poor wretch, who was twining round their spears like an eel! . . . even at this hour I cannot reflect on the transactions of that horrid day without shedding tears.

Apart from the notable exceptions of Henday and Hearne, the Hudson's Bay Company displayed the same unimaginative approach to the exploration of the continent as it did toward the fur trade. The St. Lawrence traders and particularly the North West Company were the innovators, the leaders and the explorers. The French missionary and fur trader probed the continent as far as Lake Winnipeg; the Nor'Westers traversed it to the Pacific Ocean.

As early as 1778, the intrepid Peter Pond, who had come to Montreal from Connecticut, pushed westward to Lake Athabaska and opened up the richest fur region yet known to the fur trade. Later, the North West Company built Fort Chipewyan on the western tip of Lake Athabaska; Alexander Mackenzie, a twenty-five years old Scot, was in charge. The transportation of furs from the Athabaska country all the way to Fort William was a long and costly journey. Mackenzie reasoned that a water route to the Pacific would give the North West Company the same geographic advantage that the Hudson's Bay Company had. A navigable water route to the Pacific would make transcontinental movement of furs unnecessary. The Pacific route would serve both as an exit for furs and an entrance for trade goods. The restlessness of youth and the beckoning unknown also played a part in Mackenzie's momentous journeys. Moreover, the Slave River running south and the Peace River running west seemed to invite the visionary Scot.

In 1789, with a party of French Canadians and Indians, Mackenzie set out along the Slave River and followed it to Great Slave Lake. From here, his party discovered a broad river which flowed westerly. Believing this river would flow to the Pacific, they followed it, but it turned northward and emptied into the Arctic Ocean. Discouraged and disillusioned, Mackenzie named it the Disappointment River. Today we know it as the mighty Mackenzie River.

MACKENZIE'S VOYAGE DOWN THE
MACKENZIE, 1789[131]

Sunday, July 5, 1789.

The information which they [the Indians] gave respecting the [Mackenzie] river had so much of the fabulous, that I shall not detail it: it will be sufficient just to mention their attempts to persuade us that it would require several winters to get to the sea, and that old age would come upon us before the period of our return: we were also to encounter monsters of such horrid shapes and destructive powers as could only exist in their wild imaginations. They added, besides, that there were two impassable falls in the river, the first of which was about thirty days' march from us.

Though I placed no faith in these strange relations, they had a very different effect upon our Indians, who were already tired of the voyage. It was their opinion and anxious wish that we should not hesitate to return. They said that, according to the information which they had received, there were very few animals in the country beyond us, and that as we proceeded, the scarcity would increase, and we should absolutely perish from hunger, if no other accident befel us. . . .

Dismayed but undaunted, Mackenzie returned to Fort Chipewyan and began planning another expedition. In 1792, he and his party set out along the westerly flowing Peace River. In the spring of 1793, they reached the junction of the Findlay and Parsnip Rivers; they followed the southerly flowing Parsnip River and proceeded overland to the turbulent Fraser. They proceeded along the Fraser until it became unnavigable. Retracing their path to the Blackwater River, they followed it as far west as they could and then journeyed overland to the Bella Coola River. In canoes borrowed from neighbouring Indians, Mackenzie and his party followed the Bella Coola River and reached the Pacific Ocean on July 22, 1793. The simple inscription "Alexander Mackenzie, from Canada, by land, the twenty-second of July one thousand seven Hundred and ninety-three" marked the spot where he had reached the Pacific. Later, Alexander Mackenzie won world recognition when *Voyages* — a journal of his exploits — was published and widely read. In 1801 he was knighted by King George III of Britain.

By the turn of the century, Spain, Russia, England and the United States had all shown an interest in the Pacific Northwest. The mouth of the Columbia River had been discovered but the river had not been explored. In 1805, President Jefferson sent the famous Lewis and Clarke expedition overland to claim the land west to the Pacific for the United States. Activity in the Pacific Northwest was mounting and the geography of the North American continent was becoming known.

The next Canadian to reach the Pacific was Simon Fraser, who like Mackenzie was an em-

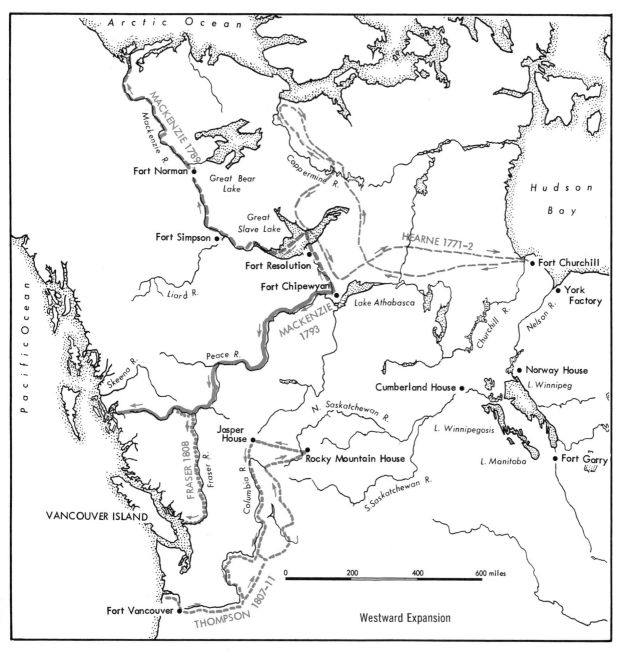

Westward Expansion

ployee of the North West Company. Following Mackenzie's route on the Peace River, Fraser crossed overland to the headwaters of the river that bears his name. He intended to explore the Columbia River which he hoped would be a practical commercial route to the Pacific. However, before he set out on his famous journey, he built a number of important trading posts. In 1805, the first trading post in British Columbia, Fort McLeod, was built. In 1806, on the shores of Stuart Lake, Fraser built Fort St. James — the oldest permanent white settlement in British Columbia.

In the spring of 1808, Fraser, two close associates, John Stuart and Jules Maurice Quesnel, and nineteen voyageurs embarked on the hazardous exploration of the Fraser River. This journey was one of the most dangerous and unbelievable in the annals of exploration. Walled in on both sides by sheer-faced cliffs of rock, Fraser and his party were flung along the swift flowing and turbulent waters of the river. At every turn, the tiny canoes were in danger of being smashed against the rocks or upset by the churning waters. Often, the party had to carry their canoes over narrow precipices high above the impossible river. These portages were every bit as daring and dangerous as was navigating the waters of the river. But Fraser and his associates were determined men. The party reached the mouth of the river.

SIMON FRASER DOWN THE FRASER RIVER[132]

Voyageurs at Dawn

Thursday, June 9, 1808.

It being absolutely impossible to carry the canoes by land, yet sooner than to abandon them, all hands without hesitation embarked, as it were *a corp perdu* [i.e., recklessly] upon the mercy of this Stygian tide. Once engaged the die was cast, and the great difficulty consisted in keeping the canoes in the medium, of *fil d'eau* [current], that is to say, clear of the precipice on one side, and of the gulphs formed by the waves on the other. However, thus skimming along like lightning, the crews cool and determined, followed each other in awful silence. And [when] we arrived at the end we stood gazing on our narrow escape from perdition. . . .

This afternoon the rapids were very bad; two in particular were worse, if possible, than any we had hitherto met with, being a continual series of cascades, mixt with rocky fragments and bound by precipices and mountains, that seemed at times to have no end. I scarcely ever saw any thing so dreary, and seldom so dangerous in any country; and at present while I am writing this, whatever way I turn, mountains upon mountains, whose summits are covered with external snows, close the gloomy scene.

Disappointment soon followed the joy of having survived the treacherous river. When Fraser took his bearing, he realized that he was not on the Columbia River at all. Nevertheless, his perilous journey gave Canada a further claim to the Pacific Northwest.

GEOGRAPHIC ADVANTAGE OF AN OUTLET
TO THE PACIFIC[133]

Harmon, at Stuart's Lake, entered in his journal observations about the benefits of a waterway to the Pacific. The two excerpts are dated May 13, 1813, and October 18, 1814 respectively:

. . . . Mr. Stuart Six Canadians and two of the Natives embarked aboard two Canoes . . . in order to go and join Mr. J. G. McTavish &c. at some place on the Columbia River, and there with them proceed down to the Sea — and should Mr. Stuart be so fortunate as to discover a water communication between this and the Columbia, we shall for the future get our yearly supply of Goods from that quarter, and send our Returns out that way, which will be shipped there directly for the China Market in Vessels which the Concern intends building on that Coast. . . .

———

This afternoon I was agreeable surprised at the arrival of . . . two Canoes, laden with Goods from the mouth of the Columbia River (Fort George) [Astoria] which place they left the latter end of August last. The Vessels from England [the *Isaac Todd* and *Columbia*] having arrived there in the Month of March & April — one of which sat sail again in the latter end of July for China (Canton) laden with furs. . . .

The exploration of the Columbia River fell to David Thompson, another employee of the North

West Company. Thompson, an orphan, had come to Canada as an employee of the Hudson's Bay Company. However, he became dissatisfied with the Company and joined the Nor'Westers. He was a meticulous surveyor and cartographer. In 1807 he set out from Rocky Mountain House, on the North Saskatchewan River. Four years later he arrived at the mouth of the Columbia. He established Kootenay House, which became his base of operation. From here, Thompson painstakingly followed the Columbia River and surveyed and mapped more than a half million square miles of the territory. In 1811 he finally reached the mouth of the Columbia and found Astoria, an established American fur trading post. Thompson was a master of his trade; his maps were so accurate that even today they are used as the basis for maps of the Northwest.

Mackenzie, Fraser and Thompson had laid claim to what is now British Columbia and, in a sense, are responsible for the transcontinental character of Canada. However, their very achievement signalled difficult days for the fur trade. It could expand no more. The western limits of the continent had been reached and the fur trade was robbed of a vital necessity — expansion.

C

THE SELKIRK SETTLEMENT

Other factors besides the impossibility of further expansion foretold the end of the fur empire of the St. Lawrence. The intense rivalry between the Hudson's Bay Company and the North West Company became ruinous. With two prospective buyers, the Indians demanded more for their furs. The cost of building and maintaining inland posts became burdensome. The dividends of the Hudson's Bay Company declined steadily in the last half of the eighteenth century. In fact, the Company paid no dividends between 1809 and 1814. The margin of profit for the partners of the North West Company also shrank as costs rose steadily. However, it was settlement — the great enemy of the fur trade — that eventually led to the defeat of the St. Lawrence-based fur enterprise.

At the turn of the century, many Scottish crofters, or peasants, were being dispossessed of their land because land owners found that sheep raising was far more profitable than renting land.

THE SORRY LOT OF SCOTTISH FARMERS[134]

Extract from evidence before committees of investigation:

We were asked by a person almost starving to go into a house. He there found on one side of the fire a very old man, apparently dying; on the other side a young man of about eighteen, with a child on his knees, whose mother had just died and been buried; and evidently both that young man and the child were suffering from want. . . . We went upstairs, and under some rags we found another young man, the widower, and turning down the rags . . . we found another man who was dying, and who did die in the course of the day. I have no doubt that the whole family was actually starving at the time.

The union of Ireland with England in 1801 had created many problems in Ireland and left in its wake hordes of poor people who could not earn a living and who faced a future of starvation and misery. The plight of the poor Irish and Highland Scots became of great concern to Lord Selkirk, a wealthy Scottish nobleman. Thomas Douglas, the fifth Earl of Selkirk, had been educated in law and displayed a good business sense that allowed him to increase the family fortunes. But Lord Selkirk, the humanitarian, could not ignore the desperate circumstances of his fellow men.

At his own expense, Selkirk undertook to settle many poor people of the British Isles in British North America. He thought that a migration of the poor to this new land would help solve some of the problems in Britain. Moreover, the resettlement of British subjects within the Empire would further strengthen the Empire. Selkirk had established a rather small but successful settlement in Prince Edward Island. Another settlement at Baldoon, near the present day city of Chatham in Ontario, proved less successful. Neither settlement, however, was of the magnitude that Selkirk envisaged. They served only as preludes to his major undertaking in the very heart of Canada — the Red River Valley.

LORD SELKIRK'S MOTIVES FOR ESTABLISHING THE RED RIVER SETTLEMENT[135]

Alexander Ross, the historian of the Red River, writing in the 1850's, lists some of "the speculative opinions" that had been advanced for the planting of the colony at Red River:

1st. According to the North West creed, his lordship planted the colony to ruin their trade . . . it was alleged . . . that Lord Selkirk . . . by means of the new colony [would] secure to the Hudson's Bay Company, and to himself, not only the extensive and undivided trade of the country within their own territories, but a safe and convenient stepping-stone for monopolizing all the fur trade of the far west; which would have been a death-blow to their [North West Co.] concern. . . .

2nd . . . a colony planted in the bosom of their own trade, must . . . be more or less dependent on them for its supplies. . . . All . . . money . . . would eventually fall back again into the Company's own hands. . . . All the surplus produce . . . articles the Company require, would by means of the colony be obtained more conveniently, cheaper, and with less risk, than by annual importation of such articles from England. . . . By supplying the Company, the settlers would have a ready market at their door, sufficient to satisfy all their wants. . . .

3rd . . . in our opinion . . . his lordship's real object, the pious and philanthropic desire of introducing civilization into the wilderness. . . . The object, then, was a laudable and charitable one, strictly in accordance with the character of such a man as Lord Selkirk . . . and also in accordance with the spirit of the Company's charter.

4th . . . Lord Selkirk's object was the good of the natives, and theirs alone . . . civilizing and evangelizing the natives . . . but as to Lord Selkirk's view of benefitting the Indians, forty years' experience has proved it . . . a complete failure.

Ironically, Selkirk had learned of the rich prairie agricultural lands from Mackenzie's *Voyages*. Settlement — the very thing that the fur trader wanted least and feared most — had its origin in the writings of the most renowned Nor'Wester. Selkirk was convinced that a hard-working population of thirty million could support itself on the prairies. The idea had become a conviction and the conviction led to a plan.

Lord Selkirk

comfortable subsistence, & they may also raise some valuable objects of exportation. . . . To a Colony in these territories, the Channel of Trade must be the River of Port Nelson.

At the turn of the century, Hudson's Bay Company shares dropped in value. Selkirk succeeded in buying enough shares to give him a controlling interest in the Company. In May, 1811 he was granted one hundred and sixteen thousand square miles of land in what is now Manitoba, Minnesota and North Dakota. Selkirk now had available for settlement a broad expanse of fertile agricultural land. But the Red River Settlement was not to be established without a struggle.

LORD SELKIRK ASSERTS THE RIGHTS OF THE HUDSON'S BAY COMPANY'S LAND[137]

On June 18, 1812, Lord Selkirk advised his traders as to their relations with the men of the North West Company:

You must give them solemn warning that the land belongs to the Hudson's Bay Company, and that they must remove from it; after this warning they must not be allowed *to cut any timber either for building or fuel. What they have cut should be openly and forcibly seized, and their buildings destroyed. In like manner they should be warned not to fish in your waters, and if they put down nets seize them as you would in England those of a poacher. We are so fully advised of the unimpeachable validity of these rights of property, that*

LORD SELKIRK POINTS OUT THE ADVANTAGES OF THE RED RIVER AREA[136]

At the western extremity of Canada, upon the Waters which fall into Lake Winnipeck [Winnipeg], & uniting in the great River of Port Nelson, discharge themselves into Hudson's Bay, is a Country which the Indian Traders represent as fertile, & of a Climate far more temperate than the Shores of the Atlantic under the same parallel, & not more severe than that of Germany & Poland. Here, therefore, the Colonists may, with a moderate exertion of industry, be certain of a

there can be no scruple in enforcing them whenever you have the physical means. If they make a forcible resistance, they are acting illegally, and are responsible for the consequences of what they do, while you are safe, so long as you take only the reasonable and necessary means of enforcing that which is your right.

The Nor'Westers very quickly understood the implications of settlement in Assiniboia, as the area of Selkirk's grant was called. To the Nor'-Westers, the establishment of a settlement was nothing more than a plot by the Hudson's Bay Company to destroy the St. Lawrence-based fur trade. The settlement would lie right across the Nor'Westers' lines of communication and supply between Fort William and the Far West. The herds of buffalo that provided the pemmican would rapidly disappear and would effectively starve the Nor' Westers out of business. The Nor'-Westers, who had surmounted every difficulty in the past, were determined not to allow settlement to disrupt their trade.

THE NORTH WEST COMPANY'S DETERMINATION TO THWART SELKIRK'S PLANS FOR SETTLEMENT[138]

From a letter by Simon McGillivray to McTavish, McGillivray and Company of Montreal, from England, dated June 1, 1811:

I have had this morning a meeting with Sir Alexander McKenzie [*sic*] and Mr. Ellice, and I am authorized to state to you and to their connexions, as our unanimous opinion, that you should immediately on receipt of this, dispatch an Express to the Interior with notice to prepare your people for a year of Trial. If possible, your posts should be strengthened with men and extra supplies of goods, and measures should be taken for a vigorous opposition. . . . We forbear to suggest the particular details of this opposition, as you will be better able to judge of them than we are, but the opposition ought to be general and followed up at almost any expense. . . . The object in view is well worth making sacrifice for. . . . The Hudson's Bay Company . . . by their grant to Lord Selkirk . . . are striking at the very root of . . . [your] Fur Trade. In short, no means should be left untried to thwart Selkirk's schemes.

Even before any of the settlers left Scotland, an anonymous letter was published and circulated in Scotland warning of the grave dangers that lay ahead. Unsafe travel, a bitter climate, constant danger of attack from hostile Indians, the destruc-tion of their crops and homes and a lonely and violent death in a lonely and violent land awaited the settlers. The anonymous letter proved to be all too prophetic.

THE NORTH WEST COMPANY WARNS PROSPECTIVE SETTLERS[139]

In a letter of June 20, 1812, to Miles Macdonell, Lord Selkirk writes about the propaganda carried on by the North West Company to dissuade prospective settlers from going to the Red River:

Our adversaries have been very busy in the Highlands & have succeeded for the present in narrowing our supply of men from that quarter. The 'Hr' ["Highlander"] continued his lucubrations in the Inverness Journal with more & more personality: & in the course of the Winter Sir Alexr [Mackenzie] & his colleagues got hold of Mff [Moncrief] Blair whom they induced to put his name to an affidavit grossly misrepresenting the transactions of Stornoway. . . . The calumnies . . . make a great impression, & deterred many from engaging in the Service.

Nevertheless, the first group of settlers, under Governor Miles Macdonell, arrived at York Factory in the fall of 1811. After a dismal winter on the desolate shores of Hudson Bay, the first Selkirk settlers set out on the seven hundred mile journey to the forks of the Red and Assiniboine Rivers. Some of the settlers continued south to the junction of the Red and Pembina, in present day North Dakota. In the summers of 1812 and 1813, new groups of settlers arrived from Scotland. Fort Douglas was built at the junction of the Red and Assiniboine Rivers where the city of Winnipeg now stands, while Fort Daer was built near the junction of the Red and Pembina.

SELKIRK'S INSTRUCTIONS ON DEALING WITH THE THE INDIANS[140]

Lord Selkirk was afraid of the impact a sudden influx of settlers might have on the Indians at Red River. His instructions to Miles Macdonell in 1811 reveal this fear as well as a desire not to alienate the Indians. At the same time, he advises a policy of firmness in order to impress the Indians with the potential might of the colony:

. . . no precaution must be omitted to obtain their [Indian] friendship as the party will not much exceed the numbers of an ordinary trading post, it may be hoped that in the first instance they will pass for such. . . . Though this idea cannot be of

Two Company Forts on the Red River, at Pembina, 1822

very long duration, it will be well to keep it up as long as possible, at least till the post is well established and fortified. When it can no longer be concealed that the establishment is to be permanent, if the jealousy of the Indians appears to be aroused, the proposal of purchasing the land must be brought forward. The purchase ought to be, in part at least and as much as possible by way of annuity, rather than a price to be paid at once. An annuity to be annually distributed among the tribes and families, who have a claim to the lands, will form a permanent hold over their peaceable behaviour, as they must be made to understand that if any individual of the tribe violates the treaty, the payment will be withheld. . . . But after all the attentions which can be used for obtaining the friendship of the Indians, it would certainly be wrong to trust very much of it, especially after the threats which have been held out. A better security will be in the awe which they will entertain for so strong a post, if they see it guarded with unremitted vigilance, and especially if they find that any proceedings in the least degree savouring of insult or encroachment is repressed with a determined vigour.

The Red River settlers lacked proper tools for breaking the soil, grasshoppers and floods ruined their crops; and early frosts caught the settlers unaware. They turned to pemmican for food. So acute had the food shortage become that in 1814 Governor Macdonell forbade the export of pemmican from the area. The Pemmican Proclamation was taken as a declaration of war by the already hostile Métis and Nor'Westers.

MILES MACDONELL'S PEMMICAN PROCLAMATION, 1814[141]

. . . it is hereby ordered that no persons trading Furs or Provisions within the Territory for the Hon'ble H. B. Co., the N. W. Co., or any individual or unconnected Traders or persons whatever, shall take out any Provisions, either of Flesh, Fish, Game or Vegetables, procured or raised within the said Territory . . . for one twelvemonth from the date hereof save and except what may be judged necessary for the trading parties at the present time within the Territory to carry them to their respective destinations and who may on due application to me obtain a License for the same. The Provisions procured and raised as above shall be taken for the use of the Colony, and that no loss may accrue to the parties concerned they will be paid for by British Bills at the customary rates.

. . . whosoever shall be detected in attempting to convey out, or shall aid or assist in conveying out or attempting to carry out any Provisions prohibited as above . . . shall be taken into custody and prosecuted . . . the Provisions so taken . . . any goods and chattels . . . taken along with them, and also the craft, carriages and cattle instrumental in conveying away the same to any part but to the Settlements on Red River shall be forfeited.

Given under my hand at Fort Daer (Pembina) the 8th day of January, 1814.

The Nor'Westers induced one hundred and forty settlers to accept transportation and resettlement in Upper Canada. Those who remained were subjected to constant harassment. Their crops and buildings were destroyed, and these loyal settlers were forced to take refuge at the Hudson's Bay post of Norway House on the shores of Lake Winnipeg.

THE NOR'WESTERS OPPOSE THE PEMMICAN PROCLAMATION[142]

From minutes of general meeting held at Fort William, July 11, 1814:

The Situation of the Concern in the Interior with the Hudsons Bay Company — and particularly the Violent & illegal seizure of all the Provisions which had been collected at the Red River — under the authority of a pretended Proclamation issued by Miles McDonell — agent to Lord Selkirk — for laying an Embargo on all Provisions which should be collected in that Department (The Red River) — It appeared that he had taken from the Hudsons Bay Company 200 Bags of Pemican & insisted on having an equal Number from the North West Company — which being very properly refused he took measures for seizing the whole — in which he succeeded. . . . The Gentlemen [Nor'Westers] of the neighboring Departments however assembled with their men & Mr. Miles was very near paying dear for his temerity . . . they entered into a compromise — that he should Keep 200 Bags & give up the remainder. Thus the matter ended for the time . . . a full determination was taken to defend the Property at all Hazards, & all the Wintering men being assembled for this purpose the true state

of the case was explained to them, and the impression it made, it is hoped will render it a dangerous service to any man who may presume to plunder them. . . .

. . . The Intentions of Miles McDonell and the Heads of the Hudson Bay Interests were evident . . . by depriving the Company of the Provisions collected in the Interior the People must have been starved and the Business totally stopped.

In 1815, Robert Semple, the new Governor, arrived with a group of new settlers from Kildonan, Scotland. The older settlers returned from Norway House and Forts Douglas and Daer were restored. However, the resentment and determination of the Nor'Westers and Métis to stamp out the colony continued unabated. In June of 1816, Governor Semple and thirty of his men intercepted a band of Indians and Métis a short distance from Fort Douglas. An argument developed and a shot was fired. Within minutes, Governor Semple and twenty of his men lay dead. The Battle of Seven Oaks, as the engagement was called, was both pitiful and tragic. The remaining settlers set out a second time for Norway House and the Nor'Westers again occupied Fort Douglas.

THE NORTH WEST COMPANY IS DETERMINED TO DESTROY THE COLONY[143]

Part of a letter from Alexander Macdonell to John McDonald, dated August 5, 1814, clearly expresses the determination of the Nor' Westers to destroy the settlement:

You see myself and our mutual friend Cameron, so far on our way to commence open hostilities against the Enemy in Red River; much is expected from us, if we believe some; perhaps too much; one thing certain, that we will do our best to defend what we consider our rights in the interior. Something serious will undoubtedly take place. Nothing but the complete downfall of the colony will satisfy some by fair or foul means. A most desirable object, if it can be accomplished; so here is at them with all my heart and energy.

Meanwhile, Lord Selkirk had been proceeding westward from Upper Canada to aid his struggling colony. At Sault Ste. Marie, he had heard of the news of the tragedy that had befallen his settlers, but he was not to be intimidated by the Nor' Westers. He hired about one hundred disbanded Swiss soldiers of the De Meurons regiment who had been engaged during the War of 1812. Resolutely and with righteous indignation, Selkirk proceeded to Fort William, the headquarters of the North West Company, and captured it. He had several officers of the Company arrested and then proceeded to Assiniboia. With all the vigour and determination at his command, Selkirk set about restoring his beloved settlement. Plans for roads, bridges and mills were made. The land was surveyed and parcelled out. Selkirk brought out Reverend John West to provide for the spiritual and educational needs of the tiny colony.

THE DE MEURONS[144]

Alexander Ross had a very poor opinion of them:

. . . They were chiefly foreigners, a medley of almost all nations — Germans, French, Italians, Swiss, and others; and, with few exceptions, were a rough and lawless set of black guards. These men had entered into written agreements with Lord Selkirk, and were to be paid at a certain rate per month, for navigating the boats or canoes to Red River. They were, further, to have lands assigned to them in the settlement, if they chose to remain; and otherwise, to be conveyed, at his Lordship's expense, either to Montreal or Europe. As the event proved, they preferred the former, and were rewarded with small grants of land, situate on a tributary stream, known as Riviere la Seine, entering on the west side of Red River, opposite to Point Douglas, which afterwards, in honour of them, took the name of German Creek. The de Meurons were bad farmers, as all old soldiers generally are, and withal very bad subjects; quarrelsome, slothful, famous bottle companions, and ready for any enterprise, however lawless and tyrannical. Under any circumstances, a levy of this character could be no great acquisition to a new settlement; and at such a juncture as we have described should never have been permitted by the Canadian Government.

Meanwhile, the North West Company had a warrant issued for the arrest of Lord Selkirk. He ignored it and, instead, attempted to have those responsible for the killings at Seven Oaks brought to trial. However, his efforts were unsuccessful, and Selkirk himself was fined £2,000 for his action against Fort William. Disillusioned and in ill health, Selkirk returned to Britain in 1817. His Red River venture had cost him £100,000 and his health. The fifth Earl of Selkirk and founder of the future province of Manitoba died in France in 1820.

ROWDYISM IN THE COLONY[145]

As related by Alexander Ross:

Governor Alexander McDonell*. . . prided himself in affecting the style of an Indian viceroy. The officials he kept about him resembled the court of an eastern nabob, with its warriors, serfs, and varlets, and the names they bore were hardly less pompous; for here were secretaries, assistant-secretaries, accountants, orderlies, grooms, cooks, and butlers. This array of attendants about the little man was supposed to lend a sort of dignity to his position; but his court, like many another where show and folly have usurped the place of wisdom and usefulness, was little more than one prolonged scene of debauchery. From the time the puncheons of rum reached the colony in the fall, till they were all drunk dry, nothing was to be seen or heard about Fort Douglas but balling, dancing, rioting, and drunkenness, in the barbarous spirit of those disorderly times. . . .

Although the Red River Settlement never fulfilled the grand expectations of Selkirk, he had firmly planted a colony in the Canadian West, a colony that was to last and endure. His vision of the settlement as the "bread-basket of the Empire" has since become a reality. Moreover, it was Selkirk's permanent settlement, rather than the transient fur trade, that gave British North America a firm and lasting claim to the Canadian West.

By 1821, competition, costs and the challenge of the settlement proved to be too much for the North West Company. The very same reasons that had led to its formation in 1787 now led the partners of the North West Company to seek consolidation with the Hudson's Bay Company. In 1821, the two companies merged under the name of the Hudson's Bay Company. British North America was finding new economic bases in lumber and wheat. New methods of transportation, new peoples, and new ideas were pushing the fur trade into the background.

* He was Governor from August, 1815, to June, 1822;

IV

EMERGENCE
FROM COLONIALISM

British North America emerged from the War of 1812 separate and distinct from the United States. The British imperial presence in North America had been preserved, and with it the likelihood of strong influences from overseas. In fact, events in Great Britain were combining to affect the next phase of development in the colonies. Crop failures, overpopulation, unemployment and the Industrial Revolution drove waves of immigrants to the New World.

Between 1815 and 1850, British North America underwent great economic and social changes as thousands upon thousands of new settlers arrived. Dense forests slowly gave way to pioneer farms, even though the new-comers had to contend with a system of land distribution that was normally inefficient and frequently corrupt. Growing villages and towns, many of them newly founded, became the bases for industrial and commercial enterprise. The Great Migration, as the flood of immigration was called, also added to the mosaic of British North America. Irishmen, Scots and Englishmen came to share half a continent with the established French, Loyalist, Indian and American population.

The system of government was once more the object of mounting pressures. The Constitutional Act of 1791 had established representative government in the Canadas. But these assemblies, and the ones previously granted in the Maritimes, were kept in check. British leaders had no intention of allowing democratic self-government which, they believed, had been the root cause of the American Revolution and Britain's loss of the Thirteen Colonies. Real political power was thus vested in the appointed royal governors and appointed councils, while the elected assemblies functioned as mere debating societies. Government became the preserve of entrenched minorities which dominated all areas of public life in the colonies.

Although conditions varied from colony to colony, the majority of inhabitants in each had sufficient grievances to demand reforms. The problem of land in Upper Canada, racial conflict in Lower Canada, the power of timber and shipping interests in the Atlantic colonies — each case involved basically a demand for greater democracy. In the Canadas, when reform was frustrated at every turn by imperial officials and the "compacts," the more radically minded reformers turned in desperation to rebellion.

The inept rebellions of 1837, in addition to diminishing radicalism as a force in Canadian politics for some time, established the fact that the colonists were largely loyal to the crown. Nevertheless, the "comic opera" rebellions of 1837 sent shock waves all the way to the British throne, where Queen Victoria had just begun her long reign, and led to an investigation by Lord Durham.

The Durham Report recommended major changes. The greatest of these was responsible government. It did not become an immediate reality; for nearly a decade the Reform leaders of British North America pressed their claims for local self-government. By 1850, however, the opposition of the British government had given way, and the problem of colonial government had found a solution. The autocratic rule of the oligarchies had been replaced by the rule of the people through their elected assemblies. Just as the American Revolution had marked the end of the First British Empire, the Canadian solution — responsible government — signalled the transformation of the Second British Empire into the modern Commonwealth.

By mid-century, British possessions in North America, isolated from one another by impenetrable wilderness, spanned the continent from the Atlantic to the Pacific. Economic development varied from area to area, each assuming its own distinctive social and cultural character. Political ferment was present everywhere; in time, it led to Confederation.

13

SOCIAL AND ECONOMIC DEVELOPMENTS

A

PRIOR TO 1815

Following the American Revolution, the Loyalist migration and the far-reaching constitutional changes of the Constitutional Act, the British North American colonies entered a period of unprecedented economic growth and development. By the beginning of the War of 1812, they had taken on economic and social characteristics that were to last well into the nineteenth century. At this point, it might be useful to survey the growth and development of the colonies as they emerged within the framework of the Second British Empire.

Of all the British North American colonies, Newfoundland was least affected by the coming of the Loyalists and the ensuing constitutional changes. Her population of 15,000 grew at a snail's pace and was generally ill-governed by naval officers. Fishing for export to Great Britain, started in the days of Cabot, continued to be the mainstay of the impoverished economic life. Well protected by the British navy, Newfoundland merchants and their indebted creditors remained aloof from the rest of British North America.

CONDITIONS IN NEWFOUNDLAND[146]

Written in 1883:

In 1804 the resident population of Newfoundland was found to be 20,380, to which may be added 4,000 employed in the fisheries, who returned to the United Kingdom at the close of the season. . . .

A very serious grievance . . . was brought under the notice of Governor Gower by a petition from the inhabitants of Fogo Island, in which they complained that "through the imposition of the merchants or their agents in Fogo by their exorbi-

ant price on shop goods and provisions, they were from year to year held in debt, so as not daring to find fault, fearing they might starve at the approach of every winter." They further stated "that the said merchants arrogate to themselves a power not warranted by any law, in selling to us every article of theirs at any price they think fit, and taking from your petitioners the produce of the whole year at whatsoever price they think fit to give. In short, let it suffice to inform Your Excellency that they take on themselves to price their own goods and ours also, as they think most convenient to them."

Except for some Highland Scots, the Maritimes did not experience any significant population growth after the Loyalist flood. The economy of the region, however, underwent drastic changes. After the American Revolution, the Navigation Acts of the old British colonial trading system were enforced with new vigour. The trade of the Empire was to be carried in the ships of the Empire. This meant that the New Englanders, who had profited so well by supplying the sugar islands of the West Indies with foodstuffs, were now excluded from this trade. It was hoped that Nova Scotia would fill the void created by the exclusion of the New England trading fleets from the imperial trading system. Fish of the North Atlantic fisheries became the article of trade, and Nova Scotian ships the vehicle. Fishing and commerce with the West Indies occupied most of the energies of Nova Scotia, but she still could not fully satisfy the demands of this trade. As a result, New England, on occasion, was allowed a share of the trade. Nevertheless, Nova Scotia enjoyed a steady, secure and protected commerce with the

West Indies. The Navigation Acts which the Thirteen Colonies had found so objectionable were working to great advantage for Nova Scotia.

THE ECONOMY OF NOVA SCOTIA, 1803[147]

Few new Settlers have come to the Province since the Loyalists — except the Highlanders to Pictou & the Gulph — also a few Irish to Halifax & the coast Westward . . . mostly come from New-foundland, make a great deal of money in the course of the Summer which they waste in Winter in idleness & drink — few take to farming as they are not well received in the interior part of the country by the Methodists & New light people, who are there prevalent & dislike them as Catholics . . . but there is no regular migration. — There are also fishermen along the Coast, East-ward of Halifax — thinly scattered along the different creeks & Harbours — these are mostly Americans. . . . The New England Schooners which fish . . . carry on a smuggling trade with these people along the Coast, which excites great jealousy in the Halifax merchants who alledge that they pick up the returns which ought to repay them for their advances to the fishermen whom they supply on credit, & who instead of paying them sell to these Smugglers. The produce of the Fishery is however the principal article of exporta-tion from Halifax — the lumber trade is also something but of no great amount, the timber in the neighbourhood being exhausted or destroyed.

Similarly, New Brunswick enjoyed great pros-perity as a result of the imperial trading system. With the tall stands of timber and the proximity to the sea, New Brunswick was particularly well equipped to supply the Empire with wooden ships and timber for Britain's shipyards. When Britain became involved in the Napoleonic Wars, she needed secure sources of timber for naval con-struction if she were to maintain her supremacy of the seas. New Brunswick, far removed from embattled Europe, was a safe source of fine timber, and Britain lowered the duty on incoming New Brunswick timber. The effect of this preferential treatment greatly encouraged the colony's timber trade. Each winter armies of lumbermen (who often farmed in the summer) felled the tall trees of the New Brunswick forests. These timbers were then shipped across the Atlantic in New Brunswick boats especially built for this purpose. The timber trade and shipbuilding soon became staples in the economy of New Brunswick. The colony had pro-fited very well from the timber boom and the protected market she enjoyed in Great Britain.

THE TIMBER BOOM IN NEW BRUNSWICK[148]

. . . . In 1806, 7,062 loads (of fifty cubic feet each) were dispatched to Great Britain, but it still could not be said that the exportation of timber for commercial purposes was more than a second-ary industry.

. . . a combination of circumstances produced spectacular results. . . . Alexander's [of Russia] compliance with the terms of the Berlin and Milan decrees meant the loss of Britain's control of navi-gation of the Baltic at a time when she was depen-dent on Baltic timber for the maintenance of her fleet . . . and the humming economy of the British Isles required extraordinary quantities of timber for building materials. The world had been searched for supplies alternative to those of the Baltic. In 1808 there were available only the virgin forests of British North America. . . .

. . . New Brunswick was able to take advantage of this rich opportunity. The country was well stocked with large pine, was intersected by many navigable rivers, and was closer to Britain than Canada was. . . . In 1807, 156 ships sailed with 27,430 tons. In 1810, 410 ships sailed with 87,690 tons. In loads the figures were 13,938 and 50,807. . . .

Large numbers of people abandoned their farms in whole or in part to enter the timber trade, which promised a quick cash return as well as a life of adventure in the woods. The decay of agriculture became a theme for moralists. In Charlotte County hundreds abandoned the fishery and moved up the St. Croix where St. Stephen became a leading centre for the assault on the forests. . . .

Only in Prince Edward Island did agriculture form the backbone of the economy. The other Maritime colonies were too busy enjoying the advantages of their preferred and protected trad-ing positions within the imperial system.

The Canadas, too, were developing economical-ly as a result of the European wars and the imperial system. The fine timber stands of the St. Lawrence and Ottawa Valleys helped supplement the supplies of timber that New Brunswick was shipping to Britain.

However, Britain also needed a safe and acces-sible source of food supplies. The Lower-Cana-dian farms, which had formerly produced only for home consumption, began producing surplus crops for export. The new Upper-Canadian farms in the fertile lands of the West also began producing foodstuffs for Britain. Although crops were always uncertain and the export of wheat was small in comparison with the gigantic fish, fur and timber trade, wheat was fast becoming a staple in the economy of the Canadas. Moreover, clearing of the timber stands and farming of the land complemented one another, and Canadians often enjoyed two cash crops — timber and wheat.

GROWTH OF THE TRADE IN THE CANADAS[149]

.... When a market for wheat developed in Lower Canada and the mother country, the Upper Canadian exporters were able to take advantage of it; although lacking adequate roads, they had at their disposal the resources of the Great Lakes-St. Lawrence route, superior in some respects to the Ohio-Mississippi route used by the farmers of the American interior. In fact, the pull of the St. Lawrence was so strong that it attracted much American trade: exports from some northern states went to market via Montreal and Quebec.

———

.... Upper Canada suffered from a lack of capital. ... An important consequence of this ... a handful of merchants first at Kingston, and later at Niagara and York and some other villages, acquired a commanding position in the province's economic life. These merchants were usually agents of large Montreal firms. ... At first the merchants were concerned only with the fur trade, but as agricultural surpluses began to accumulate and as trees were cut, they began to deal in wheat and flour and potash and lumber. Also, they were receiving manufactured items from their Montreal principals, who in turn had imported them from overseas. ...

Unlike the Maritimes, where immigration had virtually ceased with the conclusion of the Loyalist migration, Upper Canada, particularly, experienced a population boom. Geographically, Upper Canada lay like a giant wedge in the path of westward American expansion. It was natural that some of the westward movement of the American people should spill over into Upper Canada. Far from preventing American settlement in Upper Canada, John Graves Simcoe, the first Lieutenant-Governor of the colony, welcomed and encouraged it. Simcoe, who had led the Loyalist Queen's Rangers during the revolution, was, like William Smith, convinced that the exposure of American immigrants to British institutions would win back their loyalty to the Crown. He undertook an extensive advertising campaign in American newspapers and offered free land to those who would settle in Upper Canada. Times were difficult in the United States. Taxes were high and good land within easy reach was scarce. In the young United States, patriotism and nationalism had not as yet fully developed. It was a simple matter for American settlers to take the oath of allegiance to the Crown and receive a free land grant in return. So successful were Simcoe's efforts that Upper Canada which had a population of 14,000 in 1791, boasted 90,000 people, most of whom were "late loyalists," at the outbreak of the War of 1812. While it is true that the loyalty of these American settlers became a subject of grave concern during the War of 1812, there is no doubt that Simcoe's policy gave Upper Canada what it needed most — people.

AMERICAN SETTLERS IN UPPER CANADA[150]

Lord Selkirk writing in 1804:

.... I passed a traveller ... who had been to see his relations in New Jersey from whence he had originally come — he was also on a specn [speculation] of buying a lot near Buffalo — I asked how he would reconcile his Oath of Allegiance, to two different Govts, he answered that the Oath to each only applied while resident within their territories — he could never take an Oath to be otherwise understood. — From what I heard ... as to people who come from the States to Canada nothing can be more evident than that they are merely induced by the facility of getting land, and that loyalty is a mere pretext. ...

Simcoe placed great faith in the oath of allegiance as a means of assuring the loyalty of the American settlers. But he mistrusted the intentions of the United States; the possibility of renewed hostilities with the Americans led him to prepare the defences of Upper Canada. As a military man, he realized the value and necessity of good means of communication. Consequently, Simcoe embarked upon an extensive road building program for which he is chiefly remembered. At the insistence of Lord Dorchester, the Governor-General, the capital of Upper Canada had been moved from Newark (Niagara), near the United States border, to York. The new capital became the hub of an extensive system of roads. The Danforth Road, together with the famous Yonge and Dundas Streets, which today form the backbone of central Ontario's highway transportation system, originated in Simcoe's time. Although these roads were little more than paths through the wilderness, they greatly aided in the defence of Upper Canada during the War of 1812.

. . . . Making roads is always a problem in a pioneer country, but it was particularly so in Upper Canada, where settlement was thinly dispersed over hundreds of miles, where the land was heavily wooded and watered by many streams, and where immense quantities of unoccupied land resulted from the Reserves, the Indian lands, and the large holdings of absentee owners. When the government did turn to road-building, its concern was to lay out a system of trunk roads, with an eye to defence requirements, even though such roads were not always of immediate economic value to the settlers. . . . Accordingly, members of the Assembly early turned to efforts to get provincial funds for roads to their communities, with the result that road-building and political manoeuvring were soon closely intermixed. Everyone complained about the roads and the lack of them, but little was done.

Lower Canada, and particularly the Eastern Townships, received about 9,000 of the post-Loyalist American settlers. At the outbreak of the War of 1812, the population of Lower Canada numbered 330,000, most of whom were French-speaking Canadians. Montreal remained the centre of the reorganized and revitalized fur trade, while Quebec became the centre of the lumbering interests.

West of the Great Lakes, the Hudson's Bay Company and the newly formed North West Company were competing vigorously for the lion's share of the fur trade and racing each other farther westward. For the time being, the great Canadian West remained the fur trader's domain, shortly to be challenged by agricultural settlement.

THE "ACCOMMODATION'S" MAIDEN VOYAGE[152]

". . . . John Molson Esq., an enterprising and spirited merchant of Montreal, now fitted out the first steamer that ever ploughed the waters of the St. Lawrence . . ."

The following extract from the "Quebec Mercury" chronicles the arrival at Quebec:

"On Saturday morning [November 6, 1809], at 8 o'clock, arrived here, from Montreal, being her first trip, the steamboat "Accommodation," with ten passengers. This is the first vessel of the kind that ever appeared in this harbor. She is continually crowded with visitants . . . her passage was sixty-six hours; thirty of which she was at anchor . . . . *No wind or tide can stop her.* . . . The great advantage attending a vessel so constructed is, that a passage may be calculated on to a degree of certainty, in point of time; which cannot be the case with any vessel propelled by sail only. . . . The steamboat received her impulse from an open double-spoked, perpendicular wheel, on each side, without any circular band or rim. . . . The wheels are put and kept in motion by steam, operating within the vessel. A mast is to be fixed in her, for the purpose of using a sail when the wind is favorable, which will occasionally accelerate her headway."

B

FROM 1815 TO MID-CENTURY

The economic and social advances of the years from 1815 to 1850 are often overshadowed by the great constitutional development that culminated with responsible government in 1849. This British North American solution to the problem of relations between mother country and colony was so profound that it eventually transformed the British Empire into an association of sovereign units sharing common traditions and interests. As a background to understanding this political achievement, however, it is useful to look briefly at changes in the life of British North America.

The Great Migration of the years following 1815 was not the first great influx of new people to British North America. In the seventeenth century, the efforts of Louis XIV on behalf of his tiny colony of New France had caused a trickle of Frenchmen to relocate on the shores of the St. Lawrence. New Englanders had poured into Nova Scotia in the middle of the eighteenth century to take up the fertile, tilled fields of the expelled Acadians. The American Revolution drove many loyal subjects of the Crown from their homes in the Thirteen Colonies to the sanctuary of British North America. Shortly thereafter, grants of free land in Upper Canada had lured many Americans northward. But just as the Conquest of 1760 had cut off the trickle of French immigration to Quebec, so also did the War of 1812 arrest the flood of Americans that had been pouring into British North America.

The border was now a reality and no longer the imaginary unmarked line to be crossed at will. The war had forced people to declare their allegiance to either the Crown or the Republic. As may be expected, American immigrants were not welcome in British North America after the war. Upper Canada instituted restrictive measures and American immigrants were prevented from owning land for a period of seven years after their arrival.

RUINS IN THE VILLAGE OF CARIHAKEN, COUNTY OF GALWAY.

SKETCH IN A HOUSE AT FAHEY'S QUAY, ENNIS.—THE WIDOW CONNOR AND HER DYING CHILD.

Conditions of the Poor in Ireland

CABIN OF PAT. MACNAMARA, VILLAGE OF CLEAR.

KEILLINES, NEAR GENERAL THOMPSON'S PROPERTY.

The northward movement of people to British North America had virtually stopped; for the first time, the British Isles became the chief source of immigrants.

In the early nineteenth century, people did not usually undertake the dangers of ocean travel and the rigours of a new land simply for the sake of change. People left what they were accustomed to only because conditions at home were intolerable. Economic conditions in Great Britain made it imperative for many people to emigrate if they were to survive.

The conclusion of the Napoleonic Wars brought an end to the great demand for war *materiel* and an economic depression settled on Britain. As production slowed down, unemployment increased. To compound the difficulties of this sudden drop in demand, many demobilized soldiers now swelled the ranks of the unemployed. The solution to the unemployment problem was often found in emigration to British North America. Further, the Industrial Revolution was gradually gaining momentum; machines were replacing men and factories were displacing cottage-industries which had previously supported so many families.

In Ireland, thousands of people starved to death when the potato crops failed in the 1840's. Potatoes were the staple of the Irish diet, but Ireland was overpopulated and could not produce surplus food supplies to feed its population in lean years. For many poverty stricken Irishmen the choice was a brutal one — starvation or emigration.

CONDITIONS IN IRELAND[153]

. . . . In every street and alley are to be seen groups of human beings in a state of half nudity; women with their almost lifeless infants struggling to obtain a portion of the scanty nutriment from their exhausted mothers, while their reckless and infuriated fathers wander the streets, lost to all hope, and maddened with hunger and despair. Nay, I have frequently seen women with the lifeless bodies of their infant children in their arms, prowling from street to street, and begging from the casual passengers the means of depositing the remains of their departed offspring in the grave!

In Scotland, the enclosure movement spread and added to the already severe unemployment problem. Large landowners turned the crofters off their land because it was found that the larger farm unit could be operated more profitably, or simply because sheep-raising brought in more income than rent from the tenant farmers.

Britain, in the first half of the nineteenth century, was hardly the land of opportunity. Many citizens were robbed of their pride by being unable to support their families and by having no future to build for their children. In the minds of many, life in British North America could possibly be better than life in Britain — but it could certainly be no worse.

ADVICE TO EMIGRANTS[154]

. . . every young farmer or labourer going out (who can pay for the passage of two) to take an active young wife with him. . . .

Unmarried Women, who have no fortunes, and are *active*, and *industrious*, *without much pride or vanity*, and who relish a quiet and *retired* life . . . have an opportunity of being well married. . . .

. . . as the settlers must scramble about in all weathers . . . stout flannels and coarse cloths . . . must not mind fashion; the best coat and breeches are those that can come farthest through the brush with fewest holes in them . . . there is not a better article for the purpose than Scotch blanket . . . called plaiding.

. . . religious and loyal prints — coloured Scriptural subjects with texts attached, home scenery of school and village churches. Portraits of Her Majesty, Prince Albert and the royal children, Wellington and Nelson, views of Windsor Castle, the House of Parliament, our cathedrals. . . .

Above all things do not take your decanter or your corkscrew. . . . You are going to a country where you may literally swim in whisky or gin, and pretty nearly in brandy and rum. But resolve never to taste either. Drinking is the great vice of the country.

Between 1815 and 1850 the population of British North America grew from half a million to slightly less than three million. Although great numbers of the immigrants merely stopped over in the colonies and then proceeded to the United States, British North America managed to retain 800,000 English, Irish and Scottish immigrants.

ADVICE NOT TO EMIGRATE TO NOVA SCOTIA[155]

In the Novascotian *of September 29, 1831, Joseph Howe takes exception to an article by William Cobbett:*

. . . . An article in a late number of his [Cobbett's Register] is devoted to the patriotic task of dissuading the people of Great Britain from emigrating to the North American Colonies, which he characterizes as a barren desert — a howling wilderness, where sterility is the parent of starvation.

. . . Nova Scotia consists of heaps of rocks, covered with fir-trees for the greater part, with a few narrow strips of clear land on the bottoms of the valleys. . . . . Everywhere the snow covers the ground for several feet deep six months of the year. So poor are these countries, that garden stuff and fruit, even cabbages, are carried from the United States by sea, to be eaten by the governors, officers of the army, and other gentle folks, who are paid out of the taxes raised on us. . . .

Old Cobbett perhaps is ignorant that thousands of bushels of Corn, such as he is trying to ripen in his garden in England, are grown every year on the worst lands of the bleak and barren North American Colonies.

In 1841, little Prince Edward Island boasted a population of 50,000 of which 30,000 were native born. The population of Nova Scotia, which was about 80,000 in 1817 (mostly New Englanders and Loyalists), rose to 200,000 by 1838. New Brunswick's growth was less dramatic but no less impressive as the population grew from 75,000 in 1824 to 160,000 in 1840. Apart from Newfoundland, Lower Canada received fewer immigrants than any other colony. Nevertheless, the population of Lower Canada, the largest of the British North American colonies, was 700,000 by 1844. Upper Canada, the newest of the British North American colonies, received most of the new immigrants; its population soared to 430,000 by 1840.

Some of the immigrants who left Great Britain

Top: Interior of the Agent's Office   **Centre:** Between Decks   **Bottom:** Departure of Steamers Carrying Emigrants

were able to pay their own passage and thus enjoyed relative comfort on passenger vessels or even steam ships, which came into limited use in the 1830's and 1840's. Frequently these immigrants, when they arrived, were able to purchase farms.

· The great majority of the immigrants, however, was desperately poor and required assistance from land companies, charitable organizations or the government. Frequently, the passage of these sponsored immigrants was paid by the town or village from which they came; the town councils found the passage fare cheaper than indefinite financial assistance to the poor and unemployed. For the sponsored immigrants, the passage to North America was a nightmare.

PAUPER IMMIGRANTS[156]

The president of the Quebec Emigrants' Society said this of them:

A pauper emigrant on his arrival in this Province is generally either with nothing or with a very small sum in his pocket . . . expecting immediate and constant employment at ample wages. . . . He has landed from the ship, and from his apathy and want of energy has loitered about the wharfs, waiting for the offer of employment; or, if he obtained employment . . . found himself, at the beginning of winter, when there is little or no employment for labour in this part of the country, discharged . . . emigrants have often accumulated in Quebec at the end of summers, encumbered it with indigent inhabitants, and formed the most onerous burthen on the charitable funds of the community.

Remarks by a Collector of Customs at Quebec:

Emigrants sent out by parishes are very generally inferior, both morally and physically, to those who have found their own way out. The parishes have sent out persons far too old to gain their livelihood by work, and often of drunken and improvident habits. These emigrants have neither benefited themselves nor the country; and this is very natural, for, judging from the class sent out, the object must have been the getting rid of them, and not either the benefit of themselves or the colony. . . .

Very often the immigrants were carried to North America in the crowded holds of timber ships that had just discharged their timber cargo in Britain. The immigrants had to carry their own food and do their own cooking in the cramped quarters below decks. Sickness was constant and death frequent. One traveler to North America tells of seeing fifty-three burials at sea during one passage. Seasickness, dysentry and cholera were common ailments and diseases that plagued the immigrants. In 1832, a great cholera epidemic broke out and spread throughout British North America. In Quebec City alone, 1,500 people died from this dreaded disease in a single month.

THE VOYAGE ACROSS THE ATLANTIC[157]

Tragedy on voyage — 1832:

We had the misfortune to lose both our little boys. . . . We were very much hurt to have them buried in a watery grave: we mourned their loss, night and day they were not out of our minds. We had a minister on board, who prayed with us twice a day: he was a great comfort to us. . . . There were six children and one woman died in the vessel.

Description of a crossing in a sailing ship, in 1835:

. . . a tub of a vessel, without a sailing point in her composition. . . . Water tanks, heaps of biscuits, barrels of pork and but one of rum; a pennant, an ensign, a skipper, a fat mate, and a superannuated lieutenant of the navy by way of agent, and a most inadequate crew, were put on board, and the transport was reported fit for sea.

Fever strikes passengers on passage of 1847:

. . . . A poor female patient was lying in one of the upper berths — dying. Her head and face were swollen to a most unnatural size, the latter being hideously deformed. . . . Her afflicted husband stood by her holding a "blessed candle" in his hand and awaiting the departure of her spirit. . . . As the sun was setting, the bereaved husband muttered a prayer over her enshrouded corpse, which, as he said "Amen", was lowered into the ocean.

When the immigrants did finally arrive in Halifax, Quebec or Montreal, they were faced with new problems, almost as monumental as the ocean voyage. Before the new settlers could start tilling the soil and fashioning a new life, they faced the problem of a long, uncomfortable voyage to the interior. Moreover, they had to purchase, in one way or another, a suitable parcel of land before they could get down to the business of farming.

Land around the settled areas proved extremely difficult to obtain. Also, large tracts of land lay in disuse reserved for the Crown and clergy. Members of the Compacts also held large blocks of arable land in speculation. This land, while available, proved to be very expensive and often beyond the means of the new immigrants. Government policy in granting land was confused and inequitable and added to the difficulties of securing good holdings in reasonable proximity to settled areas. The chaotic land distribution system coupled with the speculative practices of the Compact members, became a severe irritant to the new settlers, particularly in Upper Canada. Later, the land problem became a major cause of discontent among the new settlers and contributed greatly to the troubles of the 1830's and 1840's. During the early stages of the great migration, the lack of available land close to the older settlements forced the new immigrants to open up new stretches of land in the interior, far removed from the established Loyalist settlements.

One of the early and more prominent land companies was that started by Colonel Thomas Talbot.

THE COLOURFUL COLONEL THOMAS TALBOT[158]

. . . . He dressed in homespun even on journeys abroad. His sheepskin coat and fur cap, celebrated wherever his name was known, was a familiar sight on the streets of York when he paid his winter visit to the provincial capital. . . . An artist friend painted a portrait of him, in the costume of the period, but with trousers of homespun in broad stripes of black and red, forming a somewhat startling and picturesque pattern. . . .

". . . . He had passed his life in worse than solitude . . . with inferiors and dependents, whose servility he despised, and whose resistance enraged him. . . . Hence despotic habits, and contempt even for those whom he benefitted; hence, with much natural benevolence and generosity, a total disregard, or rather total ignorance, of the feelings of others — all the disadvantages, in short, of royalty, only on a smaller scale. . . ."

. . . . Talbot used to say that a man who drank in the early morning was sure to die a drunkard. To show the sincerity of his belief, and his resolve not to expose himself to this danger, he placed a mark on an out-building, showing where the sun would cast his shadow at 11 o'clock. Long before the hour, the Colonel would sit in his armchair gazing intently at the moving shadow. Precisely when it reached the mark, [his servant] was ordered to produce the decanter. . . . To have ample time for this dissipation, he had an inflexible rule that no business should be transacted after 12 o'clock. . . .

Talbot, a testy ex-army officer, managed to secure 65,000 acres along the north shore of Lake Erie. He ruled his private domain like a feudal lord and tolerated no opposition. Nonetheless, the Talbot settlement boasted 50,000 people by 1837.

Land companies that had come into existence after the turn of the century assisted in the settling of the new immigrants. Usually, an enterprising individual or group would secure a large tract of land beyond the settled areas. This land was often purchased from the Crown at bargain prices in exchange for the promise of settling the land and building roads, bridges, schools and other improvements. The land company would then bring out immigrants who were usually desperately poor. The companies frequently had to assist the new immigrants and to supply them with tools and provisions to get them settled. After a few years, when the new settlers could earn money from the sale of surplus crops, they would then begin purchasing the land from the land company.

In 1823 the Canada Land Company was formed under the secretariat of a talented Scotsman, John Galt. He was a novelist of renown, a philanthropist and an excellent businessman. Under his direction, the Company was able to obtain a grant of 2,500,000 acres of land lying between the present city of Galt and Lake Huron. New immigrants poured into the Huron Tract, as the Canada Land Company's holding was called, and the towns of Goderich, Galt and Stratford soon became the centres of settlement.

In 1833 Galt left the Canada Land Company and formed the British North American Land Company, which undertook the settling of people in the Eastern Townships of Lower Canada. In the meantime, in 1831, the New Brunswick and Nova Scotia Land Company was formed to bring out settlers to the Maritimes.

The land companies, in their pursuit of profit, served very useful purposes. Poverty-stricken immigrants were given the opportunity of owning land with little or no cash investment. Vast stretches of land, particularly in Upper Canada, that might have gone untouched for decades were opened for settlement. In many respects, the land companies were not unlike the chartered companies of New France; they also undertook to assist immigrants in developing and settling the land.

LETTERS FROM THE NEW SETTLERS[159]

I really do bless God every day I rise, that he was ever pleased, in the course of his providence, to send me and my family to this place Lanark County, Upper Canada. Were you here and seeing the improvements that are going on among us, you would not believe that we were once Glasgow weavers!

Urge my brothers to come out if ever they wish to free themselves from bondage . . . this is the land of independence to the industrious — the soil will repay the labourer for the sweat of his brow.

Pioneer life in British North America during the first half of the nineteenth century differed very little from the pioneer life of New France a century earlier. People were still basically concerned with earning an existence from the land, clearing the forests, adjusting to the climate and securing food, clothing and shelter. Moreover, the frontier exercised the same influences. Class barriers broke down and the wilderness bred a spirit of freedom in its inhabitants.

Initially, a settler undertook the construction of a house, usually a log cabin with a thatched roof and dirt floor covered with rushes or straw. Eventually, saw-mills provided lumber for frame houses with insulated walls and well-fitting windows and doors. In some areas where good building stone was available, spacious and comfortable stone houses made their appearance.

Once the pioneer had his log cabin, the next step was to clear the forest so that he could work the soil. Clearing the land was not an easy task.

CLEARING LAND, 1820[160]

John Howson, after spending two years in Canada, made these observations:

After the trees have been felled, the most suitable kinds are split into rails for fences, and the remainder, being cut into logs twelve feet long, and hauled together into large piles, and burnt. The land cleared in this manner is sown with wheat, and harrowed two or three times, and in general an abundant crop rewards the toils of the owner.

After the felling, dividing, and burning the timber have been accomplished, the stumps still remain, disfiguring the fields, and impeding the effectual operation of the plough and harrow. The immediate removal of the roots of the trees is impracticable and they are therefore always allowed to fall into decay, which state they are generally reduced in the space of eight or nine years. Pine stumps however seem scarcely susceptible of decomposition, as they frequently show no symptoms of it after half a century has elapsed. . . .

In the early days, when horses and oxen were scarce, the pioneer relied on his own muscles. He felled the trees or at times simply burned the forests and sold the potash extracted from the ashes. In breaking the land he used oxen, if he had them, to pull the home-made plowshares; otherwise, he used a hoe. Reaping the crop was no less difficult for the pioneer who used a scythe to cut the grain. Milling the grain on the "hominy block" was a slow and tedious task.

Household effects and clothing were of the

Between Cobourg and York, Upper Canada, 1838

simplest type. Though a few newcomers managed to retain some cherished piece of furniture, most fashioned their furniture from the materials found on the frontier. The stump of a large tree served as the all-purpose table. Beds were simply constructed of four uprights connected by four poles across which were tied strips of elm bark. The clothing too was unpretentious. All clothing was made from the wool of the pioneer's sheep or from the leather of his animals. Tanning leather was as necessary a skill for a man as weaving was for a woman. Indeed, the pioneer constantly employed ingenuity to provide shelter, food and clothing.

If the pioneer had to be a rugged individualist, he also had to be co-operative with his neighbours. By himself he could, probably, eke out a primitive existence; but if he wanted the luxury of a barn he had to depend on his neighbour's help. Such mutual cooperation brought neighbours together not only for work but also for such rudimentary social life as was possible in the backwoods.

FRONTIER LIFE IN UPPER CANADA, 1828[161]

. . . . In Scotland a parish has its character to support; but let it behave in Canada as it may, few will find fault. No one will there blame you for not attending the church, nor care whether you educate your children or no. . . . If you like to live in elegance, no one will care, nor praise your house furniture, or say unto thy Turkey carpet that it is beautiful. Nay, Jonathan will squirt tobacco-juice at thy splendid fender. . . . Preachers may preach, and schoolmasters teach, but what avails it? The way to Heaven is considered by no means very complex, when people think little about it; and as for Latin and Algebra, yea even common English and the multiplication table, they are not respected. . . .

. . . there are more mills erected, in many instances, than there seems to be work for. . . . A

Launch of the **Royal William**, Quebec, 1831

distillery is a thing quite indispensable, so that *raw grain* whisky may be produced . . . the flavour of which is qualified by frosty potatoes and yellow pumpkins. Such *aqua* is extremely delicious; and those who know what *Glenlivet* is, may perhaps, touch it with a long stick, confining their nostrils at the time. . . . A tannery is also an appendage; while a store may finish the list. . . .

. . . There is a particular charm about the name whisky. . . . But look at the affair. A Scotchman plants himself down in the *bush,* but often thinks of his old habits in the old country. A yankee comes about with whisky to sell: — can Donald withstand this? No; he would drink it — he would drain it to the dregs, were it fire and brimstone; and it is a distillation little better — made of frosty potatoes, hemlock, pumpkins and black mouldy rye. No hell broth that the witches concocted of yore, can equal it.

This life on the fringe of the wilderness bore little semblance to the life in the established towns. In Halifax and York, garrison towns, small groups of soldiers and civil servants aped the manners of fashionable European society. These town dwellers, usually educated, Anglican and more prosperous, had little in common with the illiterate Non-Conformist (non-Anglican) pioneer backwoods farmer. The subsequent struggle of the Compacts against the rustic democrats stemmed, to a large extent, from this difference in class structure.

The way was opened for social and political progress by improvements in communication. In Upper Canada, as in the rest of British North America, land transportation had been primitive. Corduroy roads — logs laid side by side — were a peculiar Canadian invention and served the backwood settlements. Except for military roads, however, public highways were non-existent. Nor were there roads going through clergy reserves or land held for speculation by friends of the Executive Council. An Englishwoman, in 1837, remarked that it took three and one-half hours to travel one stretch of seven miles on the road between Hamilton and London.

Waterways, rather than roadways, impressed the people of the Canadas as their best hopes for progress and prosperity. Accordingly, with the backing of Montreal merchants, the governments of Upper and Lower Canada initiated a series of canal systems. The Lachine Canal, which opened in 1824, went around the treacherous rapids. The Welland Canal, completed in 1829, by-passed Niagara Falls. In 1832, the Rideau Canal, connecting Lake Ontario with the Ottawa River, was financed by the British government as an alternate water route in the event of an American seizure of the St. Lawrence.

The canal systems created a seaway which contributed to the expansion of the carrying trade. Steel vessels, powered by steam, gradually replaced the wooden sailing ships. The "Royal William," built by Samuel Cunard, was the first to cross the Atlantic under steam power. More rapid travel by steamships not only expanded immigration and commercial development but also strengthened Canadian connection with the mother country — now that it took only twenty-five days to cross the Atlantic.

14

THE ROAD TO REBELLION

A

THE COMPACTS AND REFORMERS

Although the Constitutional Act was intended to meet the demands of the English minority in Quebec without disturbing the overwhelming French majority, the Act contained within it the seeds of discontent. The colonial government had executive authority placed in the Governor, assisted by the Executive and Legislative Councils. In both Upper and Lower Canada the provisions of the Act gave rise to oligarchic rule; very soon, the Councils came to be controlled by small governing cliques — the Family Compact* in Upper Canada and the Chateau Clique† in Lower Canada. A minority of powerful, well-entrenched commercial interests predominated over the agrarian population.

The Compacts, whose memberships were relatively small, had virtual control over all phases of life in the colonies. Members of the Compacts held large tracts of land for speculation, owned the banks and financial institutions and dominated commerce and transportation. They used their position in the Executive Councils to formulate government policy for their own benefit, to add to their land holdings by awarding public lands to themselves and to control patronage—all appointments to public office. Through the judges, appointees of the Executive Councils, the Compacts controlled the judiciary and the administration of justice. The Compacts used the Legislative Councils to curb the activity of the Legislative Assemblies. Since no measure could become law without the consent of the Legislative Councils, the Compacts could thwart any attempt by the Legislative Assemblies to limit the privileges of the oligarchies.

THE FAMILY COMPACT[162]

ᵃ*Lord Durham in his* REPORT:

. . . . Successive Governors . . . submitted . . . or . . . yielded to this well-organized party [Family Compact] the real conduct of affairs. The bench, the magistracy, the high offices of the Episcopal Church, and a great part of the legal profession, are filled by the adherents of this party: by grant or purchase, they have acquired nearly the whole of the waste lands of the Province; they are all-powerful in the chartered banks. . . .

———

ᵇ*William Lyon Mackenzie, from the United States, in a letter to a friend shortly after the Rebellion of 1837:*

. . . . I had long seen the country in the hands of a few shrewd, crafty, covetous men under whose management one of the most lovely and desirable sections of America remained a comparative desert. . . .

The influence of the Compacts extended to the religious and educational life in the Canadas. The Church of England was either part of the Compacts or their active supporter. Control of the Clergy Reserves not only gave the Anglican Church additional financial support but also made it an ally of the government. This status established the Church of England as the dominant Protestant denomination in the Canadas. In Upper Canada, Archdeacon John Strachan, the spokesman of Anglicanism and member of the Legislative Council, advanced Anglican-controlled education at all levels. In Lower Canada, the Institute for the Advancement of Learning, an Anglican institution, for a time controlled education.

---

* They were usually Loyalists or of Loyalist descent, members of the Church of England and citizens of wealth and privilege.

† The Legislative Council in Lower Canada often included some French-Canadian seigneurs and upper clergy, but for the most part, members of this council were drawn from the Loyalist Chateau Clique or Scotch Party.

Court House and Jail, York, Upper Canada, 1829

The Compacts repeatedly avowed their loyalty to the Crown. They did not hesitate to accuse all who opposed them of disloyalty and republicanism. Such appeals to loyalty gained them the support of Loyalist elements, civil servants and retired army officers.

THE FAMILY COMPACT[163]

Sir Francis Bond Head in a dispatch to the Colonial Office, 1837:

It appears, then, from Lord Durham's own shewing, that this "FAMILY COMPACT" . . . is nothing more nor less than that "social fabric" which characterizes every civilized community in the world. It is that social fabric, or rather fortress, within which the British yeoman, farmer, and manufacturer is enabled to repel the extortionate demands of his labourers; and to preserve from pillage and robbery the harvest of his industry after he has reaped it!

"The bench," "the magistrates," "the clergy," "the law," "the landed proprietors," . . . and "the supporters of the Established Church," form just as much *"a family compact"* in England as they do in Upper Canada, and just as much in Germany as they do in England. . . .

The *"family compact"* of Upper Canada is composed of those members of its society who, either by their abilities and character have been honoured by the confidence of the executive government, or who, by their industry and intelligence, have amassed wealth. The party, I own, is comparatively a small one; but to put the multitude at the top and the few at the bottom is a radical reversion of the pyramid of society which every reflecting man must foresee can end only by its downfall.

Soon after the Constitutional Act was implemented, criticism was voiced against certain provisions of the Act and desires for reform were expressed. But during the War of 1812, while the Canadas were engaged in resistance against the American invaders, demands for reform were set aside. After the war, agitation for reform was resumed. All those who actively disapproved of existing conditions joined a loosely formed movement for reform.

The reformers wanted improved conditions for the pioneer farmers. They advocated land grants that would be more easily obtainable by the average settler, better roads to connect the scattered settlements and more schools to educate the young. They intended to achieve such improvements through government legislation. However, this proved difficult, since measures passed by the Legislative Assemblies, where the reformers had adequate representation and at times were in the majority, could be blocked by the Legislative Councils.

BOND HEAD'S OPINION OF THE REFORMERS[164]

To Lord Glenelg, the Colonial Secretary, June 22nd, 1836:

As the Republicans in the Canadas generally mask their designs by professions of attachment to the mother country, I think it important to record this admission [Mackenzie's letter to Joseph Hume of Dec. 1835] on the part of McKenzie of the traitorous object which the Reformers in this province have in view.

From a dispatch to the Colonial Office, 1837:

. . . . The idle, the profligate, and the unprincipled, see that democracy in the United States is rapidly hurrying to anarchy, and they well know, or rather they reckon, that anarchy, or in other words, *plunder,* is the shortest method of obtaining wealth.

The reform movement evolved into a struggle against the entrenched oligarchies which had the power to stifle the will of the Assemblies. In Upper Canada, the movement attracted the Methodists, under the leadership of Egerton Ryerson, and other Protestant groups who resented religious domination by the Church of England. In Lower Canada, the reform movement, although it had some English-speaking adherents who sought constitutional reforms, championed French-Canadian nationalism — which expressed itself in the attempt to preserve a rural way of life against the more progressive English-dominated commercial community. In Lower Canada the movement for reform became a struggle by the French-Canadian-controlled Legislative Assembly to gain supremacy over the obstructionist English-dominated Legislative Council.

DURHAM — ON THE POLITICAL STRUGGLE IN LOWER CANADA[165]

. . . it apears upon a careful review of the political struggle between those who have termed themselves of the loyal party and the popular party . . . each class [is] assuming false designations and fighting under false colours — the British professing exclusive loyalty to the Crown of England, and the Canadians pretending to the character of Reformers. Nay, I am inclined to think . . . that the British (always excluding the body of officials) are really desirous of a more responsible Government, while the Canadians would prefer the present form of Government, or even one of less democratic character. . . .

B

THE REFORM MOVEMENT IN LOWER CANADA

Basically, the struggle for reform became a conflict between the wishes of the people which found expression in the Assemblies, and the privileged oligarchies which controlled the Councils. But in Lower Canada the struggle for reform had racial* undertones as the French-controlled Legislative Assembly was pitted against the British-controlled Councils.

CONDITIONS IN LOWER CANADA, *1804*[166]

Observations of Lord Selkirk during his travels in British North America:

. . . They [the French Canadians] have never been reconciled to the British institutions that have been introduced among them. . . .

The English at Quebec and Montreal cry out . . . & are surprised at the natural & universally experienced dislike of a conquered people to their conquerors & to every thing which puts them in mind of their subjection. . . . The English Govt. certainly seems never to have acted with any system as to Canada—the only chance of reconciling the people would have been either to use every effort to change them entirely in language & institutions & make them forget that they were not English — or keeping them as French to give a Government adapted to them as such, & keep every thing English out of sight — neither of these plans has been followed, & the policy of Govt. has been a kind of vibration between them. . . .

Early signs of the reform movement in Lower Canada appeared in 1805. In order to raise additional revenue for public works, the government, supported by the merchants, proposed a tax on land which would hit the small farmers. Instead, the majority in the Assembly increased tariffs on imports and instituted a sales tax. Thus the burden would fall mainly on the predominantly English commercial class. The business interests claimed that the French Canadians were using their majority in the Assembly to assert their domination over the English minority. Thus a racial character was injected into a routine government matter. This racial rift was aggravated with the founding of *Le Canadien,* in 1806, by Pierre Bedard. This newspaper advocated French-Canadian nationalism — the preservation of French institutions and rights. *Le Canadien* became the organ of the reform movement in Lower Canada.

Soon political conflict arose over the position of judges in the Councils and in the Assembly. In 1806, the Assembly passed a bill which would ban judges from membership in the Legislative Assembly, but this measure was rejected by the Legislative Council. Again, in 1810, the Assembly passed a similar bill and also voted to bar one of its members, a judge, from the Assembly. Sir James Craig, the Governor, felt that the Assembly was exceeding its authority, and he dissolved it. *Le Canadien* criticised the Governor's action. The presses of the newspaper were seized and the printer jailed. In the election that followed, French-Canadian nationalism asserted itself — the group that had dominated the Assembly was re-elected with a greater majority. Now the lines were drawn; the struggle was between the Governor and his Councils and the Legislative Assembly.

* The word "racial" is used in the generally-accepted · Canadian sense of "ethnic" or "national".

GOVERNOR CRAIG'S ATTITUDE TOWARDS THE FRENCH CANADIANS[167]

Part of a dispatch to the Colonial Office:

Quebec 1st May 1810

The first and most obvious remedy that presents itself, is to deprive them of the constitution, as they term it, that is of that representative part of the Government which was unquestionably prematurely given them — neither from habits, information or assimilation, with the Government of England, were they prepared for it. . . .

——

Short of the decisive step of taking away the House altogether . . . or . . . of reuniting the Provinces . . . the enactment of a qualification with respect to the Representatives seems to be indispensably necessary. It . . . appears to me an absurdity, that the Interests of certainly not an unimportant Colony, involving in them, those also of no inconsiderable portion of the Commercial concerns of the British Empire, should be in the hands of six petty shopkeepers, a Blacksmith, a Miller, and 15 ignorant peasants who form part of our present House, a Doctor or Apothecary, twelve Canadian Avocats, and Notaries, and four, so far respectable people that at least they do not keep shops, together with ten English members compleat the List: there is not one person coming under the description of a Canadian Gentleman among them.

In Lower Canada the reform movement was inextricably tied to Joseph Louis Papineau, who gave it meaning and direction. After the end of the War of 1812, when the conflict between reformers and the oligarchy resumed after the respite of the war years, Papineau was the dominant figure in the movement for reform. He came from a well-to-do family and was himself a seigneur. Well educated, trained in the legal profession and versed in British constitutional law, Papineau was a dedicated French-Canadian nationalist and an eloquent speaker. In 1808, at the age of twenty-six, he was first elected to the Assembly, and was its Speaker almost continuously from 1815 to 1837. He worked closely with John Neilson, the leader of the small group of English reformers in Lower Canada, until 1834, when they disagreed on major policy. Papineau also kept in touch with the reform movement in Upper Canada.

Papineau was aware of the entrenched oligarchy which rode roughshod over the Assembly. Nevertheless, he decided to use the Assembly, as weak and as ineffective as it was, to press demands for reform. He employed the power of the purse — the traditional authority vested in British Legislative Assemblies — to assert the supremacy of the Assembly. Certain revenues, of course, such as customs duties, provided for in the Quebec Revenue Act of 1774, were at the disposal of the Governor. Yet the Governor depended on additional funds from the Assembly to meet the full cost of government. The Governor could command the spending of public funds without the Assembly's approval, but British tradition recognized the right of the Legislative Assembly to authorize the spending of public money. Papineau's goal was to control all revenue and expenditure, enabling the Legislative Assembly to be in a stronger position to control the Governor and his Councils.

A VIEW OF PAPINEAU[168]

Excerpts from a private letter written by T. F. Elliott, the Secretary to the Gosford Commission, to his friend Henry Taylor at the Colonial Office in London:

The truth is, that Papineau, with all his faults, is rather a fine fellow. I dare say we shall find him perverse and suspicious, and that if ever he quarrels with us, he will be coarsely abusive. Still the good points of his character are not to be denied. He seems to be irreproachable in his private life; in social intercourse he is mild and gentlemanlike; and if, in politics, he is too hot and unmeasured in his proceedings, I do not find that reasonable men accuse him of being dishonest. His principal faults are violence, a want of the plainer sort of sense, and, I fear, an inveterate prejudice against the English. Whatever else he be, it is impossible to set eyes upon him and not perceive that he is by nature, as much as by station he has won for himself, the first of the French Canadian race.

In 1819, the Assembly refused to vote supply — funds for government expenditure — unless the Assembly was given full control over all revenue and expenditure. The Legislative Council, in turn, rejected the budget prepared by the Legislative Assembly. The Legislative Council then proposed to surrender control of all revenue to the Legislative Assembly, but only in return for a permanent civil list which would assure the salaries of the Governor and his appointed officials. The Assembly turned this down. This wrangle over voting supply continued year after year.

In 1820, Lord Dalhousie, the new Governor, attempted to obtain a permanent civil list for the lifetime of the king. The Assembly refused, since in making such provisions for the salaries of all government officials the Assembly would surrender the little power it did possess for pressing its demands.

The financial stalemate deepened. The English commercial group closed ranks to resist the stubborn Assembly, which refused to vote money for the development of the St. Lawrence trading system. The French Canadians refused to vote public money because they believed that the already powerful English commercial interests would benefit most. French Canadians wanted political reforms in line with British institutions. They sought supremacy of the Legislative Assembly where they could use their majority to assure the French-Canadian way of life. The English wanted vast changes in the transportation facilities to strengthen their economic position against American competition.

In 1822, the English "party" in Lower Canada used its influence in London to press for a reunion of the Canadas. The English minority — 40,000 out of a population of 427,500 — demanded a union of Upper and Lower Canada as a means of revitalizing the St. Lawrence trading system. Furthermore, such a union would diminish the power the obstreperous French Canadians were wielding in the Lower-Canadian Legislative Assembly.

"THE ENGLISH PARTY" AND "FRENCH PARTY"
IN LOWER CANADA[169]

From T. F. Elliott's letter to Henry Taylor:

Quebec, October 24, 1835.
. . . ["The English party"] is composed of almost all the Merchants, with an admixture of considerable Landholders, and of some of the younger and more intelligent Civil Officers. It possess much intelligence, much wealth and still more credit . . . and unity of purpose . . . they know better than any other people how to confer on political association. . . . Yet I do not like the English party. It is fully as ambitious of dominion as the French party, and in my opinion, prepared to seek it by more unscrupulous means . . . but depend upon it that if ever these heats in Lower Canada should go as far as to hazard the connection with the Mother Country, the English will be the foremost to cut the tie. They . . . are by far the best disposed to sympathize with Republican principles; and, I must add, the most capable to wield Republican Institutions. They are the most rancorous, for they remember the power they have lost, and hate their rivals as a sort of usurpers. . . . The "French party" . . . consists mainly of Advocates, Physicians and Farmers, the last very ignorant of politics and indifferent to them and ambitious of their Seats . . . the bulk of the Assembly is inert, and that the few Members possessed of activity and

intelligence, work in entire subordination to Papineau, of whom they stand in profound awe.
. . . there appears to me to be a deeper motive calculated to bind the French party together, and to give general direction to their policy.
. . . . Looking to the circumstances, I cannot think that the French Canadians would be very unreasonable to dread some future extinction of their own tongue and peculiar habits . . . it is not to be doubted that some amongst them fear a lapse into insignificance.

The British House of Commons proposed a bill to bring about the union of Upper and Lower Canada, with one Legislative Assembly for the United Province. A proposed high property qualification would disenfranchise most French Canadians. Within fifteen years of the proposed union, English would be the sole language in government. Also, pending the approval of a permanent civil list by the Assembly, all revenue would be controlled by the Crown. Although Catholics would continue to have the rights of their religion, some limitations were to be placed on the freedom of the Roman Catholic Church. Obviously, the proposed union aimed to smother French-Canadian nationalism.

A storm of protest arose in Lower Canada, and French-Canadian bitterness against the English minority increased. Anti-Unionists held public meetings in Montreal and committees were drawn up from all parties to resist the proposed union, to safeguard French-Canadian privileges, and to avert domination by the English commercial minority. Resentment and fear were expressed to the British government in a petition with 60,000 signatures. The proposed union also drew opposition from other quarters. Neilson and his group of English reformers collaborated with Papineau against the union. Others objected to the arbitrary action of the British Parliament which did not consult Canadians about the union. Some disliked the undemocratic nature of the restricted franchise. Even the Legislative Council feared the difficulties that such a union might arouse.

FRENCH-CANADIAN OBJECTIONS TO THE
PROPOSED UNION OF 1822[170]

Joseph Papineau, in a letter to R. Wilmot, a British Member of Parliament, vehemently objects to insinuations made in certain British quarters about the French Canadians:

Montreal, 16th December 1822
. . . assertions that the opposition manifested in this Province on the part of the population . . .

is the effect of prejudices alone, alluding to their [French Canadian] supposed attachment to France and to French principles; calling them foreigners; (foreigners in their native land!) The Bill in question, say these friends of the Union, being so well calculated to Anglify the country, which is to be ultimately peopled by a British race.

———

The preposterous calumny against the Canadians of French origin, as to their supposed attachment to France, requires no other answer than what is derived from their uniform conduct during the wars, and the loyalty evinced by them on every occasion. They are not foreigners in this land of their birth; they claim rights as British subjects, in common with every other subject of His Majesty in these Colonies. These are their birth rights. . . .
By what they call Anglifying the country is meant the depriving the great majority of the people in this Province of all that is dear to men; their laws, usages, institutions and religion. An insignificant minority wish for a change, and are desirous of ruling against every principle of justice by destroying what they call the Canadian influence, that is to say, the influence of the majority. . . . Is it just or reasonable, or even sound policy, that she [Great Britain] should on this occasion, wound the feelings of a loyal population for the purpose of satisfying the prejudices of a few? . . .

In the face of this concerted opposition, the proposed union was dropped, and only the commercial provisions dealing with regulation of customs duties and trade between Upper and Lower Canada were embodied in the Canada Trade Act of 1822. But the episode accentuated French-Canadian resentment and fear of British designs. French Canadians were determined to safeguard their political strength in the Legislative Assembly. More than ever, they concentrated their efforts upon gaining supremacy for the Legislative Assembly.

No sooner had the turmoil over the proposed union subsided when a scandal rocked Lower Canada. In 1823, the treasury was found to be short £100,000. The Assembly held the British Government and its representative — the Governor — responsible. Papineau violently attacked Dalhousie and transformed the quarrel into one between the Governor and the Assembly. By 1827, with the Assembly repeatedly refusing to vote supply, Dalhousie dissolved the Assembly. In the election of that year, Dalhousie was very active in an effort to obtain a favourable majority that would pass a permanent civil list. It was a bitter election campaign in which both sides resorted to acrimonious denunciations. Papineau's party won an overwhelming victory. The new Assembly chose Papineau as Speaker. But Papineau was unacceptable to Dalhousie, who prorogued the Assembly two days after it met.

PAPINEAU'S COMPLAINTS[171]

In letters to his friend and collaborator, John Neilson, Papineau expressed his views on the injustice and discrimination French Canadians lived under in Lower Canada:

The injustice done to my country revolts me, and so perturbs my mind that I am not always in a condition to take counsel of an enlightened patriotism, but rather inclined to give away to anger and hatred of our oppressors.
It is odious to see every office and position closed against our people when the laws do not exclude them; to see them contributing nine-tenths of the revenue and receiving but one-tenth, and to feel that the possession of influence in this country is a passport to persecution.

The British government was anxious over the events that were unfolding in Lower Canada. In 1828, a Committee of the British House of Commons investigated Canadian affairs and made several recommendations. It suggested that all judges except the Chief Justice be barred from the Councils, and that all revenues and expenditures be under the control of the Assembly, in return for a permanent civil list. In a move to conciliate the French Canadians, membership in the Councils would be widened to include more French Canadians. Dalhousie was transferred to India; his successor, Sir James Kempt, accepted Papineau as Speaker of the Assembly. Still, the Assembly refused to grant a permanent civil list.

The British government was in a conciliatory mood. In 1831, Papineau and Neilson were offered seats on the Executive Council, but they refused. The same year, the British government transferred most of the revenue to the Assembly, but the Assembly still refused to grant a permanent civil list and demanded control over all revenue. Furthermore, the reformers wanted an elected Legislative Council, modelled after the American Senate. Such a trend toward an American-style democracy was contrary to the British government's view of colonial administration.

During the election of 1832, troops fired on a crowd in Montreal, and three French Canadians were killed. This "Montreal Massacre" heightened resentment against the English and Papineau used

Louis Joseph Papineau

George, Earl of Dalhousie

this incident to arouse the sympathy of many French Canadians who had hitherto stood on the side-lines of the reform movement. An outbreak of cholera in 1833 among newly-arrived British immigrants was seized upon by certain French-Canadian nationalists to oppose further British immigration into the colony. An appeal was sent to the British government to cancel the charter of the British American Land Company which had acquired land in the Eastern Townships for British immigrants.

In 1834, the Assembly adopted the Ninety-two Resolutions which were drawn up under Papineau's guidance. They included a lengthy list of grievances and extensive criticism of the English oligarchy imposed upon the French-Canadian majority. There were also demands for the control of all revenue by the Assembly, an elected Legislative Council, a "responsible" Executive Council and the same rights and privileges for the Legislative Assembly as the British House of Commons enjoyed. The Resolutions had an undertone of admiration for American institutions and veiled threats of force to gain reforms. Papineau's radicalism and the republican tone of the Ninety-two Resolutions frightened the moderate reformers, such as Neilson, and increased the clergy's opposition to the reform movement. But in the elections of 1834, Papineau and his followers won a sweeping victory. The opponents of the Resolutions, including Neilson, were defeated.

In 1835, Lord Aylmer was replaced by Lord Gosford as Governor of Lower Canada. Gosford was instructed to seek harmony between the executive and the Assembly. He was also to head a commission which would advise the British government on a course of action for Lower Canada. But the reformers mistrusted Gosford and his commission. The report of the commission confirmed French-Canadian fears; Gosford made no concessions regarding an elected Legislative Council and reaffirmed the British government's stand on a permanent civil list in exchange for all revenue. The Assembly turned down the proposals and voted supply for only six months, and later refused to vote any. The Assembly, for the first time, demanded that the Executive Council be made responsible to the Assembly — that is, responsible government for Lower Canada. Papineau's radical followers formed the *Patriotes* to fight the British government's designs for Lower Canada. Boycott of British goods and talk of republicanism spread in the colony. In the face of this, the English minority drew closer together and organized the Constitutional Society to resist the demands of the reformers.

In 1837 the Colonial Office abandoned the policy of conciliation and Lord John Russell drew up the Ten Resolutions for Lower Canada. Among other things, the Resolutions rejected the demands for an elected Legislative Council and again offered the Assembly control of all revenue

Attack on St. Charles, 25th November 1837

in return for a permanent civil list. At the same time, Lord Russell authorized the Governor, if necessary, to make provisions for supply without the authorization of the Assembly — an outright challenge to the reformers. Papineau and his radical followers saw no hope of gaining reforms by constitutional means. Only the use of force would convince Britain of French-Canadian determination. There was talk of revolt.

LORD JOHN RUSSELL'S TEN RESOLUTIONS, MARCH 6, 1837[172]

aRussell's instructions to the Governor:

8. That for defraying the arrears due on account . . . it is expedient, that . . . the Governor of the said province be empowered to issue from and out of any other part of his Majesty's revenues, in the hands of the Receiver-General of the said province, such further sums as shall be necessary to effect the payment of the before-mentioned sum of £142,160.14s.6d.

bPapineau on the Russell Resolutions, in an address at St. Laurent on May 14th, 1837:

The Russell resolutions are a foul stain; the people should not and will not submit to them; the people must transmit their just rights to their posterity, even though it cost them their property and their lives to do so.

cAddress of Assembly of Lower Canada, August 26, 1837:

It is our duty, therefore, to tell the Mother Country, that if she carries the spirit of these resolutions into effect in the Government of British America, and of this Province in particular, her supremacy therein will no longer depend upon the feelings of affection, of duty and of mutual interest which would best secure it, but on physical and material force.

It is, therefore, our ardent wish that the resolutions adopted by the two Houses of Parliament may be rescinded, as attacking the rights and liberties of this Province, as being of a nature to perpetuate bad Government, corruption and abuse of power therein, and as rendering more just and legitimate the disaffection and opposition of the people. . . .

The Assembly was prorogued on August 26, 1837. Mass meetings, fiery speeches, outbursts in the press — all indicated a revolutionary spirit. *Les Fils de la Liberté* (a group similar to the Sons of Freedom of the Boston Tea Party during the American Revolution) at a rally at St. Charles on October 23 passed resolutions which, in their radicalism, went beyond Papineau's demands for reform. It seems that the movement passed into the hands of the extremists, and Papineau, even had he wanted to, could not stem the revolutionary tide. In Montreal, members of the English Constitutionalists (Doric Club) clashed with the French-

Canadian *Fils*. The situation deteriorated into a racial struggle between two extremist groups. The English, violently anti-French, wished to keep Lower Canada English; the French Canadians, imbued with nationalism, wanted to preserve their culture and way of life.

In the meantime, because of the gravity of the situation, almost all the troops from Upper Canada were dispatched to Lower Canada. Gosford, anxious to avoid open rebellion, suppressed the Constitutional Society and decided to arrest the leaders of *Les Fils*. To avoid trouble, Papineau and some of his associates left Montreal. The authorities, interpreting their departure as an attempt to stir revolt in the countryside, issued warrants for their arrest. Armed *Patriotes* obstructed the troops who were sent to carry out the warrants. This led to a clash and bloodshed at St. Denis on November 23. Papineau fled to the United States. Two days later, resistance at St. Charles was broken. In December at St. Eustache, north of Montreal, a determined rebel stand was mercilessly crushed by soldiers and English militia. The rebellion was over.

PAPINEAU'S OBSERVATION ON THE REBELLION[173]

In 1839, Papineau made the following observation in his history of the insurrection:

I defy the government to contradict me when I assert that none of us had ever organized, desired, or even anticipated armed resistance . . . not that an insurrection would not have been legitimate, but we had resolved not to resort to it as yet.

The rebellion failed for several reasons. It lacked widespread support because the withdrawal of the moderates split the reform movement. Furthermore, the clergy openly cautioned the population about resorting to rebellion. Gosford had the army ready but the rebellion was ill-prepared. Papineau's flight after the first engagement at St. Denis left the rebels leaderless in a valiant stand against superior forces.

AFTERMATH OF THE REBELLION IN LOWER CANADA[174]

Stewart Derbishire, a London barrister who had turned journalist, though not connected with the Durham mission, sent Durham a report of conditions in Lower Canada. Below is an excerpt from a conversation Derbishire had with Denis Viger, Papineau's cousin:

Quebec, May 24, 1838

. . . He [Viger] told me that the spirit of persecution & lawless vengeance had run so high against all of the french party who had been conspicuous in politics that he had not ventured to leave his house for several month. I had noticed that the plate bearing his name had been taken down from the street door. He cautioned me to be discreet . . . as . . . the "Volunteers" . . . at present dragooned the City & exercised summary jurisdiction upon whomsoever they pleased to consider as enemies to the State. I did not need the caution; for I had already seen enough of these gentlemen to know that they permitted no man to hold an opinion different from theirs. He told me that the outrages, insults, and destruction of property by the "Volunteers" had left wounds in the minds of the Canadians that would never be healed.

. . . The Disorders complained of to me were the shooting of men as they stood in the door ways of their wooden dwellings long after all opposition had ceased; the firing of houses and barns by parties of Volunteers. . . . The most exaggerated statements of these matters are spread through the Country for the purpose of inflaming the minds of the *habitants*. . . . I . . . heard a Volunteer state at a public dinner table at Montreal that he had with his own hand fired fifteen [dwellings] . . . however . . . for weeks prior to the . . . military operations against the places above named, the "Patriots" had lived at free quarters in the houses of the Royalists, driving away the Owners, whose lives they sought, & appropriating their property of every description to the supply of bands which were gathering and arming as they alleged for the extirpation of the British race in Canada.

C

THE REFORM MOVEMENT IN UPPER CANADA

The reform movement in Upper Canada expressed itself in opposition to the privileges established and perpetuated within the framework of the Constitutional Act. Reformers wanted the same powers for the Legislative Assembly as the House of Commons enjoyed in Britain, an equitable land granting policy, local improvements and wider educational opportunities. These demands, assiduously pursued by the reformers and determinedly resisted by the entrenched Family Compact, led to strife, impasse and eventual rebellion.

There were mute grumblings and isolated expressions of criticism of the oligarchy, but coherent and open criticism of the Family Compact may be attributed to Robert Gourlay. A Scottish immigrant employed as a land agent, Gourlay had hoped to obtain land grants for prospective British immigrants. But he was frustrated by the Executive Council which controlled land grants. This did not deter him, and he began agitation against the oligarchy.

In 1817, Gourlay circularized a questionnaire in the form of a letter in which he asked settlers what, in their opinion, retarded the development of their areas. This statistical study revealed a widely held view that the progress of the colony was hindered by the large tracts of land that lay idle as clergy and crown reserves.

HOW WASTELANDS HINDERED SETTLEMENT[175]

Lord Durham quotes the chief agent for emigrants in Upper Canada:

. . . These blocks of wild land place the actual settler in an almost hopeless condition; he can hardly expect, during his lifetime, to see his neighbourhood contain a population sufficiently dense to support mills, schools, post-offices, places of worship, markets, or shops; and without these, civilization retrogrades. Roads under such circumstances can neither be opened by the settlers, nor kept in proper repair, even if made by the Government. The inconvenience arising from want of roads is very great. . . . I met [in 1834] a settler from the township of Warwick . . . returning from the grist mill at Westminster, with flour and bran of thirteen bushels of wheat; he had a yoke of oxen and a horse attached to his waggon, and had been absent nine days, and did not expect to reach home until the following evening . . . he assured me that he had to unload wholly or in part several times, and, after driving his waggon through the swamps, to pick out a road through the woods where the swamps or gulleys were fordable, and to carry the bags on his back and replace them in the waggon . . . [from] Warwick to Westminster and back — a distance less than 90 miles. . . .

John Strachan, the Church of England minister at York and John Beverly Robinson, the Attorney-General — spokesmen of the Family Compact — regarded Gourlay's activities as incitement of discontent. Gourlay countered their accusation with an attack on Strachan. In 1818, Gourlay called a convention of township representatives at York, where the pioneer farmers could express their opinion and choose delegates to present their

grievances directly to the British government. The Family Compact instituted an unsuccessful libel suit against Gourlay. But Gourlay was re-arrested and tried under an old law — the Alien Act of 1804. He was found guilty of seditious libel, and in 1819 was banished from Upper Canada. The Family Compact rid itself of Gourlay but, at the same time, revealed a fear of exposure and criticism. The Gourlay episode was a stark display of the Compact's power to stifle free expression of opinion in the colony.

JOHN STRACHAN ON ROBERT GOURLAY[176]

Extracts from letters by Strachan of December 1 and 8, 1818:

There has been here for a year past a Mr Gourlay from Fifeshire trying to set us by the Ears. He has done a great deal of mischief in the Colony by seditious publications exciting discontent among the people. I saw through him at once & opposed him with my usual vigour upon which the Press groaned with his abuse of me. By this he destroyed much of his influence. . . . A character like Mr Gourlay in a quiet Colony like this where there is little or no spirit of inquiry & very little knowledge may do much harm & notwithstanding the check he has rece[i]ved he has done harm by exciting uneasiness irritation & exciting unreasonable hopes. I tried to infuse some energy into the administration but it was too feeble till General [Peregrine] Maitland came out [as Lieutenant-Governor]. Things are now falling Back to their peaceful state and as we have in truth no grievances the people are beginning to discover that it is so. . . .

In regard to Mr Gourlay he [Maitland] has taken that line of conduct which I had urged our feeble Administrator in vain to adopt and the man is sinking fast into Insignificance. He denounced him & his foolish Adherents in the Speech from the Throne. An Act* was passed declaring Conventions illegal. . . .

At times, the Family Compact used its control of the Assembly to expel members who were critical of the oligarchy. Yet the reform movement grew. As early as 1820, criticism of the government was voiced in the Assembly and proposals for reform advanced. In 1821, Barnabus Bidwell, an American who had taken the oath of allegiance, was disqualified from sitting in the Assembly

* AN ACT TO PREVENT CERTAIN MEETINGS IN THE PROVINCE OF UPPER CANADA, passed on November 27, 1818.

Rev. Dr. Egerton Ryerson

John Strachan, Bishop of Toronto

because he was considered an alien. Later, his son Marshall Spring Bidwell, a Reformer and member of the Assembly, was also expelled on the same grounds. These expulsions were serious since they raised two issues in the alien question: the political rights of the many American settlers in Upper Canada and the right to hold land and own titles to their land.

In the 1824 election the Reformers won a majority in the Assembly and chose Marshall Bidwell as Speaker. The Assembly passed a bill allowing Methodist ministers to solemnize marriages — a right hitherto exercised only by the Church of England. Strachan accused the Methodists of harbouring republican tendencies and he insisted on Anglican dominance. The bill was thrown out by the Legislative Council. Two years later, the Reformers unsuccessfully sought to secularize the clergy reserves and use the proceeds from the sale of land for public education. The Family Compact, through the Legislative Council, had blocked the will of the Assembly. In advancing the cause of religious equality, the Reformers gained the valuable support of the Methodists, the fastest growing Protestant denomination.

In the election of 1828, Egerton Ryerson, the leader of the Methodists and editor of his church paper *The Christian Guardian*, aligned his followers with the reformers. He rallied opinion against the clergy reserves, for the rights of all Protestant denominations and against Anglican monopoly of higher education.* The election was important, not only because Methodist support gained the

Reformers a majority in the Assembly, but also because it brought to the fore William Lyon Mackenzie, who was destined to play a prominent role in the reform movement in Upper Canada.

WILLIAM LYON MACKENZIE—HIS PERSONALITY[177]

After an interview with Mackenzie, in 1836, Bond Head gave the following opinion of him:

Afraid to look me in the face, he [Mackenzie] sat, with his feet not reaching the ground, and with his countenance averted from me . . . with the eccentricity, the volubility, and indeed the appearance of a madman, the tiny creature [Mackenzie was just five feet tall] raved in all directions about grievances. . . .

―――――

Goldwin Smith's opinion:

. . . a wiry and peppery little Scotchman, hearty in his love of public right, still more in his hatred of public wrongdoers, clever, brave, and energetic, but, as tribunes of the people are apt to be, far from cool-headed, sure-footed in his conduct, temperate in his language, or steadfast in his personal connections. . . .

Mackenzie had come from Scotland in 1820, at the age of twenty-five. In 1824, he founded the *Colonial Advocate*, which soon became a force in

* The Anglicans received a charter and established King's College in 1827.

moulding public opinion against the privileges of the Family Compact. The *Colonial Advocate* became the organ for reform and Mackenzie gained the undying hatred of the Family Compact. In 1826, his printing shop was destroyed by a mob of Tories, as the supporters of the Family Compact were called. In the law-suit that followed, the court awarded him sufficient damages to purchase new presses. This act of hooliganism made him a prominent figure in the riding of York. Upon his election to the Assembly in 1828, he soon became the leading agitator for reform. As the spokesman of the common man and the frontier pioneer in Upper Canada, he continued his attack on the small but influential oligarchy.

Bidwell, as Speaker of the Assembly, still gave the Reformers leadership, and Robert Baldwin, later so effective a spokesman for reform, was now a young member in the Assembly. But it was Mackenzie, the agitator, writing his furious editorials and haranguing the Assembly with denunciations of the Family Compact, who forged the leadership of the reform movement.

The Reformers used their majority in the Assembly to pass legislation to secularize clergy reserves, remove judges from the legislature, give the Assembly complete control over revenue and reform the Legislative Council as a step towards responsible government. The Legislative Council rejected all these measures. In doing so, it showed the ineffectiveness of the Legislative Assembly.

W. L. MACKENZIE ON THE LEGISLATIVE COUNCIL[178]

The most extraordinary collection of sturdy beggars, parsons, priests, pensioners, army people, navy people, place-men, bank directors, and stock and land jobbers ever established to act as a paltry screen to a rotten government. They cost the country about £40,000 a year and the good laws by which it might benefit, they tomahawk. They don't like to be called a *nuisance*.

The death of King George IV in 1830 was the occasion for an election in Upper Canada. Mackenzie led the Reformers with a program which demanded an elected Legislative Council and an Executive Council responsible to the people. Sir John Colborne, the popular Governor, called the voters to show their loyalty to the Crown by electing an Assembly which would work in harmony with the Councils. The Governor's appeal for loyalty gained him a majority in the Assembly. The reform movement suffered a temporary setback and for the next four years the Family Compact had full control of the government.

W. L. MACKENZIE, ANSWERS CHARGE OF DISLOYALTY[179]

From a speech made in the summer of 1830:

. . . . The people of this Province neither desire to break up their ancient connection with Great Britain, nor are they anxious to become members of the North American confederation [U.S.A.]: All they want is a cheap, frugal, domestic government, to be exercised for their benefit and controlled by their own fixed land-marks; they seek a system by which to insure justice, protect property, establish domestic tranquility, and afford a reasonable prospect that civil and religious liberty will be perpetuated, and the safety and happiness of society effected.

The new Assembly supported the Governor and, in 1831, passed a permanent civil list in return for control of all revenue. Mackenzie attacked the government both inside the Assembly and in his newspaper. A hostile Assembly, by majority vote, expelled him in 1831, but he was re-elected by the voters of York. Altogether, he was expelled four times on the ground that he was unsuitable to hold his seat in the Assembly, and each time he was re-elected by his constituents. With each expulsion his popularity grew and he became the hero of the masses. When the town of York became the city of Toronto in 1834, Mackenzie was elected its first mayor.

Internal dissension between moderates and radicals divided the loosely-knit reform movement. By 1833, Ryerson withdrew the Methodist support because he disagreed with the radical course the reform movement had taken under Mackenzie's leadership. Mackenzie denounced Ryerson as having sold out to the Tories for a share in the clergy reserves. Other moderate reformers looked to the cautious Baldwin for leadership. Nevertheless, the Reformers in the 1834 election regained the majority in the Assembly.

W. L. MACKENZIE ON RYERSON[180]

From the COLONIAL ADVOCATE *of October 30, 1833:*

ANOTHER DESERTER!

The *Christian Guardian* under the management of our reverend neighbour, Egerton Ryerson, has gone over to the enemy, press, types, and all, and hoisted the colours of a cruel, vindictive Tory priesthood. . . . The Americans have their Arnold and Canadians have their Ryerson. . . . But he and his allies, the church and state gentry shall now have me on their rear. . . .

In 1835, a committee of the Legislative Assembly under Mackenzie's direction drew up the Seventh Report on Grievances and submitted it to the British government. The Report included complaints about the clergy reserves, the disposition of public lands, the privileges of the Church of England, the Canada Land Company, and the power of the banks. The Report demanded two basic constitutional reforms: an elective Legislative Council and an Executive Council responsible to the Legislative Assembly.

Mackenzie's' demand for an elected Legislative Council like the United States Senate smacked of American republicanism. Baldwin, politically more astute than Mackenzie, realized that the British government would not consent to such a surrender of its control over the colonial government. Instead of stressing an elected Legislative Council, Baldwin advocated an Executive Council responsible to the Legislative Assembly — the British Cabinet system. Baldwin wished to pursue reforms along the British, rather than the American, model.

In 1836 Sir Francis Bond Head replaced Colborne as Governor. Head was instructed (as was Gosford in Lower Canada) to free himself from the control of the Councils and to use his power and influence to attain harmony between the Assembly and the executive. The reformers, at first, were pleased with Head, who seemed sympathetic to them. Head even appointed Baldwin and Dr. John Rolph — two reformers — to the Executive Council. But this interlude of goodwill was short-lived. The Governor made several appointments to public office without seeking the advice of the Executive Council. The Councillors protested that it was the Governor's responsibility to consult them about the appointments. Head claimed that his responsibility was only to the Colonial Office. All the Executive Councillors, including the Tories, resigned. A new Executive Council was appointed, but the Assembly expressed lack of confidence in the new appointees and refused to vote supply. Head immediately dissolved the Assembly.

The election of 1836 was a fateful one for Upper Canada and, indeed, for the future of Canada. The Governor plunged into an energetic campaign that was marked by rowdyism and intimidation. He used all means to assure the election of an Assembly that would do his bidding. As in Colborne's time, loyalty to Britain became the issue. The electors, Head claimed, had to choose in favour either of maintaining the British ties and institutions, or of establishing republicanism and inviting absorption by the United States. He openly accused the reformers of republicanism and disloyalty to the Crown. Head's anti-American outcry drew support from Loyalist Tory elements,

some recent British immigrants and Orangemen. Ryerson threw the support of the Methodists behind the Governor. Voting by open ballot favoured the Governor who used his power of patronage to intimidate the voters. The reformers suffered a crushing defeat.

THE *1836* ELECTION IN UPPER CANADA[181]

^aBond Head's reply to an Address from Electors of Toronto, March, 1836:

... can you do as much for yourselves as I can do for you? ... It is my opinion that you cannot! It is my opinion that if you choose to dispute with me, and live on bad terms with the Mother Country, you will, to use a homely phrase, only quarrel with your "bread and butter."

―――――――

^bMackenzie writing in the CONSTITUTION: *August 1, 1836:*

Ye false Canadians! Tories! Pensioners! Churchmen! Spies! Informers! Brokers! Gamblers! Parasites, and Knaves of every caste and description, allow me to congratulate you! ... You may plunder and rob with impunity — your feet are on the people's necks. ...

Head's victory, the economic depression in the colony and the outbreak of the uprising in Lower Canada spurred the radical reformers to rebellion. Mackenzie's plan was to capture the city hall and the arms stored there and to overthrow the government. On December 7, 1837, armed rebels marched from their headquarters at Montgomery's Tavern, in the northern outskirts of the city, towards the city hall. Loyal volunteer militia prevented the insurgents from reaching the city hall and the rebels retreated to Montgomery's Tavern, where a skirmish took place. Shots were fired; the rebels dispersed; and the rebellion was over.

MACKENZIE'S HANDBILL FOR REBELLION, NOVEMBER 27, 1837[182]

BRAVE CANADIANS! God has put into the bold and honest hearts of our brethren in Lower Canada to revolt—not against "lawful" but against "unlawful authority". ...

CANADIANS! Do you love freedom? ... Do you hate oppression? ... Do you wish perpetual peace and a government founded upon the eternal heaven-born principles of the Lord Jesus Christ — a government bound to enforce the law to do to

William Lyon Mackenzie

Sir Francis Bond Head

each other as you would be done by? Then buckle on your armor, and put down the villains who oppress and enslave our country. . . . One short hour will deliver our country from the oppressors; and freedom in religion, peace, and tranquility, equal laws, and an improved country will be the prize. . . .

Up then, brave Canadians! Get ready your rifles, and make short work of it . . . now's the day and the hour! Woe be to those who oppose us, for "In God is our trust."

In Upper Canada, the loyal militia sought revenge through cruel suppression of known and suspected rebels. Two rebels were hanged and many were jailed; those who could, fled to the United States. Mackenzie himself had crossed the border and organized a government in exile on Navy Island near Buffalo. He hoped to gain support and to carry on the rebellion from the United States. Even here he was not secure. The Upper Canadian militia burned his ship, the *Caroline,* in American waters. This violation of American sovereignty created ill-feeling between the United States and Great Britain. But at the same time the diplomacy of Lord Durham and United States President Van Buren settled the incident and ended Mackenzie's hopes for continuing the rebellion from American soil.

The rebellion in Upper Canada was no better led nor more widely supported than the one in Lower Canada. Both rebellions failed, but the desire and need for reforms continued. The rebellions made the British government aware of the discontent which drove loyal British subjects to insurrection. The British government recognized the need to remove the cause of discontent. The appointment of Lord Durham to search for solutions to the problems paved the way to eventual colonial self-government in all of the British North American colonies.

MACKENZIE'S OBSERVATIONS AFTER THE REBELLION[183]

A letter to a friend written in the United States shortly after the Rebellion:

. . . . At nine-and-twenty I might have united with them [Family Compact], but chose rather to join the oppressed, nor have I ever regretted that choice, or wavered from the object of my early pursuit. So far as I or any other professed reformer was concerned in inviting citizens of this Union to interfere in Canadian affairs, there was culpable error. So far as any of us, at any time, may have supposed that the cause of freedom would be advanced by adding the Canadas to this Confederation [U.S.A.], we were under the merest delusion.

The Seventy-First Highland Light Infantry Conducting
Prisoners, c. 1837

*His regrets for Past Actions. A Letter to Earl
Grey, Feb. 3, 1849:*

A course of careful observation, during the last
eleven years, has fully satisfied me that, had the
violent movements in which I and many others
were engaged on both sides of the Niagara proved
successful, that success would have deeply injured
the people of Canada, whom I then believed I was
serving at great risks. . . . No punishment that
power could inflict, or nature sustain, would have
equalled the regrets I have felt on account of much
that I did, said, wrote, and published; but the past
cannot be recalled. . . .

D

THE REFORM MOVEMENT IN THE MARITIMES

In the Maritimes, the struggle for reform never
was as bitter as in the Canadas. The problems of
clergy reserves and the racial issue which plagued
the Canadas were absent in the Atlantic colonies.
Nor could a Maritime Governor inject the loyalty
issue in his struggle with the reformers, most of
whom were of Loyalist descent. Unlike in the
Canadas, the Assemblies of the Maritime colonies
readily agreed to a permanent civil list, often
without receiving full control over revenue. Another distinctive feature was the Legislative Councils, which also served as the Executive Councils.
The reformers demanded and obtained the separation of the Councils — New Brunswick, in 1832;
Nova Scotia, in 1837; and Prince Edward Island,
in 1839. Most significant, the British Colonial
Office paid heed to the moderate demands of the
Maritime colonial Assemblies. This may, to some
extent, account for the peaceful attainment of reforms in the Maritime colonies.

In Nova Scotia, as in the Canadas, an oligarchy
controlled every aspect of life in the colony. The
wealthy merchants in Halifax, retired army and
naval officers and government officials sat in the
Assembly and were appointed to the Councils.
The Church of England — part of the oligarchy
— controlled religion and education. Thus, the
backwood farmers and coastal fishermen had been
ruled from Halifax by a firmly-entrenched oligarchy ever since 1758, when Nova Scotia was
granted representative government.

Joseph Howe was closely associated with the
reform movement in Nova Scotia. He began his
public life in 1828, as editor of the *Nova Scotian.*
Like William Lyon Mackenzie in Upper Canada,
Howe, in his newspaper, attacked and exposed the
undue privileges of the oligarchy. An article in
which he accused the Halifax magistrates —
appointees of the oligarchy — of corruption became the centre of a celebrated libel suit in 1835.
The oligarchy hoped to silence its most outspoken
critic. But Howe conducted his own defence and
won an acquittal. His victory not only marked an
important decision for freedom of the press but
also made Howe a popular figure. The following
year he was elected to the Assembly and he soon
assumed the leadership of the reform movement
in Nova Scotia.

EXCERPTS FROM JOSEPH HOWE'S SIX AND ONE-
QUARTER HOURS ADDRESS TO THE JURY IN HIS
LIBEL TRIAL[184]

March 1, 1835:

. . . . Will you permit the sacred fire of liberty,
brought by your fathers from the venerable temp-
les of Britain, to be quenched and trodden out on
the simple altars they have raised? . . . I conjure
you to judge me by the principles of English law,
and to leave an unshackled press as a legacy to
your children. . . .

. . . . Nor is there a living thing beneath my roof
that would not aid me in this struggle; the wife
who sits by my fireside; the children who play
around my hearth; the orphan boys in my office,
whom it is my pride and pleasure to instruct from
day to day in the obligations they owe to their
profession and their country, would never suffer
the press to be wounded through my side. We
would wear the coarsest raiment; we would eat

the poorest food; and crawl at night into the veriest hovel in the land to rest our weary limbs, but cheerful and undaunted hearts; and these jobbing justices should feel, that one frugal and united family could withstand their persecution, defy their power, and maintain the freedom of the press. Yes, gentlemen, come what will, while I live, Nova Scotia shall have the blessing of an open and unshackled press. . . .

Howe pressed for the separation of the Councils, and when this was achieved in 1837, he advocated an elected Legislative Council. To check the powers of the Executive Council, he wanted members of the Executive Council to be chosen from the Legislative Assembly. In this struggle for reform, he ceaselessly attacked the economic and political power of the oligarchy and the special privileges, which the Church of England enjoyed in religion and education.

In New Brunswick, the timber trade and ship-building dominated the economic life of the colony. The local oligarchy consisted of a small group of wealthy landowners, holders of vast timber stands. As in the other colonies, this influential group also dominated the executive, legislative and judicial powers of the colony. The reform movement revolved around the main issue of the large forest preserves on the Crown lands. The Assembly, often controlled by rival timber interests, offered a permanent civil list for control of the Crown lands. The government, however, had been deriving sufficient revenue from the Crown lands and repeatedly rejected such offers. The reformers, under the leadership of Lemuel Allan Wilmot, were successful in 1837 in obtaining control of the Crown lands and revenue in return for a permanent civil list.

THE STRUGGLE FOR THE CROWN LANDS IN NEW BRUNSWICK[185]

[New Brunswick] followed the now notorious Upper Canadian procedure of establishing a committee on grievances and taking evidence from those who had suffered at the hands of the government. . . .

Seven of the eight resolutions introduced [March 8, 1833], following the report of the committee on grievances concerned the Crown lands. . . .

. . . . By September 10 [1836] a note of panic crept into his [Lord Glenelg, the Colonial Secretary] dispatches as he ordered Campbell [Sir Archibald, Lieutenant-Governor of New Brunswick] to speed

Joseph Howe

the legislative process by which the Crown lands were to be handed over to legislative control. . . .

. . . . Wilmot was on his way home from London [early summer, 1837], bearing the palm of final victory for the legislature in the struggle for the Crown lands. . . .

This summer session that saw the passing of the Civil List bill with its attendant legislation opened a new dispensation in the constitutional development of New Brunswick . . . [the previous] policy of selling land in large blocks to capitalists was abandoned. Land could now be sold only in 100-acre lots for the purpose of genuine settlement. What the timber trade had always wanted, the throwing open of the whole Crown domain on terms of cheap annual leases, had been won. . . .

The situation in Prince Edward Island differed somewhat. The oligarchy was comprised of absentee English landlords who owned the fertile agricultural lands. These wealthy landed proprietors wielded power through their agents, who controlled the Assembly and the Councils. Ownership of the land of the colony was the chief grievance. The local oligarchy headed the reform movement by exploiting the bitterness of the people against the absentee landowners. The reform movement became a struggle in which the Assembly sought to control land and to open it for local land speculators.

Lord Durham's observations:

. . . [Prince Edward Island's] past and present disorders are but the sad result of that fatal error which stifled its prosperity in the very cradle of its existence, by giving up the whole Island to a handful of distant proprietors. Against this system, this small and powerless community has in vain been struggling for some years: a few active and influential proprietors in London have been able to drown the remonstrances, and defeat the efforts of a distant and petty Province. . . .

Newfoundland was unique among the British North American colonies. Over a long period, the Island was merely Britain's fishing outpost, ruled by a series of naval captains. It was not until 1825 that the first civilian Governor was appointed, and not until 1832 that the Island was granted representative government. In St. John's, the merchants — who also controlled the marketing of fish, the colony's only significant staple — formed the local oligarchy which also dominated the colony's political life. The Reformers, following the example of their mainland counterparts, were demanding more democratic government.

Written in 1883:

. . . [During] The years which followed the introduction of representative government. . . . Political conflicts arose, and were carried on with much virulence for many years. . . . Rancor, hatred, and all the selfish passions had full swing, and the press teemed with fierce and unscrupulous manifestoes. . . .

. . . . The House of Assembly was composed of representatives of the people . . . and claimed to exercise the same functions as those of the British House of Commons. The Council was composed of nominees of the Crown, selected exclusively from the merchant class, who . . . held the principal offices. . . . The House of Assembly, in which the executive was not represented, found itself to possess powers of debating, passing measures, and voting moneys: but the Council could throw out all their measures, and were irresponsible to the people. Assembly and Council were at once found to be in antagonism, the one passing bills, the other swamping them; so that the new Constitution was out of gear from the first. Harmonious action under such an arrangement was almost impossible.

15

RESPONSIBLE GOVERNMENT: ITS MEANING AND ACHIEVEMENT

A

LORD DURHAM'S REPORT

The rebellions of 1837 forced the British government to take a serious look at conditions in the Canadian colonies. Vigorous criticism of its colonial policy had made the party in power fearful of political defeat. Under great pressure, the British Prime Minister, Lord Melbourne, appointed a commission with sweeping authority to investigate the causes of the rebellions and to make recommendations. The man chosen to head this commission was one of England's most notable political figures — John George Lambton, Earl of Durham.

Lord Durham was admirably qualified for the challenging assignment. He was an aristocrat, married to the daughter of a former Prime Minister, Lord Grey. Throughout more than twenty years in politics he had earned the reputation as a reformer with a first-class, if somewhat unpredictable, mind. Durham's belief in democracy went far beyond that of most of his contemporaries and his conviction that the Empire could be preserved through greater freedom of its parts was similarly unusual. His appointment as Governor-General and Lord High Commissioner of British North America was assurance that far-reaching recommendations would be made for the troubled Canadian colonies.

As part of his preparation for the mission to Canada, Durham enlisted several talented aides. Charles Buller, a brilliant, young, reform-minded M.P., was named chief secretary. Gibbon Wakefield joined the mission as an expert on economics, particularly concerning the colonies, and as an advocate of planned emigration for Britain's surplus population. Thomas Turton was chosen to act as adviser on legal and constitutional matters. The appointments of Wakefield and Turton turned out to be unwise politically; Wakefield's prison term for abduction of an heiress years before had not been forgotten; Turton's reputation had been stained fifteen years earlier by a divorce scandal. Both men thus provided ammunition for enemies of Durham and of the unstable British government.

Durham's arrival in Canada was, nevertheless, auspicious. On May 29, 1838, the new Governor and his retinue paraded in grand fashion through the streets of Quebec to the official residence, the Castle of St. Louis. The initial enthusiasm aroused in the capital increased with Durham's first official acts. He declared intentions of wholesale reform and replaced the Chateau Clique with a council composed mainly of his own staff members. An envoy was sent to Washington, where the United States government agreed to co-operate in restraining raids into Canada by Americans sympathetic to the unsuccessful rebels of 1837-38. Commissions were set up to inquire into such particular matters as crown lands, education, laws and municipal government.

During most of his tenure Durham remained in Quebec City where, in addition to performing administrative duties, he studied representations from many people on the causes of discontent and on possible remedies. Many of his impressions about general conditions came from reports of his assistants and from his brief tour in July to Montreal and Upper Canada as far as Niagara.

LORD DURHAM'S VIEW OF LOWER CANADA[188]

In a dispatch to Glenelg, the Colonial Secretary, Durham gave his assessment of the situation in Lower Canada. The dispatch bore the mark "Secret & Confidential", dated at "Castle of St. Lewis, Aug. 9, 1838":

ANIMOSITY BETWEEN THE FRENCH AND ENGLISH

This hatred of races is not publicly avowed on either side. On the contrary, both sides profess to be moved by any other feelings than such as belong to difference of origin; but the fact is . . . the great bulk of the Canadians and the great bulk of the British appear ranged against each other . . . the mutual dislike of the two classes extends beyond politics, into social life, where, with some trifling exceptions again, all intercourse is confined to persons of the same origin. Grown-up persons of a different origin seldom or never meet in private society; and even the children, when they quarrel, divide themselves into French and English like their parents . . . high and low, rich and poor, on both sides . . . though they use different language to express themselves, yet exhibit the very same feeling of national jealousy and hatred. . . .

Lord Durham

FRENCH CANADIANS STRUGGLE FOR SELF-PRESERVATION

. . . . Notwithstanding the division of Canada into two provinces, for the purpose of isolating the French, the British already predominate in French Canada, not numerically of course, but by means of their superior energy and wealth, and of their natural relationship to the powers of Government.

It was long before the Canadians perceived that their nationality was in the course of being over-ridden by a British nationality . . . I have no hesitation in asserting that of late years they have used the Representative System for the single purpose of maintaining their nationality against the progressive intrusion of the British race. They have found the British progressing upon them at every turn, in the possession of land, in commerce, in the retail trade, in all kinds of industrious enterprise, in religion, in the whole administration of government, and though they are a stagnant people, easily satisfied and disinclined to exertion, they have naturally resisted an invasion which was so offensive to their national pride.

ANNEXATIONIST SENTIMENT AMONG THE ENGLISH (IN LOWER CANADA)

. . . Their [British inhabitants in Lower Canada] main object . . . has been to remove the obstacles which the ignorance, the apathy, and the ancient prejudices of the Canadians opposed to the progress of British industry and enterprize; to substitute, in short, for Canadian institutions, laws and practices, others of a British character . . . Deeply offended at every measure or decision of the Imperial Government which thwarted their own British or Anti-Canadian views, they are also wanting in . . . respect for the supreme authority. . . . With less antipathy, no doubt, & more caution, but also with far more self-reliance, they are as little loyal as the Canadians. . . . I am assured that the leaders and their followers, one and all,

are in the habit of declaring that, rather than be again subject to the French (meaning rather than see another majority of Canadians in the Assembly) they should much prefer a union with the United States; & that if they are deserted by the British Govt. (I use their own expression) they shall find a way to take care of themselves. . . . And this is not all: for the sentiments expressed are enforced by deliberate arguments, such as, — that the Americans, if they had possession of this country, would quickly dispose of Canadian supremacy . . . institutions of America, being favourable at all events to industrious enterprize are well-suited to a People of British descent . . . & would be infinitely preferable to Canadian feudalism. . . .

That such views are currently expressed amongst the British party, there can be no doubt; and I am the more disposed to believe them sincerely entertained. . . .

On the surface, Durham was armed with virtually dictatorial powers for his assignment in British North America. Yet throughout his five months in the colonies, he operated under the shadow of attack from London. There the political enemies of the British government, prepared to use every device to embarrass the Cabinet, harped on the reputations of Wakefield and Turton. It was Durham's handling of a potentially explosive issue — the fate of men imprisoned for taking part in the rebellion — that led to the sudden termination of his mission.

The difficulties of the situation seemed to demand a special solution. The rebels, one hundred and sixty one in number, could not be kept in jail indefinitely without some proceedings by the government. The goodwill of French Canadians might be won by a liberal decision, and the attitudes of hostile Americans might be softened also. Yet some show of British authority was essential, and the English of Lower Canada expected no less. Durham became convinced that regular British judicial procedure was futile in a province where juries would probably be either sympathetic French Canadians or vengeful English. He hoped to meet all possible objecttions with his ordinance of June 28, whereby he granted an amnesty to all but the eight most serious offenders. These were persuaded to admit their treasonous behaviour and accept banishment to Bermuda under penalty of trial and possible execution should they return to Canada.

In spite of being generally accepted in Canada, Durham's action led to an uproar in the British Parliament. The legality of the banishment was so vigorously attacked that the government decided, in the interests of self-preservation, to disallow the ordinance. Durham took the decision as a blow against his authority and a censure of his whole mission. Canadians by and large condemned the British government for playing politics at a time when the whole future of British North America was at stake. The Governor, whose *Report* would help prepare the way for colonial self-government, resigned and returned to England on November 1, 1838.

A VIEW ON LORD DURHAM[189]

Because of severe criticism of his actions in the House of Lords, Durham decided to resign. Charles Buller, a member of Durham's staff in Canada, wrote a confidential letter to John Stuart Mill. In the following extract Buller gives an intimate glimpse of Durham:

Most Private

Quebec, Saturd[y], Oct[r] 13th, 1838
. . . You have I suppose learnt that Ld. Durham has publicly expressed his intention of resigning. . . . The private ones [reasons] I will now tell you. But you are to shew this to no earthly soul except my Father & Mother. . . . For I would not have any one else know that I find any faults in one for whom I have so sincere a regard as Lord Durham.

The truth is that Ld. D's health & character utterly unfit him for such a service as the one he is now on. He would do it better than any other of our public men, because he is thoroughly honest, & has larger & better views than any of them. But he is so anxious and so nervous that he literally cannot bear the burden of *distant responsibility*. . . . In his place I as Governor Gen would not have resigned. . . .

I, in his place would have gone on just as he did before — legislated boldly. . . . But he would not have gone on boldly. He has plenty of boldness: — boldness of an admirable kind. But he has no *constancy.* How can a man whose whole frame is bedevilled by liver & rheumatism be steady & firm?

The Durham Report, prepared under Durham's direction with the assistance of his leading advisers, was submitted to the Colonial Secretary on January 31, 1839 — approximately two months after Durham's return to England. The Report achieved two main purposes: analysis of conditions in British North America, and proposals for extinguishing the bases for discontent. The first part, consisting of four sections, discussed Lower Canada at great length, Upper Canada more briefly, the Eastern provinces and Newfoundland, disposal of public lands, and emigration. Finally, Durham put forth his ideas for reform.

Among the many problems observed, Lord Durham stressed two critical ones. The lack of harmony between the Councils and the Legislative Assemblies underlay the Canadian rebellions and explained the tension evident in the other colonies. Furthermore, the political strife in Lower Canada was a product of the unprogressive nature of the French Canadians.

OBSERVATIONS ON LOWER CANADA
IN THE REPORT[190]

. . . . I expected to find a contest between a government and a people: I found two nations warring in the bosom of a single state: I found a struggle, not of principles, but of races. . . .

. . . . The French majority asserted the most democratic doctrines of the rights of a numerical majority. The English minority . . . allied itself with all those of the colonial institutions which enabled the few to resist the will of the many. . . .

. . . . The entire wholesale, and a large portion of the retail trade of the Province, with the most profitable and flourishing farms, are now in the hands of this numerical minority [English] of the population. . . . The great mass of the Canadian population, who cannot read or write . . . were obviously inferior to the English settlers. . . .

. . . . Never again will the present generation of French Canadians yield to a loyal submission to a British Government; never again will the English population tolerate the authority of a House of

Assembly, in which the French shall possess or even approximate a majority.

――――

. . . . The error . . . is the vain endeavour to preserve a French Canadian nationality in the midst of Anglo-American colonies and states.

The union of Upper and Lower Canada, a policy considered as early as 1822, was proposed for the special purpose of assimilating, or "Anglicizing," the French Canadians. A united Legislative Assembly with representation by population (Rep. by Pop.) would give English Canadians a clear majority that would be increased by planned emigration from Great Britain. Of comparable importance, union was basic to the success of Lord Durham's most significant recommendation — Responsible Government.

DURHAM'S SUGGESTION FOR A UNION OF THE CANADAS[191]

. . . . I believe that no permanent or efficient remedy can be devised for the disorders of Lower Canada, except a fusion of the Government in that of one or more of the surrounding Provinces. . . .

――――

. . . and I have little doubt that the French, when once placed, by the legitimate course of events and the working of natural causes, in a minority, would abandon their vain hopes of nationality. . . .

――――

. . . a Parliamentary Commission should be appointed, for the purpose of forming the electoral divisions, and determining the number of members to be returned on the principle of giving representation, as near as may be, in proportion to population. I am averse to every plan that has been proposed for giving an equal number of members to the two Provinces, in order to attain the temporary end of out-numbering the French, because I think the same object will be obtained without any violation of the principles of representation, and without any such appearance of injustice in the scheme as would set public opinion, both in England and America, strongly against it; and because, when emigration shall have increased the English population in the Upper Province, the adoption of such a principle would operate to defeat the very purpose it is intended to serve. . . .

The smooth functioning of government in Canada required, in Durham's view, that the management of people's affairs be given to an Executive Council having the elected Assembly's confidence.

To eliminate, as much as possible, the dangers of conflict between the colonial government and the British government, Durham advised a division of power between the two. Imperial authority should continue in such matters as the colonial constitution, foreign relations and disposal of crown lands.

DURHAM SUGGESTS RESPONSIBLE GOVERNMENT[192]

. . . . It needs no change in the principles of government, no invention of a new constitutional theory, to supply the remedy which would, in my opinion, completely remove the existing political disorders. It needs but to follow out consistently the principles of the British constitution. . . .

――――

. . . . Every purpose of popular control might be combined with every advantage of vesting the immediate choice of advisers in the Crown, were the Colonial Governor to be instructed to secure the co-operation of the Assembly in his policy, by entrusting its administration to such men as could command a majority. . . . This would induce responsibility for every act of the Government, and, as a natural consequence, it would necessitate the substitution of a system of administration, by means of competent heads of departments, for the present rude machinery of an executive council. . . .

The Canadian government should handle the internal government of the Colony — such things as the construction of roads and canals and education. The Governor was to select Executive Councillors who had majority support in the Assembly. He should administer the colony according to the advice of the Executive Council, regardless of his own view or the views of the British government.

DURHAM'S SUGGESTION FOR SEPARATION OF POWERS[193]

. . . . I admit that the system which I propose would in fact, place the internal government of the colony in the hands of the colonists themselves; and that we should thus leave to them the execution of the laws, of which we have long entrusted the making solely to them. . . . I know not in what respect it can be desirable that we should interfere with their internal legislation in matters which do not affect their relations with the mother country. The matters, which so concern us, are very few. The constitution of the form of government, — the regulation of foreign relation, and of trade with the mother country, the other British Colonies, and foreign nations, — and the disposal of the public lands, are the only points on which the mother country requires control. . . .

The scope of the Report is illustrated by Durham's suggestions on a variety of topics, all related in one way or another to his basic objectives and recommendations. In return for a civil list, the Assembly would gain control of revenues. Municipalities would serve to prevent too great a concentration of political power and arouse citizens to a more active part in the management of public affairs. A widespread system of public education was needed generally; specifically, it would encourage the French Canadians to learn English. Durham recommended security of tenure and income to assure the independence of judges, and a supreme court for all British North America. An intercolonial railway from Halifax to Quebec would encourage trade and communication between colonies, and ultimately a union between Canada and the Atlantic provinces.

The Durham Report is open to criticism on many grounds. Lord Durham had been in Canada for five months, hardly long enough for the kind of investigation he had in mind, especially when much of his time was devoted to administration and interrupted by dealings with the government in London. The portion on Upper Canada reflected the bias of the reformers, who had influenced Charles Buller's accounts, on which Durham based his conclusions.

BALDWIN'S PLEA FOR RESPONSIBLE GOVERNMENT[194]

From a letter to Lord Durham:

Toronto 23 August, 1838

. . . . I would ask Your Lordship, would the people of England endure any system of Executive Government over which they had less influence than that which at present exists? Your Lordship knows they would not. — Can you then expect the people of these colonies with their English feelings & English sympathies to be satisfied with less — If you do Your Lordship will assuredly be disappointed — They can see a reason why their relations with foreign countries should be placed in other hands; but none why their domestic concerns should not be managed upon similar principles as those applied in the administration of the Imperial Government . . . you must give those in whom the people have confidence an interest in preserving the *system* of your Government, and maintaining the connection with the Mother Country, and then you will hear no more of grievances because real ones will be redressed imaginary ones will be forgotten — But short of this all your efforts to produce harmony and all your exertions to preserve that connection will I am satisfied be wholly unavailing —

More seriously, Durham's assessment of the French-Canadian way of life was unfair. Imbued with the spirit of material progress common to his English-speaking contemporaries, he could not see merit in a society content with living as it had for generations. Durham also overestimated the importance of the racial factor as a cause of discontent in Lower Canada. Within a decade, the alliance of Robert Baldwin and Louis Lafontaine had been instrumental in the winning of responsible government. This result was made possible by racial co-operation rather than by Anglicization. Nor could he see the futility of the Anglicization he was recommending. French-Canadian society had deep roots, and any forceful policy to change it would only strengthen the French-Canadian desire for cultural survival.

DURHAM ON THE FRENCH CANADIANS[195]

. . . . I entertain no doubts as to the national character which must be given to Lower Canada; it must be that of the British Empire . . . and to trust its government to none but a decidedly English Legislature.

———

. . . . It is to elevate them [French Canadians] from that inferiority that I desire to give to the Canadians our English character. I desire it for the sake of the educated classes. . . . I desire the amalgamation still more for the sake of the humbler classes . . . [who] are doomed, in some measure, to occupy an inferior position, and to be dependent on the English for employment. . . .

———

. . . . A people so circumstanced must alter their mode of life. . . . Were the French Canadians to be guarded from the influx of any other population, their condition in a few years would be similar to that of the poorest of the Irish peasantry.

There can hardly be conceived a nationality more destitute of all that can invigorate and elevate a people, than that which is exhibited by the descendants of the French in Lower Canada, owing to their retaining their peculiar language and manners. They are a people with no history, and no literature. . . .

The greatness of the Report lies in Durham's realization that British North America was emerging from its stage of colonial dependence. His recognition of the value of free institutions in the colonies enabled him to devise a method of preserving ties between colony and mother country. His solution pointed the way to evolution from Empire to Commonwealth.

Joseph Howe's opinion, taken from the NOVA-SCOTIAN, *April 11, 1839:*

We have risen from the perusal of this admirable exposition of the state of the British Colonies in North America, with a higher estimate of the powers of the noble Lord and . . . anticipation of the ultimate termination of Colonial misrule than we have ever ventured to form. We did not believe that there was a nobleman in Britain, who had the ability and the firmness to grapple with the great question committed to Lord Durham's care, in a spirit so searching, and yet so frank; nor a man who, in one short summer, could collect and digest so much information, and drawn from it such a volume of instruction. . . . The remedy for the local executives, which prevails or has prevailed in all the Colonies, has two prime recommenda-tions, being perfectly *simple* and eminently *British.* It is to let the *majority* and not the *minority* govern, and compel every Governor to select his advisers from those who *enjoy the confidence of the people,* and can *command a majority in the popular branch.*

———

A French-Canadian opinion, expressed by F. X. Garneau in his HISTORY OF CANADA:

. . . in London, Quebec, and Montreal, it was plain . . . that Lower-Canadian interests were about to be sacrificed . . . intimating that he [Durham] wished to impress on Lower Canada an entirely British stamp; to accord to its people a free constitution with responsible government . . . had no comfort in it for the French-Canadians; for whom fine words about "liberty" and "a more noble and vast nationality," foreshadowed the coming annihilation.

B

THE MEANING OF RESPONSIBLE GOVERNMENT

The "tea-pot" rebellions of 1837, in addition to destroying radicalism as a force in Canadian politics for some time, had established the fact that the people of the British North American colonies were largely loyal to the crown. British North America, unlike the Thirteen Colonies, was destined to find a solution to its political problems through responsible government within the context of the British Empire.* The struggle for responsible government proved to be a ten-year contest between the Governor of the United Province, acting upon the advice of the Colonial Office, and the Reformers bent upon establishing the supremacy of the elected Legislative Assembly over the appointed Legislative and Executive Councils. When the contest had ended, the problem of colonial government had found a solution, and autocratic rule of the oligarchies had given way to rule by the people of Canada through their elected Assembly. Just as the American Revolution marked the end of the First British Empire, the Canadian solution — responsible government — signaled the transformation of the Second British Empire into the modern Commonwealth.

In his famous Report, Durham had defined responsible government as "the entrusting the management of public affairs to persons who have the confidence of the representative body." This would mean that decisions on policy and care of administration would be left to those who had the support of the elected representatives of the people. Apart from certain restrictions on self-government specified in the Report, Lord Durham probably meant that Canada should have the full Cabinet system enjoyed by Great Britain. But whatever his meaning, the implementation of the principles of cabinet government became the goal of the Reformers. The Reformers were as much intent upon winning responsible government as the British government was intent upon witholding it.

TWO VIEWS ON RESPONSIBLE GOVERNMENT[197]

[a]*Goldwin Smith, writing in 1891:*

. . . . By responsible government they [Reformers] meant that the government should be carried on, not by an executive nominated by the governor and independent of the vote of parliament, but, as in England, by a cabinet dependent for its tenure of office on the vote of the Commons. They meant, in short, that supreme power should be transferred from the Crown to the representatives of the people. It was nothing less than a revolution for which they called under a mild and constitutional name.

[b]*Charles Poulett Thomson (Sydenham), in a letter to a friend, December 12, 1839:*

I am not a bit afraid of the responsible government cry, I have already done much to put it down

* It must be pointed out that the "responsible-government solution" to the problem of colonial government was not available to the people of the Thirteen Colonies. Moreover, the British Colonial Office of the eighteenth century seemed to have lacked the services of such an ardent advocate of colonial self-government as Canada found in Lord Durham.

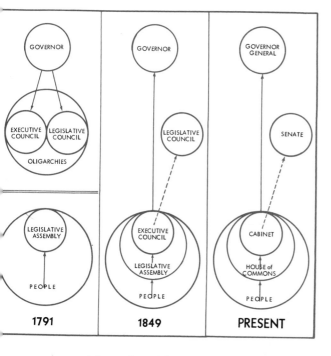

A Comparison of Constitutional Systems

1791   1849   PRESENT

Lords, the Executive Council in the Cabinet and the Legislative Assembly in the House of Commons. It was the eighteenth-century balanced constitution with the monarchical, the aristocratic, and the democratic elements represented. However, there the parallel ends; the operation of the government in the colonies differed markedly from the British model.

Generally, the governing of the colonies under the Constitutional Act served to frustrate the popular will expressed through the Legislative Assembly as well as to promote, encourage and extend the power of the Compacts. The Governor, appointed by the Colonial Office, was not only the representative of the Crown but also his own Prime Minister. It was he who appointed the Legislative and Executive Councils, formulated government policy, administered imperial policy and called elections. The Governor usually listened to the advice of his Executive Council although he was not bound to follow that advice; he could dismiss his Councillors just as easily as he could appoint them.

The primary functions of the Executive Council were to advise the Governor and to execute the policies formulated by him. In practice, the members of the Executive Council, drawn from the Compacts, were appointed for life. Since the Governor was only a temporary visitor on the Canadian scene, he relied heavily on the Executive Council for the formation of policy for the colony. Thus government policy, presumably beneficial for the colony as a whole, served only the interests of the oligarchies. Indeed, much of Canada's political troubles can be attributed to the peculiar position of the Governor who found it necessary to rely to such a large extent on the Executive and Legislative Councils.

As for the Legislative Council, its members were also drawn from the Compacts and appointed for life. The functions of this Council were to review and vote on legislation passed by the lower house — the Legislative Assembly. In practice, however, the Legislative Council stifled any measure that even slightly challenged the privileged position or the interests of the Compacts.

in its inadmissible sense; namely, the demand that the council shall be responsible to the assembly, and that the governor shall take their advice, and be bound by it. In fact, this demand has been made much more *for* the people then *by* them. . . . I have told the people plainly that, as I cannot get rid of my responsibility to the home government, I will place no responsibility on the council; that they are *a council* for the governor to consult, but no more. . . .

While the British government sought to maintain the status quo as far as it was possible, the Reformers aspired to institute the self-government recommended in the Report. It is, therefore, advantageous to view the governing of the British North American colonies at two extremes — the oligarchic system emanating from the Constitutional Act and the colonial self-government dramatized by the signing of the Rebellion Losses Bill in 1849.

The Constitutional Act had, in theory, blessed the British North American colonies with a system of government which was "the image and transcript of British parliamentary practice." The British model and the Canadian copy were similar in that both had equivalent institutions of government. The Governor had his counterpart in the Monarch, the Legislative Council in the House of

DURHAM ON THE RULE OF THE OLIGARCHY[198]

The reformers . . . discovered that success in the elections ensured them very little practical benefit. For the official party not being removed when it failed to command a majority in the Assembly, still continued to wield all the powers of the executive government, to strengthen itself by its patronage, and to influence the policy of the colonial Governor and of the Colonial Department at home. By its secure majority in the Legislative Council, it could effectually control the legislative powers of the Assembly. It could choose its own moment for dissolving hostile Assemblies; and could always ensure, for those that were favourable to itself, the tenure of their seats for the full term of four years allowed by the law. Thus the reformers found that their triumph at elections could not in any way facilitate the progress of their views, while the executive government remained constantly in the hands of their opponents. . . .

The elected Legislative Assembly was constantly opposed by the sweeping powers of the appointed Councils. The Assembly — the sole expression of the popular will — was the least effective government organ. It had no voice in Council appointments, exercised incomplete control over finances and suffered daily the frustration of having its legislative measures vetoed by the Legislative Council, the Governor or the Colonial Office.

THE ROLE OF THE LEGISLATIVE ASSEMBLY[199]

Lord Durham's observation about the Assembly in Lower Canada applies also to Upper Canada:

. . . I look on the conduct of the Assembly as a constant warfare with the executive, for the purpose of obtaining the powers inherent in a representative body by the very nature of representative government. It was to accomplish this purpose, that it used every means in its power . . . and being denied its legitimate privileges, it endeavoured to extend its authority in modes totally incompatible with the principles of constitutional liberty.

By way of contrast, it is useful to examine the operation of government after responsible government was achieved. After 1849, the Governor accepted advice from the Colonial Office on matters affecting foreign relations and trade, disposition of Crown lands and the form of government in the colony. On all other matters he accepted the advice of the Executive Council. In practice, he no longer appointed members to either Council nor did he formulate government policy. In short, the Governor no longer acted as the Prime Minister; he had withdrawn from politics and had left control over matters of internal concern to Canadians. The Executive Council was now selected from the Legislature* by the Prime Minister — the leader of the largest group in the Assembly. No longer did Executive Councillors hold office for

Lord Sydenham

life. They were in office only as long as they enjoyed or could command majority support in the Assembly; if they lacked the confidence of the Assembly they had to resign. Furthermore, now the Executive Council executed the will of the Assembly and not the will of the Governor.

The Legislative Council remained an appointed body, but its relations with the Executive Council were changed. The Executive Council was now dependent on the majority party in the Legislative Assembly. The Legislative Council was detached from the Governor because the position of Governor had risen above politics and because appointments to the Legislative Council were made on the recommendation of the Executive Council. The composition and functions of the Legislative Council remained the same, but its influence declined.

The Legislative Assembly finally took on the legislative jurisdiction proper to a body whose authority came from direct election. Subject to the will of the people at election time, the Assembly now had control over the Executive Council and full powers of the purse.

From the comparison of the operation of government before and after responsible government,

* The legislature consists of the Legislative Assembly (House of Commons) and the Legislative Council (Senate). Nowadays, the Prime Minister usually appoints one or two Senators to the Cabinet to act as liaisons between the Upper House (Senate) and the Lower House (House of Commons). For the same reason, after 1849, it was considered good practice to appoint some Legislative Councillors to the Executive Council.

four points, essential to the meaning of responsible government, emerge:

1. The Governor, the representative of the British government, is above politics.
2. The Governor must accept the advice of his Executive Council on local matters.
3. The Executive Council is chosen from the Legislature by the leader commanding a majority of votes in the Assembly (in practice, from the party that has the majority).
4. The Executive Council holds office only so long as it can command majority support in the Assembly. Failing this, the Executive Council must resign.

C

THE ACHIEVEMENT OF RESPONSIBLE GOVERNMENT IN CANADA

Government between 1839 and 1849 lay somewhere between the extremes of rule by the oligarchies and rule under responsible government. The process by which British North America gained responsible government was an evolutionary movement and its eventual achievement had a profound effect on the whole Empire. Responsible government, as developed in British North America, set the pattern for colonial government in the far reaches of the British Empire.

Following the precipitous resignation of Lord Durham, the Whig government of Lord Melbourne, through the Colonial Office headed by Lord John Russell, appointed Charles Poulett Thomson to the post of Governor of British North America. Thomson, later Baron Sydenham for his work in accomplishing the union of the two Canadas, came to British North America well prepared for his task. He was financially successful, having been actively engaged in the Baltic lumber trade and in the excitement of industrial England. He was knowledgeable in practical politics and experienced in administration, having served as a cabinet minister in Grey's government and as Vice-President of the Board of Trade. Sydenham was able to draw on his great experience and apply practical solutions to practical economic problems. Furthermore, he was probably the ablest administrator ever to set foot in Canada. His governorship in British North America was a peculiar mixture of broad, far-sighted economic policies, and narrow, political ones.

The first task that Sydenham undertook upon his arrival in October 1839 was the thorny question of the union of the Canadas. His instructions were to secure the approval of the Canadians before the British government translated the plan for union into legislation. These instructions were significant in that the British government now saw the advisability of consulting the people of the Canadas in matters of basic concern to the colonies.

The plan of union which the British government proposed to implement differed basically from the one recommended by Lord Durham. The Durham plan specified that members of the united Assembly be elected on the basis of Representation by Population. The purpose of the Durham plan was clear and emphatic — the French were to be drowned in the mainstream of the "superior" British culture. The French majority which might temporarily result from Representation by Population was the small price that had to be paid until Durham's detailed plan of English immigration would ultimately erase the French character of Canada.

The British plan, however, called for equal representation in a single Assembly even though the population of Lower Canada exceeded that of Upper Canada by some 200,000.* Such representation would give the English a majority since 150,000 people of Lower Canada were Anglo-Saxon. However, the assumption upon which this reasoning rested was false since the English of both provinces never coalesced to submerge the French in the Assembly. The gap between Anglo-Saxon Tories and Reformers of Upper Canada was much greater than the gap between the Anglo-Saxon and French Reformers of Upper and Lower Canada respectively.

The British plan was to create a legislative union in which there would be one Executive Council, one Legislative Council and one Legislative Assembly. Such a union would assume the debts of the two Canadas, although the debt of Upper Canada was far larger than that of Lower Canada.† Official records would be kept in English but French could be used in Assembly debates, and all revenues with the exception of a limited

* At the time of the Union, the distribution of population was 600,000 in Lower Canada and 400,000 in Upper Canada.
† The debt of Upper Canada exceeded £1,000,000; Lower Canada's debt was negligible.

civil list would be placed under the control of the legislature. In addition, the laws of Upper and Lower Canada* were to remain untouched.

On the question of union, Sir James Craig secured the opinion of a certain "Gentleman" of Lower Canada. Part of the observations of this gentleman which were transmitted by Craig to Lord Liverpool on June 1, 1810:

. . . there cannot I think, be any doubt, but that great strength would be derived to the Government from the reunion [of the Canadas]. Neither could anything be so calculated to destroy, at once, the favourite wish and aim, of the Canadians, to keep themselves *a distinct nation.* . . . This measure, moreover, tho' it would not be very unwelcome to the Canadians, would not be so unwelcome, as depriving them of their *Representation,* because it might be conceived to proceed upon grounds of *general* policy, equally affecting the Interests of both Provinces. It would have less the appearance of *Punishment,* it would be less *humiliating* and *disgraceful,* it would less hold them up to the *world,* as a people utterly *unworthy* of the benefits they have received.

While there is evidence to support the contention that the British government had decided upon Union long before the Durham recommendation, the French saw the Union as the prelude to the assimilation of which Durham had spoken. To the French of Lower Canada, the plan of union, already stigmatized with Durham's avowed intent of assimilation, was patently unfair. The task of getting the French to agree to a plan of union whose purpose was to assure English ascendency seemed virtually impossible. Lord Sydenham was able to cut this Gordian knot by simply not asking for such consent. He won approval, instead, from the Special Council which had handled the affairs of Lower Canada since 1837 when the constitution had been suspended. Such approval was easily forthcoming since this Special Council wore the colours of the Chateau Clique.

[a]*The Earl of Gosford, the former Governor of Lower Canada, objected to the proposed union of the Canadas. From his speech during the debate in the British Parliament in 1840:*

. . . . I cannot but regard the meditated union . . . as a most unjust and tyrannical measure, proposed in view of depriving the lower province of its constitution . . . the sure effect of the project being, to deliver into the hands of a section of the community, the great majority of their fellow-colonists, the former being bitterly inimical to the latter! . . . I ought to declare, once again, my conviction that the unjust financial arrangement I now denounce, is due to a mercantile intrigue. . . .

[b]*Lafontaine said this of the Union, in a speech during the election of 1841:*

It is an act of injustice and of despotism, in that it is forced upon us without our consent; in that it robs Lower Canada of the legitimate number of its representatives; in that it deprives us of the use of our language in the proceedings of the legislature against the faith of treaties and the word of the governor-general; in that it forces us to pay, without our consent, a debt which we did not incur. . . .

In Upper Canada the task of gaining acceptance of the proposed union proved more formidable. The Tories saw in the plan the disappearance of their privileged position and the loss of their effective control of government. But Upper Canada was in serious debt; it suffered from a severe depression and it needed funds for rapid development in order to keep pace with the United States. With the promise of a British loan of £1,500,000, Sydenham was able to win sufficient Tory support for the proposed Union.

The Reformers of Upper Canada, also enchanted by the prospect of the return of prosperous times, saw in the Union the end of oligarchic rule. Union would enable them to unite with the Reformers in Lower Canada for the purpose of winning responsible government. Sydenham readily secured the support of the Reformers of Upper Canada, and the Act of Union, passed by the British Parliament in 1840, came into effect in February, 1841.

Eye-witness accounts of the intimidation, bribery, and physical force used during the election. Sydenham actively interfered in the election. On the Island of Montreal, Sydenham placed the polling-booth in New Glasgow which was a predominantly Scottish settlement.
Adamson, an eye-witness, describes the polling:

On Saturday afternoon, the 20th of March, the Orangemen from Chatham Gore arrived to the

---

* After the Union, called Canada West and Canada East respectively.

number of about 150, with banners, armed with bludgeons, about three feet long. . . .

_____

After mid-day Sunday, the 31st the stone breakers arrived from Montreal and a large number from various parts of the district all well armed with bludgeons. . . .

_____

A large number of the bludgeons issued by Dr. McCulloch's Bullies had the appearance of being made by mechanical skill. Some were turned round, some had eight sides and some four square and many of them filled with nails on the head end. Bayonets were seen in Mr. John Walker's house. . . .

Archibald Sieverwright, Captain of militia . . . advised the men armed with bludgeons on Monday morning early the day of election — To occupy the heights and let the Canadians come down the hill and then they could kill them in the hollow. . . .

_____

Interesting evidence of Wm. Turnbill:

He replied that he had come along with them, [Gore men] that his name was Masson, that his uncle was Surveyor-General of the Province, that he [Sydenham] had promised to give the men of the Gore fifty acres of land each to come down and gain the election for Dr. McCulloch and that he had been two months surveying the land for that purpose, under orders from his uncle the Surveyor-General. . . .

After the election of 1841, in which he took an active part, Sydenham sought to accomplish two things: to return economic prosperity to the United Province and to stave off theoretical considerations of responsible government. He was largely successful in both.

Fortified by the large British loan, Canada West and Canada East embarked upon an ambitious plan to develop the St. Lawrence. In the 1840's a rash of canal digging and road building occurred — all designed to place the United Province in a more favourable position to compete with the United States.

Sydenham sought a solution for the irksome problem of the Clergy Reserves during the 1840's. These Reserves were divided among the various Protestant denominations and the revenue from them was to be used for educational purposes. Sydenham's District Councils Act of 1841 laid the foundation of municipal government; municipal government of Ontario is still guided by this Act. Through the efforts of the Colonial Office during the Sydenham administration, the tension which had existed for some years along the Maine-New

Brunswick border was brought to an end when the Webster-Ashburton Treaty was concluded in 1842.* Through popular measures as these, Sydenham was able to gain and maintain a considerable following in the Assembly. Even some Reformers supported him, although Sydenham was not prepared to yield on the basic issue of responsible government.

The policy of consultation and moderation which Sydenham had employed in winning colonial approval for the Union was further strengthened by a number of dispatches from Lord John Russell. These categorically rejected the concept of responsible government as envisaged by the Reformers. Good, sound government based on the "well understood wishes of the people" was to be the half-loaf with which Canadians had to be content. However, these same dispatches conceded that the old practice of appointing Executive Councillors for life should give way to a policy of changing the Executive Councillors as often as the "motives of public policy" suggested. The intent of this measure was to free the Governor from the Compacts and allow him to dismiss Councillors who disagreed with his policies. At the same time, it established the precedent that Executive Councillors could be dismissed.

RUSSELL'S OPPOSITION TO RESPONSIBLE GOVERNMENT[203]

Lord John Russell to Charles Poulett Thomson:

14th October, 1839.

It appears . . . that you may encounter much difficulty in subduing the excitement which prevails on the question of what is called "Responsible Government." I have to instruct you, however, to refuse any explanation which may be construed to imply an acquiescence in the petitions and addresses upon this subject. . . .

_____

. . . . It is obvious that the executive councillor of a colony is in a situation totally different [from that of a minister in England]. The Governor under whom he serves, received his orders from the Crown of England. But can the colonial council be the advisers of the Crown of England? Evidently not, for the Crown has other advisers. . . .

It may happen, therefore, that the Governor receives at one and the same time instructions from the Queen, and advice from his executive council, totally at variance with each other. If he is to obey his instructions from England, the parallel of constitutional responsibility entirely fails; if,

_____

* The Maine-New Brunswick boundary dispute was temporarily settled by Durham.

on the other hand, he is to follow the advice of his council, he is no longer a subordinate officer, but an independent sovereign.

In order to govern with the "well understood wishes of the people," Sydenham realized that his policies must have support in the Assembly. Accordingly, he appointed his Executive Councillors from all factions of the Assembly — though he largely ignored the French. His aim was to obtain broad-based support so that his policies would seem to reflect the popular will, and to follow policies that met the needs of the people. Even Robert Baldwin accepted the post of Solicitor-General; he served for a time but he resigned before the session of 1841 even convened. Baldwin was convinced that Sydenham was not prepared to yield on the issue of responsible government; therefore, to serve in Sydenham's multi-party Executive Council would have conflicted with Baldwin's concept of responsible government.

Baldwin attempted to force the issue by introducing a series of resolutions in the Assembly. These proposals stated that Executive Councillors were to be chosen from the Assembly and that they were to be accountable or responsible to the Assembly — the essence of responsible government. Lord Sydenham countered by having his own set of proposals introduced by one of his loyal supporters, S. B. Harrison. The Harrison Resolutions, as they came to be known, agreed that Executive Councillors "ought to be men possessed of the confidence" of the Assembly. However, the Resolutions skilfully avoided the issue of accountability of Executive Councillors. The Harrison Resolutions were carried, since, at the time, Sydenham's economic and administrative policies endowed him with wide Assembly support. While the Resolutions yielded on the point of the Executive Councillors having the confidence of the Assembly, omitting mention of accountability implied that Executive Councillors were to continue to be responsible to the Governor and not to the Assembly.

METCALFE'S COMMENTS ON THE HARRISON RESOLUTIONS[204]

. . . [Lord Sydenham] in composing his Council of the principal executive officers under his authority, in requiring that they should all be members of the Legislature, and chiefly of the popular branch, and in making their tenure of office dependent on their commanding a majority in the body representing the people, he seems to me to have ensured with the certainty of cause and effect, that the Council of the Governor should regard themselves as responsible, not so much to the Governor as to the House of Assembly . . . he rendered it inevitable that the Council here should obtain and ascribe to themselves, in at least some degree, the character of a Cabinet of Ministers . . . [Sydenham] carried into practice that very theory of Responsible Colonial Government which he had pronounced his opinion decidedly against.

Sydenham's career as Governor of Canada came to an abrupt end in September, 1841, when he died as a result of injuries sustained in a riding accident. His short governorship had witnessed the union of the colonies, the return of economic prosperity, and some notable advances towards responsible government—although his purpose had been to avoid such advances. By 1841, the precedents had been established that Executive Councillors no longer held office for life and that they had to have support in the Assembly. However, Sydenham had been very much his own Prime Minister; he had continued to formulate government policy and he, rather than the leader of the largest group in the Assembly, had appointed Executive Councillors. As for his Executive Council, it was a council to be consulted and nothing more; he was not bound by its advice.

Lastly, Sydenham had left a legacy of problems to his successor. The French, whom he distrusted, were sullen and resentful of the union that had been forced upon them. Throughout this period, Francis Hincks, the brilliant strategist and proponent of colonial self-government, was welding the followers of Baldwin and Lafontaine into a recognizable political party.

BAGOT'S CRITICISM OF SYDENHAM'S ADMINISTRATION[205]

Bagot to Stanley, September 26, 1842:

. . . . Towards the French Canadians his [Sydenham's] conduct was very unwise. He made enemies of them unnecessarily, at a time when he should have propitiated them and diminished their objections to the Union. He treated those who approached him with slight and rudeness, and thus he converted a proud and courteous people, which even their detractors acknowledge them to be, into personal and irreconcilable enemies. He despised their talents, and denied their official capacity for office . . . the cutting off the suburbs from the electoral Districts of Quebec and Montreal . . . [Sydenham's] alleged reason was to give a commercial representation to these two towns; his real reason, well known to his Council, was to secure

Louis H. LaFontaine

Robert Baldwin

the exclusion of the French from the representation and the acquisition of four supporters to his Government. . . .

The mode in which several of the Elections were carried in both Provinces, but especially in Lower Canada, weakened his position with the honest and uncompromising Reformers of the Upper Province, and gave even Sir Allan McNab [a Tory] a pretext for annoying and opposing him. . . .

In England, the Whig government had given way to the Tories, and Lord Stanley became the new Colonial Secretary. Sir Charles Bagot, a Victorian gentleman of the pre-industrial era, succeeded Sydenham as Governor of Canada. A quarter of a century earlier, he had negotiated the Rush-Bagot Agreement which limited armaments on the Great Lakes. Bagot's instructions from Lord Stanley were to carry on as Sydenham had done; the British government still could not accept the idea of colonial self-government, which to them was tantamount to colonial independence.

Bagot soon realized the impossibility of his instructions in the light of the realities of the Canadian situation. By personal command of majority support in the Assembly, Sydenham had achieved harmony in government. However, Sydenham's policies of economic reconstruction were nearing completion and the forces in the

Assembly were solidifying against the existing Executive Council which Bagot had inherited from Sydenham's administration. Bagot soon saw that in order to have majority support, he had to rely on the French. Sydenham had alienated the French but had been able to command majority support without them; Bagot could not. Ably led by Baldwin and Lafontaine, the Reformers had gained in strength to the point where the Sydenham ministry no longer commanded majority support. The harmony between the Executive Council and the Assembly that Sydenham had created was fast disappearing. Bagot realized that his support of this weak ministry would be a violation of the principle of governing according to the "well understood wishes of the people." The only course open to Bagot, consistent with the precedent established by his predecessor, was to dismiss Councillors who lacked the confidence of the Assembly.

Bagot, aware of the necessity of French support, invited Lafontaine into the Executive Council. Lafontaine successfully insisted upon Baldwin's inclusion — a sign that the alliance of English and French Reformers was working.* In September, 1842, five Reformers replaced five Executive Councillors, hold-overs from Sydenham's ministry, who lacked the support of the Assembly. It should

* Louis Lafontaine was, in the modern sense, the first Prime Minister of Canada.

Charles Bagot

Sir Charles T. Metcalfe

be noted that the inclusion of the Reformers in the Executive Council was only a reorganization of an existing Executive Council.

BAGOT ON RESPONSIBLE GOVERNMENT[206]

Bagot to Stanley, September 26, 1842:

Your Lordship's letter . . . led me to expect, if I had not before anticipated it, that this change of policy will be both startling and distasteful to the Government and perhaps to public opinion in England. I regret it, and most exceedingly do I regret the necessity which has compelled me to adopt it. . . .

―――――

. . . . There was but one way to avoid it — by appointing a new Executive Council prepared to act without the sympathy and against an overwhelming majority of the House of Assembly: but by denying *in toto* the principle of Responsible Government, and refusing to act upon it, at a crisis which would immediately have brought the question to an issue unfavorable to the Government . . . I was not prepared to adopt such a policy. The consequences would have been most disastrous. The Assembly would have stopped the supplies about to be voted — the questions which led to the former troubles of Canada would have been revived — all attempts to resist the power of the Assembly and the tide of public opinion would have failed, and Canada would have again become the Theatre of a wide spread rebellion, and perhaps the ungrateful separatist or the rejected outcast from the British Dominion.

Bagot's ill-health, which led to his death in 1843, forced him to leave much of the formulation of government policy in the hands of the Executive Council. He invariably followed the advice of his Executive Council. It is not certain, however, that he was prepared to do so in all matters. Nevertheless, during his governorship, the Executive Council to a large extent functioned as a Cabinet, responsible to the Assembly and not the Governor. But Bagot did not institute full responsible government — the Executive Council was heterogeneous and was not composed solely of members from the majority party in the Legislative Assembly. Bagot's actions as Governor failed to establish the precedent that the Governor must always follow the advice of his Executive Council.

Bagot had gone much further in acquiescing to the demands of the Reformers than his instructions warranted, and much further than the British government thought necessary. Reluctantly, the British government accepted Bagot's actions because it feared the consequences of reversing his measures. From Bagot's point of view, he had merely accepted the consequences of his predecessor's administration.

The British government was not too pleased with the course of events during Bagot's administration. In an attempt to close the flood-gate that Bagot had opened, Lord Stanley sent Sir Charles Metcalfe to British North America in 1843. Metcalfe had spent thirty-seven years as an administrator in India and recently had completed a tour of duty as Governor of Jamaica. He had been accustomed to autocratic rule and, like Sydenham and Bagot, he was an able administrator.

Metcalfe's instructions were that he was to recover the reins of government that Bagot had in part relinquished and to achieve harmonious government in the same fashion Sydenham had done. The Governor was to formulate policy, treat the Council as an advisory body and command a personal majority in the Assembly. These instructions necessitated the Governor's return to the political arena.

METCALFE ON RESPONSIBLE GOVERNMENT[207]

. . . . I am not perfectly satisfied with my Council, chiefly because they are under the influence of party views, and would, if they could, drag me on with them in the same course. The only effectual remedy would be to dismiss them, or such of them as are most in the extreme on this point, and form another Council. But the consequence to be expected would be, that a cry would be raised accusing me of hostility to Responsible Government. . . .

My objects are to govern the country for its own welfare, and to engage its attachment to the parent State. For these purposes it is my wish to conciliate all parties; and although this might be difficult, I do not perceive that it would be impracticable, if the Governor were free to act thoroughly in that spirit; but the accomplishment of that wish seems almost impossible when the Governor is trammelled with a Council deeming it necessary for their existence that their own party alone should be considered. Sooner than abandon myself as a partisan to such a course, I would dismiss the Council and take the consequences. . . .

Difficulty between Metcalfe and the Executive Council, headed by Lafontaine and Baldwin, was inevitable. When Metcalfe made an appointment to public office without the knowledge or consent of the Executive Council, the Lafontaine-Baldwin ministry resigned and an election was called. As it turned out, the election of 1844 was the ugliest in Canadian history. The unpopularity of some legislative measures* proposed and suported by the Reformers in the Assembly, bribery, strong-arm tactics and cries of disloyalty levelled against the Reformers won for the Tories a small majority in the Assembly. Metcalfe could now boast that his policies had popular support and that this was responsible government. Indeed, he had returned to the ways of Sydenham, much to the satisfaction of the British government. Incurable cancer cut short his governorship in British North America. His retirement was followed shortly by his death.

The *inter-regnum* between Metcalfe and his successor was filled by the Earl of Cathcart who was the Commander-in-Chief of the British military forces in British North America.

Events in Britain now became the determining factor in the struggle between the Governor and the Reformers in British North America. The Corn Laws and the Navigation Acts, which had formed the backbone of the old mercantilist system, were replaced in 1846 and in 1849 respectively. Britain, whose manufactured goods were in great demand all over the world, became a free-trade country. Colonial raw materials, which had previously received preferential treatment in Britain, had to compete with raw materials of other countries. The view of the Empire as a closed trading area was discarded. Restrictions placed on colonial trading for the good of the Empire which had benefited British colonies were lifted. Now that colonial trading was free of British restriction, there seemed little need to control colonial political life.

Following the return to popularity of the Reformers, the death of Lord Metcalfe, and the advent to power of the free-trade ministry of Lord John Russell in Britain, British North America received responsible government and the problem of colonial self-government was solved.

This fundamental evolution of the Empire into a number of self-governing colonies, bound to the mother country by ties of "loyalty and affection," can be attributed in large measure to Lord Grey, the Colonial Secretary, and Lord Elgin, the new Governor of Canada. Lord Grey was a brother-in-law to Lord Durham and Lord Elgin was a son-in-law. Both men were bent on vindicating the memory of Lord Durham and both saw clearly the necessity of rewriting the relationships between colony and mother country in the light of Britain's new free-trade policy.

Elgin's instructions were clear: Canada was to have the full measure of responsible government. His opportunity to give credence to the new British thinking came in 1848, when public disaffection with the ruling Tories gave the Reformers a large majority in the election. In accord with his instructions and the meaning of responsible government, Elgin called on Lafontaine and Baldwin to form an Executive Council (Cabinet). They, in turn, appointed Councillors from their own ranks in

---

* The University Bill sought to secularize the Anglican King's College headed by Bishop Strachan.
  The Secret Societies Bill aimed to curb the activities of the Loyal Orange Order, a society of Irish Protestants, that was closely allied with the Tories.

Lord Elgin

Lord Grey

the Assembly, and this Council, with the approval of the Assembly, was to formulate government policy.

ELGIN ON RESPONSIBLE GOVERNMENT[208]

. . . . My course in these circumstances, is, I think, clear and plain. It may be somewhat difficult to follow occasionally, but I feel no doubt as to the direction in which it lies. I give to my ministers all constitutional support, frankly and without reserve, and the benefit of the best advice that I can afford them in their difficulties. In return of this, I expect that they will, in so far as it possible for them to do so, carry out my views for the maintenance of the connexion with Great Britain and the advancement of the interests of the province. On this tacit understanding we have acted together harmoniously up to this time, although I have never concealed from them that I intend to do nothing which may prevent me from working cordially with their opponents, if they are forced upon me . . . it is indispensable that the head of the Government should show that he has confidence in the loyalty of all the influential parties with which he has to deal, and that he should have no personal antipathies to prevent him from acting with leading men.

I feel very strongly that a Governor-General, by acting upon these views with tact and firmness, may hope to establish a moral influence in the province which will go far to compensate for the loss of power consequent on the surrender of patronage to an executive responsible to the local Parliament. . . .

The crucial test for responsible government came in 1849. The Assembly had passed the Rebellion Losses Bill, which would recompense persons who had suffered property damage in Lower Canada during the rebellion. A similar measure had been passed for Upper Canada during Metcalfe's administration. However, the present bill seemed to the Tories to be compensating some of the people who had actually engaged in rebellion. The Tory cry became "No pay to rebels." Elgin, although he did not personally favour the bill, signed it, on the grounds that as a "Responsible" Governor he was bound to follow the advice of his Council. In signing the bill, Elgin did two things. First, he established the full acceptance of the system of colonial self-government that Durham had envisaged. Second, his signing unleashed a reign of terror by the worst Tory elements. Stones, eggs and vegetables were hurled at the Governor's carriage; homes of some Reformers were burned; and on April 25 the parliament buildings in Montreal were razed.

THE 1849 RIOT AND ARSON IN MONTREAL[209]

An eye-witness account of the disorders in Montreal, on April 25, 1849, following Lord Elgin's assent to the Rebellion Losses Bill:

The account was written by Rev. William Rufus Seaver, a Congregational minister who was also a shopkeeper in Montreal:

. . . when it was finally announced that he [Elgin] had really given the Royal Sanction to the Bill, then there was *trouble* — as his Excellency left the House for his carriage at the door he was

Burning of the Houses of Assembly, Montreal, 1849

assailed with stones, clubs, & rotten & good eggs by thousands, and he was struck in the face with an egg, his carriage windows broken etc. but by the speed of his horses he was enabled to escape with no injury except to his carriage and his equipage — I stop here for the cry is raised that the *Parliment House* is on fire-fire-fire is the cry — and from my shop door I see the red flames light up the Heavens — I go — more after I see what the row is —

. . . about 8 o'clock [in the evening] while Parliment was still sitting a mob (it can be called nothing else tho' composed of some of our most worthy citizens) assembled around the House, and commenced the destruction of the building, by breaking windows etc. Soon the doors were broken open and a stout fellow sprang into the speakers chair with the exclamation, "*I dissolve Parliment*" This was the Signal — and immediately in the face of the members, and an immense multitude

of spectators the Gas Pipes were fired in a dozen places, and the building wraped in flames. . . . All was lost, nothing saved, and the structure now is but a heap of smoking ruins. . . .

In 1849 the Tories and commercial interests in Montreal issued the Annexation Manifesto advocating the severance of all ties with the Empire and the annexation of Canada by the United States. The Manifesto stemmed primarily from the worsening of the economic conditions as a result of the end of mercantilism within the Empire. Loyalty to the Empire — the often avowed protestations of Toryism — was scuttled by economic self-interest. Like the rebellions of 1837, the Tory outbursts and the Annexation Manifesto lacked anything that might be termed "popular support." Responsible government was now a reality.

D

RESPONSIBLE GOVERNMENT IN THE MARITIMES

The coming of responsible government in Nova Scotia differed considerably from the path followed in the Canadas. First, the transition from oligarchic rule to responsible government was

peaceful and free of the agonies of rebellion that rocked the Canadas. Second, the French-English division that aroused bitter feelings in Canada East did not exist in Nova Scotia. Assertions of

"Passing the British Flag to Uncle Sam" **Punch** Magazine's View of the Annexationists

Anglo-Saxon loyalty to the monarchy as a bastion against French disloyalty and republicanism could not be injected into Nova Scotian politics. Third, the issue of loyalty, often successfully raised against Reformers in Canada West, was seldom used in Nova Scotia. Such smears would have proven ineffective in Nova Scotia since both Tories and Reformers could claim Loyalist ancestry; the attachment of both groups to the mother country

HOWE DECLARES HIS LOYALTY[210]

Extract from a speech by Howe to the Nova Scotia Assembly urging the adoption of the Twelve Resolutions, Febr. 11, 1837:

I know that in suggesting an elective Council I shall hear the cry of republicanism and danger to the constitution. . . .

The idea of republicanism, of independence, of severance from the mother country, never crosses my mind. . . . I wish to live and die a British subject, but not a Briton only in the name. Give me — give to my Country, the blessed privilege of her Constitution and her laws; and as our earliest thoughts are trained to reverence the great principles of freedom and responsibility, which have made her the wonder of the world, let us be contented with nothing less. Englishmen at home will despise us, if we forget the lessons our common ancestors have bequeathed.

was unquestioned. These factors may have influenced the British government's more sympathetic consideration of Nova Scotia's demands that loyal British subjects should enjoy the "rights of Englishmen." Joseph Howe expressed this sentiment in his famous four open *Letters to Lord John Russell* in 1839,* shortly after the publication of Durham's *Report*. Howe questioned the denial to loyal British subjects of the same government that the people of Britain enjoyed.

HOWE CRITICAL OF SUBJECTION OF GOVERNORS TO THE EXECUTIVE COUNCILS[211]

First of four letters written to Lord John Russell. It appeared as a supplement to the NOVASCOTIAN, *October 10, 1839:*

Halifax, September 18, 1839.
. . . a responsible Executive Council as recommended by Lord Durham . . . the principle of responsibility to the popular branch must be introduced into all the Colonies without delay . . . It is a mere mockery to tell us that the Governor himself is responsible. He must carry on the government by and with the few officials whom he finds in possession when he arrives . . . I never knew one, who, even with the best intentions . . . was able to contend, on anything like fair terms, with the small knot of functionaries who form the Councils, fill the offices, and wield the powers of the Government. . . . It is indispensable then, to the dignity, the independence, the usefulness of the Governor himself, that he should have the power to shake off this thraldom, as the Sovereign does if unfairly hampered by faction; and by an appeal to the people, adjust the balance of power. Give us this truly British privilege, and Colonial grievances will soon become a scarce article in the English market.

Russell's 1839 instruction to Sydenham to govern "in accord with the well understood wishes and interests of the people" was viewed by Nova Scotia's Reformers as a first step towards responsible government. Lieutenant-Governor Sir Colin Campbell, in spite of his objections, was persuaded by Sydenham to include Reformers in the Executive Council. Three Reformers including Howe were appointed to the Council. Although this was not full responsible government, it opened the way by setting the precedent that members of the

* These letters were Howe's reply to Lord John Russell, the Colonial Secretary, who claimed that responsible government as recommended by Durham was inadmissible in a colony.

Executive Council need not be drawn solely from the oligarchy.

From here on, the achieving of responsible government proceeded more rapidly. Between 1843 and 1846, Governor Falkland was forced to rule precariously with a weak ministry; all his efforts to bring the Reformers into a coalition failed. Lord Grey, the Colonial Secretary in Lord John Russell's government, doubted the wisdom of Falkland's rule; in 1846, Sir John Harvey, a former Governor of New Brunswick, replaced Falkland. The new Governor was instructed to act as the representative of the British government, free from partisan political involvement. This made possible the creation of a one-party ministry with a Prime Minister at the head.

When Harvey failed to attract Reformers into the ministry, he called an election in 1847. The Reformers scored a decisive victory. In accord with the new spirit of colonial self-government enunciated by Lord Grey, the Governor called upon the Reformers to form a ministry. In January 1848, J. B. Uniacke, a defector from the Tory ranks, formed an all-Reform government. That is, Uniacke, as leader of the majority party in the Legislative Assembly, chose his Executive Councillors from the ranks of the Reformers — the majority party in the Assembly. Nova Scotia achieved responsible government before the Canadas.

In New Brunswick and Prince Edward Island, the dispute between the Legislative Assembly and the Executive Council centred around the control of land. In New Brunswick, the clash was over control of Crown lands — valuable timber stands. The Assembly wanted control of these lands. The dispute, in reality, was between two rival groups interested in the timber trade. In Prince Edward Island, the oligarchy that controlled the Legislative Assembly wanted the land held by absentee landlords reverted to the Crown; local land speculators, members of the oligarchy, would benefit. In neither colony was there overt enthusiasm for responsible government. However, after Nova Scotia was granted responsible government, it was not long before it was extended to the other Maritime colonies — New Brunswick in 1848, Prince Edward Island in 1851 and Newfoundland in 1855.

16

Newfoundland, for many years a collection of fishing stations, felt the force of changes occurring in the other Atlantic colonies. By the end of the 1820's, the population, largely concentrated in St. John's but increasing in pockets along the coastline, exceeded 60,000. The colony's prosperity was temporarily enhanced by expansion of the seal industry, which produced new jobs. In 1854, the Reciprocity Treaty with the United States opened up prospects for better times.

SEAL HUNTING OFF NEWFOUNDLAND[212]

Written in 1883:

.... A blow on the nose from the gaff [a pole six or seven feet in length which serve as a club] stuns or kills the young seal. Instantly the sculping-knife is at work, the skin with the fat adhering is detached with amazing rapidity from the carcass, which is left on the ice still quivering with life, while the fat and skin alone are carried off. This process is called "sculping," a corruption no doubt of scalping. In skinning, a cut is made through the fat to the flesh, a thickness of about three inches from the throat to the tail....

Fancy two or three hundred men on a field of ice carrying on this murderous work, their persons smeared with sanguinary evidence of the wholesale slaughter; the ice stained with the gore and covered with skinless carcasses of the slain; "the shivering seals' low moans" filling the air like the sobbings of infants in distress; the murderers every minute smiting fresh victims, or dragging the oleaginous prizes to the vessel's side! .... The poor mother seals, now cubless, are seen popping their heads up in the small lakes of water and holes among the ice, anxiously looking for their young.

Poverty and a diverse population inhibited the growth of any cultural life, even the simplest type of formal education. Religious animosity, already a problem between Anglicans and Catholics, was augmented by the arrival of the British Methodists, whose influence was exerted mainly in the outposts.

Church and charitable organizations provided what little education there was in the outposts — usually rudimentary instruction in reading, writing, arithmetic and religion. In St. John's the merchant class could hire tutors or send their children to a private grammar school. The wealthy often sent their children to Boston, New York or London for higher education.

EDUCATION IN NEWFOUNDLAND[213]

An account written in 1883:

It was not till the year 1843 that the Legislature took any action in connection with the promotion of education in the colony. Previous ... all educational efforts proceeded from religious bodies or individuals ... education was in a low condition, and in the widely-scattered settlements many of the young had grown up ignorant of the very rudiments of knowledge....

In 1843 the initiatory step was taken by a Legislative Act granting a sum of £5,100 annually ... one-half ... in support of Protestant and one-half ... of Roman Catholic schools. Educational districts were defined, and a Board appointed for each....

In connection with the cause of education in Newfoundland grateful acknowledgment is due to "The Colonial and Continental Church Society," by whose instrumentality schools have been maintained in the island for more than half a century, and most valuable educational work has been done, especially at a time when the need of the poor inhabitants was sorest ... their [the Society's] efforts having been acknowledged and aided by an annual grant from the funds of the colony. In fact, the beginning of common school education in the island may be said to date from 1823, when the "Newfoundland School Society" was founded in London by Samuel Codner, a Newfoundland merchant. . . .

At mid-century, Newfoundland lagged behind the populous colonies of British North America in economic growth, immigration, education and constitutional reform. Although responsible government was to come in 1855, the colony remained largely dependent on Great Britain, even for its internal affairs.

By 1850, Nova Scotia's population of 277,000 had developed a sense of identity matched in the rest of British North America only by the French Canadians in Lower Canada. Since the building of Halifax as an imperial garrison in 1749, the military connection between Nova Scotia and Great Britain had been strengthened by cultural and economic ties. The ultimate achievement for talented men from this colony was high office in the imperial forces, business success in London or even election to the British Parliament. Nova Scotia, and particularly Halifax, was a vital link in a global empire — and leading colonials took pride in the fact.

Geography, too, played its part in creating the maritime flavour of the colony. The land frontier was not unimportant; thousands farmed in the river valleys, and, wherever good soil was available, settlers advanced into the hinterland. But communication was largely confined to coastal areas, where large towns evolved and commerce flourished. Most Nova Scotians, wherever they lived in the peninsula, felt close to the sea and knew their lives were bound up with it.

The Loyalist traditions, preserved and embellished through time by sons and grandsons of Loyalists, were central to public life in Nova Scotia. By the 1850's, the thousands of Irish, Scots and others who survived the ocean voyages during the Great Migration outnumbered the earlier inhabitants. Yet the newcomers, for the most part, gravitated to Cape Breton Island and the remote northeastern areas of the peninsula. The established society of Halifax and the larger towns, where descendants of Loyalists held prominence, maintained leadership in politics, shipbuilding, overseas trade and other aspects of colonial life.

The Church of England, to which most Loyalists belonged, persisted as an important force in the colony. For many years the Anglicans had exercised almost complete control over religion and education; non-Anglicans suffered limitations concerning schools, the right to hold public office and the performing of marriages. Accommodation, however, was necessitated by the coming of many Presbyterians, Baptists, Methodists and Roman Catholics during the Great Migration. Non-Anglicans came to enjoy full religious and civil freedom through modification of law and custom.

Formal education underwent similar changes. First the Church of England, then the other denominations, provided private schools for those who could afford the fees. By 1864, a public school system had evolved. Supported by taxation and supervised by provincial inspectors, schools were conducted by teachers trained in normal schools. Higher education, however, remained a service sustained by the churches. Although Lord Dalhousie, when he was Lieutenant-Governor, was largely responsible for the founding of government-supported Dalhousie University in 1818, the Anglicans built King's College in Halifax. The Baptists started Acadia College in Wolfville in 1832, while Roman Catholics began St. Francis Xavier in 1854 in Antigonish. After 1862, Methodists crossed the border to attend Mount Allison in New Brunswick.

EDUCATIONAL PROGRESS IN NOVA SCOTIA[214]

From an account written in 1863:

Sixty and even forty years ago, an old soldier, who could read, write, and "cipher as far as the rule of three" — a broken-down merchant, or an accountant, whose habits had become so unsteady that he could no longer serve with efficiency in the counting-house, would be hired as a schoolmaster. Now it is only the graduates of our provincial normal college for the training of teachers, that can command any of our best common schools. It is not half a century since the "New England Primer" . . . "Tutor's Assistant," the *ferule* [rod or ruler] and the *birch* [switch or whip] were accounted the orthodox and all-potent instrumentalities for teaching. . . . At present our schools are supplied with the latest and best British and American text-books, and corporal punishment . . . is resorted to but very seldom, and that in extreme cases.

The beginning of a provincial literature was further evidence that the colony was maturing culturally. Considerable credit was due to newspaper publishers, such as Joseph Howe of the *Novascotian,* who promoted local writing in papers. The most notable author was Thomas Chandler Haliburton, whose publications included an early history of Nova Scotia and a novel, *The Clockmaker, or the Sayings and Doings of Sam*

Tandem Club, Assembling in front of Dalhousie·College, Halifax, c. 1837

Slick of Slickville, which found a wide readership even in England.

ENCOURAGEMENT OF LITERATURE IN NOVA SCOTIA[215]

Joseph Howe remarks about his contribution to the encouragement of literary talent. From the NOVASCOTIAN, *December 30, 1841:*

The growth of literature in every country depends a good deal on the enterprise and liberality of its publishers. In this branch of my profession I have endeavoured, I trust, to set a good example. Most of the Works which have had a tendency to elevate the character of the country — to make it known at home and abroad — and to lay the foundation of a Provincial Literature, that have appeared within the past twelve years, have issued from The Novascotian Press. . . . I would perhaps have attempted to do more, but while I have published a volume a year for every year that I have been in business — by none of them making much, and by some of them losing heavily, I trust I have done something, to point the way towards a field which will bye and bye admit of more brilliant and profitable cultivation.

Prince Edward Island had developed a way of life somewhat different from those in the other colonies. Good land had made agriculture the main industry; yet the problem of land ownership infected all branches of endeavour. The island was insulated from its neighbours by turbulent water in summer and treacherous ice in winter. Small and insular as it was, the Island was no "melting pot" for immigrants. The population was drawn from many sources, including Acadian French, pre-Revolutionary settlers from the Thirteen Colonies, Loyalists, Scots and Irish. No ethnic group dominated the other; all retained distinctive characteristics. Political and social progress was slow, but the economic well-being enjoyed by most of the inhabitants made them generally satisfied with their lot.

Proprietary land grants were made as early as 1767 to men in England in the hope that they would promote settlement. Over the years the so-called "absentee land owners" were content to retain their large tracts of land, without concern for the development of Prince Edward Island. The result was that the land question came to dominate public affairs, even after Confederation.

DURHAM ON CONDITIONS IN PRINCE EDWARD ISLAND[216]

. . . . This island, most advantageously situated for the supply of the surrounding Colonies, and of all the fisheries, possesses a soil peculiarly adapted to the production of grain; and, from its insular position, is blessed with a climate far more genial than a great part of the continent which lies to the southward. Had its natural advantages been turned to proper account, it might at this time have been the granary of the British Colonies, and, instead of barely supporting a poor and unenterprising population of 40,000,* its mere agricultural resources would . . . have maintained in abundance a population of at least ten times that number. Of nearly 1,400,000 acres contained in the island,

* The population numbered 55,000 in 1851.

The Green at Fredericton, c. 1840

only 10,000 are said to be unfit for the plough. Only 100,000 are now under cultivation. No one can mistake the cause of this lamentable waste of the means of national wealth. It is the possession of almost the whole soil of the island by absentee proprietors, who would neither promote nor permit its cultivation, combined with the defective government which first caused and has since perpetuated the evil. . . .

Farmers in Prince Edward Island, whether they had obtained title to their land or not, were blessed with fertile soil. And though many of the Islanders left to seek their fortunes in the lumber camps of New Brunswick or Maine, the farms of Prince Edward Island produced potatoes and oats for export. Strong farm horses were also sold to the neighbouring colonies.

For several decades, the development of New Brunswick had been based on the timber trade and related industries. The great pine forests had suffered severe depletion through heavy and often wasteful cutting, and terrible fires, such as the one which ravaged the Miramichi Valley in 1825, had taken their toll. Yet the colony's staple industry provided thousands of jobs in the lumber camps, the sawmills and the shipyards. Agriculture, the heart of Prince Edward Island's economy, lagged

behind in New Brunswick. Fishing did not rank in importance as it did in the colony across the Bay of Fundy. Nor did efforts to tap mineral resources approach the efforts already evident in Nova Scotia during the 1850's.

Settlement was concentrated on the Bay of Fundy, especially in the St. John Valley, where the 25,000 people of St. John made it almost as large as Halifax. Up the river lay the capital, Fredericton, similarly well-populated by descendants of Loyalists. Separated by extensive stretches of wilderness from the main centres, the Acadian French lived in settlements along the border of Quebec and on the North Shore. During the Great Migration, this latter region received many of the Irish immigrants, whose cultivation of the potato proved to be a major stimulus to the province's agriculture. At the same time, many Lowland Scots joined their countrymen who had earlier established towns on the Miramichi River.

PROGRESS OF POPULATION IN NEW BRUNSWICK[217]

The total population of New Brunswick, in 1824, was 74,176 souls; in 1834, it was 119,457 souls; in 1840, it was 154,000 souls; and in 1851 (in the last census), it was 193,800 souls. At present [1863] the population is estimated at 210,000 souls, and upwards.

AN ACCOUNT OF THE NUMBER OF IMMIGRANTS
ARRIVED IN THE PROVINCE OF NEW BRUNSWICK
BETWEEN THE YEARS 1844 AND 1860

Year	No. immigrants arrived
1844	2,605
1845	6,133
1846	9,765
1847	14,879
1848	4,141
1849	2,724
1850	1,838
1851	3,470
1852	2,165
1853	3,762
1854	3,440
1855	1,539
1856	708
1857	607
1858	390
1859	230
1860	323

Life in the outlying areas of scattered settlements had the frontier qualities of harshness and simplicity. As settlers occupied themselves with securing food and shelter, the rum merchants found a ready market among those who liked to fortify themselves against long hours of work. The churches, of which the Roman Catholic, Anglican and other Protestant denominations had comparable membership, were active in trying to promote a more elevated spiritual life. One effect was the importation of a temperance movement from the neighbouring state of Maine. So aggressive did it become that the province's Legislative Assembly passed a bill, introduced by the same Leonard Tilley who later led New Brunswick into Confederation, to prohibit the sale of liquor. Public opinion had evidently been misjudged, however, because within four months a vigorously contested election had returned an anti-temperance majority and prohibition was repealed.

TEMPERANCE MOVEMENT IN NEW BRUNSWICK[218]

One powerful prejudice that for a time forced all others into the background startled New Brunswick. . . . Quite suddenly during the legislative session of 1852, a monster petition with 9,000 signatures was presented to the house of assembly requesting that the importation of alcoholic beverages should be prohibited. For five years the Sons of Temperance had been gathering strength, organizing their forces in the unpretentious little churches that dotted the countryside. . . . Their activities had commenced at St. Stephen in 1847, and branches had mushroomed up all over the southern part of the province. They possessed some of the mysticism of secret societies, but frequently they indulged in outward shows of their faith: processions with plumed horses, garish banners, and brass bands. Teas, picnics, and steamboat excursions helped to cement the bonds. All members of the family could be included, for there were also Daughters of Temperance and Cadets of Temperance. . . . Harnessed to politics their power could be fearsome. Their leader was Samuel Leonard Tilley of Saint John.

To the astonishment of the sophisticated, the bill passed and became law, to take effect on January 1, 1853. . . .

The cultural life of the colony was slow in developing, but there were signs of change by the 1850's, at least in Fredericton and St. John. In 1859, the University of New Brunswick was instituted as the successor to King's College. Its graduates contributed to, and were part of, a new spirit that produced such poets as Charles G. D. Roberts and Bliss Carman in the early years of Confederation.

Education followed much the same pattern as in the other colonies. An interesting exception was the introduction in the 1820's of the "Madras Schools," based on a method used by the British in India. In such schools, a single teacher could give education to a large number of pupils by training senior students to act as instructors. The churches, of course, provided an important educational service in the early years. As early as 1816, a provincial act provided for aid to grammar schools. In 1847, the Executive Council was authorized to act as a Board of Education and to set up normal schools for the training of teachers. A fully tax-supported system of public schools was put into operation following the School Act of 1871.

As the only Atlantic province with long borders on the continental land mass, New Brunswick was eventually faced with important reasons for connections with the interior — that is, with Canada. For one thing, the long border with the United States was only settled in 1842, and the need for defence against a potential threat from the American side could not be ignored. And although New Brunswickers regarded the Province of Canada as a faraway land of rebels and money-hungry businessmen, some could consider the advantages of railway connections that would open up New Brunswick and stimulate trade with the St. Lawrence Valley.

The United Province, created by the union of Upper and Lower Canada in 1841, experienced a burgeoning prosperity in the 1840's. This resulted from the infusion of new immigrants and investment capital. The Province, especially the Great Lakes-St. Lawrence Lowlands region, contained the bulk of British North America's population, industry, banking and commerce. The early network of railroads extended through this region from Quebec to Sarnia and touched on the important ports on the seaway.

The new frontier areas of Canada West (formerly Upper Canada) and the older established settlements of Canada East (formerly Lower Canada) concentrated upon the production of surplus grain crops for export. Timber continued as another important export staple, and the timber towns and ports were kept busy. New industries were established to produce a wider variety of goods than had formerly been imported.

By mid-century, the expansion of the 1840's slowed down. This resulted primarily from Britain's adoption of free trade, which deprived Canada of her protected and preferential market in the United Kingdom.

THE ECONOMY OF THE UNITED PROVINCE
OF CANADA[219]

Harold A. Innis surveys the state of the economy at mid-century:

The rapid increase in the importance of agricultural produce and especially wheat precipitated the problem of the upper St. Lawrence. Steamships, canals, and wheat involved the financial support of the state. Wheat, unlike lumber, was faced with competition from New York and in turn involved railways as supplemental to water transportation. . . .

The decline of wooden sailing vessels and of the market for timber from Great Britain, the rise of Montreal as a rival to Quebec, and the coming of the iron steamship and the railway coincided with the depletion of forests in the eastern states, the growth of cities, and the migration of sawmills to the Ottawa and the district north of Lake Ontario. Water power and steam power made their impact on the lumbering industry. . . .

The rise in importance of wheat and agricultural products, and the emergence of steamships, canals, and railways coincided with and implied . . . the establishment of new devices for finance. The upper St. Lawrence waterways . . . now demanded, under a wheat economy, continued support. Capital investment on a large scale necessitated more direct responsibility and supervision and more adequate methods of finance. . . . Eventually the difficulties of finance . . . provided a powerful driving force toward Confederation and the creation of a new institution to carry the burden of debt of the united province.

The growing Province had settled down to the reality of the Union, and the two major groups — Protestant English-speaking and Catholic French-speaking — resigned themselves to a form of co-existence. Although the Anglican Church still maintained its dominance among the English-speaking people, the other Protestant denominations had emerged as important influences in the religious, cultural and educational life of the Province. The French-speaking people clung to the privileges assured them in the Quebec Act and adhered to the Catholic Church where they fulfilled their cultural and educational needs.

The school system that had evolved in the Canadas before the Union of 1841 set the pattern for the educational system of the United Province. In Lower Canada, the elementary schools were denominational — the local parishes set up schools — and in 1829 began receiving government grants. In Upper Canada, the Common School Act of 1816 had given government support to elementary education. Secondary education, however, remained in the hands of private grammar schools and academies where students paid tuition.

In the United Province, the parish schools of Canada East were converted into public schools, and Protestant and Catholic schools were set up in Montreal and Quebec. These schools were financed by local taxes and government grants. Similarly in Canada West the dual school system was recognized and provisions made for the subsequent government support of separate schools.

THE STATE OF SCHOOLS IN THE
BROCK DISTRICT, 1849[220]

Taken from a report by W. H. Landon, public school inspector, dated at Woodstock (Canada West), October, 1849:

. . . . The School Houses in many instances, (although not all) are miserable Shanties, made of Logs, loosely and roughly put together; the interstices filled with clay, portions of which are from time to time crumbling down, filling the place with filth and dust. Under your feet are loose boards, without nails, across which, when one walks, a clatter is produced equal to that heard in a lumber yard. Over your head are the naked rafters, stained with smoke and hung with cobwebs and dust. Two or three little windows, generally half way up the walls, admit the light; and a rough door, which does not fit the opening, creaks upon its wooden hinges. . . . The writing Desks are generally long, sloping shelves, pinned up against the walls, as high as the breasts of the

Upper Canada College, 1835

Pupils who sit before them. The Seats are without backs and from eighteen inches to two feet high. Sometimes, in addition to these, we have a Master's Desk, but awkwardly constructed, for the most part, — too high for the sitting posture, and too low for the standing. This completes the articles of furniture. We have no Black Boards, no Maps, and no illustrative Apparatus of any kind.

When we enter one of these Schools we behold a picture of discomfort and misery. The children are perched upon the benches before described; but as they have no support for their backs, and as only the taller of them can reach the floor with their feet, marks of weariness and pain are visible in their features and postures. . . .

By mid-century higher education was served by several well-established colleges. King's College, the Anglican institution founded by John Strachan in 1827, became the University of Toronto in 1848. Through the efforts of Egerton Ryerson, the Methodists established Victoria University; the Presbyterians began operating Queen's University at Kingston. In Montreal, McGill University was endowed by a wealthy local financier, James McGill.

SUPPLEMENTARY ELEMENTARY EDUCATION AGENCIES IN CANADA EAST[221]

There are two Asylums for the deaf and dumb in Lower Canada. The first, for boys, was established near Montreal by the Rev. Abbé Lagorce, in 1849; and the second for girls, was established in Montreal by Mgr. Bourget, Roman Catholic Bishop of Montreal, in 1853. In these two asylums there are eight teachers and about sixty pupils. An asylum of the same description was established by Donald McDonald Esq., at Quebec, in 1832, under the authority of a special act of Parliament. . . . The law, however, having expired in 1836, it was never revived, and the Asylum was closed.

The Reformatory school for juvenile criminals was established at the Isle aux Noix, near the frontier, and at the head of the Richelieu river, in 1858. Being an old military post, it was again deemed necessary to occupy it, and the Reformatory was removed to St. Vincent de Paul near Montreal, in 1861. There are now [1863] about fifty inmates in the institution.

The need for newspapers was felt early in the century. Although many newspapers and periodicals sprang up, a good number of them lasted only a short while. But such well-known publications as *Le Canadien* in Quebec and the *Colonial Advocate* in Toronto were widely read. The *Christian Guardian*, a Methodist publication, made Ryerson one of the best known figures in Upper Canada. George Brown launched his own political career with his newspaper the *Globe*. These publications, with their potpourri of political controversy, lengthy personal columns, patent medicine advertisements, news from abroad and local gossip, relieved the loneliness of pioneer life in the far-flung settlements.

By mid-century, the United Province reflected — on either side of the Ottawa River — the cultural characteristics which put a distinctive imprint on the future provinces of Ontario and Quebec.

In the West, the merger of the Hudson's Bay and North West Companies in 1821 ended the fur trade rivalry which had plagued the Red River Settlement in the early years. At the time, the sparsely settled colony sprawled along both banks of the Red River. The total population was 419: 221 Scottish colonists around Fort Douglas and northward along the west bank of the river, 133 Canadians in St. Boniface on the east side of the river, and 65 de Meurons and Swiss Catholics, also in St. Boniface along the small Seine River. At Pembina, to the south, were 500 Métis, many of whom later moved to St. Boniface.

The Red River colony experienced very small growth. The disastrous flood of 1826 practically wiped out the colony. Many of the de Meurons, restless, non-peasant stock, unaccustomed to the pioneer environment, hardships and heartbreak of farming, left the colony for the United States. The Scots and Métis, who had moved to higher ground during the flood, returned to farm their plots when the floodwater receded.

A FLOOD DESTROYS THE COLONY[222]

Alexander Ross gives an eye-witness account of the disastrous flood in May, 1826:

. . . . The people had to fly from their homes for the dear life, some of them saving only the clothes they had on their backs. The shrieks of children, the lowing of cattle, and the howling of dogs, added terror to the scene. . . . The families were all conveyed to places of safety, after which, the first consideration was to secure the cattle, by driving them many miles off, to the pine hills and rocky heights . . . the country presented the appearance of a vast lake. . . .

While the frightened inhabitants were collected in groups on any dry spot that remained visible above the waste of waters, their houses . . . and every description of property, might be seen floating along over the wide extended plain, to be engulfed in Lake Winnipeg. Hardly a house or building of any kind was left standing in the colony. Many of the buildings drifted along whole and entire; and in some were seen dogs, howling dismally, and cats, that jumped frantically from side to side of their precarious abodes. The most singular spectacle was a house in flames, drifting along in the night, its one half immersed in water, and the remainder furiously burning. This accident was caused by the hasty retreat of the occupiers. . . .

Up to 1834, the Selkirk family, assisted by appointed councillors, ran the government of

Assiniboia, as the Red River colony was known. The Governor of Rupert's Land, an appointee of the Hudson's Bay Company, was the Company's overseer and kept close watch on the activities of the Council of Assiniboia. In 1834, when the Hudson's Bay Company re-purchased Assiniboia from the Selkirk family, the Company retained the administrative organization of the Council of Assiniboia.

The economic basis of the colony was the buffalo hunt, furs and agriculture. The buffalo hunt — seasonal expeditions conducted primarily by the Métis — made life semi-nomadic; agriculture on the fixed lots along the rivers was combined with hunting buffalo and fur trading. The Scottish settlers in Kildonan, on river plots northward along the river from Fort Douglas, were determined to rebuild their shattered lives. They had a farm background; they stuck to farming and struggled to establish a new community in a new land.

The isolation of the colony and the restrictive trade regulations of the Hudson's Bay Company impeded the growth of the settlement. The colony had only York Factory on the Bay as an outlet to the outside world. The other outlet, the overland route to St. Paul, held great promise, but this was thwarted by the Hudson's Bay Company. Using its authority of the Council of Assiniboia, the Company imposed monopolistic restrictions on trade.

All furs and surplus farm products were to be sold to the Company, which in turn provided the settlers with supplies. The colonists complained about the Hudson's Bay Company's controls on markets and prices. To evade these commercial limitations, enterprising traders developed a clandestine trade with the Americans at Pembina and St. Paul, where prices for furs were higher and goods cheaper. A climax came in 1849 with the trial of Guillaume Sayer, a Métis, charged by the Hudson's Bay Company with illegal fur trading. Sayer was found guilty, but in the face of a hostile demonstration by armed Métis at the courthouse, he was not imprisoned. The Company's monopoly over the economic life of Red River, it was now clear, had ended.

LE COMMERCE EST LIBRE[223]

An extract from the celebrated case of "Hudson's Bay Company versus Sayer." Alexander Ross gives an account of the trial which took place on May 17, 1849:

At the moment Sayer entered [the courthouse], about twenty of the half-breeds, all armed, took

Fort Garry

up their station at the courthouse door, as senti-
nels. . . . At the outer gate of the court-yard,
about fifty others were placed as a guard, and
couriers kept in constant motion going the rounds,
and conveying intelligence of the proceedings in
court to the main party outside, so that a moment's warning, had anything gone wrong a rush
was to have been made to rescue Sayer . . . from
the fangs of the law. . . . Sayer confessed the fact
that he did trade furs from an Indian. A verdict
of guilty was recorded against him, upon which
Sayer proved that a gentleman named Harriott,
connected with the fur trade, had given him
permission to traffic, and on this pretext he was
discharged. . . .
. . . one of the jurymen, on reaching the court
door, gave three hearty cheers, and in a stentorian
voice bawled out, "Le Commerce est libre! Le
commerce est libre! Vive la liberté!" . . .

Henceforth, the colony carried on unhampered
trade with St. Paul. Now the tripmen — those
engaged in the transport of freight in cart-trains
— traveled the seven hundred miles of prairie
roads to and from St. Paul. In time, steamboats,
such as the *Anson Northrup,* plied the waters of
the Red River to the Forks.

From the beginning, the Red River Settlement
had a duality in population, language, religion and
education. In 1818, St. Boniface was established
as a Roman Catholic mission. The Church hoped
to stabilize the semi-nomadic Métis, but the nature
of their existence, dictated by the buffalo hunt,
forced the priest to follow the hunter. Within the
settlement, the Church ministered to its French-
speaking parishioners and ran the mission school
which, by 1827, became the College of St.
Boniface. Education of girls began in the 1820's
with instruction in wool carding, weaving and
household arts. By the 1840's, the teaching orders
— the Grey Nuns for girls and the Oblate Fathers
for boys — supplied the teachers for the French-
Catholic schools.

The first Anglican school was established in
1815 by John Matheson. He stayed only for a
short while because his work was disrupted by
the North West Company. In 1820, Reverend
John West came to Rupert's Land and established an Anglican mission and ministered to the
needs of the colonists. Anglican missions, such as

St. John's and St. Andrew's, spread down the river bank from Fort Douglas. St. John's school was established in 1827, became the Red River Academy in 1833 and evolved into St. John's College in 1849. Although these schools were associated with the Anglican Church, they were private ventures. Only the mission schools for Indian and half-breed children were church supported. It was also in 1849 that the Presbyterians started a school in a private home. This school was maintained by voluntary contributions on a sliding scale according to ability to pay.

MERIT RATING FOR TEACHERS IN THE RED RIVER COLONY[224]

. . . . Certificated teachers were, of course, unheard of, and besides oral examinations attended by the whole district, the matter of the success or failure of a teacher was decided by the inspection and report of the trustees aforesaid. As these trustees were for the most part "plain, blunt men," whose . . . "dialect" was more or less affected by Gaelic, Salteaux, Cree and French influences, the lot of the teacher was not always a happy one. When Inkster [founder of the Presbyterian school] was teaching in '49, the trustees came in to inspect, and one of them gave to the leading class in the school the word "pekilar" to spell. It had never been heard of up to that time, and so proved a "poser" for the whole class from head to foot, whereupon the trustee grew somewhat indignant and threatened to dismiss the teacher whose leading class could not spell "pekilar." The teacher, however, asked to see the word, and saved his official head by pointing out that it was pronounced "peculiar," which latter word was triumphantly spelled by the class, who thus vindicated the scholarly attainments of their teacher.

During this time, Lord Selkirk, and later the Council of Assiniboia, recognized the duality of religion and language. The two separate school systems developed and they were equally supported by the Hudson's Bay Company and the Council of Assiniboia. This duality of religion, language and education was accepted, recognized and carried on when Manitoba became a province.

For half a century the Pacific Northwest had been the scene of rivalry for furs among the Hudson's Bay Company and the companies from the United States and Russia. By the Convention of 1818, the British and American governments had agreed to joint occupancy of the territory north of the Columbia River. In 1825, Russia agreed to restrict its sphere of influence to territory north of latitude 50°40′. Dr. John McLoughlin, Chief Factor for the British Company, promoted the idea of agriculture and settlement as well as the fur trade, in the hope of resisting American economic advance. Farm products were even raised for sale to the Russian traders, whose claims on the coast were not considered a threat. The policy of diversification failed, however, and the declining fur trade was an insubstantial basis for permanent occupation.

In 1846 the Oregon Treaty fixed the northern limits of the United States at the forty-ninth parallel. Growing numbers of Americans had followed the "Oregon Trail" to settle in the region above the Columbia River. As part of its orderly retreat, the Hudson's Bay Company co-operated with the British government in establishing Vancouver Island as a Crown Colony in 1849.

Not until immigrants began arriving after 1849 did the need for education arise. The Anglican chaplain in the employ of the Hudson's Bay Company arrived in 1849 and was paid to provide a stern form of instruction for the children of the Company employees. Then the efforts of Governor James Douglas persuaded the Company to pay a schoolmaster's salary for a boys' school at Victoria in 1852. In the following fifteen years, several denominational schools on Vancouver Island, including schools for girls, were superseded by non-sectarian ones. However, problems of organization, financing and staff continued to plague both the Island and Mainland for some years to come.

THE BEGINNING OF SCHOOLS IN BRITISH COLUMBIA[225]

James Douglas (later Sir) was first Governor of Vancouver Island, later of British Columbia.

. . . . Elementary schools were needed, Douglas wrote . . . to provide "a proper moral and religious training" and to prevent children from "growing up in ignorance and the utter neglect of all their duties to God and to Society". For each of two schools "intended for the children of the labouring and poorer classes", he asked the Company to find "a middle-aged married couple . . . of strictly religious principles and unblemished character capable of giving a good sound English education and nothing more". By persuading the Company to pay the salary of the schoolmaster and the parents to pay an annual fee, he succeeded in opening a boys' day school at Victoria and a girls' day school at Colwood Farm in 1852. . . . In [1853] . . . after children of miners at Nanaimo were discovered by Douglas to be "growing up in ignorance of their duties as Christians and as men", a school was opened at the mines.

At mid-century, when the gold rush originating in California extended to the Fraser River Valley in the 1850's, the stage was set for the "birth of British Columbia." Gold attracted fortune hunters, many of whom remained to establish a permanent British — and ultimately Canadian — claim on the Pacific.

V

THE CREATION OF A NATION:
1849-1867

The concept of a united British North America did not originate with the Fathers of Confederation: it was almost as old as the British rule in Canada. Not until the 1860's however, did circumstances favour serious efforts for implementing such a union. In all the colonies, stresses from within and pressures from without had created problems whose solutions were too difficult for any one colony. While the Maritimes considered their own regional legislative union as a way out, the United Province of Canada sought a wider union embracing all British North America.

Confederation emerged as the only plan capable of meeting the challenge of the time. Colonial leaders were influenced in their acceptance of the scheme by a variety of considerations: political deadlock in Canada, economic conditions, the need for railways, opportunities for politicians in a larger union, fear of aggression from the United States and pressure by the British government. There was also a genuine desire to keep the British North American colonies within the Empire. To some, Confederation meant eventual nationhood.

The Fathers of Confederation included some capable and colourful personalities. John A. Macdonald — the political manager — was acknowledged by his colleagues as the driving force behind Confederation and history has confirmed this judgment. George Brown — the champion of Upper Canadian Protestants — was statesman enough to join his political and religious opponents and break the political deadlock. George E. Cartier — the pacifier of French-Canadian fears — overcame French-Canadian reluctance and brought Canada East into the union. Alexander T. Galt — the financial expert — drew up the economic blueprint for Confederation. D'Arcy McGee — the eloquent orator — stimulated men to think of a glorious nation from the Atlantic to the Pacific. Dr. Charles Tupper — the crafty politician — successfully withstood concerted opposition to Confederation in Nova Scotia. Leonard Tilley — the promoter of Confederation in unpredictable New Brunswick — overcame personal political defeat and led his province into the union.

Equally capable and colourful opponents of union also played their part in the Confederation drama. Antoine A. Dorion — the relentless French-Canadian nationalist — saw Confederation as an Anglo-Saxon plot to sub-jugate French Canada. Joseph Howe — the formidable Nova Scotian nation-alist and imperialist — was determined not to sacrifice his beloved Nova Scotia for the sake of Canada. But the sincerity and skill of the critics were no match for the political ingenuity and tactical advantages of the pro-Confederationists. Nor were the obstacles to Confederation as great as the forces in its favour.

The British North America Act, an Act of the British Parliament, made Confederation a reality. The Act created a federal system in which British parliamentary institutions would function in both the central and provincial governments. The division of powers between the federal and pro-vincial governments was made in such a way as to ensure the authority of the central government. Thus the Fathers of Confederation hoped to preserve federal powers against future provincial challenges which might disrupt the union.

The B.N.A. Act was not intended as a complete "written" constitution, nor was it expected to prevail unaltered for all time. Yet the Act, together with British and Canadian traditions, other statutes and legal decisions has served as a flexible constitution for over a hundred years.

17

CONFEDERATION:
ITS BACKGROUND AND ACHIEVEMENT

A

POLITICAL DEADLOCK

During the struggle for responsible government, organized political parties in the modern sense did not exist. But the advocates of governmental reform, called the Reform Party, were united by their cause. Similarly, their opponents, the Tories, found common ground in their opposition to reform. Once responsible government had been achieved, the basis for these political groupings disappeared. Consequently, the 1850's was a time of peculiar political alignments. Out of the confusion emerged a radical group in both Canada West and Canada East, and a politically conservative organization — an amalgamation of Tories and moderates from both sections of the Province of Canada.

In Upper Canada, while the moderate reformers followed the more conservative program of Hincks and Morin — successors to Baldwin and Lafontaine — the radicals associated with the Clear Grits. This new agrarian party in Upper Canada came under the leadership of George Brown in the late 1850's. Their program stressed more democratic government and opposition to "big business" and French-Canadian "domination." In Lower Canada, the radicals — known as *Rouges* — followed the lead of A. A. Dorion. Although similarly opposed to English commercial interests — Grand Trunk Railway, Bank of Montreal and the land companies — the *Rouges* drew support from French-Canadian nationalists intent upon preserving their way of life.

VIEWS ON GEORGE BROWN AND HIS CLEAR GRITS[226]

[a]*Historian J. M. S. Careless:*

. . . [Brown's] opposition to Roman Catholic "threats" was not the simple anti-Popery of the Orange Order. It went back to his belief in the total separation of church and state. . . . Churches should keep free of state entanglements, and neither accept public grants nor seek special legislation to support their own denominational schools. Still further, the principle of the separation of church and state was an integral part of Brown's political Liberalism. . . .

[b]*Historian F. H. Underhill:*

For the essential thing about the *Globe* and the movement it led is that it represented the aspirations and the general outlook on life of the pioneer Upper Canadian farmer. The "Clear Grit" party in Upper Canada was an expression of the "frontier" in our Canadian politics. . . . Though Brown himself sat for one of the Toronto seats from 1857 to 1861, the Grits never succeeded in capturing the main urban centres. Toronto, London, Hamilton, and Kingston pretty steadily elected supporters of the Macdonald-Cartier coalition.

Neither faction could ever by itself control the Assembly, yet the stubborn stand of each seemed to rule out effective co-operation in forming a government.

The Liberal-Conservative Party, which created Confederation, developed under the leadership of practical men like John A. Macdonald of Upper Canada and G. E. Cartier in Lower Canada. Trained in law and business, they worked to realize the commercial potentialities of the St. Lawrence trading community. Macdonald was instrumental in bringing together the various groups with a financial stake in the Province of Canada. In Upper Canada, Sir Allan Macnab, the extreme Tory, and Macdonald, the moderate conservative, joined their followers of Upper Canada with

Sir John A. Macdonald

Sir George Etienne Cartier

Cartier's Lower Canadian moderate conservative *Bleus* to form the Liberal-Conservative Party.

The Liberal-Conservative Party, although a conglomeration of special interest groups, was kept in power because it managed to keep the government in operation. English conservatives co-operated with groups which would advance the commercial development of the St. Lawrence. Sufficient numbers of French Canadians saw that alignment with English conservatives would be commercially beneficial and would safeguard French-Canadian privileges. Both had to abandon ingrained prejudices — the English had to give up their desire to submerge the French-Canadian Catholic society, and the French Canadians had to shed their resistance to English commercial ambitions.

GEORGE CARTIER REJECTS "REP. BY POP."[227]

From a speech to the Legislative Assembly, June 9, 1858:

Did Upper Canada conquer Lower Canada? If not, by virtue of what right can it ask for representation based on population in the aim of governing us? Everyone knows that the union of the two provinces was imposed on Lower Canada

which did not want it at any price. But Lower Canada has carried out the Union loyally and sincerely with the determination of upholding it on the present basis.

———

I have indeed ascertained the aim of the Honourable member from Toronto [Brown] in proposing representation based on population. He demands it with the great clamour because he hopes thereby to produce for himself enough supporters to control Lower Canada. . . .

———

. . . I may say, in the name of all the members from Lower Canada, except one, that Lower Canada will adopt other political institutions before accepting the yoke of a man like the Honourable member from Toronto.

The Clear Grits and *Rouges* found political co-operation more difficult. The Clear Grits, who often commanded a majority in Canada West, lacked the Lower-Canadian allies necessary to form a government in the United Province. Brown's insistence on Rep. by Pop. and his adamant anti-French attitude hindered effective co-operation with the *Rouges*. Furthermore, the anti-clerical tendencies of the *Rouges* drove moderates into the camp of the Liberal-Conservatives

Hon. George Brown

A. A. Dorion

The presence of independent members — "loose fish" — in the Legislative Assembly complicated the intricate political alignments. Because of their slender majorities, ministries often had to rely on the support of independents, who frequently held the balance of power in the Assembly. Concessions and special privileges had to be granted to gain such support. At best, it was difficult to control the "loose fish" and to assure a stable majority; a shift of their allegiance could very well bring a government to defeat.

There was another difficulty — the practice of Double Majority. Although the Act of Union gave the United Province a single legislature, in reality the Act assured a dual system based on racial groups. Each ministry had not one but two leaders — one each from Canada East and Canada West. The custom developed that on important issues a majority from each section had to be obtained. Thus a majority in either section could check the demands of the other. Sectional conflict often blocked necessary legislation and brought government to a standstill.

The political instability which developed, especially in the 1860's, led to political deadlock which paved the way to Confederation. The Assembly of the Province of Canada during the years 1849 to 1864 became a forum for political manipulation. But not even the deftness of a Macdonald or a Cartier could do more than postpone the day when a new governmental framework would have to be created.

THE POLITICAL DEADLOCK[228]

[a]*John A. Macdonald speaks of the political deadlock.* CONFEDERATION DEBATES, *February 6, 1865:*

. . . . We had election after election, — we had ministry after ministry, — with the same result. Parties were so equally balanced, that the vote of one member might decide the fate of the Administration, and the course of legislation for a year or a series of years. This condition of things was well calculated to arouse the earnest consideration of every lover of his country, and I am happy to say it had that effect. None were more impressed by this momentous state of affairs, and the grave apprehensions that existed of a state of anarchy destroying our credit, destroying our prosperity, destroying our progress, than were the members of this present House; and the leading statesmen on both sides seemed to have come to the common conclusion, that some step must be taken to relieve the country from the deadlock and impending anarchy that hung over us. —

[b]*Prof. Frank H. Underhill discusses the economic reason for political deadlock:*

. . . The essence of the struggle which produced the political deadlock of the 1860's. . . . It was primarily a struggle of West against East; the then West being, like the modern West, in its social structure largely agricultural and its geographical position a long way from its markets;

and the East, then as now, being dominated by the transportation, banking and manufacturing interests which centred in Montreal.

The Lafontaine-Baldwin ministry, 1849-1851, a Reform government, managed to institute some worthwhile legislation. It did reform the system of elementary education and turn King's College, an Anglican institution, into the non-sectarian University of Toronto. The Hincks-Morin ministry that followed, also a Reform government, is best remembered for the promotion of the Grand Trunk Railway.

After the elections of 1854, no group had a clear majority. Through the efforts of J. A. Macdonald in Canada West, and Cartier in Canada East, the moderate conservative forces brought the Macnab-Morin ministry into being — the first of a series of such political alliances that characterized the pre-Confederation period. Sir Allan Macnab, a Family Compact man, joined forces with Morin, the Reformer, to put the Liberal-Conservatives in power and keep the radical Clear Grits out of office. Changes within the ministry took place. Morin gave way to Etienne Pascal Taché to form the Macnab-Taché government. In 1856, J. A. Macdonald replaced Macnab, and in 1857, Cartier replaced Taché and the Macdonald-Cartier ministry resulted. One fact was becoming clear — J. A. Macdonald was the real leader in Canada West and G. E. Cartier his counterpart in Canada East.

In the election of 1857, the Clear Grits' majority in Canada West was more than matched by the success of the *Bleus* in Canada East. The Macdonald-Cartier ministry was returned. Canada was going through a depression, and the government had to subsidize the Grand Trunk Railway to keep it operating. Brown attacked this move as proof of alliance between government and private industry and deplored the practice of such subsidies to strengthen the power of the already powerful financial interests. But it was the question of the location of the capital city that toppled the government in 1858. The likely choice for the capital was either Toronto or Quebec. In the Assembly, opinion was divided on sectional lines, and the matter was referred to Queen Victoria. She chose Ottawa. The Assembly was displeased with the choice and passed a resolution of regret. The government regarded this as a vote of non-confidence and resigned.

The Clear Grits and the *Rouges,* unlikely allies, formed the Brown-Dorion ministry. It lacked support and lasted only two days. The Liberal-Conservatives returned to office and, by a devious political manoeuvre that became known as the "Double Shuffle,"* the Cartier-Macdonald ministry was reconstituted. Alexander Tilloch Galt, a successful Montreal financier deeply involved in railways, transportation and land speculation, entered the cabinet. His conditions for entry were that Canada would consider federation of all the provinces and would build an intercolonial railway connecting Canada with the Maritime colonies. The same year, he and Cartier went to London to seek British aid for these projects. The Colonial Office displayed no interest in the scheme. The protective tariffs which Galt had recently introduced were one of the major reasons for the British government's unresponsive attitude towards Canada's request. Furthermore, the Colonial Office suspected federation as Macdonald's device to rescue his government from local political difficulties.

MACDONALD'S INVITATION TO GALT TO BECOME A CONSERVATIVE[229]

November 2, 1857, from Toronto:
My dear Galt:
. . . . You call yourself a Rouge. There may have been at one time a reddish tinge about you, but I could observe it becoming by degrees fainter. In fact you are like Byron's Dying Dolphin, exhibiting a series of colours — "the last still loveliest" — and that last is "true blue", being the colour I affect.

Seriously, you would made a decent Conservative, if you gave your own judgment a fair chance and cut loose from Holton and Dorion and those other beggars. So pray do become true blue at once: it is a good standing colour and bears washing.

Yours always,
John A. Macdonald.

---

* According to a normal British practice, a cabinet minister, upon receiving a new portfolio, resigned his seat in the legislature and sought re-election. Because of the frequent changes of ministries, Canada had adopted an act which allowed a minister, under certain conditions, to change portfolios without a by-election. Macdonald took advantage of this act to recall the entire cabinet. Macdonald first gave his men different offices, but within two days "shuffled" them back to their original posts. Thus he avoided having some of his chief members absent from the Assembly and prevented the risks of defeat by the Opposition.

The action was legal but left a bad taste. Many felt that Macdonald had used undue political trickery to discredit Brown and keep the Liberal-Conservatives in office.

The Clear Grits, too, adopted federal union of the Canadas as part of their platform. Other ideas favoured at their Convention of 1859, included annexation of the Northwest, a redivision of Canada into two provinces and Rep. by Pop. Writing in the *Globe*, Brown — never one subject to restraint — bluntly stated that federation would "at once draw the teeth and cut the claws of Lower Canada." The Grit leader saw in a federal system the ideal formula for subordinating French Canada forever. A provincial government would give Canada West control of its own local affairs; the federal Parliament based on Rep. by Pop. would give English Canada control of national affairs; annexation of the Northwest would give Canada West room for unlimited expansion.

THE GRIT CONVENTION, NOV. 9, 1859[230]

George Sheppard advocated "dissolution of the union" which meant to split the United Province back into its original components:

. . . . I want to know how you are to carry federation with the consent of Lower Canada — especially when it is based on the recognition of the principle of representation by population? But suppose Lower Canada says we won't grant you federation, what are you to do? Are you to continue under this union because Lower Canada says you shall? I put it to the advocates of federation if dissolution is not their only alternative?

―――――

George Brown's argument against dissolution and for federation:

. . . [federation] would secure us free access to the ocean and every facility for trading with Lower Canada — while dissolution would place us in both respects at the mercy of Lower Canada. Are you content to hand over the entire control of the St. Lawrence, to have custom-house officers stopping our railroad cars and our steamers at certain points in their downward journey and overhauling all the passengers as if entering a foreign country? . . .

In the election of 1861, the Cartier-Macdonald government was returned with a slight majority. The eruption of the American Civil War, meanwhile, had produced incidents which irritated American-British relations. The Cartier-Macdonald government attempted to bolster Canadian defence by introducing the Militia Bill of 1862. The French-Canadian members in the Assembly balked at the proposed expenditure of half a million dollars and defeated the bill. The government resigned.

The government passed into the hands of the moderate Reformers led by John Sandfield Macdonald, a Catholic from Canada West, and L. V. Sicotte, of Canada East. The new ministry pushed through the Separate Schools Act for Canada West without the support of the majority of the Upper-Canadian members. This government had violated the principle of Double Majority. The resulting criticism of the government's action prompted the dissolution of the Assembly. Dorion replaced Sicotte, and in the election that followed, the Sandfield Macdonald-Dorion ministry was successful. In 1864, because of lack of support in the Assembly, the government resigned. Sir Etienne Pascal Taché and John A Macdonald formed a Conservative government. Within three months it collapsed.

A dozen ministries in fifteen years, two elections and four ministries between 1861 and 1864 seemed to demonstrate the futility of government in the United Province. Sectional conflict, racial and religious division, frequent shuffling of ministries, the awkward practice of Double Majority and the unpredictable independent members — all contributed to instability. Affairs of state had reached an impasse and government had bogged down in political dissension.

At this point of crisis, the Great Coalition — an event of far-reaching importance — came into being. Brown persuaded the Assembly to set up a committee to analyze the reasons for the political deadlock. As a result of the committee's findings and the constant encouragement of Lord Monck, the Governor, leaders of the Clear Grits and the Liberal Conservatives, in spite of their long-standing differences, agreed that they must co-operate in order to form a durable coalition government. George Brown again eased the way by entering into a coalition with Macdonald and Cartier, his bitter political opponents.

THE GREAT COALITION[231]

George Brown explains his reasons for entering into a coalition in a speech to the Assembly, June 22, 1864:

. . . . For ten years I have stood opposed to the Hon. gentleman opposite in the most hostile manner it is possible to conceive of public men arrayed against each other in the political arena . . . if a crisis has even arisen in the political affairs of any country which would justify such a coalition as has taken place, such a crisis has arrived in the history of Canada . . . party alliances are one thing and the interests of my country are another. . . .

... if I never have any other parliamentary success than that which I have achieved this day in having brought about the formation of a Government more powerful than any Canadian Government that ever existed before, pledged to settle, and to settle forever, the alarming sectional difficulties of my country, I would have desired no greater honour for my children to keep years hence in their remembrance than that I had a hand, however humble, in the accomplishment of that great work. . . .

Macdonald's skillful diplomacy welded the coalition into a workable team. But Brown and Cartier were the men directly responsible for the creation of the coalition. Without the adherence of either the Grits or the *Bleus* a coalition would have been impossible. The Brown-Macdonald-Cartier government, in which the Grits were given three seats in the cabinet, was formed. This strong government, capable of commanding a majority in the Assembly, set out to make Confederation a reality.

B

PROBLEMS OF TRADE

British North America, like other colonies in the Empire, enjoyed many benefits within Britain's mercantilist system. From the time of the Napoleonic Wars, British preference for colonial goods helped establish timber and wheat as new British North American staples for export. The favourable reception of colonial products in the United Kingdom between 1815 and 1850 stimulated British North American economic expansion.

Canada's privileged position was enhanced in the 1840's by a British preference on flour shipped from Canada. Heavy capital investments were made in milling facilities, which sprang up almost overnight in port towns and cities along the St. Lawrence. Even American grain was bought for Canadian mills to meet the ever increasing British demand for flour. The milling industry and the flour export trade soon became an important part of the Canadian economy.

But is was not too long before the Canadian economy got a severe blow. Rapid industrialization forced Britain to seek expanded markets for her surplus manufactured goods. Free trade — a sharp departure from mercantilism — to increase foreign trade was advanced by British industrialists. The population growth in the United Kingdom and the potato famine in Ireland added further pressure for removal of import duties. In 1846, Sir Robert Peel's administration repealed the Corn Laws. Reduction of duties on wheat, to bring in low-priced grain, was followed by the reduction of duties on other primary products — the very colonial exports which had enjoyed preferential treatment. Britain had embarked on a course of free trade and abandoned her mercantilist system.

The partial loss of colonial preference reduced Canada's export trade and caused an economic depression. Colonial wheat and timber had to compete in an open market with products from other countries. Resulting low prices and shrinking markets made agriculture unprofitable, and many hard-working farmers abandoned their farms to start life anew in the American West. The newly-constructed flour mills became idle, and the railway boom that accompanied the prosperity of the 1840's came to a temporary halt.

The milling, transportation and timber enterprises — all in the hands of powerful financial interests — suffered heavy financial losses. Canada's commercial leaders — usually Tories and self-appointed "guardians" of the British connection — now felt abandoned by the mother country. These selfsame "loyal" Tories, who had once unhesitatingly smeared their liberal opponents as republican traitors, drew up the Annexation Manifesto in 1849.

Lord Elgin viewed the annexationist sentiments of Canadian businessmen with alarm. He firmly believed that only reciprocity with the United States, affording opportunities for trade, would prevent annexation to the United States. Shortly after the Corn Laws were repealed, Canada had made unsuccessful overtures to the United States for reciprocity. Now, Canada again looked for better trade relations with her prosperous neighbour to the south. Here was a potential market which could supplement Canada's dwindling trade with Britain. But the United States, to protect her infant industries, had erected tariff barriers. The problem for Canada was how to penetrate these tariff barriers and enter the American market.

ANNEXATIONIST SENTIMENTS IN CANADA[232]

From a letter by Lord Elgin to Lord Grey, March 14, 1849:

There has been a vast deal of talk about 'annexation', as is unfortunately always the case here

London Bazaar: Victoria, B.C., c. 1860

when there is anything to agitate the public mind. If half the talk on this subject were sincere, I should consider an attempt to keep up the connection with Great Britain as Utopian in the extreme. For no matter what the subject of complaint . . . annexation is invoked as the remedy for all ills, imaginary or real. A great deal of this talk is, however, bravado, and a great deal the mere product of thoughtlessness. Undoubtedly it is in some quarters the utterance of very sincere convictions; and if England will not make the sacrifices which are absolutely necessary to put the colonists here in as good a position commercially as the citizens of the States — in order to which *free navigation and reciprocal trade with the States are indispensable* — . . . the organs . . . of the Government and of the Peel party are always writing as if it were admitted fact that colonies, and more especially Canada, are a burden, to be endured only because they cannot be got rid of, the end may be nearer at hand than we wot it.

The fisheries of the Maritimes proved the deciding factor in securing reciprocity with the United States. The limited inshore fishing rights granted the United States in the Convention of 1818 had long been disputed by the Maritimes and the United States. Lord Elgin, representing the British government, personally conducted negotiations in Washington. He offered the United States wider privileges in the British North American fisheries in exchange for reciprocity. In 1854, he concluded the Reciprocity Treaty — an agreement for reciprocal trade between the United States and the British North American colonies.

The agreement was to run for ten years, after which it could be renewed or ended by either side. Either party could terminate the treaty by giving one year's notice. Most important to British North America, the agreement provided free entry for the natural products of each country into the markets of the other. In addition, both the United States and British North America gained free access to each other's fisheries. In exchange for free navigation by Canada on Lake Michigan, the United States obtained similar privileges on the St. Lawrence River.

Canadian grain and timber, as well as Maritime fish, timber and coal now had a new market. The early period of reciprocity coincided with the Crimean War, which created a European demand for Canadian wheat. British North America enjoyed an economic boom. Transportation and shipping, combined with feverish railway construction, gave employment to many; farming and fishing increased; and numerous lumber towns and sawmills sprang up in Canada, especially in Canada West.

The end of the Crimean War in 1856 aggravated the depression which had recently set in. To protect the recently established industries, the Canadian government in 1859 imposed the Galt Tariffs on goods entering Canada. Meanwhile, the American market, expanded by the Civil War which broke out in 1861, created additional demands for British North American goods.

Soon the bitterness of the Civil War and the unfriendly relations between Britain and the Northern States stirred American feelings against British North America. As early as 1862, shortly after the *Trent* affair, there was agitation in the North to end reciprocity. British North America, it was claimed, gained most of the benefits from the reciprocity agreement; indeed, the British colonies owed their prosperity to reciprocity. Many Americans in the North earnestly believed that an end to reciprocity would create such economic chaos that Canadians would gratefully welcome annexation to the United States. The American government, in 1865, indicated its intention to terminate the Reciprocity Treaty.

THE NEED FOR INTERCOLONIAL TRADE[233]

Alexander T. Galt saw in Confederation the means of instituting extensive intercolonial trade. CONFEDERATION DEBATES, *February 7, 1865:*

. . . . Intercolonial trade has been, indeed, of the most insignificant character; we have looked far more to our commercial relations with the neighbouring — though a foreign country, — than to the interchange of our own products, which would have retained the benefits of our trade within ourselves; hostile tariffs have interfered with the free interchange of the products of the labour of all the colonies, and one of the greatest and most immediate benefits to be derived from their union, will spring from the breaking down of these barriers and the opening up of the markets of all the provinces to the different industries of each. . . .

If we have reason to fear that one door [reciprocity with the United States] is about to be closed to our trade, it is the duty of the House to endeavor to open another; to provide against a coming evil of the kind feared by timely expansion in another direction; to seek by free trade with our own fellow-colonists for a continued and uninterrupted commerce which will not be liable to be disturbed at the capricious will of any foreign country. . . .

The unfriendly attitude both of the American government and of responsible American newspapers aroused Canadian fears that reciprocity would end, and with it the prosperity in British North America. The colonies intensified efforts to establish intercolonial trade in British North America to offset the loss of the British market and the impending loss of the American market. A union of the colonies could remove the tariffs and trade barriers which had in the past obstructed intercolonial trade. Furthermore, a unified nation would be in a better position to make commercial agreements with other countries and to attract the foreign investments so vital to national growth. Confederation seemed the only solution to the problems of trade.

ECONOMIC ASPECTS OF CONFEDERATION[234]

George Brown spoke of the economic advantages from Confederation. CONFEDERATION DEBATES, *February 8, 1865:*

. . . . I am persuaded that this union will inspire new confidence in our stability, and exercise the most beneficial influence on all our affairs. I believe it will raise the value of our public securities, that it will draw capital to our shores, and secure the prosecution of all legitimate enterprise. . . .

———

. . . . I go heartily for the union, because it will throw down the barriers of trade and give us the control of a market of four millions of people. What one thing has contributed so much to the wondrous material progress of the United States as the free passage of their products from one State to another? . . . . I am in favor of a union of the provinces . . . because it will make us the third maritime state of the world. When this union is accomplished, but two countries in the world will be superior in maritime influence to British America — and those are Great Britain and the United States. . . .

C

RAILWAYS

The St. Lawrence was a natural avenue for trade among the colonies. Yet, movement of goods all year-round required an overland link between Canada and the Maritimes. Freight railway across the vast wilderness that separated the St. Lawrence communities from the ports on the Atlantic had to travel on American lines. Because of the Civil War, the United States government was threatening to withdraw this privilege.

THE ADVANTAGES OF AN INTERCOLONIAL RAILWAY[235]

a*From speeches at a banquet in Halifax, September 12, 1864. George Etienne Cartier:*

. . . . Halifax through the intercolonial railroad will be the recipient of trade which now benefits Portland, Boston, and New York. . . . It is as evident as the sun shines at noon that when the intercolonial railway is built — and it must necessarily be built if that confederation takes place — the consequence will be that between Halifax and Liverpool there will be steamers almost daily leaving and arriving at the former — in fact it will be a ferry between Halifax and Liverpool. . . .

John A. Macdonald:

. . . this railway must be a national work, and Canada will cheerfully contribute to the utmost extent in order to make that important link, without which no political connection can be complete. What will be the consequence to this city, prosperous as it is, from that communication? Montreal is at this moment competing with New York for the trade of the great West. Build the road and Halifax will soon become one of the great emporiums of the world. All the great resources of the west will come over the immense railways of Canada to the bosom of your harbor. . . .

———

b*George Brown speaks of the need for a railway.* CONFEDERATION DEBATES, *February 8, 1865:*

. . . . I am in favor of this union because it will give us a sea-board at all seasons of the year. It is not to be denied that the position of Canada, shut off as she is from the sea-board during the winter months, is far from satisfactory — and should the United States carry out their insane threat of abolishing the bonding system, by which our merchandise passes free through their territory, it would be still more embarrassing. The

Maritime Provinces are equally cut off from communication inland. Now, this embarrassment will be ended by colonial union. The Intercolonial Railway will give us at all times access to the Atlantic through British territory. . . .

Another pressure for an intercolonial railway stemmed from the difficulties of the Grand Trunk Railway Company. During the railway boom of the 1850's, the Company had constructed rail lines between Sarnia and Rivière du Loup, west of Quebec City. Promoters had failed to anticipate the expenses of constructing and operating the Grand Trunk, and expected profits did not materialize. The threat of bankruptcy drove investors, both Canadian and British, to seek a way that would make the Grand Trunk a paying proposition. To start with, an extension of the railway from Canada to the Maritimes would bring increased traffic. Eventually, a transcontinental railway reaching from the Atlantic to the Pacific would carry freight from the Orient — a Northwest Passage on rails of steel. This was not an idle dream. In 1863, a company associated with the Grand Trunk Railway Company purchased the Hudson's Bay Company and thus controlled the western territory across which such a railway would run.

CONFEDERATION AS "A GRAND TRUNK JOB"[236]

A. A. Dorion saw "Big Business" behind Confederation. CONFEDERATION DEBATES, *February 16, 1865:*

. . . . This project [Intercolonial Railway] having failed, some other scheme had to be concocted for bringing aid and relief to the unfortunate Grand Trunk — and the Confederation of all the British North American Provinces naturally suggested itself to the Grand Trunk officials as the surest means of bringing with it the construction of the Intercolonial Railway. Such was the origin of the Confederation scheme. The Grand Trunk people are at the bottom of it; and I find that at the last meeting of the Grand Trunk Railway Company, Mr. WATKIN did in advance congratulate the shareholders and bondholders on the bright prospects opening before them, by the enhanced value to their shares and bonds, by the adoption of the Confederation scheme and the construction of the Intercolonial as part of the scheme. I repeat, sir, that representation by population had very little to do with bringing about this measure [Confederation]. . . .

A transcontinental railway had far-reaching implications. Extending the railway went hand in hand with the opening of the West to British immigrants and securing the land from American encroachment. Otherwise, the colonies at Red River and on the Pacific Coast, separated from each other and from eastern colonies by formidable geographic barriers, were in danger of succumbing to the pull of an expanding United States. The Americans were building another transcontinental railway which would run close to the 49th parallel and which would serve the people of British Columbia and of the Red River.

ANNEXATIONIST SENTIMENTS IN
BRITISH COLUMBIA[237]

From a letter to the BRITISH COLONIST *[1870]:*

It is the patriotic duty of British Columbia to assist the over-burdened taxpayer by casting herself off from the Mother Country. . . . We would feel at home with the United States. Without railways British Columbia might as well be confederated with the Pyramids of Egypt. Canada could not defend a Pacific province in case of war with the United States. Would you expect a Canadian Hannibal to lead an army across the mountains to our rescue?

The British government saw many advantages in an ambitious railway policy for British North America. Under pressure from British banking interests and the Grand Trunk promoters, by 1862 the Colonial Office indicated a willingness to guarantee a loan for the construction of an inter-colonial railway between Canada and the Maritimes. The problem of defence imparted further urgency to the project. A railway could carry troops from the Maritimes to Canada in the event of an emergency such as occurred in 1861, at the time of the *Trent* crisis.

A RAILWAY AS A MEANS FOR DEFENCE[238]

Alexander T. Galt, in a speech at Halifax, September 12, 1864:

. . . . But the railway is not to be looked upon as a question of cost, but as a bond of union that will unite us in peace and in time of need. . . . We can only trust that nothing may arise to break up the friendly relations that exist between us [Canada and the United States]; but at the same time, it is our duty to provide against all contingencies. If ill-feeling should arise, then the intercolonial railway would be of the highest importance to us. It would enable the strength of the Maritime Provinces to be available for Canada, and allow us to obtain that assistance from Great Britain which she will ever accord us when we need it. . . .

Disagreement between the British and colonial officials over a suitable route produced a temporary delay. But essentially the problem was financial. The costly railway projects required backing by either the British government or private British investors. The separate colonies were already drastically in debt over railway building; no single colony could attract the investment still needed. But a united British North America — which Confederation could accomplish — might gain British confidence for extensive railway construction. Confederation would, at least, provide a single colonial government with which the British could deal more effectively on railways and other important matters.

D

THE AMERICAN THREAT

The American Civil War threatened not only British North American trade but also the very fact of a British presence on the continent. Against a background of traditional American hostility toward European influence in the Western Hemisphere, relations between the United States and Great Britain deteriorated between the years 1861 and 1865. A series of incidents irritated the Northern States and fed an expansionist mood — the spirit of Manifest Destiny — which resumed with the victory over the South in 1865.

The United States government was, in fact, more occupied with reconstructing than expanding a nation. Nevertheless, statements in the

American press, and even in Congress, about annexation of the region to the north were enough to convince John A. Macdonald and D'Arcy McGee that a foreign danger existed. And no effective resistance seemed possible as long as the British North American provinces remained separated.

THE THREAT FROM THE UNITED STATES[239]

D'Arcy McGee's speech about the danger from the United States. CONFEDERATION DEBATES, *February 9, 1865:*

. . . . These are frightful figures [referring to the numbers of soldiers and guns possessed by the United States] for the capacity of destruction they represent, for the heaps of carnage that they represent, for the quantity of human blood spilt that they represent, for the lust of conquest that they represent, for the evil passions that they represent, and for the arrest of the onward progress of civilization that they represent. . . .

. . . . They [the United States] coveted Florida, and seized it; they coveted Louisiana, and purchased it; they coveted Texas and stole it; and then they picked a quarrel with Mexico, which ended by their getting California . . . had we not the strong arm of England over us, we would not now have had a separate existence. . . .

The *Trent* affair in 1861 dramatized the predicament of British North American defence as the colonies became caught in the strife between the United States and Great Britain. When two Southern agents were forcibly removed from the British steamer *Trent* in the Gulf of Mexico and taken captive aboard a ship of the American navy, public opinion in the United States was aroused. Demands for annexation of British North America prompted the British to dispatch nearly 14,000 troops to St. John, New Brunswick. With the St. Lawrence frozen and no railway connection to Canada, the troops had to make an arduous and time-consuming overland march; had an invasion occurred, the Province of Canada might have fallen before help arrived.

After further incidents had seemed to indicate the sympathy of British North Americans for the cause of the South (the Confederate States), the most serious episode of all occurred in the fall of 1864 — the St. Alban's raid. In October, while the Fathers of Confederation were meeting at Quebec for the second of the Confederation Conferences, a band of Southern soldiers attacked and robbed the town of St. Alban's, Vermont. Fleeing to Canadian soil, they were arrested and tried in Montreal; but the magistrate set them free. Charging that Canada could not police its own borders, the United States government threatened such action as terminating the Rush-Bagot Treaty of 1817 and placing gunboats on the Great Lakes and Lake Champlain.

MILITARY PREPAREDNESS IN THE FACE OF THREAT FROM THE UNITED STATES[240]

George Brown, in the CONFEDERATION DEBATES, *February 8, 1865:*

. . . . But not only do our changed relations towards the Mother Country call on us to assume the new duty of military defence — our changed relations towards the neighboring Republic compel us to do so. For myself, I have no belief that the Americans have the slightest thought of attacking us. . . . But . . . there is no better mode of warding off war when it is threatened, than to be prepared for it if it comes. The Americans are now a warlike people. They have large armies, a powerful navy, an unlimited supply of warlike munitions, and the carnage of war has to them been stript of its horrors. The American side of our lines already bristles with works of defence, and unless we are willing to live at the mercy of our neighbors, we, too, must put our country in a state of efficient preparation. War or no war — the necessity of placing these provinces in a thorough state of defence can no longer be postponed. . . . And how can we do this so efficiently and economically as by the union now proposed? . . . .

When the Civil War ended in the spring of 1865, what was there to prevent a battle-hardened United States army from conquering British North America? The Fenian raids in 1866 showed that the British colonies had good reason to wonder. The Fenians, whose ranks included Civil War veterans, were Irish-Americans intent on striking a blow at "British tyranny" by conquering Canada. The raids along the Niagara River and the New Brunswick border, which the United States government did little to stop, could hardly be considered an invasion. Yet the fact that marauders, lacking both numbers and organization, could terrorize border communities was an indication of how vulnerable the British North American provinces were. Union could mean both a stronger and more efficient militia for home defence and a stronger voice in dealing with Washington.

Fear of losing the West was perhaps the most realistic reason for concern about the United

Military Review, Champ de Mars, Quebec, c. 1864

States. Promoters of the Grand Trunk Railway saw a railway to the Pacific giving them Oriental trade that would save the company from bankruptcy. At the same time the prairies would be opened to British and Canadian settlement. A railway and a growing population would help preserve the West for the Empire at a time when American settlers were moving westward. In addition to the practical reasons, the idea of a Canada stretching "from sea to sea" was beginning to fire the imaginations of the George Browns and the D'Arcy McGees.

What was to be done about the isolated prairie region, stretching for hundreds of miles between the lakes and barren bushland of the Canadian Shield and the Rockies? The Hudson's Bay Company could not preserve it much longer for the fur trade alone, although as long as its monopoly continued the Company would discourage immigration. Yet the Company's monopoly was not a guarantee of either law and order or of resistance to American advance. Settlers at Red River found the rule of a commercial company unsuited to the needs of a growing community, and began to demand changes and even union with Canada. But Red River was developing a dependence on the American centres of Minneapolis and St. Paul for supplies, trade and transportation. By the 1860's the possibility of annexation by the Americans was very real. The alternative was to transfer control of the territory to a government of unified

British North American colonies. Such a government could raise the money to purchase the Hudson's Bay Company's monopoly and, perhaps, extend control over the land.

Especially difficult was the problem of preserving the two British crown colonies on the Pacific Coast — British Columbia and Vancouver Island. The gold rush of the 1850's in the Fraser River valley had brought a temporary prosperity to the area. Governor James Douglas of Vancouver Island extended his authority to the Fraser, where he maintained law and order and supervised such vital public works as the Cariboo Road. His policy was confirmed by the British decision to make British Columbia a crown colony in 1858. However, the cost of building roads and providing other essential services meant that the colonial governments accumulated considerable debts, which remained to be paid when the boom subsided and most of the gold-seekers departed.

THE DANGER OF LOSING BRITISH COLUMBIA
TO THE UNITED STATES[241]

As expressed in the WEEKLY BRITISH COLONIST, *Victoria, B.C., April 30, 1867:*

In writing thus, we know we speak the mind of nine out of every ten men in the Colony — men who after struggling for years to awaken the Home Government to a sense of the wrongs under the

Barkerville, Interior of B.C., c. 1860

weight of which we are staggering, have at last sat down in despair at the gloomy prospects before them. . . . The people — disgusted, disheartened and all but ruined — are loud in their expression of a preference for the stars and stripes. The sentiment is heard on every street corner — at the theatre — in the saloons . . . and the feeling is growing and spreading daily.

The British government simplified administration and reduced its expense by joining the two colonies as British Columbia, with Victoria as the capital, in 1866. But the danger of the United States expanding northward through settlement, as it had done in Oregon Territory, was ever present. Closer economic ties with the Pacific Northwest of the United States promised prosperity to the colony. A strong annexationist movement was developing among settlers, who felt neglected by the British authorities and isolated from the rest of British North America. Confederation, and the construction of a transcontinental railway, could provide the link between east and west and serve the interests of men on both sides of the continent.

E

CONFEDERATION ACHIEVED

The failure of the 1841 legislative union in the Province of Canada, where political deadlock was the result, did not deter the Maritimes from considering such a union for themselves. The British government regarded Maritime union as a possible preliminary step to a wider union and, therefore, approved an initiative by Nova Scotia to arrange a conference. Favourable resolutions were passed by the legislatures of Nova Scotia and New Brunswick. The selection of Charlottetown as the site of the meeting induced Prince Edward Island to follow suit.

When the delegates convened on September 1, 1864, they were joined by eight members of Canada's coalition cabinet, led by John A. Macdonald and Georges Cartier. Through the co-operation of

Charlottetown Conference, September 1864

Canada's Governor, Lord Monck, and the Colonial Secretary, the Canadian representatives had sought and obtained an invitation to state their arguments for a larger association of British North American colonies. They arrived in Charlottetown with hope of success aroused not only by the official British attitude, but also by the friendly reception they expected and received. A hundred Canadian politicians (including D'Arcy McGee), businessmen and journalists had just completed a tour of Maritime centres in August. The social encounters between people of both regions had lowered barriers and made co-operation more likely.

THE CHARLOTTETOWN CONFERENCE[242]

George Brown's letter to his wife about the Charlottetown Conference, September 13, 1864, from Halifax:

Our party from Quebec consisted of Cartier, John A. [Macdonald], Galt, McDougall, Campbell, Langevin, McGee and myself. . . . We had great fun coming down the St. Lawrence — having fine weather, a broad awning to recline under, excellent stores of all kinds, an unexceptionable cook, lots of books, chessboards, backgammon, and so forth. . . .

. . . . Having dressed ourselves in correct style, our two boats were lowered man-of-war fashion — and being each duly manned with four oarsmen and a boatswain, dressed in blue uniforms, hats, belts, etc., in regular style, we pulled away for shore and landed like Mr. Christopher Columbus who had the precedence of us in taking possession of portions of the American continent. . . .

The Canadians used well-prepared arguments to point out the advantages of the larger union over the Maritime plan. Economic growth through expanded markets and increased investment, aid for completing an intercolonial railway, improved defence and greater opportunity for Maritime politicians were attractive possibilities of the Canadian plan. Maritime union was consequently set aside, and the delegates agreed to meet at Quebec to examine more fully the advantages and problems of a union of all British North America.

GEORGE BROWN ASKS THE MARITIMES TO JOIN CONFEDERATION[243]

From a speech delivered at a banquet in Halifax, September 12, 1864:

. . . . It has been said . . . that we only come now seeking union with these provinces to escape from our sectional difficulties at home . . . the existing coalition was formed expressly for the purpose of settling justly and permanently the constitutional relations between Upper and Lower Canada. . . . We are pledged as a government to place before parliament at its next session a bill giving effect to the conditions of our compact. . . . You will therefore clearly perceive that we have not come here to seek relief from our trouble, — for the remedy of our grievances is already agreed upon, — and come what may of the larger scheme now before us, our smaller scheme will certainly be accomplished. Our sole object in coming here is to say to you: 'We are about to amend our constitution; and before finally doing so, we invite you to enter with us frankly and earnestly into the inquiry whether it would not be for the advantage of all the British American Colonies to be embraced under one political system. Let us look the whole question steadily in the face: if we find it advantageous let us act upon it; but if not, let the whole thing drop . . . .'

The Quebec Conference, beginning on October 10, was attended by delegates from all the Atlantic colonies, including Newfoundland, and the Cabinet ministers of Canada's coalition government. To promote frank discussion and to prevent revealing, as far as possible, any serious divisions which might develop, the delegates decided to follow the practice of cabinet secrecy and closed the meetings to the public and the newspapers.

The politicians were only too well aware of the many formidable obstacles to union, including the diverse and often antagonistic demands of the different regions, tariff barriers among the provinces, strong local pride and the fear of every colony or culture that it might lose more than it would gain. The pressures for union were immediate and forceful, but only a spirit of compromise and patience could make possible the creation of a national system of government that could accommodate the aspirations of French Canadians, the individuality of Prince Edward Island, the urge of Upper Canadians for westward expansion and all the other special interests.

The nature of the union was the fundamental question. John A. Macdonald was the principal advocate of a legislative union, which would provide one government sovereign over all affairs not under the jurisdiction of the British government. He was deeply concerned about the importance of a strong government that could ensure the endurance of the union. The United States, he believed, was suffering a terrible civil war because it had a federal system in which the states had too much power and the central government too little. French-Canadian spokesmen, such as Cartier, were opposed, however, on the grounds that their rights of law, language and religion would be in jeopardy. Prince Edward Island, and the other Atlantic colonies too, protested that their interests and ways of life could not be protected under a unitary system. Only a federation of provinces, each with its own government for local affairs and a central government to administer matters of common concern, held the promise of joining together an area so large and diverse as British North America.

THE NATURE OF THE UNION[244]

ªJohn A. Macdonald saw the need for a strong central government, October 12, 1864:

. . . . In framing the constitution, care should be taken to avoid the mistakes and weaknesses of the United States' system, the primary error of which was the reservation to the different States of all powers not delegated to the General Government. We must reverse this process by establishing a strong central Government, to which shall belong all powers not specially conferred on the provinces. . . . A strong central Government is indispensable to the success of the experiment we are trying. . . .

ᵇGeorge E. Cartier saw the need for the retention of the monarchy and for the rejection of democratic principles, February 7, 1865:

. . . . They [the United States] had founded Federation for the purpose of carrying out and perpetuating democracy on this continent; but we, who had the benefit of being able to contemplate republicanism in action during a period of eighty years, saw its defects, and felt convinced that purely democratic institutions could not be conducive to the peace and prosperity of nations. . . . In our Federation the monarchical principle would form the leading feature, while on the other side of the line, judging by the past history and present conditions of the country, the ruling power was the will of the mob, the rule of the populace. . . .

The Seventy-two Resolutions, sometimes referred to as the Quebec Resolutions, were finally approved by the conference as the basis of Confederation. They proposed a federal system, with authority divided between a new central government and the provincial governments. With the United States' experience in mind, they tentatively resolved the thorny question of dividing power by limiting provincial authority to matters believed to be of strictly local concern. The central government, besides its specified powers, would have authority over matters that were found not to have been allocated to either level.

The British connection and parliamentary government were to continue. The federal government would be bicameral, with an appointed Upper House and an elected Lower House. In return for annual subsidies, the provinces would turn both their rights to collect customs duties and their debts over to the federal government. An intercolonial railway was to be completed "without delay."

VIEWS ON SUBMITTING THE SEVENTY-TWO
RESOLUTIONS TO THE ELECTORATE[245]

ªGeorge Brown was against submitting the RESOLUTIONS to the voters. CONFEDERATION DEBATES, February 8, 1865:

. . . . An appeal to the people of Canada on this measure simply means postponement of the question for a year — and who can tell how changed ere then may be the circumstances surrounding us? Sir, the man who strives for the postponement of this measure on any ground, is doing what he can to kill it almost as effectually as if he voted against it. . . .

_____

bA. A. Dorion *insisted upon a vote by the people,* CONFEDERATION DEBATES, *March 6, 1865:*

. . . . Everywhere [in Lower Canada] this scheme has been protested against, and an appeal to the people demanded; and yet, in defiance of the expressed opinions of our constituents, we are about to give them a Constitution, the effect of which will be to snatch from them the little influence which they still enjoy under the existing union . . . I shall oppose this scheme with all the power at my command, and insist that under any circumstances it shall be submitted to the people before its final adoption.

_____

cThe Hamilton TIMES, *a Reform newspaper, held a different view:*

If their [the people's] *direct* decision on the confederation question is unnecessary, we know of no question that has arisen in the past, we can imagine none in the future of sufficient importance to justify an appeal to them. The polling booths thereafter may as well be turned into pig-pens, and the voters lists cut up into pipe-lighters.

Having devised a plan generally acceptable to themselves, the delegates had to secure the approval of their respective provinces and the blessing of the British government. Agreement of the provincial legislatures would be taken as sufficient indication that people in the different areas supported Confederation. But events soon proved the existence of opposition strong enough to delay, if not destroy, Confederation.

SUPPORTERS OF CONFEDERATION[246]

Views expressed in CONFEDERATION DEBATES, *1865: Etienne P. Taché, February 3, 1865:*

. . . in a Federal Union . . . all questions of a general nature would be reserved for the General Government, and those of a local character to the local governments, who would have the power to manage their domestic affairs as they deemed best. If a Federal Union were obtained it would be tantamount to a separation of the provinces, and Lower Canada would thereby preserve its autonomy together with all the institutions it held so dear, and over which they could exercise the

watchfulness and surveillance necessary to preserve them unimpaired. . . .

_____

J. Dufresne, March 10, 1865:

. . . . I accept them [the Seventy-two Resolutions] for many reasons, but chiefly as a means of obtaining the repeal of the present legislative union of Canada, and securing peaceable settlement of our sectional difficulties. I accept them, in the second place, as a means of obtaining for Lower Canada the absolute and exclusive control of her own affairs. I accept them, thirdly, as a means of perpetuating French-Canadian nationality in this country. I accept them, fourthly, as a more effectual means of cementing our connection with the Mother Country, and avoiding annexation to the United States. I accept them, fifthly and lastly, as a means of administering the affairs of the colony with greater economy. Such are my reasons for accepting the Confederation scheme submitted to us by the Government. . . .

OPPONENTS OF CONFEDERATION

Antoine A. Dorion, March 6, 1865:

. . . . I am opposed to this Confederation in which the militia, the appointment of the judges, the administration of justice and our most important civil rights, will be under the control of a General Government the majority of which will be hostile to Lower Canada, of a General Government invested with the most ample powers, whilst the powers of the local governments will be restricted, first, by the limitation of the powers delegated to it, by the *Veto* reserved to the central authority, and further, by the concurrent jurisdiction of the general authority or government. . . .

_____

Christopher Dunkin, February 27, 1865:

. . . . They [the French Canadians] will find themselves a minority in the General Legislature, and their power in the General Government will depend upon their power within their own province and over their provincial delegations in the Federal Parliament. They will thus be compelled to be practically aggressive, to secure and retain that power . . . there will certainly be in this system [Federal Union] the very strongest tendencies to make them practically aggressive upon the rights of the minority in language and faith, and at the same time to make the minority most suspicious and resentful of aggression. . . .

George Brown went to England in the spring of 1865 to obtain British acceptance, and he was successful. His main talking point was the fact that the Canadian legislature had voted favourably in March. That vote was an important victory, but it had not been easily won. English-speaking Canada West had, of course, responded. Its representatives saw the opportunity of eliminating political deadlock, of acquiring the Northwest, of financing canals and roads and of submerging French Canada to some extent in an Anglo-Saxon country. On the other hand, strong opposition came from Canada East. The English-speaking minority feared for its future in a French-Canadian province, and Alexander Galt was hard-pressed to assure his fellow members that minority rights would be safeguarded. French Canadians, especially the *Rouges* led by A. A. Dorion, claimed that Confederation would mean the end of their way of life. Some even attacked the idea as a thinly disguised English-Canadian plot. Cartier replied that Confederation, providing as it did for provincial control of provincial matters, was the best possible guarantee of cultural survival for French Canadians. In the end, the coalition ministry had its way, and the legislature voted in favour of Confederation.

CONFEDERATION DEBATES IN THE CANADIAN ASSEMBLY[247]

The STRATFORD BEACON *(March 17, 1865) observed the effects of the long intensive Confederation Debates in the Canadian Assembly. This account refers to the atmosphere just before the Assembly approved the Quebec Resolutions:*

. . . the House was in an unmistakably seedy condition, having, as it was positively declared, eaten the saloon keeper clean out, drunk him entirely dry, and got all the fitful naps of sleep that the benches along the passages could be made to yield. . . . Men with the strongest constitutions for Parliamentary twaddle were sick of the debate, and the great bulk of the members were scattered about the building . . . impatient for the sound of the division bell. It rang at last, at quarter past four [in the morning], and the jaded representatives of the people swarmed in to the discharge of the most important duty of all their lives.

The story in the Maritimes was considerably more complicated. New Brunswick, geographically necessary to any union, became even more significant with the troubles of Premier Leonard Tilley. As the legislature was due to expire within a few months, his opponents hoped to gain office by attacking Confederation. Tilley and his Lieutenant-Governor decided that an early election, called before the anti-Confederates had built up a following among the voters, might return a sympathetic Assembly. But surprisingly, Tilley

and his supporters were swept out of office. This result encouraged the critics in Nova Scotia, where even Joseph Howe had decided to take a stand against Confederation. In his "Botheration Letters," Howe lent his considerable prestige to the opponents of the scheme, and the uproar was so great that Premier Charles Tupper dared not submit the Seventy-two Resolutions to the legislature. All he could do was wait and hope that circumstances would soon improve. Prince Edward Island rejected Confederation and Newfoundland showed little interest.

ANTI-CONFEDERATION SENTIMENTS IN THE MARITIMES[248]

[a]*W. H. Needham speaking in the House of Assembly of New Brunswick, April 3, 1865:*

When I forget my country so far as to sell it for Confederation, may my right hand forget its cunning, and if I do not prefer New Brunswick, as she is, to Canada with all her glory, then let my tongue cleave to the roof of my mouth. When the day comes when we shall have . . . Confederation deposited in the grave, those that will be there will not be there as mourners, but as glorifiers, and they will sing, with hearts elate with patriotic joy:

> Then safely moored, our perils o'er,
> We'll sing the songs of Jubilee,
> For ever and for ever more,
> New Brunswick, Land of Liberty.

———

[b]*A sample of Joseph Howe's "Botheration Letters," a mocking criticism of the Confederation idea, published in a Halifax newspaper a few months after the Quebec Conference:*

Where there are no cohesive qualities in the material, no skill in the design . . . unite what you will and there is no strength. . . . Was there strength when the new wine was united to the old bottle, or the new cloth to the old garment? Is union strength when a prudent man, doing a snug business is tempted into partnership with a wild speculator? Was Sampson much the stronger when the false Delilah got him confederated, bound him with cords and cut off his hair?

———

[c]*An anti-Confederation ditty current in Newfoundland:*

Hurrah for our native isle, Newfoundland!
Not a stranger shall hold one inch of its strand!
Her face turns to Britain, her back to the Gulf.
Come near at your peril, Canadian wolf!

Ye brave Newfoundlanders who plough the salt
    sea
With hearts like the eagle, so bold and so free,
The time is at hand when you'll all have to say
If Confederation will carry the day.

———

Would you barter the rights that your fathers
    have won,
Your freedom transmitted from father to son?
For a few thousand dollars of Canadian gold,
Don't let it be said that your birthright was sold.

The British government viewed these developments with some alarm. Relations between Great Britain and the United States had been severely strained by events during the Civil War, and there was no lessening of American hostility when the war ended. Many British leaders argued that troubles with the United States stemmed mainly from complications involving British North America, whose defence was a heavy burden on the British treasury. If the colonies expected to enjoy responsible government and the right to establish their own tariffs, there was no reason why they should not assume an increasing proportion of the costs of their own defence. Confederation would improve the ability of British North America to undertake such responsibility. In fact, some British leaders questioned the value of colonies and saw Confederation as a step to freeing the mother country from her burdensome colonies.

The British government began an active effort to press the cause of union. Lord Monck, the Governor of Canada, was already an enthusiastic agent of the policy. Lieutenant-Governor Gordon of New Brunswick, known to prefer Maritime union, was advised to use his influence on behalf of Confederation. Sir Fenwick Williams, a Nova Scotian who had won fame in the imperial army, was sent out from London as Lieutenant-Governor of his native province with orders to follow the same plan.

THE BRITISH GOVERNMENT URGES THE ATLANTIC
PROVINCES TO ACCEPT CONFEDERATION[249]

In a dispatch to the Lieutenant-Governors of the four Atlantic colonies, Edward Cardwell, the Colonial Secretary, urged them to do their utmost to influence the respective colonies to accept Confederation:

June 24, 1865

Looking to the determination which this Country has ever exhibited to regard the defence of the Colonies as an Imperial concern, — the Colonies must recognize a right and even acknowledge an obligation incumbent on the Home Government

to urge with earnestness and just authority the measures which they consider to be most expedient on the part of the Colonies with a view to their own defence [i.e., Confederation]. . . .

I am aware that this project so novel as well as so important, has not been at once accepted in Newfoundland [nor in P.E.I., N.S., N.B.] with that cordiality which has marked its acceptance in the Legislature of Canada; but Her Majesty's Government trust that after full and careful examination of the subject in all its bearings, the Maritime Provinces will perceive the great advantages which in the opinion of Her Majesty's Government the proposed Union is calculated to confer upon them all.

In New Brunswick, Gordon used pressure to bring about an election in the spring of 1866. The aim was to give Tilley a chance to regain the office of Premier. No effort was spared in his campaign and support came from many quarters: railway promoters who were anxious to build the Intercolonial; British financiers hopeful of rescuing investments; shipping and timber interests. Even the Canadian government contributed to Tilley's election fund. The threat of Fenian raids, meanwhile, was used to dramatize the need for union and to make support for Confederation seem a patriotic duty. The result was Tilley's return to power and the new Assembly's approval of concluding union with the other provinces.

With the persistent efforts of Lieutenant-Governor Williams and the favourable trend in New Brunswick, Tupper felt sure enough to test the legislature of Nova Scotia. After he was successful in getting Confederation approved in principle, he joined Tilley in urging the Canadians to complete the work of union while conditions were favourable. Although the Canadians spent the summer preparing for the division of their province and fending off Fenian raids, delegations were ready for the final conference.

The London Conference began meeting in December, 1866, under the chairmanship of John A. Macdonald. The representatives from Canada, Nova Scotia and New Brunswick had to revise the Quebec Resolutions so that they could be accepted by the British government and passed as an Act of Parliament. This accomplished, the delegates agreed on the name "Canada" for the new union. The only seriously considered alternative was "Kingdom of Canada," a name which Macdonald and others thought would properly suggest the continuation of strong ties with Britain and stress the importance of the monarchy in the new union's government. The British government scotched the idea, however, because the word "kingdom" would have provoked strong reaction from the republican United States.

In a letter to Lord Knutsford, dated at Rivière du Loup, July 18, 1889, John A. Macdonald explains why the "Kingdom of Canada," which would impress the monarchical ties with the mother country, was rejected:

. . . . The Union was treated by them [Duke of Buckingham, the Colonial Minister, and Lord Monck, the Governor-General] as if the B.N.A. Act were a private Bill uniting two or three English parishes. Had a different course been pursued — for instance, had united Canada been declared to be an auxiliary Kingdom, as it was in the Canadian draft of the Bill — I feel sure (almost) that the Australian Colonies would, ere this, have been applying to be placed in the same rank as 'The Kingdom of Canada.'

———

P.S.—On reading the above over, I see that it will convey the impression that the change of title from Kingdom to Dominion was caused by the Duke of Buckingham. This is not so. It was made at the instance of Lord Derby, then foreign Minister, who feared the first name would wound the sensibilities of the Yankees. . . .

H.M. Queen Victoria and H.R.H. Prince Albert

The British North America Act was passed by the British Parliament in March with a minimum of debate; not even the exertions of the tireless Joseph Howe had aroused any serious opposition. Queen Victoria signed the Act on March 29, 1867. The Dominion of Canada, consisting of Ontario and Quebec (formerly the Province of Canada), and Nova Scotia and New Brunswick, was to begin its formal existence on July 1, 1867.

Opening the First Parliament of the New Dominion of Canada, 1867

18

THE BRITISH NORTH AMERICA ACT

The British North America Act is the "written" portion of Canada's constitution. British parliamentary principles, customs and later legislation and court decisions make up what is referred to as the "unwritten" part of the constitution.

*What is a constitution? One could consider it as the basic rules by which a country is governed. The following statement offers a comprehensive definition:**

The word "constitution" is used with several different meanings of which only four need concern us. The four meanings are distinct but allied. In the first sense, the constitution of a state is its supreme law or theory of government. In the second meaning, it is the body of laws that are considered of basic importance and to which all other laws and institutions are, by law or by custom, subordinate. Since such laws usually define the structure and functions of the essential organs of government, the third sense of "constitution" denotes these structural laws. And in the fourth meaning, a constitution is the body of laws (whether basic or not), conventions, and institutions that make up the government of the state, that is, the structure and organization of the state.

The constitution . . . is the supreme law of the land defining the fundamentals of government and delimiting the functions of the principal institutions. . . .

THE BRITISH NORTH AMERICA ACT, 1867
30 & 31 VICTORIA, C.3

An ACT for the Union of Canada, Nova Scotia, and New Brunswick and the Government thereof; and for Purposes connected therewith.

(29th March, 1867)

Whereas the Provinces of Canada, Nova Scotia, and New Brunswick have expressed their Desire to be federally united into One Dominion under the Crown of the United Kingdom of Great Britain and Ireland, with a Constitution similar in Principle to that of the United Kingdom:

And whereas such a Union would conduce to the welfare of the Provinces and promote the Interests of the British Empire:

And whereas on the Establishment of the Union by Authority of Parliament it is expedient, not only that the Constitution of the Legislative Authority in the Dominion be provided for, but also that the nature of the Executive Government therein be declared:

And whereas it is expedient that Provision be made for the eventual Admission into the Union of other Parts of British North America:

Be it therefore enacted and declared by the Queen's most Excellent Majesty, by and with the Advice and Consent of the Lords Spiritual and Temporal, and Commons, in this present Parliament assembled, and by the Authority of the same, as follows:

The preamble outlines the general purposes of the Act — to establish a federal union, which the Fathers of Confederation had already agreed to at the Quebec Conference of 1864; to provide a constitution based on British principles (that is, parliamentary government) as well as British rights and freedoms enshrined in such statutes as the Magna Carta and the Bill of Rights; and finally, to allow for the expansion of the Dominion in the expectation of including other provinces and territories.

* from Peter J. T. O'Hearne, *Peace, Order and Good Government: A New Constitution for Canada* (Toronto: The Macmillan Co. of Canada, Ltd., 1964), pp. 9-11.

I. PRELIMINARY

1. This Act may be cited as the *British North America Act, 1867*.

II. UNION

3. It shall be lawful for the Queen, by and with the Advice of Her Majesty's Most Honourable Privy Council, to declare by Proclamation that, on and after a Day herein appointed, not being more than Six Months after the passing of this Act, the Provinces of Canada, Nova Scotia, and New Brunswick shall form and be One Dominion under the Name of Canada; and on and after that Day those Three Provinces shall form and be one Dominion under the Name accordingly.

5. Canada shall be divided into Four Provinces, named Ontario, Quebec, Nova Scotia, and New Brunswick.

6. . . . The Part which formerly constituted the Province of Upper Canada shall constitute the Province of Ontario; and the Part which formerly constituted the Province of Lower Canada shall constitute the Province of Quebec.

7. The Provinces of Nova Scotia and New Brunswick shall have the same Limits as at the passing of this Act.

8. In the general Census of the Population of Canada which is hereby required to be taken in the Year One thousand eight hundred and seventy-one, and in every Tenth Year thereafter, the respective Populations of the Four Provinces shall be distinguished.

OPTIMISM ABOUT CANADIAN FEDERALISM[251]

Pierre Elliott Trudeau takes the positive view:

Of the countries of the world, Canada has the eighth oldest written constitution, the second oldest one of a federal nature, and the oldest which combines federalism with the principles of responsible government.

Yet some of our fellow Canadians have an even more illustrious record as pioneers in constitution-making: the Confederation of Six Iroquois Nations was founded in 1570, or thereabouts, and is still in existence today. Anthropologists and sociologists have marvelled at the keen political sense of Canada's earlier inhabitants. And the question arises whether historians will have the same opinion of the subsequent settlers!

If it be true that the first hundred years are the hardest, I see no cause to despair of the future of Canadian federalism. . . .

The effective date for Confederation was declared, by Queen Victoria's proclamation in May, to be July 1, 1867.

An interesting point about the terms of the union is that the creation of the Dominion is placed first in Section 3. Then follow the terms for dividing Canada into provinces, and for separating the Province of Canada into Ontario and Quebec. In other words, the unity of Canada is emphasized and the division into parts is made secondary.

III. EXECUTIVE POWER

9. The Executive Government and Authority of and over Canada is hereby declared to continue and be vested in the Queen.

10. The Provisions of this Act referring to the Governor General extend and apply to the Governor General for . . . carrying on the Government of Canada on behalf and in the Name of the Queen. . . .

11. There shall be a Council to aid and advise in the Government of Canada, to be styled the Queen's Privy Council for Canada; and the Persons who are to be Members of that Council shall be from Time to Time chosen and summoned by the Governor General and sworn in as Privy Councillors, and Members thereof may be from Time to Time removed by the Governor General.

13. The Provisions of this Act referring to the Governor General in Council shall be construed as referring to the Governor General acting by and with the Advice of the Queen's Privy Council for Canada.

15. The Commander-in-Chief of the Land and Naval Militia, and of all Naval and Military Forces, of and in Canada, is hereby declared to continue and be vested in the Queen.

16. Until the Queen otherwise directs, the Seat of Government of Canada shall be Ottawa.

The principle of monarchy is clearly affirmed. The Queen, represented by the Governor-General, is declared to be the source of executive authority. Taken literally, the terms of the Act appear to assign almost autocratic powers to the Governor-General during both peace and war.

It should be noted that responsible government, in local affairs, was already operative in 1867 and was in no danger of being discontinued after Confederation. The men who devised the B.N.A. Act thus felt no need to provide any guarantee in the "written constitution." The execution of the affairs of the Canadian government — those not affecting the Empire — actually rested with the Prime

Minister and his cabinet, even though neither is mentioned in the Act.

The position of the Governor-General was, however, much different in 1867 from what it is today. Canada was still a colony, subject to the laws which Great Britain applied to the Empire as a whole. The Governor-General represented the might and splendour of the Empire, over which the British government remained supreme in matters of defence and foreign affairs. He was also expected to exert influence in Canadian affairs when the occasion arose. In the intervening years, as Canada acquired its autonomy, the position of Governor-General decreased in power and took on symbolic value instead. Today, the man filling the office is the Queen's personal representative, in no way an agent of the British government.

Vincent Massey was the first Canadian to be appointed Governor-General, in 1952. His successors have been, and will likely continue to be, Canadians. No longer are they selected by Britain; rather, the monarch formally appoints the person chosen by the Canadian cabinet.

IV. LEGISLATIVE POWER

17. There shall be One Parliament for Canada, consisting of the Queen, an Upper House styled the Senate, and the House of Commons.
20. There shall be a Session of the Parliament of Canada once at least in every Year, so that Twelve Months shall not intervene between the last Sitting of the Parliament in one Session and its first Sitting in the next Session.

The legislature is said to be bicameral because it contains two "Houses." Such a legislature permits representation of all the people in the House of Commons, and representation of special interests in the Senate. Parliament is required to meet at least once a year so that it can account to the people for its actions.

The Senate

21. The Senate shall, subject to the Provisions of this Act, consist of Seventy-two Members, who shall be styled Senators.
22. In relation to the Constitution of the Senate Canada shall be deemed to consist of Three Divisions:—
   1. Ontario;
   2. Quebec;
   3. The Maritime Provinces, Nova Scotia and New Brunswick; which Three Divisions shall (subject to the Provisions of this Act) be equally represented in the Senate as follows: Ontario by Twenty-four Senators; Quebec by Twenty-four Senators; and the Maritime Provinces by Twenty-four Senators, Twelve thereof representing Nova Scotia, and Twelve thereof representing New Brunswick. . . .
23. The qualifications of a Senator shall be as follows:
   1. He shall be of the full age of Thirty Years:
   2. He shall be either a natural-born Subject of the Queen, or a Subject of the Queen naturalized by an Act of the Parliament of Great Britain, or of the Parliament of the United Kingdom of Great Britain and Ireland, or of the Legislature of One of the Provinces of Upper Canada, Lower Canada, Canada, Nova Scotia, or New Brunswick, before the Union, or of the Parliament of Canada after the Union:
   3. He shall be legally or equitably seised as of Freehold for his own Use and Benefit of Lands or Tenements held in Free and Common Socage, or seised or possessed for his own Use and Benefit of Lands or Tenements held in Franc-alleu or in Roture, within the Province for which he is appointed, of the Value of Four thousand Dollars, over and above all Rents, Dues, Debts, Charges, Mortgages, and Incumbrances due or payable out of or charged on or affecting the same:
   4. His Real and Personal Property shall be together worth Four thousand Dollars over and above his Debts and Liabilities:
   5. He shall be resident in the Province for which he is appointed:
   6. In the Case of Quebec he shall have his Real Property Qualification in the Electoral Division for which he is appointed, or shall be resident in that Division.
24. The Governor General shall from Time to Time, in the Queen's Name, by Instrument under the Great Seal of Canada, summon qualified Persons to the Senate; and, subject to the Provisions of this Act, every Person so summoned shall become and be a Member of the Senate and a Senator.
26. If at any Time on the Recommendation of the Governor General the Queen thinks fit to direct that Three or Six Members be added to the Senate, the Governor General may by Summons to Three or Six qualified Persons (as the Case may be), representing equally the Three Divisions of Canada, add to the Senate accordingly.
29. A Senator shall, subject to the Provisions of this Act, hold his Place in the Senate for Life.

In the United States Senate, every state was given two representatives. One purpose was to make the Senate the protector of smaller states. The same principle was embodied in the Canadian Senate, where regions of smaller population were assigned blocks of seats to balance those given to Ontario and Quebec. In addition to protecting the interests of the different regions of Canada, the Senate was expected to serve other functions. It was to continue the role of the Legislative Councils as they had operated in the colonies during responsible government. It assured, in its provisions for membership, that men of property and position had a legislative body to offset the democratically elected House of Commons. The Fathers of Confederation, living in an age when leaders feared democracy might lead to mob rule, believed that some power must be reserved for men of "substance."

The number of seats in the Senate naturally increased as new provinces joined the Dominion. The Senate now contains 102 members, but the principle of regional representation has been maintained.

One important amendment, passed in 1965, changed the terms of tenure; instead of holding office for life, senators appointed since 1965 will retire at the age of seventy-five. Otherwise, the section of the B.N.A. Act dealing with the Senate has remained substantially unaltered, in spite of the fact that, many times since Confederation, cries for reform or abolition of the Senate have been raised.

SENATE REFORM[252]

The following was written more than forty years ago, in 1926: Clearly, Senate reform has been one of the most lasting issues in Canadian politics.

The problem of a second chamber recurs annually in Canada. . . . Of late years it has become the fashion to attack the Senate as the foe of public ownership because it has interfered with several bills for the construction of railways by the Dominion. The Senate as a "Home for the Aged", as a refuge for old warriors, and as a means of rewarding contributors to the party war chest, is the continual butt of newspaper wits. And yet, for all its unpopularity, the Senate continues on its dignified way, little changed from what it was half a century ago.

The reform of the Senate has been in the air almost since the federation of 1867. In 1875 the subject was introduced and debated at length for the first time in Parliament. Since then the debate has been reopened many times in both Houses. . . .

The House of Commons

37. The House of Commons shall, subject to the Provisions of this Act, consist of One Hundred and eighty-one Members, of whom Eighty-two shall be elected for Ontario, Sixty-five for Quebec, Nineteen for Nova Scotia, and Fifteen for New Brunswick.

38. The Governor General shall from Time to Time, in the Queen's Name, by Instrument under the Great Seal of Canada, summon and call together the House of Commons.

39. A Senator shall not be capable of being elected or of sitting or voting as a Member of the House of Commons.

44. The House of Commons on its first assembling after a General Election shall proceed with all practicable Speed to elect One of its Members to be Speaker.

46. The Speaker shall preside at all Meetings of the House of Commons.

48. The Presence of at least Twenty Members of the House of Commons shall be necessary to constitute a Meeting of the House for the Exercise of its Powers, and for that Purpose the Speaker shall be reckoned as a Member.

49. Questions arising in the House of Commons shall be decided by a Majority of Voices other than that of the Speaker, and when the Voices are equal, but not otherwise, the Speaker shall have a vote.

50. Every House of Commons shall continue for Five Years from the Day of the Return of the Writs for choosing the House (subject to be sooner dissolved by the Governor General), and no longer.

51. On the Completion of the Census in the Year One Thousand eight hundred and seventy-one, and of each subsequent decennial Census, the Representation of the Four Provinces shall be re-adjusted by such Authority, in such Manner, and from such Time, as the Parliament of Canada from Time to Time provides, subject and according to the following Rules:
1. Quebec shall have the fixed Number of sixty-five Members:
2. There shall be assigned to each of the other Provinces such a Number of Members as will bear the same Proportion to the Number of its Population (ascertained at such Census) as the Number Sixty-five bears to the Number of the Population of Quebec (so ascertained):

52. The Number of Members of the House of Commons may be from Time to Time increased by the Parliament of Canada, pro-

vided the proportionate Representation of the Provinces prescribed by this Act is not thereby disturbed.

The House of Commons was given the same name as its British counterpart as a symbol of the continuity of the British precedent. The House of Commons was to continue as the chief law-making body in Parliament, as the Legislative Assembly had done in the past.

Seats were apportioned on the basis of representation by population, with Quebec assigned the fixed number of 65 seats and the other provinces given proportionate representation. The Act also provided for redistribution of seats after each decennial census as well as for increasing the total number of seats. An amendment of 1952 changed the method of computing distribution, although the original principle of representation by population and proportional representation has been retained. After the 1961 census membership of the House of Commons stood at 265.

Money Votes; Royal Assent

53. Bills for appropriating any Part of the Public Revenue, or for imposing any Tax or Impost, shall originate in the House of Commons.
54. It shall not be lawful for the House of Commons to adopt or pass any Vote, Resolution, Address, or Bill for the Appropriation of any Part of the Public Revenue, or of any Tax or Impost, to any Purpose that has not been first recommended to that House by Message of the Governor General in the Session in which such Vote, Resolution, Address, or Bill is proposed.
55. Where a Bill passed by the Houses of the Parliament is presented to the Governor General for the Queen's Assent, he shall declare, according to his Discretion, but subject to the Provisions of this Act and to her Majesty's Instructions, either that he assents thereto in the Queen's Name, or that he withholds the Queen's Assent, or that he reserves the Bill for the Signification of the Queen's Pleasure.

The fact that money bills must originate in the House of Commons is a continuation of a British practice established in British North America as part of responsible government. Only the elected representatives of the people have the right to authorize the imposition of taxes and the spending of revenue obtained.

The phrase "according to his Discretion" in Section 55 empowers the Governor-General to use his judgment as to whether or not he will sign a bill to make it law. In practice, however, Governors-General have not witheld royal assent. Although they have advised Prime Ministers on proposed legislation and other important matters of government, once a bill passes both Houses of Parliament the representatives of the Crown do not disregard the "will of the people."

V. PROVINCIAL CONSTITUTIONS

Executive Power

58. For each Province there shall be an Officer, styled the Lieutenant Governor, appointed by the Governor General in Council by instrument under the Great Seal of Canada.
60. The Salaries of the Lieutenant Governors shall be fixed and provided by the Parliament of Canada.
66. The Provisions of this Act referring to the Lieutenant Governor in Council shall be construed as referring to the Lieutenant Governor of the Province acting by and with the advice of the Executive Council thereof.
68. Unless and until the Executive Government of any Provinces otherwise directs with respect to that Province, the Seats of Government of the Provinces shall be as follows, namely, — of Ontario, the City of Toronto; of Quebec, the City of Quebec; of Nova Scotia, the City of Halifax; and of New Brunswick, the City of Fredericton.

Legislative Power

69. There shall be a Legislature for Ontario consisting of the Lieutenant Governor and of One House, styled the Legislative Assembly of Ontario.
71. There shall be a Legislature for Quebec consisting of the Lieutenant Governor and of Two Houses, styled the Legislative Council of Quebec and the Legislative Assembly of Quebec.
88. The Constitution of the Legislature of each of the Provinces of Nova Scotia and New Brunswick shall, subject to the Provisions of this Act, continue as it exists at the Union until altered under the Authority of this Act . . .

Parliamentary government was also extended to the provincial legislatures. Provincial Premiers, each with his cabinet selected from the respective legislatures, directed the affairs of the provinces as did the Prime Minister the affairs of the Dominion as a whole.

Quebec retained the bicameral legislature specified in the Act until 1969, when the Legislative

Council was abolished. Ontario's single-house legislature, however, has been the example followed by all the other provinces.

The Lieutenant-Governors corresponded to the Governor-General. They represented the Crown in the provinces. However, the Act indicates that they might also be the "agents" of the federal government, which was involved in their appointment and paid their salaries. Today, the office of Lieutenant-Governor, like that of Governor-General, is symbolic.*

VI. DISTRIBUTION OF LEGISLATIVE POWERS
Powers of the Parliament

91. It shall be lawful for the Queen, by and with the Advice and Consent of the Senate and House of Commons, to make Laws for the Peace, Order, and good Government of Canada, in relation to all Matters not coming within the Classes of Subjects by this Act assigned exclusively to the Legislatures of the Provinces; and for greater Certainty, but not so as to restrict the Generality of the foregoing Terms of this Section, it is hereby declared that (notwithstanding anything in this Act) the exclusive Legislative Authority of the Parliament of Canada extends to all Matters coming within the Classes of Subjects next herein-after enumerated; that is to say,
1. The Public Debt and Property.
2. The Regulation of Trade and Commerce.
3. The raising of Money by any Mode or System of Taxation.
4. The borrowing of Money on the Public Credit.
5. Postal Service.
6. The Census and Statistics.
7. Militia, Military and Naval Service, and Defence.
8. The fixing of and providing for the Salaries and Allowances of Civil and other Officers of the Government of Canada.
9. Beacons, Buoys, Lighthouses, and Sable Island.
10. Navigation and Shipping.
11. Quarantine and the Establishment and Maintenance of Marine Hospitals.
12. Sea Coast and Inland Fisheries.
13. Ferries between a Province and any British or Foreign Country or between Two Provinces.
14. Currency and Coinage.
15. Banking, Incorporation of Banks, and the Issue of Paper Money .
16. Savings Banks.
17. Weights and Measures.
18. Bills of Exchange and Promissory Notes.
19. Interest.
20. Legal Tender.
21. Bankruptcy and Insolvency.
22. Patents of Invention and Discovery.
23. Copyrights.
24. Indians, and Lands reserved for the Indians.
25. Naturalization and Aliens.
26. Marriage and Divorce.
27. The Criminal Law, except the Constitution of Courts of Criminal Jurisdiction, but including the Procedure in Criminal Matters.
28. The Establishment, Maintenance, and Management of Penitentiaries.
29. Such Classes of Subjects as are expressly excepted in the Enumeration of the Classes of Subjects by this Act assigned exclusively to the Legislatures of the Provinces.

And any Matter coming within any of the Classes of Subjects enumerated in this Section shall not be deemed to come within the Class of Matters of a local or private Nature comprised in the Enumeration of the Classes of Subjects by this Act assigned exclusively to the Legislatures of the Provinces.

Exclusive Powers of Provincial Legislatures

92. In each Province the Legislature may exclusively make Laws in relation to Matters within the Classes of Subjects next hereinafter enumerated; that is to say, —
1. The Amendment from Time to Time, notwithstanding anything in this Act, of the Constitution of the Province, except as regards the Office of Lieutenant Governor.
2. Direct Taxation within the Province in order to the raising of a Revenue for Provincial Purposes.
3. The Borrowing of Money on the sole Credit of the Province.
4. The Establishment and Tenure of Provincial Offices and the Appointment and Payment of Provincial Officers.
5. The Management and Sale of the Public Lands belonging to the Province and of the Timber and Wood thereon.
6. The Establishment, Maintenance, and Management of Public and Reformatory Prisons in and for the Province.
7. The Establishment, Maintenance, and Management of Hospitals, Asylums, Chari-

* As recently as 1961, the Lieutenant-Governor of Saskatchewan reserved a provincial bill for Ottawa's consideration. In this act of "reservation," the Lieutenant-Governor asserted his authority as a representative of the federal government in this province.

ties, and Eleemosynary Institutions in and for the Province, other than Marine Hospitals.

8. Municipal Institutions in the Province.

9. Shop, Saloon, Tavern, Auctioneer, and other Licenses in order to the raising of a Revenue for Provincial, Local, or Municipal Purposes.

10. Local Works and Undertakings other than such as are of the following Classes:—

(a) Lines of Steam or other Ships, Railways, Canals, Telegraphs, and other Works and Undertakings connecting the Province with any other or others of the Provinces, or extending beyond the Limits of the Province;

(b) Lines of Steam Ships between the Province and any British or Foreign Country;

(c) Such Works as, although wholly situate within the Province, are before or after their Execution declared by the Parliament of Canada to be for the general Advantage of Canada or for the Advantage of Two or more of the Provinces.

11. The Incorporation of Companies with Provincial Objects.

12. The Solemnization of Marriage in the Province.

13. Property and Civil Rights in the Province.

14. The Administration of Justice in the Province, including the Constitution, Maintenance, and Organization of Provincial Courts, both of Civil and of Criminal Jurisdiction, and including Procedure in Civil Matters in those Courts.

15. The Imposition of Punishment by Fine, Penalty, or Imprisonment for enforcing any Law of the Province made in relation to any Matter coming within any of the Classes of Subjects enumerated in this section.

16. Generally all Matters of a merely local or private Nature in the Province.

Education

93. In and for each Province the Legislature may exclusively make Laws in relation to Education, subject and according to the following Provisions:—

1. Nothing in any such Law shall prejudicially affect any Right or Privilege with respect to Denominational Schools which any Class of Persons have by Law in the Province at the Union:

2. All the Powers, Privileges, and Duties at the Union by Law conferred and imposed in Upper Canada on the Separate Schools and School Trustees of the Queen's Roman Catholic Subjects shall be and the same are hereby extended to the Dissentient Schools of the Queen's Protestant and Roman Catholic Subjects in Quebec:

3. Where in any Province a System of Separate or Dissentient Schools exist by Law at the Union or is thereafter established by the Legislature of the Province, an Appeal shall lie to the Governor General in Council from any Act or Decision of any Provincial Authority affecting any Right or Privilege of the Protestant or Roman Catholic Minority of the Queen's Subjects in relation to Education:

4. In case any such Provincial Law as from Time to Time seems to the Governor General in Council requisite for the due Execution of the Provisions of this Section is not made, or in case any Decision of the Governor General in Council on any Appeal under this Section is not duly executed by the proper Provincial Authority in that Behalf, then and in every such Case, and as far only as the Circumstances of each Case require, the Parliament of Canada may make remedial Laws for the due Execution of the Provisions of this Section and of any Decision of the Governor General in Council under this Section.

Agriculture and Immigration

95. In each Province the Legislature may make Laws in relation to Agriculture in the Province, and to Immigration into the Province; and it is hereby declared that the Parliament of Canada may from Time to Time make Laws in relation to Agriculture in all or any of the Provinces, and to Immigration into all or any of the Provinces; and any law of the Legislature of a Province relative to Agriculture or to Immigration shall have effect in and for the Province as long and as far only as it is not repugnant to any Act of the Parliament of Canada.

Distribution of legislative powers was a difficult problem facing the Fathers of Confederation. Their basic plan was to separate federal from provincial jurisdiction, hoping that the central government would be strong and that provincial governments would control local affairs. In spite of the detailed enumeration of powers assigned the two levels of government, no perfect separation was possible. Generally, sweeping powers were given to the federal government in Section 91, and only limited powers to the provinces in Section 92.

Sections 91 and 92, though carefully prepared, have been the basis for many difficulties in government over the years:

. . . . Although the authors of the B.N.A. Act were relatively painstaking in delineating the powers assigned to the two levels of government, the language they used to define those powers was still, of necessity, general and abstract. Phrases such as "peace order and good government," "trade and commerce" and "property and civil rights," which appear in Sections 91 and 92, the vital sections for the division of legislative powers, are obviously replete with ambiguities. Even though some of the other subject-matters of legislation are more precisely described, the list, taken as a whole, could never anticipate the enormous range and complexity of problems which through the course of time have concerned Canadian legislators. . . .

Section 91 begins by authorizing the Dominion Parliament "to make Laws for the Peace, Order, and Good Government of Canada, in relation to all Matters not coming within the Classes of Subjects by this Act assigned exclusively to the Legislatures of the Provinces." Even in such specifically provincial powers as education (Section 93), federal authority is not excluded. The power of remedial legislation seems to establish the Canadian Parliament as the guardian of privileges conceded to minorities at the time the B.N.A. Act was passed.

Section 95, by placing "concurrent powers" with the Dominion, further strengthened the central government. In matters of agriculture and immigration, both levels of government may make laws. However, in case of dispute, Parliament's will would prevail.

To provide for occasions when conflict might arise, and for future subjects of legislation not anticipated in 1867, the Act placed the "residual" powers with the federal government. Item 29 of Section 91 re-emphasizes that powers not specifically allocated to the provinces belong to the federal government.

Provisions of Sections 91 and 92 reflect a fundamental weakness in Canada's "written constitution;" namely, that they establish no machinery for amending the B.N.A. Act. This is understandable since the B.N.A. Act is an act of the British Parliament for what was, in 1867, one of its colonies. Nevertheless, amendments by the British government have customarily been made upon the request of the Canadian Parliament.

After Canada had achieved the status of an autonomous country, its leaders recognized the need for independent power over the Canadian constitution. In 1949, an amendment to Section 91* opened the way to general amendment of the B.N.A. Act:

The amendment from time to time of the Constitution of Canada, except as regards matters coming within the classes of subjects by this Act assigned exclusively to the Legislatures of the provinces, or as regards rights or privileges by this or any other Constitutional Act granted or secured to the Legislature or the Government of a province, or to any class of persons with respect to schools or as regards the use of the English or the French language or as regards the requirements that there shall be a session of the Parliament of Canada at least once each year, and that no House of Commons shall continue for more than five years from the day of the return of the Writs for choosing the House: provided, however, that a House of Commons may in time of real or apprehended war, invasion or insurrection be continued by the Parliament of Canada if such continuation is not opposed by the votes of more than one-third of the members of the House.

In spite of efforts in recent years, Canadians have not been able to agree on a formula for recovering the powers of amendment that have been left with the British Parliament. The British, as well as the Canadian leaders, will be relieved when the "Canadian" constitution is finally repatriated.

VII. JUDICATURE

96. The Governor General shall appoint the Judges of the Superior, District, and County Courts in each Province. . . .

97. . . . the Judges of the Courts of those Provinces appointed by the Governor General shall be selected from the respective Bars of those Provinces.

98. The Judges of the Courts of Quebec shall be selected from the Bar of that Province.

99. The Judges of the Superior Courts shall hold Office during good Behaviour, but shall be removable by the Governor General on Address of the Senate and House of Commons.

* The amendment became Item No. 1 of Section 91, and the previous Item No. 1 was re-numbered 1A.

Top left: Settlers' Log Cabin, Tartique River, P.Q., c. 1865

Top right: H. R. Biggar and his Survey Party,
Maritimes, Intercolonial Railway, c. 1870

Centre: E. B. Eddy Store, Hull, P.Q., 1873

Bottom right: On a Picnic, Elora, Ontario, c. 1856

Bottom left: Timber Coves at Sillery near Quebec

100. The Salaries, Allowances, and Pensions of the Judges of the Superior, District and County Courts (except the Courts of Probate in Nova Scotia and New Brunswick), and of the Admiralty Courts in Cases where the Judges thereof are for the Time being paid by Salary, shall be fixed and provided by the Parliament of Canada.

101. The Parliament of Canada may, notwithstanding anything in this Act, from Time to Time, provide for the Constitution, Maintenance, and Organization of a General Court of Appeal for Canada, and for the Establishment of any additional Courts for the better Administration of the Laws of Canada.

The Governor-General-in-Council appoints all judges except those in minor provincial courts. Parliament pays their salaries and, in exceptional cases, may remove judges by means of a vote in both the House of Commons and the Senate.*

The Judiciary is not, however, a branch of Parliament. Fair interpretation and application of the laws of Canada require that judges be free from political influence and other pressures. Therefore, judges have been accorded a special status that other officials of the government do not enjoy. To safeguard the independent position of judges, the B.N.A. Act provides that they "hold Office during good Behaviour" — which, until the amendment of 1961, meant appointment for life. Now Superior Court judges retire at the age of seventy-five.

The federal system of courts and federal jurisdiction over criminal law are the main unifying forces in the country. The Supreme Court of Canada, created in 1875, has become the final court of appeal for all of Canada.

VIII.   REVENUES: DEBTS: ASSETS: TAXATION

102. All Duties and Revenues over which the respective Legislatures of Canada, Nova Scotia, and New Brunswick before and at the Union had and have Power of Appropriation, except such Portions thereof as are by this Act reserved to the respective Legislatures of the Provinces, or are raised by them in accordance with the special Powers conferred on them by this Act, shall form One Consolidated Revenue Fund, to be appropriated for the Public Service of Canada in the Manner and subject to the Charges in this Act provided.

107. All Stocks, Cash, Banker's Balances, and Securities for Money belonging to each Province at the Time of the Union, except as in this Act mentioned, shall be the Property of Canada, and shall be taken in Reduction of the Amount of the respective Debts of the Provinces at the Union.

108. The Public Works and Property of each Province, enumerated in the Third Schedule to this Act, shall be the Property of Canada.

109. All Lands, Mines, Minerals, and Royalties belonging to the several Provinces of Canada, Nova Scotia, and New Brunswick at the Union, and all Sums then due or payable for such Lands, Mines, Minerals, or Royalties, shall belong to the several Provinces of Ontario, Quebec, Nova Scotia, and New Brunswick in which the same are situate or arise, subject to any Trusts existing in respect thereof, and to any Interest other than that of the Province in the same.

111. Canada shall be liable for the Debts and Liabilities of each Province existing at the Union.

121. All Articles of the Growth, Produce, or Manufacture of any of the Provinces shall, from and after the Union, be admitted free into each of the other Provinces.

Confederation required elaborate financial arrangements. The federal government assumed the provinces' debts as well as their assets, including money and such public works as canals, lighthouses, railways, customs houses and military establishments. The original four provinces were left in possession of their natural resources. To replace the sources of revenue which they relinquished, the provinces were to receive a fixed annual grant sum and an annual grant based on eighty cents per head of population. This same formula in future years was applied to new provinces joining the Dominion.

The removal of intercolonial tariffs, stipulated in Section 121, was one of the chief objects of the Fathers of Confederation. Now the way was clear for the development of trade on east-west lines, which could produce an expanding economy across the continent.

* In March, 1967, a Senate-Commons committee recommended the removal of Mr. Justice Leo Landreville of the Ontario Supreme Court as "unfit for the proper exercise of his judicial functions."

IX. MISCELLANEOUS PROVISIONS

129. Except as otherwise provided by this Act, all Laws in force in Canada, Nova Scotia, or New Brunswick at the Union, and all Courts of Civil and Criminal Jurisdiction, and all legal Commissions, Powers, and Authorities, and all Officers, Judicial, Administrative, and Ministerial, existing therein at the Union, shall continue in Ontario, Quebec, Nova Scotia, and New Brunswick respectively, as if the Union had not been made; subject nevertheless (except with respect to such as are enacted by or exist under Acts of the Parliament of the United Kingdom of Great Britain and Ireland) to be repealed, abolished, or altered by the Parliament of Canada, or by the Legislature of the respective Province, according to the Authority of the Parliament or of that Legislature under this Act.

133. Either the English or the French Language may be used by any Person in the Debates of the Houses of the Parliament of Canada and of the Houses of the Legislature of Quebec; and both those Languages shall be used in the respective Records and Journals of those Houses; and either of those Languages may be used by any Person or in any Pleading or Process in or issuing from any Court of Canada established under this Act, and in or from all or any of the Courts of Quebec.

The Acts of the Parliament of Canada and of the Legislature of Quebec shall be printed and published in both those Languages.

Note that laws passed by the British Parliament applicable to Canada could not, until fairly recent times, be "repealed, abolished, or altered" by Canada. The *Statute of Westminster* in 1931, which recognized Canada and other British Dominions as fully self-governing members of the Empire (Commonwealth), authorized Canada to repeal any British laws that formed part of the laws of Canada.

The use of the French language, respected since the Conquest, was not accorded official status in the Quebec Act. Section 133 of the B.N.A. Act accorded the right to use the French language in the newly created Parliament of Canada, and in federal courts.

The Report of the Royal Commission on Bilingualism and Biculturalism recommends clearer definition of language rights:

416. Section 133 is the only one in the Act specifically referring to the use of the English and French languages. But in this section the guaranteed usage of both languages is limited to debate in the Parliament of Canada and in the legislature of Quebec, official publication of statutes in Ottawa and Quebec, and pleadings and processes of all federal and Quebec courts. . . .

. . . It is our opinion that section 133 should be amended so as to state clearly that English and French are the two official languages of Canada, and to provide rules for the application of the principle of equality at the provincial level and in bilingual districts. . . .

X. INTERCOLONIAL RAILWAY

145. Inasmuch as the Provinces of Canada, Nova Scotia, and New Brunswick have joined in a Declaration that the Construction of the Intercolonial Railway is essential to the Consolidation of the Union of British North America, and to the Assent thereto of Nova Scotia and New Brunswick and have consequently agreed that Provision should be made for its immediate Construction by the Government of Canada: Therefore, in order to give effect to that Agreement, it shall be the Duty of the Government and Parliament of Canada to provide for the Commencement within Six Months after the Union, of a Railway connecting the River St. Lawrence with the City of Halifax in Nova Scotia, and for the Construction thereof without Intermission, and the Completion thereof with all practicable Speed.

An intercolonial railway was one of the main inducements offered by the United Province of Canada to the reluctant Maritimes during the Confederation conferences. The importance of the railway is indicated by its inclusion in the Canadian constitution — perhaps the only constitution in the world that contains such a clause. Construction was begun within the prescribed time, and by 1876 the Intercolonial Railway connected Halifax with Rivière du Loup on the St. Lawrence. Once the railway was completed, the clause had no meaning, and Section 145 was repealed in 1893.

146. It shall be lawful for the Queen, by and with the Advice of Her Majesty's Most Honourable Privy Council, on Addresses from the Houses of the Parliament of Canada, and from the Houses of the respective Legislatures of the Colonies or Provinces of Newfoundland, Prince Edward Island, and British Columbia, to admit those Colonies or Provinces, or any of them, into the Union, and on Address from the Houses of the Parliament of Canada to admit Rupert's Land and the North-western Territory, or either of them, into the Union, on such Terms and Conditions in each Case as are in the Addresses expressed and as the Queen thinks fit to approve, subject to the Provisions of this Act; and the Provisions of any Order in Council in that Behalf shall have effect as if they had been enacted by the Parliament of the United Kingdom of Great Britain and Ireland.

147. In Case of the Admission of Newfoundland and Prince Edward Island, or either of them, each shall be entitled to a Representation in the Senate of Canada of Four Members, and (notwithstanding anything in this Act) in case of the Admission of Newfoundland the normal Number of Senators shall be Seventy-six . . . but Prince Edward Island when admitted shall be deemed to be comprised in the Third of the Three Divisions into which Canada is, in relation to the Constitution of the Senate, divided by this Act, and accordingly, after the Admission of Prince Edward Island, whether Newfoundland is admitted or not, the Representation of Nova Scotia and New Brunswick in the Senate shall, as Vacancies occur, be reduced from Twelve to Ten Members respectively, and the Representation of each of those Provinces shall not be increased at any Time beyond Ten, except under the Provisions of This Act for the Appointment of Three or Six additional Senators under the Direction of the Queen.

INTERPRETING THE CANADIAN CONSTITUTION[255]

A Canadian authority comments on the problems of interpreting the constitution of Canada, and argues in favour of the legal, rather than the political, approach:

. . . By following the sentimental route, many authors have interpreted our constitution not as it really is but rather as each one of them has desired that it should be. . . .

Unfortunately most speeches on constitutional subjects are delivered with the thought of pleasing the electorate and winning votes, whether in the House or on the hustings.

There is not much use in invoking the spirit of the constitution or in trying to guess what was in the minds of the Fathers of Confederation if the majority can quote the letter of the law and the decisions of the Privy Council.

The shifting sands of sentiment cannot destroy the solid rock of a law which might perhaps be altered in a different way if the cause be just and the necessity of such alteration made evident.

Problems have a better chance of solution if the remedy proposed is suggested in a dispassionate way and not by politicians trying to pass on as truths the prejudices which necessarily exist in different parts of the country.

As was outlined in the preamble to the B.N.A. Act, the Fathers of Confederation intended the union of 1867 to be only a prelude to a nation "from sea to sea." They expected that the remaining colonies and territories of British North America would, within a short time, join Confederation.

VI

THE MACDONALD ERA: EXPERIMENT IN NATION BUILDING 1867-1896

When the Dominion of Canada was created, Sir John A. Macdonald (knighted by Queen Victoria for his efforts in bringing about Confederation) became the first Prime Minister of the new Dominion. He held this office until the year of his death in 1891, with the exception of the Liberal interlude between 1873 and 1878. His skill in keeping the Conservatives in power — they were not ousted until five years after his death — is recognized in that the period 1867-1896 is often referred to as the Macdonald Era.

In 1867 only a small part of British North America was in the Union. Outside the Dominion were the colonies of Newfoundland, Prince Edward Island and British Columbia. The Northwest, stretching from Lake Superior to the Rockies, and under the control of the Hudson's Bay Company, had yet to be acquired by Canada. The Macdonald era witnessed one of the chief aims of the Fathers of Confederation — the extension of the Dominion from sea to sea. Only Newfoundland, which delayed its entry until 1949, resisted the pull of unification. Also, the transcontinental railway provided a continuous link from Nova Scotia to British Columbia and facilitated a growth of pride and a sense of identity in the young country.

But the Macdonald era was a stormy period. It was a time of recurring crises in which the very survival of the new Dominion was often in doubt. The Washington Treaty rejected Canadian attempts for reciprocity and, thereafter Canada resorted to a protectionist tariff policy. The Pacific Scandal nearly destroyed the Conservative Party and threatened Macdonald's political career. Rebellion in the West inflamed racial and religious animosities and endangered the fragile unity that Confederation had achieved. Sectionalism and the struggle for provincial rights challenged the wide powers which the British North America Act had ostensibly vested in the central government. Economic difficulties raised talk of annexation to the United States; moderates advocated commercial union with either the United States or Britain or with both.

Macdonald's statesmanship kept the Conservative Party in power and was a vital force in preventing the disintegration of the Union. After his death political difficulties and economic depression combined to end the long Conservative regime. A new figure, Wilfrid Laurier, appeared on the political horizon and, like Macdonald, dominated Canadian political life.

19

DOMINION "FROM SEA TO SEA"

A

TROUBLE WITH NOVA SCOTIA

Nova Scotia posed the first serious threat to the newly created Dominion. The province felt that it had been herded into Confederation by British and Canadian politicians with no regard for the wishes of its people. The first federal election in September, 1867, gave the voters a chance to express themselves on their new status as Canadians. Enough were satisfied to give Macdonald an election victory, but Nova Scotia rejected the Conservatives — Joseph Howe's anti-Confederationists captured eighteen of the province's nineteen federal seats. In view of the election results, Macdonald carried on with a coalition cabinet in the hope of guaranteeing representation from all sections and groups of the country.

Howe began a campaign to protect the interests of his province, which was suffering economic depression because of the end of reciprocity. He not only blamed the federal government for Nova Scotia's economic distress, but also accused it of forcing unfair financial arrangements on his province. In the provincial election of 1868, Howe's Liberals won thirty-six of the thirty-eight seats. The new legislature passed a resolution for the repeal of the B.N.A. Act. Howe headed a delegation to London to present the repeal resolution. The British government refused to consider it. In Nova Scotia there was talk of defying the British government, of secession, and even of annexation to the United States.

As was the case in the Canadas during the 1830's, Loyalists and moderates pledged their support to the British connection. Howe, a persistent opponent of Confederation, was a staunch imperialist and an adamant foe of annexation. He insisted that changes in Nova Scotia's status take place within the British Empire. Therefore, he decided upon a course of collaboration with the Dominion government to obtain better financial terms for Nova Scotia.

NOVA SCOTIA'S THREAT OF WITHDRAWAL[256]

D'Arcy McGee's reaction to Nova Scotia's attempt to withdraw from Confederation, in a speech to the House of Commons April 6, 1868:

. . . I have every confidence that we will similarly wear out Nova Scotian hostility by the unfailing exercise and exhibition of a high-minded spirit of fair play. We will compel them by our fairness and our kindness. . . . Our friends, Sir, need have no fear but that Confederation will ever be administered with serene and even justice. To its whole history, from its earliest inception to its final triumphant consummation, no stigma can be attached, no stain attributed. Its single aim from the beginning has been to consolidate the extent of British North America with the utmost regard to the independent power and privileges of each Province, and I, Sir, who have been, and who am still, its warm and earnest advocate, speak here not as the representative of any race, or of any Province, but as thoroughly and emphatically a Canadian, ready and bound to recognize the claims, if any, of my Canadian fellow-subjects, from the farthest east to the farthest west, equally as those of my nearest neighbour, or of the friend who proposed me on the hustings.

Macdonald was prepared to pacify a dissatisfied Nova Scotia. In 1869, Ottawa agreed to increase Nova Scotia's annual grant for a period of ten years. By yielding to Nova Scotia's demands, the federal government set a precedent for federal-provincial relations. In the future, provinces would exert pressure on the federal government to obtain revisions on agreements between the two levels of government.

"BETTER TERMS" FOR NOVA SCOTIA[257]

In a letter of January 12, 1869, Sir John A. Macdonald writes to Joseph Howe:

. . . . We shall have our own difficulties with the General Parliament in carrying *any* concessions. Already has George Brown, through the *Globe*, protested against any pecuniary advantages being given to Nova Scotia, beyond those secured to them by the Union Act. This course will not at all deter us here from agreeing to what is reasonable, and staking our existence upon it in the Legislature.

The Province of Quebec . . . will, we fear, attempt to put on the screws for additonal pecuniary aid if it is granted to you. So you see that we must take great care as to every step we take.

. . . whatever you agree upon must be kept strictly a secret. If divulged prematurely, the Opposition press in Ontario will protest against any additional charges being put upon the people of that Province. . . . In Quebec, the united press will demand a slice for that Province, and all the anti-papers in Nova Scotia will denounce the arrangement as being altogether insufficient and unsatisfactory, and you will have the usual charge brought against you of "selling you heritage for a mess of potage", & c. . . .

Sir John A. Macdonald

By a clever political move, Macdonald further diminished Nova Scotia's recalcitrant attitude. He enticed Howe into the federal cabinet by offering him a ministerial post. Followers of the long-time "Voice of Nova Scotia" were bewildered; they raised the cry of bribery, treachery and betrayal. But Howe's removal from Nova Scotia's political scene had left the anti-confederationists without a leader, and their vociferous agitation soon subsided. Thus the crafty Macdonald managed to keep Confederation intact.

B

MANITOBA BECOMES A PROVINCE

Bringing the West into Confederation proved a far more difficult task than the pacification of Nova Scotia. The reasons for acquiring the territory between the Great Lakes and the Rockies were bound up with the original drive for Confederation. South of the Red River settlement lay Minnesota, which became a state in the American Union in 1858; by 1865, it had a population of 300,000. With the westward movement of American settlers, a "peaceful invasion" of the Canadian West seemed imminent. In the eyes of the Colonial Office and Sir John A. Macdonald, Canada must either acquire the Northwest or lose it to the United States. What began as a mere transfer of land was forced, by unexpected events, to include the creation of Manitoba as the Dominion's fifth province.

At the request of the Canadian Parliament, the British government began preparations in 1868 to transfer the Northwest to the Dominion. In the fall, Cartier and William McDougall went to London to take part in the final negotiations. The following year, the Hudson's Bay Company agreed to give up its governing authority and land. The Company was to receive £300,000 ($1,500,000), and retain approximately 45,000 acres of land around its trading posts, as well as one-twentieth of the total fertile land. Britain was to receive the land, transfer it to Canada and guarantee Canada a loan for the purchase.

The official date set for the transfer was December 1, 1869. Arrangements were almost completed, and still the settlers of the Northwest were neither consulted nor advised about the terms and date of the transfer. This is not entirely surprising, since the whole of the Northwest contained no more than 12,000 people, most of whom resided along the Red River. Of these, some 10,000 were Métis engaged in hunting, trading and some agriculture. There were also English-speaking half-breeds, British settlers, a few Americans, and a small group of immigrants from Ontario. These English Canadians, a self-important group who called themselves the Canadian Party, agitated for union with Canada as a means of opening the West for settlers of their own kind. The leader, Dr. John Christian Schultz, used the *Nor'Wester* — a newspaper founded in 1859 — to champion the cause of the Canadian Party.

JOHN CHRISTIAN SCHULTZ[258]

Alexander Begg discusses Schultz:

.... This bold, ambitious and aggressive man [John Schultz] had become the focus of all the dislike and distrust of Canadians and things Canadian in Red River. Schultz was the outspoken advocate of Canadian annexation . . . he would himself be a beneficiary of the transfer. . . . The handsomest of men, tall, solid, and quick in movement, he was yet reserved, studious and low-voiced; able but not popular; winning men, if at all, by force of intellect, not by the power of affection. His reputation amongst the leading men of Red River was that he was a selfish and unscrupulous adventurer; his friends thought him a champion of popular rights and a Canadian patriot. . . .

.... In 1864 Schultz was a leader in the formation of the Order of Free and Affiliated Masons. And in 1867 he married Anne Campbell Farquharson when that lady had just been baptized as a convert to Roman Catholicism. The marriage put an end to the conversion . . . the dislike and distrust with which he was viewed by the clergy and *métis* may well have been intensified by his adherence to Free Masonry and the circumstances of his marriage.

The Dilemma Facing Nova Scotia

Rumors about the future of the Northwest had already begun to circulate when, in September, 1868, surveyors arrived to lay out the Dawson Road — a highway from Lake of the Woods to Fort Garry. The settlers, especially the Métis, became alarmed that their land might be taken away by the Canadian government. The Métis fears were substantiated in the following year, when another group of surveyors arrived. The Canadian government, while still negotiating the purchase of the Northwest, had decided upon an advance survey to prepare for the expected rush of settlers into the new territory. Division of the land on the American plan of rectangular townships necessitated trespassing on the strip farms — adapted to Red River from the system on the St. Lawrence.

When the terms of the transfer became known, the Canadians in the colony approved the idea of union with Canada and envisioned a large influx from Ontario. The Métis, however, were filled with a sense of uncertainty about their future. The isolation of the prairies had enabled them to develop a separate identity and a semi-nomadic way of life. All this, the Métis believed, would come to an end if hordes of strangers were to come to the Northwest. In their anxiety about the fate of their language, religion and unconfined existence, the Métis turned to Louis Riel for leadership.

Louis Riel, an able and well educated Métis born in St. Boniface, had studied in Montreal for the priesthood. Riel was only twenty-five years old when he took up the Métis cause and became their spokesman. His fluency in both French and English and his sense of mission concerning the rights

Riel and his Councillors, 1869-70

of the settlers of Red River made him the natural leader of resistance to Canada's designs for the Northwest.

This episode is related by Begg:
Tuesday, 11th January, 1870

Weather biting cold.
All the escaped prisoners except two have been recaptured — one of them W. F. Hyman had his feet so badly frozen that it is feared he will lose his toes. Mr. Riel who was present while the doctors were cutting and working at the injured parts on the man's foot had to leave the room — and as he afterwards remarked to a friend ["] I pitied that young man — what a position mine is to have to bear all this — but I cannot help myself.["]

The Dominion government was not unaware of the mood in the colony. The Anglican Bishop of Rupert's Land had informed Ottawa of his concern. Bishop Alexandre Antoine Taché, in October, 1869, on his way to the Ecumenical Council in Rome, had warned Cartier about unrest in Red River. The federal government showed little concern.

October 11, 1869, may be taken as the beginning of resistance to the Dominion government. On that day, Riel and a group of his followers stopped a government survey party near Red River. A more serious challenge to Ottawa took place at Pembina, on the United States border. William McDougall, the appointed Lieutenant-Governor for the Northwest Territory, had travelled by way of the United States to the Red River colony. On October 21, a few days after his arrival at Pembina, he was prevented from entering the

colony by members of *Comité National des Métis* — an organization created by Riel only five days before. It was an embarrassing situation for an official of the Dominion government to be stranded in the United States and prevented from entering into what was shortly to become Canadian territory.

Riel sensed that the Canadian Party might persuade McDougall to attempt an immediate takeover of the colony. He decided to forestall this in order to give the other settlers a position of bargaining strength with the federal government. On November 2, he seized Fort Garry, the Hudson's Bay Company fort, strategically located at the junction of the Red and Assiniboine Rivers, with its stores of weapons.

Riel worked to obtain support among English-speaking settlers as well as from the Métis for a provisional government and a "Bill of Rights" to be presented to Ottawa. The restive McDougall, from Pembina, decided to force the issue on December 1, the date originally set for the official transfer of the Territory to Canada. In the absence of further instructions from Sir John A. Macdonald, and not knowing what was transpiring in Ottawa, McDougall took matters into his own hands and proclaimed his authority over the Northwest. His announcement was ineffective; he had no reason to believe it could be enforced. More serious still, his action was unwittingly premature. Macdonald had stopped proceedings in the transfer of the Territory until the Hudson's Bay Company could guarantee law and order. But the Company's ailing Governor, William Mactavish, felt his jurisdiction ended with McDougall's proclamation.

Sir John A. Macdonald in a letter to Hon. John Rose, from Ottawa, December 31, 1869:

. . . . McDougall has made a most inglorious *fiasco* at Red River. When he left here he fully understood that he was to go as a private individual to report on the state of affairs at Red River, but to assume no authority until officially notified from here that Rupert's Land was united to Canada. . . .

Notwithstanding this, from mere impatience at his uncomfortable position at Pembina, and before he could possibly have received instructions in answer to his report of being stopped on the way, he chose to assume that, on the 1st of December, the surrender was made by the Company and the Order in Council passed by the Queen. . . . He issued a proclamation under the Great Seal of the new province, formally adding it to the Dominion. . . .

All this has been done in the direct teeth of instructions, and he has ingeniously contrived to humiliate himself and Canada, to arouse the hopes and pretensions of the insurgents. . . .

Into this void stepped Riel. On December 8, he set up a provisional government to provide law and order and to give the settlers an Assembly to which they could elect their representatives. A Bill of Rights embodying the people's demands was drafted.

INAUGURATION OF THE PROVISIONAL GOVERNMENT[261]

Alexander Begg's account:
Friday, 10th December, 1869

It was the opinion of certain residents in the town that the settlement would have to go in for the Provisional government for self protection. . . . The French to-day hoisted the Provisional Government flag . . . and fired off a volley of small arms and salutes from the cannon at Fort Garry . . . the band of St. Boniface . . . had played several tunes. . . . Three cheers were given for the Provisional Government — three for the leaders and three for the band — followed by three groans for Mulligan — late chief of police now a prisoner at Fort Garry. Mr. Riel addressed the French at Fort Garry and in the course of his speech hoped his men were all loyal to the Queen. Thus was inaugurated the Provisional Government of Red River under Bruce & Riel. How long it will last remains to be proved.

News of the activities in Red River aroused sympathy in Quebec and hopes of annexationists in the United States. The powerful anti-Catholic Orangeman organization in Ontario, supporters of the Canadian Party in the colony, agitated against the privileges sought by the Métis. The federal government, at last, abandoned its policy of ignoring the Métis grievances.

AMERICAN ANNEXATIONISTS AT RED RIVER[262]

John Wickes Taylor was one of several United States officials who worked to turn discontent at Red River, especially among the Métis, into a movement for union of the colony with the United States. An American historian gives this account of him:

Taylor, formerly state librarian of Ohio, was the greatest American authority on western British

"The Situation" Brother Jonathan (U.S.) Watching Miss Winnie Peg, while Miss Canada Extends Arms

America and he peddled his knowledge to advantage. During the period of the revolt the Department of State employed him as a secret agent to keep [the United States' Secretary of State] posted on Red River affairs; at the same time he was also serving as informant and publicist for [prominent American railway interests]. Taylor, however, was more than a hack for special interests. He believed sincerely in the mutual benefits and the ultimate inevitability of annexation. He knew all of the groups of expansionists, commuted between the centers of agitation, and became the liaison man for the movement. Its failure was not due to any lack of ability or effort on his part.

The Canadian government dispatched its negotiators, headed by Donald A. Smith, the chief representative of the Hudson's Bay Company in Canada, to negotiate with the provisional government. At mass-meetings in January, held outdoors in temperatures of twenty below zero, Smith presented Canada's case. The settlers agreed to deal with Canada's representatives and established a Legislative Assembly representing French- and English-speaking settlers, with Louis Riel as President. The oft-revised Bill of Rights was again amended and a delegation chosen to proceed to Ottawa to discuss the new Bill of Rights with the federal government.

Sir John A. Macdonald was unwilling to recognize the Red River delegates as envoys of a legal government. When negotiations finally began late in April, the delegates were accepted only as representatives of the people of Red River. Agreement was reached for the colony to enter the Dominion as a province and for Riel to hand over his authority to a Lieutenant-Governor to be appointed by the Dominion. It was also decided to send troops to the colony to assure order and to facilitate the establishment of a new government.

DONALD SMITH ADDRESSES MEETING IN RED RIVER[263]

THE NEW NATION, *January 21, 1870, reports the meeting held on Wednesday, 19th January, 1870:*

MASS MEETINGS
Mr. Smith Canadian Commissioner,
before the People
OFFICIAL DOCUMENTS
(Reported for THE NEW NATION)

A grand mass meeting of the inhabitants of the Settlement, was held at Upper Fort Garry on the 19th inst. So many were present that the assembly had to be held in the open air, and this, when the thermometer stood at about 20 deg. below zero. The meeting lasted some five hours. . . .

In opening the meeting the chairman [Mr. Thos. Bunn] expressed it as his opinion that this was the most important meeting ever held in the Settlement. The most vital interests were at stake, and he therefore hoped that the utmost order and good humor would prevail. . . .

The Chairman introduced to the meeting Mr. Donald A. Smith, who came forward and reading the following document, which he said, had been handed to him in Canada. . . .

Alexander Begg notes in his entry of 19th January, 1870:

At the close of the meeting Mr. John Burke jumped up and demanded the release of the prisoners. Mr. Riel said not just now. Some . . . cried out yes! yes! They must be released. On this the French flew to their arms and there was a general skidaddle amongst a good many of the English — the act was premature on the part of Burke — but everything was quieted down and the meeting separated quietly.

On May 12, 1870, the federal government passed the Manitoba Act creating the Province of Manitoba as of July 15, 1870. The Act embodied most of the major clauses of the Bill of Rights drawn up by Riel's Provisional Government. Of the land acquired from the Hudson's Bay Company, a small portion became the Province of Manitoba; the rest of the North West Territory was to be governed by an appointed Governor and Council. In the new province, the settlers were given rights to their land, but public land remained the property of the Dominion government.* Both

French and English were to be official languages in the debates and records of the legislature. The dual school system — denominational Catholic and Protestant schools — already in existence would continue. The provincial government was set up, with a bicameral legislature, a Lieutenant-Governor and Executive Council.† Manitoba was to receive an annual subsidy of $30,000 and a yearly grant of eighty cents per head of population until it reached 400,000.

The "birth of Manitoba" was not the only product of the insurrection at Red River. Throughout Canada, relations between French- and English-speaking Canadians — the fundamental issue in the creation of Confederation — was further embittered by events which unfolded in the colony.

The Canadian Party of Dr. John Schultz had resisted Louis Riel from the beginning of his leadership of the Red River Métis. Shortly after proclaiming the Provisional Government in December 1869, Riel had thrown Schultz and some of his followers in jail. Donald A. Smith had arrived and was conducting his discussions with the Provisional Government when Schultz escaped and began to stir up English-speaking settlers to attack Fort Garry to free the other prisoners. Thomas Scott, an Irish Canadian, mobilized a band of sixty men from the Canadian settlement at Portage la Prairie and joined Schultz in Kildonan. As the atmosphere in the colony grew tense, a skirmish involving Métis and several of the Canadian Party resulted in death to one of each side. Cooler heads prevailed for the moment, and the expected fight did not develop. Riel decided that the Provisional Government's authority must be demonstrated; the Portage men, including Thomas Scott, were imprisoned.

TENSION AT RED RIVER[264]

The following refers to the tension between French and English at Red River at the beginning of December, 1869, shortly before Dr. Schultz and some of his followers were jailed:

Dame rumour now began to use her power, and it must be said that she added greatly to the complications of the time. Reports began to fly about in all quarters and on all subjects; and it was greatly owing to this that the excitement was kept up to such an extent as it was. One of these injurious reports, circulated about this time, was to the effect that the Canadians in Winnipeg were going to make a dash upon Fort Garry, and take it out of the hands of the French. There was no

---

* The Dominion government later used grants of land to promote settlement in the West, and to subsidize railway-building.

† The Legislative Council was disbanded in 1876.

foundation for this rumour; but the consequence of its being afloat caused the French to be more on the alert, and to have suspicions of those who had not joined them, and tended to widen the breach then existing between the two sides of the Settlement. . . .

Scott, an Orangeman from Ontario who had come out the year before to work on the Dawson Road, was contemptuous of Riel and anxious to overthrow the Provisional Government. He had previously escaped from jail in Fort Garry and was known to the Métis as one of the most militant men in the Canadian Party. As a prisoner a second time, he showed a foolhardy lack of concern for his life by abusing the Métis guards and threatening Riel's life. The result was a council, consisting of seven Métis and presided over by Riel's chief aide, Ambroise Lépine. Accused of hostility toward the Provisional Government, abuse of his guards and inciting the other prisoners to violence, Scott was condemned and the following day, March 4, 1870, was shot.

EXECUTION OF THOMAS SCOTT[265]

Alexander Begg's account:
Tuesday, 1st March, 1870

. . . . Scott one of the prisoners is in irons for having been indiscreet in the use of his tongue while in prison.

Friday, 4th March, 1870

This morning the news spread that Thos. Scott one of the prisoners was condemned to be shot to-day at twelve O'Clock — this was not believed at first by anyone but some time after when it became known that the lumber and nails had been procured for his coffin people began to realize it. Rev. Geo. Young at the request of Scott went and stayed with him to prepare him for his end. Paper pens and ink were furnished the doomed man to write to his friends. At about twelve O'Clock a.m. a large crowd gathered around the side door leading into Fort Garry. Scott was then brought out — it is said he prayed as he walked — a bandage was then put over his eyes and he knelt. . . .

On a given signal four of the guns were fired (two missing fire) and Scott fell forward pierced in four places — he was not yet dead but struggled on the ground. The Canadian [Métis] then went up and shot Scott — the ball from the revolver passed in at the ear of the unfortunate man and passed out at his mouth. The corpse was then put into a rough coffin and placed in one of the bastions. A deep gloom has settled over the settlement on account of this deed.

Whatever the justification for the act, the execution of Scott raised a storm of angry protest in Ontario, where anti-French and anti-Catholic feeling flared up anew. In Quebec, the shooting of Scott was considered to be a necessary part of the Métis struggle for French-Canadian rights. In Ottawa, Sir John A. Macdonald came under considerable pressure to send troops to Red River in order to crush the "rebellion" and protect English Canadians.

The dispatch of troops took place sooner than had been planned. British regulars and militia from Ontario and Quebec, a total of 1200 men under Colonel Garnet Wolseley, began the long journey to the Red River colony. The federal government also enlisted the aid of Bishop Taché, who was on his way back from Rome, to assist in an orderly transfer of governmental authority. After a ninety-six-day arduous trek across the rugged terrain of the Canadian Shield, the troops entered the newly created province on August 23rd. Riel, fearing for his life since an anticipated amnesty had not yet been granted by the federal government, fled to the United States.

Manitoba, the first province to be created by Canada, came into being much sooner than it would have if there had not been an insurrection. Because of Riel's leadership, the federal government was compelled to recognize the existence of a small but flourishing community at Red River. But the tragedy of racial hatred that accompanied the establishment of Manitoba was to have long-lasting repercussions. To some, Riel was a murderer whose hands were stained with Protestant blood; to others, he was a patriot who fought for and secured the rights of his people.

C

BRITISH COLUMBIA ENTERS CONFEDERATION

In 1867, the British Columbia legislature passed a resolution favouring a union with Canada. Nothing was done about it at the time, since the Hudson's Bay Company territory lay between the

Rockies and Canada and made it physically impossible to accomplish such a union. However, once the Northwest became part of Canada, the prospects for including the Pacific colony in the

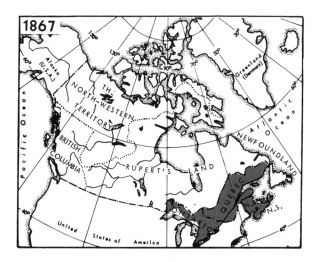

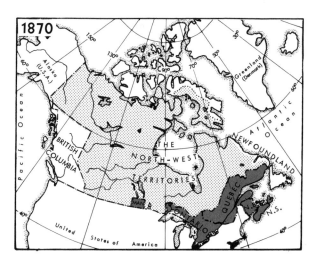

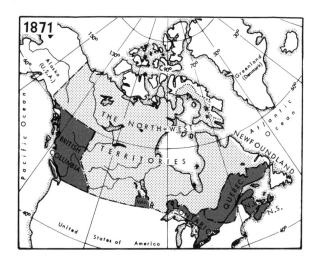

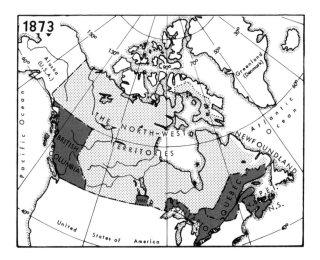

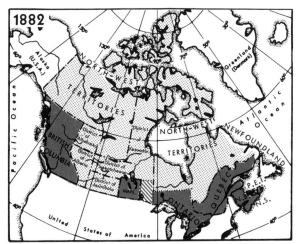

Dominion became brighter. The key to Confederation for British Columbia was a railway to connect it with Canada.

British Columbians had diverse views on the future of the colony. A small but influential British group — officials of the Hudson's Bay Company and the government — favoured continuation as a Crown colony under a Governor and representative government. Commercial interests saw their destiny with the American Northwest; they received considerable support from annexationists in the United States. A Canadian element whose

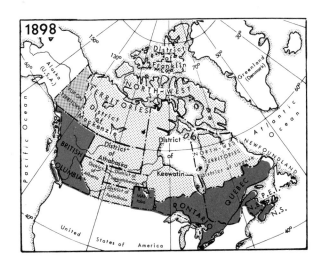

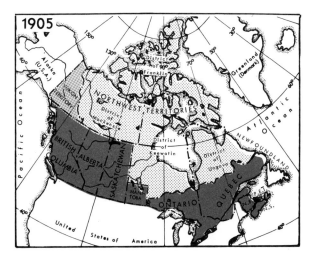

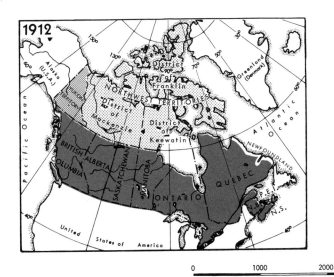

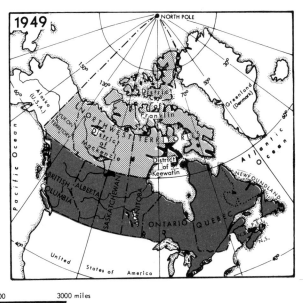

0   1000   2000   3000 miles

The Growth of Canada, 1867-1949

leaders saw the benefits of provincial status and responsible government stood for Confederation.

VICTORIA, B.C. ABOUT 1870[266]

A description of Victoria:

Its population is less than 5,000; but almost every nationality is represented. Greek fishermen, Kanaka sailors, Jewish and Scotch merchants, Chinese washermen, French, German, and Yankee restaurant-keepers, English and Canadian office-holders and butchers, negro waiters and sweeps, Australian farmers and other varieties of the race, rub against each other, apparently in the most friendly way. The sign-boards tell their own tale;

"Own Shing, washing and ironing;" "Sam Hang," ditto; "Kwong Tai & Co., cigar store;" "Magasin Francais;" "Teutonic Hall, lager beer;" "Scotch House;" "Adelphic" and "San Francisco" saloons; "Oriental" and "New England" restaurants; "What Cheer Market," and "Play Me Off at Ten-pins," are found within gunshot, interspersed with more common-place signs.

The most articulate of the pro-Confederationists was William Alexander Smith, a native of Nova Scotia, who assumed the *nom de plume* of Amor de Cosmos. He used his newspaper, *The British Colonist*, to promote his cause. In September, 1869, he organized a convention at Yale, B.C.,

Amor de Cosmos

Victoria Harbour, B.C., c. 1870

where resolutions were passed for union and responsible government. The colonial officials denounced the rally and termed its demands disloyalty and treason. The annexationists, on their part, sent a petition, bearing only 104 signatures, to President Grant requesting the absorption of British Columbia within the United States. The net result of the anti-Confederation activities was to arouse wider support for union with Canada.

Conditions within the colony moulded a favourable opinion for Confederation — British Columbia had a population of only 36,000, financial difficulties, economic depression and a huge debt. Also, in 1867, the United States' purchase of Alaska from Russia imparted to British Columbians a feeling of American encirclement. Only union with Canada appeared to offer hope of survival.

A PRO-CONFEDERATIONIST IN
BRITISH COLUMBIA[267]

The Hon. Mr. Robson speaks on Confederation in the Legislative Council of British Columbia, March 9, 1870:

. . . . Ten years ago the Colony had a very much larger population than now, and very much larger commerce. Are we, then, under these circumstances, to ask the people to wait and work out their own salvation? . . . we are told in a State paper that we are not to be allowed to hang on the skirts of Great Britain, like a mendicant's child. I can hardly reconcile the position of manly independence with the position of hanging on to unwilling Imperial skirts. Rather than that, I would ask for Union with the Sandwich Islands, or with Hindostan. British Columbia has tried long enough to get on by herself. After fifteen years hard struggle, she finds herself worse off than she was at the beginning. Her progress has been like that of a crab — backward.

. . . . Apart from its being the policy of the British Government to unite all the British American Colonies in one great Federation, if we persist in remaining alone we shall be told by the Imperial Government that we are not fit for liberal institutions, and not prepared for self-government . . . we are not fit for Responsible Government, and that we ought to confederate.

There is no difficulty in showing that Confederation will be beneficial to British Columbia; that is to say, Confederation on proper terms. . . . The public works proposed would make the population of the colony double what it is now . . . the construction of the Railway alone would bring a very great increase to our labouring and productive population.

The British government regarded British Columbia's entrance into the Dominion as the best assurance for keeping the colony within the Empire. In 1869, the death of Governor Frederick Seymour, a persistent opponent of Confederation, opened the way for the appointment of Sir

Anthony Musgrave. The new Governor arrived with instructions to promote the Imperial Government's hopes for the colony.

In the summer of 1870, a delegation from British Columbia negotiated the colony's entry into the Dominion. Sir John A. Macdonald promised the construction of a railway to the Pacific to meet the prime condition for British Columbia's entry. Macdonald did so in spite of the fact that few in Canada believed that the Dominion possessed the resources for such an ambitious undertaking. In fact, many dismissed the project of building a railway through the seemingly insurmountable Canadian Rockies as sheer folly.

On July 20th, 1871, British Columbia became the sixth province of the Dominion. The Pacific colony entered Confederation on the promise that a railway to the coast would be begun in two years and completed within ten. British Columbia was to receive provincial status, an annual subsidy of $35,000 and a yearly per capita grant of eighty cents until the population reached 400,000. The federal government also assumed the new province's debt. Canada now stretched from the Atlantic to the Pacific, physically united "from sea to sea."

<hr>

D

PRINCE EDWARD ISLAND JOINS THE DOMINION

The reluctance which kept Prince Edward Island out of Confederation in 1867 soon gave way to a more realistic attitude. While Canada showed signs of growth, Prince Edward Island was stagnating. Along with the traditional problem of the absentee landlords, the colony contracted a huge debt because of an over-ambitious railway building program. The Island also experienced difficulties in raising funds; its credit was very low in the financial houses of New York and London. In 1872, Sir John A. Macdonald again proposed that Prince Edward Island enter Confederation. She could not resist the financial inducements offered her. On July 1, 1873, Prince Edward Island became part of the Dominion.

PRINCE EDWARD ISLAND'S PROPOSED ENTRY INTO CONFEDERATION[268]

Sir John A. Macdonald in a letter of December 13, 1872, to Sir John Rose:

. . . . The matter stands thus: Governor Robinson of Prince Edward Island has written privately, and as if off his own bat, to Lord Dufferin, saying that he thought that he could bring round his Government to consider the subject of Union, if Canada were still inclined in that direction. He wrote beyond a doubt at the instigation of his Council. . . . Since then, Robinson telegraphed in cypher to know whether he was to understand that the island railway debt would be taken into consideration. The answer was, that the railway debt was a proper subject for negotiations, and that any proposition with regard to it would be carefully considered here.

Prince Edward Island received full provincial status and annual grants similar to those given Manitoba and British Columbia. In addition to assuming the heavy debt of the colony, Canada contributed $80,000 to assist in the purchase of land from the absentee landlords. The federal government took over the Island's railway lines and undertook to guarantee communication with the mainland through a telegraph system and a year-round ferry service between Prince Edward Island and Nova Scotia.

Within six years of Confederation, seven of the ten provinces of modern Canada had been created. The Northwest Territory seemed fated to remain a vast preserve for great herds of buffalo, roaming Indian tribes and enterprising fur traders. But with large scale immigration at the turn of the century, the provinces of Alberta and Saskatchewan were soon carved out. With the belated entry of Newfoundland in 1949, only the Yukon and the new Northwest Territories remain as potential provinces of the Dominion.

20

EXPERIMENT IN PERIL

A

THE WASHINGTON TREATY

A number of issues arising out of the American Civil War strained relations between the United States and Britain. Canada — closely tied to Britain for defence, and dependent on the United States for trade — did not escape the anti-British feelings prevalent in the United States. Britain and the United States had set up a Joint High Commission to meet at Washington to discuss the outstanding issues causing a deterioration of relations not only between the United States and Britain but also between the United States and Canada. Since matters affecting Canada were to be agreed upon, Sir John A. Macdonald was appointed one of the five British commissioners. Ostensibly, his duties were those of a commissioner and not of a Prime Minister of Canada.

From the outset it was evident that Britain was mainly interested in establishing cordial relationships with the United States. In view of this British attitude, Macdonald was faced with the difficult task of obtaining the best possible terms for Canada. Whereas the United States wished to combine all the issues — the *Alabama* claim, the San Juan boundary dispute and the Canadian inshore fisheries controversy — and refer them to arbitration, Macdonald sought separate consideration of each. Thus he hoped that matters of concern to Canada would not be sacrificed in a general agreement. In spite of his efforts, all the issues were interwoven, to a large extent, in the discussions.

J. A. MACDONALD ON THE WASHINGTON TREATY[269]

In a series of letters from Washington to Dr. Charles Tupper, Sir John A. Macdonald remarked on the proceedings of the conference:
March 17, 1871

. . . . Having nearly made up my mind that the Americans want everything, and will give us

nothing in exchange, one of my chief aims now is to convince the British Commissioners of the unreasonableness of the Yankees. This they are beginning to find out, and are a good deal disappointed.

————

April 1, 1871

I must say that I am greatly disappointed at the course taken by the British Commissioners. They seem to have only one thing on their minds — that is, to go home to England with a treaty in their pockets, settling everything, no matter at what cost to Canada.

A favourable outcome of the dispute over the Canadian inshore fisheries was of primary importance to Canada. When reciprocity ended in 1866, Canada claimed that the fishing rights expanded by Elgin in 1854 should revert to the privileges accorded by the Convention of 1818. American fishermen, upon payment of license fees, were still allowed to fish in Canadian waters. By not excluding the Americans entirely, the door was kept open for future negotiations in the hope of gaining renewal of reciprocity. But the United States showed no desire to change its stand on reciprocity, and Canada began to enforce fishing regulations more rigidly. Unlicensed American fishing boats were seized by Canadian coastal patrols. The Americans were highly incensed by these actions and threatened retaliation. When the Commission met at Washington, the fisheries were one of the main subjects of discussion.

The fisheries were Canada's trump card in the negotiations with the United States; there was no doubt that Macdonald considered the possibility of exchanging fishing rights for reciprocity. The United States, however, under pressure from its high tariff protectionists, dismissed all suggestions of reciprocity, but did offer a token reciprocity — free entry on several items — in return for inshore fishing rights. Macdonald refused the offer and negotiations were deadlocked. Britain, more anxious to settle the *Alabama* claim, gave only feeble support to Canada on the fisheries issue. Macdonald soon realized that the British delegates were ready to make concessions to the United States even at the expense of Canadian interests.

Eventually agreement was reached. Citizens of the United States were given the right to fish in Canadian waters for a period of ten years; in return, Canadian fish could enter the American market duty-free. Also, the amount to be paid for this fishing privilege was to be determined by a commission. In 1877, such a commission met at Halifax and set the payment at $5,500,000 — an award very favourable to Canada.

Macdonald also sought compensation for damages caused by the Fenian raids. The United States claimed that this topic was not on the agenda and refused to discuss it. Britain, however, desirous of avoiding friction — so anxious was she to please the Americans — offered to compensate Canada for the damages she suffered in the Fenian raids!

MACDONALD ON THE FENIAN CLAIMS[270]

To Dr. Charles Tupper, dated at Washington, April 16, 1871:

To-day he [Lord de Grey, one of the British Commissioners] informed me . . . in strictest confidence, that H.M. Government, if all other matters were settled . . . would agree to pay to Canada a sum of money for the Fenian claims, if the United States did not. If, however, other matters were not settled, this understanding would go for nothing.

Another contentious issue was the boundary in the Portland channel separating Vancouver Island from the mainland. The Oregon Treaty had stated that the boundary followed the channel of communication. But there were two channels and between them lay the island of San Juan. Both Britain and the United States claimed possession of this island, where extensive sheep raising was carried on. The ambiguous, if not incorrect, wording of the treaty had to be clarified. The Washington Commission decided to refer the dispute to the German Kaiser for arbitration. He awarded the island to the United States.

The question of the waterways along the American-Canadian border, of mutual interest to both countries, was quickly and amicably settled. Agreement was reached for free navigation of the St. Lawrence by the United States and the same privileges for Canada on Lake Michigan and on the rivers in Alaska.

At the Washington Conference Britain was mainly interested in settling the *Alabama* claim. The *Alabama* was a cruiser built in Britain for the South, who used it to raid Northern shipping during the Civil War. The United States held Britain responsible for the losses sustained because of the ship's activities. The dispute was handed over to a Commission at Geneva which, in 1872, awarded $15,500,000 damages to the United States. In this dispute, it seems that the American negotiators took full advantage of Britain's desire to gain American friendship and of the disagreements between Macdonald and the British delegates.

In the face of Britain's attitude and Canada's impotence, Macdonald reluctantly signed the treaty. Upon his return to Canada he was severely criticized both in the press and in Parliament for agreeing to the terms of the treaty. Canadians felt that Britain sacrificed Canadian interests for the sake of American friendship. Canadians became convinced of the need for Canada to look after her own foreign policy.

MACDONALD RELUCTANTLY SIGNS THE TREATY[271]

To Sir John Rose, dated at Washington, May 11, 1871:

I at first thought of declining to sign the treaty. That would have been the easiest and most popular course for me to pursue. . . . But my declining to sign might have involved such terrible consequences that I finally made up my mind to make the sacrifice of much of my popularity and position in Canada, rather than run the risk of a total failure of the treaty.

Nevertheless, the Washington Treaty was an important milestone in the history of Canada. Although Sir John A. Macdonald did not represent Canada as its Prime Minister, his inclusion on the commission was a recognition of Canada's growing stature as a nation. The treaty eased frictions between Canada and the United States, and established the principle of arbitration as a means of resolving international conflicts.

SIR JOHN A. MACDONALD'S SENSE OF HUMOUR[272]

Part of Sir John A. Macdonald's charm, to political foes and friends alike, was his ability to look on the light side:

[At the negotiations (1871) leading to the Treaty of Washington, during an official excursion on the Potomac to which he had come early and alone, the wife of an American senator fell into conversation with Sir John:]

'I guess you come from Canada?'
'Yes, Ma'am.'
'You've got a very smart man over there, the Honorable John A. Macdonald.'
'Yes, Ma'am, he is.'
'But they say he's a regular rascal.'
'Yes, ma'am, he's a perfect rascal.'
'But why do they keep such a man in power?'

'Well, you see, they cannot get along without him.'
'But how is that? They say he's a real skalawag, and . . .'
Just then her husband, the Senator, stepped up and said:
'My dear, let me introduce the Honorable John A. Macdonald.'
The lady's feelings can be imagined, but Sir John put her at her ease, saying: 'Now don't apologize! All you've said is perfectly true, and it is well known at home.'

B

THE PACIFIC SCANDAL AND LIBERAL INTERLUDE

In the 1872 general election, the Conservative government faced widespread criticism. Canadians blamed Macdonald for his submission to American demands and for the failure to obtain restitution from the United States for the Fenian raids. In Ontario he was berated for allowing Riel to escape punishment. Nevertheless, Macdonald was returned to office, though with a reduced majority.

The new government planned to start work on the railway to the Pacific in fulfillment of the promise to British Columbia. Two rival firms had competed for a charter to form a railway company; it was understood that the successful bidder would receive the contract to build the railway. The Pacific Railway Company, headed by Sir Hugh Allan, owner of the Allan Line of Ocean Steamships, was granted the charter.

In April, 1873, in the House of Commons, L. S. Huntington, a Liberal member from the province of Quebec, accused the Conservatives and certain cabinet members of accepting $325,-000 in campaign funds for the 1872 election from Sir Hugh Allan. Macdonald admitted that his party had received the funds but he insisted that these contributions were neither to bribe him nor to influence him in the final granting of the railway contract. Furthermore, he claimed that contributing to election funds was an accepted practice indulged in by all political parties. Although there was never evidence that any of the money went into Macdonald's pockets, the cry of "bribery" was on everyone's lips. Parliament moved a vote of censure, but before the vote was taken Macdonald resigned. The Conservative Party, rocked by the scandal, could not weather this political storm. Lord Dufferin, the Governor-General, asked Alexander Mackenzie to form a government. Thus the first Liberal government came into office. The Pacific Scandal brought the downfall of the Conservative government, almost wrecked Macdonald's political career and postponed the building of the railway.

THE PACIFIC SCANDAL[273]

In an address in the House of Commons, Sir John A. Macdonald asked for a vindication of his conduct. Excerpt from the speech of November 3, 1873:

. . . I have fought the battle of Confederation, the battle of union, the battle of the Dominion of Canada, I throw myself upon this House; I throw myself upon this country; I throw myself upon posterity, and I believe that I know that, notwithstanding the many failings in my life, I shall have the voice of this country and this House rallying round me. And, sir if I am mistaken in that, I can confidently appeal to a higher court — to the court of my conscience, and to the court of posterity. I leave it with this House with every confidence . . . I know, and it is no vain boast for me to say so, for even my enemies will admit that I am no boaster — that there does not exist in Canada a man who has given more of his time, more of his heart, more of his wealth, or more of his intellect and power, such as they may be, for the good of this Dominion of Canada.

Edward Blake's reply to Macdonald's plea for vindication of his conduct:

When he (Sir John Macdonald), was called upon by reason and argument to sustain his course at the last general election, and to prove his title to the confidence of his country, it was not to these high and elevating sentiments he appealed,

"Isn't that a dainty dish to set before the King?"

it was not upon the intelligent judgment of the people he relied, but it was upon Sir Hugh Allan's money which he obtained by the sale of the rights of the Canadian people which he held in trust.

Mackenzie carried on the government for a short while and then, in 1874, called an election. The Pacific Scandal was the main issue. The Liberals scored a decisive victory. Mackenzie's administration coincided with a world-wide depression. Canada suffered hard times which were aggravated by poor crops and the dumping of low-priced goods on the Canadian market. In 1874, George Brown was sent to Washington to seek renewal of reciprocity. In spite of significant tariff concessions he was willing to make, he failed in his mission. Faced with severe depression, the Liberals — firm believers in reciprocity and free trade — were forced to resort to protective tariffs. The government increased the duties on goods entering Canada in order to protect home industry and to raise needed revenue.

Economic conditions forced Mackenzie to pursue a policy of frugality. This reflected itself most strikingly in his railway program. The promise to begin a railway within two years of British Columbia's entry into Confederation was not fulfilled — Mackenzie believed that in time of depression it was unwise to undertake such an

extravagant project. British Columbia protested loudly. Instead of spending large sums on a transcontinental railway, the liberal government wanted rather to construct short railway links to waterways. When Mackenzie sought to revise the railway agreement with British Columbia, the legislature rejected his offer and threatened secession. Lord Dufferin took it upon himself to go to British Columbia, where he soothed the irate populace.

ALEXANDER MACKENZIE'S FRUGALITY[274]

In a speech in 1877, Mackenzie explained why his government did not undertake building a railway to the Pacific. Instead, short railway links were built. He expressed the need for frugality:

. . . . I know that some people imagine that in a period of depression the Government can do a great deal to resuscitate business and induce prosperity; but any prosperity we may now have is owing, not to legislation, but to hard work, the industry, the productive powers and energy of our people; and any attempt to bolster our manufacturers by giving them an extravagant amount of protection would simply amount to the imposition of a heavy tax upon the farmer. The farming interest is the one which sustains this country. . . .

The government proceeded with its modest railway program. A line was built from Winnipeg to the American border to join with the American railroad from St. Paul and Minneapolis. The Intercolonial Railway was completed in 1876 as a government project. In 1878, a line was in progress from Fort William to Winnipeg. A wagon road and a telegraph line from the east were being completed. Some short lines of track were laid in British Columbia, but there was no construction of a railway to the province.

The economic depression obscured many accomplishments of Mackenzie's Liberal government. His administration passed some significant political reforms, some of which enlarged Canada's self-governing powers. The Election Act of 1874 contained several clauses that improved Canada's antiquated and inadequate election practices; the secret ballot and voting on a designated day throughout the country minimized corruption and voting irregularities. Also, to avert any possible recurrence of scandals like the Pacific Scandal, it was required that candidates keep records of election expenses. The removal of the property qualification for members in the House of Commons offered wide opportunities for public service.

Alexander Mackenzie

The government also turned its attention to the West. In Manitoba, the Royal North West Mounted Police was formed to patrol the area against the Americans who were carrying on an illicit trade. To encourage western settlement, the Homestead Act made provisions for the distribution of land held by the Dominion government, and the Northwest Act set up government administration for the Territory.

Although Mackenzie did not specifically demand autonomy (self-government) certain developments set Canada on the road towards self-government. In 1875, the Supreme Court of Canada was established to hear appeals from Canadian courts and thus to reduce the number of cases taken to the Privy Council in London. The Royal Military College was founded in Kingston in 1874 to train Canadian officers for the militia. Also, Mackenzie insisted that when Canadian interests were involved in negotiations conducted by the British government with other powers, Canadian representatives should be included.

The most significant expression of Canadian independence was the limiting of the powers of the Governor-General. Lord Dufferin had recommended to the Imperial Government that the death sentence of Ambroise Lépine, who had been convicted of the murder of Thomas Scott, be commuted to life imprisonment; and he had quietened British Columbian resentment over the railway. But the Canadian government felt that in both instances the Governor-General was meddling in Canadian affairs. Upon the insistence of the Canadian government, the British Parliament

curtailed, to some extent, the powers of the Governor-General. Henceforth pardons would be granted only upon the recommendation of the Canadian cabinet. In all other matters, the Governor-General, although he still represented the British Parliament, had to act in accordance with the wishes of the Canadian cabinet. He still commanded prestige and retained ceremonial functions as the Queen's representative.

ALEXANDER MACKENZIE AND LORD DUFFERIN[275]

A heated argument between Mackenzie and Lord Dufferin about railway construction in British Columbia:

After a lengthy discussion . . . he [Lord Dufferin] turned to me and in a very excited tone said: "I call upon you to answer this question. I have a right to call upon you as Prime Minister to answer me now, and I insist upon an answer. I call upon you to tell me distinctly what you meant by 'compensation for delays' in your minutes referring to the Island Railway." [railway between Nanaimo and Esquimalt].

I replied that I had no objection to answer any question properly put, but that he had no right in a verbal discussion to demand an answer in such a manner. I said that if he desired any information to write down what he wanted and I would of course furnish it. . . .

His Lordship after this scene spoke more calmly, and I embraced the opportunity to tell (him) that Lord Carnarvon [the Colonial Secretary] and he must remember that Canada was not a Crown Colony (or a Colony at all in the ordinary acceptation of the term), that 4,000,000 of people with a government responsible to the people only could not and would not be dealt with as small communities had been sometimes dealt with; that we were capable of managing our own affairs, and the country would insist on doing it, and that no government could survive who would attempt, even at the insistence of a Colonial Secretary, to trifle with Parliamentary decisions.

Mackenzie may not have been as spectacular or colourful a personality as Sir John A. Macdonald, but he did give Canada honest and frugal government. He has been blamed for irritating British Columbia by not proceeding with the construction of the railway, but with hard times and a depleted treasury a railway to the Pacific seemed too risky an undertaking for the cautious Mackenzie.

Related by Rev. Dr. Clark, in Zion tabernacle, Hamilton, at the time Mr. Mackenzie died:

From 1865 to 1868, while stationed at Sarnia, I had the privilege of being intimately acquainted with the late ex-Premier. I remember on one occasion having charge of a missionary enterprise, and applying to Mr. Mackenzie for a donation. It happened to be just prior to the dissolution of Parliament, and Mr. Mackenzie's reply to my request was: 'We are expecting an election before long, and it is a rule with me never to give, or promise to give, for charitable or other purposes when we are near an election.' After the election was over we were surprised to receive from Mr. Mackenzie a substantial cheque for our missionary scheme. He was a man of broad sympathies. He was not connected with our denomination. . . .

C

NATIONAL POLICY

Although Mackenzie's government instituted a modest tariff policy, Canadian manufacturers were clamouring for still higher tariffs to protect their industries. In planning for a return to power, John A. Macdonald took careful note of this protectionist sentiment. He adopted the National Policy as an answer to both American rejection of reciprocity and erection of tariff walls against Canadian goods.

Much of the program of the National Policy was borrowed from the Canada First movement — Canadian nationalism in the economic, political and cultural fields — which sprang up in the 1870's. The National Policy advocated high protective tariffs to protect infant Canadian industries, to boost the domestic market for Canadian farm products, to create employment and to end the economic depression. It also was ready to lower tariffs on British goods if Britain would extend similar preference to Canadian goods in British markets.

THE NATIONAL POLICY[277]

On March 7, 1878, J. A. Macdonald introduced the Conservative Party's National Policy:

I move: . . . that this House is of the opinion that the welfare of Canada requires the adoption of a National Policy, which, by a judicious readjustment of the Tariff, will benefit and foster the agricultural, the mining, the manufacturing and other interests of the Dominion; that such a policy will retain in Canada thousands of our fellow countrymen now obliged to expatriate themselves in search of the employment denied them at home, will restore prosperity to our struggling industries, now so sadly depressed, will prevent Canada from being made a sacrifice market, will encourage and develop an active interprovincial trade. . . .

In the election campaign of 1878, Macdonald made the National Policy the platform of the Conservative Party. He blamed the Liberals for the depression, for the failure to build the railway to the Pacific and for the discontent in British Columbia. He pointed out the inadequacies of the Liberal administration and its failure to develop the West and protect Canadian industries. The National Policy promised something to everyone — high tariffs, extensive railway construction, industrial development and an end to the depression. Macdonald plunged into active and imaginative electioneering; political rallies, personal appearances at picnics and ample funds were used in the campaign. Support for the Conservative cause came from various quarters. The Orangemen, a great political force in Ontario, resentful over the amnesty granted Riel and his followers by the Mackenzie government, backed the Conservatives. Financial support came from industrialists, financial institutions, railway companies and liquor interests who opposed Mackenzie's Temperance Act.* The Conservative Party was returned to power.

The Conservative government proceeded with its tariff policy. Manufacturers and others interested were invited to Ottawa to present their views. In 1879, Tilley, the Finance Minister, imposed tariffs to satisfy the demands expressed at the meeting. Two distinct tariffs were instituted. Protective Tariffs were high duties placed on articles which were imported but which could be produced in Canada. Revenue Tariffs were lower duties imposed on articles which were imported and were not, generally, manufactured in Canada. These two strengthened the position of the Canadian manufacturers and supplied the needed revenue.

---

* This Act gave municipal governments the right to prohibit the sale locally of intoxicating beverages.

The protracted economic depression which had plagued Canada since 1873 came to an end shortly after Macdonald's return to office. Improved world conditions, good crops and general prosperity brought better times. Naturally, the Conservatives attributed this to the National Policy. After the cautious, depression-ridden years of Mackenzie's administration, Canada was ready for the boldness of Macdonald and his National Policy; he injected a spirit of optimism and imagination into the country. Now he was ready for his most ambitious project — the building of the Canadian Pacific Railway.

Sir John A. Macdonald Addressing the People in the Amphitheatre, Toronto, 1878

D

BUILDING THE CANADIAN PACIFIC RAILWAY

Once the political union of Canada had been achieved, it was necessary to achieve physical union. A railway had to be built not only to bind the country together but also to fulfill the agreement with British Columbia. The return of good times encouraged investment in a railway. George Stephen, president of the Bank of Montreal, and Donald A. Smith, a high official of the Hudson's Bay Company, headed the newly-formed Canadian Pacific Railway Company. Concessions had to be made to the company as an inducement to start construction. The proposed contract was presented to Parliament in 1880. In return for building the railway line, the company was to own and operate it. In addition, it was to be granted $25,000,000 in cash, twenty-five million acres of fertile western land, perpetual tax exemption and an assurance that for twenty years, west of Lake Superior, no competing railway line would be built south of the Canadian Pacific Railway. Also, approximately 700 miles of railway lines that had already been completed by the Canadian government at an estimated cost of $35,000,000 were to be transferred to the Canadian Pacific Railway Company. The transcontinental railway was to be completed by 1891.

The Liberal opposition in the House of Commons attacked these terms as far too generous. Some said that much of Canada's best land was being given away to the railway interests. Some objected to handing over a railway built with the people's money to a private company. However, the Conservative majority disregarded the criticism and approved the contract.

William Cornelius van Horne was engaged as chief engineer in charge of construction. The line was laid across the rocky terrain along the north shore of Lake Superior. By 1882, the section from Fort William to Winnipeg was completed and the railhead was being pushed across the prairies. In 1883 the company announced that it needed more funds, and the government supplied the money to keep construction going. Again in 1885, more money was needed. The constant pouring of public funds into the Canadian Pacific Railway project dismayed even Macdonald and his supporters; there was danger that construction might have to be suspended for lack of funds.

WILLIAM CORNELIUS VAN HORNE — HIS CHARACTER[278]

J. H. E. Secretan, an engineer on van Horne's staff, tells of his first interview with van Horne at Moose Jaw Creek:

. . . Van Horne sent for me and announced in a most autocratic manner that he wanted *"The shortest possible commercial line"* between Winnipeg and Vancouver, also that he intended to build *five hundred miles* that Summer, lay the track and have trains running over it. In discussing the projected location, I pointed out that such a line would often run through an infertile country, and made other objections; but he was adamant and said he did not care what it ran through. He was evidently bound to get there. . . .

I doubted if he could possibly construct five hundred miles in a short Summer (it was then probably about April) but he scowled at me fiercely, and before I left "the presence" he informed me that "nothing was *impossible* and if I could show him the road it was all he wanted, and if I *couldn't* he would have my scalp." Thus ended a short but characteristic interview with the great magician! As a matter of fact, he did lay about four hundred and eighty miles of track that Summer.

The Northwest Rebellion of 1885 was the railway's salvation. The partially completed railroad was used to move troops from the east to crush the rebellion. Parliament became convinced of the value of the railway and voted the necessary loan to proceed with construction.

AN ANECDOTE ABOUT THE C.P.R.[279]

Sir John A. Macdonald is reported to have said upon one occasion in the House of Commons, when making a speech upon the subject of the Canadian Pacific Railway: "Mr. Speaker, although I may not live to see the completion of this great Transcontinental highway, I hope I may someday look down and see the two oceans united by a band of steel." Mr. Alexander Mackenzie, then the leader of the opposition, interjected the remark: "Perhaps the Right Honourable gentleman will be looking *up*."

On November 7, 1885, the railway was completed at Craigellachie when the line from the Pacific Coast was linked with the one from the east. Donald Smith, in an impressive ceremony, drove in the last spike to mark the completion of the railway.

THE LAST SPIKE[280]

Sanford Fleming gives this account in the CANADIAN ALPINE JOURNAL, *1899:*

It was indeed no ordinary occasion; the scene was in every respect noteworthy, from the groups which composed it and the circumstances which had brought together so many human beings in this spot in the heart of the mountains, until recently an untracked solitude. Most of the engineers with hundreds of workmen of all nationalities who had been engaged in the mountains were present. Everyone appeared to be deeply impressed by what was taking place. . . .

"The Last Spike" Staged by C.P.R. Construction Crew that Missed the Official Ceremony

The blows on the spike were repeated until it was driven home. The silence however continued unbroken. . . . It seemed as if the act now performed had worked a spell on all present. Each one appeared absorbed in his own reflections. . . . Suddenly a cheer spontaneously burst forth, and it was no ordinary cheer. The subdued enthusiasm, the pent up feelings of men familiar with hard work, now found vent. Cheer upon cheer followed as if it was difficult to satisfy the spirit which had been aroused. . . .

It was a tremendous accomplishment for such a young country. Passing the almost impenetrable barrier of the Canadian Shield and tunnelling through the challenging mountains of the Cordillera was an engineering feat, indeed. And this all-Canadian railway — the world's longest at that time — took only five years to complete!

CONSTRUCTION OF THE C.P.R. IN BRITISH COLUMBIA[281]

Onderdonk [contractor for the B.C. line of the C.P.R.] found the white labour that he had got from San Francisco — the only source of supply at the moment — consisted for the most part of clerks out of employment, broken-down bartenders and other of that ink, men who had never handled a shovel before and who often appeared on the scene attired in fashionable garments in a rather tattered state, who might even be seen in the cuttings with patent leather shoes, much the worse for wear and trousers sprung over the foot. So he determined to import a lot of Chinamen . . . and he got two ship loads, 1,000 men each. They came in very bad weather and had to be kept below hatches most of the way, so as soon as they got upon the work and began to take violent exercise, they developed scurvy and were decimated, fully one-tenth of their number dying. Being fatalists, as soon as a man was stricken with scurvy the others would not wait upon him or even give him a drink, and the government agent at Yale had great difficulty in getting them buried when they died. In fact many of their bodies were so lightly covered with a few rocks and a little earth that one became unpleasantly aware of the fact while walking along the line.

Chinese at Work on the C.P.R. in the Mountains, 1884

E

THE SASKATCHEWAN REBELLION

The wilderness of the Northwest had long been the Indian's preserve when white explorers and traders made their intrusion about the year 1700. Over the course of the next century and a half, only the scattered and often abandoned trading posts and missions bore witness to the advances of European civilization. The enterprising Englishmen had come from the Company's forts on Hudson Bay; the adventurous French, over the routes of La Vérendrye from Montreal; the hardy Scots and their French-Canadian voyageurs, from the East by way of Fort William. But they were not interested in permanent settlement, and by the time of the Red River uprising, the land stretching beyond to the Rockies was still essentially the home of the Cree, the Saulteaux, the Assiniboines and the Blackfoot — and the seemingly inexhaustible herds of buffalo.

Yet two kinds of bases for settlement did exist. Small numbers of whites were gathered at Hudson's Bay Company posts such as Cumberland House and Fort Carlton, not far from the confluence of the North and South Saskatchewan Rivers, and at Fort Pitt and Fort Edmonton in present-day Alberta. Catholic missions, such as Prince Albert, St. Laurent (near Batoche) and St. Albert attracted the Métis who traveled west in increasing numbers to hunt and trap.

HOTEL RULES IN THE CANADIAN WEST[282]

At Fort Macleod, where the Mounted Police had their first headquarters in western Canada, the hotel of "Kamoose" Taylor had the following rules for its guests:

1. Guests will be provided with breakfast and dinner, but must rustle their own lunch.

2. Spiked boots and spurs must be removed at night before retiring.
3. Dogs not allowed in bunks, but may sleep underneath.
4. Towels changed weekly, Insect Powder for sale at the bar.
5. Special rates to "Gospel Grinders."
6. Assaults against the cook are strictly prohibited.
7. Only registered guests allowed the special privilege of sleeping on the Bar Room floor.
8. To attract attention of waiters, shoot a hole through the door panel. Two shots for ice water, three for a deck of cards.
9. In case of fire the guests are requested to escape without unnecessary delay.
10. Guests are requested to rise at 6 A.M. This is imperative as the sheets are needed for tablecloths.

After the insurrection at Red River and Manitoba's creation (as a "postage stamp province"), the Métis in Manitoba received grants of 240 acres each, in recognition of being descendants of the original inhabitants. Rather than try to contend with the growing number of settlers from the East, however, many of the Métis sold their land to speculators and drifted northwest to the banks of the Saskatchewan. Here they joined other Métis who had occupied strips of land on the pattern of earlier settlements at Red River. Their hope of a life free from outside interference was, however, as futile as it was natural.

News about the construction of the Canadian Pacific Railway made eastern landseekers more aware of the opportunities for cheap land and easier access to the once remote prairies. Expecting a heavy migration westward, the Dominion government sent out teams of surveyors, who laid out townships divided into 160-acre plots, as surveyors had done at Red River. Once again, the government was guilty of serious mismanagement, and this time the situation was more dangerous.

The Métis on the Saskatchewan began to demand payments of money and land such as had been made in Manitoba. Those who had already given up a life of wandering and settled on plots of land insisted they be given clear and official titles. White settlers joined in protests against the government's failure to complete the survey and to provide for registration of claims to land.

The Indians had grievances too, although some progress was made with them in the 1870's. Before losing office over the Pacific Scandal, Sir John A. Macdonald had established the North West Mounted Police. Stationed at Fort Macleod, Fort Edmonton, Calgary and other strategic points, members of the new police force drove out the whiskey runners who had been exploiting the Indians* and discouraged the Indians from fighting among themselves. Moreover, through a series of treaties, the Dominion government set up a system of reservations and guaranteed the Indians assistance in adjusting to changed conditions, in return for a surrender of their ancestral claims to the land. By the mid-1880's, however, many tribes had not accepted the new mode of life; the government's attempts to sponsor agriculture and education had been unsuccessful. The disappearance of the buffalo, which had been slaughtered in incredible numbers within a few years, deepened the natives' plight. Famine spread; there was not sufficient aid from the authorities; and an ominous restlessness spread among the Indians.

THE DISAPPEARANCE OF THE BUFFALO[283]

The senseless slaughter of buffalo:

The last remnant of the great, brown living blanket that had once grazed the plains from Canada to Texas was now [in the years 1879-1880] concentrated in Montana, and, to a lesser extent, in northwestern Dakota Territory. And there the professional hunters went to work with a skill that had been drawn fine with several years of practice. The grass to the north of the herd was burned over to discourage the beasts from migrating northward into Canada. The buffalo, surrounded on all side, were helpless before the hunters, whose equipment now included telescopic sights. . . .

The northern herd was much smaller than the

Buffalo Hunt on the Prairies

huge masses of buffalo that had ranged in the south. . . . By the end of 1883 about all that did remain were the carcasses. . . .

A political crisis among the settled population loomed in the early 1880's. Besides the land problem, grievances accumulated over crop failures, falling prices for grain and the high costs of transportation and shipping freight on the railway. Meetings among both whites and Métis resulted in a series of petitions being sent to the federal government. Ottawa's reaction was indecision and delay. By the spring of 1884, a common feeling of desperation among all groups of settlers led to a meeting in the Prince Albert district, where a resolution was passed to invite the assistance of Louis Riel.

The name "Riel" was still magic to the Métis. In their minds, he was still the leader who had forced the government in distant Ottawa to recognize the aspirations of his people at Red River. Why could he not repeat his success, this time for the benefit of Métis on the Saskatchewan? He was living not far away, in Montana — surely he would answer an invitation to serve once more a cause to which he had proven himself so devoted.

What was not important to the Métis was the story of Riel's life in the years since the Red River insurrection. In 1871, it was true, Riel had earned a public expression of appreciation from Manitoba's Lieutenant-Governor Archibald for offering to help defend the province from a threatened Fenian raid. He had even been elected Member

---

* Fort Whoop-up, located near the present city of Lethbridge, Alberta, had been a distributing point for smuggled American liquor.

Gabriel Dumont

Big Bear

Poundmaker

of Parliament for Provencher constituency in the elections of 1873 and 1874. But Riel was never allowed to take his seat in the House of Commons; in fact, he had traveled to Ottawa under the danger of arrest by Ontario police for the execution of Thomas Scott. Following his expulsion from the House of Commons, he was granted a partial amnesty, but only on condition of being banished from Canada for five years. The anxiety Riel experienced as a result of these events was too much. He spent nearly two years in an asylum in Quebec, before drifting to Montana, where he earned a living by trading and teaching school.

SONG OF THE METIS MAIDEN[284]

This is a translation of a song written by Louis Riel, probably in early 1870, when he was at the height of his power:

1. I am a maid of the small Métis nation
    And with great pride this heritage I share;
    I know that God when He shaped His creation
    Made every race with equal love and care.
    Though the Métis are not many in number,
    Great is the destiny which they command;
    Proud of the hate that the world heaps upon
        them,
    Yet they have played a great role in this land.

    Chorus:

    Oh! if some day perchance I should be
        courted
    Gladly I'd love without shame or demand

A soldier brave from the little detachment
So proudly led by our chief-in-command.
Gladly I'd love a soldier brave
So proudly led by our chief-in-command.

repeat

2. When on that night, the seventh of December,
    They captured Schultz and his troop all in one,
    The fading sun, like a guardian angel,
    Hung in the sky until the task was done.
    Then morning came on the eighth of
        December,
    One never saw a day so bright and fair;
    And the Métis in their moment of triumph
    Fell to their knees in a heart-warming prayer.

3. Have I not seen, I, a timid young maiden,
    The Métis troops in the Fort and the town,
    Eight hundred strong in defence of their
        country,
    Risen as one with no thought of renown?
    Oh! wondrous sight to behold our proud
        soldiers,
    Sons of the plain where man is free to roam,
    With their heads bowed in a most humble
        gesture
    Praying for help to save their land and homes.

4. Then a fine priest, a brave and saintly pastor,
    For Ottawa set out one morning bright
    At every turn he met with disaster
    But he had God aiding him in his fight.
    Six months of toil had given us a Province
    Happily wrought of his faith and his dreams;
    While McDougall who envisioned a kingdom
    Had to forego his devilish schemes.

When the delegation arrived from the Northwest, Riel saw in their request a chance to serve his people. In July 1884 he joined the Métis at Batoche. Soon a petition was dispatched to Ottawa. It outlined the grievances and made such requests as self-government, representation for the Northwest in the federal government, guarantees of land titles and a railway linking the region with Hudson Bay.

The federal government showed little sign of having learned from the troubles at Red River fifteen years before. In the face of Ottawa's inaction, the Métis decided to use force to gain their goals. Reflecting the mental imbalance that had grown worse with the years, and convinced that he was the "David" that would lead the Métis out of their troubles, Riel established a provisional government at Batoche in March, 1885.

The white settlers, wanting no part in a rebellion, withdrew their support. The clergy opposed Riel's behaviour as extremist, and discredited his claim of being God's instrument chosen to lead the Métis nation. Undeterred, Riel prepared his followers for violence. Gabriel Dumont, a skilful buffalo hunter widely known on the prairies, was appointed military commander. The loyalty of the Métis was assured, and several Indian leaders were asked for aid.

In an atmosphere of rising tension, the Northwest Rebellion was ignited by a clash between a force of North West Mounted Police and a band of Métis led by Gabriel Dumont. On their way to retrieve supplies and ammunition stored at Duck Lake, the Mounted Police were intercepted and, after a brief but terrible fight, ten of them lay dead. The Métis then destroyed Fort Carlton, just after the white inhabitants had fled to Prince Albert.

The Métis success set in motion a number of Indian attacks and raised the fear of a general Indian uprising. The Crees of Chief Poundmaker laid siege to the town of Battleford, a major white settlement.* Within a few days, Big Bear's Indians sacked the hamlet of Frog Lake and killed several of its inhabitants, before burning down Fort Pitt.

The federal government quickly dispatched troops and volunteers to put down the rebellion.

SOLDIERS ON WAY TO SASKATCHEWAN REBELLION[285]

Lieutenant Colonel Montizambert, commanding the artillery, describes the passage around the north shore of Lake Superior:

Here began the difficulties of passing gaps on the unconstructed portion of the road. About 400 miles . . . had to be passed by a constantly varying process of embarking and disembarking guns and stores from flat cars to country team sleighs, and vice versa. There were sixteen operations of this nature in cold weather and deep snow . . . on the night of the 30th March the roads were found so bad that it took the guns seventeen hours to do the distance (thirty miles). . . . On from there . . . by team sleighs and marching twenty-three miles further on; on flat cars (uncovered and open) eighty miles, with thermometer at 50 degrees below zero . . . by alternate flat cars on construction tracks; and, teaming in fearful weather round the north shore of Lake Superior. . . . The men had no sleep for four nights.

More than five thousand troops traveled west on the partially completed Canadian Pacific Railway. Within two weeks, troops from the Maritimes, Ontario, Quebec and Manitoba, as well as volunteers from western settlements, joined the Mounted Police to fight the rebels.

General Middleton, commander of militia in Canada, was in charge of operations. His strategy was to launch a three-pronged attack on the areas of disturbance in order to localize the Indian violence as well as suppress the Métis. Middleton led the main force from his base at Qu'Appelle, and after an initial setback and a stout defence directed by Dumont, he gained control of Batoche. Another column, under Colonel Otter, headed from Swift Current to Battleford. Otter was fortunate to avoid being trapped by Poundmaker's Indian warriors when news reached the chief of the Métis defeat at Batoche and the capture of Riel. Poundmaker surrendered to Middleton within a few days. Colonel Strange moved a third column from Calgary to the vicinity of Frog Lake, where the last Indian resistance was scattered.

A DESCRIPTION OF CHIEF POUNDMAKER[286]

An officer present at General Middleton's camp at the time of Poundmaker's surrender wrote as follows:

Ere long the renowned Cree Chief appears before us . . . Captain Hughes and myself receive the braves at the gate of our fortress with becoming dignity. Poundmaker is accompanied by some 15 sub-chiefs and councillors, and the appearance of the band is very picturesque and striking. The Great Chief himself is a very remarkable-looking man: tall, very handsome and intelligent-looking, and dignified to a degree. He wears a handsome war-cap made of the head of a cinnamon bear, with a long tuft of feathers floating from it, and

---

* Battleford was the capital of the Northwest until 1883, when the government moved headquarters to Regina.

Gun Pit   Northwest Rebellion, 1885   Asleep in the Trenches

a leather jacket studded with brass nails and worked with beads, long beaded leggings coming up to his hips, and brightly coloured moccasins, while over his shoulders hangs(?) a very gaily coloured blanket. The others dressed in much the same manner, and all are elaborately painted. Poundmaker shakes hands with us without dismounting or uncovering. But all the others get off their horses and take off their caps before they approach us. After a short talk we send the party on to the General.

Riel had tried unsuccessfully to challenge the Canadian government as he had done at Red River. He had not recognized the changes which had come to the Northwest in the interval of fifteen years since Manitoba became a province — the Mounted Police, the railway, increasing numbers of white settlers. Decisive action by the Canadian government, much more purposeful in suppressing the Rebellion than in preventing its outbreak in the first place, dramatized Riel's lack of planning, even for short-term success. A few Indian tribes had joined the Métis (they had not at Red River), but neither showed much will to fight. Indians who remained loyal during the rebellion were well rewarded with presents and supplies; those who had fought in the Rebellion were dealt with harshly by the courts. The Métis were scattered by the Rebellion that was supposed to secure their rights, even though a number did receive payments and grants of land.

The effects of the Rebellion extended to Ontario and Quebec, where furious debate resulted. In Ontario, Riel was still remembered as the murderer of Thomas Scott, and his execution was demanded. In Quebec, French Canadians were equally emotional in defending Riel as a hero of their cause in the West. Against this background

of strong feeling, Riel and several others were committed to trial. Eight Indians were tried and hanged for murdering settlers. Riel was convicted of treason and given the death penalty. A storm of protests followed from Quebec. Requests for a pardon for Riel reached Ottawa from citizens in the United States, Great Britain and France. Riel's lawyers appealed the verdict all the way to the Judicial Committee of the Privy Council, and the execution was delayed. Macdonald appointed a "medical commission" of three to investigate Riel's sanity, while the cabinet pondered the problem.

RIEL'S "DEFENCE" AT HIS TRIAL[287]

Riel's address to the court at his trial. His lawyers pleaded insanity but Riel contradicted their defence:

Your Honors, Gentlemen of the Jury: It would be easy for me to-day to play insanity. . . . Under the excitement which my trial causes me would justify me not to appear as usual, but with my mind out of its ordinary condition. . . .

―――――

. . . . I know that through the grace of God I am the founder of Manitoba; I know that though I have no open road for my influence, I have big influence concentrated, as a big amount of vapour in an engine. I believe by what I suffered for 15 years, by what I have done for Manitoba and the people of the North-West that my words are worth something. . . .

―――――

As to my religion what is my belief? What is my insanity about that? My insanity, Your Honors, Gentlemen of the Jury, is that I wish to leave Rome aside inasmuch as it is the cause of division between the Catholics and Protestants. . . .

. . . . My condition seems to be so helpless that they [the lawyers] have recourse to try and prove insanity to try and save me that way. If I am insane, of course I don't know it, it is a property of insanity to be unable to know it. . . . It is said that I had myself acknowledged as a prophet by the Half-breeds. The Half-breeds have some intelligence. . . . It is not to be supposed that the Half-breeds acknowledge me as a prophet if they had not seen that I could see something into the future. . . .

I am glad that the Crown have proved that I am the leader of the Half-breeds in the North-West. I will perhaps be one day acknowledged as more than a leader of the Half-breeds, and if I am I will have an opportunity of being acknowledged as a leader of good in this great country. . . .

. . . . If it is any satisfaction to the doctor to know what kind of insanity I have, if they are going to call my pretensions insanity, I say, humbly, through the grace of God I believe I am the prophet of the New World. . . .

The political pressure from Ontario, combined with the belief among cabinet members that Riel deserved the extreme in punishment, led the government to decide against interfering with the conviction. Riel was hanged in Regina on November 16, 1885.

ONTARIO'S ANTI-FRENCH FEELINGS[288]

Ontario's anti-French feelings are bluntly expressed in an editorial of the Toronto EVENING NEWS, *of April 20, 1885, while rebellion was raging in Saskatchewan:*

Ontario is proud of being loyal to England.

Quebec is proud of being loyal to sixteenth century France.

Ontario pays about three-fifths of Canada's taxes, fights all the battles of provincial rights, sends nine-tenths of the soldiers to fight the rebels [Riel's], and gets sat upon by Quebec for her pains. . . .

Hundreds of thousands of dollars are spent in maintaining the French language in an English country. . . .

An anti-French party is springing up in all the Provinces except Quebec. . . .

If we in Canada are to be confronted with a solid French vote, we must have a solid English vote. . . .

If she is to be a traitor in our wars, a thief in our treasury, a conspirator in our Canadian household, she had better go out.

She is no use in Confederation. . . .

Riel Addressing the Jury in the Courthouse, Regina

As far as we are concerned, and we are concerned, and we are as much concerned for the good of Canada as any one else, Quebec could go out of the Confederation to-morrow and we would not shed a tear except for joy.

If Ontario were a trifle more loyal to herself she would not stand Quebec's monkey business another minute.

The rebellion on the Saskatchewan demonstrated, as no campaign of publicity could have done, the value of the Canadian Pacific Railway to the Dominion. The Canadian government had thrust its power into the Northwest to restore law and order. And if the railway could transport thousands of troops in record time, then it could do the same with settlers and freight. Riel's execution, however, bore much more immediate results. Many English-speaking Canadians hailed the event as a triumph for justice and order; French Canadians saw Riel as a martyr, a victim of Protestant hatred. Politicians and others in public life stood ready on both sides to take advantage of the fears and suspicions which the blood-spilling in the Northwest had aroused.

HONORE MERCIER'S SPEECH ON RIEL'S DEATH[289]

On November 22, 1885, Mercier gave his famous speech at the mass rally attended by over 50,000 people on the Champ de Mars in Montreal. The following is an extract from the speech:

Riel, our brother, is dead, the victim of his devotion to the Métis cause of which he was the leader, the victim of fanaticism and treason: of the fanaticism of Sir John [A. Macdonald] and of some of his friends; of the treason of three of ours [the three French Canadians in the Macdonald cabinet] who, in order to save their portfolios, have sold their brother.

By killing Riel, Sir John has not only struck our race at the heart but also struck the cause of justice and humanity which, represented in all languages and sanctified by all religious beliefs, demanded mercy for the prisoner of Regina, our poor brother of the North-West.

In the face of this crime, in the presence of these failings, what is our duty? We have three things to do; unite ourselves in order to punish the guilty; break the alliance that our deputies have made with Orangeism and seek, in a more natural and less dangerous alliance, the protection of our national interests.

Mercier's Dream of the Future Map of the Dominion

F

DOMINION-PROVINCIAL RELATIONS

Sectionalism, a major problem for the Fathers of Confederation, remained a central fact of Canadian life after the Dominion had been brought into being. In 1868, within a year after the British North America Act was passed, Nova Scotia sought better terms through a petition of withdrawal — a portent of troubles to come. The British North America Act did set forth the conditions of union, as well as the division of powers between central and provincial governments. But creating a legal document was one thing; using it as the basis for administering a new country was quite another.

As political leaders got down to the practical matters of preparing legislation, raising and spending money, and exploring the limits of their authority, conflict between the Dominion government and the provinces was to be expected. Friction between provinces, French-Canadian nationalism and threats of secession by provinces added a variety of complications. Where politicians failed to resolve their inter-governmental disputes, the Judicial Committee of the Privy Council — the final court of appeal in the British Empire — made settlements. Generally the judicial decisions favoured the provinces at the expense of the Dominion government, and thus strengthened provincial pretensions.

Ontario's battle with the federal government was led by Oliver Mowat, the Liberal Premier of the province from 1872 to 1896. Once an articled student in Macdonald's law office in Kingston, Mowat, as the leader of Canada's strongest province, became a formidable opponent of the Prime Minister. To press his claims that Ontario must be a partner, not a satellite, of the government in Ottawa, Mowat carried many cases to the courts. A particular subject of contention was the Dominion's use of disallowances of provincial laws which the federal government thought were detrimental to the welfare of the country as a whole.

MOWAT ON RIGHTS OF THE PROVINCE OF ONTARIO[290]

At a mass reception at Queen's Park, Toronto, on September 16, 1884, Mowat spoke of the favourable decision of the Judicial Committee of the Privy Council in London on Ontario's claim on the southwestern boundary with Manitoba:

Now, why is it that we are so anxious that the limits of our province shall not be curtailed? First, and foremost, is because we love Ontario, we believe in Ontario, and we know from past experience that it is in the interest of the Dominion, as well as of the provinces composing the Dominion that the limits of Ontario should not be restricted. Ontario is, in fact, the "back-bone" of the Dominion; and we desire that that should continue to be the position of our province; that it should not be brought down to be one of the least of the great provinces; that there should be an extent of country ample enough to admit of its development, so that, as the other provinces develop, Ontario should develop also.

Ontario and Manitoba experienced a quarrel over their mutual border, where possession of a large tract of public land, with its timber and mineral rights, was at stake. The Dominion Government fixed a boundary between the two provinces in 1881. Ontario demanded a settlement more favourable to itself, and took its claim to court. The Privy Council ruled in favour of Ontario. Similar decisions were handed down on other provincial legislation disallowed by the federal government: in 1883, the temperance legislation, which asserted Ontario's authority over the sale of beer, wine and liquor in the province; in 1884, the Rivers and Streams Bill, which protected public rights on the waterways of the province.

The decisions of the Privy Council seemed to confine the powers of the federal government to those enumerated in Section 91 of the British North America Act, and to limit the residuary power to matters of a strictly federal nature. Ontario's campaign on behalf of provincial rights, attacked by Sir John A. Macdonald as destructive of the Dominion's unity, was nevertheless meeting with success. Other provinces, in the meantime, were finding it in their interest to follow Ontario's lead.

In Quebec, Macdonald's government had lost a pillar of strength with the death of Sir George Etienne Cartier in 1873. Yet the Conservatives retained the very important loyalty of church leaders, largely because the only alternative was the *Parti Rouge*, an organization of liberals and radicals who often questioned the power of the church in public affairs. Another reason for Conservative strength in Quebec was the party's apparent support for French-Canadian minority rights in the rest of Canada, including Manitoba and the Northwest.

The hanging of Louis Riel, however, was bitterly condemned throughout Quebec as proof that the Conservatives were really the party of English Canada, and particularly of Ontario Protestant bigotry. To exploit this feeling, Honoré Mercier formed the *Parti National*, to which French-speaking Liberals and many Conservatives were drawn. He then led his party to victory in the

provincial election of 1886. Once in office, he set out to win acceptance by the clergy and to establish his image as defender of the Catholic religion and French-Canadian rights.

Troubled relations between the Maritime provinces and the Dominion government stemmed from disappointment with Confederation in those provinces. The halcyon days of the sailing ship were passing, and the effect was a decline in the ship-building industry and the carrying of goods to overseas markets. The construction of the Intercolonial Railway neither enabled Maritime producers to compete successfully in the markets of Ontario and Quebec, nor produced a sufficient flow of goods to Halifax and other ports to encourage the development of steamship companies. Failing to fulfill the early promises of promoting trade between the Atlantic provinces and the rest of Canada, Confederation was blamed for the depressed region's persistent economic problems. In 1886, the legislature in Nova Scotia went so far as to pass a resolution favouring secession from Canada. Although nothing came of this action, it did indicate the extent of discontent.

British Columbia's exasperation over the delays in the building of the Canadian Pacific Railway, and the Northwest Rebellion involved expression of deep dissatisfaction in the western parts of Canada. In Manitoba the Conservative government of John Norquay voiced the people's resentment of the Dominion's ownership of provincial public lands. More serious was the agrarian criticism of the C.P.R.'s monopoly and of the high freight rates. As farmers demanded more railway lines, the Manitoba Legislature issued charters for the construction of railways to link up with American lines. The federal government disallowed the provincial acts as violating its grant of monopoly to the C.P.R. By 1887, agitation in Manitoba was reaching a peak.

As the federal government found itself embroiled in problem after problem with the provinces, Honoré Mercier invited the provincial premiers to meet at Quebec to discuss their grievances. Thus, in October, 1887, five premiers — those from Prince Edward Island and British Columbia did not attend — met in the first interprovincial conference. The conference echoed with expressions of sectional discontent; such outstanding issues as federal disallowance, tariffs and freight rates were discussed. What emerged, however, was the fact that the provinces had few specific interests in common. Macdonald dismissed the affair as a Liberal Party conspiracy, in spite of the presence of Manitoba's Conservative Premier. Yet the problem of Canadian unity, after twenty years of Confederation, stood out more vividly than ever.

G

ECONOMIC PROBLEMS

Prosperity during Macdonald's first term under the National Policy enabled the Conservatives to make progress in building the railway and to sweep the election of 1882.* But the latter part of the decade was a time of economic difficulties throughout Canada. World trading conditions had not recovered from the depression of the 1870's, and the Dominion's inter-provincial commerce was not fulfilling the expectations aroused at the time of Confederation. Western expansion, in particular, was disappointing, falling prices for farm products and declining immigration interfered with the movement of settlers to the prairies. Many farmers abandoned their homesteads and joined in the exodus from all parts of Canada to the United States.

Proximity to the United States was a dilemma for Canada in many ways. The dynamic republic provided so great a range of opportunities that it attracted the waves of immigration from Europe and drew the discontented from Canada as well. The same was true of capital investment, which flowed from London and other financial centres to help finance the American industrial revolution. The absence of a Canadian-American reciprocity agreement, which did not seem to interest the United States, meant that Canada was forced to compete with much more advanced countries for American markets. Canadian manufacturers, who had fared well in the first years of the National Policy, found themselves with limited export trade and slumping markets within the Dominion. Production in such industries as iron-making and textiles slowed down, and job insecurity became a problem for many workers.

In response to the troubled conditions of the times, many organizations sprang up to promote the interests of special groups. The Trades and Labour Congress of Canada, a trade union of skilled workers, was organized in 1886. The next year the Canadian Manufacturers' Association was formed. The Farmers' Protective Union in Manitoba demanded abolition of high tariffs, lower freight rates and a secure market for farm products.

Many cures for the failing economy were advanced. Imperial union — closer economic ties with Great Britain — was urged by a group of men who formed the Canadian branch of the Imperial Federation League. Men of strong pro-British sentiment, such as George Parkin, principal of Upper Canada College, Principal G. M. Grant

of Queen's University, Colonel Denison and D'Alton McCarthy, a member of Parliament from Ontario, looked back to the days of British preference for Canadian goods. Their hopes were not dimmed by the fact that Britain had followed a policy of free trade for some forty years, since they could point to a renewal of imperialist thinking in Britain and in English Canada. Perhaps the bonds of empire, grown slack in recent decades, should be strengthened now that Great Britain was engaged with Germany, France and other European powers in a struggle for new colonies, particularly in Africa. Bonds of trade could both help the mother country and rescue Canada's sagging economy.

IMPERIAL FEDERATION LEAGUE[291]

In a leaflet, in 1890, this organization outlines its program:

The Imperial Federation League is an organized body, with many branches in the United Kingdom, Canada, Australia, New Zealand and South Africa.

The following are its objects, viz: —

1. To promote the discussion of means whereby the permanent unity of the British Empire may be maintained.

2. To further the development of the resources and promote the interchange of the products of the several parts of the Empire.

3. To resist any measures tending to disintegration.

It is not, as many suppose one of the functions of the League to propound a new constitution for the British Empire. No scheme worthy of the name is possible, without consulting every interest by properly constituted authority, after obtaining the fullest information respecting the wants and wishes of the several communities concerned.

The duty of inquiry comes within the sphere of the League, and it is felt that the Canadian Branches will do well by consultation and all proper means, to ascertain what is best for the Dominion.

* Constituency boundaries were redistributed in 1882 with the result that Liberals tended to be concentrated in fewer ridings. Macdonald was accused of "gerrymandering" in order to increase his party's chances of winning more seats.

Others advocated commercial union with the United States. This proposal, widely regarded as being almost the same thing as annexation, had the support of noted anti-imperialist historian Goldwin Smith and a number of leading businessmen and newspaper editors in Toronto. Commercial union, which would mean the removal of all tariff barriers between Canada and the United States, also appealed to many farmers, who wanted an opening to American markets and the chance to purchase cheaper American farm machinery. Many Liberals saw commercial union as an alternative to Macdonald's National Policy, although the party was divided on the issue at the time of the federal election of 1887.

UNION WITH THE UNITED STATES[292]

Goldwin Smith sets out his reasons for the need of a union of Canada with the United States:

That a union of Canada with the American Commonwealth, like that into which Scotland entered with England, would in itself be attended with great advantages cannot be questioned. . . . Canadians almost with one voice say that it would . . . bring with it a great increase of prosperity. The writer has seldom heard this seriously disputed, while he has heard it admitted in the plainest terms by men who were strongly opposed to Union on political or sentimental grounds. . . . The case is the same as that of Scotland or Wales in relation to the rest of the island of which they are parts, and upon their union with which their commercial prosperity depends. The Americans, on the other hand, would gain in full proportion as England gains by her commercial union with Wales and Scotland. . . . Canadians who live on the border, and who from the shape of the country form a large proportion of the population, have always before their eyes the fields and cities of a kindred people, whose immense prosperity they are prevented from sharing only by a political line, while socially, and in every other respect, the indentity and even the fusion is complete.

The confusion in Liberal ranks helped the Conservatives survive the election, in spite of discontent on every side. The government then made a bid for reciprocity with the United States. The occasion was a British-American joint commission in Washington on the long-standing fisheries question between the United States and Canada. Sir Charles Tupper, the Canadian member of the British delegation, tried unsuccessfully to use the fisheries to gain reciprocity.

Rebuffed by the Americans, Macdonald then reverted to his stand in favour of protective tariffs. The Liberals, meanwhile, had officially decided for unrestricted reciprocity as the only hope for ending the depression. Such were the opposing positions of the two parties during the election campaign of 1891, the last of Sir John A. Macdonald's incredible political career.

ANECDOTES ABOUT JOHN A. MACDONALD[293]

When the city of Vancouver was in its infancy, or rather, before there was a city there at all, Lady Macdonald one day expressed the wish to purchase two lots on what is now the town site, and asked Sir John's permission to do so.

Said she, 'I don't want any money; I have three or four hundred dollars of my own, and the Colonel (her brother) will give me three or four hundred more.'

'No, my dear,' he replied, 'you had better not!'

'Why?' said Lady Macdonald.

'Well, if you were to buy any lots out there, the first thing I should know would be that a post-office or a custom-house was put on them without my knowing anything about it, and I should have it thrown at me in Parliament that you had been paid for them ten cents more than they were worth.'

So the lots were never bought.

———

Sir John Macdonald always observed his birthday, and liked others to remember it. . . . Among many congratulatory letters he received [on his last birthday] was one from an unknown little maiden, who wrote him a childish note to announce that her birthday was on the same day as his [January 11th]. She added a hope that he would not follow the 'mean' example of a small boy of her acquaintance, who had not answered a letter she had written him. To this youthful epistle Sir John replied: —

'Earnscliffe, Ottawa, January 6, 1891.

'MY DEAR LITTLE FRIEND,

I am glad to get your letter, and to know that next Sunday you and I will be of the same age. I hope and believe, however, that you will see many more birthdays than I shall, and I trust that every birthday may find you strong in health, and prosperous, and happy.

I think it was mean of that young fellow not to answer your letter. You see, I have been longer in the world than he, and know more than he does of what is due to young ladies.

I send you a dollar note, with which pray buy some small keepsake to remember me by, and,

Believe me your sincerely,

John A. Macdonald.'

———

. . . . It is related that, many years ago, Sir John was present at a public dinner, at which he was expected to deliver a rather important speech. In the conviviality of the occasion he forgot about the more serious part of the duty of the evening, and when at a late hour he rose, his speech was by no means so luminous or effective as it might have been. The reporter, knowing that it would not do to print his notes as they stood, called on Sir John next day, and told him that he was not quite sure of having secured an accurate report. Sir John received him kindly, and invited him to read over his notes. He had not got far when he interrupted him: 'That is not what I said.' There was a pause, and Sir John continued, 'Let me repeat my remarks.' He then walked up and down the room, and delivered a most impressive speech in the hearing of the delighted reporter, who took down every word as it fell from his lips. Having profusely thanked Sir John for his courtesy, he was taking leave, when he was recalled to receive this admonition: 'Young man, allow me to give you this word of advice. Never again attempt to report a public speaker when you are drunk.'

H

THE BREAKDOWN OF CONSERVATIVE LEADERSHIP

Sir John A. Macdonald's agile leadership had enabled the Conservative Party to maintain almost uninterrupted control during Canada's first two decades of life. The mounting storms of economic adversity, rebellion, Dominion-provincial conflict and racial tension seemed only to demonstrate the indispensability of the first Prime Minister and the party he had built. But a chain of crises was in the making; Macdonald's career was near an end; and the Liberal Party was becoming unified under a new leader, Wilfrid Laurier.

For twenty years after Confederation, the Liberals failed to develop a cohesive party capable of representing an effective alternative to Macdonald's party. The Pacific Scandal had helped carry the Liberals into office, where Alexander Mackenzie gave honest and diligent, if unimaginative, administration for a term. But following defeat in the election of 1878, the ailing Mackenzie was inadequate to the task of leading the opposition. Deferring to the wishes of his colleagues, he resigned in favour of Edward Blake. The brilliant Blake, for all his intellectual talent, lacked the temperament for political leadership. He was an enigma to both friend and foe, uncomfortable with the routine of political life, and he lacked the sense of humour and personal warmth that make for success in public life.

Weary from the campaign of 1887 and self-critical over yet another failure at the polls, Blake carried out the last of his several attempts to give up the leadership of the Liberal Party. A caucus of the party agreed to accept Blake's own choice, Wilfrid Laurier, as his successor. Little acclaim greeted the new leader, for most Liberals in Ontario would have preferred one of their own; even in Quebec, not to mention the English-speaking provinces, a French Canadian had many obstacles to face in moulding a national Liberal organization. A courtly manner and a reputation for parliamentary oratory in both French and English seemed to be inadequate recommendation for a man who could well be the country's next Prime Minister.

The Conservatives had been unable to retain provincial power in Quebec. Honoré Mercier exploited French-Canadian feeling over the Riel affair to gain the premiership. Within a few months he moved to broaden his support, and possibly to provoke federal interference in Quebec that might discredit the Conservatives. In 1888 the Quebec Legislature passed the Jesuits' Estates Act, which was designed, among other things, to compensate the Jesuits for property seized by the Crown after the British conquest of 1763. To settle the rival claims of the recently revived Jesuit Order and of the Roman Catholic bishops, the government of Quebec had called upon the assistance of the Pope. The strong reaction in English Canada, especially in Ontario, was predictable.

D'Alton McCarthy, the Ontario Conservative and imperial federationist, assumed the leadership of the extremist opposition to the Act. He denounced it in the House of Commons and demanded that Macdonald use the Dominion power of disallowance. However the Prime Minister refused to adopt a policy that would only engender more religious and racial bitterness and further diminish his support in Quebec. The motion of disallowance introduced by an associate of McCarthy was decisively defeated. Only thirteen members — seen by one side of the argument as the "noble thirteen," by the other as the "devil's dozen" — voted in favour.

Just as Mercier had fashioned himself the defender of French-Canadian rights, McCarthy became the hero of many English Canadians. As organizations in Quebec entered the public controversy, the Equal Rights Association was formed in Toronto to mobilize public sentiment behind McCarthy. He unleashed a campaign of venom against French and Catholic privileges and called upon English-speaking Protestants to fight to keep Canada an English country. The accusation that Sir John A. Macdonald was allied with Catholic French Canada undoubtedly undermined his party outside Quebec.

REACTION TO THE JESUIT ESTATES ACT[294]

a*Protestant view as expressed in an editorial in the* TORONTO MAIL, *March 14, 1888:*

If the British and Protestant element in Quebec will not save itself, we must try to save it for our own sakes. That the abandonment of Quebec to the Ultramontane and the Jesuit will be the death of Canadian nationality is clear enough. But Ontario will not be safe. Our eastern gate has already been opened by the perfidious hand of the vote-hunting politician, and French and Roman Catholic invasion is already streaming through. . . .

b*Catholic view as expressed by Honoré Mercier on St. Jean Baptiste Day, June 24, 1889:*
. . . . The moment to speak has arrived and as a representative authorized by the province of Quebec . . . with the sense of responsibility attached to my words, I declare in the name of all that we have remained and shall remain Catholics and French. Love of religion and nationality of our fathers is impressed in our hearts, and no one, not even the most powerful of tyrants, will be able to tear this love away from us.

This province of Quebec is Catholic and French and it will remain Catholic and French.

Yet in spite of the mounting problems and the challenge from Laurier, in spite of the National Policy's apparent failure and charges of corruption in Sir Hector Langevin's federal department of public works, the Conservatives hung on to office in the national election of 1891. They based their campaign on an appeal to loyalty to "the old man, the old flag, the old policy." The Liberals were condemned for being ready to sell out to the United States, as if their program of unrestricted reciprocity were the first step to severing ties with Great Britain. Those ties would be secure only under a Conservative administration. Macdonald's sentimental plea to the voters was dramatized by his declaration, "A British subject I was born — a British subject I will die." Although the Conservatives lost seats in both Ontario and Quebec, the loyalty of the West and the Maritimes provided a narrow margin of victory.

Sir John A. Macdonald, c. 1890

MACDONALD'S LAST ELECTION CAMPAIGN[295]

Macdonald's appeal in the elections of 1891 in which he attacked the Liberal Party's policy of unrestricted reciprocity:

. . . . For a century and a half this country has grown and flourished under the protecting aegis of the British Crown. . . . Under the broad folds of the Union Jack, we enjoy the most ample liberty to govern ourselves as we please, and at the same time we participate in the advantages which flow from association with the mightiest Empire the world has ever seen . . . shall we endanger our possession of the great heritage bequeathed to us by our fathers, and submit ourselves to direct taxation for the privilege of having our tariff fixed at Washington, with a prospect of ultimately becoming a portion of the American Union? . . .

As for myself, my course is clear. A British subject I was born — a British subject I will die. With my utmost effort, with my latest breath, will I oppose the 'veiled treason' [unrestricted reciprocity] which attempts by sordid means and mercenary proffers to lure our people from their allegiance . . . I appeal . . . to give me their [the people's] united and strenuous aid in this, my last effort, for the unity of the Empire and the preservation of our commercial and political freedom.

Macdonald had fought and won his final battle. In his seventy-sixth year, exhausted from the fight, he died three months after the election. And now the Conservative Party was faced with the challenge that everyone knew must come, and most

Hon. Joseph Abbott, 1892

Sir Mackenzie Bowell

dreaded its coming — finding a successor to "Sir John A." The first to follow was Sir John Abbott, virtually drafted from the Senate. In 1892, unhappy in office and troubled by ill health, he resigned. The next Prime Minister, Sir John Thompson, was a man of great ability who had been a brilliant Halifax lawyer and judge and an able Minister of Justice in Macdonald's cabinet. But Thompson died suddenly in London at the end of 1894, just when the question of schools in Manitoba was about to become the next crisis in federal politics.

TRIBUTES ON THE DEATH OF SIR JOHN A. MACDONALD[296]

[a]*Laurier's eulogy of his political opponent, delivered in the House of Commons, June 8, 1891:*

... although we were prepared for the sad event, yet it is almost impossible to convince the unwilling mind that it is true that Sir John Macdonald is no more, that the chair which we now see empty shall remain for ever vacant, that the face so familiar in this Parliament for the last forty years shall be seen no more, whether in solemn debate or in pleasant and mirthful tones. . . . Sir John Macdonald now belongs to the ages, and it can be said with certainty, that the career which has just been closed is one of the most remarkable careers of this century. . . . I think it can be asserted that, for the supreme art of governing men, Sir John Macdonald was gifted as few men in any land or in any age were gifted. . . . As to his statesmanship, it is written in the history of Canada. It may be said without any exaggeration whatever, that the life of Sir John Macdonald, from the date he

entered Parliament, is the history of Canada, for he was connected and associated with all the events, all the facts which brought Canada from the position it then occupied . . . to the present state of development which Canada has reached. . . . He was fond of power, and he never made any secret of it. Many times we have heard him avow it on the floor of this Parliament, and his ambition in this respect was gratified as, perhaps, no other man's ambition ever was. . . . Today, we deplore the loss of him who, we all unite in saying, was the foremost Canadian of his time, and who filled the largest place in Canadian history. . . .

[b]PUNCH, *the English journal of humour, carried this poem on June 20, 1891:*
Punch sympathizes with Canadian sorrow
For him known lovingly as 'Old To-morrow.'
Hail to 'the Chieftain'! He lies mute to-day,
But fame still speaks for him and shall for aye.
'To-morrow — and to-morrow' Shakespeare sighs.
So runs the round of time; man lives and dies.
But death comes not with mere surcease of breath
To such as him. 'The road to dusty death'
Not 'all his yesterdays' have lighted. Nay,
Canada's 'Old To-morrow' lives to-day
In unforgetting hearts, and nothing fears
The long to-morrow of the coming years.

Sir John Thompson's speech delivered on the occasion of the unveiling of a statute to Sir John A. Macdonald, at Hamilton, Ontario, on November 1, 1893:

. . . . As time goes on other statues will be raised to his memory in various parts of Canada, and yet the grandest thing for his memory will be that

Sir John Thompson

Sir Charles Tupper

his fame needs no monument to extend or to preserve it. At the time of his death it was poetically and truthfully said, 'his work — a nation — stands his monument.' Of no man of any period can it be more truly said that he was the father and founder of his country. . . . The history of Sir John Macdonald is the history of a long and successful struggle with the greatest difficulties . . . but Sir John lived to see, as the fruits of work in which he took a leading part, nearly all British North America united under one system of government, and connected by railways and other means of communication unequalled in their completeness in any part of the world. . . . In the first place, Sir John's love of Canada and his desire to serve her must be put far in the front of all his characteristics. His daily thought might be expressed in Webster's words: 'Let our object be our country, our whole country, and nothing but our country'. . . . In the next place, I must mention his wonderful devotion to the interests of the Empire. . . . When he died, the Queen knew that her wreath upon his coffin covered the breast of as faithful a servant of the Crown as ever lived within her realm of England. . . . Another feature of Sir John's character that we, who knew him best, will long delight to remember, was the great amiability and gentleness of his nature. His patience was most remarkable. . . . He was a parliamentarian in the true sense of the word — in the sense in which that word has been applied to some of the great men who have adorned the Parliament of Great Britain. . . .

A false estimate of Sir John's character is formed by those who regard him as having been selfish, or even as having been actuated by mere love of power. . . .

. . . . It was not mere love of power which kept him to those daily and nightly tasks. It was devotion to a duty which became more pressing and unavoidable as years rolled by. He could be replaced when he was no more, but while his services could be had no man could replace him. . . .

How did the Manitoba Schools Question become an issue of national importance? On the surface, it concerned only a small fraction of Canada's population far removed from the main centres of the country. Yet the Schools Question proved to be a part of long-standing religious, cultural and political controversies that knew no local limits. Once again the conflicts between French Canadians and English Canadians, between Catholics and Protestants, between champions of dualism and of uniformity, were to be re-enacted. Would English-Canadian ways prevail in Manitoba, or would there be a dual society in which both English and French languages and institutions would flourish? Would the outcome influence the whole Confederation experiment?

When Manitoba became a province of the Dominion in 1870, the tiny population was fairly evenly divided between people who spoke English and those who spoke French. Schools for the English-speaking inhabitants were operated by the Protestant churches; the Roman Catholic church looked after education for the French. Hence the Manitoba Act perpetuated the dual system by allowing the educational rights existing "by law or practice at the union." The French and English languages were both legally recognized in the province.

In the twenty years that followed, however, an influx of English-speaking Protestants destroyed the racial balance in the population. By the late 1880's the feeling was growing among the majority that separate, church-run schools should be replaced by a system of public schools. Many reasons were given to support the contention: public schools would encourage the democratic spirit and foster provincial unity. French Catholic schools were a privilege, not a right, in a pioneer land; the sparsely settled province could not afford to support two school systems.

Public debate began to mount as newspapers took up the question. In southwestern Manitoba, a stronghold of the Orange Lodge and assertive Protestantism, the *Brandon Sun* published editorials in May, 1889, calling for the abolition of separate schools. At this point, the old battle between Ontario Protestants and Quebec French-speaking Catholics was injected into Manitoba by D'Alton McCarthy.

A CALL FOR ABOLITION OF SEPARATE SCHOOLS IN MANITOBA[297]

From the second of two editorials in the BRANDON SUN, *May, 1889:*

We are glad to know that The Sun's course in opening the attack on the separate school system of this province is meeting with almost universal approval. It is scarcely necessary to point out or even say that the system is a vicious one. The creation of classes by the state is a very grave error that can only result in harm. Particularly in a new country should there be no distinction. We cannot afford to divide our effort: we must husband our resources in every way. Until our population is materially increased, there must be great difficulty in many parts in maintaining our schools with any degree of efficiency. Until our revenues are very considerably increased our schools must suffer for lack of financial support, or an excessive burden of taxation must be imposed. But what seems to us as worse than these considerations is the fact that a separate school system creates and perpetrates class distinctions that should never be known in a well organized state. Why should Catholics be selected out of the body of citizens, and laws enacted that give them a very decided advantage over the other religious bodies. . . .

In August, 1889, at Portage la Prairie, McCarthy personally introduced his anti-Catholic, anti-French campaign to Manitobans. He had a ready audience, for many Protestants had already been urging the Liberal government of Premier Greenway to abolish French-Canadian rights in the province. Furthermore, he was joined on the platform by the Attorney-General, Joseph Martin, who expressed the view that Manitoba should discontinue separate schools and the privileges of the French language. This apparent forecast of the government's policy was borne out in 1890, when legislation was passed to establish a single secular educational system. Separate schools were no longer to receive financial support from the government.

Roman Catholics called upon Macdonald to employ disallowance, but he refrained from risking the charge of interference in provincial affairs. Then they appealed to the courts, claiming that the Public Schools Act was contrary to provisions in the Manitoba Act. The Privy Council, however, ruled against them. A subsequent appeal, launched under Section 93 of the British North America Act, requested that the federal government pass remedial legislation. This time the Privy Council decided that such federal action was possible.

ANTI-CATHOLIC SUPPORT FROM AMERICAN ORANGEMEN[298]

A letter to Premier Greenway from an American Orange Lodge Council:

Washington D.C.
April 1, 1895
No. 631, F.st.nw.

Hon. Greenway
Premier of Manitoba

Sir —

I see by many newspapers, that the Pontifex Maximus, thro' his minions in Canada, is still pressing vigorously to destroy your Public Schools. I thank God that Protestantism is standing up manfully for its rights. I cannot believe that the Gov. Genl. has any legal or moral right to interfere in the way he has.

I am a Past Prest. of a Council of the great A.P.A., now numbering about 3,000,000 of voters in the U.S.A., one plank of whose platform demands the maintenance of one general, unsectarian, free-school for all; and you may be *sure* of our active sympathy for your cause. We feel that *your* cause is *ours*, and we shall aid you, I believe, with a 100,000 men and millions of dollars, if war should be forced upon you by the Pope and his emissaries for the destruction of your school system; for we feel that your defeat would certainly strengthen the hands of our enemies in the United States.

We should be pleased to hear from you directly;

and we should be glad to receive copies of any newspapers or other documents throwing any light upon the situation.

Yours truly,

Chase Roys, Sec.
W-m Council No. 3, D.C.

N.B. I use the seal of
my council merely as a
guarantee of good faith.

R.

Mackenzie Bowell, former Grand Master of the Orange Lodge, had succeeded Thompson as Prime Minister. The mediocre Bowell, who obtained the high office because the Conservative party had no acceptable leader of talent available, resolved to intervene in the question of Manitoba schools. The decision, announced in the Speech from the Throne in January, 1896, split his cabinet. French-Canadian members had, of course, been demanding a remedial act. The English-Canadian ministers, however, refused to co-operate with Bowell.

TROUBLES IN THE CONSERVATIVE CABINET, 1895-96[299]

Richard Cartwright, a senior Liberal in the House of Commons, was noted for his sarcastic wit. As Mackenzie Bowell struggled to keep his government intact, Cartwright ridiculed the Conservatives:

. . . we are here in the presence of the Royal Ottawa Low Comedy Troupe, and we should be grateful for . . . the amusement they have afforded, not only to us, but to all Canada . . . what we have been listening to, after all, has really been a series of rehearsals. We had No. 1 rehearsal — because I can hardly count the little episode of the hon. member for Pictou (Sir Charles Hibbert Tupper)* as one — a sort of undress rehearsal . . . when three members of the Cabinet went out, and one of them . . . stayed out. Then we have lately had what I may call a full dress rehearsal, when seven members went out and practically seven came back. . . . Now, these hon. gentlemen being nearly letter perfect, we can have the rest of the performance, which will not be long delayed, when all of them go out and none come back. . . .

---

* The son of Sir Charles Tupper. The younger Tupper had resigned for a few days in March, 1895. Though he returned to the Cabinet as Minister of Justice, he never accepted Bowell as his leader. He was one of the seven who later "went out," and helped force Bowell to resign in favour of the senior Tupper before the election of 1896.

YE GOOD KNYGHTE AND YE WICKED GIANT.

Picture of ye good knyghte, Sir Charles Tupper, bravely putting his shield between the wicked giant and the suffering minority.

Sir Charles Tupper's Stand on the Manitoba Schools Question, 1896

The veteran Conservative from Nova Scotia, Sir Charles Tupper, returned from his post as Canada's High Commissioner* in London to become Prime Minister.

VIEWS ON THE REMEDIAL BILL[300]

The proposed remedial legislation under Section 93 of the British North America Act aroused heated debate. Several views are here presented:

aFather A. Lacombe to Laurier, expresses the Church's position, January 20, 1896:

. . . . It is in the name of our bishops, of the hierarchy and the Catholics of Canada, that we ask the party of which you are the very worthy chief, to assist us in settling this famous question, and to do so by voting with the government on the Remedial Bill. . . .

If, which may God not grant, you do not believe it to be your duty to accede to our just demands, and if the government, which is anxious to give us the promised law, is beaten and overthrown while keeping firm to the end of the struggle, I inform you, with regret, that the episcopacy, like one man, united with the clergy, will rise to support those who may have fallen in defending us. . . .

---

* The post of High Commissioner had been created in 1880 to give Canada a direct representative in Great Britain. Alexander Galt was the first Canadian to hold the position.

. . . . So long as I have a seat in this House, so long as I occupy the position I do now, whenever it shall become my duty to take a stand on any question whatever, that stand I will take not upon grounds of Roman Catholicism, not upon grounds of Protestantism, but upon grounds which can appeal to the conscience of all men, irrespective of their particular faith, upon grounds which can be occupied by all men who love justice, freedom and toleration. . . .

———

[c]*Sir Charles Tupper states the government's position, March 3, 1896:*

. . . . It is not a question of separate schools, it is a question of the constitution of the country. The progress and the prosperity and the future development of Canada depends upon that constitution being sacredly maintained, and that all the rights that are guaranteed under it, whether to the central or the provincial government, shall be sacredly guarded. . . .

———

[d]*William Mulock to Laurier, April 3, 1895:*

. . . Manitoba must be left alone. . . . All these fine-spun arguments of legal rights seem to me quite beside the question of public policy. . . . Suppose the Dominion Parliament were to pass a Remedial Act establishing separate schools in Manitoba and the people there were to withhold the necessary machinery for giving effect to such legislation what good would the Catholics of Manitoba take by such legislation? Why it would involve further legislation and agitation the end of which no one can foresee. If we now establish a precedent we shall encourage appeals to Ottawa from every province. . . .

The remedial bill was successfully stalled by its opponents in Parliament, who prolonged debate with lengthy speeches. Before a vote could be taken, the five-year term of Parliament had expired, and the Manitoba Schools Question became a major issue in the federal election. The disorganized Conservative Party went down to defeat after eighteen years of power. Wilfrid Laurier began a new era in Canadian politics.

VII

THE LAURIER ERA: A MATURING NATION, 1896-1911

As the nineteenth century ended, Sir Wilfrid Laurier summed up the general mood of Canadians with his declaration that the twentieth century would be "Canada's century." Prosperity, the promise of Confederation, seemed at last to be attainable. Nearly a half-century before, Canadian leaders had pointed to the West and said that its development was the key to Canadian prosperity. Now the greatest immigration in the history of the northern half of North America was opening the West, creating the "wheat boom" and helping to build the larger and more varied economy needed for progress.

Two new transcontinental railways were built to complement the C.P.R. in binding the Dominion together more surely with "bonds of steel." Mining and forestry provided the products necessary for Canada's industrial revolution, and hydro-electric power was harnessed to the needs of new and growing industries.

Great changes in the life of a nation are invariably accompanied by the need for major adjustments, as new problems frequently appear. Canada in this period was no exception; such groups as farmers and workers in industry felt that they were not sharing fully in the benefits of the new age. Organizations were formed to promote the interests of agriculture and labour, and businessmen responded by forming organizations of their own.

The Laurier Era was also a time of developments in Canada's status within the British Empire. Some British leaders were anxious to strengthen the mother country's control over the self-governing colonies. Canada, however, was anticipating greater freedom, not less, in running its own affairs. From the time of the Colonial Conference in 1897 until the Naval Issue which helped defeat him in the election of 1911, Laurier was faced with pressures from the British Government. He ably defended Canada's right to determine its own policies when called upon to contribute to the military and financial power of the Empire. By so doing, he fostered a new concept of empire, later embodied in the Commonwealth, in which unity would be founded on co-operation.

The series of crises in imperial affairs caused strains within Canada as well. Many of British origin spoke of "Anglo-Saxon unity," and insisted that Canada show its loyalty to Great Britain in tangible ways. French Canadians did not feel the same attachment. They particularly denied any obligation to participate in wars where Canada's interests did not appear to be at stake. Laurier's policies of compromise, combined with his emphasis on national unity, served to soften hostile feelings and to preserve the opportunity for later co-operation.

Canadians were beginning to be proud of their accomplishments. They enjoyed the role as leader among the self-governing colonies of the Empire, but many believed that colonial status was no longer suitable. The Alaskan boundary dispute reinforced this attitude, and seemed to illustrate that the association between Canada and the United States would be more harmonious if it did not involve Great Britain at every turn.

21

CANADA'S ECONOMIC GROWTH

A

THE ELECTION OF 1896

In spite of the disarray of the Conservative opponents, Liberal victory in the election of June, 1896 was not a foregone conclusion. The wily Tupper had a lifetime of political experience to guide him in the campaign; he and his Tory colleagues would not be easily dislodged. Laurier's acceptance outside Quebec was questionable, and in his own province the Roman Catholic bishops condemned him for his stand on the Manitoba schools controversy.

THE 1896 ELECTION[301]

John W. Dafoe outlines the tactics used in the election campaign of 1896:

The Conservatives decided upon a line of action which seemed to them to have the maximum advantage. They would go in for remedial legislation. In the English provinces they would say that they did this reluctantly as good, loyal, law-abiding citizens obeying the order of the Queen delivered through the Privy Council. From their experience with the electors they had good reason to believe that this buncombe would go down. But in Quebec they would pose as the defenders of the oppressed, loyal co-operators with the bishops in rebuking, subduing and chaining the Manitoba tyrants. . . .

. . . . He [J. Israel Tarte] foresaw that the issue in Quebec would not be made by the government nor by the bishops, it would be whether the French Canadians, whose imagination and affections had already been captured by Laurier, would or would not vote to put their great man in the chair of the prime minister of Canada. . . .

Laurier persisted in his view that "the sunny way" was preferable to federal coercion of the Manitoba government. The rights of the Roman Catholic minority were important, he agreed, but they could more likely be secured through discussion aimed at co-operation. He denounced remedial action on the matter of education because it seemed to be an infringement of provincial rights. In Quebec, French Canadians responded to the idea of having one of their own become the Prime Minister of Canada; moreover, the Conservative leaders and their policies had become suspect. Former Conservatives such as Israel Tarte put their influence to work for the Liberal Party. Quebec elected forty-nine Liberals and only sixteen Conservatives.

LAURIER'S "SUNNY WAY" SPEECH[302]

From an address delivered at Morrisburg, Ontario, October 8, 1895:

Well, sir, the government are very windy. They have blown and raged and threatened and the more they have raged and blown, the more that man Greenway [the Premier of Manitoba] had stuck to his coat. If it were in my power, I would try the sunny way. I would approach this man Greenway with the sunny way of patriotism, asking him to be just and to be fair, asking him to be generous to the minority, in order that we may have peace among all the creeds and races which it has pleased God to bring upon this corner of our common country. Do you not believe that there is more to be gained by appealing to the heart and soul of men rather than by trying to compel them to do a thing?

Sir Wilfrid Laurier

Trade was another issue in the election. Here again the Liberals were successful. They attacked the old National Policy of protective tariffs. As an alternative they promoted partial reciprocity with both the United States and Great Britain. In Ontario, discontent over prolonged economic depression and resentment over the Conservatives' religious policy helped give the Liberals half of the eighty-six seats. When the Maritimes vote split and the West generally rejected the old government, the Liberals had a comfortable majority. The election result in Manitoba was puzzling. Here the voters apparently had every reason to support Laurier — but four of the six successful candidates were Conservatives.

In July, Laurier was sworn in, along with an impressive team of cabinet ministers. Sir Oliver Mowat from Ontario, W. S. Fielding from Nova Scotia and A. G. Blair from New Brunswick had all been successful provincial premiers. J. Israel Tarte, the master political strategist and former *Bleu* who had changed sides in time to organize Liberal victory in Quebec, was appointed Minister of Public Works.* Sir Richard Cartwright, who had served in Mackenzie's cabinet twenty years before, received the Trade and Commerce portfolio. Representing the West in the cabinet was Clifford Sifton; the member from Brandon, Manitoba, was made Minister of the Interior, with responsibilities for western expansion.

SIFTON ENTERS THE CABINET[303]

John W. Dafoe speaks of the tasks confronting Clifford Sifton upon entering the cabinet:

Tasks of great complexity and much public importance were awaiting the attention of the young minister. Conditions called loudly for the re-organization of the department entrusted to his charge. Of the Department of Interior at that time Mr. Sifton himself once gave this description: "The crying complaint was that it was a department of delay, a department of circumlocution, a department in which people could not get business done, a department which tired men to death who undertook to get any business transacted with it." . . . An organization had to be built up capable of securing immigrants in Great Britain, the United States and the continent of Europe.

The case of Manitoba schools still headed the list of important problems and Laurier lost little time in arranging a settlement. Before the end of the year, discussions between Mowat, the Minister of Justice, and Manitoba representatives had produced a compromise. Public financial support for separate schools was denied, but the right of Roman Catholics to religious instruction was recognized. Where the number of pupils in a public school was sufficiently large — forty in a town or ten in a rural school — the school could employ a properly qualified Catholic teacher. Religious instruction in public schools by a clergyman was permitted in the last half-hour of each school day. In any school where ten or more pupils spoke French, or any language other than English, instruction could be given in their native tongues when requested by the parents. This Laurier-Greenway agreement evoked some opposition; the bishops in Quebec were particularly incensed. Laurier then sent a delegation to Rome to call on the Pope, who appointed the youthful Cardinal Merry del Val to visit Canada. The result of the Cardinal's report was a papal recommendation to the bishops for more moderate tactics on behalf of Roman Catholic rights. The question of schools was dropped, for the time being, from federal politics. Laurier's government turned to other business.

ORANGEMEN OPPOSE CONCESSIONS TO CATHOLICS[304]

The following is a copy of a resolution passed by the members of L.O.L. No. 1583 at a regular meeting held in McNaughton's Hall, Killarney, Manitoba, March 18, 1897:

Moved by Bro. Wm Hodgins seconded by Bro. Geo. S. Walker that we the members of L.O.L.

---

* This portfolio, ironically, had been the one held in the Conservative government by Hector Langevin. Tarte had played a large part in exposing the scandals in Langevin's department.

No. 1583 view with great apprehension the proposed amendments to the Public School Act of 1890, We do hereby enter our most emphatic protest against any such amendments believing them to be detrimental to the best interest of our Public School educational system as well as to the peace harmony and goodwill that should be fostered and practised by the people of a young and rising Province like Manitoba. We also view with alarm and shame the abject humiliation the people of this Glorious Dominion of Canada are subjected to by sending an embassy to Rome to consult a foreign Potentate in matters pertaining to the Dominion pure and simple.

We do hereby urge upon our government to resist by all lawful means every attempt, no matter from what source it comes, to make the proposed changes to our Public School Act of 1890.

Signed

Herbert B. Dangerfield
Rec. Sec. L.O.L. No. 1583

B

SETTLING THE WEST

When the Dominion acquired the Northwest shortly after Confederation, it was hoped that the development of the prairies would be the key to the growth of a truly national economy. The West could yield many benefits for the country as a whole — a wider range of products for consumption at home and for export, traffic for the C.P.R., a home market for manufactured goods from Ontario and Quebec, as well as an outlet for natural products from the Maritimes.

But the completion of the transcontinental railway was accompanied by very modest results. The West opened up only very slowly, and the last quarter of the nineteenth century was for Canada a time of unfulfilled dreams. The explanation lay essentially with international conditions over which Canadian leaders had no control. Most important, Canada was neighbour to the United States, which, in the twenty-five or thirty years since the industrialized north had triumphed in the Civil War, had experienced a national growth unmatched in history. Men and money from overseas were drawn to the United States, whose employment and investment opportunities and western lands had become a legend in the Old World.

The Laurier era coincided with a return to prosperity in Canada and throughout the world. Industrialization and urbanization in Britain and continental Europe set up a demand for foodstuffs, especially wheat, for the growing factory towns. The growing cities in the United States required much of the wheat it produced and left little for the export market. Russia, another large grain producing country, also needed most of her wheat to feed her own people. Thus, Canada was in a favourable position to enter the world wheat markets. Yet, vast stretches of the Canadian prairies lay languishing — unoccupied and uncultivated. In 1891, Canada's wheat export was only 2,000,000 bushels, and in 1900, the territory which later comprised present day Manitoba, Saskatchewan and Alberta produced only 25,000,000 bushels of wheat.

The Laurier government began an immigration policy to populate the open spaces of the Canadian West. Clifford Sifton, a westerner who had entered the cabinet in 1897 as Minister of Interior, was put in charge of immigration. Sifton recognized that potentialities of the West could only be realized by bringing in large numbers of immigrants. Sifton plunged into his task of promoting western settlement, and brought out suitable immigrants irrespective of their place of origin. He looked to the experienced farmers in the United States and central Canada, to the land-hungry people in the United Kingdom and to the landless peasants of eastern Europe as sources.

THE CHOICE OF IMMIGRANTS[305]

Clifford Sifton, in an article in MACLEAN'S MAGAZINE, *April, 1922, describes the policy of his department as to the selection of immigrants:*

.... In those days settlers were sought from three sources; one was the United States. The American settlers did not need sifting; they were the finest quality and the most desirable settlers. In Great Britain we confined our efforts very largely to North of England and Scotland ... they were the very best settlers in the world. ...

.... Then, came the continent — where the great emigrating center was Hamburg. ... If one should examine twenty people who turn up at Hamburg to emigrate he might find one escaped murderer, three or four wasters and ne'er-do-wells, some very poor shopkeepers, artisans and laborers and there might be one or two stout, hardy peasants in sheep-skin coats. Obviously the peasants are the men that are wanted here.

.... I think a stalwart peasant in a sheep-skin coat, born on the soil, whose forefathers have been farmers for ten generations, with a stout wife and a half-dozen children, is good quality. A Trades Union artisan who will not work more than eight hours a day and will not work that long if he can help it, will not work on a farm at all and has to be fed by the public when work is slack is, in my judgment, quality and very bad quality. I am indifferent as to whether or not he is British born. It matters not what his nationality is; such men are not wanted in Canada and the more of them we get the more trouble we shall have. ...

Sifton's campaign to lure immigrants to the West was intensive. Advertisements in American and British newspapers, especially in weekly and farm papers, spoke glowingly of the benefits of settling in the West. A flood of literature — circulars, pamphlets, booklets, illustrations, handbills and pictorial displays — was circulated in eastern Europe. His agents offered a quarter section — one hundred sixty acres — of free land to all comers; the Hudson's Bay Company, the C.P.R. and other land companies set up offices to sell good land at low prices to prospective settlers.

SEEKING IMMIGRANTS IN THE UNITED STATES[306]

F. Pedley, Superintendent of Immigration, explains his department's activities in the United States in 1900:

With regard to the work in the United States, I only wish to say that ... the advertising that is done by the department in the United States is pretty extensive. We have advertised in over 7,000 American newspapers having an aggregate circulation of about 7,000,000. ...

In the United States we also have a system of sending delegates to inspect Manitoba and the Northwest and to make their report to the section of the country from which they come. These delegates in the majority of cases are chosen at a meeting of farmers called together by one of the agents ... the department ... asks ... the Canadian Pacific Railway ... to give these delegates free transportation from the boundary line to the point they wish to visit in Manitoba and the Northwest Territories. ...

At a time when there was plenty of free or cheap land in Canada, the United States had reached a point of exhaustion of its free land. In 1890 the American Department of Interior stated officially that there was no longer a frontier in that country. A large number of Americans

"Come to Stay." Canada Welcoming Immigrants

crossed the border and took up homesteads. The influx of Americans, openly boasting that their presence in Canada would make annexation to the United States inevitable, worried Canadian and British politicians. They began urging large scale British migration to offset the American influence and insure this land for the Empire. They deplored the fact that many from the British Isles went to the United States; these, they argued, should be persuaded to go to Canada. At the same time, Canadians from the eastern provinces did settle by the thousands in the west.

From eastern Europe came a flood of non-English-speaking immigrants, who would have gone to the United States if free land had been available there. To this sturdy farm element, who had always lived on the fringe of poverty and under national or religious persecution, the offer of free land was sufficient incentive. Many sold their meagre belongings to pay passage, and thousands of these "men in sheepskin-coats" came to the Canadian West.

It was not the first time that non-English immigrants from eastern Europe had come. Such earlier migrations, however, were only a trickle compared with the tide of settlement opened by Sifton. In 1874, Mennonites — a German Protestant sect who had resided in Russia — came to Manitoba. They left their homeland because the Czarist regime ordered them to serve in the army; bearing arms was contrary to their religious beliefs. The Canadian government, anxious to have these hardy peasants settle in the West, granted them homesteads and in addition guaranteed them exemption from military service and allowed them their own schools. By 1879, 6,000 Mennonites had

Immigrants wait to go ashore at Quebec, P.Q., c. 1911.

settled in Manitoba, centred around the town of Steinbach.

The Mennonites were soon followed by Icelanders who came from the colony at Kinmount, near Toronto, in 1875. Many of these were experienced deep-sea fishermen, and the abundance of fish in Lake Winnipeg prompted them to relocate on the northwestern shores of the lake. In the same year, a volcanic eruption in Iceland devastated much of the arable land and set the Icelanders in search of a new homeland. In 1876, a large group of these joined the earlier settlers in New Iceland, as the colony on Lake Winnipeg was called. Some 1,500 of the newcomers settled on farms along the lake with Gimli as the principal town. The word "Gimli" is Icelandic for Paradise, but their early experiences were far from heavenly. They had difficult times — a small-pox epidemic took its toll, poor crops threatened famine and hostility from neighbours made life unpleasant. But they managed to overcome these early difficulties and became part of the fabric of Canada.

The third distinct ethnic group coming to the West were the Jews. Prior to 1880, there were a few Jews in Winnipeg engaged in the purchase and export of furs for the American market in St. Paul, Minnesota. In 1882, 271 Russian Jews who had fled religious persecution reached Winnipeg. Some of these worked on railway construction; others proceeded further west to outlying farming districts to start agricultural colonies; the rest remained in Winnipeg where they, like the Icelanders before them, were housed in the temporary wooden immigration barracks while waiting for land grants. Other groups of Jews arrived, took up homesteads or remained in the growing city of Winnipeg.

Starting in the early 1890's, Ukrainians from Russia and Slavs from the Austro-Hungarian Empire — Bukovinians, Ruthenians, Galicians — settled in the West. By 1914, over 100,000 had entered the Dominion, most of whom settled in the prairies. All these were classified as "Galicians," a word which for many years denoted the contempt in which these immigrants were held by their Anglo-Saxon neighbours who regarded themselves superior to the poor, uneducated and often illiterate peasants who "jabbered" in a foreign tongue. It took many years before the "Galicians" were referred to as Ukrainians.

VIEW ON NON-ANGLO-SAXON IMMIGRANTS[307]

Excerpts from an address by Rev. W. D. Reid from Pre-Assembly Congress *of the Presbyterian Church in Canada:*

. . . . Of the Anglo-Saxon we are not in the least afraid, but when we consider that last year [1912] over twenty-one per cent of all the incomers to Canada were non-Anglo-Saxons . . . then we begin to understand what a task is ours as a nation. . . .

. . . . From southern Italy fifty-six of every hundred are illiterate. The illiteracy of the Russian Jew runs about twenty-three per cent, and he is perhaps the hardest of all to assimilate. He is industrious, hardworking and sober, but from the viewpoint of national digestion is like Jonah of old, still indigestible.

All authorities agree that intemperance is the great curse of the Slav wherever you find him. . . .

. . . . In many cases they [the foreigners] bring with them a sort of atheistic socialism which casts a blight of death over any country where it takes root. Often they underbid the labor market, driving out the white man. They raise vexing municipal questions, they strain our charitable organizations sometimes to the breaking point, they expose healthy people to disease, and often herd themselves together in certain localities of the cities, constituting a real problem of the slums. . . .

How should we receive the immigrants? . . . we must inaugurate more stringent rules at our entry ports, for keeping out undesirables. . . .

The question we have to ask ourselves seriously at this moment is, will the foreigner paganize us or shall we Christianize him? . . .

They settled on homesteads north of the C.P.R. land, often poorer land, and began to create a life for themselves and their children. Their lot was not easy. They broke the land with primitive tools and they lived in sod huts. In the off-season, many worked in lumber and mining camps and on railway construction to supplement their meagre farm

First Party of Doukhobors, a Day's Journey from Yorkton, Saskatchewan, Spring 1899

income. Their circumstances made them a source of cheap labour and they were exploited to the limit. Their sweat and toil built much of the West.

From Russia came another group, the Doukhobors — a religious sect which broke away from the Orthodox Church in the eighteenth century. Like the Mennonites before them, they left Russia because service in the army was against their religious beliefs. The Dominion government was so anxious to have these settlers in the West that three-quarters of a million acres of land were set aside for Doukhobor settlements and an Order-in-Council exempted them from military service. In 1899, 7,427 of them took up homesteads in the Northwest around Yorkton, Prince Albert, Blaine Lake and Langham, in what is now Saskatchewan. The Doukhobors, however, refused to comply with Canadian regulations to register the individual homesteads, and between 1909 and 1912 more than 5,000 of them left for British Columbia where they purchased land for their settlements.

CLIFFORD SIFTON DEFENDS DOUKHOBORS AND GALICIANS[308]

From a letter by Sifton, November, 1901:

The cry against the Doukhobors and Galicians, is the most absolutely ignorant and absurd thing that I have ever known in my life. There is simply no question in regard to the advantage of these people. The policy of exciting racial prejudice is the most contemptible possible policy, because it is one that does not depend upon reason. You can excite the prejudice of one nationality against another by simply keeping up an agitation. . . . All you have to do is to keep hammering away and appealing to their prejudices, and in the course of time you will work up an excitement; but a more ignorant and unpatriotic policy could not be imagined.

Western Canada grew rapidly with the influx of immigrants. The west was being settled. Manitoba and the Northwest, which had only 22,000 settlers in 1897, had 419,512 people in 1901, and by 1911, the three prairie provinces had a population of 1,322,709. Although many immigrants had used Canada as a stop-over on their way to the United States, Canada's population rose from 5,371,000 in 1901 to 7,204,527 in 1911.

The rapid growth of the Northwest was responsible for the creation of two new provinces — Saskatchewan and Alberta — which entered Confederation in 1905. The Northwest Territories, governed since 1875 by a Lieutenant-Governor and Council, had been given an elected Assembly in 1888 and responsible government in 1897. Now Saskatchewan and Alberta received full provincial status, except that the federal government, as was the case in Manitoba, controlled public lands. Each province received an annual subsidy of $50,-000 and eighty cents per capita grant until the population reached 800,000. In addition, each was given a special annual grant of $100,000 for a period of five years. Since these provinces were free of debt, they were to receive additional allowances. The federal government allowed these new provinces to maintain the separate schools that had existed in the Northwest Territories. Furthermore, religious minorities had the right to channel their portion of school taxes to support the schools of their denominations. The provision for separate

Threshing in Western Canada, 1910

schools evoked controversy in the Dominion and was partly responsible for Clifford Sifton's resignation from the cabinet.

THE GROWTH OF POPULATION IN THE WEST[309]

1901

Province	Total Population	Immigration
Manitoba	255,211	11,254
Saskatchewan	91,279 ⎫	14,160
Alberta	73,022 ⎭	
British Columbia and Yukon	178,657	2,600
TOTALS	598,169	28,014

1911

Province	Total Population	Immigration
Manitoba	461,394	34,289
Saskatchewan	492,432	40,076
Alberta	374,295	44,091
British Columbia and Yukon	392,480	52,786
TOTALS	1,720,601	171,242

The West was changing. Small villages dotted the prairie landscape. Many of these were block settlements of religious groups such as Mennonites and Doukhobors, or of ethnic groups such as Ukrainians, Poles, Germans and Jews. All settlers — British, Canadian, American, and European — put the land under cultivation and made the west the *Granary of the Empire*. By 1911, the wheat harvest was 197,000,000 bushels. The drastic decline in freight rates made large scale movement of goods much easier and cheaper. Grain replaced timber as the major staple export and the wheat boom brought general prosperity to Canada. Grain elevators silhouetted the prairie skies and huge terminal elevators at the lake ports received the bountiful harvests. Here, automatic loaders filled the lake freighters which carried the large quantities of wheat to the ocean ports for export.

It was fortunate for Canada that at a time when there were ready markets for her wheat, circumstances favoured wheat production and, with it, the development of the West. The western farmers did not have to go through the back-breaking task of chopping a clearing from the forested wilderness; the fertile prairie soil needed only planting, and soon the full ears of golden wheat were swaying in the prairie breeze. At first, Red Fife "hard" wheat, suitable for the short-growing season of the Canadian West, was generally grown. Europeans found this wheat ideal for mixing with their own cheaper soft wheats to produce high quality flour. In 1903, after years of painstaking research, Charles Saunders, a cerealist in the employ of the Canadian Department of Agriculture, developed Marquis wheat, which ripened eight days earlier than the Red Fife. Marquis wheat not only beat the killing effect of early frost but also pushed the prairie wheatlands farther north. Thus, more land was made available for wheat.

Other developments aided Canada's agricultural economy. Developments in farm machinery helped cultivation, and improvements in farming methods made it possible to grow crops on dry prairie lands. In addition, drier land, especially in southern Alberta, was turned into grazing areas for large herds of cattle. Before long, Canadian beef cattle, hogs and horses found their way to world markets. But it was the boom in wheat which increased Canada's foreign trade and encouraged industry and railway construction.

Immigration resulted in profound changes. The coming of the immigrants not only put the plough to millions of untouched acres of fertile prairie land, but also led to the general development of Canada. In the West, where the concentration of the foreign population was highest, newly established towns were given European place names. Names such as Komarno, Bruderheim, Elfros, Hofer, Esterhazy, Hirsch and Odessa became common and accepted. In the cities, islands of foreign groups crowded into separate sections. Cities had their Ukrainian, German and Jewish quarters, as well as their Chinatowns. It was not unusual, on the streets of cities, to hear a half-dozen different languages.

English-speaking Canadians were concerned about the flood of "foreigners" into their midst. The newcomers, it was feared, would not be easily assimilated into the Canadian way of life. However, all these people from various foreign backgrounds became Canadians and loyal citizens, though still preserving their cultural backgrounds. The many non-English national groups formed, in the future, a third segment between the two so-called founding nations; Canadian bi-nationalism became multi-nationalism.

C

NEW TRANSCONTINENTAL RAILWAYS

A new spirit of optimism, fostered by economic recovery and the development of the West, led to the construction of two new transcontinental railways during the Laurier period. Settlement along the C.P.R. had been so successful that the increase in the production of wheat and the spread of population had created the need for more railway facilities.

The very good fortunes of the C.P.R. had aroused fears of monopoly and led to the willingness on the part of the Liberal government to support new railways rather than simply extend the old. Moreover, Laurier and his colleagues became convinced that Canada's potential development demanded rapid completion of competitive systems.

The most colourful figures associated with the new age of railways were the shrewd and enterprising William Mackenzie and Donald Mann. After some early experience working for the C.P.R., the two men formed a partnership and secured financial aid from the governments of Canada and Manitoba to build a line from Gladstone to Dauphin in Manitoba.

Then, with lavish support from federal and provincial governments, they extended their lines within the province and into Saskatchewan, calling their railway the Canadian Northern. Between 1903 and 1915, the railway was completed westward through Yellowhead Pass to Vancouver. Eastward, from Port Arthur the lines extended to North Bay, Ottawa, Montreal and Quebec. The whole enterprise was made possible by continued government subsidies and guarantees of bond issues. Mackenzie and Mann built a financial empire without having to invest any money of their own. The weakness of the operation lay in the accumulation of huge amounts of interest on the money borrowed. Only a large and continuous revenue could prevent eventual financial distress and possible disaster.

OPTIMISM ABOUT THE FUTURE OF THE CANADIAN NORTHERN RAILWAY[310]

The following comments were made by an editor in Winnipeg in 1912:

. . . . Canada long since outgrew the facilities of a single transcontinental railway. . . . It will tax the utmost resources of the three transcontinental systems, when the two now under construction are finished, to meet the demands upon them.

What will particularly impress the reader of the interesting story of the Canadian Northern will be the wisdom and conservatism with which its builders have followed legitimate lines of development throughout the country and the foresight with which they have endeavored to create outlets for the produce of the various provinces.

The three outstanding features marked by a study of this vigorous growth of the Canadian Northern system are first, the wise location of the Canadian Northern lines; second, the construction of them in accordance with the needs of the localities served; and third, a corresponding economy in management.

Both the C.P.R. and the Canadian Northern had been possible only through co-operation between government and private enterprise; governments offered financial grants and guarantees while individual companies provided the talents for building and management. The third transcontinental involved an even more active role for the government, which undertook to construct the eastern section.

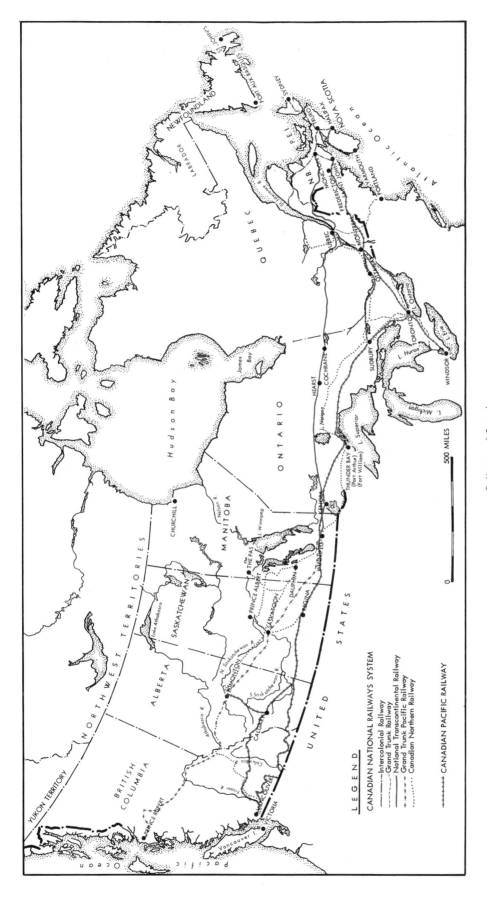

Railways of Canada

LEGEND

CANADIAN NATIONAL RAILWAYS SYSTEM

Intercolonial Railway
Grand Trunk Railway
National Transcontinental Railway
Grand Trunk Pacific Railway
Canadian Northern Railway

CANADIAN PACIFIC RAILWAY

G.T.R. Engine 618 and Train, c. 1910

The Grand Trunk Company, one of Canada's pioneers in railway building, had developed a network of lines in central Canada and a number of links with American railways. By 1903, the directors had decided that extension from coast to coast was the only answer to competition from the C.P.R.

The Dominion government was anxious to open other areas not serviced by the C.P.R. or included in the plans of the Canadian Northern. Consequently, it agreed to build the National Transcontinental from Moncton, New Brunswick to Quebec, across the Clay Belt of Quebec and through northern Ontario to Winnipeg. The plan was to lease the line on a long-term basis to the Grand Trunk Railway's subsidiary, the Grand Trunk Pacific. The new company undertook to lay rail lines from Winnipeg along the same northern route chosen by the Canadian Northern to Yellowhead Pass. From here, the road led northwest in the hope of making Prince Rupert an important terminal on the Pacific coast.

Even before the new transcontinentals were fully in use, the outbreak of World War 1 curtailed the flow of immigration and increased the costs of construction and operation. The Dominion government could not afford to allow the railway companies to collapse because both the taxpayers' money and the country's reputation were involved. Temporary assistance was given and, in 1916, a royal commission was appointed to investigate the problem of transportation and to recommend solutions.

The report of the commission urged that the government take over the troubled companies.

The very complicated procedure was begun under Prime Minister Robert Borden and completed in 1923, when Mackenzie King's Liberal party was in power. The Canadian National Railways, as the new combination was called, incorporated almost all the railways in Canada not belonging to the C.P.R. Management was entrusted to a board of directors appointed by Parliament. When taking over the railways, the Canadian government also assumed their debts. The C.N.R. remained a problem in the years to follow.

REPORT OF RAILWAY COMMISSION IN 1917[311]

. . . . We think the question, whether there should be one body or more, is answered by the facts that we have already recited. The Canadian Northern is weak in the East. The Grand Trunk, with the inadequate prairie branches of the Grand Trunk Pacific, would be almost powerless to compete in the West with the Canadian Northern and Canadian Pacific. The natural tendency of the Grand Trunk and Canadian Northern organizations, if left separate, would be for each to invade the territory of the other. Remaining separate, the Canadian Northern system would need to spend many millions of dollars to obtain an adequate hold on the East in competition with the Canadian Pacific and Grand Trunk. Remaining separate, the Grand Trunk and Grand Trunk Pacific system would need to spend many millions of dollars on new branches in the West, in order to hold its own with the Canadian Pacific and the Canadian Northern. And this money would be needed at once, for till it was spent neither organization would possess a complete system. Canada cannot afford all these new railways, and does not need three competitive systems. We recommend therefore that the three undertakings, the Canadian Northern, the Grand Trunk, and the Grand Trunk Pacific be united in one system. To whom then should the management be entrusted?

The pre-World War 1 "railway boom" resulted in the completion of more than 20,000 miles of track, the stimulation of the Canadian economy and the opening of the West. But there had been much unnecessary railway building, entailing tremendous outlay by the Dominion. The Laurier government has, therefore, often been criticized for catering to the railway promoters and for failing to establish a national policy for transportation.

D

DEVELOPMENT OF NATURAL RESOURCES

The Laurier era was also a period of expansion of Canada's mineral and forest resources, water-power and industry. The land of forests and muskeg of the Canadian Shield, long the preserve of the fur trade, came under the probing eye of the lonely prospector. The development of the natural resources brought prosperity to many parts of the Dominion and laid a foundation for Canada's industrial development.

As early as 1883, the copper-nickel deposit of the Sudbury district was discovered while a road-bed was being blasted for the C.P.R. A mine was opened and a smelter constructed at nearby Copper Cliff. It is ironic that the presence of nickel in the ore created difficulties for the company's officials. This "nuisance" metal finally came into its own when Dr. Ludwig Mond developed a process for separating the nickel from the copper. In time, increased uses of nickel gave Canada a virtual world monopoly in this versatile metal and made Sudbury the "Nickel Capital" of the world.

In the far West, the Yukon gold rush started when gold was found on the Klondike River, a tributary of the Yukon. The lure of gold attracted tens of thousands of fortune seekers from all parts of the world. The sudden riches, the tales of heroic exploits, the tragedies and disappointments, the shady characters and the rowdiness of the mining frontier have been immortalized in poems and songs: "The Trail of '98," "Dangerous Dan Mc-

Grew," "Soapy Smith" and "Lady Lou" became part of Canada's legends and folklore.

THE SPELL OF THE YUKON[312]

From a ballad about the Yukon by Robert Service:

I wanted the gold, and I sought it;
   I scrabbled and mucked like a slave.
Was it famine or scurvy — I fought it;
   I hurled my youth into a grave.
I wanted the gold, and I got it —
   Came out with a fortune last fall, —
Yet somehow life's not what I thought it,
   And somehow the gold isn't all.

———

You come to get rich (d----d good reason);
   You feel like an exile at first;
You hate it like hell for a season,
   And then you are worse than the worst.
It grips you like some kinds of sinning;
   It twists you from foe to a friend;
It seems it's been since the beginning;
   It seems it will be to the end. . . .

In southern British Columbia, towards the end of the nineteenth century, extensive mining operations were carried on — silver, lead and zinc in the Kootenay district, copper in the Sullivan mine, gold around Rossland. At Trail a giant smelter was erected to refine the ore of neighbouring

Paying with Gold Dust, 1899

A Prospector and Companion, Klondike, 1898

mines. So important was this region, that the C.P.R. built a railway through it, and British and Canadian investors poured capital into the many mining ventures. Southern British Columbia prospered; flourishing communities were established because of the mining activities.

When the Klondike rush was petering out, a sensational silver find near Cobalt, Ontario, set off a mining boom. The Temiskaming and Northern Ontario Railway was being built to Clay Belt, an isolated pocket of agricultural land in the Canadian Shield north of Lake Nipissing, which was to be opened for settlement. In 1903, Fred La Rose, a worker on the railroad, came upon a rich silver deposit. Thousands of prospectors and speculators rushed into the district and staked claims. Mining operations were soon started and Canada became a major silver producer.

The find at Cobalt touched off a flurry of prospecting throughout the Shield. Within a few years large deposits of gold were found in the Porcupine district and at Kirkland Lake. A challenging new frontier — a mining frontier — was unfolded to wrest the hidden base and precious metals from their hiding places within the ancient pre-Cambrian rocks.

Although other provinces did not experience the hustle and bustle of sudden mining booms, they did carry on important mining activities. In Quebec, asbestos was being mined, but it had only a limited market. The expanding use of electricity for home and industry created such an enormous demand for this insulating material that Canada became the world's chief supplier of asbestos. Coal mining in Nova Scotia supplied over half of Canada's coal. In Alberta, coal was mined near Lethbridge and Drumheller. Lesser coal deposits were worked in other parts of Canada. Intensified explorations opened new mining areas, especially gold, in the bushland in Quebec and Manitoba.

Forestry may not have had the romance and glitter of the mining rushes, but it contributed continually to Canada's foreign trade. The square timber trade gave British North America an era of prosperity during the first half of the nineteenth century. Towards the end of the century, world requirements for the products of the forests placed increased demands on Canadian timber.* During the first decade of this century, the white pine, mainly from the vast timber stands of Ontario, was in great demand as a building material in Canada, United States and other parts of the world. The production of lumber to meet this profitable market was on such a large scale that the pine tree stands were almost depleted. British Columbia, too, enjoyed prosperity from its forests. Douglas fir, spruce and cedar made excellent lumber for the growing cities and towns, for barns

and for grain elevators. In addition, British Columbia's forests supplied foreign markets, especially the Orient. Canadian timber found a large domestic market in ties for railway tracks, poles for hydro and telephone lines and timber for mines.

Pulpwood from Ontario, Quebec and New Brunswick had an almost unlimited market in the United States because of the rising demand for newsprint. Huge investments were made by Canadian, British and American firms to assure adequate supplies of pulp. Production of pulpwood spread into many areas of Canada and paper mills were constructed to produce newsprint; as a result, a sizeable paper industry was established in Canada. The softwood forests made Canada the world's leading exporter of newsprint.

Profit from the forests was the overriding consideration; the more trees felled, the higher the profits. Aside from some limited efforts at forest-fire prevention by the federal and provincial governments, very little was done to stop the indiscriminate logging practices. Neither public authorities nor lumbermen paid heed to conservation, forest management, or reforestation. Forests were chopped out recklessly as if trees were an inexhaustible resource. This wanton destruction continued and became so alarming that, belatedly, conservation measures were initiated to assure a future for Canada's forest resources.

The expanded mining and wood pulp industries created increased demands for an economical source of power. The immense water power resources of the Canadian Shield were harnessed to produce hydro-electric power. Soon surplus electricity was available, and this was drawn along hundreds of miles of transmission lines into factories and homes. So important was this valuable energy source, that the public demanded government ownership lest the production, distribution, and sale of electricity fall into the hands of profit-seeking monopolies. As a result, the Hydro-Electric Power Commission of Ontario was created in 1906 as a publicly-owned utility. Other provinces followed Ontario's example and instituted government ownership of hydro-electricity.

DEMAND FOR PUBLIC OWNERSHIP OF
HYDRO-POWER[313]

A resolution passed by representatives of seventy Ontario municipalities, April 11, 1906:

That the municipalities now present and represented in the City Hall, Toronto, having an urban and rural population of over one million, respect-

* Demand was especially great for timber planks, known as "deals."

fully urge upon the Lieutenant-Governor-in-Council of the Province of Ontario the necessity of safeguarding the peoples' interest by originating as a Government measure legislation enabling the Lieutenant-Governor-in-Council to appoint a permanent provincial commission with power to take, where considered by it advisable, the following action: The construction, purchase or expropriation of works for the generation, transmission and distribution of electrical power and light; to arrange with any existing development company or companies for power at a reasonable price, so as to be transmitted and sold by the Government to municipalities or others; also to vest in it the powers necessary to enable it to regulate the price at which electricity can be sold to all and every customer, whether municipal, corporate, or private.

E

GROWTH OF INDUSTRY

The wheat boom, the flow of immigrants and the development of the hitherto untapped natural resources laid the foundation for industrial expansion. Most of the industrial growth was confined to the manufacturing centres in Ontario and Quebec. The West and the Maritimes remained primary producers whose products were channelled to the factories of central Canada.

DEVELOPMENT OF AGRICULTURE AND INDUSTRIES
IN CANADA[314]

	1901	1911
Area of occupied farms, in acres	63,422,338	108,968,715
Production of wheat in bushels	55,572,368	132,077,547
Value of live stock	$268,651,026	$ 615,457,833
Export of wood and wood products	$ 33,099,915	$ 56,334,695
Mineral production	$ 65,797,911	$ 103,220,994
Gross value of manufactured products	$481,053,375	$1,165,975,639

Canadian manufacturers, following the example of the United States, though not on as large a scale, merged small companies into large combines which completely controlled specific industries. Conditions in Canada favoured such mergers; Canada had ample raw materials and manufacturers could count on high tariffs to protect their industries. The protective tariff of the National Policy, with the exception of slight downward adjustments on certain farm implements and supplies, was continued by the Laurier government.

The Canadian Manufacturers' Association (C.M.A.), founded in 1885 to promote tariff protection, was reorganized in 1899. It became the powerful spokesman of industry and carried on widespread propaganda to convince Canadians that high tariffs were necessary to protect existing industries and to develop new ones. To the government and to the public, the C.M.A. constantly stressed the need to prevent American interests from acquiring Canadian natural resources. Obviously, the C.M.A. was the voice of Big Business and because of this drew the lasting opposition of farmers' organizations and labour unions.

THE CANADIAN MANUFACTURERS' ASSOCIATION[315]

G. M. Murray, Secretary of the C.M.A., on February 9, 1910, states the growth and influence of his organization:

The reorganized Canadian Manufacturers' Association is like a young giant ignorant of its own power. By the exercise of these powers it could, if it chose, bring several millions of people to the verge of starvation, or paralyze the industry of the whole Dominion. From the half-hearted 132 who comprised the total membership of the Association in 1899 (the year of reorganization) it has grown with such strides that now in 1910 the members number more than 2,500.

Canadian industry and finance became concentrated in a few hands; this resulted in gigantic corporations. Huge intertwining companies controlled the production and distribution of such products as steel and iron, farm implements, electric power, pulp and paper, textiles, cement, flour, meat, and petroleum products. "Dominion Steel", "Steel Company of Canada," "Algoma Steel," Canada Cement," "Maple Leaf Milling," "Dominion Textiles," "Imperial Oil," and "Massey Harris" became household names.

Monopolies emerged as a result of buying out or merging smaller competing companies. This was considered more efficient; it enabled the companies to compete in expanding markets. But in fact the mergers eliminated competition and enabled the large corporations to maintain fixed high prices and to reap the highest profits possible from the Canadian consumers. Big business found the government most helpful; high tariffs kept out lower priced foreign manufactured goods and Canadians had no choice but to buy Canadian products.

Foreign investors — British and American — invested heavily in Canadian industrial enterprises to reap profits from the lucrative Canadian market. Large American firms opened branches in Canada to market electric appliances, farm machinery and petroleum products. American capital flowed freely into the development of natural resources. Although such investments were encouraged as a blessing for the development of untapped natural resources, many Canadians deplored the placing of so much of Canada's natural wealth under foreign control.

The common man was suspicious of these industrial empires; he feared their economic power and resented their political influence. Canadians realized that these super-powerful companies controlled production and distribution of their products and fixed prices; they demanded anti-trust laws, similar to those of the United States, where government legislation forced some of the largest monopolies to break up. In Canada, an act was passed in 1889 to check the growth of combines, but the mergers which followed proved the ineffectiveness of the act. Pressure of public opinion prompted the Laurier government to pass the Combines Investigation Act in 1910, to control the growth of monopolies. The government was empowered to investigate complaints of abuses and fine companies conducting business as combines against the interests of the consumers. But this Act, like its predecessor of 1889, was not very effective. Big industries grew bigger and new mergers swallowed or eliminated competition; the public remained helpless and continued to pay high prices fixed by monopolies.

THE COMBINES INVESTIGATION ACT[316]

Mackenzie King introduced the Combines Investigation Act *in the House of Commons on January 18, 1910:*

. . . . The legislation differs in some particulars from legislations of a like nature which has been introduced in other countries in that it is not aimed against combines or mergers as such, but rather against the exercise on the part of combines, mergers or monopolies, in an unfair manner, of the powers which they may get from that form of organization. . . . A highly organized industry should, from the facilities it has of improving production, lead to greater efficiency and economies of one kind and another, which should, on the whole, benefit the consuming public. But, we know that . . . organizations have not always used their corporate powers to the advantage of the consumers, but have taken, in some cases, possibly, an unfair advantage to themselves. This measure seeks to afford the means of conserving to the public some of the benefits which arise from large organizations of capital for the purpose of business and commerce. It is organized society which alone makes the organization of capital and industry possible, and the people have a right to expect and to look to the government to see that their rights shall be conserved and that their liberties shall not be curtailed by privileges which they permit others to enjoy. . . .

F

FARM ORGANIZATIONS

The early Canadian agricultural societies came into being mainly to assist farmers in improving agricultural practices. In time, farm organizations were founded to improve the conditions of the agrarian population. When agriculture became the mainstay of Canada's economy, farmers became suspicious of big business in Ontario and Quebec, which reaped most benefits from Canada's agricultural prosperity. Several farm organizations came into existence between 1900 and 1911 to protect the farmers against what they regarded as the rapacity of big business.

The Grange, a fraternal organization brought into Canada from the United States in the 1870's, primarily intended to raise the cultural level of farmers. Unlike certain Granges in some of the American states, the Canadian offshoot did not involve itself in politics. But soon the Grange began to press the federal government to look into freight rates and the costs of storing grain.

In 1889 the Patrons of Industry was organized in Ontario. This new farmers' organization did essentially what the Grange had done, but more actively, and also started some co-operative ventures which were not too successful. It also participated in politics — some of its members were elected to the Ontario legislature in 1894. Through political action, the Patrons of Industry aimed to improve the farmers' lot. From these earlier farm organizations sprang others such as the Farmers' Association in Ontario in 1902. In 1907 it joined the Grange. In the west, farm organizations arose to press for a better deal from elevator and railway monopolies. The Patrons of Industry declined; in 1902 the Territorial Grain Growers Association, the latest farm organization, spread in Manitoba and Saskatchewan. A similar organization, the United Farmers of Alberta, was formed.

More powerful organizations evolved — the Grain Growers' Grain Company (G.G.G. Co.) in Manitoba and Alberta and the Saskatchewan Co-operative Elevators in Saskatchewan. The G.G.G. Co. became a very influential pressure group. It was behind the move which turned the Bell Telephone Company into the provincially owned and operated Manitoba Telephone System. In 1908, through pressure of the Manitoba government, the G.G.G. Co. gained a seat on the Winnipeg Grain Exchange to handle the sale of the farmers' grain. Pressure for an equitable and accurate grain grading system resulted in the establishment of the federal Board of Grain Commissioners. In the same year, the G.G.G. Co. began to publish the *Grain Growers' Guide* to express the views of the farm organization and its members.

The growth and influence of the farm organizations were indications of the importance of Canadian agriculture. The various farm associations in the provinces were, to some extent, successful in forcing provincial governments to pass favourable agricultural legislation. In 1909, with the formation of the Canadian Council of Agriculture, the unified pressure of Canadian farmers was exerted on the Dominion government. The Council was not a political association but a pressure group to force the federal government to adopt measures for the benefit of Canadian farmers.

What did the farmers want? Mainly, they wanted reciprocity, which they believed would provide a large market for Canadian agricultural products in the United States. Farmers objected to the high tariff policy which protected Canadian manufacturers at the expense of the consumers. They saw in reciprocity a means of obtaining cheaper farm machinery and manufactured goods from the United States; Canadian manufacturers would thus be forced to lower their prices.

The Canadian Council of Agriculture became impatient with the inaction of the federal government, which turned a deaf ear to the farmers' demands. In December, 1910, the Council organized the "Siege of Ottawa" — a delegation of

Erecting an Elevator for Storing Grain

almost one thousand, representing the farmers of the prairie provinces and Ontario. The delegates gave the Laurier government an account of agrarian discontent. The protest of so many farm representatives was a dramatic demonstration of the strength of the agrarian community.

"THE SIEGE OF OTTAWA," 1910[317]

The resolutions presented by the delegates of the Canadian Council of Agriculture:

We come, asking no favors at your hands. We bear with us no feeling of antipathy towards any other line of industrial life . . . but in view of the fact that the further progress and development of the agricultural industry is of such vital importance to the general welfare of the state that all other Canadian industries are so dependent upon its success, that its constant condition forms the great barometer of trade, we consider its operations should no longer be hampered by tariff restriction. . . .

. . . we strongly favor reciprocal Free Trade between Canada and the United States. . . .

———

. . . it is the opinion of this convention that the Hudson's Bay Railway and all terminal facilities connected therewith should be constructed, owned and operated in perpetuity by the Dominion government. . . .

... we ... request that the Dominion government acquire and operate ... the elevators of Fort William and Port Arthur, and immediately establish similar terminal facilities ... at the Pacific Coast. ...

... that the new Bank Act be so worded as to permit the act to be amended at any time and in any particular.

... it is desirable that cheap and efficient machinery for the incorporation of co-operative societies should be provided by Federal legislation during the present session of parliament.

The government be urgently requested to erect the necessary works and operate a modern and up-to-date method of exporting our meat animals.

That the Board of Railway Commissioners be given complete jurisdiction in ... matters of dispute between the railways and the people, and to enable them to do this that the law be more clearly defined.

The government took no concrete immediate action, but it could not help but be impressed by the growing influence of Canadian agriculture. To get the farm vote, the Laurier government recognized the farmers' demands in the Liberal party's election platform of 1911. But many farmers were convinced that their organizations, as mere pressure groups, were not effective enough to wring concessions from the government; only political action could achieve their goals. It was not until the post-World War I period that farmers entered politics, at first through their own provincial political parties and, eventually, in the federal field through the Progressive Party.

G

LABOUR ORGANIZATIONS

The growth of industry brought the growth of organized labour. Early labour unions were mutual aid societies rather than bargaining agents for their members. It was not until 1872, after a successful strike of the Toronto Typographical Society against the *Globe* for a nine-hour work day, that the Macdonald government passed legislation which gave legal recognition to trade unions. Prior to this, unions were considered illegal organizations subject to prosecution.

In the early 1880's, the Knights of Labour, which had gained considerable success in the United States, moved into Canada. This organization aimed to attract all kinds of labourers, both skilled and unskilled. Although the Knights flourished, many of its locals joined the Trades and Labour Congress of Canada (T.L.C.) when it was organized in 1886. The T.L.C. affiliated itself with the American Federation of Labour (A.F. of L.) of the United States, and both worked to obtain better wages and improved working conditions. In 1902, the remnants of the Knights of Labour were excluded from the T.L.C. and formed the Canadian Federation of Labour, a Canadian-based craft union.

Unions spread mainly in the industrial sections of central Canada. In Quebec, however, unionization was hindered by the influence of the Roman Catholic Church and by French-Canadian sentiments against Anglo-Saxon domination and American affiliation of the existing unions. French Canadians organized Catholic unions, closely tied to the French-Canadian scene and to the Church. On the west coast, a radical American union, the Industrial Workers of the World (I.W.W.) or "Wobblies" as they were called, gained adherents among the lumber workers.

THE CANADIAN WORKING CLASS[318]

View of a European in 1907:

The workers have begun the work of organizing themselves according to American methods, but have been retarded greatly by all their differences of race, religion, etc. In imitation of what has been done in the United States, they have established in most of the towns special Trade Unions for each trade; the different Trade Unions in each locality take part frequently in Trade and Labour Councils. ...

These Unions have until now devoted themselves principally to professional ends—the securing of higher wages, the reduction of the hours of labour, the improving of the conditions of employment either through their own action or by means of amicable negotiations with employers or through the mediation of the State. ... The tendency of the Trades and Labour Congress is undoubtedly to exercise influence over the social legislation of the country. Some of the Unions, chiefly in British Columbia, are of a distinctly Socialistic character, but these are the exception. ...

Coming now to the political side of the matter, we find that the Canadian workers, in spite of

Labour Day Parade, Winnipeg, 1914

in industrialized Canada. In 1900, the federal Bureau of Labour was reorganized as the Department of Labour under William Lyon Mackenzie King, the youthful Deputy Minister. He regarded labourers as an important segment of the Canadian people and he firmly believed that they should have a voice in conciliation and settlement of industrial disputes with employers. He was instrumental in drafting the Industries Disputes Investigation Act, or Lemieux Act, which was passed in 1907. The Act provided for conciliation and negotiation by an arbitration board of three —"representing respectively the interest of labour, the employer and the public" — rather than lock-outs or strikes in industrial disputes. At the time it was hailed as progressive legislation to settle labour disputes. Although the findings of such boards were not binding on either management or labour, quite often such decisions settled disputes and avoided strikes. The Department of Labour became a separate ministry, and after Mackenzie King was elected to parliament in 1908, he became Minister of Labour in 1909.

some isolated victories at the polls, have not yet succeeded in constituting themselves a Third Party. . . . In a new country, prospering and developing rapidly, the general interests of all classes are too interlaced and interdependent for it to be easy to organize a class policy; the policy of national prosperity comes before all else.

In the beginning of the present century, unions were fairly well established but they represented only a small portion of Canadian Labour. Hostility of industry and splits in the labour ranks resulted in a rather slow growth of unions; skilled workers were well organized, but semi-skilled and unskilled labour had little representation.

With the growth of population and industrial expansion, the labour force grew and, with it, union membership. The period between 1900 and 1914 was a time of industrial strife; strikes, lockouts, work stoppages and violence were common. Since most of the unions were affiliates of American organizations, the cry of "foreign influence" was raised against labour unions generally and against those on strike particularly. The antiforeign cry was raised to divert public attention from the real issues — poor wages and unsatisfactory working conditions.

The government became aware of labour's role

THE INDUSTRIAL DISPUTES INVESTIGATION ACT[319]

In a letter of November 12, 1908, to J. D. Cameron, Laurier expressed his private view of this Act:

The Lemieux Act [Industrial Disputes Investigation Act] was not passed with the object of conciliating the labour vote. It was passed with the sole object of preventing the untold misery and mischief wrought by strikes. When the Bill was under discussion some sections of the railway organization fought it most strenuously, and they may perhaps attack it again next session, certainly during the present Parliament; notwithstanding this view of the most important class, I persist in believing that the Act is a most meritorious piece of legislation.

The unions were not political organizations; their members supported the old parties. The unions' chief function was to represent labour effectively in bargaining with employers. As union membership grew, neither the political parties nor government — federal or provincial — could ignore the voice of labour. The provinces enacted progressive labour legislation which set minimum wages, limited the hours of work, forbade child labour and provided workmen's compensation for those injured on their jobs.

22

PROGRESS TOWARDS NATIONAL STATUS

A

CANADA AND THE EMPIRE PRIOR TO 1896

Sir Wilfrid Laurier* was "the right man at the right time" in much the same way as Sir John A. Macdonald. British North America had been fortunate that such a man as Macdonald was present and in a position to apply his insight and many talents to the challenge of building the basic structure of a Canadian nation. Laurier was Prime Minister at a time when Canada had reached another threshold in its development, as internal strains and external pressures held great potential for good or ill.

A central problem within the Dominion was relations between French- and English-speaking Canadians. The Manitoba Schools Question had been the most recent manifestation of this problem. Related to this racial and religious tension was the growth of French-Canadian nationalism and of English-Canadian devotion to the bonds with Great Britain. The result was divided feelings toward the British Empire, in which Canada was the principal colony. Relations with the United States, meanwhile, were complicated by the recurring problems of boundary, trade and fishing rights. Throughout the Laurier era, Canadians moved toward some definition of their national identity.

Canada, it must be remembered, was still a colony, even though responsible government in matters of internal concern had been recognized before Confederation. As a colony it did not have diplomatic relations with other countries in the same sense that Canada and other nations do today. When treaties were arranged between a foreign country and any member of the Empire, the actual settlements were concluded by British diplomats.

Yet in the years following Confederation, the growth of autonomy was distinctly evident. Macdonald was included in the British delegation that made the Treaty of Washington with the United States in 1871. The office of Canadian High Commissioner to London was created in 1880 to facili-

tate discussion of mutual interests between Great Britain and Canada. Canadian representatives of both Liberal and Conservative governments had taken the initiative in seeking reciprocity with the United States — even though an actual treaty would have required the official participation of the British Foreign Office in Washington. In 1887 and 1894, conferences of colonial Prime Ministers and British cabinet ministers signified that the colonies were growing up and that their wishes were being considered before the British government introduced policies affecting all parts of the Empire.

Canadian leaders of both French and English descent professed their attachment to Britain and to British ideals of justice, social progress and liberty. French Canadians looked upon the imperial government, and such laws as the British North America Act, as important to survival in a continent where English-Canadian domination and American annexationism were equally unacceptible. Yet many Canadians of all backgrounds expected that their country would keep moving in the direction of nationhood, and that independence would come some day in the distant future. The attitudes of British government for several decades had encouraged the trend toward greater colonial freedom and reduced imperial responsibility for government defence.

British attitudes began to change subtly in the latter 1880's. Then in the next decade, Great Britain became engaged in a steadily rising competition with Germany, France and others for colonies around the world, but particularly in Africa. One result in England was renewed inter-

---

* A knighthood was conferred on Laurier when he attended Queen Victoria's "Diamond Jubilee" in 1897. For the sake of convenience, Laurier will be referred to as Sir Wilfrid Laurier from the beginning of the chapter.

est in its older, self-governing colonies, such as Canada. Joseph Chamberlain, who accepted the post as Colonial Secretary in 1895 in the hope of advancing his vision of empire, exploited this interest. He took every occasion to urge that the administration of the British Empire be more centralized. Greater control concentrated in London would give the Empire an image of greater strength and unity in world trade and defence.

In Canada, too, imperialist notions were flourishing. The assumption of Anglo-Saxon superiority appealed to men who preferred to be identified with a glorious empire rather than with an obscure colony. The Conservative Party attracted such men; so did organizations such as the British Federation League, which stood for stronger ties between parts of the Empire. Recent British immigrants, numbering in the hundreds of thousands at the turn of the century, and descendants of United Empire Loyalists, had strong affection for England, the heart of the Empire. An outburst of patriotic literature from England nurtured these feelings.

"Lip-Loyalty vs. Loyalty that Acts"   Cartoonist's View of Imperial Preference

B

IMPERIAL PREFERENCE

Trade was one of the first subjects demanding the Laurier government's attention. The Liberal Party in opposition had expressed preference for closer economic relations with the United States. It had officially espoused reciprocity and attacked Macdonald's National Policy. The American government had been erecting high tariffs of their own, however, and had displayed no interest in lowering them for the sake of Canada. Moreover, the majority of Canadians had apparently accepted the Conservatives' warning that reciprocal trade with the United States could lead to Canada's annexation. All things considered, Laurier decided against any radical changes in the tariff.

The first budget, brought down by Finance Minister William S. Fielding, in April, 1897, was noteworthy as the budget of "Imperial Preference." The Liberals retained the basic structure of the National Policy, and defended their action largely with the argument that tariffs were still needed to provide government with revenue, and to afford some protection to Canadian manufacturers. A limited number of reductions in tariff were, nevertheless, provided in the hope of promoting trade. Far more important, the budget specified an "Imperial Preference," which would allow imports from Great Britain to enter Canada at much lower tariff rates than those applied to goods from other countries.

This policy was naturally praised by men of imperialist sentiments in Canada and in England.

A BRITISH COMMENT ON IMPERIAL PREFERENCE[320]

Lord Farrer, a leading advocate of free trade in England, commented on the Fielding tariff:

No reasonable free trader wishes to see a system of protection which has been in force for many years, and under which industries of various kinds have grown up, abolished at a single blow. Such a step would be both unjust and unwise. They wish to see the colonies abandon protection as a theory and gradually reduce the most obnoxious of their present protective duties. This would probably, by increasing importation itself, increase revenue and make further reductions possible. . . . This is what we may hope for under the new régime in Canada. . . . So far as Canada is concerned, it is not complete free trade, but it is a step from protection towards free trade. . . .

Free traders also had words of approval, at least for the clauses that lowered tariffs. The British government could not respond with reciprocal treatment for Canadian products, of course, since it had been committed to free trade for a half-century. Americans did not feel that their interests would be much affected by increased Anglo-Canadian trade. Therefore, there was no sign given that the United States would reconsider the idea of reciprocity with Canada. But Canadians had greater hope of expanded trade with both of their main trading partners.

C

THE COLONIAL CONFERENCE OF 1897

Queen Victoria's "Diamond Jubilee," marking the Queen's sixty years on the throne, was held a few months later, in the summer of 1897. London was the gathering place for representatives from British possessions all round the world. Bemedalled dignitaries and brilliantly attired troops from exotic places — India, Hong Kong, Jamaica — joined in a festive celebration of Empire and of imperial power. Along with the other colonial Prime Ministers, Laurier was a feted guest.

As Prime Minister of the leading colony, Laurier was accorded the special favour of a knighthood. He was treated to the splendour of London's aristocratic social life and flattered with personal attention and compliments. For his part, Laurier responded with glowing public speeches in which he paid tribute to the British Empire and counted the blessings for Canada of its membership. The occasion called for rhetoric, and Laurier disappointed no one.

The practical opportunities of the "Jubilee" had not escaped the attention of Joseph Chamberlain.

THE DIAMOND JUBILEE OVERWHELMS LAURIER[321]

John W. Dafoe believed that Laurier was greatly affected by the adulation showered upon him in England:

To be translated from the humdrum life of Ottawa to a foremost place in the vast pageantry of the Diamond Jubilee, there to be showered with a wealth of tactful and complimentary personal attentions was rather too much for Laurier. The oratorical possibilities of the occasion took him into camp; and in a succession of speeches he gave it as his view that the most entrancing future for Canada was one in which she should be represented in the imperial parliament sitting in Westminster. "It would be," he told the National Liberal Club, "the proudest moment of my life if I could see a Canadian of French descent affirming the principles of freedom in the parliament of Great Britain." This, of course, was nothing but the abandonment of the orator to the rhetorical possibilities of the situation. . . .

The man responsible for directing colonial affairs had planned a Colonial Conference to coincide with the pageantry. Encouraged by Canada's new "Imperial Preference" and Laurier's recent enthusiastic oratory, the Colonial Secretary was convinced that he had an ally in his plans for strengthening the Empire. When the private meetings of the Conference were convened, however, Laurier was the cautious politician.

Chamberlain proposed an imperial council, which would include representation from the self-governing colonies and serve to reinforce their political bonds with the mother country. Laurier resisted by pointing out the difficulties inherent in devising such a council, in fixing representation and in determining methods of operation. He finished by supporting a resolution which described existing arrangements as "generally satisfactory."

Concerning defence, Chamberlain tried to convince the Premiers that the imperial navy and army were being maintained at their present level because of the colonies' needs. He singled out Canada to illustrate the importance of imperial protection for the colony in the past. Therefore, he said, Canada should contribute to the financial support of the British navy. Again Laurier disagreed, arguing that Canadian money was needed more urgently for development at home.

The topic of trade, which Canada was more willing to explore, was not promoted as forcefully by Chamberlain because England's policy of free trade prevented him from offering privileges to the colonies — at least for the time being. Laurier recognized the futility of pressing for reciprocal British preference. As with other issues involved in imperial relations, he was content to leave things as they were.

Laurier's confrontation with Chamberlain may be seen as another advancement in the development of Canadian autonomy, even though Laurier's actions were essentially defensive. The trend toward greater freedom of action might have been reversed if Chamberlain's plans had been accepted by the colonies. By resisting as he did, Laurier had helped establish Canada's determination to defend its own interests.

D

THE SOUTH AFRICAN WAR

British pressure on Canada did not lapse at the end of the Colonial Conference of 1897. In the following year, Chamberlain took another step toward closer unity in defence by appointing Lord

Minto as Governor-General of Canada and Major-General Edward Hutton as commander of the Canadian militia.

Lord Minto was a military man and an ardent

Canadian Contingent, Ready to Board the **Milwaukee**, Halifax, and Leave for South Africa, 1899

imperialist. He had served in the army in Afghanistan, had been military secretary to the Canadian Governor-General, Lord Lansdowne, between 1883 and 1885, and had acted as chief of staff to General Middleton during the Riel uprising in 1885. When his friend, Colonel Wolseley, requested Canadian voyageurs for service in the Sudan in 1884, Minto personally enlisted a force of Canadians.

Hutton, a specialist on imperial defence, had strong views on colonial participation in imperial service. By the beginning of 1899, he had effected reforms in the militia in a manner that annoyed Canadian officials. The authority that the British officer assumed was resented by the Canadian government as contrary to the spirit of responsible government.

The South African War (1899-1902) was the crisis that brought Canada's relations with Great Britain to a head. At the same time, it provoked trouble between French- and English-speaking Canadians, and convinced Laurier of his prime responsibility. He must place harmony and progress in Canada ahead of all other considerations, including the performance of duties in imperial affairs.

The war in South Africa was a contest between British imperialism and Boer nationalism. The Boers, descendants of Dutch settlers who had

arrived before the British, lived in the republics of Transvaal and the Orange Free State. They had fallen under British control in the 1870's, but had been allowed to remain republics with local self-government. However, two developments created pressure for incorporating them in a federation which would be dominated by Britain's Cape Colony. First, fabulous discoveries of diamonds and gold made the Boer territories more desirable, and attracted immigrants and huge investments from Great Britain. Secondly, empire-builders such as Cecil Rhodes shared Joseph Chamberlain's dreams of "painting Africa red"* from the Cape to Egypt in the north. The opportunity for imposing stronger control over Transvaal and the Orange Free State arose when British nationals claimed, with some justification, that the Boer governments were collecting heavy taxes and fees while refusing to grant any political rights.

When conditions for war were ripening, Chamberlain inquired about the possibilities of Canadian troops serving in Africa. Laurier doubted that Canada's Militia Act allowed for troops to be used outside Canada unless Canada itself was in danger of attack. In July, Chamberlain notified the

---

* Red was the colour used on maps to indicate the British Empire.

Governor-General that war with the Boers was probable, and that an offer of Canadian troops would be helpful. Lord Minto then advised Laurier to consider a "spontaneous offer of soldiers."

When the expected war did erupt on October 12, 1899, Laurier found himself in a difficult position. Aside from the repeated urging by imperial officials, he was under public attack from Conservative leader, Sir Charles Tupper, and from many English Canadians, especially newspaper editors. They claimed he was giving in to French Canada by witholding support for the British Empire in an hour of need. French Canadians, including Laurier's colleague in the cabinet, Israel Tarte, opposed participation in a war in which Canada's interests were not involved. The situation was a new one for a Canadian Prime Minister, for never before had a Canadian government needed to make an official decision on the question of military support for Great Britain.*

A QUEBEC POLITICIAN WRITES ABOUT HIS FELLOW FRENCH CANADIANS[322]

Israel Tarte, writing in 1900 to John Willison, editor of the TORONTO GLOBE, *analyzes the difference between French Canadians and English Canadians:*

. . . The French-Canadian population do not belong, if I may speak that way, to the same civilization as their fellow-countrymen of English origin. The French genius is not the same as the Anglo-Saxon genius. We are French, you are English. Would you permit me to add that we are Canadians to the fullest extent of the word while, on many occasions, you are more British than Canadians. If there is any trouble in future, the trouble will come out of that difference.

The reluctance of the French Canadians to taking part in the Transvaal war had for its cause the earnest desire of the French population not to be involved in continental conflicts. . . . Is it not our right, not to love that infernal war in South Africa? And why should we be accused of disloyalty because we don't like the war? We think that in minding our own business we could be a very happy people. The English and the French of this continent would very soon become close friends if there was a real, genuine national sentiment.

Do not believe that we are backward: very far from it: we want to go forward, we want to be a nation, which, you will grant, is a legitimate ambition.

Laurier and his cabinet decided on a compromise. The decision taken was that Canada was not bound to commit an official force to a British war not directly involving the colony. However, in view of the number of Canadians who had volunteered for service in South Africa, the government would provide equipment and transportation for those who wanted to join the British army. By the end of October, without calling Parliament into session, the government had arranged for the departure of the first thousand volunteers. All told, some eight thousand Canadians enlisted, including those in the cavalry, the Strathcona Horse, whose expenses were borne by Lord Strathcona (Donald Smith), now Canada's High Commissioner to London.

LAURIER'S BOER WAR CRISIS COMPROMISE[323]

The skillfully worded order-in-council authorizing participation in the Boer War:

The Prime Minister, in view of the well known desire of a great many Canadians who are ready to take service under such conditions, is of opinion that the moderate expenditure which would thus be involved for the equipment and transportation of such volunteers may readily be undertaken by the Government of Canada without summoning Parliament, especially as such an expenditure under such circumstances, cannot be regarded as a departure from the well-known principles of constitutional government and colonial practice, nor construed as a precedent for future action.

In military matters Laurier asserted Canadian autonomy in two ways. First, Canadian troops were organized in units to serve in British regiments, rather than attached individually as the Australians were. Secondly, Laurier arranged for the recall of the over-zealous General Hutton, in February, 1900, in spite of the opposition of Chamberlain and Lord Minto.

Canadian troops conducted themselves with distinction in the fighting. Whatever the merits of the war, Canadians drew acclaim for their country. The names of Paardeberg, Mafeking and other battles in which they took part became household words among Canadians who were proud of their countrymen's exploits. English-Canadian boys played war games in which the heroes were the "RCR's" — the newly formed Royal Canadian Regiment — and the enemy was led by Kruger, the hated symbol of the Boers.

Canadian public opinion was, however, badly divided by the war, and Laurier's compromise had satisfied very few. English-language newspapers

---

* There was no question of declaring war, since a colony had no such power. Officially, all parts of the Empire were at war when Great Britain declared war. But actual participation, and the amount of it, was a decision open to a colony.

questioned the Prime Minister's loyalty to Canada and the Empire, and attacked French Canadians as foreigners. When Parliament met in February, 1900, the Conservatives began their campaign for the election of that year with bombastic speeches against Laurier's actions. Then, as the English Canadians charged Laurier with doing too little about the war, French Canadians accused him of doing too much, of submitting to British pressure. Henri Bourassa, the brilliant young grandson of Joseph Papineau, left the Liberal Party. He introduced a motion in the House of Commons insisting on the sovereignty of the Canadian Parliament and declaring that Canada's contribution to the South African War was not a precedent for smiliar action in the event of future imperial wars. Although the motion was resoundingly defeated, Bourassa had seized the opportunity in the debate to assert that Canada's autonomy had suffered a severe blow.

BOURASSA ON THE SOUTH AFRICAN WAR[324]

In a letter to Laurier in November, 1899, Bourassa explains his opposition to Canadian participation in the South African War:

. . . . Note that I am much less ferocious on this question of imperialism than you think. I have never been and I am not now in favour of independence — at least not for the moment and for a long time to come. It seems to me that we can remain in our present state of transition for some time yet. Chamberlain wants to get us out of that stage. That megalomaniac's fixed intention is to go down in history as the *Builder of the Empire.* He could well become the *loosener of the Empire.* . . . However, Chamberlain is not the Empire, nor even England, and I think that we ought to ponder the matter a bit before executing his orders. . . .

Laurier did what he could to answer critics on both sides. To those who pointed up his lack of enthusiasm for the war, he replied, "I have no sympathy for that mad, noisy, dull-witted and short-sighted throng who clamours for war." But he noted that once a decision had been taken, no time was lost in getting troops to South Africa. To Bourassa, Laurier defended his policy as an attempt to minimize racial disunity. Canadian autonomy had not suffered, he declared. The Canadian government had decided on its own policy, in response to wishes expressed by its own citizens.

If the government's policy had earned little praise, it was better received in all parts of Canada than its vocal critics predicted. The election of 1900 gave the Liberals an increased majority, and except for a slight drop in support from Ontario, the party had stronger representation from the various regions of the country.

LAURIER'S DEFENCE OF HIS ACTIONS IN THE BOER WAR CRISIS[325]

Laurier answers Bourassa's charges that Canadian autonomy had suffered:

I put this question to my honourable friend. What would be the condition of this country to-day if we had refused to obey the voice of public opinion? It is only too true that if we had refused our imperative duty, the most dangerous agitation would have arisen, an agitation which, according to all human probability, would have ended in a cleavage in the population of this country upon racial lines. . . .

The unity of Canada had not been destroyed by the crisis over the South African War, but it had been seriously tested. Laurier had seen the effect of imperial pressure on the thin fabric of Canadian nationalism. He had seen the strength with which English Canadians identified themselves and their country with the Empire, and the vehemence with which they could denounce fellow citizens who saw the Empire differently. For French Canadians, true Canadianism meant asserting national sovereignty in opposition to British domination.

In London, Chamberlain was more convinced than ever by 1902 that an imperial council with strong powers was necessary to maintain Great Britain's position in the world. He called another Colonial Conference; this time the coronation of Edward VII would provide the background of pageantry. Encouraged by the support given by the colonies during the Boer War, Chamberlain mistakenly believed that the time had come for imperial federation.

CHAMBERLAIN AT THE COLONIAL CONFERENCE OF 1902[326]

Joseph Chamberlain's melodramatic appeal to sentiment:

. . . . Gentlemen we do want your aid. We do require your assistance in the administration of the vast Empire which is yours as well as ours. The weary Titan staggers under the too vast orb of its fate. We have borne the burden for many years. We think it is time that our children should assist us to support it. . . .

Chamberlain's response to Canada's claim that public opinion would not support a system of imperial military reserves:

. . . . I am bound to say that in my opinion, public opinion in these colonies must be very backward.

I think it will have to progress, especially as the dangers which lie all around you are better appreciated. . . .

If Chamberlain was more aggressive and demanding than he had been five years before, Laurier was even more determined to resist. With Canada's refusal to submit, imperial federation was finished. Canada's control over it own affairs would continue to grow as Canadians of all backgrounds developed pride in their own country and its achievements at home and abroad.

E

THE ALASKAN BOUNDARY DISPUTE

Relations between Canada and the United States had been generally satisfactory since Confederation. Nevertheless, irritations had arisen periodically over such problems as trade, boundaries and fishing rights in coastal areas and common inland waterways. Canada's lack of freedom to make decisions on foreign policy complicated the negotiations between the two countries. This lack of freedom was part of a deep dilemma. Canada, on the one hand, had traditionally relied on the protective "umbrella" of British power to resist northward expansion by the United States. On the other hand, there was always the danger that British actions elsewhere, such as in Latin America, would draw Canada into an Anglo-American conflict. Conversely, Great Britain might sacrifice Canadian interests in order to maintain cordial relations with the United States.

In 1898 the three members of the English-speaking "triangle" began a series of meetings that would deal with several problems — including one major crisis. Fishing rights in eastern coastal waters and the Pacific seal industry were irksome issues, but they were resolved in time. Trade, or reciprocity, was a special matter on which the Canadian voters would later pronounce a verdict. The question of the Alaskan boundary, however, was crucial for Canada's relations with both the United States and Great Britain.

The boundary between Canada and the Alaskan Panhandle, the narrow, jagged strip of land and islands that cut northern British Columbia off from the sea, was not clearly defined. The original boundary was vaguely set out in 1825 in a treaty between Russia, then the owner of Alaska, and Great Britain.

From Portland Channel at the fifty-sixth parallel, the line was to run north along the summits of mountains located parallel to the coast. Where the summits lay more than ten leagues inland, the boundary would continue at that distance from the coast. The boundary was not precise, since there were many mountains, but no chain clearly running parallel to the coast; the sinuous coastline could only add to the uncertainty. However, at that time, neither country required a more precise definition. When the United States purchased Alaska in 1867, it felt no urgency to examine the accuracy of the provisions of 1825.

The boundary suddenly became an urgent matter in 1898, when gold was discovered in the Klondike region of Canada's Yukon. Canada clearly had the important gold fields in its territory, but it did not so clearly have access to them from the Pacific. Although Sir Clifford Sifton had considered the incredible scheme of a railway to the Yukon, water transportation was the only practicable means of linking the Yukon with the rest of Canada. The United States and Canada both claimed several islands and the coastal strip, including the port of Skagway, which had become a boom town because of the gold rush.

American President Theodore ("Teddy") Roosevelt, who took office in 1901, followed a diplomatic policy of "walking quietly but carrying a big stick." Once having decided what American interests were in a given situation, he was usually ready to employ force. The United States had recently established a dominating influence in the Caribbean and had acquired Hawaii and the Philippines as a consequence of victory in the Spanish-American War. Roosevelt was in the process of "taking Panama" for the purpose of building the canal there. The pattern of intervention in the affairs of other nearby countries led to the president's declaration, in 1904, that the United States was the "policeman" of the Western Hemisphere. The assertiveness of the Americans had been directed at Latin America, but Canada's treatment would not be substantially different.

In 1903 the dispute over the Alaskan boundary was referred to a joint commission of six officials, three from the United States and three appointed by Great Britain. The British government named two Canadians to the tribunal; the third was a high-ranking British judge, Lord Alverstone. Although the agreement was that each side would appoint "impartial jurists of repute," Roosevelt appointed men who were widely known to oppose any compromise with Canada. Furthermore, the Americans were acting under instructions from Roosevelt, who had informed the British privately of the verdict he expected — or else he might have to send American troops to conduct a survey of the boundary.

In a letter to his son, October 20, 1903, President Roosevelt explains the United States' success:

I am very much pleased over what has just been accomplished in the Alaska Boundary award. I hesitated sometime before I would consent to a commission to decide the case and I declined absolutely to allow any arbitration of the matter. Finally I made up my mind I would appoint three men of such ability and such firmness that I could be certain there would be no possible outcome disadvantageous to us as a nation; and would trust to the absolute justice of our case, as well as to a straight-out declaration to certain high British officials that I meant business, and that if this commission did not decide the case at issue, I would decline all further negotiations and would have the line run on my own hook. I think that both factors were of importance in bringing about the result. That is, I think that the British Commissioner who voted with our men was entitled to great credit, and I also think that the clear understanding the British Government has as to what would follow a disagreement was very important and probably decisive.

As the only member of the tribunal who had apparently not made up his mind beforehand about the merit of the rival claims, Lord Alverstone was in a difficult position. If he agreed with the American demands, he would annoy the Canadian government at a time when Britain — especially Joseph Chamberlain — hoped for Canadian co-operation in strengthening the bonds of empire. If he seemed to favour the Canadian view, he would offend the United States at a time when many other leading nations were hostile toward Britain over its treatment of the Boers. Alverstone finally decided to support a settlement which gave the United States basically what it had demanded, and in fact, which seemed closest to the orginal treaty.

Canadians were loud in their protest over the result, and they accused Lord Alverstone of betraying Canadian interests. Canadians were not so much concerned about the Americans' success in winning their claims* as about the manner in which it was accomplished. The build-up of anti-Americanism was to leave a residue of strong memories, as Laurier discovered to his regret in the election of 1911.

Another lasting result was the feeling among

Street Scene in Skagway, Alaska, 1897

Canadians that Great Britain had served its own interests — conciliating the United States — at the expense of Canada. Many expressed the conviction that Canada could look after its own welfare properly only if it obtained the power to conduct its own foreign policy.

[a]*Sir Clifford Sifton describes his disappointment over the result:*

As you have no doubt already sized the matter up, the British Government deliberately decided about a year ago to sacrifice our interests at any cost, for the sake of pleasing the United States. . . .

It is, however, the most cold-blooded case of absolutely giving away our interests, without even giving us the excuse of saying we have had a fight for it. . . . My view, in watching the diplomacy of Great Britain as affecting Canada for six years, is that it may just as well be decided in advance that practically whatever the United States demands from England will be conceded in the long run, and the Canadian people might as well make up their minds to that now.

[b]*Sir Wilfrid Laurier's comments in the House of Commons:*

. . . . I have often regretted also that we have not in our own hands the treaty-making power which would enable us to dispose of our own affairs . . . Our hands are tied to a large extent . . . obliging us to deal with questions affecting ourselves through the instrumentality of the British ambassador. . . .

* Historians seem to agree that the Americans did have the stronger claim.

It is important that we should ask the British parliament for more extensive powers so that if ever we have to deal with matters of a similar nature [Alaskan Boundary Dispute] again, we shall deal with them in our own way, in our own fashion, according to the best light we have.

F

FURTHER STEPS TOWARD SELF-GOVERNMENT IN FOREIGN AFFAIRS

The need for a special department of government for foreign affairs was apparent by the time of the Alaskan boundary dispute. Canadian officials, trying to gather information and relevant documents about the case, found that little was available in the records of Canada's government; what did exist was either scattered in several departments or filed away in the Colonial Office in London. Sir Joseph Pope, the Under-Secretary of State and former assistant to Sir John A. Macdonald, began a campaign for the creation of at least a "housekeeping" department. Two men who were readily convinced were the Governor-General, Lord Grey, and the British ambassador to Washington, both of whom found the confusion in settling Canadian-American differences frustrating. Another was the Minister of Labour, Rodolphe Lemieux, who experienced the complexities of diplomacy in 1907, when he travelled to Japan to negotiate a restriction on immigration to Canada. Finally, in 1909, Laurier introduced the bill that established the Department of External Affairs.

The modest functions of the new department were administrative, such as collecting files, copying documents of the British Foreign Office, developing a trained staff and acting as a central body for communications among departments of the Canadian government respecting external affairs. Needless to say, these affairs involved principally Great Britain and the United States. The department was not intended for policy-making, which remained the business of the British Foreign Office. Official contacts with other countries still proceeded through the office of the Governor-General. However, this small and limited department was a stage in Canada's progress toward controlling its own foreign relations.

The International Joint Commission, also set up in 1909, was designed to facilitate direct Canadian-American negotiations on mutual problems. The Commission was to include three Canadians, appointed by the Crown on the recommendation of the Canadian government, and three Americans. It was decided to hold annual meetings in Washington and Ottawa. Each section was to have its own chairman, with Canadians and Americans alternating in presiding over joint meetings. The responsibilities of the Commission included international waterways, boundaries and any other subject submitted to it by the governments of the two countries.

THE CREATION OF A PERMANENT JOINT HIGH COMMISSION[329]

O. D. Skelton comments on the importance of the Commission:

. . . . In its explicit recognition of Canada's international status, in the optional provision for reference to the commission of any subject whatever in dispute between the two countries, in the permanent character of the joint body, and, not least, in the adoption for the first time in international practice of the far-reaching provision that individual citizens of either country might present their cases direct, without the State acting as intermediary, the experiment was a distinctive North American contribution toward a sane international polity.

G

THE NAVAL ISSUE

When Laurier returned to London for the 1907 conference with British officials and colonial Prime Ministers, he was the senior delegate in more ways than one. Besides representing the most important of the colonies, he was the only remaining leader from the two previous conferences. Joseph Chamberlain, the driving force in the past, was now out of politics and seriously ill. Laurier was no longer on the defensive about Canada's place in the Empire. He could decisively reject the still lingering British proposals of imperial federation and Canadian contributions in support of the British navy. He could even recommend, successfully, that the name of the meeting be changed from Colonial Conference to Imperial Conference. Thus he gained some recognition for his view that all governments assembled, including the British, were meeting as partners, not as a family where the mother country's world was law.

By 1909, however, Great Britain and Germany

H.M.C.S. **Rainbow**

H.M.C.S. **Niobe:** Canada's First Warship

were engaged in a naval-building race, and a special conference of Colonial delegates was called in London. Britain claimed she needed financial help; without it, Germany's navy would soon be larger, and the whole Empire would be in danger. Laurier agreed to change his long-standing policy. The only question was whether to make direct contributions of money to the British Admiralty or to build a Canadian navy. Laurier chose the latter course.

In January, 1910, the Prime Minister introduced his plans to the House of Commons. They called for the establishment of a Canadian naval college and the recruitment of men, and the construction of five cruisers and six destroyers to be built in England. Although the ships were to be part of the Canadian navy, Parliament could place them under the direction of the British Admiralty in the event of war.

THE NAVAL QUESTION[330]

[a]On January 12, 1910, Sir Wilfrid Laurier introduced the Naval Bill in the House of Commons:

The Bill . . . provides for the creation of a naval force to be composed of a permanent corps, a reserve force, and a volunteer force on the same pattern absolutely as the present organization of the militia force. . . .

The Act provides also, that . . . in case of war . . . the force may be called into active service. There is also an important provision . . . that while the naval force is to be under the control of the Canadian government . . . yet, in case of emergency the Governor in Council may place at

the disposal of His Majesty for general service in the royal navy the naval service or any part thereof and any ships or vessels of the naval service and any officers or men serving on these vessels or any officers or men of the naval service. . . .

[b]In LE DEVOIR, *Bourassa denounced Laurier for his naval policy:*

He [Laurier] assumes the air of a Chamberlain, of a Rhodes, of a Beers, of a gold speculator, or of an opium merchant creating a conflict in South Africa or in the Orient, in the Mediterranean or on the Persian Gulf, on the shores of the Baltic or on the banks of the Black Sea, on the coasts of Japan or in the seas of China — we are always involved, in any case, with our gold and with our blood.

The Naval Service Bill appeared to be a satisfactory way for Canada to meet its obligations for imperial defence and reflected a recognition of threatening world conditions. But the reasonableness of the Bill did not appeal to Bourassa and his supporters in Quebec. They claimed that the proposed Canadian navy would only encourage Great Britain, which was already on the verge of war with Germany, and would draw Canada into European conflicts. As expected, many English Canadians again accused Laurier of being lukewarm toward Great Britain, and they ridiculed his "tin pot navy." The Conservative Party led by Robert Borden insisted, instead, that Canada could be far more helpful by giving outright contributions of money to the British. The naval issue was a major factor in the 1911 election.

H

THE ELECTION OF 1911

Both of the main issues in the election of 1911 involved relations with other countries. The naval issue was another of the crises in imperial affairs;

reciprocity was the latest development in Canadian-American relations. The combination evoked so much opposition that, along with the recent poor administrative record of the government, it drove the Liberals out of office and ended the Laurier Era.

Reciprocity with the United States had been the goal of Canadian politicians ever since the original agreement had been terminated, just before Confederation. Finally, in the spring of 1910, the government of the United States expressed willingness to remove duties on such natural products as grain, fruit, vegetables and livestock, Laurier then embarked on a summer tour of the western provinces, where he found farmers everywhere asking him to give them prosperity by opening up the markets to the south. Farmers from Ontario made similar requests.

LAURIER'S VIEW ON RECIPROCITY, 1902[331]

In a letter to Wharton Barker, October 12, 1902, Laurier rejects the idea of reciprocity:

. . . . In my estimation, a movement [reciprocity] such as you suggest, would not meet with any favour in Canada, and, personally, I would be opposed to it. You are aware that the Liberal party carried on a campaign in favour of a policy of unrestricted reciprocity between Canada and the U.S. some few years ago. You are likewise aware that our efforts in that direction were received with no sympathy in your country. For my part, I valued very highly the importance of the American market for Canadian products, but failing to make an impression in that quarter, we directed our efforts elsewhere [Great Britain], and I am glad to say that they have been successful beyond expectations.

This movement in favour of unrestricted reciprocity on our part had its *raison d'être* some 12 years ago: in the present condition of our trade, its *raison d'être* has ceased to exist.

Negotiations went forward and an agreement was arranged. Once the American Congress had given its approval, in April of 1911, the Liberals had only to obtain the expected acceptance of the Canadian Parliament. However, a massive campaign to kill reciprocity had been launched by manufacturers, railway interests, banks and others who saw it as the beginning of the end of protection. The Conservatives seized on reciprocity, and made it their chief election target outside Quebec. "No Truck or Trade with the Yankees!" they declared, for reciprocity would be only the first step toward the annexation of Canada by the United States. Certain American politicians and newspapers made irresponsible statements which seemed to give some substance to the idea.

A BRITISH IMPERIALIST ON CANADA AND THE 1911 ELECTION:[332]

Rudyard Kipling, famous British poet and imperialist, supported the Conservative Party in Canada's election of 1911. He wrote as follows in a Montreal newspaper:

It is her own soul that Canada risks today. Once that soul is pawned for any consideration Canada must inevitably conform to the commercial, legal, financial, social and ethical standards which will be imposed upon her by the sheer admitted weight of the United States.

Why, when Canada has made herself what she is, should she throw the enormous gifts of her inheritance and her future into the hands of a people who, by their haste and waste, have so dissipated their own resources that even before national middle age they are driven to seek virgin fields for cheaper food and living?

Whatever the United States may gain, and I presume that the United States proposals are not wholly altruistic, I see nothing for Canada in reciprocity except a little ready money, which she does not need, and a very long repentance.

In Ontario, the Atlantic provinces and parts of the West, the Conservatives struck the ever reliable chord of anti-Americanism, much of it still lingering from the Alaskan boundary dispute. With election funds swelled by large contributions from business and industrial interests, they unleashed a campaign against reciprocity. It was, they declared, a deliberate attack on Canada's ties with Great Britain by the French-Canadian Prime Minister.

AN AMERICAN COMMENTS ON RECIPROCITY AND ANNEXATION OF CANADA[333]

[a]*Champ Clark, Speaker of the House of Representatives, was one of those Americans who in 1911, called for annexation of Canada. Before the 1911 election in Canada:*

We are preparing to annex Canada. . . . I am for the bill [reciprocity] because I hope to see the day when the American flag will float on every square foot of the British North American possessions clear to the North Pole.

[b]*After the 1911 election in which Canadian voters rejected Laurier:*

Clark claimed in a speech early in November, 1911 that "nine-tenths of the people of the United States favoured annexation". "I don't care who hears me say that," the Missourian added. "Moreover I'm willing to make this proposition: You let me run for President on a platform for the annexation of Canada, in so far as this country can accomplish it, and let President Taft run against me opposing annexation — and — well, I'd carry every State in the nation."

In Quebec, Bourassa diverted a great deal of French-Canadian support from the Liberals with his virulent attacks on Laurier's naval policy. F. D. Monk, leader of the Quebec Conservatives, joined with Bourassa in what the Liberals described as an "unholy alliance." Together, the Conservatives and Bourassa's Nationalists denounced the navy as proof that Laurier had surrendered to the British imperialists. Fearful that Canadian autonomy had been sacrificed, many French Canadians believed the suggestion that a vote for the Liberals was a vote for conscription into British wars all over the world.

LAURIER'S APPEAL IN THE 1911 ELECTION[334]

From an address delivered at St. John:

I am branded in Quebec as a traitor to the French, and in Ontario as a traitor to the English. In Quebec I am branded as a Jingo, and in Ontario as a Separatist. In Quebec I am attacked as an Imperialist, and in Ontario as an anti-Imperialist. I am neither. I am a Canadian. Canada has been the inspiration of my life. I have had before me as a pillar of fire by night and a pillar of cloud by day a policy of true Canadianism, of moderation, of conciliation. I have followed it consistently since 1896, and I now appeal with confidence to the whole Canadian people to uphold me in this policy of sound Canadianism which makes for the greatness of our country and of the Empire.

When the bitterly-fought election of 1911 was over, the Laurier Era had ended. The Liberals won only 87 seats; the Conservatives captured 134, including 73 in Ontario and a gain of 19 in Quebec. Sir Robert Borden, the former lawyer from Nova Scotia and leader of the opposition in the House of Commons since 1900, was the new Prime Minister.

LAURIER ON HIS DEFEAT IN THE ELECTION OF 1911[335]

A letter to a Prince Edward Islander:

Ottawa, October 5, 1911.

It is the province of Ontario which has defeated us. Our losses elsewhere were not very serious and would simply have reduced our majority, but Ontario went solid against us. It is becoming more

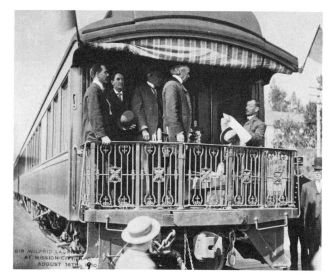

Sir Wilfrid Laurier in Mission City, B.C., August 16th, 1910

and more manifest to me that it was not reciprocity that was turned down, but a Catholic premier. All the information which comes to me from that province makes this quite evident.

The election had shown that the Liberal Party, after fifteen years in office, had declined in vigour. The men who helped build the Party were nearly all gone, and the magic of Laurier's leadership had not been enough to carry off another victory. The performance of some departments had recently been clouded by weak administration and rumours of scandal. Sir Clifford Sifton, once a powerful figure in the Liberal Party, had struck a telling blow against his former leader by heading a revolt of eighteen prominent Ontario Liberals into the ranks of the Conservatives.

CANADA AND THE 1911 ELECTION[336]

O. D. Skelton discusses the conditions in Canada which worked against reciprocity:

. . . . Canada, after years of looking to Washington, had determined to work out her own salvation, and had succeeded beyond her dreams. Why risk this prosperity, why disturb the whole national basis of the business that had been built up? Laurier prosperity thus proved its own undoing. Much play was made of the precarious basis of the bargain; after Canadian industry had been adjusted to the new market, Congress could, at a moment's notice, abrogate the agreement, and leave the Canadian producer stranded. . . . The farmer, the miner, the lumberman, might think they would gain, but that hope was illusory: the

United States itself was a greater exporter of farm and mine and forest products; the Canadian truck-farmer and fruit-grower would lose their early market; the dozen countries with most-favoured-nation treaties could pour in their products; preference in the British market would be barred.

The strategy of the Conservatives had been as masterful as it had been unscrupulous. In Quebec, the cynical co-operation between Tories and anti-imperialists was used to promote an appeal that was, in an important sense, the very opposite to the one used in the rest of Canada. Among English Canadians they had converted reciprocity into an emotional issue. Rejecting reciprocity was, to many Canadians, the same as rejecting American domination and asserting Canadian sovereignty.

VIEWS ON LAURIER'S CHARACTER[337]

aClifford Sifton, in 1909:

. . . he is, despite his courtesy and gracious charm, a masterful man set on having his own way, and equally resolute that his colleagues shall not have their way unless this is quite agreeable to him. I had a good many experiences of the difficulty in getting my policies accepted and acted upon where they did not make a special appeal to him. . . .

bA Nationalist critic:

He [Laurier] will ask this minister and that his view, and then he gives his own; he never asks what is ideally best, but merely what is the best that will work.

LAURIER'S OPINIONS[338]

aOn the attachment to Great Britain. In his Paris speech, 1899:

. . . . I am told that here in France there are people surprised at the attachment which I feel for the Crown of England and which I do not conceal. . . . We are faithful to the great nation which gave us life [France], we are faithful to the great nation [England] which has given us liberty.

During the Naval Question crisis, 1910:

I do not pretend to be an imperialist. Neither do I pretend to be an anti-imperialist. I am a Canadian first, last and all the time. I am a British subject by birth, by tradition, by conviction, by the conviction that under British institutions my native land has found a measure of security and freedom it could not have found under any other régime. . . .

On Militarism. His stand on war, during the Boer War crisis:

Sir, I have no hesitation in admitting that I was not enthusiastic for that war or any war. I have no sympathy for that mad, noisy, dull-witted and short-sighted throng who clamour for war, who shouted "On to Pretoria".

On Imperial defence, 1902:

. . . there is a school in England and in Canada . . . which wants to bring Canada into the vortex of militarism which is the curse and the blight of Europe. I am not prepared to endorse any such policy.

On Bourassa. From a letter to a Bourassa supporter, November 20, 1907:

No one recognizes Bourassa's talent better than I do . . . but he fights his friends with the same violence as his enemies; he becomes intoxicated with his own words . . . allows himself to be drawn along unconsciously from friendly criticism to open warfare.

On the knighthood he received in 1899. From a letter to a colleague, August 31, 1901:

. . . . Notwithstanding my course at the time could not have been else. I have often had occasion to realize that this conferring of a title on me . . . was a serious political error, and I have never ceased to regret it.

On Canadianism. Canadian unity was the reason for his action in the Boer War. From an address to the House of Commons, February, 1900:

. . . if there is anything to which I have given my political life, it is to try to promote unity, harmony, and amity between the diverse elements of this country.

bOn a Canadian nation. From a speech at Arichat, N.S., August 15, 1900:

. . . . As long as I live, as long as I have the power to labour in the service of my country, I shall repel the idea of changing the nature of its different elements . . . I want the sturdy Scotsman to remain the Scotsman; I want the brainy Englishman to remain the Englishman; I want the warm-hearted Irishman to remain the Irishman; I want to take all these elements and build a nation that will be foremost amongst the great powers of the world.

VIII

A NATION ON TRIAL, 1911-1939

At the turn of the century, several factors made war in Europe seem almost inevitable: intensive commercial and naval rivalry between Germany and Britain; Austrian and Russian rivalry in the Balkans; French desire to avenge her humiliating defeat in the Franco-Prussian War of 1870; impassioned nationalism within the Austro-Hungarian Empire; propaganda in the press; and an ever-growing armaments race. The major European powers aligned themselves into two armed camps — the *Triple Alliance* of Germany, Austria and Italy against the *Triple Entente* of Great Britain, France and Russia. The hostile atmosphere was punctuated by several serious crises.

Then, on June 28, 1914, the assassination of the heir to the Austrian throne, Archduke Ferdinand and his wife, at the little-known town of Sarajevo, set off a series of events which plunged the world into a bloody war. Austria declared war on Serbia on August 1, and immediately all the European powers were engulfed in conflict.

Everyone expected it to be a short war — as many of the previous wars had been. However, it lasted four long years, during which time millions died in battle, cities were devastated and the map of Europe reshaped. Canada, as part of the British Empire, could not stay aloof from the European conflict. She made her contribution on the battlefield and on the home front, proportionately far in excess of her small population.

The postwar period brought many changes in Canada. A temporary depression created industrial strife and agrarian discontent. The Progressive Party arose to challenge the lethargic Conservatives and Liberals, but with the return of prosperity, it soon dissipated.

The twenties — the "Roaring Twenties" — were a period of unprecedented prosperity which affected every aspect of Canadian life. The economy soared to new heights; technological advances in transportation and mass communication further shattered long-accepted morals, manners and habits.

The carefree twenties came to an abrupt end with the financial crash of 1929. The cruel economic depression of the thirties followed, which palled Canadian life. The poverty and distress brought forth new political parties—the Co-operative Commonwealth Federation (C.C.F.), Social Credit and *Union Nationale* — which gained a considerable following. The political leaders of the old parties were unable to find a workable formula for coping effectively with the depression. Both Conservative and Liberal governments of the "Dirty Thirties" were forced to embark upon a policy of federal intervention in the field of social welfare — an area they both had long considered outside the government's domain. In spite of palliatives, the depression continued, and only ended with the outbreak of war in 1939.

For Canada, the years between World Wars I and II were a period of important constitutional developments. Canadian nationalism, forged on the battlefields of World War I, gained momentum in the twenties. Canada pointed to her war effort and the sacrifices Canadians had made as proof that she had earned the right to nationhood. The British government could not disregard the sentiments of the Dominion, and Canada was granted a new status as a self-governing nation — an equal partner within the British Commonwealth. As a sovereign nation, Canada was faced, for the first time in her history, with the responsibility of making decisions in a troubled world.

23

CANADA AND WORLD WAR I

A

CREATION OF A CANADIAN ARMY

When German troops marched into Belgium and violated her neutrality, which had been guaranteed by European powers including Britain and Germany, Great Britain declared war on Germany on August 4, 1914. Canada, as a part of the Empire, was automatically at war, and decided to fulfill her obligation as a colony to aid the mother country. Most Canadians favoured Canada's entry into the war; Laurier and even Henri Bourassa supported Canada's decision to aid Britain. This unity of purpose is remarkable when one considers the multi-national composition of the Canadian population — English, French and immigrants from many non-British countries, even enemy countries.

At the outbreak of war, Canada had a standing army of only 3,000 men and a fledgling navy. The Canadian Parliament met and immediately allocated $50,000,000 to outfit troops. In October, 33,000 men of the Canadian Expeditionary Force — the First Canadian Infantry Division — were dispatched to Britain, where they were to undergo further training. By the following February, some of these troops were already in action in France. Volunteers flocked to the colours. By April, 1915, 100,000 had enlisted; by the end of the year, 212,000 men were under arms. By the end of 1916, enlistment had reached 434,000. In all, 620,000 Canadians were mobilized in the armed forces; 425,000 went overseas — a remarkable effort for a country of only eight million people.

The casualties on the battlefields of Europe demanded increased reinforcements. Towards the end of 1916, it became evident that voluntary enlistment was no longer adequate. There were persistent demands for conscription to insure a continued flow of men into the armed forces. Such demands were viewed differently by French and English Canadians. The English accepted the view that if Britain was at war, Canada was at war; if

Germany was a threat to Britain, then Germany was also a threat to Canada. The French Canadians had a different opinion. The majority saw the destiny of their ancestral homeland on the St. Lawrence within the British Empire, but their long estrangement from France and their lack of sentimental attachment to Great Britain bred a feeling of isolation from European entanglement.

Initially, a good percentage of the Canadian contingent was French Canadian, but many people in other parts of Canada felt that Quebec was lukewarm in its war effort. Many French Canadians saw no reason why they should be involved in Britain's imperialistic war. Nationalists like Bourassa at first restrained their criticism of Canada's war policies, but were soon provoked to declare French-Canadian opposition to the war. They pointed to the denial of French as a language of instruction in Ontario primary schools, as laid down in Regulation 17 of the Ontario Department of Education in 1913, as proof of Anglo-Saxon designs against French Canadians. The abolition of French as a language of instruction in Manitoba by the Education Act of 1916 reinforced their argument. Why should French Canadians fight for a cause that was not theirs?

In the meantime, political controversy continued unabated; the Borden government was under constant attack. The Liberals proclaimed the right, in spite of the unity the war demanded, to expose war profiteering and fraud in munition contracts. Col. Sam Hughes, the Minister of Militia, was criticized for alleged ineptitude and for irregularities in awarding lucrative war contracts to friends and acquaintances. Under pressure from the opposition, Hughes resigned in 1916.

Since the term of the Conservative government

was to end in 1916, Borden asked for an extension to avoid a "khaki" election. The Liberals supported a petition to the British Parliament to amend the B.N.A. Act, and the life of the Canadian Parliament was extended for one year. At the same time, the Liberals declared their right to be consulted concerning the war effort. In face of Liberal strength, there was talk of a coalition government — but Laurier's role in such a government posed a problem.

In February 1917, Borden went to the Imperial Conference in London. He insisted on Canada's having a voice in the planning of the war and in the disposition of Canada's troops on the battlefields. To meet these demands and the strong nationalistic feelings of the Dominions, the Imperial War Cabinet was formed, consisting of Great Britain's cabinet and the Prime Ministers of each of the self-governing Dominions. This principle of consultation established a new status for the Dominions within the Empire — equal partnership with the Prime Minister of Britain. Sharing responsibilities with the mother country led to greater rights for the Dominions, and eventually led to Canada's conducting her own foreign affairs.

THE 1917 IMPERIAL WAR CONFERENCE[339]

Borden's comments on Resolution 9 of the Imperial War Conference of 1917 as a way for the future of Canada as an autonomous nation:

. . . . I say this with a full understanding that it is unwise, having regard to the lessons of the past, for any of us to predict absolutely the developments of the future. But, nevertheless, the line of development which has been noticeable during the past twenty or twenty-five years seems to point unmistakeably to that conclusion. Indeed, the action of the Dominions in this war has made the spirit of nationhood splendidly manifest. The fact that one million men in the Dominions have taken up arms for the defence of the Empire's existence and the maintenance of its future influence, is so significant a lesson that one would be unwise not to have it constantly in mind. I believe that the Dominions fully realise the ideal of an Imperial Commonwealth of United Nations and one should not forget the importance of the Crown as a tie between the Dominions and the Mother Country. . . .

Borden returned to Canada convinced that only through conscription could the heavy casualties suffered by the Canadian Corps in Europe be

replaced. He announced his conscription policy and asked for the co-operation of his political opponents. Laurier brushed aside all suggestions for a coalition government if it meant agreeing to conscription. He dared not risk any association with a policy so hated in Quebec, for fear of losing French Canada to Bourassa's extremists. The 1917 session of Parliament proved stormy indeed.

The government passed the Military Voters Act which extended the franchise to all men and women, regardless of age or citizenship, in the armed forces and denied it to conscientious objectors. This Act was followed by the War Times Election Act, which gave the vote to the widows, wives, mothers and adult daughters and sisters of Canadians serving overseas. Citizens from enemy countries who had been naturalized since 1902 were disenfranchised. These Acts were preparations for the forthcoming elections. The Liberals accused Borden of manipulating the vote to assure the election of a pro-conscriptionist Conservative government.

CRITICISM OF THE WAR TIMES ELECTION ACT[340]

The Halifax MORNING CHRONICLE, *September 13, 1917:*

No more partisan measure that this freak scheme to corral votes for a discredited Government, has ever been presented to, much less passed by, the Parliament of Canada. It is subversive of the fundamental principles of democracy. . . . It is, in effect, Prussianism and not the British sense of justice and fair play which is the guiding spirit. The War Time Franchise Bill would more properly be described as a Win-the-Election Measure, regardless of good faith and national honour — win at any cost and any price.

———

The Vancouver BRITISH COLUMBIA FEDERATION-IST, *September 14, 1917:*

The Ottawa high priests of political depravity have nobly risen to the occasion by incubating a "War Times Election Act" that has anything in the line of impudent chicanery and clumsy cunning that was ever perpetrated, beaten to a standstill.

On July 11, 1917, the government introduced the conscription act which it claimed was necessary to keep Canada's four divisions in Europe at full strength. The whole conscription issue was pervaded with prejudice and passion; extremist French Canadians were pitted against equally extremist pro-British imperialists. To the English-

Henri Bourassa

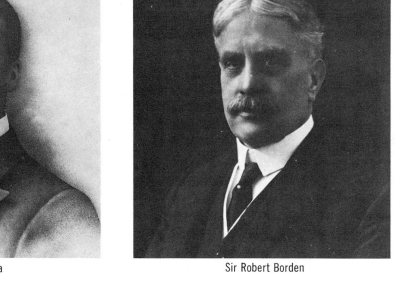

Sir Robert Borden

speaking leaders, conscription was an equitable measure which assured an equal share in the war effort. This view was not necessarily shared by many farmers and organized labour; they did not consider conscription of manpower alone as "equality of sacrifice." To the French Canadians, conscription meant forcing their sons to fight foreign wars of neither Canada's making nor concern.

Laurier tried to occupy a middle ground between the conflicting factions. He contended that conscription would drive French Canadians into the camp of radicals like Bourassa. He suggested a referendum in which Canadians would have the opportunity to express their views on the whole conscription issue. Western Liberals, however, supported Borden; Laurier's conscription referendum proposal was defeated. Many influential Liberal newspapers also supported conscription. The Military Service Act was passed on August 28, 1917, making military service compulsory for all able-bodied male British subjects between the ages of twenty and forty-five with the exception of those in vital industries, conscientious objectors and those to whom service would pose "serious hardship."

THE 1917 CONSCRIPTION ISSUE[341]

aPremier Brewster of British Columbia expressed his view in a letter to Rowell, August 23, 1917:

We may as well face the fact that in this western Province the wealthy classes and the big business interests in the East are prefectly willing to see the poor man put all his capital, that is to say, his blood and sinews on the altar to aid in winning the war, but unquestionably is putting up a strenuous fight to block every organization and legislative procedure that would entail equivalent sacrifices of conscription of wealth and material resources. . . . I am of the opinion that if steps are taken to enforce the conscription of manpower alone, it will be met with resistance and in many parts of Canada we shall see exhibitions of violence and possibly bloodshed, with other consequences too serious to contemplate with any measure of complacency, although I am a firm believer in the principle of selective conscription.

bHenri Bourassa's stand against conscription:

It is the exact truth. All Canadians who want to fight conscription . . . must have the courage to say and repeat everywhere: *"no conscription! no enlistment: Canada has done enough."*

Another question arises with regard to the fairness of our allies: *How many soldiers would France, and even England, send to America if Canada were attacked by the United States?*

What England needs most are not soldiers, but bread, meat, and potatoes.

Another measure of conscription, which would be vital long before conscription itself . . . [is conscription] of capital and industry. . . .

It is useless to disguise the truth: *two million French-Canadians are united against conscription. . . .*

[c]*Laurier on conscription, from his election address, November 4, 1917:*

As to the present Military Service Act my policy will be not to proceed further under its provisions until the people have an opportunity to pronounce upon it by way of a Referendum. . . . It is a fact that cannot be denied that the voluntary system, especially in Quebec, did not get a fair trial . . . it is no answer to say as is now often said, that we must have Conscription or "quit". . . . Australia rejected Conscription and Australia did not "quit". Australia is still in the fight under the voluntary system. . . .

―――――

Rev. S. D. Chown, General Superintendent of the Methodist Church of Canada, wrote in support of the Union Government and conscription a few days before the election of 1917:

To me it is as clear as the day that if we defeat conscription we cannot possibly get the last available man and fulfil our promise to Great Britain. . . .
. . . . I believe . . . that under any conditions it [conscription] is the fairest, most democratic, most expeditious and least expensive method of raising an army in this country: and under present conditions it is the only possible way of fulfilling our obligations to Christian civilization. I also believe that socially considered it is the most moral and profoundly religious method of doing our national duty. . . .

Borden included Liberals in his cabinet and formed a Union government to give the country a sense of unity in the war effort. Elections were called for November; conscription was the issue. The Conservative platform appealed to patriotism and war hysteria with a "Win the War" slogan. Seventy-seven year old Laurier conducted a vigorous campaign from coast to coast. He criticized the government for denying the people the right to express themselves on conscription. He insisted that Canada had not fully exhausted the possibilities of raising troops through voluntary enlistment. In Quebec, Bourassa organized anti-conscriptionist meetings which the Conservative government branded as acts of disloyalty.

Although the Union government mustered a majority, Quebec showed its displeasure by giving Laurier sixty-two of the province's sixty-five seats. In spite of Laurier's entreaties to obey the conscription act, violence, anti-draft meetings and riots took place in Quebec. Generally, conscription failed to raise the manpower for which the act was passed* and left a feeling of hostility between French and English Canadians that lingered for many years.

Recruiting Poster, World War I

THE ELECTION OF 1917[342]

[a]*In a letter to W. D. Gregory, December 27, 1917, Laurier gives his views on the defeat of the Liberals:*

The result in Ontario did not surprise me. With the press of the province almost unanimous against us, it would have been difficult to hope for victory, or even a fair show. What the press failed to achieve the women and parsons completed.

It has been my lot to run the whole gamut of prejudices in Canada. In 1897 I was excommunicated by the Roman priests and in 1917 by Protestant parsons. Let us take it cheerfully, however, and be prepared to continue the fight for the good cause.

―――――

* It should be noted that upwards of 80,000 men were conscripted, with only a few seeing active service. Had the war lasted longer, conscripts might have been important to the Canadian Corps.

Borden's post-election statement to the Canadian people, December 18, 1917:

It was not a partisan victory in any sense. The splendid elements of the Liberal party who worked so strenuously and with such magnificent results in every Province except one are to be congratulated equally with the Conservatives. Equally fine was the spirit of the Conservatives who, regardless of party affiliations, supported and elected Union-Liberal candidates in many ridings. It was a notable test of democracy. The Canadian people, after more than three years of heroic devotion and untold sacrifice, were called upon to say whether Canada's effort in the War should be maintained. In the midst of the campaign the test of compulsory military service had to be applied. No more severe trial of the self-endurance of a democracy was ever made.

CANADIANS ON THE BATTLEFIELDS

The first Canadian troops, the Princess Patricia Canadian Light Infantry, were in the trenches in France by January, 1915. In the second battle of Ypres, a little Belgian town, in April and May, Canadians were subjected to poisonous chlorine gas attacks — a new method of warfare. Previously, French colonial troops had withered under the gas attacks. But the Canadians held the line and prevented a German breakthrough to the Channel ports.

THE GAS ATTACK AT YPRES[343]

Major-General Victor W. Odlum, commander of a Canadian battalion during the second Battle of Ypres, which began on April 21, 1915, recalls the gas attack. From the WINNIPEG TRIBUNE, *March 9, 1967:*

I saw the whole picture of the gas attack as probably no one else did. I have never been in a battle — and I have been in many — where the men were suffering in such numbers that their crying and groaning could be heard all over the battlefield.

There were some who ran away, French, British and Canadians. These were individuals. They were young and they were terrified.

They had never seen gas before. None of us had — it was the first gas attack in history.

But not a single unit skipped out — some individuals, yes, but formations, no. In every battle someone runs away. I saw it wherever I was.

In front of us was the 8th (Canadian) Battalion: to the right were the British battalions and way to the left were French-African troops.

Suddenly we saw the gas rolling up in a brownish-yellowish bank. It was between four and 12 feet high and it wouldn't rise higher unless it was puffed up by the wind.

We saw the French-Africans running away choked with gas, not as a body, but as individuals. We paid no attention to them. We were sorry for them.

I went over to where the line had been broken and where there was confusion. No Canadian troops were running.

The gas was dreadful and suffering was immediate. The only thing we could do was soak our handkerchiefs in urine and hold them over our noses.

Thousands were lying around gasping and crying. They were being drowned by the gas. They didn't know how to protect themselves.

But we held our position.

The same year, the two army divisions were formed into the Canadian Corps which was augmented by the Third Division in January, 1916. These troops, under the command of the British General Byng, distinguished themselves in the Battle of the Somme. This allied offensive, which was halted by the autumn mud, was costly: allied and enemy casualties were close to one million. No wonder the Germans appropriately called the Battle of the Somme the *Blutbad* — the Blood Bath.

At Vimy Ridge, the exploits of the Canadian Corps drew praise of the Allies. This important ridge, which commanded a wide front, was the object of three previous attacks by allied soldiers. Seasoned German troops repulsed the attacks. The Canadian Corps finally captured it after months of careful planning. They struck on April 9, 1917 — Easter Monday. It was a cruel struggle and a costly victory. The Vimy Memorial, the monument to the Canadian dead, enshrines the memory of the thousands of Canadians who died there.

After Vimy, Major-General Arthur Currie, a Canadian, took over the command of the Canadian Corps. Later, in the fall, the Canadians took

Tank Advancing with Infantry at Vimy, April 1917

Paschendaele, in the Ypres sector, after a fierce battle and high casualties.

THE BATTLE OF VIMY RIDGE[344]

An eye-witness account:

Easter Sunday, the eve of the battle, was fine and sunny. . . . All was peaceful to the eye, as unit by unit took its way in ordered leisure up the slopes and spurs which are the talons of the claw-like Ridge. . . .

Wonderful in their work and in their secrecy had been the Engineers. For months they delved underground. . . . The tunnel system ran sheer into and up the Ridge, to open at the very feet of the Germans when "Zero" hour struck. . . .

Through these subways . . . passed every man of the tens of thousands who played a part in the battle. . . . Sleep, in the rare moments throughout the hectic week . . . was so only if one stood flat against the wall. . . .

Meanwhile, as night wore on, the historic Easter Monday was dawning to snow and wind and rain. . . . So we caught him [the enemy] napping his soundest, and for this occasion the elements, foul as they were for us, were fouler for him. . . .

. . . . Our barrage which opened at 5.30 a.m., involved a gun to every 25 yards of the Bosche front, and was regular as a clock and as sweet as a sewing-machine. Nothing human could stand against it, and, combined with the gale, it sent the Hun helter-skelter for cover. . . .

So, from Monday's dawn till midnight of Friday the battle raged. . . . Throughout the week, with us had raged the storm, at times at blizzard strength, so that hourly the toil had become harder, and snow and mud made every step purgatory. But we were masters of our fate, filthy but triumphant, and had scored a signal victory as ever crowned Canadian arms.

Canadian troops were hurled into the counter-offensive of 1918. It was a fateful year. In 1917, the United States had entered the war, but Russia had withdrawn to strengthen the revolution at home. With the pressure removed from the Eastern front, German leaders were able to shift forces to western Europe. A powerful offensive was planned to defeat the Allies before the full strength of the Americans would be effective.

Canadian troops played an important part in frustrating the German plan. The period between August 4 and November 11, 1918, became known as Canada's "Hundred Days." Canadian troops in the Amiens sector broke the fortified German Hindenburg Line and captured Cambrai on October 9, and then pushed across the Belgian border. On Armistice Day, November 11, 1918, the Canadians entered Mons.

Even after the war had come to a halt, Canadian troops remained in Europe. They crossed the Rhine into Germany to share in the allied occupation and remained there until the spring of 1919 while the peace treaty was negotiated. A small Canadian contingent was at Archangel, taking part in the futile allied intervention to crush the Bolshevik Revolution.

In the latter stages of the war, Canadian troops fought as a national unit, and paid a heavy price for their victories. Many Canadians, however, served with the British and allied armies. Canadians had joined the Royal Flying Corps — the forerunner of the Royal Air Force — and the British Navy. As a reservoir for manpower and a storehouse for the Allies, Canada developed specialized units utilizing special skills. The Canadian Railway Construction Corps enlisted railway workers who built rail communication behind the British lines. The Canadian Forestry Corps supplied the timber that was so widely used in the trench warfare on the western front. The Canadian Medical Corps enlisted doctors and nurses for the field hospitals. The Atlantic Coastal Patrol relieved the British Navy from duty around Canadian Atlantic waters. Towards the end of the war, the Canadian Air Force was organized.

There are 51,000 Canadians in the carefully tended war cemeteries in Europe — a reminder of Canada's contribution to the war. With the returning troops came 175,000 wounded, some of whom never fully recovered.

C

CANADIANS ON THE HOME FRONT

Canada, essentially an agricultural country, under pressure of war, expanded her factories for wartime production. A munition industry soon started; shipyards were enlarged to replace losses inflicted by enemy submarine activity. Food, a prime necessity in war and peace, was constantly being shipped to Britain, brought to the brink of starvation by German submarine blockade. The Food Control Board was established to expedite the production, conservation and shipment of food to the Allies in Europe. The Munition Board directed the production of arms and ammunition. Other control boards supervised other phases of production. The railway transportation system was appropriated for war. The government even subsidized the privately-owned Grand Trunk and Canadian Northern Railways, much to the displeasure of the West, which harboured an old grievance against the high freight rates maintained by these railway companies. By the end of the war, the federal government had purchased these railways and integrated them later with the Intercolonial Railway into the government owned and operated Canadian National Railway.

Canadian workingmen played an important role in Canada's war effort. Labour produced the weapons of war from the products of forests, fields and mines. Railway workers transported the goods to the thriving Atlantic ports for shipment overseas. When there was a shortage of workers, women were employed in the factories where they worked side by side with the men; there was hardly an industry in which women were not engaged. Labour realized its importance, and during the war years labour unions enjoyed a marked increase in membership. The unions protected the rights of workingmen and revealed flagrant war profiteering in the munition industries.

VIEWS ON WAR PROFITEERING[345]

R. E. Watters, President of the Trades and Labour Council of Canada, gave labour's view, June 14, 1917:

The greatest service that Canada can render the Allies . . . is to conscript (not borrow) the wealth of the nation, to take over and operate the mines, railroads, munition works and other establishments necessary to the prosecution of the War (including the Banking system), to eliminate the last vestige of profiteering, thus giving the nation the benefit, instead of the profiteer, of the work done. . . .

Sir Joseph Flavelle, a Canadian industrialist and financier, in a speech on November 25, 1918, defended the profits made in the manufacture of munitions:

I have been unable to understand why there has been such a depth of feeling, so widely expressed, and apparently so commonly held, against the manufacturers in Canada who have made munitions. They accepted contracts to produce materials greatly needed for the War, at prices fixed by the Board, under contract conditions of the most arbitrary character. They have brought honour to Canada and great wealth and we owe them much.

The funds for war production and for the conduct of the war were raised by bond sales and loans. Such expenditures left Canada with a tremendous national debt. She had to resort to various forms of taxation to finance the war. Under pressure of organized labour, the Business Profits War Tax Act placed taxes on profits made on war contracts. In 1917, the Income War Tax Act was passed, which imposed a tax on income.

A Sales Tax was also instituted on consumer goods. Thus the people were saddled with new tax burdens. The Patriotic Fund, to which individuals contributed voluntarily to aid widows and dependents of soldiers, was inaugurated. Numerous patriotic organizations, charitable organizations and the Red Cross conducted fund-raising campaigns.

Wartime caused emotional outburst. Labour accused industrialists of war profiteering. The prolonged war, with its heavy casualties, generated hostility against those of German descent; riots occurred in several Canadian cities where over-zealous self-appointed patriots resented the use of the German language. Some Canadian cities with German names renamed them, usually after war heroes. The Manitoba Legislature, taking advantage of the wartime patriotic mood, passed the Education Act of 1916 which did away with the language privileges of the 1897 Laurier-Greenway compromise and made English the only language of instruction in the schools.

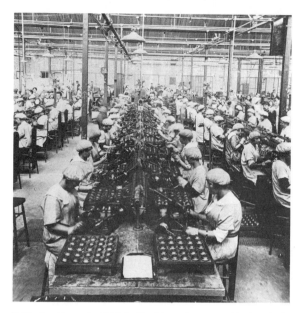

Soldering Fuses in British Munitions Company, Verdun, P.Q., during World War I

AN EXPRESSION OF ANTI-FRENCH SENTIMENT[346]

John W. Dafoe bitterly denounced French Canadians for their attitude towards the war, in a letter to Thos. Coté, January 1, 1918:

The trouble between the English and French Canadians has become acute, because the French Canadians refused to play their part in this war — being the only known race of white men to quit. They try to excuse themselves by alleging that they have domestic grievances which should first be righted. The excuse, if true, would be contemptible. In the face of any emergency like this domestic questions have to stand.

Do not flatter yourself with the idea that English Canadians are disturbed by your attitude of injured innocence or your threats of reprisals. You can do precisely as you please; and we shall do whatever may be necessary. When we demonstrate, as we shall, that a solid Quebec is without power, there may be a return to reason along the banks of the St. Lawrence.

The women of Canada, because of their part in the war effort, intensified their drive for political, economic and social equality. By World War I, women's organizations across Canada were demanding the right to vote and to hold political office. But they seldom resorted to violence as their counterparts in England were doing. The movement for the franchise for women was led by such able women as Mrs. Gordon Grant in British Columbia, Mrs. Nellie L. Mclung

and Miss Frances Beynon on the Prairies, Dr. Stowe-Gullen in Ontario, Professor Carrie M. Derick in Quebec and Mrs. W. F. Hatheway in the Maritimes. In their work they could count on help from many prominent men in Canada. However, there were also those who rebuffed all claims and demands for women's rights. But the suffragette movement, in spite of obstacles, made steady progress. Led by Manitoba, shortly followed by Saskatchewan and Alberta — they all granted women the vote in 1916 — the provinces conceded political equality to women.

THE STRUGGLE FOR WOMEN'S RIGHTS:[347]
SUPPORTERS OF WOMEN'S RIGHTS

[a]*Sir John A. Macdonald on vote for women, as expressed in his speech introducing the Franchise Bill, in 1885:*

. . . . I believe that is coming as certainly as came the gradual enfranchisement of woman from being a slave of man until she attained her present position as almost equal of man. I believe that time is coming, though perhaps we are not, any more than the United States and England, quite educated up to it. I believe the time will come, and I shall be very proud and very glad to see it, when the final step towards giving women full enfranchisement is carried in Canada.

[b]*From an address by Miss Barbara Wylie, a suffragette leader, Montreal November 4, 1912:*

Don't be submissive. Don't be docile. Don't be ladylike. Don't dread being conspicuous. Now is the time for deeds not words. Remember you are fighting for liberty. . . . Concentrate all your efforts on the Dominion Parliament. Insist that the Federal Elections Act of '97 be repealed. . . . Go to Mr. Borden in your thousands and demand votes for women at this Session — not at some long distant future, but now.

___

The following advice to Canadian women was given by the noted suffragette, Miss Frances Beynon, in GRAIN GROWERS' GUIDE *of January 29, 1913:*

Be as moderate as possible and be careful not to promise the millenium as soon as women get the vote, because it is too big an order for us to live up to. Also there is nothing to be gained by railing at men. . . . They are, in the main, mighty decent people and if they are approached reasonably and the subject presented to them sanely are amazingly easy of conversion.

___

Part of Borden's speech in the House of Commons, March 22, 1918, in moving second reading of Bill Number Three, giving franchise to women:
. . . . I do not even base it on the wonderful and conspicuous service and sacrifice which women have rendered to the national cause in the war. Apart from all of these, I conceive that women are entitled to the franchise on their merits, and it is upon this basis that this Bill is presented to Parliament to its consideration. It is our belief that the influence of women exercised in this way will be good influence in public life. We believe that beneficial results have ensued wherever the franchise has been granted them. . . .

OPPONENTS OF WOMEN'S RIGHTS

Record of the Roblin Government in Manitoba Premier Roblin of Manitoba, January 27, 1914:

It is in the home that her influence is best felt and exercised. Home is the type of every national excellence. . . . I believe Women's Suffrage would be a retrogade movement, that it would break up the home, that it would throw the children into the arms of the servant girls.

___

Other expressions against equal rights for women:

The majority of women are emotional and very often guided by misdirected enthusiasm, and, therefore, if possessed of the franchise, would be a menace, rather than an aid.

___

Temperamental differences of men and women makes it impossible to place them on an equal footing in political life.

___

Placing women on a political equality with men would cause domestic strife. Sex antagonism would be aroused. It is an easy flame to fan. It can be no more disregarded than the operation of any other natural law can be set aside.

___

Jean Joseph Denis voiced his opposition to Bill Number Three, in the House of Commons, April 11, 1918:

. . . . I say that the Holy Scriptures, theology, ancient philosphy, Christian philosophy, history, anatomy, physiology, political economy, and feminine psychology, all seem to indicate that the place of women in this world is not amid the strife of political arena, but in her [sic] home. . . .

The war brought some significant changes in the economic, social and political life in Canada. Wartime industrialization demonstrated the importance of the workingman, and the need of the government to pay heed to demands for "equality of sacrifice." Industrialization also brought women into the factories, and the social impact of freeing women from the kitchen laid lasting foundations for the rights of women. The movement of manpower in the armed forces and in industry offered Canadians an opportunity of seeing the various parts of Canada; many, for the first time, saw themselves as part of a larger Canada. Wartime conditions taught Canadians to accept rationing, restrictions on individual liberties and heavy taxation. Participation in the war, whether on the battlefields of Europe or on the home front, gave Canadians a sense of accomplishment in a gigantic national effort — Canadians, together with other nations of the world, had fought a war "to end all wars."

24

CANADA IN THE TWENTIES

A

THE ECONOMICS OF PROSPERITY

The end of World War I brought a short-lived economic slump to Canada. The demand for war supplies fell off, wheat prices dropped and the brisk trading boom of the war years slackened. But in 1923 Canada embarked upon an age of economic prosperity that was to last until 1929, when the world's financial structure came tumbling down with a resounding crash and ushered in the Great Depression of the 1930's. The boom years of Laurier's administration had rested upon a threefold foundation — immigration, wheat farming, and railway construction. These were again very much in evidence during the twenties.

Immigration, which had been curtailed during the war, resumed in the 1920's. Although immigration reached a peak of 165,000 in 1929, it never did become the flood it had been the 1890's. No longer did the Canadian government undertake extensive advertising and recruiting campaigns. Immigrants now had to purchase farms and Canada's postwar immigration policy became selective. The end of the farm frontier was in sight.

THE IMMIGRATION POLICY OF THE 1920's[348]

Briefs presented to the Committee on Agriculture and Colonization, in 1928.
Resolution of the United Farmers of Canada, Saskatchewan Section, passed at Moose Jaw, in 1927:

Resolved: That the United Farmers of Canada in convention assembled do not approve of a vigorous immigration policy on the part of the government until our own unemployed are cared for and those brought out in former years are assimilated and stabilized. . . . And further that no one political party nor religious body nor corporations should be allowed to solicit or dump

immigrants indiscriminately within the Dominion of Canada but that all immigration activities should cease until the whole question has been thoroughly examined on a scientific and economic basis.

———

E. W. Beatty, President of the C.P.R.:

. . . . I agree with others that our ambition should be to admit, first from Great Britain, for very obvious reasons, and afterwards from the United States and selected continental countries, men who are physically fit and able and willing to follow agricultural pursuits. . . .

———

. . . increasing prosperity will follow increased population, not only in the general wealth of the country through extension of its agricultural activities but through the increased markets thereby provided to its manufacturing and other industries, it seems fairly obvious that immigration policies should be vigorously prosecuted.

Wheat farming also suffered in the immediate postwar years. In 1920, the government abandoned the Wheat Board which had been set up for the orderly marketing of Canadian grain and for maintaining of a uniform high price. Moreover, wartime price controls were removed and farmers had to pay more for their manufactured goods at a time when wheat prices were falling. As we shall see later, the farmers' discontent expressed itself in political action.

Nevertheless, a variety of circumstances developed in the twenties that created a new demand for Canadian wheat and launched the greatest wheat boom that Canada had ever known. War-ravaged Europe was in obvious need of food-stuffs. The United States loaned and gave large sums of money to war-torn countries, which in turn purchased Canadian wheat with American currency. The confusion in Russia following the Revolution of 1917 eliminated that country as a grain-exporting nation for a number of years. The surplus of wartime ships and low import duties reduced the overhead costs of Canadian wheat. In Canada itself, reduced freight rates helped to make the price of Canadian wheat attractive in European countries. So great was the demand for Canadian wheat that Canada became the largest wheat-exporting nation in the world. In 1928, Canada harvested 567,000,000 bushels of wheat, which sold at $1.60 a bushel.

The railways also shared in the prosperity. The privately-owned C.P.R. continued to show profits and to declare dividends to its shareholders. In fact, it was only during the depression of the 1930's that the C.P.R., for the first time in its history, failed to pay a dividend on its outstanding common stock. The publicly-owned C.N.R. had not fared as well, and in the slump of the early postwar years it had difficulty meeting the interest payments on its loans. In an attempt to solve the difficulties that plagued the C.N.R., the government engaged Sir Henry Thornton as president of the Company. Thornton, a man of boundless energy and foresight, had enjoyed successful railroad careers in Britain and the United States. For a time, he was able to raise the sagging fortunes of the C.N.R. Non-paying lines were abandoned, roadbeds were improved and obsolete rolling stock was replaced with modern equipment.

Both railways enjoyed the financial prosperity. Luxurious parlor cars were introduced and each company vied with the other in the building of palatial hotels. In 1928, the C.P.R. opened the Royal York Hotel in Toronto. In other major cities across the country, C.P.R. and C.N.R. hotels became familiar landmarks. Between 1924 and 1929, both railways spent over 700,000,000 dollars in building new branch lines and modernizing rolling stock. Canadian railways became world-famous for their comfort, elegance and service. As long as the wheat continued its trans-continental movement to the grain elevators of the East, the railways prospered.

However, the newly created prosperity of the twenties grew more out of new advances and directions than out of wheat farming and railways. The automobile, the aeroplane, paved roads, the oil industry, metal alloys, hydro-electric power, base metal mining and the gigantic pulp and paper industry became the giants of the new economic prosperity.

Moving Camp on the Provincial Highway, North of Parry, Saskatchewan, 1923

A HISTORIAN REMARKS ON THE PROSPERITY OF THE TWENTIES[318]

D. G. Creighton regards the unequal distribution of prosperity in Canada as a cause for sectional grievances:

. . . . Without any question, Canada was in many ways a more favoured and stronger country in an age of electricity, alloys, and airways than she had been in the era of steam, steel, and rail. And yet, though the economic life of the whole country unquestionably grew richer and more varied, the bounty of the post-war period seemed unequal in its distribution . . . the new staples almost seemed to encourage the unfortunate process of regional division. In the pre-war age, wheat had been the one great export staple, round which the whole economic life of the country had centred; but now there were half a dozen distinct staple-producing regions, each with its own important export specialty or specialties, each with its regional interests in markets outside Canada, each with its individual successes and misfortunes. While some provinces . . . profited superlatively from the new enterprises, others . . . benefited only moderately, and still others . . . gained little advantage at all. . . .

By the end of the twenties, one out of every two Canadian families owned an automobile, whereas in 1911 there had been fewer than 25,000 cars and trucks in the whole of Canada. Although many different companies had attempted to manufacture automobiles in Canada, they all eventually were swallowed up by the Big Three — Ford, Chrysler and General Motors. By far the most popular automobile was Ford's Model T which sold for under $400. Available in black only, awkward looking and boasting a full twenty horsepower, Model T's could be seen bouncing over dusty roads throughout the land.

Log Pile: Laurentide Pulp Co., Grandmere, P.Q., 1926

Automobile manufacturing became so important that by 1929 it ranked fourth among the manufacturing industries in Canada.

The growth of automobile production naturally stimulated road construction and the petroleum industry. Only six small refineries were in operation in Canada before the war. By 1929, twenty-five modern refineries were producing a hundred million dollars' worth of petroleum products a year, and networks of service stations began lining the major roads of Canada. But Canada had not yet really experienced an oil boom. Search for oil reserves had been undertaken in the 1920's, but except for the deposits in Turner Valley, no major finds were made. For the moment, Canada continued to import 95 per cent of her crude oil.

Road building inevitably received great stimulus from the increased automobile production. In the early years of the decade, rain often proved to be the most unwelcome visitor on a journey by car: the dirt roads became quagmires of mud. In the winter months, only the venturesome dared drive, even in the cities. However, by 1929, there were over 75,000 miles of roads in Canada and of these, 10,000 were paved. The building of roads in Canada, prompted by the "Good Roads Association," proved to be a boon not only to the motorist but to the economy as well. The advent of the automobile and the building of good roads bolstered the Canadian tourist trade. As early as 1929, four million American visitors spent over three hundred million dollars in Canada as they enjoyed the vast wonderland of unspoiled beauty.

Perhaps the greatest single new contributor to the prosperity of the twenties was the pulp and paper industry. The United States had depleted much of its own soft wood timber stands. Moreover, the end of the war saw an unprecedented growth in daily newspapers, magazines, advertising and cardboard packaging. Nature had en-dowed Canada with ample soft wood timber stands in the Canadian Shield and the United States had given her the largest market in the world. So spectacular was the growth of the pulpwood industry in Canada that in the year 1920 the price of newsprint rose from $65 to $120 per ton. The export trade was so great that the Canadian government had to insist that producers keep enough pulpwood in reserve for Canada's needs. By 1929, Canada was exporting more pulpwood products than the rest of the world combined.

The tremendous growth of the pulpwood industry also stimulated the development and use of hydro-electric power. The numerous rivers of the Canadian Shield were harnessed to produce the electric power required by the pulpwood industry. However, the use of hydro-electricity was not restricted to the pulp and paper industry. In Quebec and Ontario particularly, the development of hydro-electric sites gave those provinces cheap and efficient supplies of electricity for home lighting and secondary manufacturing.

Cheap and abundant supplies of hydro-electric power and extensive development and use of metal alloys gave rise to a substantial secondary manufacturing industry in Canada. Electric appliances, automobile parts and chemicals were extensively produced. The development of secondary industries alongside the great primary industries of wheat and pulpwood gave a certain balance and health to the Canadian economy.

Another important advance during the twenties was the development of the great mineral wealth of the Canadian Shield. The aeroplane provided the answer to the problem of transportation in the Shield and made it possible to discover and develop the mineral wealth. "Bush flying" became popular and no part of the Shield remained inaccessible to man. Canada soon led the world in air freight traffic as the bush pilots of the age transported machine parts, men and minerals. The decade also saw the development of some of Canada's greatest mining ventures, such a Noranda Mines and the Hudson Bay Mining and Smelting Company.

THE CANADIAN ECONOMY[350]

In January, 1925, Sir John Aird, President and General Manager of the Canadian Bank of Commerce, assessed Canada's economy:

. . . . The striking development of Vancouver as a port for wheat shipments is providing cheaper access to the seaboard for the farmers of Alberta and western Saskatchewan. . . .

It has been predicted that Canada is likely to become the leading producer of minerals in the

Mail is transferred from plane to dog train, at Fort Smith, N.W.T. First Regular Flight, 1929

world . . . Canada contains 16 per cent of the world's known coal reserves, and has greater asbestos, nickel and cobalt deposits than any other country . . . Ontario is the greatest mineral-producing province in Canada. . . . In the Hollinger mine Ontario possesses the third greatest producer of gold in the world. British Columbia also achieved in 1924 new records for that province in the output of lead, zinc, silver and copper.

. . . . From her vast area of forests she [Canada] is already providing the means of paying for her large purchases of iron and steel and coal from the United States. The production from her forests is second in value only to that from her farms. . . . The combination of her water powers with her timber . . . makes it possible for her to reduce the overhead charges of manufacturing to a point which should enable her to compete with any other country in the world. . . .

Her fisheries are also exceptional in their fertility. . . . They are found on both Atlantic and Pacific coasts, as well as in her vast expanse of inland waters. In the value of the production of the fisheries the province of British Columbia ranks first, followed by Nova Scotia and New Brunswick in the order named.

The period from 1923 to 1929 was one of great economic advances in Canada, but prosperity was unevenly distributed. The Maritimes suffered from their chronic problem — insufficient natural resources. Although the Prairies enjoyed a wheat boom, they could not keep pace with the rich provinces of Quebec, Ontario and British Columbia. Under these circumstances — uneven growth and wealth in the provinces — the nationalism that had pervaded Canada during Laurier's time gave rise to a rebirth of sectionalism.

B

THE POLITICS OF PROSPERITY

Before World War I, the Dominion government had worked vigorously in fulfilling the aims of the National Policy. The federal government, as land agent, had successfully encouraged large scale immigration, which was so necessary for the East-West trade and for the settling of the West that the National Policy envisaged. The government had worked hand-in-hand with the large and powerful railway interests in order to encourage and finance the building of new lines that would open up new farm areas. It fostered East-West trade and maintained the tariff at a high enough level to encour-

age and protect Canadian industry and manufacturing.

During the war, the Canadian government had weathered the conscription crisis and had led a united country to victory. On the home front, the Canadian people had worked hard to produce the foodstuffs and material required for the war effort. Canadian troops had fought in the bitterest campaigns of the war with valour and distinction; throughout the war, Canadian statesmen had vigorously asserted Canadian independence and nationalism.

After the war, the Canadian government could look back on its work of the past two decades with justifiable pride and satisfaction. The immediate postwar demobilization problem had been accomplished with dispatch and efficiency. The only dark cloud was the faltering economy. Prices shot up, wages remained stable and international trade slackened. However, the government could look upon the troubled economy as one of the inevitable slumps in the business cycle that was accentuated by the transition from wartime to peacetime production. If left to itself, the Canadian free-enterprise economy would recover from its present dislocation and again surge upward. And that was exactly what happened.

In a sense, the Dominion government had finished its work and no new national goals appeared. People started to look towards their provincial governments as the trustees of their destiny. The prosperity of the twenties, which affected the various provinces unevenly, contributed no more to the rise of sectionalism than the Dominion government's inactivity during the same period. Without national goals and programs, the role of the Dominion government declined.

However, new forces were at work in the political arena in the decade following the war. The Canada that had taken its place among the nations of the world in the war was not the Canada of the 1890's. Conditions were changing. Life in Canada was changing. Ideas about government were changing. The days of easy expansion into a vast and rich western farm land were at an end. In 1920, Canada evolved from a rural to an urban nation. The "war to end all wars" created a demand for new goals in politics. People began to feel that the efforts of government should be directed towards bettering the lot of the masses rather than towards acting as the handmaiden of big business. The new frontier in a democratic political society should be social justice and equality for all. Every citizen should have the right to seek his "place in the sun" protected and aided by a benevolent government. Freedom from want; health and old age care were birthrights of free men in a democratic society. Government policies must, above all, favour the masses rather than the few men of wealth. The war which had been fought to "make the world safe for democracy" had given rise to an upsurge of democratic feeling.

THE METHODIST "SOCIAL GOSPEL"[351]

In 1918, the Methodist Church adopted these rather radical resolutions to reform society:

1. *Special Privilege Condemned:* We declare all special privilege, not based on useful services to the community, to be a violation of the principle of justice, which is the foundation of democracy.
2. *Democratic Commercial Organization:* . . . labor to have a voice in the management and a share in the profits and risks of business. . . .
3. *Profits of Labour and Capital:* We declare it to be un-Christian to accept profits when laborers do not receive a living wage, or when capital receives disproportionate returns as compared with labor.
4. *Old Age Insurance:* We recommend Old Age Insurance on a national scale. . . . This would protect all citizens from the fear of penury in old age. . . .
5. *Unearned Wealth:* We condemn speculation in land, grain, food-stuffs, and natural resources. . . .
7. *Nationalization of Natural Resources:* We are in favor of the nationalization of our natural resources . . . the means of communication and transportation, and public utilities on which all the people depend. . . .

A growing labour movement provided another force in Canadian life. Before the war, union membership had remained small, but with the growth of industry union membership doubled. The high prices, low wages, long hours of work, and unemployment of the immediate post war period gave rise to discontent and labour unrest.

Although trade unions were by no means new in Canada, in 1919 the labour movement blasted its way onto the front pages of the nation's newspapers. In March, labour delegates from the prairie provinces and British Columbia met in Calgary to form a branch of the One Big Union (O.B.U.). It was an offspring of the International Workers of the World, which espoused the Marxist doctrine that the working class could throw off the shackles of big business only by organizing into one large powerful union. Such a union must then, by peaceful means if possible or violent means if necessary, take over industry and the government to create a society in which those who produced reaped the benefits of their labour. The I.W.W. appeared to many to be advocating the same sort of violent and bloody revolution that had swept Russia in 1917. In the United States, the "Wobblies" were ruthlessly hunted and ill-treated during the "Big Red Scare" — an outburst of national hysteria and fear of Bolshevism.

At the Calgary convention, the cause of the O.B.U. was put forward by speaker after speaker in terms of the familiar Marxist doctrine. R. B. Russell of Winnipeg assured the delegates that "a Revolution is about to take place in Canada in which the workers will triumph and the capitalists will be in the same position as those in Russia." Much was said of class struggle between the capitalists and workers. Canadian democracy with all

General Strike, Winnipeg, Manitoba, June 21, 1919

its capitalist trappings was damned; the Russian rule of the proleteriat was extolled. All the catch phrases of Marxism were quoted at length. The convention ended by drawing up a constitution for the O.B.U. The delegates also called for general strikes to take place simultaneously in many western cities and ultimately to spread to every city in Canada. Faced with a complete withdrawal of the services of labour, the government, business and industry would soon be forced into capitulation.

On May 15, 1919, Canada's first and only general strike began in Winnipeg; 30,000 men had left their jobs in sympathy with the metal workers who were striking for a shorter work-week and for higher wages. Only the railway workers refused to strike. Virtually all other labour services were withdrawn. Factories, stores and warehouses closed. Essential public employees such as milkmen, garbage collectors, meat processors, bakers, firemen, hydro employees and transit workers were on strike. Three of the leaders, R. B. Russell, Ernest Robinson, and the Reverend William Ivens became the "Winnipeg Soviet." After a time, the Strike Committee, in the interests of the public well-being, permitted some essential public service employees to return to their jobs.

THE 1919 WINNIPEG GENERAL STRIKE[352]

May 17, 1919, in the WESTERN LABOUR NEWS, *organ of the Strike Committee:*

There is great cause for congratulation during this struggle, in that until the present moment the participants are more orderly than a crowd of spectators at a baseball game. . . . There has been evolved a weapon of great power — orderliness.

May 17, 1919, in the WINNIPEG CITIZEN, *organ of the employers:*

It is to the general public of Winnipeg that we speak in stating without equivocation that this is not a strike at all, in the ordinary sense of the term — it is revolution.

It is a serious attempt to overturn British institutions in this western country and to supplant them with the Russian Bolshevik system of Soviet rule. . . .

May 23, 1919, W. R. Plewman, TORONTO STAR:

It must be remembered that this (Winnipeg) is a city of only 200,000, and that 35,000 persons are on strike. Thus it will be seen that the strikers and their relatives must represent at least fifty per cent of the population. In the numerical sense, therefore, it cannot be said that the average citizen is against the strike . . . there is no soviet. There is little or no terrorism.

Rev. Dr. John MacLean, a Methodist minister, noted in his diary, on May 20, 1919:

We are under the sway of Bolshevism in the city. Everything is quiet, but there are some ugly rumours floating around, and the Home Defence Guards are all ready for action at a given signal. . . .

The situation was explosive. Mounted police patrolled the streets lined with striking workers. The attention of the nation was focused on Winnipeg and the newspapers decried the strike as "plain ugly revolution." But the people of Winnipeg refused to panic. Except for one brief outbreak of violence, in which a young boy was accidentally killed, the city remained tense but peaceful. Civic and industrial leaders refused to yield; after six weeks of tension, workers began to drift back to their jobs when it appeared that further resistance was futile. The strike was breaking up by the time the federal government stepped in and arrested ten of the strike leaders. This action evoked a great outcry of public protest.

Of the ten arrested, seven were sentenced to a year in jail. J. S. Woodsworth, one of the acquitted, later became the leader of Canada's first socialist party. Professor W. L. Morton, in his book *The Kingdom of Canada,* says this of him: "More than any other Canadian public man he helped transform Canadian politics from the politics of special and sectional interests to the politics of collective concern for the welfare of the individual in a society collectively organized." Three of those sent to prison — John Queen, George Armstrong and William Ivens — were elected to the Manitoba Legislature while they were still serving their prison sentences.

In assessing the General Strike, it has been argued that it was a Communist-inspired plot to overthrow the Canadian democratic system. However, the facts show otherwise. One must look at the conditions of the day and the men who organized the strike. Many returning soldiers were unable to find work; prices were high and wages were low; men worked long hours under poor conditions and had little recourse against industrial abuses. Moreover, the Communist Revolution in Russia was a very recent historical event, and the Calgary delegates saw the Soviet system idealistically without understanding or appreciating its real character. The Winnipeg General Strike was led by men who were motivated by the welfare of mankind rather than by Marxist ideology. The strike foretold the growing role of the labour movement as a force in Canadian politics.

VIEWS ON THE 1919 WINNIPEG GENERAL STRIKE[353]

a*J. S. Woodsworth, in a letter dated August 25, 1921:*

The strike has been entirely misrepresented. I know the details intimately. Without hesitation I say that there was not a single foreigner in a position of leadership, though foreigners were falsely arrested to give colour to this charge. . . .*

In short, it was the biggest hoax that was ever 'put over' any people! Government officials and the press were largely responsible. . . .

---

b*H. A. Robson, K.C., who headed the Royal Commission investigating the strike:*

It is too much for me to say that the vast number of intelligent residents who went on strike were seditious or that they were either dull enough or weak enough to be led by seditionaries . . . but the cause of the strike . . . was the specific grievance [the refusal of collective bargaining] . . . and the dis-satisfied and unsettled condition of Labour at and long before the beginning of the strike.

. . . it is more likely that the cause of the strike is to be found under the other heads [other than unemployment], namely, the high cost of living, inadequate wages . . . profiteering. . . .

. . . . If Capital does not provide enough to assure Labour a contented existence with a full enjoyment of the opportunities of the time for human improvement, then the Government might find it necessary [to step] in and let the state do these things at the expense of Capital.

Of no less importance in Canadian politics was the rise of the Progressive movement, particularly among the farmers of western Canada. The farm revolt, as the Progressive movement has been called, took shape immediately after the war. The Wheat Board had been abolished, resulting in declining wheat prices. The high tariff wall (which meant that farmers had to pay high prices for imported goods and machinery) was a constant source of irritation and concern to the farmers. Both the Liberals and the Conservatives talked at length about the tariff but neither did very much about lowering it. It seemed that the farmer was being sacrificed to the business and industrial interests of the East. Farmers were also dissatisfied with the high freight rates and the high fixed rates of interest on bank loans and mortgages. It became clear to the farmers that they would not find solutions to their problems in the old parties that were wedded to big business. Political action was clearly necessary.

In 1918, the Canadian Council of Agriculture issued a blueprint for political action in a document that came to be known as the "New National

* Section 98 of the Criminal Code was passed in 1919 to provide for the deportation of aliens who advocate the overthrow of the Canadian government.

Mackenzie King

Arthur Meighen

Policy." It expressed some of the exciting new political ideas of the times, such as public ownership of essential utilities and social legislation in the form of old age pensions and widows' allowances. Understandably, it attacked the high tariff and the power of the wealthy financial interests. Farmers quickly organized themselves and translated the new program into political action.

The farmers' program had widespread appeal. In 1919, the United Farmers of Ontario (U.F.O.) won a majority of seats in the provincial election and formed a government with E. C. Drury as Premier. The United Farmers of Alberta (U.F.A.) won the election in that province two years later. In 1922, the United Farmers of Manitoba (U.F.M.) also came to power. Although the initial success of the farm revolt occurred in eastern Canada, Progressivism was to have more lasting effects in the West. The U.F.O. was defeated in the election of 1923; the United Farmers of Alberta were able to remain in office until 1935. United Farmers' parties sprang up in every western province and, to a lesser extent, in the Maritimes.

In 1920, the Canadian Council of Agriculture called a convention in Winnipeg at which a new party, the National Progressive Party, came into existence. Having the New National Policy as its platform, the support of the United Farmers' groups, and T. A. Crerar as its leader, the National Progressive Party rose to challenge the Liberals and the Conservatives in the federal election of 1921.

In 1920, Robert Borden retired and Arthur Meighen succeeded him as Prime Minister. Meighen, who, as a member of Borden's Union cabinet, had guided the Military Service Act and the War Time Elections Act through parliament, was now faced with the task of resurrecting Conservative Party fortunes in the face of the disintegration of the Union government and the rise of the Progressive movement.

A year earlier, after Laurier's death, William Lyon Mackenzie King assumed the leadership of the Liberal Party. Perhaps no Canadian politician has ever been so well groomed for the task of leadership as Mackenzie King. He was a graduate in political science and law from the University of Toronto; he also held degrees from the Universities of Harvard and Chicago. For eight years he had served as Deputy Minister of Labour during which time his skill as a conciliator in industrial disputes won him wide respect. Moreover, he had mastered the intricate details of public affairs and had written widely on labour and social problems. When he was first elected to the House of Commons in 1908, King was made Minister of Labour in Laurier's government. With great skill and patience, King was able to weld the remnants of the pre-war Liberal Party. The election of 1921, except for the interest created by the Progressives, lacked clear cut issues. The Liberals won 118 seats, the Conservatives 50 and the Progressives 65.

Two more elections in the 1920's failed to produce a majority government. King and his party managed to form a minority government and relied on support from Progressives and the two Labour members from Winnipeg to keep the Liberals in office. King was able to argue, with some justification, that his own policies were closer to those of the Progressives than were the Conservatives' policies. The Progressives themselves were content to work with the Liberals, and in doing so lost much of their own sense of direction and purpose.

PROGRESSIVE PARTY PLEDGES SUPPORT TO LIBERALS[354]

The following resolution was passed by the Progressive Party in 1922:

That this meeting of western supporters of the National Progressive party, having taken under consideration the existing political situation in Canada and the course the Progressive party should follow, is of opinion that the gravity and importance of our many national problems call for a strong government;

That the first consideration of the Progressive party will be to support the legislation the country needs, both in the economic and the administrative sense, and in the larger sense of promoting and developing the spirit of Canadian national unity, and will extend to the Hon. Mr. King's government all reasonable co-operation and support in any efforts it may make to enact into legislation those economic and administrative reforms which have been advocated by the National Progressive party, while at the same time maintaining the complete identity and organization of the Progressive party.

The marriage of the Liberals, Progressives and Labour brought about a modest old age pension and slight reductions in the tariff on farm implements. Progressivism, however, declined rapidly as a national force; many of its members, including Crerar, were absorbed in the Liberal Party.

THE ORIGIN OF OLD AGE PENSION LEGISLATION[355]

[a]*The two Labour MP's, representing Winnipeg constituencies, realizing the strength of their position, wrote the following letter to Prime Minister Mackenzie King on January 7, 1926:*

Dear Mr. King:

As representatives of Labour in the House of Commons, may we ask whether it is your intention to introduce at this session (a) provision for the Unemployed; (b) Old Age Pensions.

We are venturing to send a similar inquiry to the leader of the Opposition.

Yours sincerely,
J. S. Woodsworth
A. A. Heaps.

[b]*Mackenzie King, seeking the support of the two Labour members, agreed to institute legislation for old age pension. On January 26, 1926, he met with Woodsworth and Heaps, the Labour MP's from Winnipeg:*

This morning at my office we accomplished a really important stroke of work. I had the members of the cabinet meet Woodsworth & Heaps & discuss old age pension legst. tho some members of the Cabinet, Lapointe in conversat'n and Robb by memo from Finlayson opposed attempting anything, when they were confronted in discussion all agreed on a bill which would apply to the Dominion as a whole, letting each province come under, on a 50-50 basis, for a non-contributory scheme applicable to persons over 70 years of age. The conference lasted over an hour and was very satisfactory. It was agreed to have a bill immediately drafted.

Canadian Senators, enjoying old age pensions of $4,000 a year themselves, objected to $20 a month pensions for destitute old people at the age of 70.

[c]*The following are speeches in the Senate, March 23, 1927, after the Old Age Pension Bill had passed in the House of Commons:*
Senator C. P. Beaubien:

This, in my opinion, is an iniquitous measure. First of all it is unhealthy in its basic moral principle. It is going to stunt the growth if it does not altogether blight and wither all incentive for thrift and providence in the land. Furthermore, it rests upon a very unsound financial structure.

Senator John McCormick:

The men who promoted the Bill do not represent a body of people in this country who are prepared to contribute to it; they are representative of a body of so-called Labour who do not want to encourage or practise thrift; they are men who work to "Burn the candle at both ends; spend all you make and when you are 65 or 70, and unable to work, go to those people who have been leading well-ordered lives, who have been practising the good old habit of thrift."...

In some measure, the unbridled prosperity between 1923 and 1929 was responsible for the decline of Progressivism just as it accounted for the momentary eclipse of the labour movement as a force in Canadian politics. Nevertheless, the spirit of Progressivism never really died in Western Canada. It enjoyed renewed activity during the depression years of the 1930's when the democratic and social ideas that Progressivism propounded took on a new meaning and were advocated with new vigor.

C

THE PEOPLE OF PROSPERITY

The decade of prosperity following World War I has been described as "The Roaring Twenties," "The Asprin Age," "The Lost Generation," and "The Era of Wonderful Nonsense." Relieved of the pressures of war and aided by new technological advances, the United States underwent a social revolution. The pre-war values of family, church, hard work and sobriety were set aside and gave way to the pursuit of material wealth and pleasure. Canadians were also affected by the prosperity of the twenties, but Canadians as a whole remained aloof from many of the less desirable aspects of the hysteria enveloping the United States.

THE PULL OF THE UNITED STATES[356]

Ralph Allen, in his book ORDEAL BY FIRE, *speaks of the influence of the United States on Canadian life in the twenties:*

To say that Canada, at this period, had a conscious desire to ape the United States would be rather like saying that the tides ape the moon when they are only yielding to its pull. . . .

Thus, in the immediate aftermath of the war, the United States had a deflationary depression and Canada had a deflationary depression too. Coal strikes broke out in the United States; coal strikes broke out in Canada. The United States embarked on prohibition; so — usually a little before, sometimes a little later — did most all the provinces of Canada. The United States spawned the prohibition gangsters; Canada spawned the prohibition rumrunners to keep him supplied. The American female developed invisible busts and hips, the boyish bob, bells on her garters, and a taste for cigarettes and gin; the Canadian female sought to do the same. . . .

Symptomatic of the social revolution was the change in the status of women. Such advances as the refrigerator, the vacuum cleaner, the washing machine and the electric iron freed women from much of their daily drudgery, enabled them to become part of the nation's working force and gave them more freedom than they had ever known. This emancipation may have been responsible for some shocking (for the day) fashions, manners and habits. The hemline, which had stood at the ankles in pre-war days, crept inexorably upward to the knees; in some instances, only decency laws prevented the hemline from going even higher. Petticoats and bustles became old fashioned; rayon and silk fabric began to be used along with cotton. The one-piece bathing suit, considered indecent only a few years before, became fashionable and adorned feminine forms on beaches throughout the continent. The widespread use of cosmetics created an enormous industry to provide the ingredients for the artificial glamour. Hair styles also changed, as bobbed and boyish cuts replaced the elaborate coiffures of an earlier age; beauty parlours sprang up all over the country.

Woman's new status also reflected itself in changing manners and habits. Cigarette smoking by women, long considered a private vice and a public sin, gained social acceptance. Rude, smart and shocking conversation became fashionable. Mixed drinking at parties, especially the consumption of bootlegged whiskey and bathtub gin, was thought to be very *avant-garde*. The social barrier between the sexes began to break down. In pre-war days, teaching and nursing were often the only employment positions open to women. In the new era, the number of working girls increased greatly as women entered occupations in retail stores, business, real estate and even politics.

In the postwar decade, the whole national outlook changed as well. The pursuit of pleasure, centering about motion pictures, the radio and organized sports, became a national goal. A shorter work week, higher wages and the new technological advances all gave the North American public more leisure time and more money for entertainment. The widespread availability of the automobile provided greater mobility than ever before. The automobile, more than any other single development, tended to break down family ties; these were further weakened by the development of organized entertainment outside of the home.

THE IMPACT OF THE AUTOMOBILE[357]

Arthur R. M. Lower, in his book CANADIANS IN THE MAKING, *devotes a section to "The great god* CAR *and his associates":*

That inventive society known in Canada as "the country to the south," could make a new goddess as quickly as it made a new car. But in making new cars, it made a new god. For the god, no better name could be found than simply — CAR!

. . . . CAR's devotees increased with the years. And no wonder. A patient, obedient god who takes you where you want to go, faster than any magic carpet. A comfortable, well-upholstered god. . . . And above all, the god of power, who multiplied man's ego manifold. Yet a ruthless god, sometimes, too, who could turn on his idolater and rend him.

CAR brought in his company a whole host of lesser godlets (most of them born of Electra), which their worshippers called 'modern conveniences' or more simply 'progress'. . . .

Meanwhile, CAR and his associates changed our society out of recognition. They scattered our homesteads far beyond the cities, so that many of us became once more, after a fashion, country dwellers. . . . CAR threatened to turn us all into nomads. . . . They invaded every urban space and threatened to destroy every blade of grass. They knocked down houses. They called imperiously for straight, wide roads to be carved out of the diminishing fertile fields. They tore up our precious peach orchards and ordained that factories for making new parts of CAR should be erected in their place.

Hollywood gained world-wide fame as the centre of the motion picture industry. The public flocked to movie houses to see their revered idols on the silent silver screen. Later, the "talkies" projected the new morality. Torrid love scenes between women of great beauty and men who epitomized masculinity, the eternal struggle between good and evil, and sweet innocence pitted against dark passion were the themes that Hollywood fed the entertainment-starved public. On Saturday afternoons, children filled the theatres to see their favourite cowboy heroes outwit, outride and' outshoot the most villainous of outlaws. Audiences laughed at the wonderful and foolish antics of slapstick comedians, or were thrilled by the daring deeds of swashbuckling adventurers.

The public thirst for entertainment gave rise to a phenomenal increase in spectator sports. Huge stadia were built to accommodate the thousands of Saturday afternoon enthusiasts who came to watch and worship their football heroes. Baseball, long popular in the United States, gained interest in Canada and many Canadians followed eagerly the batting averages of their baseball idols. Professional boxing, in such disrepute today, enjoyed great popularity during the twenties, and boxing fans could count on a good fight between well matched contestants. Hockey and rugby-football

C.P.R. Ladies' Lounge in the New Solarium Car, 1920's

were followed by Canadians from coast to coast; curling and golf emerged as participator sports.

THE 1924 CANADIAN OLYMPIC HOCKEY TEAM[358]

W. A. Hewitt, father of the well-known hockey broadcaster Foster Hewitt, was honorary manager of the Toronto Granites hockey team which represented Canada at the 1924 winter Olympics at Chamoix in the French Alps. He recounts an incident in the final game against the United States team:

The sun had another effect on play. At times, it shone so brightly that the team facing it had difficulty tracing the movement of the puck; and the glare forced the goalkeeper to be very alert lest a long looper elude his vision.

. . . . The choice of ends had not been decided, and the European referee called the two captains, Munro of Canada and Small of the United States, to the centre of the ice. The captains presumed there would be a coin toss of some kind and were preparing to call, when suddenly the official turned to Munro and enquired, "How old are you?" Dunc told him he was twenty-one. Then the referee asked Small, "How old are you?" The American answered, "I'm twenty-eight." The referee nodded as he explained, "Thank you. The older man will have the choice of ends." So, because Munro was younger, the Canadians were forced to play with the sun in their faces for the first and third periods. It was a rather unusual verdict.*

* The Canadian team scored a 6-1 victory and won the Olympics hockey championship.

Broadcast of Madge Macbeth's Play **Superwoman** from Radio Station CNRO, Ottawa, 1920's

The advent of radio brought entertainment into the home. Thousands of local broadcasting stations came into existence during the twenties. Broadcasts of sports events were an immediate success with the male population; Foster Hewitt's "Hockey Night in Canada," first broadcast in 1923, became an enduring Canadian tradition. The housewife listened to the news of the world and followed the many serialized and never-ending human dramas of the afternoon "soap-operas." Of course, commercials frequently interrupted the suspense-filled dramas.

In the frenzy of the age, a spicy scandal could capture public attention just as fully as Charles Lindberg's famous solo flight across the Atlantic. Fads swept the nation: college students took to swallowing live goldfish, six-day bicycle races were the rage and the Charleston spread like wildfire. Newspapers were often sensational and a tantalizing murder trial could push the news of the world off the front pages for weeks. Jazz and happy, light-hearted, fast-moving songs were the music of the hectic age. The song "Happy Days Are Here Again" aptly expressed the incurable optimism of "The Era of Wonderful Nonsense."

Any consistency that the North American public might have shown during the twenties, was in its reverence for affluent businessmen. The wealthy capitalist was looked upon with respect and admiration. Unfettered by government interference, he had, in the American tradition, fought his way to the top. He could buy his way into the highest social circles of the land as easily as he could buy favours from many government officials. In an age of unbridled prosperity in which traditional values had been set aside, it did not seem to matter whether the man of wealth was honest or principled.

Dabbling in the stock market became yet another activity of the people. Many, in all walks of life, bought common stocks as the market climbed steadily upward. The great brokerage firms of Wall Street in New York, Bay Street in Toronto, and St. James Street in Montreal did an unprecedented volume of business. So certain was the stock market and so confident the public that the band-wagon of prosperity would keep rolling along, that buying "on margin" became far too prevalent. People would put a down payment on stocks hoping to pay the balance out of the profits that might result. Credit soon became dangerously overextended but the big "bull" market kept soaring skyward, and tales of quick fortunes made overnight whetted the appetite of the public for a share in the prosperity.

DABBLING IN THE STOCK MARKET[359]

The prospects of profits and quick riches prompted many Canadians to "play" the stock market:

The middle twenties were the days of 'Coolidge Prosperity'. . . . Signs of disaster were plain to be seen, but neither the people nor the government heeded the signs.

Canada followed in the trail of its big neighbour like a wobbly-kneed puppy after a Great Dane. Canadian stock-exchanges did proportionately as much business as those in the United States. Most of the issues traded in were those favoured by speculators across the line. As an instance of this aberration, one of the favourites of the time was a taxicab company! One day, it was this stock, the next, it was something else. Everybody made money, on paper, because stocks always went up.

Although many church and civic leaders decried the weakening of the moral fibre of the nation during the reckless twenties, few people suspected the disaster that lay just around the corner. Indeed, in an age of plenty and steadily growing prosperity, it was sheer lunacy to predict anything but the brightest future.

Canadians sang the songs of the age, revered the idols of the silver screen, enjoyed jazz, adopted the new styles and listened to the radio. However, the changes which did come in Canada were more gradual and Canadians did not partake of the new fads and fancies with the same intensity as their southern neighbours. Perhaps the social revolution was less drastic for Canada because it was a small nation; perhaps Canadians were conservative by nature. Although styles, manners and habits changed in Canada, they never became a matter of moral concern.

Church membership and attendance in Canada increased. People flocked to the churches of their faith — perhaps as a reaction against the loose morality. In 1925, a significant advance in church unity occurred when the United Church of Canada was formed by the union of several Protestant denominations. In the first four years of its existence the United Church claimed over 50,000 new members.

ON CHURCH UNION[360]

Rev. Dr. George C. Pidgeon, Chairman of the Presbyterian Committee on Church Union, gives his views on the value of such a union, March 1, 1923:

. . . . The most valuable feature is that it will be a Canadian Church, arising out of the experience of our people, adapted to their needs and committed to the solution of their problems. The heritage of the Gospel we have in common with fellow-Christians the world over, but we have also the heritage of the Canadian spirit and this will find in the new Church an expression and an instrument peculiarly its own. The Churches now at work in Canada have come to us from without. They sprang out of conditions strange to us, and were built up to deal with the circumstances and meet the needs of other lands. . . . Whereas the union movement aims at a church distinctively Canadian. . . . It is the greatest Spiritual enterprise of one hundred years.

————

Organized opposition to the union proposal was confined to the Presbyterian Church. Presbyterians felt church union would spell the end to the Presbyterian Church:

No one has ever yet had the temerity to propose a merging of the soprano and the bass. You cannot build a choir in that style. You will ruin your orchestra if you do not keep your strings and winds apart. Amalgamation spells destruction. There is no merging of the great final and inviolable essentials of music or of faith. You can associate them, but you cannot merge them.

————

. . . and the world will be poorer if the voice of age-long Presbyterianism is merged in the voice of any other, no matter how rich and true that voice may be.

Canadians of the twenties were not without their vices. From the Maritimes to the Rockies, rumrunning became a lucrative enterprise. Prohibition in the United States forbade the manufacture, importation and sale of alcohol. In Canada, even though many provinces had not removed their wartime prohibition laws, the production of alcohol for export was legal. Many Canadians made fortunes by manufacturing whisky and exporting it (unhindered by the high tariff wall) to the large and thirsty American market. The only hindrance to this lucrative north-south trade was the United States Customs Service, but, with thousands of miles of common border, enterprising Canadians had little difficulty in smuggling their products across the boundary. Rumrunning was a prominent feature of Canadian life in the twenties.

RUMRUNNING IN THE TWENTIES[361]

In a discussion in the House of Commons about liquor smuggling across the border, the Canadian Minister of National Revenue, W. D. Euler, spoke of his own experience:

I was offered safe conduct by a liquor exporter and went out on a launch on the Detroit River. I could see the United States customs office on the other shore and I could see it was not very difficult to detect any boats that left the Canadian shore to go to the American side. While in Windsor I got into conversation with a man engaged in the business of exporting liquor. I asked him 'Do you cross in the daytime?' He answered, 'Yes, quite often.' I said, 'How is it they do not get you?' He replied with a smile, 'It just happens that they are not there when we go across.'

Canadian faith in the continued prosperity of the nation abounded. Who could foresee or even imagine the terrible days of the Great Depression of the 1930's?

25

THE GREAT DEPRESSION OF THE 1930's

A

THE ECONOMICS OF THE DEPRESSION

In 1929, Canadians joined their American neighbours in a wave of over-optimism. They were to share with them the painful after-effects. It was to be Canada's "sobering decade," when the "happy-go-lucky" youth of the twenties experienced the staggering problems of mature nationhood.

The Canadian economy had three distinguishing features. First, it rested on exports — primarily grain, pulp and paper, and mineral resources. Canada prospered when there were buyers, but what if there were none? Secondly, Canada was bound closely to the economy of the United States. Here Canada sold 40 per cent of her exports and here Canadians borrowed money to build and expand. What would happen to the Canadian economy if Americans stopped buying or bonding? Third, Canadians had over-expanded, pouring millions of borrowed dollars into production. What if Canadians stopped buying? There had been storm warnings — the record crop of 1928 could not be sold — but they had gone unnoticed, until the thunder struck. The stock market crash of October, 1929, burst the bubble of prosperity. Between September 3 and the end of October, the value of Ford of Canada stock dropped more than 50 per cent of its market value. In those two months alone, Ford lost sixty-two million dollars. And Ford was only one such company. The depression, soon to be worldwide, had begun.

The Canadian economy got a stunning blow. Shrinking markets and drastic drops in the world prices of primary products slashed Canada's foreign trade. To increase home production, the United States, Canada's largest customer, raised tariffs to their highest level ever. Canadians found it almost impossible to sell in the United States, while the European countries, unable to earn money by selling to the Americans, retaliated by raising their tariffs and cutting purchases. In 1930 Mackenzie King's Liberal government was forced to adopt a policy of high tariffs as a counter-measure to the barriers created by other countries. This move was aimed mainly at the United States whose Hawley-Smoot Act — high protective tariffs — had had such a devastating effect on Canada's agricultural exports. Competition from Argentina, Australia and Russia, coupled with reduced purchases by European countries, brought wheat prices to an appalling level. In Winnipeg, by the end of 1932, the price of wheat dropped to 38 cents per bushel from a high of $1.60 in 1929!

THE DECLINE IN PROVINCIAL
PER CAPITA INCOMES[362]
1928-1933

From the Rowell-Sirois Report:

	1928-29 average $ per capita	1933 $ per capita	Per- centage Decrease
Saskatchewan	478	135	72
Alberta	548	212	61
Manitoba	466	240	49
Canada	471	247	48
British Columbia	594	314	47
Prince Edward Island	278	154	45
Ontario	549	310	44
Quebec	391	220	44
New Brunswick	292	180	39
Nova Scotia	322	207	36

Read It in the Morning While It Is News

The Globe.

THE WEATHER
Probabilities: Fair and cool
Sun rises at 6.44 a.m. and sets at 5.30 p.m.

VOL. LXXXVI. NUMBER 24,904. TORONTO, FRIDAY, OCTOBER 25, 1929. 24 PAGES.

Stock Speculators Shaken in Wild Day of Panic

Erratic Wheat Prices Churn Market

Your Paper

IN ACCORD with its daily custom, The Globe this morning carries the official figures of the trading in all stocks on the New York Exchange at yesterday's record session. As a result of the panic of trading, the ticker did not catch up with the transactions until nearly 8 o'clock last night, after which the official computations had to be concluded. The Globe utilized two leased wires direct from the offices of the New York Times in the race against time in order that its readers might have the complete tables, as usual, in this morning's issue.

SLANDER CAMPAIGN IN SOUTH ONTARIO CHARGED BY SINCLAIR

"Contemptible Tactics" Vigorously Attacked by Liberal Leader

SPEAKS IN OWN RIDING

(Canadian Press Despatch.)

Port Perry, Oct. 24.—Claiming a campaign of slander is being wager against him in his own riding, William E. N. Sinclair, Liberal Leader, tonight addressed a large meeting here. Apart from one or two matters, however, he declined to reply to the allegations of F. G. Mason, Conservative candidate, and his supporters.

"My position in the riding," he said, "does not require me to answer any of the small stuff being handed out by my opponents. One of the charges dealt with was that of a Conservative speaker, who said: 'If the Liberals of this riding, and Mr. Sinclair himself, would lay their permits on the table the consumption of liquor would drop enormously.'

"Ladies and gentlemen, I have no permit, and never had one," declared Mr. Sinclair. "And I leave it to the people to judge of the man making that statement."

The Liberal Leader said one of the men who signed the nomination papers

BODIES AND FLOTSAM MUTELY TELL OF FATE MET BY 50 ON FERRY

Life-Belted Remains of Sailors Found in Lake Michigan

WATCH TIMES DISASTER

No Evidence Found to Support Story of Erie Foundering

(Special and A. P. Despatches.)

Milwaukee, Oct. 24.—Four bodies picked up on Lake Michigan and the sighting of a dozen others floating on the rough waters gave definite evidence tonight that the car ferry Milwaukee had gone to the bottom with her crew of fifty men.

Two of the bodies were recovered late this afternoon. Tonight, the coast guard at Kenosha found two more which were identified as those of Captain Robert McKay of Detroit and Purser A. R. Sadon, Grand Haven, Mich.

Because of the extreme roughness of the lake, salvaging operations were suspended until tomorrow.

The motorship Steel Chemist picked up two bodies eleven miles off Kenosha, and, five miles farther out in the lake, the white pilot house with "Milwaukee" printed on it. The lifebelts on the bodies bore the name Milwaukee.

Two more bodies were recovered ten miles off shore tonight by Coast Guardsmen.

A watch on one of the bodies stopped at 9.35, indicating that the ferry went down Tuesday night, six hours after it steamed out of the Kinnickinnic River with 27 loaded freight cars aboard, bound for Grand Haven, Mich. Captain Robert McKay, Grand Haven, veteran skipper of the Grand Trunk fleet, was in command.

In Face of Gale.

The Milwaukee sailed in the face of a violent gale, which some marine men described as the worst in the last 16 years.

An investigation into the disaster, the largest on Lake Michigan in 49 years, will be made immediately, Captain W. A. Collins, Federal Steamboat Inspector here, said tonight.

Exactly what happened to the Milwaukee probably will never be known.

Marine men here were of the opinion that the 27 freight cars were torn from their moorings. The weight of the shifting cars probably centred on one side of the ship, tipping it just as the boat was caught in the trough of the waves. Once on her beam-ends, it is believed she went down like a shot, the water pouring into the open stern end

New Records Set

Total sales on the New York Stock Exchange reached 12,894,000 shares, 4,000,000 shares more than the previous record day.

Total sales on the Toronto Stock Exchange reached 277,000 shares and on the Montreal Stock Exchange 382,521 shares, outstripping all previous records.

Shares from all parts of North America were dumped on the New York Stock Exchange by necessitous sellers, by people selling out of panic, and by "short" sellers who later covered, resulting in the worst breaks in quoted values since the war panic of 1914.

Bankers and responsible brokers in the United States and Canada consider the debacle yesterday was the inevitable result of too much speculation, and that it has "cleared the air."

There was a noticeable recovery in values in the last hour of trading, though the losses were still severe as compared with the previous day's close.

Brokerage loan totals, announced at the end of trading, showed a decrease of $167,000,000.

Frantic scenes were also witnessed in grain markets of Winnipeg and Chicago as grain prices crumbled, with a considerable recovery in final trading.

CANADIAN SITUATION ECONOMICALLY SOUND, SAY FINANCIAL CHIEFS

President A. E. Phipps of Bankers' Association Sees No Reason to Be Troubled About General Business Conditions — Local Stock Market Weathers Test Well

"DIP" FORESEEN BY OBSERVERS

Banking and brokerage authorities in Toronto yesterday were in agreement that the sweeping declines on New York, Montreal and Toronto Stock Exchanges were more or less "coming" to the market; that too much stock had been carried by people who were weak financially and who had made too little investigation as to the soundness of values, and that those who had made sound commitments within their means had little reason to fear. The bankers especially, though regretting the losses to small traders who had put up their all as margin, and could not come through with more funds, felt that there was no reason to be troubled about general business conditions. One high banking

Giant of Yesteryear

(Special Despatch to The Globe.)

NORTH BAY, Oct. 24. — Remarkable in size, symmetry and the soundness of its wood, a white pine tree, which has been lying 50 years or more on the farm of Norman Reid on Coulonge Lake, near Westmeath, was utilized this week for wood, and yielded seventeen cords. The pine measured 145 feet from the tip to the base, with a diameter of 5 feet 10 inches. The stump bears evidence that the tree was felled either completely or partly possibly half a century ago. The wood was perfectly sound.

SOCIALIST MAY LEAD NEXT PARIS CABINET

President to Confer With Newly Elected Radical Leader

MAELSTROM OF PANIC AS VALUES PLUNGE, THEN LEAP UP AGAIN

Chicago, Then Winnipeg, Subjected to Ruthless Smashes

SMALL MAN SQUEEZED

Turn of Finger as Signal Scales Millions From Total

(Associated Press Despatch.)

Chicago, Oct. 24.—The bottom dropped out of the wheat pit today in a scene reminiscent of war panic days. Frantic traders heaped their holdings of wheat into a market already overflowing with selling orders, and, under tremendous pressure, support crumbled and prices dropped 12 cents a bushel below yesterday's closing levels.

By noon the avalanche had spent its force, and with the stock markets rebounding, wheat, too, came back to finish 4⅝ to 5⅜ cents lower than Wednesday.

The final prices were: December wheat, $1.20¼ to $1.20½; March, $1.28⅛ to $1.28⅝, and May, $1.31¼ to $1.31½.

Other grains were strong in contrast, corn recovering from a small decline to end ¾ to 1½ cents higher, and oats losing only ¼ to ½ cent.

Maelstrom of Panic.

The wheat pit was a maelstrom of panic as millions of bushels were dumped. Traders swarmed, shouted and gesticulated wildly in their effort to unload on the falling market. The pace was too fast to execute stop-loss orders. The flying hands and fingers that signal bids and sales on fluctuations of an eighth or a quarter cent each day were talking of half cents and cents today, and the turn of a finger scaled a million dollars from the wheat crop.

The break started early in the day with a drop of five cents. Then as the stock market break grew in proportions, embarrassed traders turned loose their offerings at any price and perspiring clerks chalked down the tobogganing quotations on the big board.

The second hour saw the bottom reached, the bottom for the day and the year. December wheat touched $1.13 3-4, March $1.21 1-4 and May $1.24 1-2.

Then came the rebound. Commis-

(Continued on Page 14, Col. 7.

Record for All Time Is Set by Wall Street In Frenzy of Selling

Most Disastrous Decline in History of New York Stock Exchange Sees 12,894,650 Shares Change Hands—Total of 974 Separate Issues Handled—Thousands of Accounts Wiped Out Before Leading Bankers Combine to Halt Slump—Losses Reported to Reach Billions of Dollars

FINANCIAL LEADERS IN CONFERENCE ISSUE REASSURING STATEMENT

Securities Markets of Country Feel Effects of Downward Movement—Chicago Prices Break in Record Day's Trading of 1,220,000 Shares — London Spends Nervous Day Watching Events Across Atlantic

(Special Despatch to The Globe.)

NEW YORK, Oct. 24.—The most disastrous decline in the biggest and broadest stock market of history rocked the financial district today. In the very midst of the collapse five of the country's most influential bankers hurried to the office of J. P. Morgan & Co., and, after a brief conference, gave out word that they believed the foundations of the market to be sound, that the market smash has been caused by technical, rather than fundamental considerations, and that many sound stocks are selling too low.

Suddenly the market turned about, on buying orders thrown into the pivotal issues, and before the final quotations were tapped out, four hours and eight minutes after the 3 o'clock bell, most stocks had regained a measurable part of their losses.

The break was one of the widest in the market's history, although the losses at the close were not particularly large, many having been recouped by the afternoon rally.

Speculators go Down.

It carried down with it speculators, big and little, in every part of the country, wiping out thousands of accounts. It is probable that if the stockholders of the country's foremost corporations had not been calmed by the attitude of leading bankers, and the subsequent rally, the business of the country would have been seriously affected. Doubtless business will feel the effects of the drastic stock shakeout, and this is expected to hit luxuries most severely.

It was by far the biggest market day in the country's history. Total sales on the New York Stock Exchange were 12,894,650 shares and on the Curb 6,337,415 shares. A total of 974 separate issues was dealt in on the exchange. This figure established a new record.

The total losses cannot be accurately calculated, because of the large number of transactions and the thousands of securities not listed. However, they were staggering, running into billions of dollars. Fear struck the big speculators and little ones, big investors and little ones. Thousands of them threw their holdings into the whirling stock exchange pit for what they would bring, and thousands of prosperous brokers and bank accounts, sound and healthy a week ago, were completely wrecked in the strange debacle, due to a combination of circumstances, but accelerated into a crash by fear.

Trading Reaches Climax

(Associated Press Despatch.)

New York, Oct. 24.—The remarkable era of avid public speculation in stocks which has swept over the country during the past five years, came to a climax today in the most terrifying stampede of selling ever experienced on the New York Stock Exchange and

CRASH IN NEW YORK ROCKS SHARE PRICES IN TORONTO MARKETS

Rush of Orders Demoralizes Communications for a Time

MINES SHARES AFFECTED

Vigorous Upswing Late in Day—Montreal Exchange Has Record Day

Unable to withstand the sudden and terrific pressure of record-breaking liquidation, prices on the Toronto and Montreal Stock Exchanges collapsed yesterday in a market which made financial history.

Vigorous Upturn.

Almost as rapidly as it had declined, the stock market turned vigorously upward in the afternoon, and many of the day's extreme declines at Toronto and Montreal were reduced by as much as 50 per cent.

Equally encouraging was the fact that the Standard Stock and Mining Exchange not only withstood the effect of selling on other markets, but losses among mining issues were largely of a minor character.

With no warning of the impending decline, exchanges at Toronto, Montreal and New York opened at approximately the same levels as at the close on Wednesday. For more than an hour the list moved irregularly, until shortly after 11 o'clock the New York ticker spelled out the first words and figures in quotations that were to become historic.

Rush to Sell.

As prices revealed declines of extravagant proportions between consecutive sales of stocks at New York, nervous traders in Toronto and Montreal rushed to sell their holdings at what they could obtain. The result was a semi-panic, in which the floor of the Toronto Stock Exchange became the focal point of interest. Frantic efforts to "unload" led to such heavy trading that the ticker soon ceased to be of any use as a guide to prices, and by noon trading almost was completely demoralized. It was during the first half of the day that most of the 227,000 shares traded in Toronto made their appearance, while at Montreal no fewer than 382,521 shares changed hands. Both were far above any previous records.

Communications Clogged.

At the height of selling, millions of dollars were curtailed from the market value of Canadian and inter-listed stocks, and the confusion was further increased by the congestion of telephone messages into Toronto brokerage houses, and in turn from Toronto brokers to their correspondents at New

Drifting Soil Covering Shrubbery Around Settler's House, Saskatchewan, 1921

Men Lined up for Food, 1930's

Other branches of the Canadian economy were affected by the slump in wheat. The railroads, carriers of grain, suffered a serious decline in revenue. The farm machinery industry fell on difficult times. Manufacturing faced a dwindling domestic market. Production was cut and men lost their jobs. Unemployment increased, purchases dropped, and so production was cut again with more people unemployed, and buying less and less. The depression moved in this vicious circle.

Hardest hit were the regions of primary producers: wheat farming on the Prairies; fishing, lumbering and mining in British Columbia; and mining and pulp and paper industries in Northern Ontario and Quebec. The Prairies suffered most. On top of disappearing markets — wheat exports were down to 25 per cent of the pre-depression sales — natural disasters struck the wheat fields. Drought parched the Prairies soil. Scorching winds piled drifting top soil into dunes, which gave the landscape the appearance of a barren desert, as indeed it was.

DROUGHT ON THE PRAIRIES[363]

Two stanzas from Anne Marriott's THE WIND OUR ENEMY:

Wind
in a lonely laughterless shrill game
with broken wash-boiler, bucket without
a handle, Russian thistle, throwing up
sections of soil.
God, will it never rain again? What about
those clouds out west? No, that's just dust, as
thick and stifling now as winter underwear.
No rain, no crop, no feed, no faith, only
wind.

Although prices of goods in Canada fell, they were still out of reach for the mass of the people who lacked the money to buy the food, clothing and household goods they so desperately needed; Canadians learned to do without these. Wheat, the mainstay of Canada's economy, because of lack of foreign markets, was choking the terminal grain elevators; surplus wheat stocks continued to accumulate at a time when millions of people the world over, including Canada, were on the verge of starvation.

Politicians spoke of "prosperity around the corner." The depression was only a normal dip in the business cycle. This had happened before, and soon the business cycle would climb to a crest. But the depression deepened. By the end of 1932, Canada had 600,000 unemployed, and by 1935, 10 per cent of Canada's population received public relief. The burden of unemployment weighed heavily on provincial and municipal governments. Although the federal government possessed wide tax-levying powers, the provinces and municipalities, with their limited revenues, had to provide many social services and assistance to the unemployed. The local governments were driven to the brink of bankruptcy.

The Liberal government was under pressure from the Conservative opposition to relieve distress in the country. In the House of Commons, in the course of a debate on the unemployment situation, Prime Minister King indicated that his government might "contribute to the relief" of several western provinces but would not give a "five-cent piece" to provinces under Tory administrations. Nevertheless, the Dominion government found it necessary to channel funds to the provinces if only to save some of them from financial collapse.

In the election of 1930, the Conservatives played up King's "five-cent piece" speech. Richard Bedford Bennett, a millionaire Calgary lawyer and leader of the Conservative Party, in a vigorous campaign, promised to aid the provinces, "blast a way" into world markets, raise tariffs to protect Canadian industry, put the unemployed back to

The Hon. R. B. Bennett and his Sister

A "Bennett Buggy"

work and end the depression. The Conservatives also attacked the Liberals for their ineffective retaliation against American high tariff policy on Canadian imports.

MACKENZIE KING'S "FIVE-CENT PIECE" SPEECH[364]

On April 3, 1930, Mackenzie King answered his critics and their attack on the government for its failure to give funds for unemployment relief to the provinces:

. . . . Every winter in this country, ever since there was a winter or a Canada, there has been unemployment and there always will be . . . we have no right to say that there is any national unemployment problem in this country.

. . . . What does the suggestion [funds for unemployment relief] amount to that is being made by those who ask us to dip into the federal treasury and take out money raised by taxation from the people of Canada as a whole to give it to certain of the provinces? . . . give it . . . to whom, if you please? . . .

. . . I might be prepared to go a certain length possibly in meeting one or two western provinces that have Progressive premiers at the head of governments —

. . . . With respect to giving moneys out of the federal treasury to any Tory government in this country for these alleged unemployment purposes, with these governments situated as they are to-day, with policies diametrically opposed to those of this government, I would not give them a five-cent piece.

Hopelessness and human suffering were the curse of the depression. In some, disillusionment bred a "what's the use" attitude. In others, the deplorable conditions aroused bitterness and resentment against the government's failure to end

the depression. Both Liberals and Conservatives appealed to the voters with promises of ending unemployment. Canadians, no longer believing the Liberals, turned in desperation to Bennett's rosy promises and voted the Conservatives into office.

Under the new Conservative government, the depression plunged to its bleakest depths. Faced with a world-wide rise in tariffs against wheat imports, Bennett's administration followed the traditional Conservative protective tariff policy. This retaliatory measure helped somewhat the manufacturing provinces, especially Ontario, but did little for the others; Canadians still had to pay high prices for goods produced by the tariff-protected industries in Canada.

The Ottawa Conference, held in the summer of 1932, was Canada's attempt to gain a larger share of the British market. An agreement was reached wherein preferential duties were to apply between Canada and Britain and the other Dominions; Canadian primary products were to receive tariff preference within the Commonwealth. In practice, however, Commonwealth countries allowed only those reductions in tariffs that were not detrimental to their own economy. Canadian trade within the Commonwealth showed a slight rise, but other countries, notably the United States, resented the exclusive character of the Ottawa Agreement and further raised duties on Canadian goods. Between 1929 and 1933 Canada's foreign trade dropped 67 per cent — hardly a course that would "blast a way" into world markets.

Protective tariffs and Commonwealth preference did little to lessen the depression. The government decided to extend aid to the farmers by buying their wheat with interim payments of five cents per bushel on the 1931 crop. Mounting mass unemployment, demonstrations and a "Red Scare" prodded Ottawa into action. Ever larger federal funds were provided the provinces for unemployment relief. A public works program gave employment to some marrried unemployed on relief.

Unemployed men, participating in "March on Ottawa", board train in Alberta, June 1935.

"Relief camps" — working camps administered by the Department of National Defence — accommodated some 20,000 unmarried unemployed men who were paid a wage of 20 cents a day — a pittance even in depression years. Understandably, very little useful work was ever accomplished by relief camp workers, but these camps served the purpose intended; thousands of unemployed young men were housed and fed and kept out of the cities where, it was feared, they might be influenced by Communist propaganda.

LIFE IN RELIEF CAMPS[365]

James H. Gray, in his book THE WINTER YEARS *describes the lot of the single unemployed in relief camps:*

Equally to blame for morale trouble in the camps was the pay of twenty cents per day. There was something about that twenty cents per day that came to symbolize everything that was wrong with the lives of everybody on relief. It affronted human dignity as little else could have done. It was just the right size to be insulting.

. . . . In addition to twenty cents per day, the men also got a tobacco allowance — based on 1.45 cents per day for each day in camp. Thus, before a new-comer was able to get a ten-cent package of tobacco, he had to get seven days of camp life behind him. . . . There was little reading material and no means of pursuing an education or a hobby. Nobody was allowed to have a camera in camp.

So they griped about the food, the clothing, the bed bugs, the overcrowding in the dormitories, the martinetish regime, the latrines, and any other grievance they could conjure up. . . . All the investigators who roamed the camp — social workers, preachers, Members of Parliament, and Royal Commissioners — were unanimous on this point: the single unemployed regarded themselves as Canada's forgotten men. They had been filed and forgotten and nobody cared if they lived or died.

Little did the government realize that these camps were to become hot-beds of discontent which led to the "March on Ottawa" and culminated in the tragic Regina Riot on Dominion Day in 1935.

THE REGINA RIOT[366]

An eye-witness account:

. . . . Dominion Day, 1935, our country's birthday, and what a birthday celebration it turned out to be. . . . There were probably four or five hundred of us on Market Square. . . . The meeting wasn't long under way . . . when four large furniture vans backed up, one to each corner of the market square . . . and out poured the Mounties, each armed with a baseball bat. . . . In less than minutes the Market Square was a mass of writhing, groaning forms, like a battlefield. . . .

.... Immediately orders were given us to build barricades, and there was plenty of material to work with.

The streets were lined with parked cars and we simply pushed them into the streets, turned them on their sides, and piled them two high. . . .

———

It was a terrible night, downtown Regina a shambles. Not a store with a window left in, the streets piled with rocks and broken glass. . . . About a hundred of our members in jail . . . forty of our comrades suffering from gunshot wounds, one man killed, scores of other casualties, of whom I think the Mounties could claim the majority. . . .

July 2, 1935, we arose from our straw to an . . . almost unbelievable sight. . . . The Exhibition Grounds at Regina were fenced in by that strong industrial fence . . . and at every entrance was a squad of Mounties with mounted Vickers machine guns. . . . It was the first Canadian concentration camp.

Government intervention — a departure from the long-held Canadian view as to the role of government — failed to cope with the mounting depression. Although the Bennett government was instrumental in passing some worthwhile legislation and was responsible for some significant developments, the gloom of the depression obscured these accomplishments. In 1932, the Canadian Radio Broadcasting Commission, renamed the Canadian Broadcasting Corporation in 1936, was set up as a government owned and operated monopoly in radio broadcasting. It was also in 1932 that a treaty was concluded with the United States for a St. Lawrence seaway, but the American Senate refused to ratify the treaty and the project was further delayed by the depression and World War II. To help agriculture, the government passed the Prairie Farm Rehabilitation Act in 1935. The same year, the Canadian Wheat Board was established to market Canadian wheat abroad and to assure farmers a minimum price for their grain. The Bank of Canada was founded in 1934 as a government agency to look after Canada's monetary system and to control private banks.

Bennett's administration was a period of important economic developments. The newly completed Hudson's Bay Railway carried prairie wheat to the port of Churchill, and the first export grain was shipped from this northern port in 1931. Turner Valley in southern Alberta and Fort Norman on the Mackenzie River became major oil producing regions. Into the northland, bush pilots flew prospectors and miners who began the exploitation of the northern mineral resources.

The government also inaugurated a transcontinental air service — the forerunner of Air Canada. The railway system was reorganized and certain competing unprofitable branch lines were eliminated. As a further economy measure, the federal government assumed control over appropriation of funds to the C.N.R., reorganized the C.N.R. and pooled passenger service with the C.P.R.

The government also probed into the reasons behind Canada's financial distress. A Royal Commission looked into many financial problems. In 1934, the Royal Commission on Price Spreads, directed by H. H. Stevens, investigated price fixing by manufacturers. Although their findings revealed startling abuses, the government had little chance to act upon the recommendations.

EVIDENCE GATHERED BY THE STEVENS COMMISSION, 1934[367]

From the Report of the Royal Commission on Price Spreads:

A large number of examples of price spreads . . . were submitted to us by our investigators and the variation in initial mark-up referred to above [in a large department store] is illustrated by the following brief extracts from these tables:

| | Laid Down | | Selling to cost |
Description	Total Cost	Initial Price	Initial Mark-up Per-cent
Men's pyjamas	$ 1.59	$ 2.98	87.42
Men's negligee shirts	0.45	0.75	66.67
Cambray Shirts	0.69	0.95	37.68
Boy's suits	3.60	9.95	176.39
Boy's Britches	0.81	1.15	41.97
Women's coats	7.08	10.74	51.69
Women's dresses	7.95	29.50	271.07
Shoulder of pork	0.11	0.10	9.09*
Beef hearts	0.04	0.08	100.00
Men's top coats	13.60	25.00	83.8
Blue waist overalls	1.19	1.49	25.2
Solid walnut end-tables	1.03	0.95	7.8*
Mercurochrome	0.10½	0.25	138.1
Lysol	0.22	0.27	22.0
*Loss			

In January 1935, with an election approaching R. B. Bennett, in a series of radio addresses to the nation, announced a sweeping program of government intervention in the nation's economy. This was Bennett's "New Deal," patterned after President Franklin D. Roosevelt's New Deal in the United States. A number of promised reforms such as unemployment insurance, social security, a minimum wage law and a shorter work week were brought in by the government. Most Canadians were skeptical of Bennett's sudden conversion to government meddling in social legislation. Why had he waited so long? The people suspected that the New Deal was a manoeuvre to gain votes for the Conservatives in the forthcoming election. The Liberals, although they had offered no constructive proposals of their own to end the depression, attacked the New Deal as a device to deceive the electorate. Mackenzie King claimed that Bennett fully realized that the New Deal laws encroached into areas of provincial jurisdiction and that the courts would declare them unconstitutional.

BENNETT'S "NEW DEAL"[368]

Excerpts from his radio addresses, January, 1935:

In the last five years, great changes have taken place in the world. The old order is gone. It will not return. . . .

———

. . . in my mind, reform means Government intervention. It means Government control and regulation. . . .

———

. . . . The dole is a condemnation, final and complete, of our economic system. If we cannot abolish the dole, we should abolish the system. . . .

———

Selfish men, and this country is not without them . . . fearful that this Government might impinge on what they have grown to regard as their immemorial right of exploitation, will whisper against us. They will call us radicals. They will say that this is the first step on the road to socialism. We fear them not. . . . We invite their cooperation . . . all the parts of the capitalist system, have only one purpose and that is to work for the welfare of the people. And when any of

those instruments in any way fails, it is the plain duty of government which represents the people, to remove the cause of failure. . . . The lives and the happiness and the welfare of too many people depend upon our success to allow the selfishness of a few individuals to endanger it. . . .

At the polls, on October 24, 1935, the Canadian people showed little faith in Bennett's New Deal; the Conservative government together with twelve of its ministers, was defeated.[*] The Liberal government, under Mackenzie King, sent the New Deal measures to the courts, where, in 1937, the Judicial Committee of the Privy Council declared most of the statutes *ultra vires* — beyond the jurisdiction of the federal government — because they affected "property and civil rights in the provinces."

Under the Liberal government the depression continued. The provinces did not have the resources commensurate with their responsibilities. They had the power but not the money, because of the separation of taxation rights in the B.N.A. Act. Bankrupt provinces, especially the western ones, and their municipal governments were expected to shoulder the crushing burden of the depression's seemingly numberless unemployed. In the end, the federal government was forced to support them by grants and loans. In response to this situation, in 1937, the government appointed a Royal Commission on Dominion-Provincial Relations known as the Rowell-Sirois Commission. The Report of the Commission, issued in 1940, was the first comprehensive inquiry into Canadian government since Confederation. It recommended sweeping changes in federal-provincial relations and pointed the way to the "welfare state."

———

[*] The results of the election: Liberals — 171; Conservatives — 39; Social Credit — 17; C.C.F. — 7; and Reconstruction — 1.

B

THE POLITICS OF THE DEPRESSION

The Conservatives were unable to solve the country's problems. As the situation worsened, new answers began to appeal to Canadians. Under the economic and social pressures of the time, a renewed sectionalism appeared, where new political parties became the voice of protest. They were but one expression of the strain placed on

the federal system by the depression. But out of this tension a stronger, more unified country emerged.

The Co-operative Commonwealth Federation took shape in 1933 at a convention in Regina, under the leadership of J. S. Woodsworth, the Methodist ex-minister who had been involved in

Maurice Duplessis in the 1930's

William S. Aberhart Addressing a Rally in St. George's Island Park, Calgary, July 1937

the 1919 Winnipeg General Strike, who combined Christian social justice with economic ideas of socialism. The Regina Manifesto, the C.C.F.'s program, called for such measures as centralized government planning, public control of financial institutions, nationalization of key industries and uniform public health services. The movement found its greatest support from farm organizations and remnants of the Progressives in drought-stricken Saskatchewan. It also gained the support of workers and labour unions who regarded the C.C.F. as the true representative of the working-man against special interests which had long been sheltered by both the Liberal and Conservative parties.

THE REGINA MANIFESTO[369]

. . . . The C.C.F. . . . is a democratic movement, a federation of farmer, labor and socialist organizations, financed by its own members and seeking to achieve its ends solely by constitutional methods. . . .

2. SOCIALIZATION OF FINANCE
   Socialization of . . . banking, currency, credit, and insurance. . . .

3. SOCIAL OWNERSHIP
   Socialization (Dominion, Provincial or Municipal) of transportation, communication, electric power and all other industries and services essential to social planning. . . .

4. AGRICULTURE
   Security of tenure for the farmer upon his farm on conditions to be laid down by individual provinces; insurance against unavoidable crop failure. . . .

James S. Woodsworth

6. CO-OPERATIVE INSTITUTIONS
   The encouragement by the public authority of both producers' and consumers' co-operative institutions.

7. LABOR CODE
   A National Labor Code to secure for the worker maximum income and leisure, insurance covering illness, accident, old age, and unemployment. . . .

8. SOCIALIZED HEALTH SERVICES
   Publicly organized health, hospital and medical services. . . .

11. TAXATION AND PUBLIC FINANCE
   A new taxation policy designed . . . to provide funds for social services and the socialization of industry. . . .

No C.C.F. Government will rest content until it has eradicated capitalism and put into operation the full program of socialized planning which will lead to the establishment in Canada of the Co-operative Commonwealth.

Over the years, the C.C.F. managed to elect a number of members of Parliament, never sufficient to form the Official Opposition. Its strength, however, was in the provincial field in the west. In 1944, under its provincial leader T. C. Douglas, the C.C.F. gained power in Saskatchewan and continued in office until 1964, when it was ousted by the Liberals under Ross Thatcher, a one-time C.C.F. member of Parliament from Moose Jaw. In 1943, the C.C.F. won enough seats to become the Official Opposition in Ontario. In Manitoba, the C.C.F. continued to elect a considerable number of members to the Legislature, and in British Columbia it has been the Official Opposition since 1951. In 1961, the C.C.F. was transformed into the New Democratic Party under the leadership of T. C. Douglas, with a lesser emphasis on doctrinaire socialism.

Although the C.C.F. never elected enough members to form the government in Ottawa, many of its socialistic proposals, often attacked as too radical, have been adopted and put into law by federal governments, both Liberal and Conservative. Because of the influence the C.C.F. has exerted on behalf of social legislation, it has been referred to as "the conscience of the House of Commons."

In Alberta, William Aberhart, a high-school principal and evangelical radio preacher, started the Social Credit Party, which based its ideas on the theories of Major C. Douglas. Social Credit blamed the depression on international bankers and attributed the plight of the western farmers to the "Eastern" financial interests. Social Credit's financial theories, derisively known as "funny money," were to counteract the socialistic appeal of the C.C.F.

Social Credit promised a cash dividend of $25.00 a month to every resident in Alberta. Placing this money in the hands of the people would enable them to buy the goods they needed. This increased purchasing power would, in turn, stimulate production and put the unemployed back to work. The money for such a give-away scheme, the Social Credit Party claimed, would be derived from the natural resources of the province.

SOCIAL CREDIT IDEAS[370]

. . . . Social Credit claims that each of these consumers [individual citizen of Alberta] has a right to a share in the production from the natural resources of the province. At the present time this great wealth is being selfishly manipulated and controlled by one or more men known as the "Fifty Big Shots of Canada.". . .

. . . regular issuance of dividends from month to month sufficient to secure for the individual citizen the bare necessities of food, clothing and shelter. . . . To enable each citizen to secure these bare necessities, each of them will receive a passbook in which at the beginning of each month will be entered the basic dividend for that month, say $25.00. . . .

The credit issued will be a charge against the Natural Resources of the Province much in the same way as the present Government Bonds are.

In 1935, Albertans grasped at this unique appeal and brought a Social Credit government into office, ending the long-entrenched United Farmers of Alberta administration which had ruled the province since 1921. Very soon, the Social Credit government passed a series of acts to put the party's theories into operation. However, since most of these measures concerned monetary matters, these laws were either disallowed by the federal government or declared *ultra vires* by the courts.

Social Credit has been ruling Alberta ever since, and when Aberhart died in 1943, E. C. Manning succeeded him as Premier. In British Columbia a Social Credit government, with W. A. C. Bennett as Premier, has been in power since 1952. Ever since 1935,* a number of Social Credit members, mainly from Alberta, have been elected to the House of Commons. In the 1962 federal election, the party made significant inroads into Quebec; of the thirty Social Credit seats, twenty-six were from Quebec. An uneasy collaboration existed between the Creditistes, Social Credit's Quebec faction led by Réal Caouette, and the Social Crediters from the rest of Canada. Although Robert Thompson was the federal leader of the party, there was no doubt that Caouette intended to dictate policy. The tenuous alliance could not withstand the strain of regional differences, and shortly after the election the party split, with Social Credit and Creditistes sitting in the House of Commons as separate opposition parties.

In Quebec, Maurice Duplessis, a former Conservative, headed a new French-Canadian nationalist party, the *Union Nationale*. He claimed that "aliens" — the English minority in Quebec — who controlled the natural resources, industry and

* In the 1958 election, Social Credit lost all seats in the Diefenbaker landslide.

finance of the province were responsible for Quebec's economic and social ills. He skillfully exploited French-Canadian discontent to attract to his party disillusioned Liberals and Conservatives as well as others disappointed in the established parties. The *Union Nationale* won the provincial election in 1936, and rooted itself firmly in Quebec's political life. But it was a provincial party and it did not venture into the federal political arena.

THE UNION NATIONALE PLATFORM[371]

PROGRAMME DE L'ACTION LIBERALE NATIONALE, 1934*

The actual crisis is due mostly to the poor distribution . . . the greed of big business, and all sorts of corruption which have been facilitated by the democractic system. . . .

L'Action libérale nationale thus offers the following overall plan which, although it is not perfect, aims towards . . . the only way of assuring a better redistribution of wealth, consequently reducing unemployment and terminating the crisis [Depression].

IV. ECONOMIC REFORMS
    1. To break, by every means possible, the stranglehold which big business has upon the province and the municipalities. . . .
VI. POLITICAL AND ADMINISTRATIVE REFORMS
    1. Good management and honesty in the public administration;
VII. ELECTORAL REFORMS
    2. Compulsory voting (measure subject to plebiscite);
    4. Identity cards in cities exceeding 10,000 souls;
VIII. FISCAL REFORMS
    6. Redistribution of federal, provincial and municipal taxes in order that the commercial corporations and certain classes of individuals, who often enjoy exemptions or unjust assessments, may contribute to the public coffers in an equitable manner.

Duplessis ran the province like a benevolent dictator and his regime lasted until his death in 1959, with the exception of the period 1939-1944. In spite of his platform against Anglo-American control of Quebec's natural resources, American investment in the province increased. Duplessis championed clericalism and French-Canadian nationalism based on special Quebec rights, and lavishly rewarded his active supporters. He considered labour unions a hindrance to the province's economic progress, and he acted swiftly, using force if necessary, against strikers in important industries. The Padlock Law of 1937 — its repressive character befitting an authoritarian state — struck at the basic rights of common citizens. It gave the provincial Attorney-General the right to padlock the premises of "subversive" organizations. The Padlock Law apparently was aimed at Communists, but "subversive" had wide interpretations and the law could be and was used against groups which the *Union Nationale* disliked.

The *Union Nationale* was firmly entrenched. Obviously, it offered what Quebeçois wanted. Duplessis, in posing as the defender of the rights of Quebec, managed to fan a narrow provincial nationalism. Quebec was to be the bastion of French-Canadian heritage in an "alien" controlled Canada.

* This became the platform of the *Union Nationale*.

C

THE PEOPLE OF THE DEPRESSION

The Thirties scarred the people with hunger, unemployment and poverty. The nation, along with the rest of the world, suffered severely. In the Maritimes, fish, the staple produce of the east coast, went to rot while children walked about hungry. In the West, where grain elevators were bursting with wheat, people lacked bread. The depression years can be aptly described as the decade of hunger and discontent.

Merciless exploitation of human labour and deplorable working conditions were the lot of the workingman during the depression. There were many hungry men out of work but very few jobs. The employer well knew this and he took advantage of a glutted labour market. The workingman, dependent on wages for his livelihood, took pay cut after pay cut and his wages bought less and less. For the unemployed worker there seemed no hope. "No Help Wanted" signs greeted his frantic search for work — any work. The unemployed were forced to rely on public charity, which was both degrading and inadequate. The clothes issued to families on relief became familiar and "reliefers" were identifiable. The efforts of many families to preserve their self-respect were heroic. Wives worked in factories at extremely low wages, a mere three or four dollars a week, to augment their husband's low pay — anything to keep off relief.

LIFE ON RELIEF[372]

Recollections of a former relief recipient:
. . . . There were the usual vexations about clothing and shoes and landlords, which everybody had all the time. . . . There usually were worse problems, all of which revolved around how to get hold of $1.50 in cash every week. . . .

We received no cash in relief, and for the first year no clothing whatever was supplied. Relief vouchers covered food, fuel, and rent, and nothing else. But we needed other things — many other things like tobacco and cigarette-papers, tooth-paste, razor blades, lipstick, face powder, the odd bottle of aspirin, streetcar fare, a movie once a week, a pair of women's stockings once a month, a haircut once a month, and a permanent twice a year. Most people tried to find twenty-five cents a week, every week for a newspaper. Unexpected needs continually cropped up, like needles and thread, darning wool, a bit of cloth for fancy work, a pattern for remaking a dress, a half-dollar every other month for a co-operative half-keg of beer for a neighbourhood party. . . . The catalogue of essential trivia differed from family to family, but it seldom added up to less than a rock-bottom minimum of $1.50 a week.

In the farming communities on the Prairies, conditions were little better. Many farmers, heavily indebted to the banks and finance companies, were unable to meet their mortgage payments and lost their farms. A bailiff's foreclosing a farm became an everyday occurrence. Flour and sugar sacks and burlap bags, boiled in strong bleach, were fashioned into towels, sheets, pillow cases, tablecloths and women's underclothing. The farmer had to endure the heartbreak of natural disasters. He could only stand by helplessly and watch his crops withered by drought or devoured by hordes of grasshoppers. Yet many endured and stayed on — there was really nowhere else to go.

THE DEPRESSION ON THE PRAIRIES[373]

From THE WIND OUR ENEMY:
The sun goes down. Earth like a thick black coin
Leans its round rim against the yellowed sky.
The air cools. Kerosene lamps are filled and lit
In dusty windows. Tired bodies crave to lie
In bed forever. Chores are done at last.

A thin horse neighs drearily. The chickens drowse,
Replete with grasshoppers that have gnawed and scraped
Shrivelled garden-leaves. No sound from the gaunt cows.
Poverty hand in hand with fear, two great
Shrill-jointed skeletons stride loudly out
Across the pitiful fields, none to oppose.
Courage is roped with hunger, chained with doubt.
Only against the yellow sky, a part
Of the jetty silhouette of barn and house
Two figures stand, heads close, arms locked,
And suddenly some spirit seems to rouse
And gleam, like a thin sword, tarnished bent,
But still shining in the spared beauty of moon,
As his strained voice says to her, "We're not licked yet!
It must rain again — it *will!* Maybe — soon —"

There was always the hope of a crop next year. They sowed again, only to have a heartbreaking repetition of the year before. The young people did not have the staying power of their parents; they left the poverty of the farm to seek a better life in the city.

Mixed farming areas of southern Ontario and Quebec and certain parts of the Maritimes fared much better. At least here they grew ample food for the family larder. In the manufacturing regions of Ontario and Quebec, some tariff-protected industries managed to continue operation, cushioning somewhat the blow of the depression. The Prairies had no such cushion.

Canadians began to leave their homes in search for work. In their wandering, hope was maintained. The news of a friend or an acquaintance finding a job in Toronto or Vancouver sparked the hope in others that in another city work could be found. Freight cars became loaded with human cargo traveling across the land in search of non-existent jobs. Most of those riding on the tops of freight cars were the young, but there were also many family men. The most wretched were the thousands of disillusioned First World War veterans. Was this the democracy they fought for in France? Was this their country's reward for their deeds on the battlefield? The search for the elusive job proved aimless and futile for most. Vancouver had its unemployed as did Winnipeg, Toronto, or Halifax. Yet, there was nothing at home, only the aggravation of seeing the family suffer. So the wandering continued.

The heavy hob-nailed work boots, rough trousers, work shirt and a packsack marked Canada's wandering youth of the depression. All one's personal belongings were in that packsack — a razor, perhaps an extra pair of socks or a set of underwear, a family snapshot, a book or a Bible obtained from the Gideon Society. These were the "hobos," penniless, filthy and hungry who rode from coast to coast, lived in "jungles" along the railway tracks and drifted from city to city.

In the city, life was deplorable. Food and shelter were a constant concern, for a hobo seldom had the fifteen cents for a meal or the ten cents for a bed in a flop-house. "Pan-handling" — begging on the streets — for cigarettes or five cents for coffee and doughnuts proved profitable for some. The popular song "Brother Can You Spare a Dime" fittingly characterized conditions during the depression. Those who could not stoop to pan-handling lined up at soup kitchens for the free food which even an empty stomach resented. There were also the mission houses where a thin soup and even thinner sandwiches rewarded those persevering enough to sit through the ritual of being "saved." The Salvation Army hostel or the local jail could be counted on for a night's lodging. Many found refuge in the public libraries. But most hobos spent their days idling on city streets.

LEISURE TIME DURING THE DEPRESSION[374]

An unemployed recalls how time was whiled away during the depression:

. . . . Sometimes we would go up town and drop in at auction sales . . . they constituted a popular form of entertainment. . . . So many people came to be amused, however, and so few came to buy. . . .

———

The pool-rooms and brokerage offices were all crowded throughout the depression, though seldom with customers. The brokerage offices supplied free newspapers and the pool-room furnished both recreation and heat . . . the unemployed congregated in such numbers that the players often had to complain to the management in order to get elbow room for their cues.

———

Those who lived within walking distance of the city police court never missed the morning show in court. . . . The high court criminal cases at the law courts drew upon a city-wide audience. . . . Sex cases and murder trials naturally got the largest crowds. . . .

———

The library . . . was a special haven for the homeless and ageing single unemployed, some of whom might spend eight hours a day, six days a week, in its warm, friendly quiet. Some of them read, some of them just sat and looked at books and magazines until they fell asleep. The librarians

Single Mens' Unemployed Association Parading in Toronto, 1930's

frowned on sleepers and would occasionally clear them out of the reading-rooms. . . .

———

Life itself could never be a bore as long as there was a working radio within earshot. Radio-listening was a passion that the unemployed shared with the employed, the rich shared with the poor. . . . For the farm families, a radio in working order was a categorical imperative. It broke the barrier of isolation. . . .

Many knocked on doors and offered to do some work in return for food. Sympathetic people gave them food and even clothing; others berated them as worthless bums who were too lazy to work. To some, hobos represented instability and a threat to decent citizens. People feared these hungry men, for hungry men are desperate men, and desperate men commit desperate acts. There is no doubt that among the derelicts of the depression were those who stole and shop-lifted, and accounts of their crimes deepened the comfortable citizen's fears.

A Westerner tells of the young unemployed transients of the depression:

Most of the time, the transients weren't really going anywhere. At first they moved out of the West in great numbers looking for work in the factory towns of Ontario, and found a welcome as cold as a Manitoba winter. . . . By 1933, the idea of getting a job had been abandoned and the legions of single unemployed moved back and forth across the country because they had nothing else to do. The railway towns of the West were overrun in the summers by young transients, who dropped off freight trains to try to exchange a day's work in a garden for a square meal or two. . . .

I had no garden to weed, but I liked to sit with them while they ate and try to get them to talk, but it was rarely we fed a talkative type. Mostly they were so young, and they just wanted to sit for a while, eat, and get on their way again. Besides, there was little of interest in their lives to talk about. They had left home in Glace Bay or Kitchener or Nelson to look for work because their families were on relief. They were often homesick but were resolutely heading in the opposite direction. They had been on the road long enough to have lost any hesitancy about asking for a meal. . . .

The depression dealt cruelly not only with the youth but also with their fathers. The father, the traditional head of the family and its provider, lost his role — no longer could he earn a living for his family. He was embittered at his idleness and helplessness as he saw his wife eke out the scanty food, his daughter suffer the humiliations of poverty and his sons leave to wander aimlessly across the land.

No wonder that those who lived through the cruel years of the depression refer to them as the "Dirty Thirties." The youth of prosperous postwar Canada cannot perceive the suffering, poverty and despair of the depression. It is not surprising that young people are irritated with their parents' stories of those horrible years; they often believe that these tales of woe are related in order to point out the extravagance of the postwar generation. Surely such conditions could not have existed in Canada! Surely a depression such as this could not have happened in Canada! It did happen, and it did happen to people alive today. And it was not too long before "the lost generation" which lived through the decade of depression was to face another catastrophe — the holocaust of war.

Some observations by R. B. Bennett's contemporaries:
[a]*As a public speaker:*

. . . ."Bonfire Bennett", as he was called in the West for his fiery style of speech, could utter 220 words a minute, as registered by a stopwatch, never missing a syllable or misplacing a predicate. Without a note to guide him, his language glowed like a purling brook. . . .

———

His work habits in his Chateau Laurier suite:

. . . he worked steadily for fifteen or sixteen hours, with a brief interruption for lunch and a leisurely dinner in his suite, where he usually consumed a pound of chocolates every night. . . . Several times a week expert massage would substitute for exercise. The Chateau barbers grew prosperous on his tips.

———

[b]*Meighen's tribute to R. B. Bennett at a farewell dinner in Toronto, January 16, 1939:*

. . . . He is not, as Laurier was, so spontaneously affable, a personality so universally gracious and engaging that one likes him, sometimes follows him though he believes him wrong. He is not, as Macdonald was, so intensely human and companiable as to be loved even for his faults. He is, as everyone knows, a different stamp of man altogether . . . he depends, and does not fear to depend, upon his achievements for his following and his fame. . . .

———

[c]*A comment on his retirement:*

. . . . How tragic it was . . . that a man who had given so much of himself to his country should in the end, when nearly seventy, quit that country for voluntary exile elsewhere [England], and still leave so few who felt any real distress at his departure.

———

An anecdote about Bennett's inefficiency:

One [secretary] employed by Bennett dictated, for Bennett to sign, a very moving letter of condolence to the lady he assumed to be the suddenly bereaved wife of a Conservative M.P. Bennett signed this letter without reading it, and was exceedingly vexed when he received from the M.P. himself a chiding letter saying that he was in fact alive, but saddened to feel that his leader had not noticed his still regular attendance at Party caucus meetings.

26

CANADA AND THE BRITISH COMMONWEALTH: 1918-1939

A

CANADA'S STATUS AT THE END OF WORLD WAR I

One of the standard judgments in Canadian history is that World War I, for all its terrible results, quickened the pace of Canadian national growth. A steadily maturing pride in domestic achievements in the years up to 1914 was suddenly translated into widespread feeling that the developing colony had earned a new place in the British Empire and in the world community. The contributions of farm and factory to the Allied war effort would have justified demands for special recognition. The memory of thousands of their young compatriots dead and buried in Europe convinced Canadians that their people had come of age, that they had "paid the price in blood."

Even before the war had ended, the British government had acknowledged the right of the Dominions to a voice in imperial war policy. While serving in the Imperial War Cabinet, Sir Robert Borden fought for formal post-war changes in Canada's status within the Empire. He was instrumental in the adoption, by the Imperial Conference of 1917, of Resolution IX. Together with a similar resolution at the Conference of 1918, Resolution IX showed that leaders of Great Britain and the Dominions generally supported the idea of changes once the war was concluded.

RESOLUTION IX OF THE 1917 IMPERIAL CONFERENCE[377]

The Imperial War Conference are of opinion that the readjustment of the constitutional relations of the component parts of the Empire . . . should form the subject of a special Imperial Conference to be summoned as soon as possible after the cessation of hostilities.

They deem it their duty, however, to place on record their view that any such readjustment, while thoroughly preserving all existing powers of self-government and complete control of domestic affairs, should be based upon a full recognition of the Dominions as autonomous nations of an Imperial Commonwealth . . . should recognize the right of the Dominions . . . to an adequate voice in foreign policy and in foreign relations, and should provide effective arrangements for continuous consultation in all important matters of common Imperial concern, and for such necessary concerted action, founded on consultation, as the several Governments may determine.

There was, at the same time, much concern that solidarity of the type displayed during the war must somehow be maintained. Borden shared this feeling, but rejected such notions as imperial federation, which held dangers for the autonomy of the Dominions. Instead, he advocated the concept of mutual consultation and periodic conferences on matters of concern to all members of the Empire.

BORDEN ON CANADA'S NEW STATUS AFTER THE WAR[378]

On September 2, 1919, Borden presented the Treaty of Versailles to the Canadian Parliament for ratification. He spoke to the House of Commons about Canada's new status in the Empire and the world:

. . . . On behalf of my country I stood firmly upon this solid ground; that in this, the greatest of all wars, in which the world's liberty, the world's justice, in short the world's future destiny were at stake, Canada had led the democracies of both the American continents. Her resolve had given inspiration, her sacrifices had been conspicuous, her effort was unabated to the end. The same indomitable spirit which made her capable of that effort and sacrifice made her equally incapable of accepting at the Peace Conference, in the League of Nations, or elsewhere, a status inferior to that accorded to nations less advanced in their development, less amply endowed in wealth, resources, and population, no more complete in their sovereignty, and far less conspicuous in their sacrifice.

The Canadian Prime Minister advanced the cause of Canadian autonomy through his part in obtaining representation at the Paris Peace Conference. Canada also gained the right to sign the Treaty of Versailles in 1919 as one of the countries which had helped bring about victory over Germany. Separate membership in the League of Nations was another achievement, which came only after other nations were persuaded that Canada's vote would not be merely an automatic British vote.

Borden's government had also been pressing for greater Canadian freedom in handling its relations with the United States. In 1918 the Canadian War Mission had been set up in Washington to facilitate wartime co-operation. In the following year, Borden submitted a plan to the British calling for the creation of a Canadian diplomatic establishment as part of the British embassy in the United States. By this plan the Canadian government would appoint its own minister, who would be in charge of communications among Canada, the American government and the British embassy in the United States.

The British agreed that some such arrangement was desirable, but preferred a compromise whereby the Canadian diplomat would be a part of the British senior staff in the United States. In this way, emphasis would be placed on the solidarity of the Empire, instead of on the separateness of the Canadian representation. The Canadian government accepted this proposal, and in 1920 announced its intention to make an appointment. Nothing was done before Borden retired a few months later and Arthur Meighen replaced him as Prime Minister, only to lose in the election of 1921 to Mackenzie King, the new Liberal leader. But the groundwork had been laid for Canada's first diplomatic office in a foreign country, even though the actual legation was not established in Washington until 1927.

Arthur Meighen represented Canada at the Imperial Conference of 1921. The main topic on the agenda was the renewal of the alliance between Great Britain and Japan. The United States had just officially informed Meighen of its strong opposition to the alliance. Meighen advised the Conference that Canada — as the member of the Empire whose interest would be most affected by American hostility — should have a hand in determining the Empire's decision. This stand by the Canadian Prime Minister was in line with the concept of a common imperial foreign policy based on consultation among parts of the Empire whose interests were involved in each case — the very concept which the British seemed to favour at the conclusion of World War I.

ARTHUR MEIGHEN'S VIEW ON CANADA'S DESTINY[379]

On November 4, 1921, Meighen argued that Canada had achieved the ideal — nationhood within the British Empire:

By tradition, by the sense of common inheritance and of common ideals, the dominion of Canada aspires to one destiny, and one only — a destiny than which there is no nobler—nationhood within the British Empire. I am convinced there is no single thing more vital than that the British Empire, as at present constituted, should be maintained. We enjoy the fullest autonomy, and that autonomy is not challenged and never shall be challenged. For the maintenance of the British Empire as a league of autonomous nations there are common burdens that all must share, but these burdens are light and the advantages abundant, in comparison with either the burdens or the advantages of any other destiny that can be conceived. Sentiment and interest are in accord in upholding British connection.

At the Conference, no conclusion was reached about the Anglo-Japanese treaty. However, Great Britain's decision to discuss the matter later in the year in the United States was seen by Canadians as proof that Meighen's influence had been of some importance. Meanwhile, the Conference pointed up how different were the interests of various parts of the Empire: Great Britain regarded Japanese friendship as important to its colonies in the Far East; Australia was intent on some British guarantee of security in the Pacific; Canada was mainly concerned about averting bad feelings with the United States; South Africa had no serious interest in the problem at all. Significantly, the Conference decided against any further meeting which might attempt to devise some new arrangement to facilitate formulation of imperial foreign policy. It was potentially a serious omission — unless the British were to decide to keep the Dominions informed, a sudden crisis might mean that one or more Dominions would decide they were not obligated in an affair on which they had not been consulted.

B

MACKENZIE KING AND CANADIAN AUTONOMY

William Lyon Mackenzie King, grandson of the leader of rebellion in 1837, had his own views on Canadian independence and a deep distrust of British politicians. Unlike his fiery ancestor, King was a shrewd and cautious individual. His early experience in politics came during the latter part of the Laurier years, and he had been impressed by Laurier's style of leadership. Many times in his career, King drew parallels between Laurier's efforts and his own in striving to maintain Canadian unity and to defend Canada's "sovereignty."

The new Prime Minister had seen the divisive effects of Canada's involvement in British and European affairs, and the damage done to the Liberal Party before and during the last war. He recognized that disruptions in the country's national life were not only dangerous to Canada but likely to mean defeat at the polls.

Borden and Meighen had both shown interest in finding some workable scheme whereby Canada could remain part of a united and strong British Empire and still exercise the necessary control over its own policy. King was skeptical about the possibilities of such a policy succeeding, and suspicious that Great Britain wished only to use the Dominions as a source of her own power.

C

THE CHANAK AFFAIR

Shortly after King took office with a minority government, events in the eastern Mediterranean led to the so-called Chanak affair, which seemed to bear out King's suspicions of the contemporary British government. The revolutionary Turkish government of Kemal Ataturk was threatening to occupy Chanak, a neutral zone at the narrows of the Dardanelles. Great Britain made ready for war to prevent Turkish control in the strategic area in defiance of the post-war treaty. Without allies in the venture, the British turned — rather unexpectedly — to the Dominions.

The British mismanaged their attempt to secure Canada's assistance. They had not followed up the Imperial Conference of 1921 by devising any system for consulting with the Dominions over foreign policy. No official information had been transmitted to Canada about the imminence of war in the eastern Mediterranean. Nevertheless, the British Prime Minister, David Lloyd George, cabled the Dominions, in September, 1922, with an inquiry about their support in a possible war. The implicit request for troops was contrary to the custom of the Dominions volunteering aid. The climax was the press release, prepared by Winston Churchill, the Colonial Secretary, in which the British government appealed over the heads of the Dominion governments to their people.

Mackenzie King, absent from Ottawa on a trip to his constituency, first learned of developments from a newspaper reporter. He was angry and determined to oppose such tactics. Certain that his French-Canadian supporters, as well as the Progressive Party — which the Liberals hoped to absorb — would be firmly opposed, he called a meeting of the cabinet. The result was a dispatch to London that "only Parliament could decide" on a matter of such importance as approving the offer of Canadian troops.

MACKENZIE KING'S THINKING AT THE TIME OF THE CHANAK AFFAIR[380]

King recorded his reaction to the Chanak affair. Referring to the British request for troops, he wrote on September 17, 1922:

I confess it [the official message] annoyed me. It is drafted designedly to play the imperial game, to test out centralization vs. autonomy as regards European wars. . . . I have thought out my plans. . . . No contingent will go without parliament being summoned in first instance. . . . I shall not commit myself one way or the other, but keep the responsibility for prlt. — . . . I do not believe prlt. would sanction the sending of a contingent. The French Canadians will be opposed. I believe most if not all our members in Ont. & the maritime provinces will be opposed. I am not sure of B.C. — I feel confident the Progressives will be opposed almost to a man. — It is the time now to bring them into the Government . . . to strengthen us in our attitude of refusing to send a contingent without sanction of prlt. . . . I am sure the people of Canada are against participation in this European war.

League of Nations, Geneva, Aug.-Sept. 1928. L to R: O. D. Skelton, Under-Secretary of State for External Affairs, Canada; Hon. Philippe Roy, Canadian Minister to France; Sen. the Hon. Raoul Dandurand; the Rt. Hon. W. L. Mackenzie King, Prime Minister of Canada; the Hon. Charles Dunning, M.P., Minister of Railways and Canals; Dr. W. A. Riddell, Canadian Advisory Officer, Geneva

The Conservative Leader of the Opposition scolded the government's inaction. Meighen declared that Canada's reply to Britain's call for assistance should have been "Ready, aye, ready; we stand by you." In Meighen's view, Canada was obliged to support the Empire in upholding peace in the Eastern Mediterranean — because Canada had taken part in the settlement less than three years before. But such a stand — however logical — had little appeal for Canadians, among whom the memories of World War I were still fresh. Mackenzie King had judged that Canadians were in no mood to run the risk of entanglement in another European war. When the situation at Chanak did not explode into war, the Prime Minister could take satisfaction from the consequences of his refusal to give unquestioning support to Great Britain.

The Chanak affair may have been a minor event, but it was one of major significance for Canada and for the British Empire. It nullified the efforts of preceding years to develop a centralized control of imperial foreign policy. It discredited the idea that Great Britain would co-operate with the Dominions in a policy of joint responsibility for foreign affairs. Of more fundamental importance still, Chanak had dramatized the fact that British interests and Canadian interests were growing increasingly divergent. Greater Canadian independence appeared to be essential, if not inevitable, to progress.

D

THE HALIBUT TREATY

On the question of Chanak, Canada had needed to play only a passive part in events that pointed the way toward greater autonomy. In the following year, 1923, the Canadian government helped create a situation which produced a further step in the same direction. To do so, Mackenzie King took advantage of the perennial problem of Canadian-American fishing rights. The subject was not a spectacular one, yet it was appropriate enough for a man who would never be accused of colourful leadership.

Officials in the United States and Canada had come to an agreement in principle on a closed season on halibut fishing in the north Pacific. Such negotiations had been conducted in accordance with the custom of many years standing, whereby Canada had the freedom to arrange commercial treaties. However, it was still standard procedure that an official of the British government would sign the final treaty before it was submitted to the Crown for ratification.

Mackenzie King had decided that the time had come for excluding the British government from Canada's treaty-making process. Just as final details were being completed, King informed the government in London of his intentions. Canada's Minister of Fisheries, Ernest Lapointe, was dispatched to Washington. He alone signed the Halibut Treaty for Canada, while the British Ambassador waited for the call that never came. The Canadian government then resisted attempts by the United States' Senate to require the participation of imperial authorities, and the Halibut Treaty became law.

CANADA'S STAND ON THE SIGNING OF THE HALIBUT TREATY[381]

A telegram from Governor-General Byng to the British Ambassador in Washington, dated at Ottawa, February 28, 1923:

Mr. Lapointe in Toronto to-day. Will proceed this afternoon from Toronto to Washington. . . . Canadian Government is of view that, Treaty being one of concern solely to Canada and the

United States and not affecting in any particular any imperial interest, signature on behalf of Canada by Mr. Lapointe, who has full powers, should be sufficient. . . .

Canada was still not a sovereign state in its negotiation of the Halibut Treaty, but the experience had nevertheless been useful. Canadian diplomats had carried out both the practical and the formal stages of an operation in foreign relations. The Imperial Conference of 1923 not only recognized the Halibut Treaty as a precedent, but also laid the groundwork for future conferences. From that time on, each Dominion had broadened powers to make its own treaties with other nations. The obligation that clearly remained was one of consultation with other members of the Empire in case they might be involved or might wish to participate.

THE 1923 IMPERIAL CONFERENCE[382]

On October 8, 1923, at the Imperial Conference, Mackenzie King delivered his statement on Canada's position:

Canada is not putting forward any new principles. . . . Canada stands on the old principle of responsible democracy. . . . For seventy years our most honoured leaders have done what they could to develop the basic principle of responsible government, and to apply it in steadily increasing measure to the whole range of domestic and foreign affairs. . . . We believe that the decision of Great Britain on any important public issue, domestic or foreign, should be made by the people of Britain, their representatives in Parliament, and the Government responsible to that Parliament. So the decision of Canada on any important issue, domestic or foreign, we believe should be made by the people of Canada, their representatives in Parliament, and the Government responsible to that Parliament.

———

Lord Curzon, the Secretary of State for Foreign Affairs, in a letter to his wife of November 8, 1923, comments on King's stand at the Conference:

The last two days have been a whirlwind of negotiations and trouble in order to get the Imperial Conference to agree to a report (written by myself) on Foreign Affairs. The obstacle has been Mackenzie King, the Canadian, who is both obstinate, tiresome and stupid, and is nervously afraid of being turned out of his own Parliament when he gets back. . . .

E

THE KING — BYNG CRISIS

The next stage in the growth of Canadian autonomy was prefaced by a constitutional crisis within Canada between Mackenzie King and the Governor-General, Lord Byng, the former commander of the Canadian Corps in World War I. The Prime Minister had called an election in October, 1925, in the hope of securing a strong majority. His expectations were dashed, however, when the Liberals lost 16 seats and the Conservatives increased their representation from 50 to 116. The Conservatives had become the largest group in the House of Commons, but they had less than a majority; besides the 101 Liberals, there were 24 Progressives, 2 Labour and 2 Independents. King, therefore, decided not to resign in favour of the Conservative leader, Arthur Meighen.

The Progressives continued their support of the Liberal government for a time, but some of their members wavered after hearing reports of wrongdoing in the Customs Department. King had to act quickly if he wished to forestall defeat under a cloud of scandal. But when he asked the Governor-General to dissolve Parliament and call an election, Lord Byng refused — on the grounds that two elections within nine months would not be in the best interests of the Canadian people. King then resigned and Meighen was asked to form a government. Within a few days, Meighen was defeated by one vote and he too asked the Governor-General for a dissolution. The request, unlike that of King's, was granted.

In the election campaign of 1926, Mackenzie King made the constitutional question the centre of his appeal to the voters. The Governor-General, he claimed, had denied the principles of responsible government by refusing King's request for dissolution. Then Lord Byng had compounded his error by granting the same request to Meighen, who had been defeated in the House of Commons. Clearly such action by the Governor-General was a threat to Canadian autonomy.

THE KING-BYNG CONTROVERSY[383]

[a]*Mackenzie King, in the House of Commons, June 30 - July 1, 1926:*

. . . . The difference between a crown colony and a self-governing Dominion is that the Governor

General of a self-governing Dominion acts upon the advice of his responsible minister . . . since this Dominion was formed, since confederation in 1867, there is not a single instance where a Prime Minister has advised dissolution and has been refused it . . . I feel we are called upon at this time to see that the principle of responsible self-government is fully carried out. . . .

Is there then no constitutional issue at stake?

---

bGovernor-General Byng to the Secretary of State for the Dominions, in a telegram of June 30, 1926.

. . . . A Governor General has the absolute right of granting dissolution or refusing it. The refusal is a very dangerous decision, it embodies the rejection of the advice of the accredited Minister, which is the bed-rock of Constitutional Government. . . . But if the advice offered is considered by the Governor General to be wrong and unfair, and not for the welfare of the people, it behoves [sic] him to act in what he considers the best interests of the country.

---

cArthur Meighen, September 1, 1926, in MAC-LEAN'S MAGAZINE:

. . . to my mind, the Governor-General acted correctly and well within his powers, and in conformity with established constitutional usage. I cannot, therefore, see that there is any real issue at all. . . .

Mr. King tried to run away from the just condemnation of himself and his Government by Parliament, but he was not permitted to do so; he thereupon hatched a constitutional issue to act as a smoke screen. That is the case in a nut-shell.

Meighen was the convenient scapegoat for King's strategy. Blamed for advising Lord Byng to act improperly, the Conservative leader bore the brunt of attacks which the Liberals shrewdly avoided making on the representative of the Crown. Meighen's denial that a constitutional crisis even existed gained little sympathy, and his campaign to make Liberal corruption the central election issue did not succeed.

The Liberals emerged victorious from the election. With the support of the few remaining Progressives, King was able to count on a majority government, and the Conservatives had been reduced from 116 to 91 members in the House of Commons. The last act of Lord Byng was to swear in the new government. The brilliant but politically unwise Meighen was defeated in his own Manitoba riding of Portage la Prairie. He was soon replaced as leader of the Conservative Party by R. B. Bennett, a Calgary lawyer.

Mackenzie King was now regarded by many of his followers as a proven political genius, as a leader who had rescued his party after years of uncertainty. The legend of his political infallibility had begun to spread across the Dominion. Jubilantly he proclaimed his successful defense of responsible government and Canadian autonomy, so recently threatened by the representative of the British government.

F

IMPERIAL CONFERENCE OF 1926

During the five years prior to 1926, a series of events had been responsible for loosening the formal bonds among the members of the British Empire. The Canadian government, in the hands of Mackenzie King, had played no small part in hastening the process of decentralization and strengthening Canada's controls over its own affairs. But the development of practical autonomy had not been matched by any constitutional changes in the Empire. The time had come for new definitions of the status of the Dominions. Fresh from the "King-Byng crisis," the Canadian government joined such members of the Empire as South Africa and the Irish Free State in requesting formal recognition on a number of matters — including a clarification of the role of the Governor-General.

The opportunity came at the Imperial Conference in 1926. The Balfour Report — named for the former British Prime Minister who acted as chairman of the Inter-Imperial Relations Committee — was the resulting description of the changed British Empire. In addition to defining the status of the Dominions, the Balfour Report dealt with a number of specific questions.

THE 1926 IMPERIAL CONFERENCE[384]

The following fundamental principles were enunciated at the 1926 Imperial Conference: Status of Great Britain and the Dominions:

. . . we refer to the group of self-governing communities composed of Great Britain and the Dominions. Their position and mutual relation may be readily defined. They are autonomous Communities within the British Empire, equal in status, in no way subordinate one to another in any aspect of their domestic or external affairs, though united by a common allegiance to the Crown, and freely associated as members of the British Commonwealth of Nations.

Position of the Governor-General:

In our opinion it is an essential consequence of the equality of status existing among the members of the British Commonwealth of Nations that the Governor General of the Dominion is the representative of the Crown . . . and that he is not the representative or agent of His Majesty's Government in Great Britain or of any Department of that Government.

The position of the Governor-General was re-defined as being that of the representative of the Crown; in no way was he to be the agent of the British government as he had been in the past. It followed that communication between the Canadian government and the government of Great Britain should take place directly, rather than through the Governor-General. In recognition of this change, Great Britain appointed a High Commissioner in 1928 to reside in Canada for the purpose of facilitating contacts between the two governments.

The Original Group of Seven: L to R: F. H. Varley, A. Y. Jackson, Lawren Harris, Barker Fairley (non-member), F. H. Johnston, Arthur Lismer, J. E. H. MacDonald, (Frank Carmichael is absent)

The Report had also recorded the principle that each Dominion government had the right to advise the Crown on all matters of its own affairs. The related question of the British government's authority to disallow Dominion laws, an authority which had not been used on a Canadian law since 1873, was not fully resolved. However, since British disallowance of Dominion laws had become a political impossibility, it was no longer an impediment to inter-imperial harmony.

G

THE STATUTE OF WESTMINSTER, 1931

The Balfour Report was both a summation of the existing nature of the Empire and a signal for more changes to come. Even before the end of 1926, within a few months of the conclusion of the Imperial Conference, Canada had appointed its first foreign minister — Vincent Massey took up residence in Washington as Canada's Minister to the United States. The Canadian legation, which began operating in 1927, was independent of the British embassy and concerned only with Canadian-American questions. Other countries seemed ready to accept the Dominions as fully self-governing in matters of trade and other international affairs. In 1927 Canada was elected as one of the non-permanent members on the Council of the League of Nations.

The Statute of Westminster in 1931 gave legal effect to the decisions incorporated in the Balfour Report and recognized the existence of the British Commonwealth of Nations in place of the old Empire. The British Crown, in the words of the preamble to the Statute, "is the symbol of the free association of the members of the British Commonwealth of Nations." No act passed by a

Dominion Parliament was to be "void or inoperative" because it was inconsistent with the law of England. Nor would any act passed by the British Parliament extend to any Dominion unless a Dominion so requested and consented.

CANADA'S ROAD TO AUTONOMY[385]

The historian A. R. M. Lower reviews Canada's advance to autonomy in the 1920's, culminating in the Statute of Westminster of 1931:

The indirect refusal to assist Great Britain over the Chanak incident, 1922, was the first notice given that Canada would make up her own mind about foreign affairs. It was followed by the still more emphatic show of independence involved in the way in which the Halibut Treaty of 1923 with the United States was signed. . . .

The [Imperial] Conference of 1926 solved the great problems of inter-imperial relationships in principle but left a good many details to be worked out. This process was completed at the next Conference, in 1930. . . .

The Statute of Westminster came as close as was practicable without revolutionary scissors to legislating the independence of the 'Dominions'. There is good ground for holding December 11, 1931 as Canada's Independence Day, for on that day she became a sovereign state. . . .

The Statute of Westminster could not properly be considered a constitution for the British Commonwealth. Most of the changes in the constitutional operation of the Commonwealth had already been established by convention and practice. Nor had the Statute granted sovereignty, in the sense of independence, to the Dominions. The British Parliament was still the only body which could possibly pass laws for the entire Commonwealth, or repeal the Statute of Westminster. Canada was not even empowered to amend the British North America Act, the heart of the Canadian constitution.

Yet the practice of Canadian independence was never in doubt in the years to follow. By 1949 legal autonomy was established, when appeals to the Judicial Committee of the Privy Council were abolished and the Supreme Court of Canada became the final court of appeal for Canada. In 1947 the Canadian government omitted "Dominion of" from the country's name so as to eliminate any reminder of Canada's relation to Great Britain as subordinate.

The matter that has remained unresolved until the present day is the Canadian constitution. Canada has still not made arrangements for "bringing the constitution home," and has followed the practice of securing amendments by advising the British government to implement the necessary changes. Conditions within Canada, and not any objections from Great Britain, have frustrated plans to place Canada's constitution under strictly Canadian control. The federal government has not been able to reach agreement with the provinces on a way to remove the British Parliament from the amending procedure. The provinces have been fearful of any change that may threaten their powers, particularly those stated in Section 92 of the British North America Act.

The Liberal government in 1964 put forward the so-called Fulton-Favreau formula.* This was the product of joint efforts by successive Conservative and Liberal administrations. Since acceptance by all the provinces was needed, the project was discarded when Quebec dissented. Later discussion has centred on the need for rewriting, or replacing entirely, the B.N.A. Act and other parts of the constitution. As later chapters will explain, recent complications in the relations between French-speaking and English-speaking Canadians and between federal and provincial levels of government have given greater urgency to the question of creating a constitution "made in Canada."

* E. Davie Fulton was Minister of Justice during the administration of the Rt. Hon. John Diefenbaker (1957-1963). Guy Favreau held the same portfolio after the Liberal Party took office in 1963 under the Rt. Hon. Lester B. Pearson.

Canadian Pavillion at British Empire Exhibition, Wembley, England, 1924

27

THE INTER-WAR YEARS: CANADA AND INTERNATIONAL RESPONSIBILITY

A

CANADA'S MEMBERSHIP IN THE LEAGUE OF NATIONS

The Armistice on November 11, 1918 marked the end of World War I. Led by Great Britain, France and the United States, the victorious nations faced the problems of a devastated European continent. The spirit of revenge, fed on the shock and revulsion over the unprecedented destruction and suffering caused by the war, expressed itself in the treatment given to defeated Germany. That country and its supporters were declared to be solely responsible for having inflicted the holocaust on the world. Terms of the Treaty of Versailles, completed in Paris after months of work, were designed to reduce Germany for all time to a condition of impotence. Never again, so the argument went, would Germany have the strength to threaten peace.

The hope of ensuring that the war of 1914 to 1918 would be "the war to end all wars" led to another important step by the delegates at Paris. This was the creation of the League of Nations. Through the untiring efforts of Woodrow Wilson, President of the United States, terms providing for the League were incorporated within the Treaty of Versailles itself. Over the objections of skeptical European leaders, an international organization dedicated to preserving peace was born.

The League of Nations was based on the principle of collective security. All members were to be responsible for co-operating against the outbreak of war. Should the security of any member be threatened, the others were to assist in preventing armed conflict. Consultation, rather than the application of force, was to be the principal service which the League could provide. The International Court of Justice was set up as a world court for passing judgment on disagreements referred to it by League members. People around the world were hopeful that justice, not force, would prevail in international affairs, and that the League would be successful in achieving its goal of universal disarmament.

The Covenant, or charter, of the League, to be realistic, had to provide at least some measures stronger than negotiation and judicial decisions. According to the controversial Article X, League members were called upon "to respect and preserve as against external aggression the territorial integrity and existing political independence of all members." Moreover, Article XVI stated that sanctions* could be imposed on a member if it went to war for a reason other than to preserve its own security. This meant that the League had the authority to isolate a belligerent member from trade with the others in order to bring it to its senses.

The weaknesses of the League were evident to many from the beginning. There was little sign that nations would co-operate any more effectively than they had in the past. Old selfish ambitions had not died in the war just fought. In fact, the war had created new problems. Traditional powers such as France and Great Britain remained anxious to maintain world leadership. Not all nations were willing to join the new organization, and no special military force was created to back up decisions made by the League.

At the League's inception, Canada's choice was not one of accepting or declining membership. Rather it was a question of membership either as part of the British Empire, with Great Britain having the principal influence in deciding policy for the Dominions as well as for itself, or of separate representation. Sir Robert Borden and his colleagues concentrated on securing the latter. Their main argument was that Canada was entitled, by virtue of its war effort, to at least the same recognition as that accorded to such smaller countries as Belgium.

---

* Sanctions could take the form of restrictions on trade or, in extreme cases, military blockade.

For Canada, then, status in the League was inseparable from status in the British Empire; each would affect the strength of the other. Imperialists in Great Britain were no less aware of the fact. In their view, a common foreign policy for the Empire would be impossible if the Dominions were given individual seats in the world organization, and the Empire would be severely weakened. Borden met this objection on Canada's behalf by affirming his belief in the need to find ways for mutual consultation among members of the Empire. If sufficient effort and imagination were forthcoming, policies based on consensus could be as effective in peacetime as they had been during the latter part of World War I.

Foreign nations, such as France, voiced a very serious objection. Membership for the Dominions could mean that Great Britain actually had multiple representation and, therefore, several votes on League matters — while all other nations would have but a single vote. Even this argument was overcome, however, by the forceful stand taken by Canada and the other Dominions.

When the Covenant of the League of Nations was drafted, the Dominions were admitted as original members. Although they were listed in association with Great Britain, and other nations continued to regard them as British colonies, the Dominions were granted a position which was substantially that of independent states. It was not immediately clear, but Canada's step toward independence was also a step toward new and potentially far-reaching responsibilities.

CANADA'S OBJECTION TO ARTICLE X, 1921[386]

J. C. Doherty, the Canadian representative at the League of Nations, objected to the responsibility imposed by Article X. From his speech on June 1, 1921:

This article is open . . . to the very gravest objections, both generally, and from the point of view of countries in the condition and stage of development of Canada in particular.

———

(a) *Generally.* — The clauses makes each one of the nation signatories of the convention the guarantor of the actual territorial possessions of all members of the League. . . .

———

(b) *Objections particular to Canada and other dominions, and nations whose conditions may be similar.* — . . . it is right that a guarantee such as proposed should be given, it does not follow that it should be given by all the states. It may be right that one class of states should give it, and entirely wrong to exact it of another. Many reasons for such distinction exist, and all of them justify Canada's being classed with those states upon which this onerous obligation should not be imposed. . . .

———

. . . . If the great powers are to be the exclusive arbiters of matters of general interests, why should they not, for the same reason, be the exclusive protectors of these general interests? . . . .

B

CANADA'S POLICY TOWARD THE LEAGUE

With the same kind of caution that had marked its imperial relations in recent decades, in the League Canada resisted automatic inclusion in actions involving threats to world peace. Thus Canada was one of the countries most critical of Article X of the League Covenant. From the time the Article was first proposed, the Canadian delegation attacked it as an unreasonable obligation for a country located in the "peaceful" Western Hemisphere. Canada — young, far from the traditional areas of military conflict and belonging to the continent protected by the United States navy — was unlikely to be the target of aggression.

The failure of the United States to join the League of Nations was, therefore, a blow to Canada. Americans had been disillusioned by their brief encounter with the troubles of the Old World and turned away from President Wilson's vision of the United States as an arbiter and moral force in world diplomacy. When Congress rejected Wilson's plea that his nation participate in the League, the United States embarked on the path of isolationism from international affairs. This development left Canada in the unenviable position as a kind of representative of North America, perhaps more liable for military commitment in far-away disputes and perhaps without the support of its powerful neighbour.

Once the United States had made its disappointing decision, Canada had even greater reason for protecting itself against foreign entanglements. Repeated attempts to have Article X deleted from the League Covenant were unsuccessful, but Canada had made its position clear. When other plans for strengthening the obligations of League members were brought forward, Canada preferred not to be involved.

Canadian leaders saw the League of Nations as a means of advancing the Dominion's autonomy, not — as was the case with many countries — as an agency vital to its own interests in the world. Canada did serve on various committees and accepted positions on the Council and other bodies of the League, but successive governments in the inter-war period were content with a limited role in the League's business. They recognized that any Canadian foreign policy had to be certain of favourable reception in London and Washington. As a North American nation having historic links with Great Britain, Canada could best hope for a world role in which it formed part of a "North-Atlantic triangle."

As the prosperous twenties passed one by one into memory, Canadians seemed to have the best of all possible worlds. Snugly secure from any danger of war and richer materially, if not spiritually, than ever before, Canada had little interest in existing or potential problems elsewhere in the world. When European nations entered into agreements to buttress the League of Nation's ability to guarantee peace, the Canadian government consistently expressed disinterest. With the watchful Mackenzie King at the helm, Canada was quite willing to be overlooked in the Geneva Protocol of 1924 and the Locarno agreements of 1925. Canada was a party to the Kellogg-Briand Pact of 1928, but that embodied a principle to which Canada could comfortably subscribe. Arranged in part by the United States, the treaty provided that nations signing it should renounce war as an instrument of national policy.

CANADA'S OBJECTIONS TO THE GENEVA PROTOCOL, 1924[387]

The Canadian representative, Senator Raoul Dandurand, expressed Canada's reluctance to be committed in advance to action on wars not involving Canada's vital interests. Note the isolationist sentiment in his statement:

The falling away of the United States who did not join the League has increased, in our eyes, the risks assumed, and the history of Europe in the past five years has not been such as to lessen that apprehension.

The heavy sacrifices to which we agreed for the re-establishment of peace in Europe led us to reflect on what the future might hold in store.

May I be permitted to add that in this association of mutual insurance against fire the risks assumed by the different states are not equal? We live in a fire-proof house, far from inflammable materials. A vast ocean separates us from Europe. Canada therefore believed it to be her duty to seek a precise interpretation of what appeared to her to be the indefinite obligations included in Article 10 of the Covenant.

C

THE OTTAWA CONFERENCE ON TRADE, 1932

The decade of the 1930's began with the economic depression that confronted leaders of the industrialized nations with a terrible dilemma: how could they bring about a recovery of sound international trade and finance? Everywhere the economic paralysis seemed to be spreading, and with it went unprecedented problems of unemployment, want and despair. As the crisis deepened, individual nations shrank from the risk of trusting others. Instead of showing willingness to cooperate, they turned to such nationalistic devices as high tariffs in the futile hope that such barriers would serve as some kind of protection.

Canada found itself with no choice but to fight with the same weapons that were used by others in attacking the problems of trade. When the Commonwealth Conference opened on a note of optimism in Ottawa in 1932, Prime Minister R. B. Bennett spoke of co-operation among Great Britain and the Dominions. The negotiations soon showed, however, that even the members of the Commonwealth were mutually suspicious, each one cautious about making concessions and each intent on hard bargaining.

Great Britain was faced with the choice of abandoning its historic insistence on free trade or of risking further Commonwealth breakdown in the face of precarious world conditions. R. B. Bennett's government gained a victory of sorts when the British agreed to raise tariffs against foreign products while admitting a wide range of Canadian goods at preferred rates. Treaties with other Dominions completed the effect of a kind of Commonwealth front against the rest of the world.

THE IMPERIAL ECONOMIC CONFERENCE OF 1932 IN OTTAWA[388]

a*Prime Minister R. B. Bennett reported to the House of Commons on October 12, 1932, the tariff agreements reached at the Conference:*

These agreements were made in good faith between friends and kinsmen. They do not represent the result of dispassionate bargaining . . . I can tell you that while naturally and properly each delegation did its best for its own country, we all realized that no agreement could be lasting or beneficial which was one-sided. . . . In the result, we have agreements which, I claim, are fair and because of their fairness, I believe, will be enduring. It is in our interest that they should be enduring, for in my view advantages under these agreements are not secured through drying up world channels of trade. On the contrary, the more profitable shall be our inter-empire trade, the greater the volume of commodities which shall pass from one country to the other, the more certain it is that Canada . . . will be the better able to reach out into other markets. . . .

――――

The Rt. Hon. Neville Chamberlain, a British delegate, was critical of Bennett's conduct at the Conference:

. . . . Most of the difficulties centred round the personality of Bennett. Full of high Imperial sentiments, he had done little to put them into practice. Instead of guiding the Conference in his capacity of Chairman, he has acted merely as the leader of the Canadian delegation. In that capacity he has strained our patience to the limit. . . .

Did Canada's stand at the Ottawa Conference represent a forward-looking approach in foreign affairs? Some would argue that the question is not a fair one, since Canada had to act in the prevailing spirit of self-defence. Others would up-

Dominion Bureau of Statistics Computer in Operation, Ottawa, 1930's

hold Canada's lead in negotiating trade agreements that demonstrated that at least part of the world — the Commonwealth — had the will to increase the mutual flow of trade. Still others would point to the hostile reaction of foreign countries, particularly the United States, and claim that the Ottawa Agreements actually reduced world trade as a whole, and thereby contributed to a worsening of the depression.

One thing is certain: Canadians were no different from others in believing that their own immediate problems deserved priority. For the masses of unemployed across the country — the idle fishermen or miners of the Maritimes, or the drought-ridden farmers of the prairies — there was enough anguish at home without worrying about the misfortunes of men in foreign lands.

―――――――――――――――――――――――――――

D

CANADA AND THE MANCHURIAN CRISIS

The political leadership of the western democracies was undistinguished in the twenties, but favourable world conditions forestalled any serious ill effects. The succeeding decade, however, brought many forms of challenge which exposed any assumption that continued progress was automatic. Wars of aggression, first by Japan and then by Italy and Germany, evoked only timid responses from other major nations until the world was faced for the second time in twenty years with global war. The democracies were tested in the 1930's and found wanting; the problems were bigger than the men who had to face them.

The first world crisis arose from Japan's invasion of Manchuria in 1931, and the subsequent

Japanese-China conflicts that merged into World War II. The major powers of the League of Nations were reluctant to intervene in the struggle between the Asian rivals, both of which were League members. The League conducted extensive investigations and sought to persuade Japan to accept conciliation. But when the Japanese refused to co-operate, neither economic nor military sanctions were invoked, although both were possible under the League's charter.

Canada followed the lead of Great Britain; R. B. Bennett's Conservative government made clear its unwillingness to become involved in military action in the Far East. Canada, in fact, shared for many months the illusions of major League members that Japan would halt its aggression to avoid alienating them. Fearful of losing trade with Japan at a time when the world depression was worsening, Canada wanted to avoid taking sides.

CANADA AND THE MANCHURIAN CRISIS, 1932[389]
C. H. Cahan, Secretary of State and the Canadian representative at the League, in his speech of December 8, 1932, echoed the sentiments of other members — not to become too involved in the crisis:

It seems to me that this assembly may not wholly disregard the emphatic statement made at the opening of this discussion by M. Matsuoka, the delegate of Japan, that the Japanese government has not at any time allowed itself to be connected with the independence movement in Manchuria, that it did not then and does not now want Manchuria, but that it only desires the preservation of its rights and interests therein.

. . . . If Japan indicates any genuine readiness to seek a solution consistent with League obligations as well as her own special interests in Manchuria, it would seem undesirable to make such a settlement difficult by precipitate action. At the same time, after having exhausted all available means for effecting the reconciliation and amicable agreement of the two parties, further delay without any clear evidence of readiness to co-operate on the part of Japan might prove most unfortunate.

By 1933 the Japanese had gone ahead with the creation of a subordinate state in conquered Chinese territory, and, in response to criticism by the League, withdrew from membership. Canada had upheld the principles of observing international agreements and peaceful settlement of disputes, but it had no policy for situations where other nations did not. Its support for disarmament was to prove similarly disappointing; conferences between 1932 and 1935 ended in failure.

E

CANADA AND THE ETHIOPIAN CRISIS

By 1935 Adolf Hilter, whose mad ambitions for power would plunge the world into another global war, was restoring Germany's military capacity. But another European aggressor would strike a first blow at international law and order. The Italian dictator, Benito Mussolini, had decided that his nation's destiny lay in recapturing the glory of the ancient Roman Empire. In the spring of 1935, the weak African country of Ethiopia fell victim to the tyrant's ambition.

The subjects of Emperor Haile Selassie fought vainly to repel the conquest; the League of Nations moved to condemn yet another aggression by one member against another. Sanctions on trade, which had not been applied against the more powerful nation of Japan, were voted with the idea of reducing Italy's ability to complete its barbaric plan. But the League did not go far enough in implementing a boycott of trade with Italy, and soon had to consider more drastic action if it wanted results.

Mussolini's war machine was dependent on supplies of imported oil, and a total ban by the League on trade with Italy would very likely have forced that country to desist. Even Great Britain and France held back from so forceful a decision. But the Canadian representative, W. A. Riddell, proposed that oil be added to the list of economic sanctions against Italy. The Canadian government was in the process of changing hands, as Mackenzie King had just defeated R. B. Bennett in the election of October, 1935. Forced by circumstances to act on his own initiative, Riddell believed that his strong recommendation was a logical result of Canada's stand up to that point on the question of Ethiopia.

CANADA AND THE DISPUTE OVER ITALY'S AGGRESSION AGAINST ETHIOPIA[390]
When the proposal of sanctions at the League of Nations was widely interpreted as a Canadian initiative, Mackenzie King promptly dismissed Riddell's action as a personal decision, and not the policy of Canada:

. . . . What was my amazement when on reading a morning paper I found that Doctor Riddell at Geneva was reported to have proposed to add oil, coal, and steel to the list of commodities which by sanctions were to be prohibited from export to Italy. No instructions whatever had been sent to him authorizing anything of the kind . . . word was immediately to be sent that no action of any kind was to be taken by Doctor Riddell without specific instructions from the government. I asked whether that communication had been sent, and was informed that it had been sent within an hour after receipt of the communication from Doctor Riddell. So that so far as the present administration is concerned I say we gave specific direction to Doctor Riddell that he was to do nothing in the matter of extending sanctions without express direction from the government itself.

News of the "Canadian proposal," as the overseas press described it, ignited furious controversy in Canada. The most pointed opposition arose in Quebec, where sympathy for Italy, the home of the papacy, was very strong and where some charged that the League's pressure on Italy was a manoeuvre by Protestant, imperial Britain. Canadian public opinion was divided, and Mackenzie King's government feared taking a stand that could not be certain of inspiring confidence among the people. Neither Great Britain within the League nor the United States outside the League seemed likely to take the risks associated with real preventative steps against Italy. The Canadian Prime Minister, therefore, refused a leadership role for his country. Although insisting that Canada would co-operate in whatever decisions the League might reach, he declared that Riddell's proposal was not the policy of the Canadian government.

The major powers seemed to take their cue from Canada, although it is likely they would have come to the same conclusions regardless, and the proposed sanctions on oil were dropped. Whatever the explanation, the League of Nations had failed at its moment of greatest challenge. If a "paper tiger" like Mussolini could flaunt world opinion and feel confident in the act of forfeiting League membership, what might be the attitude of men heading a government equally militant but commanding far more power?

F

CANADA AND NAZI AGGRESSION

While Mussolini was successfully defying the League of Nations, Nazi Germany was rapidly emerging as a far greater threat to Europe and the world. After introducing conscription, forbidden by the Treaty of Versailles, Hitler dramatically violated the settlement of 1919 by marching troops in to reoccupy the Rhineland. The date was March, 1936. In October of the same year, Hitler and Mussolini concluded the treaty which established the "Rome-Berlin Axis." The League's vacillating handling of the Ethiopian crisis, by trying to avoid antagonizing Mussolini, had neither prevented the alliance of dictators nor discouraged their further irresponsible behaviour.

Through 1937, the Nazis supported the Nationalists in the Spanish Civil War (1936-1939), perfected brutality as an instrument of power within Germany and plotted territorial expansion. Early in 1938, Austria succumbed to Nazi terror and was ruthlessly annexed by Germany. Hitler had satisfied himself that, with Italy as an ally and Great Britain and France standing back ostrich-like from the sorry proceedings, he had virtually a free hand in central Europe. Next he turned his attention to Czechoslovakia, where the population included a large German minority. The pretext he gave to the rest of Europe was his desire to unite the German-speaking peoples and to obtain *Lebensraum* — living-space — for the growing population of Germany.

Germany's appetite for expansion seems, in retrospect, to have been so clearly exposed by the fall of 1938 that no one could have failed to recognize it. Great Britain and others did, in fact, begin to increase spending for rearmament. But the fear of war and its consequences was so deeply embedded in the thinking of most men that the most acceptable policy for a government to adopt was appeasement — grant Hitler his demands and hope that his ambitions would soon be satisfied. Consequently, Great Britain and France signed an agreement at Munich in September, 1938, by which Germany could occupy the part of Czechoslovakia known as Sudetenland provided that the rest of the country remain free.

Neville Chamberlain, Prime Minister of Great Britain, returned home from Munich to receive the acclaim of his citizens for having won "peace in our time." The relief which people felt in the democracies was short-lived, however, as Hitler followed up his success by seizing the remainder of Czechoslovakia early in 1939. The hopeless policy of appeasement was finally abandoned as the rest of Europe scrambled to prepare for the war that most men had refused even to contemplate. Following the signing of a non-aggression pact with the Soviet Union in August, Hitler sent his armies rolling into Poland on September 1, 1939. Two days later, Great Britain and France declared war on Germany.

Since regaining office in 1935, Mackenzie King had done little to arouse Canadians to serious thinking about foreign affairs. As crisis followed crisis in Europe, King remained evasive about the government's plans in the event of a major war. With a regularity that struck his critics as monotonous, the Prime Minister repeated his round-about replies that Canada was a peace-loving nation and could contribute little to resolving foreign disputes by pronouncing judgments on them. Canada would approach each situation on its merits and, should a case arise where the country was confronted with the choice of peace of war, "Parliament would decide."

KING'S STATEMENT TO THE HOUSE OF COMMONS ON CANADIAN FOREIGN POLICY[391]

On January 25, 1937, Mackenzie King stated Canada's foreign policy and praised Great Britain's appeasement policy:

. . . . In any action this parliament takes, we shall do well to have regard for the world situation as it is to-day and for the way in which our action may be viewed by other parts of the world. If ever there was need for unity on the part of nations and peoples who hold certain cherished ideals of freedom and liberty, that need exists to-day. We have need for unity in our own country. Nothing can do this country more injury than internal disruptions and differences. We have need for unity as between all parts of the British commonwealth of nations. I for one believe that the British commonwealth to-day is exercising a greater influence for peace than any other force in the world. . . . What Britain has done to appease antagonisms in the last few years is something that the rest of the world hardly begins to appreciate. What, I wonder, would be the condition of Europe to-day if Britain had not endeavoured, as she has at every moment, to avert or circumscribe conflict? She has been the great pacifier.

The nearest the Canadian Government came to a declaration of policy was the support given at the Imperial Conference in 1937 to Great Britain's strategy of appeasement. Following the Conference, King made a trip to meet Adolf Hitler and came away convinced that the German leader was not a man to fear as an aggressor. Even when Hitler's behaviour clearly became a menace, King clung desperately to the notion that peace could still be preserved.

King's dilemma was a product, in large part, of his fear that a clear-cut policy might cause a serious division in Canadian public opinion. Remembering the tragic conflict between French-speaking and English-speaking Canadians during World War I over conscription and other issues, King was wary of making any commitments that might lead to another domestic feud. Preserving national unity was the responsibility the Prime Minister placed above all others. Canada's best hope for continued peace within the country was to avoid involvement in an overseas war. If a war did erupt

A Section of Halifax Harbour, N.S., 1930

and Canada's future was clearly at stake, Canadians would forget their differences and meet the challenge in a common spirit of determination.

KING CONGRATULATES CHAMBERLAIN ON THE MUNICH AGREEMENT[392]

Mackenzie King showed the false optimism shared by many in the Western world when he congratulated the British Prime Minister on concluding the ill-fated Munich agreement with Adolf Hitler in September, 1938:

The heart of Canada is rejoicing tonight at the success which has crowned your unremitting efforts for peace. May I convey to you the warm congratulations of the Canadian people and with them an expression of their gratitude that is felt from one end of the Dominion to the other? My colleagues in the government join with me in unbounded admiration at the service you have rendered mankind. Your achievements in the past month alone will ensure you an illustrious and abiding place among the great conciliators which the United Kingdom, the British Commonwealth, and the whole world will continue to honour.

On the very brink of chaos, with passions flaming and armies marching, the voice of reason has found a way out of the conflict which no people in their hearts desire but none seemed able to avert. A turning point in the world's history will be reached if, as we hope, tonight's agreement means a halt to the mad race of arms and a new start in building a partnership of all peoples. May you have health and strength to carry your great work to its completion.

IX

THE MODERN NATION: CANADA, 1939-1968

With its declaration of war on Nazi Germany, Canada joined the Allies in defence of freedom against the forces of repression. The feeble policy of appeasement, to which Canada had adhered until all hopes for peace had vanished, had only encouraged the dictators of Europe and contributed to the outbreak of World War II. Once committed to the war, which Canadians had prayed would never come, Canada contributed unstintingly to the Allied cause.

On a scale even greater than its effort twenty-five years before, Canada served as the "arsenal of democracy" for embattled Britain. Foodstuffs, war materials, arms and ammunition were transported across the Atlantic in spite of the German naval threat. Canada's manpower was mobilized for both war production and the armed services. On the high seas, in the skies over Europe and on the battlefields, Canadians served with distinction. Names such as Dieppe, Ortona and Normandy evoke poignant memories of Canadian sacrifice.

On the home front, Canadians contended successfully with other challenges. Another conscription crisis tested national unity but Mackenzie King found a way through the difficulty. Canadians endured limitations on their rights as citizens and submitted to high taxes and rationing. As never before, Canada recognized its destiny as a North American nation and turned to greater co-operation with the United States.

Canada's economy, expanded and diversified during the war, made a relatively smooth transition to peacetime production. The nation enjoyed a prolonged postwar prosperity, based in large measure on development of newly-discovered resources of oil and iron. The federal government, reflecting the increased activities of government at all levels, prepared the way for the "welfare state." But the increasing complexity and cost of government, along with the mounting cost of living, put many strains on Canada's federal system.

The Liberal Party, under Mackenzie King and his successor, Louis St. Laurent, maintained its political dominance at the national level in the early postwar years. However, long years in power had made many Liberals think that they alone had the talents, indeed the right, to govern the country. The image of arrogance, high-handed law-making and apparent unconcern for public opinion had much to do with the Liberals' defeat in the election of

1957 — after a 'reign' of twenty-two years. The Diefenbaker 'landslide' of 1958 appeared to usher in another long regime in Ottawa, but the Progressive Conservatives were reduced to a position of minority government in 1962. In the following year, the Liberals returned to power, but elections in 1963 and 1965 failed to give them the majority for which the Prime Minister, Lester B. Pearson, appealed.

As a fully sovereign nation, Canada departed sharply from its pre-war concern with isolationism and took on heavy international responsibilities. When the Cold War divided the world into groups of nations associated either with the United States or the Soviet Union, Canada took an active part in the North Atlantic Treaty Organization. Meanwhile, Canada also joined the United Nations as one of its founding members. Among the many duties performed in the world organization has been service by Canadian contingents in the United Nations Emergency Force.

After decades of working for decentralization of the British Empire, Canada has now dedicated itself to preserving the new Commonwealth of Nations. As the senior member, Great Britain no longer has the power to dominate its former colonies; yet many of the new African and Asian members of the Commonwealth are uncertain of what their relations with the former mother country should be. Canada, regarded by many of these states as a "big brother," may have an opportunity to foster co-operation between the new and the old members of the Commonwealth.

While the traditional concern with imperial relations has diminished in importance since 1945, Canada's relations with the United States have become more vital than ever. Besides dependence for defence, Canada has come under increasing American influence in other ways. Businessmen from the United States have invested large sums in Canada and established "branch plant" subsidiaries of American companies. This trend has aroused fears that foreign ownership of Canada's recources and foreign domination of both Canadian business and labour may eventually lead to the loss of Canadian independence. Television has vastly increased Canada's exposure to American ideas and customs. Some Canadians regard the closer integration of Canada and the United States as an inevitable part of the world-wide trend toward interdependence. Others feel that Canada must strive to maintain a distinctive cultural identity and a separate political existence.

Following the conscription issue of 1944 and the end of the war, the recurring Canadian problem of national unity returned to its place just below the surface of public controversy. There it remained during Maurice Duplessis' long tenure as Premier of Quebec. Once the Liberal government of Jean Lesage took office, the "revolution tranquille" (the "Quiet Revolution") erupted. Where the Church and a limited number of politicians and businessmen had formerly dominated public opinion in Quebec, the province now had many voices — including those of "separatists," who demanded various degrees of autonomy for Quebec. Sweeping reforms in education, health services, industry and government released pent-up energies that began to work for greater independence for the province, as well as for greater opportunities for French-Canadian citizens.

Canadians celebrated the one hundredth birthday of their country in 1967. It was a year of celebrations, festivals and centennial projects that ranged from new libraries and parks in hundreds of small towns to EXPO '67 in Montreal. In all parts of the nation, people recalled the achievements of the Fathers of Confederation and reflected with pride on a century of growth. Even during the festivities, however, Canadians could not ignore the deep sectional differences that still strain national unity.

28

CANADA AND WORLD WAR II

A

CANADA DECLARES WAR

The "peace in our time," which Neville Chamberlain believed he had secured at Munich in 1938, proved to be only wishful thinking. At dawn on September 1, 1939, the German air force (*Luftwaffe*) unleashed a devastating attack on Poland, while tanks and armoured vehicles rolled across the frontier into Poland. Britain's last minute diplomatic efforts failed to persuade Hitler to halt the invasion. On September 3, Great Britain and France declared war on Nazi Germany.

Although Britain's declaration of war did not necessarily mean Canada's commitment, there was little doubt that Canada would, once again, align herself with Britain. True, Canada's advance to autonomy had followed a cautious course in regard to a possible future entry into a war; Prime Minister King had repeatedly proclaimed that only the Canadian Parliament would decide upon a war declaration. On September 7, Parliament met in special session. The following day, in reply to the Speech from the Throne, Prime Minister King clearly stated that his government would stand by the side of Great Britain, and "if this house will not support us in that policy, it will have to find some other government to assume the responsibilities of the present." At the same time, he pledged that "no such measure [conscription] will be introduced by the present administration." Mackenzie King did this to assure Canadian unity and to avoid a repetition of the 1917 conscription crisis. Ernest Lapointe, the federal Minister of Justice, assuming the role of spokesman for Quebec, promised full support in the prosecution of the war, but cautioned that under no circumstances would he or Quebec consent to conscription for overseas service.

For three days the House of Commons debated the war issue. Several Quebec members asked for Canada's neutrality. J. S. Woodsworth, the leader of the C.C.F., courageously affirmed his, but not necessarily his party's, pacifist conviction and uncompromising opposition to war. His was the only voice of dissent against Canada's entry into the European conflict. On September 10, King George VI, upon the advice of the Canadian cabinet, announced that Canada had declared war.

VIEWS ON CANADA'S WAR DECLARATION[393]

In the House of Commons on September 8 and 9, 1939, Canadian leaders expressed their views on Canada's entry into the war:

Prime Minister Mackenzie King, for the Liberal Party:

I have never doubted that when the fatal moment came, the free spirit of the Canadian people would assert itself in the preservation and defence of freedom, as it did a quarter of a century ago. I have, however, been anxious that when the inevitable hour came, our people should be as one from coast to coast in recognizing the magnitude of the issue which was presenting itself, and as one in their determination to meet it with all the strength and power at their command. I have made it, therefore, the supreme endeavour of my leadership of my party, and my leadership of the government of this country, to let no hasty or premature threat or pronouncement create mistrust and divisions between the different elements that compose the population of our vast dominion, so that when the moment of decision came all should so see the issue itself that our national effort might be marked by unity of purpose, of heart and of endeavour.

R. J. Manion, for the Conservative Party:
. . . we are bound to participate in this war. We

are British subjects, we are part of the British empire. . . .

––––––––

. . . we are fighting in a war for justice, for honour and for liberty. We in Canada . . . have no selfish motives and no desire for profit. . . . We are fighting, or will be fighting, against policies and principles which are anti-christian and anti-democratic . . . barbarous and brutal. . . .

––––––––

M. J. Coldwell, for the C.C.F. Party:
. . . the Co-operative Commonwealth Federation recognizes that Canada is now implicated in a struggle which may involve the survival of democratic institutions. . . .
. . . . Canada should be prepared to defend her own shores, but her assistance overseas should be limited to economic aid and must not include conscription of man power or the sending of any expeditionary force.

––––––––

Ernest Lapointe's warning against conscription:
. . . . The whole province of Quebec — and I speak with all the responsibility and all the solemnity I can give to my words — will never agree to accept compulsory service or conscription outside Canada. I will go farther than that: When I say the whole province of Quebec I mean that I personally agree with them. I am authorized by my colleagues in the cabinet from the province of Quebec . . . (Mr. Cardin) . . . (Mr. Power) . . . to say that we will never agree to conscription and will never be members or supporters of a government that will try to enforce it. Is that clear enough?

––––––––

J. S. Woodsworth's opposition to the war:
I would ask, did the last war settle anything? I venture to say that it settled nothing; and the next war into which we are asked to enter, however big and bloody it may be, is not going to settle anything either. . . .
. . . personally I cannot give any consent to anything that will drag us into another war. . . . I have every respect for the man who, with a sincere conviction, goes out to give his life if necessary in a cause which he believes to be right; but I have just as much respect for the man who refuses to enlist to kill his fellowmen and, as under modern conditions, to kill women and children as well, as must be done on every front. . . .

In 1914, as a colony, Canada had been automatically at war alongside Great Britain. In 1939, the Dominion, as an autonomous member of the British Commonwealth of Nations, decided her own course of action. Canada's independent declaration was an unmistakable sign of her maturity as a nation.

But Maurice Duplessis, the Premier of Quebec, asserted that Canada's declaration of war did not reflect the wishes of French Canada. Within two weeks of Canada's entry into the war, he dissolved the provincial legislature and called an election with the war as the main issue. Duplessis relied on the isolationist sentiment of the French Canadians in Quebec to repudiate the Dominion's war policy. Prime Minister King viewed the election as a challenge to national unity and considered it imperative to defeat Duplessis' attempt to disrupt Canada's war effort. Four influential French-speaking Liberal cabinet ministers from Ottawa actively campaigned in support of Adelard Godbout, the provincial Liberal leader. Ernest Lapointe, the elder statesman respected and trusted in Quebec, appealed to the voters to reject Duplessis and his *Union Nationale* administration. He threatened that he and his three French-Canadian colleagues would resign — leaving Quebec with no representation in the federal cabinet — if Duplessis were returned to power. Lapointe pledged to exert his influence against any attempt to introduce conscription; he promised his own resignation from the federal cabinet if conscription were even contemplated by the Dominion government. On October 26, the voters of Quebec swept the *Union Nationale* Party out of office. The Liberals hailed the victory as a triumph for Canadian unity.

A few months later, the Dominion government was again challenged, this time by Mitchell Hepburn, the fiery Liberal Premier of Ontario. Hepburn, long known for his hostility towards the federal government, was instrumental in passing, in the Ontario legislature, a resolution condemning Prime Minister King's prosecution of the war as ineffectual. Mackenzie King decided to meet this serious accusation and personal abuse head-on. Parliament convened on January 25, 1940, in what was promised to be a full session. However, the Prime Minister obtained dissolution, bringing on an election on March 26, to give the people of Canada the opportunity of passing judgment on his government's conduct of the war effort.

King was too busy with his wartime duties for extensive campaigning, and he made his appeal to the country in several radio broadcasts. Canadians generally resented Hepburn's abusive outbursts against the Prime Minister. In the ensuing election, the voters unhesitatingly approved the government's wartime policies by returning the Liberals to power with a large majority. This endorsement by the people convinced King that he should reject

Conservative demands for a coalition government. For the sake of wartime unity, he offered to include several Conservatives in his cabinet. This the Conservatives refused; they continued to insist upon a coalition government. King, with his large majority, saw no reason for sharing political power, and the Liberals carried on their administration for the duration of the war.

B

CANADA — ARSENAL OF DEMOCRACY

At the beginning of the war, it was assumed that Britain's factories would produce the needed war material. In fact, British manufacturers withheld plans, blueprints and processes from Canada. At the time, Canada had neither the skilled workers nor the factories for extensive production of war supplies. The existing factories, many of which had been idle throughout the Great Depression, had to be converted to war industry. As a consequence, Canada's productive capacity was only partially utilized and industry proceeded at a rather leisurely pace.

But Germany's lightning war (*Blitzkrieg*) in Western Europe altered the whole situation. A desperate Britain, reeling from her disaster at Dunkirk and facing constant aerial attack from the *Luftwaffe,* turned to Canada for both military aid and war material. A sense of urgency pervaded the whole country and Canada geared her manufacturing capacity for war production. The newly-created War Supply Board was put in charge of all phases of production. In June, 1940, the National Resources Mobilization Act was passed to marshal Canada's resources for an all-out war effort. The Department of Munitions and Supply (D.M.S.) replaced the War Supply Board and the new agency began a frantic build-up of Canada's industry. Government corporations were set up to manage the many publicly-owned industries which were often operated by private companies. Private enterprise was granted favourable depreciation allowances and other incentives for establishing new factories. Under the guidance of the Department of Munitions and Supply new industries were started and old ones expanded.

PRODUCTION OF WAR MATERIALS[394]

On June 17, 1940, in the House of Commons, C. D. Howe spoke of the methods used by his department to obtain maximum production:

. . . . Where a peace-time operation can efficiently carry on war-time work, we believe it is in the best interests of the country to develop that peace-time industry for the purposes of the war rather than start a new enterprise, government-owned, for the same purpose.

We have used the powers indicated in the bill to dictate the prices at which people shall undertake work. We have gone into a plant and said, "We want this article. . . . If you are not satisfied with that price you can take your case to the exchequer court." We have done that on a few occasions; as the need grows more urgent, we will use this power very extensively. We are getting to the point where, if a manufacturer has a thing which the government needs, we preempt it; we pay him what we think is a fair price, and if he does not think so he has, as I have said, an appeal to the courts. In many instances we have imposed our price.

To offset the loss of sources of strategic supplies such as rubber and tin resulting from the Japanese occupation of the Dutch East Indies, factories which produced synthetic rubber and plastics were hurriedly constructed. The War Time Bureau of Technical Personnel, a government agency, called upon the talents of Canadian scientists and technicians to build and operate the new industries. The National Research Council was actively engaged in developing new processes and products.

To insure adequate manpower for the busy factories, the National Selective Service Act was passed in 1942. This Act empowered the government to direct workers to essential jobs. To minimize the loss of productivity because of industrial disputes, regulations against strikes and lockouts were passed. In spite of such regulations, many strikes did occur, and in 1944 the government established the Federal Wartime Labour Relation Board to settle industrial disputes by conciliation.

To assure a steady supply of war materials, production of non-essential consumer goods was curtailed. Products of mine, forest and farm were appropriated for the war industries in order to channel maximum supplies into war production. To direct the gigantic war industries, the government drew on the most capable individuals, all experts in their respective fields, and appointed them as advisors to cabinet members to assist them in the operation of their departments. In fact, the experts became part of the civil service, and

Hon. C. D. Howe, Minister of Munitions and Supply, accepts the 500,000th Canadian military vehicle at the General Motors Plant, Oshawa, Ontario, June 21, 1943.

they synchronized manpower, supplies and production for maximum output of war supplies.

It would be a great oversight to omit the name of Clarence Decatur Howe, the minister in charge of the Department of Munitions and Supply. He was responsible for mobilizing Canada's manpower and industrial facilities for war production. This required almost unlimited authority, which was readily given him — the power to control allocation of raw materials, place war contracts and administer the manufacture of war supplies for Canada and her Allies. To this task Howe brought his extensive engineering knowledge and experience as well as his enormous organizational skill. He pursued his task ruthlessly, and for this he was often accused of authoritarianism.

Under the watchful eye of the Department of Munitions and Supply, a steady stream of war supplies was pouring out of Canadian factories. Canada built merchant vessels, corvettes, minesweepers, aircraft and armoured vehicles, and produced small arms, machine guns, artillery pieces, ammunition, synthetic rubber, aviation fuel — all so vital to the conduct of the war. Over one million workers were employed directly or indirectly by the Department of Munitions and Supply.

THE DEPARTMENT OF MUNITIONS AND SUPPLY[395]

C. D. Howe, on November 19, 1945, assessed the accomplishments of the Department of Munitions and Supply:

The impact of the demands of war has brought about tremendous expansion of industry in Can-

ada. Approximately 60 per cent of all production in Canada during the past six years was for war uses . . . slightly less than 70 per cent of all war production was for export. In addition to the private investment in war production facilities estimated at five hundred million dollars, the Department of Munitions and Supply has invested approximately seven hundred and twenty million dollars in land, plant and equipment. Almost five hundred million dollars of this represents investment in new war plants wholly owned by the Crown. . . .

————

. . . . At peak production, there were one million, one hundred and eighty-six thousand employed in direct and indirect war industry, or one in every twelve persons of our population.

Often contracts were awarded on a "cost-plus" basis which guaranteed a set mark-up on costs. Thus, manufacturers were making their share of profit on war material. Howe's department was criticized for this; it was argued that "cost-plus" not only encouraged inefficiency but also rewarded it. Undoubtedly, urgency bred inefficiency and greed. The C.C.F. was most critical of such profiteering and called for the imposition of a 100 per cent excess profit tax to eliminate undue profits from production of war material. The C.C.F.'s proposal was looked upon as a possible deterrent to maximum production; and profits, it was argued, were only part of the enormous cost of war.

Producing war materials created financial hardships for Canada. Large quantities of supplies, parts and machine tools had to be purchased from the United States, and Canada lacked American currency to pay for such purchases. Something had to be done lest production be curtailed. At this juncture, Prime Minister Mackenzie King and President Franklin Delano Roosevelt met at Hyde Park, New York, on April 20, 1941. They reached an economic agreement providing for an interchange of supplies between Canada and the United States to ease Canada's shortage of American funds. To her southern neighbour Canada would sell war supplies, such as small arms, ammunition, aeroplane parts and explosives which Canada produced in large quantities. Such sales would offset some of the purchases made in the United States and would help Canada's economy.

The Hyde Park Agreement provided for close collaboration with the United States. This co-operation made possible the continued Canadian economic contribution to Britain. Co-operation with the United States made possible planned

Churchill Addressing the House of Commons during Visit to Ottawa, 1941

production for maximum and efficient manufacture of war supplies. The United States, outwardly neutral in the war, had been assisting the Allies by giving "aid short of war." The United States viewed with alarm Germany's initial successes, and, if only for American self-interest, deemed it desirable to help the Allies. American lend-lease aid was given unstintingly to the Allies. Canada received no such aid from the United States. Instead, she set up her own system of lend-lease which supplied over four billion dollars' worth of materials and foodstuffs to her Allies. It can be truly said that Canada, together with the United States, was the arsenal of democracy.

C

CANADIANS ON THE BATTLEFIELDS

World War II began with the attack on Poland which later felt the full fury of *Blitzkrieg*. A modern German mechanized war machine of infantry, tanks, armoured cars and motor vehicles made short work of the Polish army of two and one-half million men. From the air, Stuka dive-bombers rained death and devastation on Poland's cities and villages, wrecked the communication system and destroyed the inadequate and antiquated Polish air force before it could even take to the air. Across Poland's eastern frontier, on September 17, 1939, Soviet troops, as previously agreed with Germany, marched westward to a predetermined demarcation line. Trapped between two advancing armies, the Polish troops were ineffective. A battered Warsaw surrendered on September 28 to German troops entering the ruined city.

In disposing of Poland, Germany achieved a primary objective — she removed the necessity of having to fight a war on two fronts. On her eastern frontier, for the time being, Germany had the doubtful neutrality, if not the security, of the Soviet Union. Now, everyone expected Germany, in the flush of her initial victory, to hurl her military might against western Europe. But throughout the autumn a lull set in on the western front, and bad weather during the winter of 1940 ruled out any possible large-scale German attack. This was the "Phony War" phase — the period of inactivity from October to April.

Britain, impressed with the military power Germany displayed in Poland, utilized the lull in the west to prepare her defences. She also dispatched an expeditionary force to the continent to support

France, especially along the Belgian border. French troops took up positions on the Maginot Line — a system of fortifications constructed in the inter-war years to protect France against possible German invasion. This defensive line stretched from the Swiss border northward along France's eastern frontier to the Belgian border. German troops also manned their less elaborate fortified line, the West Wall, named the Siegfried Line by the British, on the Rhineland facing the Maginot Line.

At the outbreak of war, the Canadian armed forces were small indeed. The army counted 4,000 officers and men and a militia of 60,000 part-time citizen-soldiers. The Royal Canadian Navy (R.C.N.) had only 1,800 men, and only 4,500 men served in the Royal Canadian Air Force (R.C.A.F.). The equipment of the three services was almost nil; very little of it could be used in modern combat. Canada began building up her forces. Volunteers flocked to the colours, and by the end of September the army's strength rose to 55,000 men. Units of the Canadian First Division sailed for England from Halifax on December 10, 1939.

The "Phony War" came to an end in the spring of 1940. On April 9, without a declaration of war, Germany struck at Norway and seized it. At the same time, German troops swarmed into Denmark and put it under Nazi occupation. The Allies regarded Norway as a country of strategic importance and shifted some troops from France to Norway in an attempt to drive the Germans out. The capture of the ports of Narvik and Trondheim was

Canadian troops en route to Britain sail from Halifax, December 1939.

the main objective. Despite a British naval victory near Narvik, Allied troops, including some Canadian army engineers, had to withdraw. Norway remained under Nazi occupation for the duration of the war.

Germany's army (*Wehrmacht*) worked with clock-like precision. On May 10, the day Winston Churchill succeeded Neville Chamberlain as Prime Minister, Germany sprung her *Blitzkrieg* against Holland, Belgium and France. Within four days, most of Holland was in German hands; two weeks later, Belgium capitulated. British and French troops made a valiant stand on the Franco-Belgian border but were no match for the *Wehrmacht*, which broke the Allied line and rushed headlong westward towards the Channel ports. The collapse of Belgian resistance placed the Allied forces in an even more precarious position. Almost 400,000 French and British troops retreated and were trapped along the Channel with the sea as the only hope for escape. German armoured (*Panzer*) columns, supported by Stuka dive-bombers, kept the Allied troops under constant attack. Then the miracle of the war occurred on the beaches of Dunkirk. Between May 27 and June 4, almost 350,000 men, mainly of the British expeditionary force, were evacuated across the Channel to England. No doubt the retreat at Dunkirk was a major disaster; but the heroic rescue of so many raised the morale of a saddened British people.

THE MIRACLE OF DUNKIRK[396]

An account of one of the many volunteer amateur sailors who rescued soldiers from the beaches of Dunkirk:

. . . . We muddled, we quarrelled, everybody swore and was bad-tempered; boats were poorly handled and broke down, arrangements were wrong.

And yet out of all that mess we beat the experts, we defied the law and the prophets, and where the Government had hoped to bring away 30,000 men, we brought away 350,000. If that was not a miracle, there are no miracles left.

———

The picture will always remain sharp-etched in my memory — the lines of men wearily staggering across the beach from the dunes to the shallows, falling into the little boats, great columns of men thrust out like human piers into the water among the bomb and shell splashes. . . . As the front ranks were dragged aboard the boats, the rear ranks moved up, from ankle deep to knee deep, from knee deep to waist deep, until, they too, came to shoulder depth and their turn.

———

The little boats that ferried from the beach to the big ships in the deep water listed drunkenly with the weight of men. The big ships slowly took on lists of their own with the enormous numbers crowded aboard. And always down the dunes and across the beach came new hordes of men, new columns, new lines.

While the evacuation from Dunkirk was going on, German armies were marching towards Paris. The French were bewildered and stunned by the speed of the German advance. Resistance seemed futile; France was on the verge of collapse. Mussolini, Hitler's Axis partner, administered the infamous "stab in the back" — he attacked a dying France on the Mediterranean front. The situation was hopeless and France had no choice but to surrender to Germany.

Having lost its principal ally, Britain with its Dominions stood alone and awaited a German invasion. Churchill, in eloquent speeches, rallied his people and expressed the determination of Britain to meet "the whole fury and might of the enemy." Reichsmarshall Hermann Goering sent wave after wave of his *Luftwaffe* across the Channel in an attempt to destroy the Royal Air Force, as a forerunner to the invasion of the British Isles. But the plucky, outnumbered R.A.F., in which many Canadians were serving, fought the German air force in the skies over England. Having failed to destroy the R.A.F., Germany, on August 25, resorted to daylight bombing of English cities. London, Coventry, Winchester and Birmingham, among others, were favourite targets. The air war continued without let-up, but the *Luftwaffe*, so far,

Royal Canadian Air Force Recruiting Poster

failed to knock the R.A.F. out of action. On September 15, Germany carried out a furious daylight raid on London in a desperate attempt to deal with the R.A.F. Hundreds of German bombers attacked the city, but the R.A.F. shot down so many aeroplanes that even the superior *Luftwaffe* could not afford such enormous losses. Henceforth, Germany was content to continue regular bombing of English cities. The Battle of Britain, as the courageous stand by the small R.A.F. become known, saved Britain and convinced Hitler to abandon his planned invasion of the British Isles. Fittingly Churchill expressed his nation's gratitude to the R.A.F.: "Never in the field of human conflict was so much owed by so many to so few."

During the period of the "Phony War," Canada stepped up recruiting to bolster her armed forces. The Second Division began arriving in England in the summer of 1940, and together with the First Division, the First Canadian Corps, under Lieutenant-General A. G. L. McNaughton, was being constituted. After the collapse of France, the Third and Fourth Divisions were being mobilized. A small Canadian force was dispatched to the West Indies to release the British garrison there for service elsewhere.

The strength of the Royal Canadian Navy was constantly increasing. By the end of 1941, 27,000 men were serving in the navy, mainly on convoy duty in the North Atlantic. After the Battle of Britain, Germany decided to starve Britain into submission by striking at Britain's sea communications and cutting her off from overseas supplies.

German submarine warfare against Allied shipping was very effective; in the first year of the war, almost one thousand ships laden with supplies destined for Britain were sunk in the North Atlantic. And the losses were mounting as a result of the U-boat activities in the Battle of the Atlantic. The Canadian navy, manning whaler-type corvettes, patrolled the convoys plying the North Atlantic and kept the life-line to Britain open.

From the few Canadians who had participated in the Battle of Britain, the R.C.A.F. grew to 100,-000 men by the end of 1941. The British Commonwealth Air Training Plan, operating in Canada, initially trained air crews only from Britain and the Dominions, but later extended the training to include Free France, Norway and Poland. Over half of the 130,000 who qualified as air crewmen during the existence of the Training Plan served in the R.C.A.F.

GERMAN VIEW OF THE R.C.A.F.[397]

Joseph Goebbels, Hitler's Minister of Propaganda, made this entry in his DIARY, *March 3, 1943, after an air bombardment of Berlin:*

I also inspected a bombed-out hospital in Luetzow Street. Several corpses were just being carried out — a touching picture. One of the nurses killed was an air-raid warden. It drives one mad to think that any old Canadian boor, who probably can't even find Europe on the globe, flies to Europe from his super-rich country which his people don't know how to exploit, and here bombards a continent with a crowded population. But let's hope we can soon deliver the proper reply. . . .

Canada plunged into an all-out war effort. The navy patrolled the sea lanes of the North Atlantic and guarded the approaches to the harbours of North America. The air force became part of the air squadrons which bombed Germany's cities and industries. The army was steadily growing and undergoing intensive battle training in both Canada and the United Kingdom.

The war with the Axis powers was spreading. In September, 1940, while the *Luftwaffe* was bombing Britain, Italian troops from Libya invaded Egypt. The strategy seemed to be the seizure of the vital Suez Canal and the opening of the road to the oilfields of the Middle East. But by November, the initial Italian advance was halted. Early in December, the Italians were driven out of Egypt. General Sir Archibald Wavell led a British offensive which, by the beginning of February, 1941, had annihilated the Italian army and had captured 130,000 prisoners and huge quantities of arms and ammunition.

Hitler sent *Panzer* divisions and *Luftwaffe* units to rescue his Ally in North Africa. The daring General Erwin Rommel was put in command of the Italo-German forces. In a twelve day, hurriedly prepared offensive in March, he regained the territory the Italians had previously lost, beseiged the important stronghold of Tobruk and advanced to the Egyptian border. Once again Suez was threatened.

Mussolini's other venture fared no better. On October 28, 1940, much to Hitler's displeasure, the Italians invaded Greece. Mussolini had expected an easy victory, but within a week the Italians were routed and the war went on through the following winter. The Italians were forced to retreat into Italian-occupied Albania. This setback worried Hitler. In March, he sent German soldiers into Greece to extricate the bogged-down Italians. Britain shifted over 50,000 troops from Egypt to Greece in an unsuccessful attempt to check the German invasion. In a lesser-Dunkirk-like evacuation, most of the British troops managed to escape by sea to Egypt. On April 27, 1941, Athens was in German hands and Greece came under Nazi occupation. The Germans followed up this victory with a lightning airborne assault on Crete and cleared the British and New Zealanders out of the island. Hitler had not only saved Mussolini but also gained full control of the Balkans.

Nevertheless, by the spring of 1941, Britain still maintained its hold of the Mediterranean, still kept the Strait of Gibraltar open to shipping, still held the strategically located island of Malta and still hung on to Suez.

On June 22, 1941, the war entered a new phase. On that day, the Soviet Union became Allies and comrades-in-arms against the Axis powers. Hitler's armies turned on the Soviet Union with a carefully planned three-pronged offensive. Through the Baltic states, German columns were heading northward towards Leningrad; in an almost straight line eastward, other German armies were racing towards Moscow; a third force was advancing across southern Poland towards Kiev, the capital of the Ukraine. The German objective was the Ukraine with its fertile wheat fields, as a first step to the oil fields of the Caucasus. Altogether, Hitler sent in almost three million troops, supported by tanks and aeroplanes, to destroy his former ally. The German armies scored spectacular victories and maintained an offensive which took them within sight of Moscow and Leningrad. Hitler was so sure of a Soviet collapse that on October 3, in an address to the German people, he said,

I declare today, and I declare without reservation, that the enemy in the East has been struck down and will never rise again. . . . Behind our troops there already lies a territory twice the size of the

German Reich when I came to power in 1933.

Hitler's declaration was premature indeed. The beleaguered cities withstood repeated attacks, and the determined Soviet troops barred the road to the Caucasus. Death and devastation descended upon the German-occupied areas, and what the Nazis failed to destroy, the Soviets did, with their ruthless "scorched earth" policy of burning and destroying everything of possible use to the enemy. Soon the autumn rains and the fields of mud slowed down the German advance. The early winter, which set in at the beginning of November, together with the stiff resistance by the Red Army, brought the Nazi offensive to a halt. In the winter blizzards the German armies were soon to meet the same fate that had befallen Napoleon's armies in 1812.

On the other side of the world, the surprise Japanese attack on Pearl Harbor on December 7, 1941, turned the European war into a global conflict. The might of the United States was now added to the Allied cause. On the same day, Canada declared war on Japan and made Canadian territory and facilities available to the United States. Canadians were soon in battle with the Japanese. In September, Canada had sent a contingent of troops, drawn from the Winnipeg Grenadiers and the Royal Rifles of Canada, to reinforce the British garrison in the Crown Colony of Hong Kong. On December 8 the Japanese attacked Hong Kong. The outnumbered garrison put up a stubborn resistance but was forced to surrender on Christmas Day. Of some 2,000 Canadians in Hong Kong, more than 500 lost their lives either in battle or in prisoner of war camps.

In Libya, during November and December, in the see-saw battles across the desert, Axis troops were finally driven back. In January, 1942, the Italo-German forces sprang back and recaptured most of the lost ground. In May, Rommel resumed his offensive, captured Tobruk, and entered Egypt. By the end of June he reached El-Alamein, only 65 miles from Alexandria. The British position seemed hopeless; the victorious *Afrika Korps* was within reach of Suez. For his incredible exploits, Hitler elevated Rommel to the rank of Field Marshal. But, in spite of his spectacular victory, Rommel halted the offensive and failed to follow up his advantage. On August 31, he resumed the offensive and was stopped by a reinforced British army, including many Australians, under its new commander, Sir Bernard Law Montgomery. Early in November Montgomery launched a counter-offensive which smashed the vaunted *Afrika Korps*.

Meanwhile, during the winter of 1941-1942, on the Soviet fronts, the German armies suffered reverses. By the end of the winter, their casualties reached almost one and one-quarter million. The spring mud slowed the fighting almost to a halt. Towards the end of August, Hitler ordered an offensive against Stalingrad, the key to the Crimea and the Caucausus. German troops, reinforced with armies of Germany's satellites and allies — Rumanian, Hungarian, Slovak, Italian and Spanish — pursued the retreating Red Army to Stalingrad.

In October, there was bitter house-to-house fighting within Stalingrad. Axis soldiers, who were rushed into the city, were decimated in the fierce, suicidal resistance of the Soviet troops. To all entreaties by his field commanders to withdraw from Stalingrad, Hitler had one answer, "no retreat," and he insisted that "Where the German soldier sets foot there he remains." In November, in a blinding blizzard, the Soviet armies opened an offensive in which the Germans surrendered in the thousands. Fierce fighting continued through January, 1943. At Stalingrad, Germany suffered a shattering defeat. British successes on the sands of Libya coupled with Soviet victory in the snows of the Ukraine marked a turning point in the war against the Axis.

Up to 1942, Canadian forces had suffered very few losses. There were casualties in the R.C.A.F. in the air war over Europe; Canadian sailors were lost at sea on their dreary convoy duty on the North Atlantic; Canadian troops died in the disaster at Hong Kong. But August 19, 1942, was a sad day for Canada.

The Allied High Command had repeatedly refused to open a second front in western Europe as demanded by the embattled Soviet Union. The time, it was felt, was not yet right for an all-out invasion of the continent. However, as a gesture of co-operation with the Soviet Allies, and as a reconnaissance in force, it was decided to undertake a raid on the German-held French coast. Units from the Canadian Second Division, together with some British commandos and American Rangers, were chosen to carry out an assault on Dieppe.

Since 1940, the Germans had fortified the French coast with the Atlantic Wall. At Dieppe, this fortification was on a cliff overlooking the beach. Barbed wire entanglements, concrete pillboxes, coastal guns and artillery emplacements had been installed. When at dawn of August 19, 1942, the Canadians attempted a landing on the beach, they were under fire from the heavily defended German positions. Many of the assault troops never landed — they were blown up on their landing craft by shore batteries. Those who did manage to get on shore were under constant fire, and many were killed before they ever reached the fortifications. Some of the troops penetrated one or two miles inland, only to be driven back. Of the 6,000 men who took part in the raid, 5,000

Dieppe, France, August 1942

were Canadians, and of these, 900 were killed, 500 wounded and 2,000 were taken prisoners.

Since the end of World War II, conflicting assessments of the value of the raid have been presented. Some claim that it was a useless slaughter; others maintain that the experience gained at Dieppe was invaluable in planning the invasion of the continent. Be that as it may, Canada paid a frightful price during the few morning hours of August 19, 1942, on the Dieppe beaches.

THE RAID ON DIEPPE[398]

[a]*The Canadian war correspondent Ross Munro describes the scene on the beach at Puys, near Dieppe, August 19, 1942:*

When I got to Puys it was just a carnage. I never saw anything like it in the remaining years of the war, following the Canadians on all their campaigns. This was the worst battle I have ever seen. . . . It was at that time, when I could see the Puys thing was gone, because the whole slope was just littered with khaki bodies of wounded and killed Royals. It was unbelievable to see that gulch just covered with Canadians. And they were lying around the beach, and the tremendous fire from the buildings and from the top of the gulch. You could see that things were in a desperate shape then, and very few people actually got up the gulch. . . .

———

[b]*The assessment of the raid was recorded by the 302nd German Infantry Division which defended Dieppe:*

The main attack was launched by the Second Canadian Division with great energy. That the enemy gained no ground at all in Puys and could take only parts of the beach at Dieppe . . . and this only for a short time . . . was not the result of lack of courage but of the concentrated defensive fire of our division artillery and infantry heavy weapons. In Puys, the efforts made by the enemy, in spite of heavy German machine-gun fire, to surmount the wire obstacles studded with booby traps on the first beach terrace are signs of a good offensive spirit. The large number of prisoners at Puys was the result of the hopelessness of the situation for the men who had landed, caught under German machine-gun, rifle, and mortar fire between the cliffs and the sea on a beach which offered no cover.

---

cOn August 19 and 21, 1942, Mackenzie King made these entries in his diary:

. . . . I question if the information gained could begin to equal the heavy losses. Moreover the enemy themselves are able effectively to represent the whole episode as a gain for themselves between the numbers taken prisoners and those who have been killed. It is a very serious blow to the Canadian forces. . . .

. . . still not too sure of the wisdom of what was attempted. It goes back, I feel, above all to the time when it was felt it was necessary to have the Canadians do something for a variety of reasons. I still have the feeling that the part of wisdom would have been to conserve that especially trained life for the decisive moment. It may, in the long run, prove to be for the best but such is war. It makes me sad at heart.

---

dMinister of National Defence J. L. Ralston, in the House of Commons, May 14, 1943:

Dieppe demonstrated the difficulties and revealed the possibilities of landing on the continent. . . . The losses were heavy; but although the price was great, when history comes to be written I believe it will be recorded that Dieppe did a service of untold benefit. . . . Dieppe was an important operation. . . . It taught our enemy that Hitler's European stronghold was not inviolable. . . . Some day it may well be considered as having sown the seeds of our final victory. . . .

At the beginning of November, 1942, while warfare flared on the deserts of Libya and the frozen fields of the Ukraine, a combined Anglo-American force, under the command of General Dwight Eisenhower, was landing on the beaches of French Morocco and Algeria. Over a quarter of a million German and Italian troops were rushed to Tunisia to prevent Eisenhower from seizing it. By the following May most of the Axis troops had become prisoners of the Allies. North Africa, from Gibraltar to Suez, was in Allied hands. The next step seemed obvious — the invasion of Italy, the "soft under-belly" of Europe, if only to meet the Soviet Union's constant clamour for a second front.

On July 10, 1943, Allied forces under cover of an air and sea bombardment landed on the southeastern tip of Sicily. The Canadian First Division, commanded by Major-General Guy Simonds, as part of the British Eighth Army under Montgomery, took part in the invasion. The Canadians advanced quickly northward, easily brushing aside Italian resistance. Only German *Panzer* units, fighting a delaying action, were able to slow down the headway made by the First Division.

On July 25, the day Mussolini was deposed by the Fascist Grand Council, Germany decided to withdraw from Sicily, across the Strait of Messina, to the mainland. Farther north, a line of defence was set up to block possible future Allied attacks. By the end of August, the Sicilian campaign was over. On September 3, Allied troops including the Canadians, facing little resistance, landed on the mainland.

CANADIANS CROSS THE STRAITS OF MESSINA TO THE ITALIAN MAINLAND[399]

Matthew Halton, a Canadian war correspondent, described the landing of the Canadians on the Italian mainland, September 3, 1943:

We are in Italy. The First Canadian Division, with brother formations of the Eighth Army, is in Italy, unopposed. We made an assault landing at dawn today, and made the first breach in the walls of Nazi Europe. . . . The role of the Canadians was to cross the straits . . . and capture Reggio. . . . It was after midnight when we went aboard our assault landing craft in Sicily. There was nothing but confidence, because we knew we were not storming the "toe" of Italy with any possibility of failure. But we were tense and silent as we went aboard, for how were we to know we were not to go ashore through curtains of bullets and shells? We sailed just after three o'clock . . . our artillery split the night with one of the most enormous barrages of this war. Hundreds and hundreds of our guns were pouring tens of thousands of shells onto the beaches where we were to land, and onto the enemy gun positions overlooking them. The horizon behind us was a staggering rippling and flashing fire and flame and the night was one enormous roar, and the Italian mainland was occasionally vomiting explosions. One hour before dawn, the pandemonium died away into the most complete silence. We were going ashore. It was our hour.

In the meantime, German troops and materials poured into Italy. Hitler decided to occupy Italy; he had little faith in the fighting abilities of the Italian armies. The Italians were secretly negotiating an armistice with the Allies. Anglo-American forces, under General Mark Clark, struck at Salerno, south of Naples, on September 9. A successful German counter-offensive threatened the Allies with another Dunkirk. Montgomery's Eighth Army and the Canadians rushed northward to Salerno, but before they had arrived Clark's army repelled the Germans and captured Naples. Henceforth, the Germans were on the defensive with a fight for every inch of ground.

The Canadians advanced slowly northward along mountain roads, clearing the mine fields left by the retreating Germans. In December, units of the First Division reached the area around Ortona, an important port on the Adriatic. The Germans had no intention of giving way. For a month the Canadians fought in the winter of mud and slush. Under their new commander, Major-General Chris Vokes, they battled their way into Ortona. But the Germans were determined, and bitter fighting took place in the rubble-strewn city; the enemy had to be dislodged in fierce house-to-house fighting. It was here that the Royal 22nd Regiment — the "Vandoos" — a French-Canadian unit, distinguished itself. By the end of December, Ortona was in the hands of the Canadians.

THE BATTLE FOR ORTONA[400]

Field Marshal Albert Kesselring, German Commander-in-Chief in Italy, expressed his view at the time:

It is clear we do not want to defend Ortona decisively, but the English have made it as important as Rome. . . . It costs so much blood that it cannot be justified. . . . You can do nothing when things develop in this manner; it is only too bad that the world press makes so much of it.

———

Major General Sir Francis de Guingand, Montgomery's Chief of Staff, wrote of Ortona after the war:

The fighting during this period had been fairly costly, and one rather wondered what we achieved. Enemy formations were certainly pulled over from opposite 5 U.S. Army, and heavy casualties had been inflicted on the Germans. With snow in the mountains and mud everywhere else, we began to think about Passchendaele. Had we gone on too long? Were the troops being driven too hard? I feel very definitely that a mistake was made in pressing the Sangro offensive as far as it was. . . .

Canadian Armoured Column, en route to Assault the Gothic Line, Italy, August 1944

The next phase in the Italian campaign was a move northward to capture Rome. Although military opinion differed as to the strategic importance of the city, both the Allies and Germans recognized the psychological value of such a move. Furthermore, a successful thrust northward might bring the Allies to the frontiers of southern Germany and Austria. Germany decided to make a stand in order to prevent the Allies from reaching Rome. The road to Rome was difficult, obstructed by extensive mine fields. The campaign slowed down to minor skirmishes. The Canadians took advantage of the lull in the fighting to rebuild their shattered battalions. On February 1, 1944, the First Canadian Corps was formed, with Lieutenant-General E. L. M. Burns in command.

In January, the Allies, mainly Americans, landed marines and paratroopers at Anzio; Rome was only 100 miles away. The town of Casino, renowned for the ancient Benedictine monastery on the mountain top, became the key position blocking the road to Rome. Units of many Allied armies fought fiercely on the slopes in unsuccessful attempts to wrest the heights. Casino was finally by-passed. On May 24, the Canadian Corps penetrated the heavily fortified Adolf Hitler Line, the last defences on the way to Rome. Allied troops entered Rome on June 4, 1944.

In the fall, the Canadian Corps smashed its way through the Gothic Line, the last German defensive position in northern Italy. It was an important campaign since over a quarter of a million German soldiers were tied down in Italy at a time when the Allies were advancing in western Europe. The Canadians remained in Italy until January 1945,

Vive la France!

General de Gaulle Visiting Ottawa, July 11, 1944. L to R: Lord Athlone, General de Gaulle, Rt. Hon. W. L. Mackenzie King, Hon. L. S. St. Laurent.

when they were transferred to the western European front to join the Canadian Army there.

In western Europe, Operation Overlord — the long awaited second front — opened on D-Day, June 6, 1944. Allied invasion armies on 4,000 landing and assault craft set out for the beaches of Normandy. Overhead, an air-umbrella of 11,000 aircraft bombarded German positions and communication lines. Guns from 800 warships shelled German coastal defences in support of the attacking troops. The magnitude of this attacking force had never before been equalled in military history. Nevertheless, the Allied landing met with fierce resistance. The landing craft were under intense fire from the entrenched German shore batteries, and many of the troops had to wade, often neck-deep, to the beaches. Thousands of soldiers died in the withering fire or drowned in the waters of the Channel. Enormous quantities of equipment, arms and supplies were lost and never reached the beaches. On the beaches, there was fierce fighting before the Allies were able to gain a firm foothold.

THE ASSAULT ON NORMANDY ON D-DAY[401]

This description is typical of the many landings on the beaches of France:

All boats were under criss-cross machine-gun fire. As the first men jumped they crumpled and flopped into the water. Then order was lost. It seemed to the men that the only way to get ashore was to dive head first in and swim clear of the fire that was striking the boats. But, as they hit the water, their heavy equipment dragged them down and soon they were struggling to keep afloat. Some were hit in the water and wounded. Some drowned then and there. . . . But some moved safely through the bullet fire to the sand, finding they could not

hold there, went back into the water and used it as cover, only their heads sticking out. Those who survived kept moving forward with the tide, sheltering at times behind under-water obstacles and in this way they finally made their landings. Within ten minutes of the ramp being lowered, A Company had become inert, leaderless and almost incapable of action. Every officer and sergeant had been either killed or wounded. It had become a struggle for survival and rescue. The men in the water pushed wounded men ashore ahead of them, and those who had reached the sands crawled back into the water pulling others to land to save them from drowning, in many cases only to see the rescued men wounded again or to be hit themselves. . . .

The Canadian Third Division landed on the beach, north of the British Army, and fought its way to Caen. To the south, around Cherbourg, the American army effected its landing. The Canadians suffered heavy losses in the face of stiff resistance from *Panzer* units. The Canadian initial objective was to close the gap between Caen and Falaise, but the advance toward Falaise stalled. In spite of this apparent failure, the Canadians in the Caen-Falaise sector held down some of Germany's best troops. This enabled the Americans to break out of Cherbourg in an encirclement movement threatening to trap the Germans in the Falaise pocket. To avoid annihilation, the Germans began to retreat, and in July, the Canadians captured Falaise.

CANADIANS FAIL TO CAPTURE FALAISE[402]

Major-General Kurt Meyer, who commanded the German 12th S.S. Division against the Canadians on this front, later wrote:

The Canadian Army of 1944 was a high-class force. . . . Every Canadian operation bore the mark of intensive planning and was built on sound tactical principles. Every opening phase was a complete success and the staff work a mathematical masterpiece. . . . The Canadian Army never followed up their opening successes to reach a complete victory. Every one of the Canadian attacks lost its punch and determination after a few miles. . . . British and Canadian planning was absolutely without risk. . . . Both used the tank more or less as an infantry support weapon. . . . They executed the operations in an inflexible, time-wasting method. Never once did speed, the most powerful weapon of armoured warfare, appear . . . the Anglo-Canadian forces stuck to their step-by-step schedule. . . .

In southern France, an American army which had landed on August 15, headed northward. From the west, Allied armies were pursuing the retreating Germans eastward. The Allies were converging upon central France. On August 25, Paris was liberated by the American and by the Free French troops of General Charles de Gaulle.

In the autumn of 1944, the Canadians under Lieutenant-General H. D. G. Crerar, moved into Belgium to clear the Scheldt estuary and free the port of Antwerp. The capture of Antwerp was of immense importance; through it could be funnelled much needed arms, ammunition, supplies and reinforcements for the Allied armies which were advancing towards the Rhine. Canadian troops fought through flooded ground and suffered high casualties before Antwerp was taken.

In the early winter, the Canadian Army in northern Europe was reinforced by the First Division from Italy. The Canadians pushed the Germans out of Holland. The campaign for the Rhineland began. Canadian troops crossed the Rhine and swung northward as far as Bremen. The Germans continued to retreat. Their armies were beaten but not destroyed. They dug in behind the West Wall in a desperate last stand to stem the Allied thrust into Germany.

By April, 1945, the German retreat became a rout. At the same time, millions of Soviet troops had pushed the Germans out of Poland, Hungary, Austria and Czechoslovakia. By the end of April, units of the Red Army were attacking the outskirts of Berlin, and soon were fighting in the ruins of the city. Hitler, in his deep underground shelter, committed suicide. The German war machine was disintegrating. The German people's will to resist was gone. On May 7, 1945, Germany surrendered unconditionally. The war in Europe was over.

However, the war against Japan was still on. Although Canadians had confined their activities mainly to Europe, they were ready to assist their American allies. In 1943, Canadians took part in the invasion of Kiska, in the Aleutians. However, the Japanese had already withdrawn when the American-Canadian force arrived. A Canadian division was also readied to take part in a contemplated invasion of Japan. But the atomic bombing of Hiroshima and Nagasaki in August 1945 brought with it Japan's surrender.

World War II was over. Again Canada counted her dead. Tablets on cemeteries in France, Italy, Belgium, Holland and Hong Kong mark the sacrifice Canadians made in defence of freedom. Canada, as a nation matured through the ordeal of war, was now ready to assume responsibility as a member of the world community.

D

CANADIANS ON THE HOME FRONT

The plight of Britain in the early years of the war drove Canada and the United States into closer relations. In August 1940, Prime Minister King and President Franklin D. Roosevelt met at Ogdensburg, New York. The Ogdensburg Agreement which emerged from this meeting established a Permanent Joint Defence Board which tied Canada militarily to the United States and placed Canada within the American defence system. In effect, the United States pledged to defend Canada against an aggressor. After Pearl Harbor, American troops were stationed in Canada. The Canadian North was made available to the United States for the construction of air fields and for the Alaska Highway to link Edmonton with Skagway. To provide American forces in the Aleutian Islands with petroleum products, the Canol Project — an oil pipe line from northern Alberta across the northland to Alaska — was undertaken by the United States.

In Canada, the conscription issue, reminiscent of 1917, arose again. English-speaking Canadians kept demanding compulsory military service for all able-bodied Canadians. French Canadians generally opposed conscription. Mackenzie King was under pressure from both public opinion and some of his ministers. He sympathized with those who saw the need for compulsory military service, but at the same time he wanted to honour his 1939 non-conscription pledge. He therefore decided to consult the Canadian people. A national plebiscite was held on April 27, 1942, in which a "Yes" or "No" vote was asked on the following:

Are you in favour of releasing the Government from any obligation arising out of any past commitments restricting the methods of raising men for military service?

An affirmative vote would release the Prime Minister from his pledge.

The vote was 64 per cent in favour of releasing the Prime Minister from his "past commitments," with English Canada voting 79 per cent "Yes" and Quebec 72 per cent "No." French Canada was resentful and viewed the plebiscite as a betrayal of a solemn pledge. The outcome of the plebiscite not only freed Mackenzie King from his "no-conscription" promise but also increased demands for conscription. The Prime Minister felt compelled to introduce Bill 80, on June 10, 1942, to amend the clause in the N.R.M. Act which had stated that no compulsion would be used to require "persons to serve the military, naval or air force outside of Canada." King sensed the danger to Canadian unity and he assured Quebec that the amendment was "not necessarily conscription but conscription if necessary." But P. J. A. Cardin, the Minister of Public Works, felt he could not go along with the government's action and, on June 12, resigned from the cabinet. Mackenzie King, the skillful compromiser, assuaged French-Canadian fears somewhat by declaring that conscripts would be used for home defence, and overseas service would continue on a voluntary basis.

This by no means ended the conscription issue; it recurred in 1944. J. L. Ralston, the Minister of National Defence, after a tour of the European theatres of war, became convinced that reinforcements were needed to replace the higher than expected casualties in the Normandy fighting. He asked that home defence conscripts be sent overseas. A. G. L. McNaughton, the former commander of the Canadian Army who had been recalled to Canada in 1943, disagreed with Ralston. McNaughton believed that conscripts could be persuaded to volunteer for overseas service and compulsion would be unnecessary. Prime Minister King favoured McNaughton's suggestion. Ralston resigned and McNaughton replaced him as Minister of National Defence.

But the expected volunteers did not come forward. McNaughton failed to gain a seat in the House of Commons in a by-election, nevertheless, he continued in his portfolio. The failure of McNaughton's appeal for volunteers forced the Prime Minister's hand — he agreed to send conscripts overseas. C. G. Powers, the Minister of Air, in fulfilment of his pledge to his Quebec City constitutents, resigned in protest. All in all, 13,000 conscripts were sent overseas.

FRENCH-CANADIAN VIEWS ON CONSCRIPTION, 1944[403]

P. J. A. Cardin — anti-conscriptionist:

. . . . For a moment, if you wish to understand me and the French Canadians, reverse the picture if you please. Try to imagine Canada as part of a French empire, with the descendants of British citizens in the minority. Can you tell me that if that French empire, of which you would be part, were in danger you would be as enthusiastic in defending that empire as would be the Canadians of French descent? To any man who would say that he would have the same views and sentiments I would reply that he is not sincere.

Hughes Lapointe — anti-conscriptionist:

. . . personally I cannot go back on the word which I solemnly gave to the people whom I represent in this house, especially when I am not convinced that this order-in-council was necessary for the winning of the war and the security of Canada. . . .

. . . I believe I truly express the sentiments of the people whom I have the honour to represent here when I tell the Prime Minister that there is no one else whom they want to see as the head of the government of Canada, but on the other hand they cannot forget the breaking of a pledge which to them was sacred. . . .

Louis St. Laurent:

. . . believing as I do that whenever the majority, after full consultation and mature deliberation, reaches a conclusion of that kind, it is proper the minority should accept it and loyally assist in carrying it out, I appeal to all the members of this house . . . to unite and to assert to the men overseas that this nation, from one ocean to the other, stands pledged to a victory that will be decisive and that will endure.

The conscription issue revealed the rift that existed between English and French Canada. Mackenzie King, like Laurier before him, was caught in the crossfire of English-French differences, and he found, as Laurier had, that compromise satisfied neither side. Nevertheless, King's policy of compromise, the exclusion of Ralston and the presence of Louis St. Laurent* in the cabinet as the representative of Quebec, helped to prevent the conscription issue from reaching the proportions of 1917.

To provide the material for war, Canadian factories operated to full capacity. Unemployment vanished — everyone was working. All branches of industry were booming. Farm income was high, and in spite of farm labour shortage essential food was produced in large quantities. The women of Canada worked side by side with the men in occupations usually regarded too difficult for or not generally undertaken by the "weaker sex." It

* After the death of Ernest Lapointe in 1941, Mackenzie King appointed Louis St. Laurent as Minister of Justice. St. Laurent was a successful lawyer, widely respected in Quebec, and his appointment was a continuation of King's policy of having Quebec represented in the government.

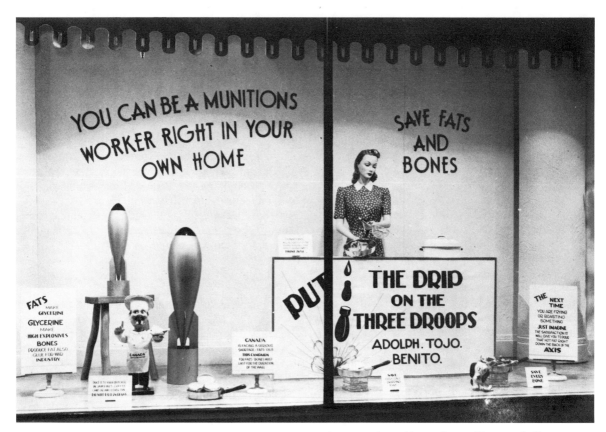

Wartime Prices and Trade Board window display urges people to save fat and bones for munitions production.

became common to see women operating rivetting hammers in shipyards, welding in aeroplane factories or driving trucks and buses on city streets. Many women enlisted in the armed services in non-combatant positions, thus releasing men for more direct participation in the war.

In October 1941, the War Time Prices and Trade Board (W.T.P.T.B.) was established to give the federal government authority to set price ceilings on consumer goods. The Board also froze rents and wages. These steps, the Board claimed, were necessary to prevent a wild spiralling in the cost of living. But the freezing of wages proved a major cause for labour unrest and industrial disputes.

In 1942, rationing of certain foods and strategic supplies was introduced. This was done to make more food and supplies available for Britain, which had been brought to near-starvation by the effective German submarine warfare. Canadians were issued ration coupons for gasoline, meat, butter, sugar and coffee. Rationing caused some discomfort but no undue hardship to the people of Canada, and it made available to every Canadian essential commodities of everyday living.

In financing Canada's war effort, the government pursued a pay-as-you-go policy — raising as much revenue as possible by taxation and less

by borrowing. To raise these funds, increased direct taxes on individuals and corporations and high taxes on luxury goods were imposed. The government still borrowed through sales of Victory Bonds. Of these, less than half were purchased by individual Canadians, the rest, by large corporations, banks, insurance and trust companies. Canadians were saddled with an enormous war debt to repay the loans and interest on them. The C.C.F. regarded this as yet another type of war profiteering, since the major portion of the interest would go on to the already wealthy corporations. The C.C.F. advocated interest-free bonds as a token "equality of sacrifice" in Canada's war effort. The government regarded the C.C.F. proposal as a noble gesture but impractical for large-scale fund raising. More Victory Bonds were sold, adding yet more to the burden of debt.

Because of wartime conditions, the federal government found it advisable to curb certain liberties of individual Canadian citizens. At the beginning of the war, the War Measure Act of 1914, on the statute books but not used over the years, was revived. This Act gave the Dominion government almost unlimited power to pass Orders-in-Council imposing controls deemed necessary for the prosecution of the war.

In September 1939, an Order-in-Council set up

the Defence of Canada Regulations — a series of wartime emergency measures. For the sake of national security, the government was empowered to institute censorship, allow search without warrant and impose other restrictions on individual liberties. As a result, known active enemy aliens and Nazi sympathizers were put in detention camps. Before the Soviet Union entered the war, Canadian Communists who had openly opposed the war as yet another "imperialist war" were also interned, and their halls were either closed or disposed of by the government.

Canadians, aware of the need for wartime security, generally accepted the infringements upon their liberties — infringements which they would not ordinarily tolerate. However, under the pretext of national security, the Canadian government committed a most flagrant violation of citizens' rights, a violation perhaps more unjust than the expulsion of the Acadians in 1755.

In June 1942, the landing of Japanese troops on the Aleutian Islands off the coast of Alaska and the presence of a Japanese submarine off the coast of Vancouver Island, heightened the anti-Japanese hysteria in British Columbia. Canadians of Japanese origin or descent, long residents of the Pacific province, were now regarded as a threat to the security of Canada. As a precautionary measure, the federal government removed the Japanese from British Columbia; some were placed in internment camps, others were dispersed throughout the Dominion. Their property was sold to eager buyers at bargain prices. The Japanese Canadians, uprooted from their homes and deprived of their livelihood, were forced to start afresh to build a new life for themselves and their families. The wartime restrictions on the Japanese were repealed in 1947. Since then, men in public life, including Prime Minister Lester B. Pearson, have expressed regret for the injustice perpetrated upon these innocent Canadian citizens.

TREATMENT OF JAPANESE CANADIANS[404]

[a]*Howard C. Green, representing Vancouver South, demanded in the House of Commons, on January 29, 1942, the removal of the Japanese Canadians from British Columbia:*

. . . . Canadians on the Pacific are entitled to and insist on getting complete protection from treachery, protection from being stabbed in the back. . . . We have at least 24,000 of Japanese origin in our province, all in the coastal area — fishermen, men working in our woods in the lumbering industry, men farming on both sides of the great Fraser river valley, which means that they are astride both of our transcontinental lines. There has been treachery elsewhere from Japanese in this war, and we have no reason to hope that there will be none in British Columbia . . . if we were Canadians in Japan, we might feel much the same; we would be only too willing to assist British troops should they attempt to land on the Japanese coast. The only complete protection we can have from this danger is to remove the Japanese population from the province. . . .

———

[b]*Mackenzie King felt that in the interest of national security, it was essential to move the Japanese Canadians from the West Coast. From his diary, February 19, 1942:*

. . . a very great problem to move the Japanese and particularly to deal with the ones who are naturalized Canadians or Canadian born . . . there is every possibility of riots. Once that occurs, there will be repercussions in the Far East against our prisoners. Public prejudice is so strong in B.C. that it is going to be difficult to control the situation; also moving men to camps at this time of year very difficult indeed. I did my best to get decisions from the Cabinet and matters sufficiently advanced to be prepared for afternoon questions [in the House of Commons].

———

[c]*Observation made in 1946 on the evacuation and internment of Japanese Canadians:*

The evacuation and resettlement of the people of Japanese ancestry living along the Pacific coast . . . has created unprecedented problems. Although more than half the Canadian Japanese were born in Canada, and although many of their parents were naturalized citizens, they were moved by arbitrary order of Ottawa, their property was sold without their consent, and their rights of citizenship were denied. Domestically, this treatment raises the question of the meaning of citizenship and of racial tolerance in Canada. Internationally, it raises complications in Canada's relations with the Far East, since Canada, as a nation of the Pacific area, must live in this "one world" with the peoples of the Orient, the Japanese as well as the others.

Although Canada was busy with the war, the government did devote some attention to social legislation. In May 1940, the Rowell-Sirois Commission presented its report. It suggested that the provinces relinquish the field of income, corporation and inheritance taxes in return for federal grants. Also, the Dominion was to take over the debts of the provinces. In order to assure a basic standard of social services in all provinces, the Commission recommended "equalization grants" — additional annual payments to the more needy provinces. Several provinces opposed the adoption of the recommendations of the Commission, and for the time being the report was shelved. In subsequent years some of the recommendations were implemented.

RECOMMENDATIONS OF THE ROWELL-SIROIS COMMISSION[405]

. . . . The striking fact . . . is that many provinces . . . are unable to find the money to enable them to meet the needs of their citizens.

———

[The Commission recommends]:
. . . the relief of the unemployed who are able and willing to work will become a federal function.

———

. . . the Dominion should assume all provincial debts . . . and that each province should pay over to the Dominion an annual sum equal to the interest which it now receives from its investments. . . .
. . . . The provincial debt of the Province of Quebec is low in comparision with the per capita debt of other provinces . . . the Dominion should take over 40 per cent of the combined provincial and municipal net debt service in Quebec.
. . . [the provinces] should surrender to the Dominion the subsidies, whatever their character, which they now receive. . . .
. . . the provinces . . . should renounce some of the taxes which they employ (or are entitled to employ) at present. . . .

———

. . . the provinces should renounce . . . the tax on personal incomes. . . .
. . . the provinces should forgo . . . those taxes imposed on corporations. . . .
. . . the Dominion should pay over to the province concerned 10 per cent of the corporate income derived from the exploitation of the mineral wealth of the province. . . .
. . . the provinces should forgo . . . various forms of succession duty. . . .

———

. . . to provide normal Canadian services . . . each province found to be in need . . . should receive it [an amount] by way of an annual National Adjustment Grant from the Dominion. . . .

During the war, the Dominion government adopted two long-needed progressive measures.

In 1940, the Unemployment Insurance Commission (U.I.C.) Fund was established to provide for those who might be temporarily unemployed. The fund was to be supported by compulsory contribution from employees and employers. However, according to the B.N.A. Act, providing unemployment insurance was a provincial jurisdiction; a constitutional amendment was required to transfer this authority to the federal government. A joint address by the Canadian House of Commons and Senate to the British Parliament, and subsequent approval by all the provinces brought the U.I.C. into being. Because of almost full employment during the war years, very little was paid out from the U.I.C. Fund and the growing funds were invested in government bonds and securities, thus helping the government's overall wartime borrowing.

Another social legislation, Family Allowance, was introduced in 1944. Parents received monthly payments from the federal government for each child up to the age of sixteen. This assistance to families aimed at raising the general standard of living of all Canadians. Unemployment insurance and family allowance, modified and expanded over the years, have endured and have become part of Canadian life.

FAMILY ALLOWANCES[406]

On July 25, 1944, Prime Minister Mackenzie King introduced a bill to establish Family Allowances:

. . . . The purpose [of social security measures] is to give special attention to human welfare and health. Within the last twenty-four hours, a bill was assented to in this parliament related to national health and welfare. . . . The measure before the house at the moment will come for administration under the Department of National Health and Welfare. . . .

This measure to provide family allowances . . . makes provision for the children of all families in a manner that helps to safeguard their economic and social needs. . . . The money that will be voted for the purposes of the bill will find its way into a demand for commodities or services that are part of the essentials of life, and as such will create employment. . . . In other words, this measure should prove an instrument that will help prevent anything like the depressions that have followed in previous periods in the wake of war. In addition, it will of course play an all-important part in furthering the well-being and welfare of the citizens of the country.

29

CANADIAN GOVERNMENT AND THE ECONOMY, 1945 TO THE PRESENT

A

THE RETURN TO PEACE

Of all the nations facing the challenge of postwar adjustment, Canada was one of the most fortunate. Its factories and farmlands, stimulated to produce as never before to meet Allied wartime needs, had escaped the ravages of bombs and cannon. Within a short time after 1945, Canadian industry was turning out consumer goods for buyers at home and abroad.

With many of the important industrial nations lying in ruin, their productive capacities crippled, the demand for Canadian products remained high. Instead of a severe economic depression — such as struck the country after World War I — Canada enjoyed a continuation of wartime prosperity.

THE GOVERNMENT CAUTIONED ABOUT ITS PLANS FOR POSTWAR PROSPERITY IN CANADA[407]

A financial critic of the day expressed the following doubts:

. . . . Those wrecked countries, formerly good customers of ours to whom we are presumably now looking for an increased consumption of our exports, will need our goods but will have no means of payment. . . . We can extend them long-term credits and we can continue "mutual aid" but we may be certain that we shall not get rich furnishing goods without getting paid for them, and that genuine recovery of our export trade must wait upon the economic restoration of those foreign markets. . . .

A short-lived crisis did, in 1947, interrupt the progress of events. Ironically, the boom in the Canadian economy was at the root of the trouble. Canada's customers, especially Great Britain and countries in Europe which were beginning the immense task of rebuilding, had been buying from Canadians as never before. However, they were making their purchases on credit. At the same time Canadian exports were not actually bringing money into the country, the buying power of Canadians was at a peak. In addition to rising wages, many Canadians had income from such sources as war bonds and veterans' allowances. Much of this money was being spent on imported goods, principally from the United States, which enjoyed an influx of Canadian dollars. A threat of national bankruptcy loomed.

The federal government, its wartime authority over the economy still intact, moved swiftly to avert calamity. It introduced emergency restrictions on a wide range of imports, including household appliances, luxury goods, even fresh vegetables and fruit. Fortunately the measures seemed to have the desired effect, and Canadians had to endure them for only a short time. The exchange crisis soon eased, and the forbidden imports were once again admitted.

In the decade which followed, the Canadian nation moved through economic expansion and development of resources to higher and higher levels of prosperity. The economy grew in complexity, and the terms "inflation" and "high cost of living" became established in the Canadian vocabulary. Although some regions of the country lagged behind others, most Canadians believed they lived in one of the "best of all possible worlds."

A REACTION TO HIGH TAXES IN CANADA AT THE END OF WORLD WAR II[408]

About high Canadian taxes in 1945, a journalist had words to say that were both typical and prophetic:

"It's tough trying to keep both my wife and the Government on one income!"

"Three days out of every six I work for the Ottawa crowd!"

When Canadians try to figure out how they're going to pay for the war, together with present and promised social legislation, they express themselves in various ways but think along similar lines. . . .

Canada stands therefore at the crossroads of financial decision — either to dig down hard now and get this mounting debt under control, or take it easy and hope that the up-and-coming generation will feel kindly and generous about footing the bill as it pyramids to even dizzier heights. . . .

B

MAJOR ECONOMIC DEVELOPMENTS

Newer types of industries, such as the chemical and electronic, and the increase in the population of Canada — that is, an increased domestic market — have continued to play a large part in Canadian expansion in recent years. But for various reasons Canadian manufacturing industries have often not maintained the spectacular advances of the immediate postwar period. Intensified foreign competition, tariff barriers and other obstacles both economic and political often lay in the way. Therefore, the discovery and exploitation of large new deposits of minerals, accompanied by giant projects in transportation and other utilities, has been vital to the nation's progress.

The Leduc oil fields, discovered near Edmonton, Alberta, in 1947, were the first of several that gave rise to the postwar oil boom. Besides providing much needed supplies of oil and natural gas for Canadians to use, these oil fields became the resource base for an expanding petroleum industry. The province of Alberta, long thought of as "next year country," a land which had thrived in large measure on hope for the future, was naturally the immediate beneficiary. Western Canada in general assumed a stronger position in the nation's economy. With the rise of new industry and increasing population, Western Canadians could look forward to the growth of new enterprises to complement the traditional reliance on agriculture.

AN OIL TOWN IN ALBERTA[409]

Shortly after the discovery of oil at Leduc in 1947, a magazine writer noted some of the changes in the town:

Six months ago a traveller always could get a room in the two-story brick hotel at Leduc, 19 miles south of Edmonton on the highway to Calgary. . . . The only day in the week when many people were around was Saturday. If a traveller visited Leduc often he probably knew by sight or name many of Leduc's 864 citizens and some of the farmers, too.

Today he'd be lucky to find anyone he knew. Citizens and farmers alike are almost lost in the dozens of men in plaid and khaki shirts, high boots, wide-brimmed hats and oil-stained overalls — wildcatters, the men who search for new oil fields.

The pool room is full of oilmen off shift, drillers and cathead men and lead tong men and derrick men. Upstairs in the hotel, past the deserted desk with its "No Rooms Vacant" sign, oilmen sit around a blanket-covered table and play quiet, dollar-limit poker. In the beer parlor below some oilmen drink beer and others drink a mixture of beer and tomato juice. The mid-European accents of the Ukrainian and Polish farmers and the clear prairie speech of the townspeople mix with the more precise English of Easterners and occasionally with the drawls of Texas and Oklahoma.

And among oilmen and farmers alike the talk is not of crops but of . . . the $130,000 Pete Hairysh got for his half section, or the $41,000 the widow Kate Malchak got for her quarter. . . .

Serious development of Alberta's new found source of wealth was made possible by the construction of a trans-Canada pipeline. In one of the great national projects of the 1950's, pipelines were completed to transport crude oil and natural gas to markets both on the west coast and in eastern Canada and the United States. Through the combination of government assistance and private enterprise, largely American in origin, the petroleum and natural gas industry had become by 1968 one of Canada's leading industries.

The mineral resources of the Canadian Shield have long been known to be vast. Major discoveries were made early in the century, and by the 1930's, mining of gold, nickel, copper and other valuable minerals was well underway. But the earlier efforts were mere trials compared to the tremendous undertakings after World War II. Contributing factors have included the demands of industry in Canada — and in the United States,

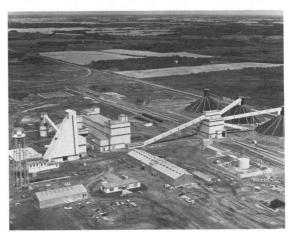

Left: Operating a Drill Jumbo: Uranium Mine, Elliott Lake, Ontario

Right: Workmen Setting Drilling Bit at Imperial Oil Co.

Centre: Aerial View of the International Minerals and Chemicals Corp. Potash Mine at Esterhazy, Saskatchewan

by far Canada's biggest customer — improved techniques for mineral exploration and extraction and the availability of investment capital from the United States.

Canada's position as one of the world's leading mineral producers has been strengthened by new ventures in every region of the country. Examples include copper mines and asbestos in British Columbia, potash at Esterhazy, Saskatchewan and the Thompson nickel mines in northern Manitoba. In mineral-rich northern Ontario, the Elliot Lake uranium deposits were tapped in the 1950's and the reserves should provide another bonanza when demands for the valuable ore increase in the near future. The Timmins area is the site of zinc-silver-copper deposits. Copper mines north of Noranda and at Murdochville in the Gaspé region are important examples in Quebec. Rock salt in Pugwash, Nova Scotia, lead-zinc mines at Bathurst, New Brunswick and asbestos at Baie Verte in Newfoundland are important to the economy of the Atlantic provinces.

The Canadian North is clearly one of the keys to the nation's economic growth. The mining frontier is being pushed into the northern reaches of the provinces and even beyond the 60th parallel. Oil in the Athabasca tar sands, lead-zinc at Pine Point near Great Slave Lake and tungsten in the Northwest Territories indicate the possible future rewards of northern development.

PROBLEMS AND PROSPECTS OF MINING IN CANADA'S NORTH[410]

William M. Gilchrist, President of Eldorado Mining and Refining, gives a realistic view:

. . . the Canadian north is a vast country, the ore deposits are scattered and far from ports, and the climate is severe. The land itself sets the limits. While the chances of coming across a rich placer stream or a fabulous outcrop of mineral wealth are still there, thus adding excitement to the hunt for northern mineral wealth, its future development today depends on large-scale capitalization. The Iron Ore Company of Canada's initial operation in the heart of Labrador-Ungava cost half a billion dollars; International Nickel's Thompson operation cost even more. To go with this massive capital investment, northern mining development, along with a high level of science and technology, will also require the right sort of labour force. Otherwise these investments will just not pay. . . .

Two Freighters on the Welland Canal

People walk along the Trans-Canada Highway in Glacier Park, B.C. to attend the opening ceremonies of the Rogers Pass Section.

The most spectacular northern mining project initiated in the 1950's was the one in the Ungava region of Quebec and Labrador. Because of the iron deposit, one of the largest known in the world, such new mining communities as Schefferville, Labrador City and Gagnon have been built, many related industries have sprung up, and a 350-mile railway was laid from Schefferville to Sept Iles on the St. Lawrence River.

THE FUTURE OF CANADA'S NORTH[411]

The note of enthusiasm expressed by a writer in 1966:

. . . . Canada's new dimension lies in the north. Canadians have so much to gain in embarking on bold plans to develop its resources.

As Canada faces her second century, her north — the Yukon and Northwest Territories — will provide not only a good living for the people of these Territories, but will give all of Canada greater depth, wealth and stature.

If all Canadians look upon the north as part of their Canadian inheritance, it can be a truly uniting factor transcending factions and fractioning tendencies into which our restive regional nationalisms so often push us. The north can be one of Canada's great sources of inspiration and unity.

This last case illustrates the extent to which resource development and advances in transportation have proceeded together. Penetration of the northern frontiers has been made possible by the extension of air freight transport, new roads and railways such as the Quebec-Labrador railway, the lines to Thompson and Lynn Lake in northern Manitoba, and the railway from Rosa, Alberta, to Great Slave Lake.

The single greatest transportation project of the 1950's was the St. Lawrence Seaway. The idea of extending the mighty St. Lawrence was not a new one. Since the beginning of the twentieth century, men in both Canada and the United States had dreamed of the day when ocean-going ships could travel to the head of the Great Lakes. In 1932 the necessary step of deepening the Welland Canal was completed by Canada. However, negotiations with the United States failed to produce an agreement for the joint construction of the Seaway.

The Canadian government finally decided, in 1951, to proceed independently. This move added to the pressures already being exerted on the government of the United States. To states bordering the Great Lakes, the Seaway would provide much needed hydro-electric power and serve as an efficient avenue for moving Quebec-Labrador iron ore to American steel mills. Grain from both sides of the international boundary could be transported in greater quantity at lower cost. An agreement between Canada and the United States was signed in 1954, and five years later the St. Lawrence Seaway was ready for operation.

The forecasted volume of shipping and of the revenues from tolls charged to meet the cost of the Seaway has proved to be optimistic. However, although the rise in traffic has been slower than expected, the trend is sufficiently encouraging to justify the project. Already it can be said that the Seaway has stimulated Canada's industrialization, its other modes of transportation and its overseas trade.

Lionel Chevrier, the first President of the St. Lawrence Seaway Authority, writing in 1959, looked back to this great achievement:

The history of the St. Lawrence and the fight for the seaway has been a history of ships. Basically it has been a battle to get bigger and bigger ships up the river, to move heavier and heavier cargoes. Now that the seaway is complete, an epoch is ended. The old dream of the pioneers has been realized. The ocean has been let into the North American heartland.

Looking at the seaway now with its gigantic locks, power-houses, dams, enormous channels cut across fields, islands, cities, with its 20,000-ton ships steaming majestically up and down the river. It is interesting to note the changes that two and a half centuries have brought to the great waterway. The ships have replaced the muscular and colourful voyageurs, heaving and straining their canoes overland past the rapids, watching for Iroquois, and dreaming of a fortune in furs from the hinterland. They have replaced the soldiers and the raft men.

Besides its value as part of Canada's transportation network, the Seaway is one of several important hydro-electric developments of recent years. In a continent where modern technology and urban centres are expanding rapidly, other sources of power — such as atomic energy — are contemplated. Nevertheless Canada's hydro-electric potential is being exploited as never before. The Columbia River, the Nelson River of Manitoba and the Churchill Falls of Labrador are but three of the locations where projects are in progress.

C

PROBLEMS AND PROGRESS TO THE PRESENT

By 1957 the postwar boom had lost its momentum. Growth of the labour force outstripped that of new employment opportunities, with added job-seekers coming from the ranks of maturing "war babies," women seeking fulltime employment, increased numbers of people moving from rural areas to the cities and men thrown out of work by automation, as well as a continuing flow of immigrants. An adverse balance of trade worsened as Canada faced intensifying competition from West Germany, Japan, France and other countries recovered from the war. Canadians' demand for imports continued unabated while the nation's exports found markets less available. Many of the enterprises that had been attracting foreign capital were completed about this time, and investors frequently turned to more attractive economic conditions in other countries.

The Diefenbaker government began a number of programs to alleviate the situation. The winter works program, in which half the costs were undertaken by the federal government, provided limited, seasonal employment. The Trans-Canada Highway, built in co-operation with the provinces between 1959 and 1962, furnished short-term financial benefits and added to the physical unity of Canada. The "roads to resources" program was a constructive beginning to plans for opening up the north, although it fell short of expectations. But the basic problem of economic difficulty remained unsolved for the nation as a whole.

The Canadian government, spending far more than it was taking in, was accumulating large annual deficits. To make matters worse, a conflict developed between the policies of the government and the Bank of Canada. After months of feuding, the Bank's Governor, James Coyne, was dismissed from office, but the "Coyne affair" had further damaged the country's economic climate. Finally, in May, 1962, the Canadian government was forced to devalue the Canadian dollar, which was pegged at 92½ cents in relation to the United States dollar in order to guard against national bankruptcy and stimulate export trade.

Fortunately the economy entered a new period of expansion at this time. Exports increased and greater spending within the country added stimulus to the trend. Yet a major reason for renewed prosperity was an influx of capital from the United States. One effect was to bring to a head the serious concern of many Canadians about American domination of such principal industries as petroleum, vital minerals and manufacturing industries of all kinds. The question was not a new one, but it seemed more pressing than ever before: if Americans continued to extend their control of the Canadian economy, how long would it be before Canadians would lose their political independence?

"The Diefendollar", 1962

The issue, for all its complexity, may be stated fairly simply. As a country whose entire history has been that of a "developing nation" with a relatively small population engaged in developing a vast territory, Canada has always relied on imported money, men and techniques. Great Britain was the chief source for these until recent times but ceased being so — at least for capital — at about the time when Canada became fully independent. With the growing importance of American capital in Canada, especially since World War II, Canadians face the problem of retaining its benefits while keeping its hazards to a minimum.

Walter Gordon, Minister of Finance in Lester B. Pearson's new Liberal government, was one of those Canadians with strong feelings on the subject. In his first budget, brought down in June, 1963, he introduced discriminatory taxation to discourage further American take-over of Canadian companies and to encourage Canadians to buy back companies already American controlled. A tax of thirty percent was to be levied on shares sold to foreigners or to foreign controlled companies. Companies with less than twenty-five per cent Canadian ownership were to pay extra taxes. Immediately a storm of opposition forced Mr. Gordon to present a revised budget, withdrawing the tax penalties. The United States made clear that it would take retaliatory action should Canada resort to unneighbourly economic behaviour in future.

Mr. Gordon remained in the Cabinet when the Prime Minister refused his offered resignation, but after the election which he recommended in 1965 did not produce a majority Liberal government,

he left office. His crusade against American economic domination did not cease, however. In 1966, his book, *A Choice for Canada: Independence or Colonial Status,* was published. In the book he detailed the extent of American economic penetration into Canada and restated the arguments behind the policies he attempted to implement while Minister of Finance.

AMERICAN INVESTMENT IN CANADA[413]

Walter Gordon points out the benefits and dangers in American investment in Canada:

Canada has benefited greatly from the investment of foreign capital, and we will need more of it. But to suggest, as is sometimes done, that it makes no difference who owns Canadian companies, is a complete contradiction of the facts. There are those who . . . see no cause for concern about the size and character of foreign investment in Canada. . . .

. . . . I suspect that some of my economist friends who try to reassure me that there are no difficulties attached to the unprecedented amount of foreign investment in our country have not fully thought through the political implications of this.

We believe, or many of us believe, that economic independence and political independence go hand in hand. In wanting to retain our independence, we are no different than the British, the French, the Swiss, the Japanese, or the people of other countries, including the United States. Some may call this nationalism, and so it is. It is a proper respect, loyalty, and enthusiasm for one's country, and a legitimate optimism and confidence about its future.

Yet even within the Liberal government, men such as Mitchell Sharp, who succeeded to Mr. Gordon's portfolio, took an opposing stand. Many of the provincial Premiers, particularly those in the West, declared themselves opposed to any schemes that might inhibit the inflow of foreign investment. During the election campaign of May and June, 1968, the New Democratic Party cited the Watkins Report,* as proof that Canada must take immediate steps to control foreign investment. The NDP proposed, among other things, the creation of the Canada Development Corporation, which was a favorite plan of Walter Gordon. The Corporation would serve as a vehicle for securing Canadian influence over companies and resources now dominated by foreigners and for initiating new Canadian business ventures. Both the Liberals and Progressive Conservatives, however, while not denying the problem, preferred to stress the harsh reality that no Canadian government could lightly risk actions that could lead to the withdrawal of American capital from Canada.

CANADA'S TRADE PROSPECTS IN A CHANGING WORLD[414]

The ECONOMIC COUNCIL OF CANADA, *in its* FIFTH ANNUAL REVIEW (*1968*), *says Canada can compete with other industrial nations if it concentrates on certain types of markets:*

What should be Canada's response to fast-growing world demands for high-technology products? Almost certainly it should not be to enter fields such as the manufacture of large jet airliners or supertankers where other countries have established major advantages. Rather, it should be . . . strengthening . . . the great resource industries in which Canada already possesses substantial comparative advantages, and . . . to seize particular opportunities arising out of world demands for technological products — opportunities which happen to suit reasonably well Canadian industrial capabilities. Canadian industry has established a good position in such "niches" as the world market for certain kinds of specialized aircraft. . . . Also, in recent years, many Canadian manufacturing industries have improved their capabilities for producing new and more advanced products in competition with imports.

* A study on "Foreign Ownership and the Structures of Canadian Industry" commissioned by the government of Canada. This Report prepared for the Privy Council Office was presented on January 12, 1968.

D

FEDERAL-PROVINCIAL RELATIONS

Of the many effects of World War II, none was more enduring than the creation of "Big Government." Expanded to meet the demands of a nation engaged in total war, government continued to grow at all levels in the complex postwar period. Canada's federal system, seeming infinitely flexible and capable of taking on new functions, has become so all pervasive that Canadians feel its influence in almost every aspect of their daily lives.

The outstanding feature of government in Canada is, nevertheless, the continual "tug o' war" between the federal government and the provinces. The nature of the problem was brought out in the first postwar meetings, in 1945 and 1946, between representatives of both levels of government. As the Rowell-Sirois Report of 1940 had made clear, the fundamental question was one of properly redefining the separate jurisdictions of federal and provincial authorities. Could this be done, then a formula might be more easily found for ensuring that governments which were expected to provide certain services would have the necessary money.

Ottawa had assumed wide taxation powers during the war as part of the central government's general assumption of authority over the nation's affairs. The provinces, some more grudgingly than others, conceded that centralization of power was natural during the wartime emergency. With the end of the war, however, the federal government was not prepared to relinquish its position of strength. As announced in its White Paper on Employment and Income, released in April, 1945, the federal government planned to use its authority as a means of managing the national economy and improving the level of prosperity in Canada. To do so, in line with the precepts of economist John Maynard Keynes, would involve the utilization of public spending when economic recession seemed imminent and the application of increased taxes in good times so as to accumulate surpluses in the federal treasury.

The provinces, particularly Ontario and Quebec, were anxious to recover some of their former powers and to enlarge their shares of government revenue. A serious clash was unavoidable. When

Ottawa proposed, in 1945, to take over succession duties — in addition to its control over income and corporation taxes — hard bargaining followed. No scheme of compensation satisfactory to all the provinces could be devised. Hence the federal government resorted to making separate "tax rental" agreements with the provinces individually.

A COMMENT ON THE DOMINION-PROVINCIAL CONFERENCES OF 1945-1946[415]

In a column of humour in its edition of January 19, 1946, SATURDAY NIGHT *magazine remarked:*

A Toronto choreographer has invented a new dance which requires the partners to go around one another while turning in opposite directions. We do not favor the suggestion that it be known as the DPC (Dominion-Provincial Conference) side-step.

What began as a temporary arrangement was renewed in similar forms in the years that followed. Out of the need for repeated meetings of the two levels of government developed a new, and distinctly Canadian, institution — the Federal-Provincial Conference. The most important are the conferences of Prime Ministers and Premiers, but dozens of meetings, involving cabinet ministers and civil servants, are held every year. The purpose of the meetings in the new era of "co-operative federalism" is to co-ordinate the many programs which now require the participation of both levels of government. The need grew acute with the multiplication of provincial responsibilities in the 1960's, and with the corresponding explosion of provincial-municipal costs, particularly in such spheres as education and health and welfare.

The Federal-Provincial Tax Structure Committee, established in 1964, is one of the more important instruments of co-operation. The Committee was set up to investigate trends in government expenditure, to consider the allocation of revenue to the different governments, and to work out the nature of federal-provincial programs and the order in which they may be introduced. Long-term progress of the Committee depends on the extent to which the government of Canada intends to follow the recommendations of the Carter Royal Commission Report on Taxation, tabled in 1967. Any comprehensive reform of Canada's system of taxation would have profound implications for federal-provincial relations.

Even more significant possibilities may emerge in the event of changes in the Canadian constitu-

tion, which came under increasing scrutiny in the 1960's. Early in the decade, attention was directed at the need for creating a strictly Canadian set of procedures for amending the constitution. Successive governments have so far been unable to devise a formula by which amendments affecting the provinces as well as the federal government can be made without invoking the aid of the British Parliament.*

Criticism of the constitution has broadened in scope, however, and raised the question of re-writing the constitution or replacing it with one more applicable to the modern Canada. Premier John Robarts of Ontario took the occasion of Centennial Year to invite the provincial Premiers to a meeting in Toronto. At the conference in November, 1967, where proceedings were given full national television coverage, the government of Canada was an observer rather than a participant. Later, in February, 1968, the federal government was host to a Federal-Provincial Conference on the constitution. In an atmosphere seemingly marked by reasonableness and a spirit of compromise, the heads of Canada's governments again spoke to each other and to national television audiences on the subjects of the constitution and the integrally linked issues of relations between governments and between Canadians of English-speaking and French-speaking backgrounds.

Since the beginning of the "Quiet Revolution" in Quebec, the question of that province's position in Confederation has become one of the main controversies in Canada. Quebec's provincial governments have promoted themselves as the guarantors of the survival of the French-Canadian culture, and have sought autonomy within Canada's federal system so as to have greater control over the province's affairs. Thus Quebec has been the source of much of the impetus for constitutional reform.

PROBLEMS OF FEDERALISM[416]

From an interview with Prime Minister Lester B. Pearson in December, 1966:

. . . . There has not been a single arrangement made in this field [of federal-provincial relations] with the province of Quebec which was not applicable to every other province. The problem arises when Quebec wishes to recover certain powers or jurisdiction and no other province does. Then you get an appearance of constitutional disunity and of special favors to one province. But it's not a

---

* Note, for example, the fate of the Fulton-Favreau formula proposed in 1964.

Federal-Provincial Conference on Confederation, Ottawa, 1968

question of special favors, it's a question of making an arrangement applicable to all provinces when Quebec is the only province that wishes to take advantage of it.

Federalism then, and I think this is important, does not involve only problems between Ottawa and Quebec, but problems that concern every province in a federal state.

The nation-wide debate that has grown up around concern over the status of Quebec and the further concern over the future of Canada,

has obscured the fact that all the provinces have sought and gained much authority which they did not possess in 1945. A federal state, more difficult to administer than a unitary one such as Great Britain or France, is a state in which the relations of its parts are dynamic and subject to change as conditions change. Since no division of powers is perfect, and new subjects of legislation will arise from time to time, not even the evolution of a co-ordinating agency to fill the role now performed by the innumerable federal-provincial conferences will ensure a future for federal-provincial relations any less complicated than their past.

E

GROWTH OF THE WELFARE STATE

An important area of government spending since 1945 has been social welfare. For most of Canada's history the prevailing attitude was that the individual, in most cases, was responsible for his own destiny. The handicapped and the indigent might be so fortunate as to receive charity or "handouts," from a church or underfinanced private agency. Often the family was expected to provide assistance for less fortunate members, especially aged parents. In general, though, in such a land of opportunity as Canada, a man was thought to be free to advance himself by his own hard work and ingenuity. Such a philosophy may

have been suitable in the days when life was simpler, but it is no longer so in the complex world of the mid-twentieth century.

In response to the changing conditions of a modern industrialized country, and the public demand for services, governments have gone a long way toward creating "the welfare state." Pressure groups on behalf of the public need have included the churches, private philanthropic agencies, farm organizations and labour unions, and at least one political party, the Co-operative Commonwealth Federation, now called the New Democratic Party.

Government in a democracy is no longer viewed

as essentially a negative institution, maintaining law and order but otherwise rarely touching the lives of citizens. Instead, it has become increasingly an instrument of social justice for all parts of the population. It is now more generally recognized that the aged, the physically handicapped, the people born in the sprawling slums of expanding cities and others less fortunately placed in society are often denied the opportunity for what used to be termed "free enterprise." It is more widely believed that society has a duty to the individual as well as vice versa. Large numbers of Canadians, wherever they live and whatever their circumstances, may be guaranteed a share in the nation's prosperity only if government acts on their behalf.

WHY GOVERNMENTS MUST PROVIDE SOCIAL SECURITY IN THE MODERN AGE[417]

The ECONOMIC COUNCIL OF CANADA, *in its 1968 report, explains:*

The vicissitudes of life being what they are, the need for direct income maintenance programs will never disappear completely. There will always be some families and individuals unable to participate fully and independently in economic life because of age, disability, ill health, or other reasons. In addition to ensuring adequate standards of living, social assistance to such people should be provided in a way that fosters their full participation in other aspects of our common life. Assistance should be extended to them as a right rather than a privilege, with no stigma attached.

Social security is, in many respects, a practical matter. In this sense, it represents the attempt on the part of a society to obtain the maximum benefits from its human resources. To work toward such a goal, governments are increasingly called upon to plan new programs for maintaining higher health standards, improved education and manpower training, better housing and working conditions and reducing the differences in living standards in the various regions of Canada.

Although old age pensions were first introduced in 1927, government responsibility for welfare in Canada really began in the 1940's — after the depression had demonstrated the need. In 1940, the federal government made arrangements with the provinces and passed an act to provide unemployment insurance. Then the Marsh Report, submitted to the cabinet early in 1943, advocated a complete program of social insurance. One of the recommendations, family allowances, was implemented in the following year.

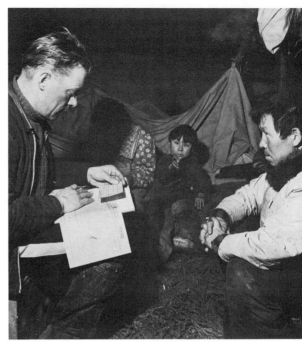

Corporal Jim Davis, during 1100 mile journey, registers Eskimos for Family Allowance at Great Whale, Quebec.

A PROMINENT CANADIAN CONDEMNS FAMILY ALLOWANCE[418]

In March, 1945, Charlotte Whitton, later mayor of Ottawa, denounced the "baby bonus" as a threat to Canada:

. . . . Not only does the cash bonus for children threaten serious repercussions for the economies of the provinces and for the over-all welfare program. . . . It is also breeding an administrative octupus of fantastic proportions whose extending arms are winding in and through and about the constitutional rights of the provinces . . . it strikes at the very basis of Confederation which precluded, in a minority state, the intervention of the central power and the thrust of its officials into the civil life and homes of the citizens. Problems of the gravest portent are attendant on the ruthless rushing ahead of Dominion officials to issue the first cheques under the statute. . . .

The old age pension scheme was altered in 1951. The new act brought in payments, without any means test, to all persons over the age of seventy with ten years' residence in Canada. In the intervening years, the monthly payments have been increased and the age for receiving benefits reduced to sixty-five by 1970. An added feature is the guaranteed income supplement, available to pensioners who lack another source of income.

Entrance to Canada Pension Plan Office

To help Canadians meet the cost of hospital care, some of the provinces granted financial aid for treatment of specific illnesses, while others, notably Saskatchewan in 1947, set up more comprehensive health insurance plans. In 1957, the Hospital Insurance Act provided that the federal government would pay approximately half the government costs of hospital insurance; by 1961 all the provinces had decided to participate. Various plans, both private and public, have come into existence to help citizens pay for such medical costs as doctors' fees. In 1962 Saskatchewan introduced compulsory medical insurance, often called "medicare," to ensure services to the entire population of the province. A federal "medicare" program has since been devised in the hope that all provinces will take part.

The Canada Pension Plan, and the associated plan in Quebec, was initiated in 1965 to provide further retirement benefits, disability allowances and survivors' benefits.

Like the Canada Pension Plan, the Canada Assistance Plan, for which the act was passed in 1966, is a comprehensive program that will eventually incorporate many existing schemes that have grown up piece-meal over recent years. Also a product of federal-provincial co-operation, it is designed to cover mothers' allowances, blind and disabled persons' benefits, child welfare, community development services and a range of other projects.

Public health services have similarly expanded since 1945. With the aid of national health grants, the provinces have materially increased the number of hospitals for general care, mental illness, medical rehabilitation and communicable diseases. Research and immunization programs have been subsidized to help reduce the incidence of disease.

CANADA MUST FIGHT A "WAR ON POVERTY"[419]

The Economic Council of Canada insists that Canada must work to eliminate poverty for both humane and practical reasons:

We believe that serious poverty should be eliminated in Canada, and that this should be designated as a major national goal. We believe this for two reasons. The first is that one of the wealthiest societies in world history, if it also aspires to be a just society, cannot avoid setting itself such a goal. Secondly, poverty is costly. Its most grievous costs are those felt directly by the poor themselves, but it also imposes very large costs on the rest of society. These include the costs of crime, disease, and poor education. They include the costs of low productivity and lost output, of controlling the social tensions and unrest associated with gross inequality, and of that part of total welfare expenditure which is essentially a palliative made necessary by the failure to find more fundamental solutions. It has been estimated in the United States that one poor man can cost the public purse as much as $140,000 between the ages of 17 and 57.

30

POLITICAL LIFE IN CANADA, 1945 TO THE PRESENT

A

THE LAST YEARS OF MACKENZIE KING

The last year of World War II, 1945, was an election year and the Liberal government was in serious danger of defeat. Liberals had fared badly in provincial elections in Ontario, Saskatchewan and Quebec. Identified across Canada with wartime restrictions, suffering from declining morale in the cabinet and in the caucus, the Liberals faced a critical situation in Quebec, where much support had fallen away over the conscription crisis of 1944.

Then VE Day, May 8, marked the end of the war in Europe, and the anti-government feeling began to subside. In the election of June 11, the Liberals managed to secure a bare majority, 125 out of the 245 seats which the House of Commons then contained. A major reason was the loyalty of Quebec, which returned 54 Liberals and rejected the many radicals who had vigorously attacked the federal government's emphasis on national unity. Otherwise the Liberals held firm in the Maritimes and Manitoba, but lost heavily to the Conservatives in Ontario, to the Co-operative Commonwealth Federation in Saskatchewan and to Social Credit in Alberta.

The aging Mackenzie King relied more and more on his ministers as the government and the nation moved into the postwar period of adjustment. The formidable C. D. Howe, labelled by the opposition as the "Minister with all the Portfolios," exhibited the same energy in organizing the return to peacetime as he had in mobilizing wartime production. Louis St. Laurent, the principal French-Canadian associate of Mackenzie King, moved over from the justice portfolio to become Secretary of State for External Affairs. He encouraged a more positive and active Canadian foreign policy through membership in such international bodies as the United Nations and the North Atlantic Treaty Organization.

When Mackenzie King announced his retirement in 1948, he had completed twenty-two years as Prime Minister, longer than anyone in the history of the Commonwealth. His career in public life spanned two world wars, and the transformation of Canada from colonial status to nationhood. Although he had never inspired his countrymen, he had used his political skills with effect in the interests of national harmony. With Canada entering a new phase of confidence and prosperity, he took the opportunity of stepping down from the highest political office in the land.

ABOUT MACKENZIE KING[420]

aHis bachelorhood:

. . . W. K. "Billy" Esling, the Conservative member for Kootenay West, was holding forth with great earnestness on the vexing Doukhobor question. "What would the Prime Minister do, I should like to know," he asked the House seriously, "if one evening he discovered three Doukhobor women in his garden?"

Like a flash King was on his feet.

"I should send for the leaders of the Opposition," he shot back, amidst laughter. (The "leaders of the Opposition" at that time were R. B. Bennett, and Robert Gardiner of the U.F.A., both of them bachelors).

———

"You ought to get married," a friend told King on one occasion. "It would do you a lot of good if you had a wife to come home to who would tell you what a poor Prime Minister you were and who would cut you down to size."

"I admit the value of marriage," said King, a trifle ruefully, "but when I was younger and might have married I didn't have the opportunity, and now nobody would have me."

"Just put an ad or two in the papers" suggested his friend, "and see how long you will last."

———

His dog:

Those who sought to humanize the Prime Minister invariably spoke of his attachment for his little Irish terrier, Pat. Pat was King's constant companion for some 17 years. He was the only one whom King could talk to in confidence. Pat probably was the repository of more state secrets over the years than one could shake a stick at. . . .

King always claimed that his dog had an uncanny political sense, that he seemed to know if the day had gone well or badly for his master. He believed that a man could learn a great deal from a dog's sense of devotion and loyalty. "That dog taught me much," he declared on one occasion.

Tobacco and food:

Because King disliked tobacco smoke, ministers made a habit of knocking out their pipes and snuffing out their cigars and cigarettes when he entered the room.

King never learned to smoke. He had an aversion to the use of tobacco in any form. Once, when he was visiting the war graves in France after World War I, an officer handed him a cigarette, and for some reason or other, perhaps to be sociable, King took it and lit up.
"He handled the cigarette as if it was a firecracker," someone who observed the incident reported.

[b]King used no tobacco, drank little alcohol and regarded himself as a model of temperance (even if he and Meighen were once seen, after a convivial banquet, standing together on a table and singing "My Old Kentucky Home" in tuneless duet). Food was another matter. King loved it like a glutton and savoured it like an epicure.

[c]*His belief in spiritualism:*

Only one of his secretaries and none of his colleagues knew that he had become a practising spiritualist. He guarded his secret with elaborate precautions lest the scoffing voters conclude that the Government was dominated by spooks or frauds. After his death, when the facts came out, his mediums agreed that his public policies had never been discussed with the dead. . . .

. . . [Before his death] King was interested only in the world to come. For his pending arrival there, he prepared himself by constant communication with the spirits of his parents, Roosevelt and his dead Irish terrier, Pat.

[d]*His humour:*

. . . when James Oastler of the Montreal *Star* was covering an election meeting he noticed King appeared to be having trouble with his teeth. His dentures seemed to be slipping and sliding about, and Oastler thought something should be done about it. So he sent one of King's secretaries a note suggesting that King should see his dentist and get a new set of teeth. On election night, after the returns were all in, Oastler received a wire from Ottawa. It was terse and to the point: "Got them!" it read.

. . . . He recalled another occasion when someone, hearing he was ill, sent him a telegraph expressing sympathy. King, not as ill as he had been reported, sent back an answering wire. It said simply: "Purely Tory propaganda!"

[e]*General observations:*

Addressing the school children at Elmira, he told them it would be a pity if they had to return to their classes and he suggested that the teacher give them the day off.
"Isn't that just typical of a Scotsman born in Kitchener," sighed Mayor C. E. Gibson, with a grin. "It's five to four now!"

After King's death and his own return to London, Athlone [former Governor-General of Canada] delivered a judgment in his jerky soldier's idiom.
"Your man King," he said to me. "Knew him well, actually. Bit of a puzzle, what? H'm — King. Great man and all that. And you know, he just missed being quite a decent feller."

B

THE ADMINISTRATION OF LOUIS ST. LAURENT

In a smooth transfer of office, Louis St. Laurent, King's own choice of successor, became leader of the Liberal Party and Prime Minister. A distinguished French-Canadian lawyer, he had given invaluable support to King's policies during the war. Although he had entered politics late in life,

Welcoming Ceremonies for Newfoundland: Peace Tower, Ottawa, April 1, 1949.

and then reluctantly, he brought a quiet dignity and a methodical approach to the administration of government. At the same time he won the affection of citizens in all parts of Canada. They called him "Uncle Louis," for his devotion to his family seemed to extend to all Canadians.

The entry of Newfoundland into Confederation was one of the first great accomplishments of the St. Laurent government. Instead of joining Canada in 1867, the proud islanders had chosen to remain a colony with direct links to Great Britain. Over the decades they saw little reason for changing that status — until struck by the depression of the 1930's. The war brought a measure of recovery, especially when the United States located important air bases there. But after the war, the people of Newfoundland faced an historic choice: remain under the commission set up a few years before, revert to the status of a self-governing British colony or become the tenth province.

Although King was still Prime Minister when most of the arrangements were made, the bulk of the negotiations were handled by St. Laurent, J. W. Pickersgill, adviser to the Prime Minister, and the dynamic "Joey" Smallwood, the most ardent Confederationist on the island of Newfoundland. Joining Canada was not the first wish of all the inhabitants; in fact, two referendums were required before the decision was made. The narrow majority was, however, enough to prepare the way for Newfoundland's union with Canada in 1949.

Storm clouds gathered on the international scene, with the explosion of the Soviet Union's first atomic bomb, the Communist victory in the Chinese civil war and the Korean War. Within Canada, however, no problems of national scope arose to disturb the order and progress of the period. Aided by a strong team of cabinet ministers, St. Laurent led the Liberal Party to a one-sided victory in the election of 1949. Canada's position as a sovereign country was further clarified by the succeeding parliament. With the termination of appeals to the Privy Council, the Supreme Court of Canada became the final court of appeal for Canadians. An act was passed authorizing parliament to amend the constitution in matters of federal jurisdiction. Vincent Massey, in 1952, became the first Canadian to be appointed Governor-General. With the coronation of Queen Elizabeth II in June, 1953, the royal title adopted in Canada was suitable to her symbolic role as head of the state and of the Commonwealth.

THE FUNCTION OF THE GOVERNOR-GENERAL[421]

Vincent Massey, the first Canadian to be appointed Governor-General, discusses the office in his memoirs:

. . . . If a schoolboy asked, 'What does the Governor-General do?', the simple answer would be, I think, that the Governor-General does two major things. It is his function to help our scattered population to gain the unity a country ought to possess, and also bring home the meaning of the Crown to the Canadian people to whom it belongs. These two objects are interwoven — they merge — because the Crown, as we have learned to realize in recent years, greatly strengthens our unity. It is not something reposing in the Tower of London but the very symbol of our own nationality, which helps to give us our individual character and draws all parts of Canada together. I cannot believe that we could remain an independent country without the Crown as a great and distinguishing feature of our life.

Stable government and extended economic growth contributed largely to the general acceptance of Liberal administration, and the election of 1953 returned more than 170 Liberals compared to the 51 gained by the largest opposition party, the Conservatives. But as well as indicating that Canadians had voted for more of the same, the election reflected the feeling that the opposition parties offered little alternative. Since losing office in 1935, the Conservatives had changed leaders several times and none had been successful in challenging Liberal power at the federal level. The Co-operative Commonwealth Federation, or C.C.F., after enjoying some gains at the end of the war, failed to become more than a "splinter" party with regional support. Social Credit remained confined to the far west. Only the Liberals could claim convincingly to be a truly national party, with support in all parts of Canada.

Signs of change did emerge in the provinces as early as 1952, when the Conservatives gained power in New Brunswick. In the same year, William A. C. Bennett nearly eliminated both of the old parties from politics in British Columbia when he led a Social Credit victory. Robert Stanfield's success in 1956 ended long years of Liberal power in Nova Scotia. Manitoba joined the trend two years later when the Conservatives, under Duff Roblin, took office.

Since the provinces, whatever parties were in office, traditionally resisted federal authority, the significance of the several changes in provincial governments did not necessarily reflect declining support by Canadians for the government in Ottawa. With its huge majority in Parliament, the St. Laurent administration encouraged many imposing development projects, including the St. Lawrence Seaway, mining and the Alberta petroleum industry.

It was the latter that led the St. Laurent government into a political crisis from which it did not recover. The "pipeline debate" of 1956 threw Canadian politics into a turmoil. The occasion was the proposed trans-Canada pipeline, to be built for transporting gas and petroleum from Alberta to eastern markets. The minister of trade and commerce, C. D. Howe, likened the pipeline to the Canadian Pacific Railway as a great boon to Canadian progress and unity. He believed that the government should do whatever necessary to ensure completion of the pipeline, and that Canadians could not fail to approve. He failed to see why peacetime tasks should not be fulfilled in the same aggressive and efficient manner as those of the war years.

A serious complication was that the company engaged to complete the pipeline was American owned. Yet much of the original cost was to be borne by the Canadian government, although the money would eventually be recovered. The introduction of the plan to Parliament in January, 1956, was followed by several months of involved negotiations. Action was delayed until the final weeks of the session. In order to guarantee passage of the necessary legislation in time for the project to proceed on schedule, the government immediately proposed a parliamentary device known as closure. This meant there would be a limited debate in which the opposition parties would have only a matter of days to scrutinize the plan.

The result was one of the most violent episodes in the history of the Canadian Parliament. The opposition hurled charges of arrogance — indeed, of dictatorship — at the government and walked out, almost in their entirety, before the vote was called. The pipeline bill was passed in the absence of the Conservative and C.C.F. Parties, and the Liberal leaders assumed that the whole affair would soon be forgotten. They counted on Canadian apathy and the expectation that Canadians would not be much affected by parliamentary wrangles over such technical subjects as procedure and high finance.

But there were many signs to the contrary, and had the Liberals been more in touch with public opinion, they would have been more likely to recognize them. Receptive to the highly critical coverage of the government's actions on the part of the nation's newspapers, and the dramatic impact of television news — then quite new in Canada — Canadians became convinced that the government was insensitive to the will off the people.

ABOUT LOUIS ST. LAURENT[422]

ᵃ*The start of a new era:*

The first Canadian to sense the meaning of his arrival [St. Laurent as new Prime Minister] may have been a nameless elevator attendant in the East Block.

After taking his oath of office, St. Laurent had worked until nearly eight o'clock and, when he started for home, was astonished to find this humble functionary awaiting his departure, as he had been instructed to await King's. The unfairness of such arrangements outraged the new Prime Minister. "From now on," he said, "you'll leave with the others at the regular time. I can walk downstairs."

———

. . . [on November 15, 1948] the new government held its first cabinet meeting. . . . Seated at the head of the table, St. Laurent drew out his silver cigarette case, fitted a cigarette into his holder, and lit it. Other ministers followed suit. That, too, was a symbolic move: under Mackenzie King, smoking had been forbidden in the Council Chamber. It was truly the end of an era.

———

ᵇ*The nicknames "Uncle Louis" and "Grandpapa Louis":*

. . . [in the spring of 1949, on his western tour] he made a point of speaking to the children present, and again received an enthusiastic response, both from them and their proud parents. Deep in the Rocky Mountains . . . one reporter from a Conservative newspaper remarked ruefully to another: 'Uncle Louis is going to be hard to beat.'

The nickname stuck, and St. Laurent had found his feet as a politican.

―――――

. . . . At a mass rally in Toronto's Maple Leaf Gardens on June 21 [1949], [his] fifteen-year old [granddaughter] Louise appeared on the platform as well, and reporters re-baptized the Prime Minister 'Grand-papa Louis'.

―――――――――――――――――――――――

C

THE DIEFENBAKER PHENOMENON

The election of 1957 produced one of the most stunning upsets in the history of Canada and ended twenty-two years of Liberal government. The supposedly invincible Liberals were reduced to 105 seats; included among their defeated candidates were nine cabinet ministers. Although the Conservatives, with 112 seats, also lacked a majority, Prime Minister St. Laurent interpreted the election results as proof that the electors had lost confidence in his government. He promptly resigned and the succeeding Prime Minister was sworn into office in June, 1957. The new leader's name was John Diefenbaker.

Few Canadians have inspired such partisan feeling or aroused such controversy as the "man from Prince Albert." Whatever his success as the leader of Canada, Mr. Diefenbaker injected a colourful brand of politics into the nation's public life. In the fall of 1956, when he was elected leader of the Progressive Conservative Party, the talented defence lawyer from Saskatchewan launched his stinging attacks that soon helped send the Liberal government to electoral defeat. What the nation would know as the "Diefenbaker phenomenon" had begun.

As the Conservatives adapted themselves to the unaccustomed role of exercising political power, the Liberal Party turned to the job of replacing the retired Louis St. Laurent. The almost inevitable choice of the convention, early in 1958, was Lester Bowles Pearson, who easily defeated his only rival, Paul Martin. An internationally known diplomat of long experience in the department of external affairs, Pearson was best known to Canadians as their chief representative at the United Nations. For his work in helping to settle the Suez crisis in 1956, he had been awarded the Nobel Prize for Peace. Now he was being called upon to serve in the hurlyburly of domestic politics, with which he had had little experience, and to lead his party in the House of Commons, where he was almost a stranger.

Within days of becoming party leader, Pearson, acting on bad advice from his colleagues, called upon the Conservatives to resign and return the reins of government to the Liberals. In this first of many encounters between the two, Diefenbaker utilized his best defence lawyer style of oratory. In a thundering, scorn-filled denunciation of the new opposition, he set the tone for the election he was about to call. With the Liberals in disarray under a new, and as yet unprepared, leader, the Conservatives plunged into the campaign with vigour and high hopes of winning a substantial majority.

What followed was the incredible Conservative landslide of March 31, in which Mr. Diefenbaker's party won 208 seats out of 265 ― a record by far ― and the Liberals survived with a mere 49. The C.C.F. held the remaining eight seats. The Diefenbaker "vision" of Canadian greatness, expounded by the master campaigner over television and at massive rallies across Canada, captured the imagination of Canadians in every part of the land. In Quebec the Conservatives won a majority of seats for the first time since Sir John A. Macdonald had done so in 1891. Elsewhere, candidates who normally would have had little chance of victory, were swept into office on the coat tails of their leader.

DIEFENBAKER'S "VISION" FOR CANADA[423]

In the election campaign of 1958, John Diefenbaker expounded a "vision" of Canadian greatness that helped the Conservatives elect 208 members. The following excerpts from his speech at the Civic auditorium in Winnipeg, on February 12, may only suggest the force of his oratory:

. . . . This national development policy will create a new sense of national purpose and national destiny. One Canada. One Canada, wherein Canadians will have preserved to them the control of their own economic and political destiny. Sir John A. Macdonald gave his life to this party. He opened the West. He saw Canada from East to West. I see a new Canada ― a Canada of the North.

―――――

Canadians, realize your opportunities! This is only the beginning. The future programme for the next five to seven years under a Progressive Conservative Government is one that is calculated to give young Canadians, motivated by a desire to serve, a lift in the heart, faith in Canada's future, faith in her destiny.

This is the message I give to you my fellow Canadians, not one of defeatism. Jobs! Jobs for hundreds of thousands of Canadian people. A new vision! A new hope! A new soul for Canada. . . .

One powerful majority government had been replaced by another, but to great numbers of his fellow Canadians, Diefenbaker was a man of the people. Born on a Saskatchewan homestead, descended from "new" immigrants as well as from Scottish pioneers he had risen from humble beginnings, triumphed over repeated failures to win elected office and used his fighting spirit to achieve the pinnacle of political success.

He extolled the great possibilities of Canada's northland, and the "roads to resources" program was begun. He promised the western farmers a fair share of Canada's prosperity, and pointed to the huge wheat sales to China as proof of his word. For the increasing number of aged people, the Diefenbaker government raised the old age pensions. For all Canadians, but especially for those which previous governments had neglected, including people whose ancestry was neither English nor French, he had Parliament approve a Bill of Rights.

DIEFENBAKER ON HIS BILL OF RIGHTS[424]

Speaking in the House of Commons, July 1, 1960:

I am a Canadian, a free Canadian, free to speak without fear, free to worship God in my own way, free to stand for what I think right, free to oppose what I believe wrong, free to choose those who shall govern my country. This heritage of freedom I pledge to uphold for myself and all mankind.

But in spite of imaginative promises and many bold beginnings, the Diefenbaker government failed to emulate its predecessor in attempting to take command of the nation's political affairs. Canadians expected much of their new, forceful Prime Minister who was backed by so large a parliamentary majority. Surely great progress lay in store. Yet policies were not forthcoming that could soften the impact of economic recession, prevent devaluation of the Canadian dollar or forestall record levels of unemployment. Mr. Diefenbaker was criticized for failing to delegate authority, while being unable to make sound decisions by himself. His defenders praised his refusal to be dominated by big business, but others feared

John Diefenbaker, 1957

that hostility between government and the business community was harmful to the economy.

French Canadians failed to be convinced that the Conservative government had any serious concern for their interests, even though Major-General George Vanier was appointed Governor-General in 1959. From the large delegation of Conservative M.P.'s which Quebec sent to Ottawa, few were chosen for the cabinet, and they were generally assigned to lesser portfolios. In Ontario as well, support fell away as disillusionment grew over the government's handling of economic difficulties. The Prairie provinces and the Maritimes generally continued their loyalty, but this heightened the impression of division within the Conservative party and the nation as a whole.

As the illusion of Conservative power was progressively exposed, the opposition parties found their chances for recovery strengthened. In 1961 the C.C.F. Party formed an alliance with the Canadian Labour Congress and drafted a program which toned down its original hard-line socialism. The name New Democratic Party was adopted and a new leader, T. C. "Tommy" Douglas, former C.C.F. Premier of Saskatchewan, was elected. In spite of comments that little had changed but the name, the Party was striving for a modern image that would draw broader support from workers and labour across Canada, including Quebec. The Social Credit Party also named a

T. C. Douglas

new leader, Robert Thompson of Red Deer, Alberta. Besides working for electoral gains in its provincial strongholds of Alberta and British Columbia, Social Credit also had rising hopes in Quebec, where Real Caouette was attracting the interest of rural voters.

The Liberal Party, meanwhile, was beginning a resurgence. The years of experience as leader of the opposition had enabled Mr. Pearson to acquire political skills. Increasing numbers of Canadians began to regard him as the next Prime Minister instead of as merely a misplaced intellectual and diplomat. Many young Canadians, particularly in the urban areas, were won over by his candour and his thoughtful approach to problems. The rebirth of party morale was paralleled by a restatement of Liberal philosophy and a rebuilding of the Party's organization, at least in Ontario and Quebec.

With the popularity of his government waning, Mr. Diefenbaker called an election for June 18, 1962. The timing was not opportune, however, as a financial crisis forced devaluation of the Canadian dollar in May during the campaign. The Conservatives lost 92 seats, the election results were almost as dramatic, in reverse, as those of 1958. Reduced to a minority position with only 118 seats — and a large proportion of those in the Maritimes and the loyal prairies — the Conservatives managed to cling to office. The Liberals had doubled their numbers, to 100 MP's, but the surprising gains by Social Credit — 26 seats — in

Quebec had forestalled a Liberal victory, while the New Democratic Party captured 19.

When Parliament was finally called into session at the end of September, the government had been forced to adopt emergency restrictions on spending. Thus hampered, and fearful of introducing measures that might lead to his defeat in the House of Commons, the Prime Minister was now clearly a man of little authority. In the latter part of October, the Cuban missile crisis threatened war between the United States and the U.S.S.R. What appeared as indecision by Canada concerning co-operation with the United States for North American defence caused further dissension in the ranks of Conservatives and doubts in the hearts of Canadians.

Early in 1963, divisions within the Conservative party were clearly exposed by the resignation of Douglas Harkness, the Minister of Defence. Convinced that the Prime Minister was not going to equip Canada's defence system with the nuclear warheads for which they were designed, and thereby renege on obligations to the United States and the North Atlantic Treaty Organization, Harkness chose to leave the cabinet. Then a non-confidence motion in the House of Commons was supported by the combined opposition. The Diefenbaker government had fallen, and an election was called for April 18. A movement by anti-Diefenbaker cabinet ministers to replace the leader failed, but the resignation of two more ministers added to the confusion among Conservatives on the eve of election.

VIEWS ON DIEFENBAKER[425]

[a]*Prime Minister Diefenbaker's admiration for Sir John A. Macdonald is illustrated by the following:*

At his office in Parliament Hill's East Block, Diefenbaker worked under a portrait and beside a full-figure statuette of Macdonald. His inkwell had once belonged to Sir John A. In the Privy Council chamber, Diefenbaker sat in Macdonald's original chair, and dried the signature on his instructions with Sir John's spring blotter. One of Macdonald's mantel clocks timed his movements and had to be carted to whichever of his three Parliament Hill offices Diefenbaker was occupying. In his official residence, at 24 Sussex Drive, Diefenbaker encircled himself even more liberally with Macdonald relics, including parts of his library, many portraits of him, his easy chair, another clock, and a medallion given to a barber who had once shaved Sir John. The most valuable item in the collection was a copy, in Macdonald's own handwriting, of the original National Policy, drawn up on January 16, 1878. . . .

Bruce Hutchison describes the theatrical nature of Diefenbaker, in the days before he became Prime Minister:

. . . . As a mimic he could bring to life the ponderous banalities of King, Lapointe's French accent and passionate gestures, St. Laurent's clipped sentences and eloquent shrug, the jumpy movements of Pickersgill and the supercilious look of Drew.

The repertoire was varied and endless. Striding up and down his little office in the Centre Block, Diefenbaker would people it with the entire Parliament from the Speaker to the page boys. His assortment of characters, inflections, expressions and grimaces would have made him a star on any stage. He could have played Hamlet or Touchstone, Macbeth or Lady Macbeth, and once, in the British Columbia Supreme Court, he fell to the floor, clutching his throat, to show how a murder had been committed, until a horrified judge rebuked him.

D

LESTER B. PEARSON AND A LIBERAL MINORITY GOVERNMENT

There were many issues in the election of 1963, but the theme which the Liberal opposition seized upon was that of leadership. Mr. Diefenbaker was charged with ineffective leadership and mismanagement that threatened to cripple the nation within and destroy the confidence of its allies, principally the United States. The Conservative leader proclaimed a program of Canadian nationalism and unity, which often took the form of a crusade against the interference of the United States in Canada's affairs. Mr. Pearson promised sound administration, a fuller recognition of the rights of French Canadians, a national flag, expanded social security and fulfillment of defence commitments involving the acquisition of nuclear warheads.

As the new Prime Minister, Mr. Pearson found himself with a minority government, holding 129 seats and facing an opposition of 95 Conservatives, 17 N.D.P., and 24 Social Credit. From the beginning, Canadians seemed to be justified in withholding a mandate for a majority government — the Pearson administration quickly acquired the label "accident prone" that would remain until its life ended. Having promised "Sixty Days of Decision," the Liberals were under public pressure from the day they took office. Before the sixty days had elapsed, the ill-fated budget of Finance Minister Walter Gordon had been announced, then amended, under a hail of criticism.

During the next two years, integration of the armed forces was one of the most explosive issues. Instituted under the direction of the Minister of Defence, Paul Hellyer, unification of the three services — army, air force and navy — was designed to eliminate duplication of functions while creating a new kind of mobile force capable of limited, but effective, action in non-nuclear warfare. As part of its "new look," the Canadian force was clothed in distinctive green uniforms. Some career officers, notably in the navy, denounced the whole policy as destructive of Canada's military strength. But the government proceeded with its plans, the wisdom of which only time may judge.

SOME DRAWBACKS OF CANADA'S NEW, UNIFIED ARMED FORCE[426]

Mr. Douglas Harkness, who served as Minister of Defence under Mr. Diefenbaker, expressed doubts about unification of Canada's armed forces. From a magazine article of December, 1966:

. . . . In the event of a large-scale war it is essential for us to have the ability to mobilize our manpower. The reorganization of our defence set-up which has been going on has undoubtedly cut down our ability to do this rapidly, due to the fact that a large number of training bases have been closed and the reserve forces, or militia, have been greatly reduced. This question of the ability to mobilize has been one of the things which has particularly concerned a number of the highly experienced and capable senior officers who have expressed their opposition to the unification plans of the present government.

Another matter which concerns those with military experience in war, is how the proposed unified Canadian force will be able to work and cooperate with the forces of our allies, which are organized on a navy, army and air forces basis. . . .

The Canadian flag debate proved to be an even more emotional case, as it became a bitter partisan issue in parliament and across the nation. In fulfillment of its election promise, the Liberal government introduced a design for a new and distinctive

Canadian flag. The problem was that many Canadians, particularly war veterans, were fiercely attached to the Red Ensign. Months of controversy followed before a parliamentary committee, representing all parties, recommended a flag design with a single red maple leaf and red borders at either end on a white background. Prolonged debate in the House of Commons ended in December, 1964, and the new flag became official on February 15, 1965.

The government's determination to establish such Canadian symbols as the maple leaf flag was part of its policy of "positive Canadianism." But there was a special side to the problem: the wish to accommodate the aspirations of French Canada. The "Quiet Revolution" in progress in the province of Quebec was making it clear that Canadian unity could be threatened unless Confederation was adjusted. Mr. Pearson was deeply concerned and sympathetic to the problems of rising government costs, not only for Quebec but for the other provinces as well.

Demands by the provinces, with Quebec most vocal, for a greater share of tax money posed a severe challenge to the federal government. The decision reached was to allow increased tax rebates to the provinces so that they would have more money with which to finance expanding programs. Along with "shared cost" programs in many fields the government adopted an "opting out" formula so that a province could have the revenues for its own use instead of participating in a federally sponsored project.

The Canada Pension Plan proved to be a turning point in federal-provincial financial relations. In 1963, soon after taking office, the Liberals began working out the details of a federal pension plan. The final product would have to be acceptable to the provinces, since constitutionally any province which felt itself financially able could bring in a pension program of its own. At a conference in 1964, Quebec, and Ontario as well, seemed determined to use the occasion for exacting greatly increased revenues from the federal government. Premier Lesage, whose government's reforms involved spending on a scale previously unimagined in Quebec, demanded that the federal government withdraw from the expanding field of social security and instead give the provinces the money needed to operate individually whatever programs each saw fit.

The government of Canada, though determined to hold the line, seemed to have little choice but to compromise if federal-provincial harmony was to be possible. To all the provinces, the federal government conceded millions of dollars in tax abatements. To Quebec in particular, the federal government granted the right to introduce the Quebec Pension Plan, on the conditions that it be identical and interchangeable with the Canada Pension Plan. Alarmed critics damned the result as another instance of "giving in to Quebec" and encouraging its progress along the path to "separate status" — or even ultimate separation. Lester Pearson, however, insisted that Canadian unity had been preserved by the compromise.

The election of November, 1965, matched the Liberal plea for a majority government against the opposition charges of government bungling and wrong-doing. The most spectacular case in 1965 — the "year of scandals" — was the Lucien Rivard affair. Rivard was being held in jail on charges of smuggling narcotics into the United States, where he was to be sent for trial. Before Parliament recessed for its 1964 Christmas holiday, a Conservative M.P. broke the story about persons close to the government who were trying to prevent the gangster from being extradited to the United States. The Liberal government reeled under opposition attacks, but reacted as best it could by appointing Frederic Dorion, Chief Justice of Quebec, to conduct a royal commission investigation. Besides finding evidence of malpractice on the part of the assistant to the Minister of Immigration, the inquiry cast doubts on the judgment of Guy Favreau, Minister of Justice, and placed the government under a cloud.

By the time the election was held, the Liberals' prospects seemed to be much improved, but they still failed, narrowly, to obtain the majority for which they had campaigned. On top of this disappointment, the Liberals became entangled in another unflattering episode early in 1966. A Vancouver postal clerk had been dismissed from his job because of his association with Soviet agents interested in buying confidential information. The opposition parties accused the government of indecision in failing to prosecute the man while at the same time ignoring his civil rights by placing him under the surveillance of the R.C.M.P.

DEBATE ON THE SPENCER ESPIONAGE CASE, IN THE HOUSE OF COMMONS, JANUARY 31, 1966[427]

Hon. Lucien Cardin, Minister of Justice:

. . . . The evidence was referred to the law officers of the Department of Justice, who were of the opinion that much of the evidence could not meet the requirements of the rules of evidence in criminal cases. Consequently they recommended against instituting criminal proceedings.

———

. . . I said, in the course of a television program, that there would be surveillance on this man as long as he remains in Canada. . . . It is for preventive reasons that surveillance, to the extent necessary, will continue in this case.

Right Hon. J. G. Diefenbaker, Leader of the Opposition:

. . . to continue a course of surveillance of this kind, continuing surveillance, is far removed from the accepted principles of police work. Indeed, it is essentially authoritarian and essentially dangerous.

. . . let Canadians be assured that what has taken place has not been of a nature which will become the pattern for the future. Let them be reassured at the same time that this man will receive the consideration to which every Canadian citizen is entitled.

Mr. T. C. Douglas, Leader of the N.D.P.:

. . . what has the government done? First, they fired this man under section 50 of the Civil Service Act so that he has no right of appeal. . . . Was this man permitted to appear before the Civil Service Commission before the commission recommended that he be fired? . . . .

Is this the way in which justice is to be administered in Canada? Even in wartime we would not permit a man to be stigmatized on the basis of evidence which, as the minister himself claims, would not stand up in court. . . .

. . . . Surely he is entitled, as any Canadian citizen is entitled, to have his day in court. Surely he is entitled to be heard. Surely he has the right under our laws to be deemed innocent until he can be proven guilty.

Parliament seemed to have degenerated into a forum dominated by partisan political warfare, rumour-mongering and a personal vendetta between Pearson and Diefenbaker. But the end had not yet come, for the beleaguered Liberals revealed their discovery of a skeleton in the Conservative closet. Diefenbaker was accused of failing to take adequate precautions in handling a potential threat to Canada's military security when he was Prime Minister. In an atmosphere of bitterness around Parliament and disillusionment among Canadians in general, an official inquiry showed that there had been a situation in which the associate Defence Minister could have been pressured to disclose secrets from his department.*

---

* In the House of Commons, on March 4, 1966, Justice Minister Cardin accused certain Ministers in the Diefenbaker government of associating with a German woman, Gerda Munsinger. This woman had been under investigation by the R.C.M.P. as a security risk.

The fact that no breach of security had actually occurred was at least some consolation to Canadians weary of the spectacle in Ottawa.

The troubles of the time obscured the fact that the Liberal government was accomplishing an ambitious program of legislation. Besides the Canadian flag and integration of the armed forces, there were the vastly expanded welfare programs, manpower training schemes, assistance to universities and technical schools, aid to regional development, a procedure for non-partisan redistribution of seats in the House of Commons and a trade agreement with the United States designed to encourage the Canadian automobile industry.

While these and other projects were afoot, Canadians were stimulated by a new spirit of excitement with the preparations for celebrating the centennial year of 1967. Communities large and small put the finishing touches on commemorative projects, ranging from such long needed public facilities as libraries in the smaller centres to the manmade islands at Montreal, where the magic of EXPO would draw Canadians from all over the nation. Countless words were written and spoken about the time-honoured subject of the Canadian identity and an awakened interest in Canadian history was further stimulated by the flow of centennial publications. As they toured the traveling centennial caravans, or thrilled to the sight of the canoe pageant retracing the routes of the fur traders, or revelled in the wonders of the World's Fair in Montreal, Canadians came to know their country as never before. For many, the new awareness that came out of the experiences of the centennial year gave at least a partial answer to the question, "What is a Canadian?"

In other parts of the world, the interest in Canada reached new levels. The death of Georges Vanier was deeply mourned, but Canadians took pride in the way that the new Governor-General, Roland Michener, played host to state visitors from abroad. The EXPO site, with its pavilions from nearly seventy nations, was an international meeting place. World tensions seemed generally far removed, with the exception of the controversy evoked by the visit of President Charles de Gaulle of France and his remarks that seemed intended to encourage separatist feeling among French Canadians.

As Canada embarked on its second century, many changes had either occurred or were anticipated in the national political parties. Robert Thompson left the dying Social Credit Party to become a successful Progressive Conservative candidate in the 1968 federal election. With the defeat of T. C. Douglas in the election, the New Democratic Party planned to select a successor.

Centennial Projects: Procession on way to the Burning of the Outhouses at Bowsman, Manitoba, 1967. Canoe Pageant: Fort St. James to Victoria, August 6-15, 1967. The 10 canoes are seen getting back into the race after an overnight stop at Quesnel, B.C.
EXPO '67: Montreal, Quebec

Both the Liberals and Conservatives chose new leaders as well, leaving the Creditistes as the only party to continue under the same management.

The Progressive Conservative Party held its national leadership convention in September, 1967. The meeting was called despite the resistance of Diefenbaker supporters, who regarded it as a deliberate move by such prominent Ontario Conservatives as national party president Dalton Camp to remove "the Chief" from the leadership. Mr. Diefenbaker did stand as a candidate, unsuccessfully, but even in defeat he provided the occasion with much of its drama by keeping the nation guessing about his intentions until the last possible moment. Then he went down fighting with his declaration in support of "one, united Canada" and his denunciation of the "deux nations" concept of Confederation which had recently found favour with Conservative policy makers.

"DEUX NATIONS" PLAGUED THE CONSERVATIVES[428]

A journalist traces back the roots of the "two-nations" idea which became a dilemma to the Conservatives during the election campaign. From the WINNIPEG FREE PRESS, *August, 1968:*

. . . the Conservatives were stuck with "two nations" no matter what meaning it might turn out to have. It was not formally adopted into party policy, but it could not be formally rejected without undercutting the Conservative candidates in Quebec.

Mr. Stanfield is understandably unhappy about the way his policy was understood.

Its ambiguity won his party the worst of both worlds. It alarmed English-speaking Canada and federalists in Quebec, without managing to appeal to Quebec nationalists, as if each of Canada's "deux nations — two founding peoples" had received the version that was meant for the other.

During the election campaign Prime Minister Trudeau got all the political mileage he could out of what he called the Conservatives' "two-policy policy".

But the roots of any public misunderstanding of the Conservative position were there long before the party's thinkers gave tentative approval to the slogan "two nations" without quite knowing what they meant by it themselves, and with no apparent understanding of what the slogan has come to mean to the Quebec nationalists who coined it.

Robert Stanfield, eminently successful as Premier of Nova Scotia, emerged as the new leader of the Conservatives. The quiet-spoken politician from Halifax had defeated eight other candidates, of whom the leading challenger was the former Premier of Manitoba, Duff Roblin.

The governing Liberal party changed leaders at the request of Prime Minister Pearson following his announcement in December, 1967, of his intention to retire. The choice of the convention in April was the dynamic Pierre Elliott Trudeau, an intellectual from Montreal who had entered the Liberal Party and the House of Commons less than three years earlier. Mr. Trudeau's election as Liberal leader was startling in many respects. Little known outside of his native province of Quebec, where he had long been identified with the socialists, an unorthodox individual whose diverse interests ranged from reading Plato to skin-diving, he had been elected in preference to candidates of long experience and power within the Liberal Party.

ABOUT LESTER B. PEARSON[429]

[a]*His many careers*

ACADEMIC

After graduating from Oxford, Mr. Pearson was appointed lecturer in history at the University of Toronto in 1923. There he impressed one student in particular, Maryon Moody, whom he married in 1925!

DIPLOMATIC AND POLITICAL

1928	Joined the Department of External Affairs.
1935	Represented Canada at the League of Nations.
1935-1941	Deputy High Commissioner to Great Britain.
1943	Canadian Ambassador to the United States.
1945	In San Francisco at the founding of the United Nations. With the U.N.'s relief agency in Europe to assist with aid to refugees.
1946	Top civil servant in the Department of External Affairs.
1948-1957	Secretary of State for External Affairs.
1956	During the Suez crisis he proposed a United Nations Emergency Force.
1957	Received the Nobel Peace Prize.
1958-1968	Leader of the Liberal Party.
1963-1968	Prime Minister.

AUTHOR, LECTURER, etc.

[b]*It was in the service that he acquired the nickname "Mike":*

It was when he transferred to the Royal Flying Corps that he picked up the nickname "Mike", which clung to him for the rest of his life. Friends who went to school with him continued to call him Lester, but those who first met him after the war called him Mike. When he presented himself for flying instruction a senior corps officer remarked: "Lester — that's not a very belligerent name for a man who wants to be a fighter pilot. We'll call you Mike."

Pearson, the lover of sports:

. . . . Lester played for one summer with the Guelph Maple Leafs [semi-pro baseball] . . . . One of his old teammates got into a dispute with him over which position he played — for memories tend to fade — denying that Lester had played third base. "He didn't have the arm to throw from third," the teammate claimed. "He was a good glove man, but not much of a batter." Pearson's enthusiasm for all sports stayed with him through his entire scholastic career. Even as prime minister he can be distracted from official duties by a baseball game on television.

Even the busy schedule of a Prime Minister did not prevent Mr. Pearson from attending sports events, especially hockey games involving his favorite team, the Toronto Maple Leafs.

The interest in sports came naturally to a man active in athletics as a youth. At Oxford he played on the varsity teams in hockey and lacrosse, and took part in international competition with both. While teaching history at the University of Toronto, he served as head coach of the hockey team.

Pearson, the Nobel Peace Prize winner:

The telephone rang. It was a call from Canadian Press.

"What comment do you have on winning the Nobel peace prize?" the reporter asked.

"What!" Pearson exploded. "You must be mistaken. It must be that I have been nominated for the prize. I've been nominated before."

"Just a minute, I'll check," said the reporter. "No, that's right, you've been awarded the prize."

"Gosh!" said Pearson. "I'll have to call my wife and let her know."

In the election of June, 1968, Mr. Trudeau proved to be as appealing to the Canadian voters as he had been to the Liberal delegates. "Trudeau-mania" was the term added to the Canadian vocabulary to describe the enthusiasm which built up during the campaign for the new Prime Minister. The almost hypnotic quality, sometimes referred to as charisma, which Trudeau projected was too much for the opposition parties. With 155 members elected, the Liberals had achieved the first majority government in Canada since 1962.

COMMENT ON THE CANADIAN ELECTION OF 1968[430]

[a]*A well-known journalist considers the extent to which television contributed to "Trudeaumania":*

. . . . His [Trudeau's] victory at the leadership convention was great television, and paved the way for Trudeaumania.

Trudeaumania, however, depended on his personal appearances, a technique as old as humanity itself. There is no record of outbursts of Trudeaumania around TV sets.

Trudeau used TV as a channel to the people — an instrument of communications superbly suited to his talents and his style. . . .

But television didn't make Trudeau. What made him was the over-all impact on the public of his ideas, and the general impression created by what people saw of him, what they read about him, and what they heard about him.

Pierre Elliott Trudeau

[b]*Political scientist, J. Murray Beck, examines the variety of support attracted by Pierre Elliott Trudeau in the election of 1968:*

Some expected Trudeau to establish clear-cut differences between the Liberals and Conservatives, but in this election he was, if anything, further to the right than Stanfield. However, it would be naive to believe that Trudeau — pragmatic on everything but the constitution — would normally differ on fundamentals from the equally pragmatic Stanfield. Crucial to Trudeau's success will be his ability to satisfy the demands of the rational exponents of Trudeauism for a new kind of politics. In the election of 1968 he employed his own contradictory qualities to attract conflicting interests and groups; will he appear equally attractive to them when the chips are down?

31

CANADA AND FOREIGN AFFAIRS

A

CANADA AND THE UNITED NATIONS

Canada's isolationism and caution in foreign affairs in the 1930's, a policy so fervently pursued by Mackenzie King, failed to keep Canada out of war. In the postwar period, Canada undertook active commitments which were indicative of a new direction in Canada's foreign policy. Canada, a wealthy country, a country which had evolved from colonialism, a country which had no imperial designs, was acceptable to the many newly-emerged nations. Canada could and did play an important role in international affairs in settling international disputes.

In San Francisco in 1945 at the founding of the United Nations (U.N.), Canada spoke out for the smaller countries and sought a status for these so-called Middle Powers. The United Nations held forth high hopes for a peaceful world — hopes not unlike those promised by the League of Nations. However, the Great Powers — the United States, the Soviet Union, the United Kingdom, France and China — steeped in practical power policies, could see world peace preserved mainly through their own efforts. The five Great Powers reserved for themselves, in the Security Council, permanent seats with veto power to set aside decisions they did not approve or which did not suit their national interests. In recognition of demands by the smaller nations for a decision-making voice in the United Nations, six non-permanent members — later increased to ten — were to be part of the Security Council. These were elected from the General Assembly, served for a two year period, but had no right of veto. The extent of Canada's worldwide reputation in the United Nations can be gathered from the fact that on three occasions — in 1948, 1958 and 1967 — Canada was elected to a seat as a non-permanent member on the Security Council. The highest honour was bestowed on Canada in 1952 when Lester B. Pearson, Canada's Secretary of State for External Affairs, was elected President of the General Assembly's seventh session.

CANADA AND THE UNITED NATIONS[431]

On April 29, 1948, Prime Minister St. Laurent spoke in the House of Commons on Canada's role as a member of the Security Council:

Our willingness to stand for, and our ability to secure, election to the security council last September was an earnest of our desire to play our full part in the united nations. . . .

The position of a power of the middle rank on the security council is under any circumstances a difficult one. . . .

. . . . The special nature of our relationship to the United Kingdom and the United States complicates our responsibilities. . . . Canada will be expected by some to follow the lead of the United Kingdom: by others to follow the lead of the United States. . . . Unfriendly observers will write us off as a satellite of both. . . . More objective observers will tend to assume that it will be hard for Canada to follow a policy of its own.. .. . . It will not be easy to secure credit for independence and honesty of argument and decision. Nevertheless we will continue to make our decisions objectively, in the light of our obligations to our own people and their interest in the welfare of the international community.

In the non-political work of the United Nations, Canada actively supported the agencies which are concerned with the elimination of hunger, disease and poverty throughout the world. The many areas of Canada's active participation in the United Nations are too numerous to describe, but

First Meeting of the General Assembly in San Francisco, April-June, 1945: L to R: Hon. Louis St. Laurent and Rt. Hon. W. L. Mackenzie King.

a few of these should serve to illustrate the extent of Canada's work.

Canadians have served in the Food and Agricultural Organization (F.A.O.) and contributed their knowledge and skill to increase food supplies for the world's hungry. In the World Health Organization (W.H.O.) Canadian doctors and medical teams, in the far reaches of the earth, are waging constant war on disease with the goal of "attainment by all peoples of the highest level of health." Dr. Brock Chisholm, an eminent Canadian doctor, was the first Director of the W.H.O. The Canadian government and ordinary citizens, especially school children, have donated money to the United Nations International Children's Emergency Fund (U.N.I.C.E.F.) to improve the health and welfare of children in the emerging countries.

Canada's membership in technical services organizations and special agencies attests her involvement in the many phases of the United Nations. Canada subscribes to the International Labor Organization (I.L.O.) in its task of bettering working conditions, and to the International Court of Justice. Canada is also a member of the International Telecommunication Union (I.T.U.), the Universal Postal Union (U.P.U.), International Monetary Fund (I.M.F.), General Agreement on Tariffs and Trade (G.A.T.T.) and the International Civil Aviation Organization (I.C.A.O.) which was established in 1947 with headquarter in Montreal. Since 1952, Canada has

been a member of the United Nations Disarmament Committee in Geneva.

Canada has given technical, economic and financial aid to developing nations in Africa and Asia. Canadian goods and equipment — ranging from road building machinery to fish hatcheries — have been channeled through United Nations agencies to the needy developing countries. Canadian experts are working for the United Nations in many countries to assist them in their economic, social and educational problems. Canadian policy has been to support the United Nations fully. Canada's willingness to adhere to the ideals of the United Nations was soon to be revealed in the Korean War.

Korea, a peninsula in northern China, had a long history of domination by foreign powers. Before World War II, Korea was a Japanese colony. At the end of the war, Korea was occupied by Soviet and American troops, with the thirty-eighth parallel of latitude as a demarcation line separating the Soviet armies north of the line from the American to the south. A United Nations Commission, of which Canada was a member, was appointed to arrange free elections for a single assembly for all of Korea. However, the Soviet authorities did not allow the Commission to enter North Korea. This led to the creation of South Korea which had the recognition of the United Nations. Eventually, the occupation troops withdrew, and the country remained divided.

On June 25, 1950, troops from the north crossed the demarcation line and invaded South Korea. The United States acted immediately; President Harry S. Truman dispatched American troops from their occupation duties in Japan. The United Nations felt obligated to come to the assistance of South Korea. While the U.S.S.R. boycotted the United Nations — eliminating the certainty of a Soviet veto — North Korea was declared an aggressor and the Secretary General of the United Nations appealed to its members to make forces available to resist this aggression.

Although the army in Korea was mainly American and commanded by an American, General Douglas MacArthur, military forces from sixteen United Nations member states took part in the fighting. Canada rallied to the support of the United Nations and placed a brigade of almost eight thousand men and units of the R.C.N. and the R.C.A.F. at disposal of the world organization. Canada's contribution to the Korean War was exceeded only by that of the United States and the United Kingdom.

The war dragged on with inconclusive thrusts across the demarcation line, and Communist China and the U.S.S.R. continued to provide North Korea with materials of war. General Mac-

Canadian Artillery in Korea Shelling Enemy Positions in Support of Infantry

Canadian Food for Ghana

Arthur advocated bombing of supply bases and communication lines in China in order to deprive the forces in North Korea of needed supplies. President Truman opposed any enlargement of the war — it was to be a limited war confined within Korea — and dismissed MacArthur. The war reached a stalemate, and, in 1953, a truce was arranged. Troops were returned to the original positions they held in 1950. Canadian forces, which suffered 1,642 casualties including 406 dead, were withdrawn in 1955.

CANADIAN FORCE FOR SERVICE IN KOREA[432]

Lester B. Pearson announced the recruitment of a special Canadian force for service in Korea. From a speech in the House of Commons, August 31, 1950:

This special force is unique in one way among the offers of military forces which have been made to the United Nations as the result of the war in Korea; and provides, I think, a valuable example and precedent. If other countries were, in the same way, to earmark a portion of their forces which might be made available to the United Nations for collective defence, there would be ready throughout the free world national contingents for a United Nations force which could be quickly brought together in the face of a future emergency. In this way the United Nations would be equipped with that military strength which it was intended in the charter that it should have at its disposal but which, in fact, it never had, largely because of the attitude of the U.S.S.R.

Canada, in her participation in the Korean War, demonstrated her faith in the United Nations. Moreover, Canada drastically departed from her traditional foreign policy. In the past, she was tied to Britain and was involved in Britain's European interests. Now, as a responsible member of the United Nations, Canada became concerned with global interests.

Canada's greatest impact in the United Nations was felt during the Suez Crisis in 1956. The trouble stemmed from the creation of the State of Israel by the United Nations on May 14, 1948. The Arab countries surrounding the newly created state struck at Israel in the hope that a military victory would set aside the United Nations decision. But Israel, fighting for its very existence, successfully resisted the attacks of the troops from seven Arab states. An armistice was arranged by the United Nations. However, the Arab states, regarding Israel as an intruder into the Arab lands, have persistently refused to recognize the existence of Israel and have maintained a "state of war." Egypt, using the state of war as a pretext, denied Israel the right to use the Suez Canal. This, Israel claimed, was contrary to the provisions of the Convention of Constantinople of 1888 which declared the Canal open to merchant and war vessels of all countries in peace and war except to those nations with which Egypt herself was at war.

Hostility reigned along the Arab-Israeli borders with repeated terrorist raids and punitive reprisals. Colonel Gamal Abdel Nasser, Egypt's head of state, who came to power in 1954, continued the state of war and intensified the raids against Israel. In July, 1956, he nationalized the Suez Canal and promised to compensate the shareholders of the internationally controlled Suez Canal Company. There is evidence that Britain and France, the major investors in the Canal, in collusion with Israel, devised a plan to regain the Canal and make it available to Israeli shipping and also to free Israel from the harassment of the Egyptian terrorist raids. In October, Israeli troops attacked Egyptian positions in the Sinai Peninsula and were heading towards the Canal. Britain and France, in an apparent show of concern, asked for a halt to the fighting and for a withdrawal by both sides from the Canal Zone; otherwise they would intervene to secure the Canal. Egypt refused to comply. British and French aircraft bombed Cairo and landed paratroopers who occupied strategic positions along the Canal. The Israelis, in the meantime, overran the Sinai Desert and dislodged the Egyptians from the area near the Gulf of Aqaba, where Egypt had maintained a blockade of the Straits of Tiran.

The United Nations plunged into a flurry of activity. The U.S.S.R. demanded immediate withdrawal of the invading forces and made veiled threats of intervention. The United States, fearful of the consequences of Soviet entanglement in the Middle East, joined the Soviet Union in condemning the aggression and in demanding immediate withdrawal of foreign troops from Egyptian soil. Afro-Asian nations, only recently emerged from colonialism, saw the Anglo-French intervention as a return to old-type colonial duplicity. The crisis threatened the United Nations, the NATO alliance, the Commonwealth, Anglo-American friendship and the unity of the non-Communist world.

The situation was critical. At this juncture, Lester B. Pearson, at the United Nations, worked feverishly for a peaceful solution. As a first step he called for an immediate cease-fire and withdrawal of foreign troops from Egypt. Pearson initiated the idea of the creation of a multinational United Nations Emergency Force to be stationed in the Gaza Strip and along the Sinai border to supervise the cease-fire and to act as a buffer separating the Egyptians from the Israelis. He made it clear that his proposals were only emergency measures; the real solution was to remove the basic causes of hostility and to create a lasting peace in the Middle East.

CANADA AND THE SUEZ CRISIS[133]

An adviser to Pearson at the U.N. described some of the diplomatic footwork done by Pearson:

. . . . Mike had always been interested in the idea of an international force. It would be foolish to say it was a unique Canadian idea, but we had been thinking along those lines, and so had the U.S. Someone had to take the initiative. The whole Assembly wanted something done, even the

UNEF Jeep in the Desert, Gaza

British and French. It was necessary to get the maximum support. Dulles [the U.S. Secretary of State] knew that if the U.S. proposed it, it would become a cold-war issue. Mike was able to do it because he was well thought of by the Israelis, he had been President of the Assembly, he knew half of the Foreign Ministers by their first names, he had the support of the U.S., and the Egyptian Minister, Fawzi, could talk to him rationally.

He had to play a double game. To get the Arabs and Asians to support it he had to make it seem that the UN was 'driving out' the British and French. At the same time he had to give the British and French a satisfactory reason for backing out: the reason that the UN was 'taking over. . . .'

The Canadian plan was adopted, and a small force was quickly recruited from member countries of the United Nations. The United Nations Emergency Force (U.N.E.F.) — the largest part of it made up of Canadians and under the command of Major-General E. L. M. Burns, a Canadian — was stationed on the Egyptian side of the Gaza Strip. Canada gained the admiration of the world and prestige as the world's peace-broker. She showed herself as a middle power, unaligned to either Britain or the United States and seeming to be the leader of the smaller nations; her voice was the voice of the lesser powers. For his efforts in the Suez Crisis, Pearson was awarded the Nobel Peace Prize for 1957.

Although Pearson's solution was favoured by the international community of nations, he was criticized in Canada by the Conservatives and by pro-British elements. They felt that Canada should have mobilized Commonwealth support for Britain instead of siding with the United States and the Soviet Union against Britain. Nevertheless, the world breathed easier and both Canada and the United Nations emerged from the crisis with strengthened reputations.

THE HOUSE OF COMMONS DEBATE ON CANADA'S ROLE IN THE SUEZ CRISIS[434]

Hon. W. Earl Rowe, November 26, 1956:

The Nasser government has made considerable headway towards turning a military defeat into a political victory. This has been made possible by the unfair criticism and the unnecessary compromises of the United Nations, and I may say, by our Canadian statesmen and those of the United States.

. . . . What is the use of Britain and France agreeing to a cease-fire or a withdrawal of troops with no assurance or guarantee of a settlement in the Middle East? What is the use of Israel withdrawing troops if Russia is to be free at any time to put its power behind Egypt and the Arab world, who collectively boast they will wipe out the state of Israel and eliminate all British and French influence in the whole Suez region and Mediterranean area?

Mr. M. J. Coldwell, Leader of the C.C.F., November 26, 1956:

. . . . I believe that in making the move into the Suez at the time she did Great Britain largely forfeited that moral leadership which she had built up laboriously over a number of years.

. . . . I want to say . . . that we are very happy indeed that it was the Canadian representative in the person of our Secretary of State for External Affairs who proposed the establishment of the United Nations force. I think that is something about which every Canadian can indeed be proud and happy.

Mr. Howard C. Green, November 27, 1956:

. . . . American foreign policy now is to build him [Nasser] up and presumably to get the United Kingdom and France out of the Middle East. Canada's policy seems to be the same. . . .

This policy of the Canadian government may well be disastrous to Canada. The United States would have far more admiration for Canada . . . if this government stopped being the United States chore boy.

. . . . It is high time Canada has a government which will not knife Canada's best friends [Britain and France] in the back.

The durable peace that Pearson had hoped for did not come about. The basic antagonism between Israel and her neighbouring Arab nations persisted. Border raids and retaliatory forays continued undiminished. Complaints were registered in the United Nations by both sides, but nothing conclusive was accomplished. In May, 1967, upon the request of President Nasser, the U.N.E.F., including the Canadian contingent, was summarily withdrawn from the Gaza strip. The situation deteriorated. On June 5, Israel attacked her Arab neighbours in what she claimed was "self defence." The Six Day War was swift; Israel defeated her enemies and occupied strategic positions in Arab territory.

The Security Council was in constant session during the fighting in an effort to bring the hostilities to a halt. On June 9, all parties agreed to a cease-fire, and by June 13, all military activity had halted. The Soviet and Arab blocks at the United Nations introduced resolutions to condemn Israel as the aggressor and to force her to withdraw from occupied Arab land. These resolutions were defeated since the majority of the members felt, as did Canada's Ambassador to the United Nations, George Ignatieff, that withdrawal in itself was not sufficient; it could not be separated from an overall settlement of the Middle East problem.

Throughout this latest Middle East crisis, Canada's declining role in the United Nations was obvious. Unlike 1956, Canada's voice now was only a whisper. Her status as spokesman for the lesser nations had dwindled over the years. In the eyes of many of the Afro-Asian countries, Canada appeared to be a satellite of the United States. Nevertheless, Canadian concern for the preservation of peace has been reflected in continued support for the objectives of the United Nations.

CANADA'S DECLINING ROLE IN THE UNITED NATIONS[345]

In his book, PEACEMAKER OR POWDER-MONKEY, *published in 1960, James M. Minifie foretold Canada's declining role in the U.N.:*

The conviction is growing in many quarters that the subordination or appearance of subordination [to the U.S.A.] . . . deprives Canada . . . its leadership of the middle powers in the councils of the world at a critical time when the small and middle powers are sweeping into the United Nations. . . .

. . . . Nobody fears Canada, since it is without territorial ambitions. Nobody harbours resentment against Canada, because it has never held sovereign control over an alien people. Nobody suspects Canada of coveting national resources — it has plenty of its own.

. . . Canada has the additional advantage of . . . independence . . . obtained . . . without recourse to force or violent revolution, and . . . unity . . . has . . . roots in Latin as well as Anglo-Saxon without an implacably bitter civil war . . . Canada culture . . . its contribution to peace in the critical days of Suez established Canadian diplomacy. . . .

These superb advantages . . . are cancelled out by the fact that Canada is still walking with the [U.S.A.]. It is caught in a too-close alliance which gives it the appearance of subordination to the United States. Indeed, the subordination is real to some degree, but even the suspicion of satellitism makes leadership unacceptable.

Hon. Lester B. Pearson

(I.C.C.) established at the Geneva Conference in 1954. Together with members from India and Poland, Canada has been supervising the observance of the terms of the agreement of the Geneva Conference regarding South and North Vietnam. Although it is not a United Nations operation, it is, nevertheless, a matter of great concern not only of the United Nations but of the world at large.

In addition to its tasks in the Gaza strip, Canada has participated in all United Nations peacekeeping operations. Canadians have been serving on truce supervision teams along the India-Pakistan cease-fire line in Kashmir. During the United Nations operations in the Congo in the early 1960's, the R.C.A.F. pilots flew transports into that war-torn country. Since 1964, Canadian troops, under United Nations auspices, have been stationed in Cyprus to maintain peace between Turks and Greeks on the island.

In Vietnam, Canadians have been serving as members of the International Control Commission

Ever since Canada's proposal for putting emergency forces at the United Nations' disposal was adopted, Canada has performed peace-keeping duties throughout the world. She has in readiness troops specifically trained for and allocated to any future peace-keeping mission. In her efforts on behalf of the United Nations, Canada has made a special place for herself among the nations of the world.

B

CANADA AND THE "COLD WAR"

Towards the end of World War II, the Great Powers agreed that the liberated countries would, through free elections, choose their postwar governments. The Soviet Union, in its successful thrust against collapsing German armies, had taken over countries in Eastern Europe and in the Baltic region, and was extending its domination still further. In 1945, a Communist-inspired revolt broke out in Greece, and only British and American intervention prevented the country from falling within the Soviet orbit. Pressure was also

exerted by the Soviet Union on Turkey and Iran. By 1947, Communist governments had been set up in Bulgaria, Hungary, Rumania and Poland. In 1948, a coup in Prague brought Czechoslovakia within the Soviet pale. This block of "satellite states" within the Soviet sphere of influence — these "people's democracies" — was what Britain's Winston Churchill referred as an "Iron Curtain" being drawn between East and West. In 1947 the Cominform, a resurrected Comintern, was formed: in Western eyes, a vehicle for further Communist expansion. In 1948, the Soviet Union imposed the blockade of Berlin in the hope of forcing the Western powers to abandon their rights to the city. All these activities were incidents in the "Cold War" — a state of friction and distrust between the West and the U.S.S.R.

One of the first dramatic indications of the Cold War was the Igor Gouzenko spy case in Canada. In September, 1945, Gouzenko, a clerk in the Soviet Embassy in Ottawa, turned over to the Canadian government evidence of an elaborate spy ring operating against Canada and other Western countries formerly allied with the U.S.S.R. The Western democracies viewed the advance of Soviet-directed Communism as a threat to the nations of western Europe. As early as 1947, Louis St. Laurent, Mackenzie King's Minister of External Affairs, spoke of a unified force to withstand Communist expansion. He was aware that the U.S.S.R. could not be checked by the United Nations, where she would surely veto any proposed action against her. The United States also favoured a concerted force for the containment of Communism. The North Atlantic Treaty Organization (NATO) was founded in Washington on April 4, 1949, for the express purpose of checking the spread of Communism. Belgium, Canada, Denmark, France, Iceland, Italy, Luxembourg, Holland, Norway, Portugal, the United Kingdom and the United States were the original members of NATO. Membership was enlarged with the entry of Greece and Turkey in 1952. To further strengthen the defence system of western Europe, the Federal Republic of Germany (West Germany) was admitted in 1955.

ST. LAURENT PROPOSES AN ATLANTIC ALLIANCE[436]

Excerpts from a speech by Louis St. Laurent to the House of Commons on April 29, 1948:

. . . . We are fully aware . . . of the inadequacy of the united nations at the present moment to provide the nations of the world with the security which they require. The realities of this situation must be faced, and the policy of the government in respect of it may be summarized very briefly.

. . . when I spoke seven months ago at the General Assembly, I stated then that . . . it is possible for the free nations of the world to form their own closer association for collective self-defence under article 51 of the charter of the united nations. . . .

It may be that the free states, or some of them, will soon find it necessary to consult together on how best to establish such a collective security

league. . . . Its purpose . . . would not be merely negative; it would create a dynamic counter-attraction to communism . . . the free democracies . . . would organize so as to confront the forces of communist expansionism with an overwhelming preponderance of moral, economic and military force and with sufficient degree of unity to ensure that . . . the free nations cannot be defeated one by one. . . . We must at all costs avoid the fatal repetition of the history of the pre-war years when the nazi aggressor picked off its victims one by one. Such a process does not end at the Atlantic. . . .

The signatories of the North Atlantic Treaty entered into a "defensive" alliance outside the United Nations, but at the same time they did "reaffirm their faith in the purposes of the Charter of the United Nations." This military alliance aimed "to safeguard the freedom, common heritage and civilization of their peoples, founded on the principles of democracy, individual liberty and the rule of law." Couched within these words was the real purpose of NATO; namely, to check the advance of Communism. Whereas Canada and the United States refused to subscribe to Article X of the Covenant of the League of Nations since the acceptance of it would involve them in wars not of their making, these same countries now made to NATO firm commitments that would require their aid to victims of aggression. This is clearly enunciated in Article 5 of the North Atlantic Treaty:

The Parties agreed that an armed attack against one or more of them in Europe or North America shall be considered an attack against them all, and consequently they agree that, if such an armed attack occurs, each of them, in exercise of the right of individual or collective self-defence recognized by Article 51 of the Charter of the United Nations, will assist the Party or Parties so attacked by taking forthwith, individually and in concert with the other Parties, such action as it deems necessary, including the use of armed force, to restore and maintain the security of the North Atlantic area.

Canada, in fulfilment of her obligations to NATO, stationed an army brigade in Germany and an air division in France. Canadian forces, together with personnel of other NATO nations, participated in joint manoeuvres and exercises. Co-operation was so close that NATO air crews had been trained in Canada by R.C.A.F. officers. Canada's contributions have been costly to the Canadian taxpayer. The N.D.P. has questioned the need of keeping these forces in Europe and

Canadian NATO Forces in Germany

has suggested their withdrawal. In the election campaign of 1968, Prime Minister Trudeau declared that Canada may have to review and reappraise her role in NATO. The Prime Minister stated that the promises of aid in the North Atlantic Treaty were made at a time when European countries, financially unstable and militarily weak, were unable to defend themselves. Now, however, these countries were quite capable of looking after themselves. Also, with the advent of nuclear warfare, the value of maintaining conventional forces in Europe is questionable. Perhaps NATO is obsolete, and the purposes of the organization and Canada's functions in it should be altered. Prime Minister Trudeau has indicated that there might be curtailment, change of emphasis or "phasing out" of Canada's military support to NATO, but there will be no abrupt pull-out as demanded by the N.D.P. Canada's future commitments will be agreed upon in consultation with her allies within NATO.

Canada, as a member of NATO, demonstrated her acceptance of international obligations. No longer did she take shelter in North American isolationism; instead she assumed responsibilities of a nation in world affairs.

C

CANADA AND THE COMMONWEALTH

Between two world wars, the British Empire evolved into a Commonwealth of nations. The 1926 Balfour Report defined the Commonwealth as a free association of autonomous nations united by a common allegiance to the Crown. The Statute of Westminster in 1931 enlarged the equal status of the Dominions with the United Kingdom and gave the Dominions control of legislative powers. However, the Commonwealth was made up of countries whose population was of European descent; the coloured nations were still colonies within the Emipre.

Following the end of World War II, former colonies within the Empire gained their independence, and some of them — India, Pakistan, Ceylon and Ghana — became republics that owed no allegiance to the Crown. The problem of the Commonwealth was how to accommodate these new countries to keep them within the Commonwealth. Through Canada's efforts, Britain, Australia and New Zealand agreed to a modified formula that would allow membership to such nations in the Commonwealth. The new Commonwealth became a combination of countries which continued allegiance to the Crown and those which wished to continue their association with Britain and the Dominions. Canada was responsible, to a large extent, for the transformation of the Commonwealth into a multi-racial association.

A Canadian teacher trains a student at Uganda College of Commerce, Kampala.

CANADA AND THE COMMONWEALTH[137]

Prime Minister St. Laurent speaks of Canada's relations with the other nations of the British Commonwealth. House of Commons, April 29, 1948:

Our relations with the United Kingdom and the other nations of the commonwealth, will . . . be characterized by what is lacking in the world today, mutual confidence and understanding, frankness and good will. . . . The present status of all members is in fact well described in the phrase, now often used, as "independence within the commonwealth."

The commonwealth relationship has, however, never been and cannot remain static. The dangers and uncertainties of the present world situation have compelled Canada to assume greater responsibilities as a North American nation. . . .

The strength of this commonwealth association rests not in exclusive defence or economic arrangements among its members. Indeed in time of peace formal defence arrangements have been singularly lacking. The greatest strength of the commonwealth bond is the adherence of its members to its common ideals, their common political heritage which assures mutual understanding without the necessity of formal instruments of association. . . . These ties persist in spite of all changes in the world situation. . . .

Commonwealth co-operation, in 1950, brought into existence the Colombo Plan. It was a program formulated by eight nations of the Commonwealth for economic aid to countries of South

and Southeast Asia. Through the Council of Technical Co-operation, with headquarters in Colombo, Ceylon, the Plan provided technical assistance to agriculture, industry, scientific research, health and training of personnel. Funds for the support of the program were originally supplied by Commonwealth nations, but the United States, soon realizing the value of the Plan, began to contribute and has continued to do so generously. The United Nations also became involved, not in financial aid but in providing expert advisers.

The Commonwealth is a large trading area in which the members enjoy a small measure of preferential treatment. Commonwealth co-operation is also extended to technical and educational fields. Canadian technicians and teachers are serving in Commonwealth countries in Africa and Asia. As part of its contribution, Canada has established schools and technical-vocational institutions in several of these countries.

But developments in the world often strain Commonwealth relations. The 1956 Suez crisis threatened to disrupt the Commonwealth. Whereas Australia and New Zealand supported the United Kingdom, Canada did not; India and other Commonwealth countries saw the Franco-British attack on Egypt as a return to an outmoded imperialism. Far more serious is the complexity of the racial problem within the Commonwealth. At the 1961 Commonwealth Prime Ministers Conference in London, African and Asian representatives pitted themselves against the Union of South Africa for its *apartheid* policy — the segregation of blacks and whites. South Africa insisted that *apartheid* was a domestic matter and no concern of the Conference. Although the United Kingdom, Australia and New Zealand were anxious to avoid the issue, Canada, represented by Prime Minister John G. Diefenbaker, decisively opposed South Africa's contention. South Africa thereupon withdrew from the Commonwealth. Canada's stand was prompted by the realization that survival of the multi-racial Commonwealth necessitated a declaration of racial equality.

In 1965, the latest racial issue in Southern Rhodesia produced a similar stand — Canada joined other Commonwealth countries in denouncing Rhodesia's racial policy. When Rhodesia cut off oil supplies to Zambia, a Commonwealth country, Canadian aircraft flew oil into that country. But many African countries feel that Britain has been too lenient on South Rhodesia and pays only lip service to racial equality. This viewpoint is strengthened by the fact that the United Kingdom herself discriminates against coloured people when she restricts immigration of non-whites as well as Hindus and Pakistanis from Commonwealth countries.

Future difficulties for the Commonwealth may arise in the event of a break in Anglo-American friendship. Canada, Australia and New Zealand, so dependent upon the United States for trade and defence, will be faced with a test of their loyalties — to the Commonwealth or to the United States. Other Commonwealth countries, which receive economic aid from the United States, will be confronted with a similar decision. Furthermore, it is very doubtful whether any Commonwealth country would sacrifice its national self-interest for the sake of Commonwealth unity. In such a widely diversified association of nations, serious clashes of interests are bound to arise, serious enough to place the existence of the Commonwealth in jeopardy.

Many people find the idea of the Commonwealth most perplexing. What is it? To many, the Commonwealth is an instrument by which Britain hopes to retain what is left of her former possessions. Obviously, those who hold this viewpoint fail to grasp the meaning of a "free association of autonomous nations." Little do they realize that the Commonwealth is neither an alliance with prescribed obligations nor a federation with binding constitutional powers. Very few outside the Commonwealth know that a Canadian, Arnold Smith, and not a Britisher, became the Commonwealth's first Secretary-General in 1965. What then is the Commonwealth? It has been truly described as a "family of nations" — perhaps with only tenuous attachment, but nevertheless a family. Such bonds may often be more far-reaching than clearly defined constitutions or clauses of treaties.

THE VALUE OF THE COMMONWEALTH[438]

Walter Gordon speaks of the importance of Canada's membership in the Commonwealth. These observations were expressed in 1966:

. . . . To some extent, our Commonwealth membership gives us a place in world councils that is denied to the United States. And because we have no axe to grind and harbour no territorial ambitions, past or present, our influence in Commonwealth proceedings can be useful and impressive. It is quite true that the Commonwealth countries do not wield much power. But they include hundreds of millions of people from all parts of the world. The Commonwealth is a forum where white and black can meet and talk together as equals and where they can often agree to compromise. As long as it can be useful in these ways, it is an institution that is well worth preserving.

D

CANADA AND THE UNITED STATES

Canada has always depended heavily on foreign investment — at first on British, and since the 1920's on American. At present, over three-quarters of all foreign investment in Canada is American. Americans, for many years, have invested heavily in Canada's primary resources, but since the end of the Second World War they have extended their interest into other fields. Canadian subsidiaries of American firms were established to benefit from the profitable Canadian market. With American investment came American management, technicians and control. Thus Canada's economy came under foreign domination. Canadians generally welcome American capital, but some resent such deep American financial penetration and control; they fear that the independence Canada had gained from Britain is being placed in economic bondage to the United States.

That 60 per cent of Canada's exports go to

the United States and 70 per cent of Canada's imports come from the United States indicate the extent of Canadian dependence on the American economy. True, the United States is Canada's best market, but at the same time Canada is one of the United States' best customers. Over half of Canadian manufacturing industries is controlled by Americans. Such vital fields as petroleum, mining and pulp and paper are largely American owned; the manufacturing of automobiles, rubber and electrical appliances is almost entirely American-owned and controlled.

ANTI-AMERICIANISM IN CANADA[439]

James M. Minifie believes there is deep-rooted anti-Americanism in Canada:

There is anti-Americanism in Canada too, a chip-on-the-shoulder inferiority complex based on the suspicion that Canadian independence, so patiently won from Britain, is being swiftly eroded by American military, economic and cultural domination.

———

. . . while Canadian resentment glows it does not flare into violence.

———

. . . nobody chalks "Yankee Go Home" on the walls. . . . So the American concludes, happily but wrongly, that there is no anti-Americanism in Canada.

Such mutual dependence could create serious problems for the Canadian economy. When imports of Canadian oil conflicted with American petroleum interests, the American government did not hesitate to impose tariffs and quotas on such imports. When Canada concluded profitable wheat sales with Communist countries, especially China, the American State Department resented Canadian trade with a country the United States has not recognized. Similar objection was expressed against Canadian trade with Cuba, with whom the United States came into dangerous confrontation, and Canada's Minister of Trade and Commerce found it necessary to assure the Americans that such trade would not include strategic materials. When Canada contemplated selling automotive vehicles to Communist China, the American State Department put pressure on the Ford Company of Canada, a subsidiary of the American parent company, to refrain from such trade. It must not be forgotten that the United States is still Canada's greatest competitor in world wheat markets.

Many Canadians are alarmed over the fact that

the United States, because of its hold on Canada's economy, might exert political pressure on Canadian national affairs to bring them into line with the thinking of the American State Department. Walter Gordon, the former Minister of Finance in Pearson's government and an ardent economic nationalist, expressed this Canadian attitude towards American investment. He did not object to American investment, nor to any foreign investment as such, but he insisted on setting controls on foreign capital to assure, as far as possible, Canadian economic independence.

THE QUESTION OF AMERICAN ECONOMIC INFLUENCE IN CANADA[440]

Walter Gordon, Canada's Minister of Finance from 1963 to 1965, has been an outspoken critic of American economic influence in Canada. He comments:

. . . . But I had not fully appreciated the depth and strength of these [American] pressures until I became Minister of Finance in April of 1963. During the two-and-one half years I held that office, the influence that financial and business interests in the United States had on Canadian policy and opinion was continually brought home to me. On occasion, this influence was reinforced by representations from the State Department and the American Administration as a whole. It was pressed by those who direct American businesses in Canada, by their professional advisers, by Canadian financiers whose interests were identified directly or indirectly with American investment in Canada, by influential members of the Canadian civil service, by some representatives of the university community, and by some sections of the press. . . .

Long-standing disagreements between the United States and Canada arose over the construction of the St. Lawrence Seaway and the development of the Columbia River. These were finally settled to the mutual satisfaction of both countries. The American government, under pressure from the Atlantic seaboard states, consistently refused to join Canada in the construction of the seaway — a project agreed upon as far back as 1932. Postwar Canada needed a seaway. In 1951, the Canadian government announced that it would proceed without the United States. The American government, unwilling to be left out of such a vital undertaking, reconsidered its earlier objections. In 1954, she became a partner in the project, which was completed in 1959.

Disagreement over the development of the Canadian portion of the Columbia River marred the harmony that characterized the numerous negotiations of the International Joint Commission since its inception in 1909. British Columbia and Ottawa had rejected the American offers for flood control and for harnessing the potential hydro-electric power of the upper Columbia River on Canadian territory. In 1964, the dispute was settled by treaty, and work on the project will be started in the not too distant future.

The most serious friction between the two countries resulted from the joint programs for North American continental defence. Aside from co-operation with the United States in NATO, Canada entered into bilateral defence projects with the Americans. Three radar detection systems were constructed across Canada: the Pinetree line across southern Canada; the Mid-Canada line built by Canada and abandoned as obsolete in 1966; and the DEW line across the Canadian Arctic completed in 1959, paid for wholly by the United States, and manned by American personnel. The United States spent vast sums in these installations, which were to give warning of approaching potential enemy aircraft — presumably Soviet bombers — before reaching the industrial heartland of the United States.

As a result of the launching of the first Sputnik in 1957 and the development of the atom and hydrogen bombs by the Soviet Union, the recently-constructed radar tracking lines, designed for the detection of conventional bombers, became obsolete. To protect the industrial areas of the United States, Canada and the United States in 1958 signed the North American Air Defence (NORAD) agreement which co-ordinated North American defence. A joint command, headed by an American and assisted by a Canadian second-in-command, was to man the intricate installations at Colorado Springs for the detection of approaching enemy bombers. Units of the Canadian and American air forces have been assigned to NORAD and have been placed on constant alert.

CANADA'S ROLE IN NORAD[441]

Walter Gordon's views on NORAD:

We should also continue to play a role in NORAD, under which Canada participates in the defence of North America. Again we have to face the facts of life. Compared with our American allies, Canada has never played anything like an equal role in NORAD. A Canadian has been named Deputy Chief of the NORAD establishment. But the Americans have contributed by far the largest share of men and equipment, and they have borne by far the largest share of the cost. Theoretically, if hostilities should break out with

DEW (Distant Early Warning)—Line Radar Installation

the Soviet Union, NORAD would retaliate after getting clearance from the President of the United States and the Prime Minister of Canada. But it is most unlikely that there would be time for serious consultation. In practice, it would be an American decision. I believe we should accept this and not pretend it could be otherwise. . . .

Because of the changing nature of the potential Soviet striking capability, the Canadian aircraft industry got a disastrous blow. Since 1953, the CF-105 Arrow supersonic interceptor, built at the A.V. Roe Co. Ltd., at Malton, Ontario, was regarded as North America's answer to the Soviet bomber threat. However, within the NORAD set-up, there was no place for the CF-105. Canada had already spent over three hundred million dollars on development, and expected to manufacture five hundred of these interceptors. In February, 1959, Prime Minister John G. Diefenbaker declared, "The Arrow has been overtaken by events," and ordered the immediate abandonment of production of the CF-105 and the scrapping of the test model. The A.V. Roe Co. thereupon dismissed over fifteen thousand employees, including a team of highly trained engineers.

The most serious crisis in Canadian-American relations arose over the installation of nuclear weapons on Canadian territory. Canada has agreed to the building of BOMARC "B" anti-aircraft missile bases at North Bay, Ontario, and La Macaza, Quebec. The United States paid for most of these bases and it was understood that these missiles would be supplied with nuclear warheads. However, according to a clause in the United States Atomic Energy Act, atomic warheads cannot be entrusted to foreign states. Therefore,

American troops would have to be sent to guard such weapons. Several ministers in the Canadian cabinet objected to the possibility of stationing foreign troops on Canadian soil — to them it was an affront to Canadian sovereignty. Still more irritating was the fact that the United States could never accept Canada's independent operation of the BOMARCS.

In February, 1962, the R.C.A.F. took over the BOMARC bases, but the missiles had no nuclear warheads. Eventually, when the American government showed a willingness to supply nuclear warheads, the Canadian government vacillated over such acquisition. Howard Green, the Minister of External Affairs, felt that the acceptance of nuclear warheads by Canada would put an end to Canada's role at the disarmament negotiations. Within the cabinet the split between the pro-nuclear and anti-nuclear groups widened. It was argued that the BOMARC was of short range and, therefore, ineffective. Moreover, expenditure on BOMARC missiles in Canada would be made at a time when the United States had abandoned them as obsolete. There was no valid reason for Canada to invest additional funds in obsolete missiles over which she had no control.

CANADA AND THE BOMARC MISSILES[442]

In the House of Commons, on February 5, 1963, Prime Minister Diefenbaker expressed his doubts about the value of the BOMARC missiles:

. . . . I have stated that the Bomarc was simply a part of the plan for North American defence and was not to defend Canada. That is not its purpose, but in its statement the state department said two Bomarc B squadrons would protect Montreal and Toronto as well as the United States deterrent force. Well, we installed these Bomarc and the decision to do so, as part of a ring to protect the nuclear strike force, was announced in September 1958.

What about the changes in between? What is the position of these things today? On the one hand the department of state says they will defend Montreal and Toronto, that they are effective today; but on the other hand, on January 31 it was reported that defence secretary McNamara suggested that Bomarc missile squadrons have only limited usefulness even against manned bomber attacks. Are they going to continue with them? Yes, they are going to continue them, and the reason given was because the United States government has already paid for them. That does not sound as if their defensive properties are very high today, simply because they have been paid for already. . . .

A sergeant works on a radar console, part of the SAGE (Semi-Automatic Ground Environment) warning system, near North Bay, Ontario, District Headquarters of NORAD.

During the Cuban crisis in 1962, neither the BOMARC missiles nor the supersonic CF 101-B Voodoo fighter aircraft had nuclear warheads. The missiles and aircraft were useless. It was evident that Canada was a subordinate partner in NORAD. True, the second-in-command is a Canadian, but his is only a title; the real decision rests with the United States and Washington is not accountable to Canada.

Canada's nuclear position in NATO had a similar fate. Although Prime Minister Diefenbaker had signed an agreement with the other NATO allies to stockpile tactical nuclear weapons as a deterrent to the Soviet Union, Canada failed to do so. In 1962, an R.C.A.F. squadron of CF-104's — the aircraft for the striking force carrying nuclear weapons — was stationed at Zweibrucken, West Germany, but they had no nuclear warheads. Nor did the Honest John surface-to-surface missiles assigned to Canadian NATO forces in Europe have nuclear warheads — they were stuffed with bags of sand!

Canada's independent conduct irritated the United States. It also strained cabinet unity so that Douglas Harkness, the Minister of National Defence, resigned. With an impending general election, Diefenbaker felt that the mood of the people of Canada was against nuclear weapons. Nuclear weapons in particular and Canadian-American relations in general became the major election issues. Was Canada going to honour its obligations to NORAD and NATO? What of the six hundred and eighty-five million dollars the Diefenbaker government had already spent on seemingly sterile missiles?

The Conservative election campaign slogan was that Canada should not accept nuclear warheads while disarmament negotiations were going on. Canada could play an important role in the negotiations only as a non-nuclear nation. Diefenbaker objected to the foisting of obsolete missiles on Canada — weapons to be triggered at American command. He argued, rather unrealistically, that Canada could acquire nuclear weapons just prior to an outbreak of war.

DIEFENBAKER DENIES THAT HE IS ANTI-AMERICAN[443]

From a speech in the House of Commons, February 5, 1963:

... there are some who say to me that if you take a stand like this [on the BOMARC missiles] it is anti-American ... it is nothing of the kind. I do not think it is other than pro-Canadian, or Canadian, to point out when something is wrong. ...

Somebody said to me that if I take this stand then we are going to suffer danger in Canada, damage to Canada, and that we are going to do harm to Canada's economic strength. I do not accept that argument. It is an unworthy one. Does anyone tell me that the United States ... would retaliate because we failed to adopt a suggestion that they offered? Such an argument ... if carried to its logical conclusion, means this, that our country has ceased to be a country wherein we have the right to make our own policies. I do not accept that.

I believe in co-operation because I believe in good relations. ... But I cannot accept the fears of those who believe we must be subservient in order to be a good ally of any country in the world. ...

Deliberately or inadvertently, an emotional anti-Americanism was injected into the election campaign.

THE BOMARC MISSILE[444]

Robert McNamara, the United States Secretary of Defence, on February 6, 1963, testified before a subcommittee of the Committee on Appropriations, House of Representatives, on the BOMARC missiles installed in Canada:

MINSHALL — ... we put somewhere between $3 billions and $4 billions into this [Bomarc] program. I just wonder if it is as ineffective as you now agree it is, why we even put any money into the operational cost of this weapon when it is so useless.

RCAF CF-104 Landing in Germany

MCNAMARA — Yes, the Bomarc looks to us to cost on the order of $20 millions a year to operate.

MINSHALL — that to me is an awful lot of money.

MCNAMARA — For the protection we get I do not believe it is an unreasonable amount.

At the very least, they would cause the Soviets to target missiles against them and thereby increase their requirements or draw missiles onto these Bomarc targets than would otherwise be available for other targets.

If there were any real amount of money to be saved, I would propose taking them out, but for $20 millions a year I think we are getting our money's worth.

FLOOD — If we scratch Bomarc, we have stuck the Canadians for a whole mess of them and we have another problem on our border.

The election campaign made many Canadians aware of Canada's perilous position in the nuclear age. Canada might well become the Belgium of North America — a buffer state between the world's two most powerful nations. Placing of missiles in Canada would expose her to attack by enemy nuclear missiles. The United States was not interested in Canada; Canada was to be the decoy to draw missiles that would otherwise land in continental United States. The most populated part of Canada would thus become a zone of indescribable destruction. Why then should Canada stake her wealth and future for the protection of the United States?

Canadians, living next door to and sharing the continent with such a powerful neighbour as the United States, are fully aware of the influence of American culture. Canadian life has, indeed, been Americanized. American magazines, or their Canadian editions, have captured the Canadian

President John F. Kennedy addresses the Canadian Parliament, May 17, 1961.

market; three of four magazines bought by Canadians are American publications. With such competition, Canadian magazines have had a constant struggle for survival. In 1961, the O'Leary Commission, appointed by the Diefenbaker government, recommended that Canadian publications be given protection against American competition. The Liberals, after they came to power in 1963, found it necessary to tax Canadian editions of American magazines.

Canadian book publishers fare no better — they are no match for the gigantic American publishing firms and their Canadian subsidiaries. The American publishing houses dominate the Canadian book market. Canadian public schools and universities tend to favour American text books. As for the average Canadian, he finds it difficult to resist the enticing offers of the Book-of-the-Month Club or of other similar American book clubs.

The advent of television had a most profound effect on Canadian life. At first, most of the programs originated in the United States, and Canadian viewers eagerly awaited the evening hours to watch television. Over the years, Canadian listeners and viewers have shown an overwhelming preference for American radio and television. The Board of Broadcast Governors, controllers of radio and television in Canada, insisted upon a 25 per cent Canadian content in programs shown in Canada. The Canadian Broadcasting Corporation (C.B.C.) has been attempting for many years to encourage and develop Canadian culture. Utilizing Canadian talent, it inaugurated excellent programs featuring drama, music, and variety shows, but most of them did not survive. Only

public affairs programs and hockey and football broadcasts managed to attract devoted followers. Canadians readily accept the worst of American television in preference to Canadian-produced programs. Perhaps Canadians show a lack of faith in Canadian talent.

American movies have also exerted a considerable influence on Canadian life. Most of the film theatres in Canada are American owned or controlled, and the multi-billion dollar Hollywood-based film industry spends huge sums in a constant barrage of publicity and advertising to maintain the interest of the movie-goers. Numerous syndicated columns, articles and reviews in newspapers and magazines blatantly grind out propaganda to maintain the Hollywood myths, and, incidentally, to boost box-office receipts. Stories of the movie stars — their success and lives often in minutest detail garnished with scandal — glorifying the movie idols, are designed to influence Canadians to go to the movies. Other devices — autographed pictures of movie stars, contests, radio and television advertising, fashions, personal appearances of actors and actresses, movie reviews by so-called experts — are frequently employed to create fans who have a loyalty or attachment to their favourite movie stars. There is no doubt that millions of Canadians — probably the largest Canadian television audience — sit in front of their television sets on Oscar Awards Night, a yearly extravaganza, when the movie industry honours those individuals who made outstanding contributions to the film industry.

Faced with such competition from Hollywood, independent Canadian film producers, limited in their financial resources, are inhibited in their activity. Even the National Film Board (NFB), a government agency which has been producing films for many years, cannot compete with Hollywood-produced films. The NFB has been successful in educational films, which are shown in Canadian public schools. Even in this field many excellent American educational films are competing, leaving the NFB free only in purely Canadian themes. Nevertheless, Canadian films are produced in ever larger numbers, and some of them have been of such high calibre that they won awards at several international film festivals.

In the field of education, Canada, who for so many years had followed the British pattern, began to accept American trends. The first major switch was to American text books. Next, educational experimentation and innovations, first tried in the United States, were adopted by Canadian schools. New courses in the sciences and mathematics, team-teaching, closed-circuit television instruction, programed learning, teaching machines and audio-visual aids — all were brought into the

Canadian school systems from the United States. Every year, more and more Canadian teachers go to the United States to learn effective application of new courses, methods and equipment. Canadian university graduates, in ever larger numbers, are pursuing post-graduate studies in American universities where facilities and financial aid are more plentiful. The influence of the United States on Canadian education is unmistakable.

The most serious aspect of American cultural influence on Canada is the loss of Canadian talent — the "brain drain" — to the United States. Enormous film and television facilities and funds in the United States beckon Canadian performing artists. Successful Canadian professionals, scientists, writers and university teachers have found rewarding employment in the United States. Only in professional sports is there a reverse trend — American athletes, especially football players, find Canada a profitable field for their talents. There is no denying that Canadians cannot resist the more lucrative American fields; only a few idealists have resisted the lure of American money and have remained in Canada to contribute somewhat to Canadian culture.

THE PROSPECTS FOR CANADA'S FUTURE[445]

[a]*In 1967, Professor Gad Horowitz, made a plea for Canadian nationalism:*

. . . . Canadian nationalism is clearly that of the small state: our relationship with the United States is analogous to the relationship of Finland with the Soviet Union. . . . The Canadians and the Finns are no threat to their great neighbours . . . there is a difference between the nationalism that disrupts established states and the nationalism that preserves or consolidates existing states . . . the nationalisms that today threaten to destroy and dismember India and Nigeria . . . are usually accompanied by bitter chauvinistic hatred of neighbouring peoples and often result in the shedding of blood. . . . But the Pan-Canadian nationalism which seeks to preserve a Canadian state in some form, and to prevent the digestion of both English- and French-Canadian societies by the United States, is an entirely different matter.

---

[b]*In 1968, George W. Ball, a former prominent member of the United States' government, predicted the inevitable American absorption of Canada:**

Canada, I have long believed, is fighting a rearguard action against the inevitable. Living next to our nation, with a population ten times as large as theirs and a gross national product fourteen times as great, the Canadians recognize their need for United States capital; but at the same time they are determined to maintain their economic and political independence. . . . But the Canadians pay heavily for it. . . . I wonder, for example, if the Canadian people will be prepared indefinitely to accept, for the psychic satisfaction of maintaining a separate national and political identity, a per capita income less than three-fourths of ours. The struggle is bound to be a difficult one — and I suspect, over the years, a losing one. . . . Sooner or later, commercial imperatives will bring about free movement of all goods back and forth across the long border. . . . The result will inevitably be substantial economic integration, which will require for its full realization a progressively expanding area of common political decision.

* Copyright 1968 by George Ball.

32

THE LATEST CHALLENGE

Who is right and who is wrong? We do not even ask ourselves that question; we simply record the existence of a crisis which we believe to be very serious. If it should persist and gather momentum it could destroy Canada. On the other hand, if it is overcome, it will have contributed to the rebirth of a richer and more dynamic Canada. But this will be possible only if we face the reality of the crisis and grapple with it in time.*

Since the Conquest more than two hundred years ago, French-speaking Canadians have faced the constant challenge of *la survivance*, cultural survival. To avoid absorption by English-speaking North America and to maintain their way of life in an alien economic and political environment, the French have embraced their church, their language and their land as instruments of survival.

Fear of Anglicization prompted French Canadians to keep their children out of Anglican controlled schools during the first two decades following the Constitutional Act. The proposed union of 1822 and the subsequent union of 1841 were attacked by French Canadians as deliberate attempts to exploit them economically and dominate them politically. To French Canadians the Durham Report was a blueprint for the annihilation of their culture. French Canada opposed Confederation as yet another assault on its heritage, and only George Etienne Cartier's assurances that a federal union would safeguard *Canadien* rights within Quebec convinced the French Canadians that they had nothing to fear from Confederation. Louis Riel's execution raised the spectre of a victorious Orange Lodge trampling French Catholic rights; the abolition of French as an official language and the problems of Catholic schools in Manitoba confirmed such fears. French Canadians even began to doubt their own leaders; led by Henri Bourassa they opposed Laurier's handling of the Boer War crisis. The conscription issues in two world wars revealed the depth of French Canada's resentment of being forced to serve what

it regarded as "Anglo-Saxon" causes. French Canadians thought of themselves as a distinctly North American people unconcerned with the ambitions of either Britain or France.

FRENCH-CANADIAN MISGIVINGS[446]

From COMMUNITY IN CRISIS: FRENCH-CANADIAN NATIONALISM IN PERSPECTIVE, *by Richard Jones:*

In the eyes of the French Canadian, we have never made a sincere attempt at building a pluralistic society in Canada, at least one in which he could declare that he was being treated with justice and fairness. He sees that the Anglo-Canadian has always been interested in building not a genuine pluralistic society but rather an Anglo-Canadian nation-state. This observation has been made real to him wherever he has met the Anglo-Canadian — in history, in politics, in the economy, in culture. Is he exaggerating? The very fact that a national minority comprehensively feels itself to be a minority and demands radical changes in all sectors of activity should give sufficient reason to suspect the existence of unsatisfactory relationship between minority and majority.

Since 1960, a new Quebec has emerged. Quebec has become caught up in the trends of postwar Canada — industrialization, urbanization, expanded educational opportunity, and the influence of mass communication, especially television. Quebec had entered the period of *la revolution tranquille* — the "Quiet Revolution" — which dispelled somewhat the long-held Anglo-Saxon concept of Quebec as a rural, backward, priest-controlled, homogeneous society. Quebec had undergone a transformation; it was no longer a province of self-sufficient families held together by parish institutions. Quebec no longer depended entirely on the Church for cultural survival; Que-

---

* From: *A preliminary Report of the Royal Commission on Bilingualism and Biculturalism,* (1965).

RIN Demonstrators, Montreal P.Q., 1967

bec now looked to the provincial government as the champion of the French-Canadian language and culture.

The election of Jean Lesage's Liberal government in June, 1960, on a program of industrial development, economic planning, increased social services and educational opportunity, gave added impetus to the "Quiet Revolution." The Lesage administration opened the floodgates of French Canada's desires, smothered during the long Duplessis regime, for a Quebec in step with the modern industrial age. Whereas Duplessis avoided government involvement in the fields of social welfare and ownership of resources and industries, the Lesage government plunged headlong into these areas.

The provincially appointed Parent Commission recommended drastic reform of the educational system which had, over the years, stressed classical and literary studies. The Commission advised, instead, that education in the province be patterned to the needs of a modern industrial society. Passed in 1964, Bill 60, which created a Ministry of Education, was an indication of the importance attached to education. Although the government favoured the recommendations of the Commission, Paul Gerin-Lajoie, the Minister of Education, had to proceed slowly because of the complexity of the problem and of opposition from existing school systems which for years controlled education in the province.

In spite of significant accomplishments, the Lesage government was defeated in the 1966 election. Many Quebeckers simply felt that the Lesage government had tried to accomplish too much too quickly. They saw the new programs of reform and development in terms of greatly increased taxation. This mood of apprehension naturally worked to the advantage of the revitalized *Union Nationale* Party under the leadership of Daniel Johnson. But the "Quiet Revolution" nevertheless continued under the new government, and ever larger numbers of Quebeckers participated in the movement for change.

THE LANGUAGE BARRIER[447]

A French-Canadian author and journalist, Solange Chaput-Rolland, writes in DEAR ENEMIES, *a book comprising an exchange of letters with an English-Canadian counterpart, Gwethalyn Graham:*

. . . If only we could talk perhaps we would understand each other better. But this joy is withheld from us. In the matter of bilingualism, will you admit the complete failure of our Confederative understanding? The two cultures vegetate side by side; they grow poorer on a diet of French and English imitations and American buffoonery because they have not yet discovered the richness of their own thinking. We are a people without

Visit of General Charles de Gaulle to Canada, City Hall, Montreal, 1967

understanding, without communication, without love. And this voluntary misunderstanding can be summed up in one question: When are we going to have the courage to accept one another?

Our country is far too large for a citizen of Halifax or Vancouver to be interested in the usage of French. But between these two extremes — universal bilingualism and a complete ignorance of the French fact — isn't there some middle road?

Gwethalyn Graham replies:

Fundamental to the solution of the problem of bilingualism is the presence of French Canadians in the schools of English Canada. That they have been almost entirely absent throughout our history, and still are, must astonish any non-Canadian. Perhaps still more important than the academic aspect of the problem is the purely human one — I can think of no single change which would lead more rapidly and effectively to a healing of the present breach between English and French Canadians and to a greater appreciation, love, and understanding of Quebec than to have the students of the nine other provinces taught French by French Canadians.

The "Quiet Revolution" had dramatized the need for a re-evaluation of the relations between French and English Canada, between Quebec and the rest of Canada. As a consequence, the very constitutional foundation of the country has been seriously questioned. A section of French Canadian society regards the B.N.A. Act as a pact between the two founding peoples. This "compact" theory of Confederation contends that the B.N.A. Act recognized the existence of *deux nations* and the equality of their languages. In practice, however, a French-speaking Canadian must have a good command of the English language to succeed in commerce, industry or the civil service. In the *deux nations* view, this constitutes discrimination, which stands in the way of French Canadians' securing top administrative and managerial positions. Further, this view holds that the English-speaking Canadians, *les Anglais*, have placed French-speaking Canadians in the category of second class citizens. The logical conclusion of this line of thought is that *les Anglais* have broken the pact of Confederation and Quebeckers must, therefore, strengthen their position within their province and amongst their compatriots living in Canada beyond the borders of Quebec. The Ministry of Cultural Affairs, created by the Lesage government, was to be the mentor of French-Canadian culture. To ensure the survival of this culture in North America, it seemed necessary to forge strong links with other French-speaking communities in the world. As an initial step, the Quebec government, signed a cultural agreement with France in 1965 to provide for exchange of students, professors and educationalists.

Premier Daniel Johnson carried this policy much further, since he believed that only Quebec could properly represent that province on educational matters, even at international conferences.* In March, 1968, Quebec's Education Minister, Jean-Guy Cardinal, upon the invitation of the tiny West African republic of Gabon, went to an educational conference attended by France and fifteen former French colonies, *la Francophonie* — the French-speaking commonwealth. Quebec's *fleur-de-lis* fluttered with the flags of independent nations. Ottawa was perturbed because Mr. Cardinal seemed to be speaking for Canada abroad. Prime Minister L. B. Pearson rebuked Gabon for its breach of diplomatic protocol. In April of the same year, Mr. Cardinal attended a meeting of French-speaking education ministers in Paris. The new Prime Minister, Pierre Elliott Trudeau, dispatched a note to the French government pointing out that Ottawa alone conducts Canada's foreign affairs. The Prime Minister unmistakably stated his view in remarks to the press: "When a foreign country wants to talk to Canada, there is only one address: Ottawa."

VIVE LE QUEBEC LIBRE[448]

An account of President Charles de Gaulle's meddling in Canadian internal affairs:

On a state visit to Canada in July 1967, during Canada's Centennial Year celebration, President Charles de Gaulle of France, a man not known for his humility, shouted from the steps of Montreal's city hall *"Vive le Quebec Libre,"* thus echoing the slogan of Quebec's active and vociferous separatist groups. After cabinet consultation and deliberation, Prime Minister Lester B. Pearson stated publicly that de Gaulle's remarks were "unacceptable." Ironically, many Canadians felt that the Prime Minister's rebuff was far too mild and applauded Mayor Jean Drapeau's judicious but firm rebuke of de Gaulle at a public dinner. The mayor of Montreal had unequivocally stated that President de Gaulle had no right to meddle in Canada's internal affairs.

Undaunted, de Gaulle once again found occasion to interfere in Canada's internal affairs. In June, 1968, in recounting his achievements for France, in an address to his strife-torn nation, de Gaulle openly boasted that he was responsible for "the beginning of the liberation of the French people in Canada."

Moreover, cultural survival depends on economic progress, and Quebec feels that the wide powers that the B.N.A. Act bestowed upon the federal government has stifled development in Quebec. Especially vexing to Quebec is Ottawa's encroachment into areas of jurisdiction, mainly social services, which the provinces have traditionally claimed to be their concerns. The extensive powers of taxation held by the federal government are equally objectionable. They have been vastly enlarged as a result of the Rowell-Sirois Commission's findings and the effects of World War II on increasing the powers of the federal government. Quebec considers all these accumulated powers as emergency measures which are no longer required now that the emergency is long past. Therefore, Quebec argues that the federal government should revamp the whole tax structure by transferring some powers of taxation, and restoring others to the provinces, where they truly belong.

DANIEL JOHNSON ON FRENCH-CANADIAN RIGHTS[449]

On April 23, 1963, Daniel Johnson, while criticizing the budget for the Province of Quebec, stated his views on provincial rights:

. . . . What *we* expect of a federal government is that it should merely look after those interests which both nations have in common. The moment it tries to fit us into a single mould, to destroy the characteristics that distinguish us from the other partner, we feel threatened in our very being. This, for us, is the overriding question: to be, or not to be.

———

In 1867, when our economy was still predominantly rural and agricultural, it was thought that ownership of the land, maintenance of our civil laws, free use of our language, and control of our schools were enough to preserve our particular culture. In 1963 these are no longer sufficient. We must also have control over our economy.

———

Now the master key to organizing and planning the economy is taxation.

———

In short, fiscal liberty produces economic liberty, upon which cultural liberty ultimately rests.

Quebec has not been alone in such demands; other provinces have taken a similar stand. However, Quebec has been most adamant in its claims. Quebec insists that if federal-provincial arrange-

* This interpretation relies heavily on Section 93 of the B.N.A. Act.

ments regarding taxing power need amendment of the B.N.A. Act, then the Act should be amended or even rewritten. At federal-provincial conferences since the end of the war, fiscal grievances have been the main topics, and the provinces have managed to gain concessions at the expense of the federal government. Also, in the face of provincial demands, Ottawa has evolved an opting out policy which allows non-participation in federal social welfare programs which provincial governments consider unsuitable for their provinces. Quebec has regarded this policy as merely the beginning of a trend toward greater provincial autonomy. Its provincial governments have attacked the B.N.A. Act as obsolete and argued that its financial terms favour English Canada and hinder Quebec.

Fear of assimilation and frustration over financial problems have reflected themselves in an emerging nationalism in Quebec, not unlike the current nationalism in emerging countries throughout the world. *Maitres chez nous* — masters in our own house, at least in Quebec — has become the slogan of French-Canadian nationalism. *Maitres chez nous* expresses a nationalism which was championed by Honoré Mercier, defended by Henri Bourassa and exploited by Maurice Duplessis. Yet Quebec nationalism differs from that of Mercier and Bourassa because theirs was essentially defensive, a fight for survival and a fight against assimilation. The new nationalism is more positive. The French-Canadian culture, having survived, must express itself, must be on an equal footing with the English and must find its own place in the sun. It is difficult to assess the extent to which the idea of *maitres chez nous* affects the majority of French-speaking Canadians. It cannot be denied, however, that many more French Canadians have of late become particularly interested in the affairs of state.

FRENCH–CANADIAN ASPIRATIONS[450]

From QUEBEC CONFRONTS CANADA, *by Edward M. Corbett:*

Yet many English Canadians remain genuinely puzzled that their French-speaking compatriots do not feel adequately protected by the individual rights all residents of the Confederation enjoy. "Just what does Quebec want" has become for French Canadians a mocking symbol of willful incomprehension. . . .

Ideally the French Canadian would like to see the day when the use of French would impose no hardship anywhere in Canada. This does not mean that all English Canadians should be required to learn French. By the same token, however, it does mean that not all French Canadians should be required to learn English. Essentially it means acceptance of the French Canadian as a full-fledged citizen regardless of his command of English. On the community level, this implies the right to development within French-language cultural institutions, the right to live and earn a living in French, where the French-speaking population is numerous enough and sufficiently compact to make its language a normal vehicle of communication. For the individual, this includes the right to be able to use his language in all official contacts and to participate in public life without sacrificing his linguistic heritage.

The "Quiet Revolution" has released among French-speaking Canadians a flood of political enthusiasm and a torrent of intellectual ferment. But there are still many economic and social ills frustrating the fulfillment of French-Canadian aspirations. Not infrequently, the anger and resentment of the French Canadians has been directed towards *les Anglais* as the root cause of French Canada's problems within Confederation. The solution acceptable to most French-speaking Canadians is special status for Quebec. But special status means different things to different people.

Varied interpretations of special status are advanced by "federalists" who wish to preserve Confederation but with special consideration for Quebec and for French-speaking Canadians in the rest of Canada. To former Premier Jean Lesage, special status meant giving Quebec as much autonomy as possible within Confederation. Quebec would have authority over social legislation and manpower, a larger share of direct taxes and the right to enter into international agreements in matters of exclusively provincial jurisdiction. Lesage maintained that French-speaking Canadians felt at home only in Quebec; in the rest of Canada they were strangers. The federal government, therefore, should make provisions which would give French Canadians a sense of belonging — a feeling that they are able to enjoy the benefits of living in Canada to the same extent as do English Canadians. Eric Kierans, the former president of the Quebec Liberal Federation, holds a similar view and asks the rest of Canada to recognize the "just aspirations of the French-Canadians." To Senator Maurice Lamontagne and Claude Ryan, the publisher of *Le Devoir*, special status means cultural equality with bilingualism throughout Canada. Such special status would not require serious alterations in the distribution of powers in the B.N.A. Act. Jean Marchand, the federal Minister of Manpower, sees special status as making Canada "more habitable to the French-speaking community." Pierre Elliott Trudeau doubts the feasibility of special status, but he agrees with Lamontagne on cultural equality, and he favours a bill of rights guaranteeing linguistic equality. Marcel Faribault, a financier, constitutional authority, and supporter of the *Union Nationale*, is a confirmed federalist who advocates decentralized federalism. Such a federalism would give all the provinces the powers Quebec seeks, but if any province wished to surrender some of these powers to the federal government, it would be free to do so. The central government in Ottawa would be left with certain essential jurisdictions. Faribault's scheme would confer special status on all provinces and still leave the federal union intact.

A sector of French Canada sees a solution in associate statehood. The leader of this movement is René Lévesque, a former cabinet minister in the Lesage government. To Lévesque, associate statehood would recognize the existence of two nations and a sovereign independent Quebec associated with the rest of Canada in an economic union, a sort of a Canadian Common Market.* The late Premier Daniel Johnson and some members of his cabinet spoke of associate statehood as an alternative if other proposed solutions failed. In their view, English Canada must recognize the existence of a French-Canadian nation and agree to write a new constitution that would make biculturalism a reality. Failing this, Quebec would have no recourse but separation from the rest of Canada.

RENÉ LÉVESQUE'S VIEWS[451]

In an interview on July 5, 1963, René Lévesque stated his position:

All our action, in the immediate future, must take two fundamental facts into account. The first is that French Canada is a true nation. It has all the elements essential to national life; it possesses unity, as well as human and material resources, including equipment and personnel, which are as good as or better than those of a large number of the peoples of the world. The second is that politically we are not a sovereign people. For the moment, the point is not whether we might or might not be sovereign; the point is simply that we *are* not.

Thus, we are a true nation, but a nation unattended by sovereignty. It is from these two premises, or in relation to these two realities, that we must work.

. . . . Those who talk to us about that legal entity, the 'Canadian nation', generally forget that a more fundamental and profound reality lies in the human, cultural, and social entity, embodied in the French-Canadian nation.

. . . . The present situation cannot and must not continue. We must have a Canada which, to begin with, takes into account the existence of two nations and the specific position, the particular needs of Quebec. . . .

As for the independence of Quebec, I am content to believe that it is a possibility: nothing more, but nothing less. . . .

The clearest and most outspoken statements on the future of Quebec have been expounded by the "separatists." The radical and extreme minority wants complete independence for Quebec. Apart from their agreement that Quebec should be a republic with French as the only official language, the separatists hold divergent opinions as to the political character of such a republic. Separatist views range from ultar-conservatism closely tied to the Church, to socialist anti-clericalism.

The separatist movement has included groups not averse to the use of violence to achieve their ends. Advocating armed revolution as the only path to independence for Quebec, the *Front de Liberation Québécois* (F.L.Q.) made headlines in the early 1960's. A rash of bombing struck military barracks, government buildings, Legion halls, and mail boxes in English residential districts. The F.L.Q.'s most telling blow at the symbols of Anglo-Saxon domination was the disruption of Queen Elizabeth's visit to Quebec City on October 10, 1964. Significantly, the occasion was the one hundredth anniversary of the Confederation Conference at Quebec.

VIEWS ON SEPARATISM[452]

aMarcel Chaput states why he is a separatist:

. . . as a free man and a French Canadian, I believe that I have the right to question the political institutions of this country and to express the wish that French Canada be soon relieved of her allegiance to the British Crown.

———

Since I naturally owe my first allegiance to French Canada, before the Dominion, I must ask myself the question: which of two choices will permit French Canadians to attain the fullest development — Confederation, in which they will forever be a shrinking minority, doomed to subjection? — or the independence of Quebec, their true native land, which will make them masters of their own destiny?

———

* Lévesque left the Liberal Party in October, 1967. Subsequently, he forged a union of separatist elements into *le Parti Québécois*.

Like so many others before us, the people of Quebec have reached the end of their patience with the arrogant domination of Anglo-Saxon colonialism.

———

We are a colonized people, politically, socially, and economically. Politically, because we do not have any hold on the political instruments necessary for our survival. Ottawa's colonial government has full powers. . . .

———

It is also economically a colony. A single statement will serve to prove it: over 80 per cent of our economy is controlled by foreign interests. We provide the labour, they bank the profits.

Socially, too, Quebec is a colony. We represent 80 per cent of the population, and yet the English language prevails in many fields. French is gradually relegated to the realm of folklore, while English becomes the people's working language. . . . The colonizers see us as inferior beings, and have no compunction about letting us know that they do.

———

. . . . There is only one way of overcoming colonialism: to be stronger than it is! Only the most far-fetched idealism may mislead one into thinking otherwise. Our period of slavery has ended.

QUEBEC PATRIOTS, TO ARMS! THE HOUR OF NATIONAL REVOLUTION HAS STRUCK!

INDEPENDENCE OR DEATH!

———

Trudeau states his opposition to separatism:

To sum it up, the Anglo-Canadians have been strong by virtue only of our weakness. . . .

———

. . . French Canadians could no more constitute a perfect society than could five million Sikhs of the Punjab. We are not well enough educated, nor rich enough, nor, above all, are there enough of us to man and finance a government possessing all the necessary means for both war and peace. . . .

———

By the terms of the existing Canadian Constitution, that of 1867, French Canadians have all the powers they need to make Quebec a political society affording due respect for nationalist aspirations and at the same time giving unprecedented scope for human potential in the broadest sense. . . .

———

Charles Lynch, a noted Canadian journalist, in a speech to the Canadian Club of Winnipeg on November 18, 1968, stated an English-Canadian view:

. . . do we want to cast our British connections into outer darkness only to replace them with French connections? Is it necessary, in speaking warmly of our French traditions, to speak harshly of our British ones? If so, it would be a poor and an unreasonable exchange, in terms of logic as well as of history and our own self interest.

The questions are endless — almost everything that is important is currently negotiable. Out of it, we are told, will come a better, freer, stronger, more distinctive and, in world terms, more lovable Canada.

It's all very unsettling, and it's all very exciting. For the first time in our history, I think, our own internal affairs are more interesting than our external involvements — and more vital.

It's unfortunate, I think, that the fate of the nation seems to have become so closely bound to the fate of one man, Mr. Trudeau, and to the fate of one political party, the federal Liberals. Perhaps this is but a momentary illusion — certainly, Mr. Stanfield would argue that it is, and so would Tommy Douglas, wherever he is. Most of the provincial premiers, no doubt, would agree with them.

If Trudeau stumbles and falls, and his programs are rejected, where do we go from there? If anybody has a positive answer to that question, I have not heard it, except perhaps from the separatists in Quebec. And their answer is one that I shall resist with all my might, in company with most English-speaking Canadians — but more importantly, I think, in company with most French-speaking Canadians, following the lead being given by the prime minister of Canada.

The terrorist activities evoked widespread revulsion throughout Canada, including Quebec, and unfortunately the erroneous impression was created in English-speaking Canada that all groups seeking changes in Quebec's status somehow approved terrorism. Thus a good deal of anti-Quebec "backlash" developed in the other provinces. More recent separatist activity has emphasized public rallies, propaganda and direct political action. Separatists claim that an independent republic in Quebec, freed of all vestiges of colonialism, would solve all problems besetting French Canada and would fulfill the destiny of French-speaking Canadians. As for those, like Kierans and Trudeau, who doubt the ability of an independent state of Quebec to survive economically, separatists are quick to point out that countries much smaller in population and far less endowed with natural resources than Quebec have managed to exist as independent nations. "Why not Quebec?" they ask.

The radical statements and views of the separatists in Quebec are often countered by equally extreme rebuttals by some English-speaking Canadians. The "compact" theory of Confederation has been rejected by many in English Canada as a myth created by French-Canadian nationalists in the 1950's and 1960's to advance their claim of equality of the two founding nations. These same English-speaking Canadians argue that the pact of Confederation was between two regions — the United Province of Canada and the Maritimes — and not between two nations. The French Canadian claim that the B.N.A. Act imposed linguistic equality on Canada is repudiated by many English-speaking Canadians who counter that Section 133 of the B.N.A. Act merely extended the use of the French language to the newly created Parliament of Canada and the federal courts. Equally unacceptable to English Canada is the insistence by certain French-speaking groups that the B.N.A. Act guaranteed French schools outside Quebec; Section 93 only assured the continuation of existing school systems in the original and future provinces of the Dominion. English Canada also disclaims the separatist charge of an insidious plot to assimilate the French-speaking Canadians. English Canadians maintain that there is not a shred of evidence of any conscious effort on their part at assimilation; they doubt the desirability or the practicability or even the possibility of assimilation. In the past, under more adverse conditions, French Canadians have successfully resisted Anglicization. Why this fear of assimilation now at a time when French-Canadian cultural activities — theatre, dance, music, writing, art, science — are flourishing across the land? Nor do English Canadians accept the argument that Anglo-Saxon discrimination, aimed at assimilation, prevents French Canadians from holding top corporate and governmental positions.

As for special status, English Canadians insist that French Canadians have enjoyed special status ever since the Conquest. The Quebec Act provided special rights in religion and laws. The B.N.A. Act extended the use of the French language to government and courts. As a result of agreements at several federal-provincial conferences, Quebec, more than any of the other provinces, has exercised the right to opt out of certain federal programs. To many English Canadians, the special status Quebec is now seeking is a prelude to separation from the rest of Canada.

Independence for Quebec, whether associate statehood or complete separation, poses the greatest threat to the survival of Canada as a nation. Understandably, movements towards an independent Quebec have caused the greatest apprehension and concern in Canada. English Canada, however, does not regard independence for Quebec as easy a transition as do the proponents of a separate Quebec. To begin with Quebec does not belong to Quebeckers alone; Quebec belongs to all of Canada and Quebec has as much a stake in Canada as has any other province of Canada.

A REBUTTAL OF FRENCH-CANADIAN CLAIMS[153]

Eugene Forsey, former Director of Special Projects of the Canadian Labor Congress, expresses his views in an article entitled, "The Constitution: Whence and Whither?":

What are the basic facts about the Constitution the Fathers gave us?

———

It was an agreement among the governments of at first five, finally three provinces. It was not a "pact" nor an agreement between "English Canada" and "French Canada".

It created a "new nation" . . . one nation. Nobody so much as mentioned two.

It provided for a limited bilingualism in the Quebec legislature and courts, and in the Dominion Parliament . . . no suggestion of extending this to the legislatures or courts of Ontario, the Atlantic provinces. . . .

It gave every province complete control over its own schools, subject to certain guarantees for the "Protestant" and "Roman Catholic" *minorities*. There was not one word about "French" or "English" schools.

It created a very highly centralized federation . . . our Founding Fathers gave the provinces only a short list of specific and rather narrow powers. . . .

———

They gave Quebec a limited special status notably by making it the only officially bilingual province. . . .

The demand for more power for Quebec, pushed far enough, could destroy Canada. . . . No English-Canadian public man who has read the Montreal St. Jean Bapiste Society's proposals on "associate states" could be persuaded to put his head into such a noose unless he was mad or drunk.

———

. . . to preserve one Canada, it can't be just our Canada. We shall have to give French Canadians more solid ground for feeling that all Canada is theirs as well as ours. . . .

We don't need a new Constitution. . . . What we do need is to use our existing Constitution with reasonable good sense patience . . . mutual knowledge, mutual charity, and real mutual respect.

Is independence to be accomplished by constitutional means or by unilateral declaration? If constitutionally, many constitutional issues have to be

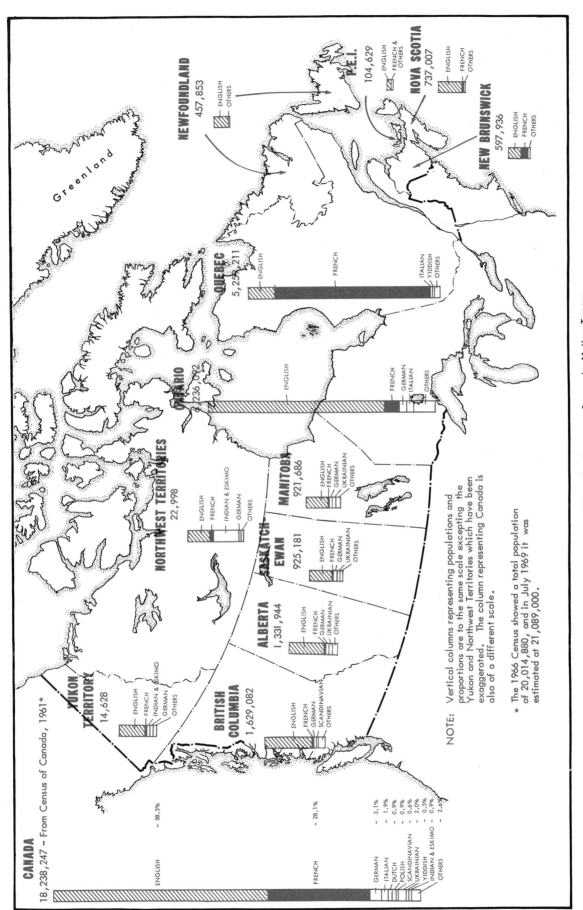

Totals and Proportions of Canadian Language Groups by Mother Tongue†

†Mother Tongue is defined as the language a person first learned in childhood and still understands.

CANADA
18,238,247 – From Census of Canada, 1961*

ENGLISH

FRENCH

GERMAN	– 3.1%
ITALIAN	– 1.9%
DUTCH	– 0.9%
POLISH	– 0.9%
SCANDINAVIAN	– 0.6%
UKRAINIAN	– 2.0%
YIDDISH	– 0.5%
INDIAN & ESKIMO	– 0.9%
OTHERS	– 2.6%

NOTE: Vertical columns representing populations and proportions are to the same scale excepting the Yukon and Northwest Territories which have been exaggerated. The column representing Canada is also of a different scale.

* The 1966 Census showed a total population of 20,014,880, and in July 1969 it was estimated at 21,089,000.

NEWFOUNDLAND
457,853

ENGLISH
OTHERS

P.E.I.
104,629

ENGLISH
FRENCH & OTHERS

NOVA SCOTIA
737,007

ENGLISH
FRENCH
OTHERS

NEW BRUNSWICK
597,936

ENGLISH
FRENCH
OTHERS

QUEBEC
5,259,211

ENGLISH
FRENCH
ITALIAN
YIDDISH
OTHERS

ONTARIO
6,236,092

ENGLISH
FRENCH
GERMAN
ITALIAN
OTHERS

MANITOBA
921,686

ENGLISH
FRENCH
GERMAN
UKRAINIAN
OTHERS

SASKATCHEWAN
925,181

ENGLISH
FRENCH
GERMAN
UKRAINIAN
OTHERS

ALBERTA
1,331,944

ENGLISH
FRENCH
GERMAN
UKRAINIAN
OTHERS

BRITISH COLUMBIA
1,629,082

ENGLISH
FRENCH
GERMAN
SCANDINAVIAN
OTHERS

NORTHWEST TERRITORIES
22,998

ENGLISH
FRENCH
INDIAN & ESKIMO
GERMAN
OTHERS

YUKON TERRITORY
14,628

ENGLISH
FRENCH
INDIAN & ESKIMO
GERMAN
OTHERS

Greenland

– 58.5%

– 28.1%

cleared away. This might well prove a lengthy, drawn-out process requiring patient bargaining, mutual agreements and treaties. Negotiations may go on for years — far too long for impatient separatists, who envisage an independent Quebec by 1970! On the other hand, independence by unilateral declaration, as in Rhodesia, may have consequences similar to those encountered by Rhodesia — violence, boycott and hostility. Many complicated factors would be involved in the birth of an independent Quebec. What would be done about assets in Quebec owned by the Dominion — railways, Air Canada installations, government buildings, Crown corporations and military establishments? What of the status of the St. Lawrence Seaway built with money of all Canadians? What of American reaction to a Canada split in two?

Equally as serious as the extreme views on an independent Quebec is the complacent attitude of a segment of the Canadian population. It is argued that separatist threats are only idle gestures. This group sees an independent Quebec as an impoverished state, politically dependent on France and susceptible to annexation by the United States, a prospect which would doom French-Canadian culture to extinction within the American melting pot.

MINORITIES AND THE MELTING POT[454]

[a]*From* COMMUNITY IN CRISIS: FRENCH-CANADIAN NATIONALISM IN PERSPECTIVE, *by Richard Jones:*

Not surprisingly, the most ardent advocates of the melting-pot are almost always members of the dominant cultures which could only be strengthened in the assimilation process. They care not a whit for the ideals of justice, wishing only to do all mankind a service by making others like themselves. They have absolutely no understanding of the rich services which the minority cultures can offer the human race.

The lesser groups are scarcely enthusiastic over such objectives. For them, community personality is a central part of their very being. Assimilation means that this personality is snuffed out. In short, this is cultural murder and they will attempt to fight it in every way possible. They may seek protection in an integral union of nation and state. Or, if justly treated, they may help to build a pluralistic society without endangering the material and social aims of an entire citizenry.

[b]*Professor J. B. Rudnyckyj, one of the Commissioners on the Royal Commission on Bilingualism and Biculturalism, submitted a separate statement*

Ukrainian Festival, Edmonton, Alberta

in the Report regarding "the other" ethnic groups. He recommended:

Consequently, the new version of the recommended amendment to section 133 of the B.N.A. Act is as follows:

5. Notwithstanding anything in this section, any language other than English and French used by 10 per cent or more of the population of an appropriate administrative district of a province or territory shall have the status of a regional language; the legislation of the provisions for regional languages shall be vested in the governments concerned.

. . . . The new recommended subsection on regional languages provides the necessary checks against any "Balkanization" of the linguistic scene in Canada, since a language to be recognized as a regional language requires the existence of a group of adherents comprising 10 per cent or more of the population in the given region and their willingness to preserve and develop their language as a means of communication and a vehicle of the respective ethnic culture. . . .

Fortunately, most Canadians subscribe to neither extreme position. Rather, most Canadians realize that the continued existence of Canada demands a spirit of toleration. There is an apparent effort to understand each other's problem and a willingness to accommodate opposing views and aspirations. At the Confederation of Tomorrow Conference held in Toronto in November, 1967, and in Ottawa in February, 1968, the provincial Premiers generally agreed to the desirability of extending bilingualism in their provinces as far as practicable. Since then, several provinces have encouraged the wider use of the French language in the public schools. The Liberal government, under Lester B. Pearson, took significant steps to smoothen existing differences. The hearings of the Royal Commission on Bilingualism and Biculturalism brought some of French Canada's grievances into the open. It is surprising how sympathetic English Canada has generally been to the Commission's recommendations for linguistic equality. The frank discussions at the Confederation of Tomorrow Conferences made large numbers of English-speaking Canadians aware, perhaps for the first time, of French Canada's hopes. The election campaign of 1968 revealed in all political parties a desire for a strong Canada with accommodation for Quebec. True, Canada has its prophets who see Confederation doomed and Canada dismembered, but the heartening signs of accommodation dispel such gloomy prophesies.

A BRIGHT FUTURE FOR CANADA[455]

Walter Gordon expresses his hopes for a bright future for Canada . . . IF:

Canadians have everything to work with — except, possibly, sufficient confidence in themselves. This we must develop. We can do anything, or nearly anything, if we try. English-speaking Canadians can benefit from the example of our French-Canadian friends. They have decided to catch up with life as it is lived in the second half of the twentieth century. French-speaking Canadians can benefit from the assistance and friendship that a great many of their English-Canadian fellow citizens are only too anxious to extend to them. Both French and English can benefit tremendously from the New Canadians who have come to Canada of their own free will. They also have a great deal to contribute, and already they have had a considerable influence on the changing pattern of our lives. We should all learn to work together. We should stop being suspicious of one another.

It would be erroneous to assume that any one or all of the recent developments is the answer to the problems facing Canada. At the same time, it must be recognized that these circumstances created a favourable climate for frank discussions. What is required is understanding. The English-speaking community must regard French Canadian claims as expressions of deep-rooted desires and not as the work of crackpots and bomb-throwing terrorists. The French-speaking community must see English-speaking Canadians as fellow citizens and not as Anglo-Saxon demons bent on destroying the culture born and nurtured on the banks of the St. Lawrence. Perhaps the two communities will come to the realization that Canada cannot do without Quebec and Quebec cannot live without the rest of Canada. Two hundred years of living together cannot be erased from the pages of history.

An Eskimo **komatic** drives towards the Midnight Sun: Aberdeen Lake, Keewatin District, West of Baker Lake, N.W.T.

APPENDIX

INTENDANTS OF NEW FRANCE

Jean Talon	1665 - 1668
Claude de Bouteroue	1668 - 1670
Jean Talon	1670 - 1672
Jacques Duchesneau	1675 - 1682
Jacques De Meulles	1682 - 1686
Jean Bochart de Champigny	1686 - 1702
François de Beauharnois	1702 - 1705
Jacques Raudot	1705 - 1710
Michel Bégon	1710 - 1726
Claude-Thomas Dupuy	1726 - 1728
Gilles Hocquart	1729 - 1748
François Bigot	1748 - 1760

BISHOPS OF NEW FRANCE

François de Montmorency Laval	1674 - 1688
Jean Baptiste de la Croix Chevrière de Saint-Vallier	1688 - 1727
Louis François Duplessis de Mornay	1727 - 1733
Pierre Hermann Dosquet	1733 - 1739
François Louis Pourroy de Lauberivière	1739 - 1740
Henri-Marie Dubreuil de Pontbriand	1741 - 1760

GOVERNORS OF CANADA

Samuel de Champlain	1612 - 1629
	1633 - 1635
Charles Jacques de Huault de Montmagny	1636 - 1648
Louis de Coulonge d'Ailleboust	1648 - 1651
Jean de Lauzon	1651 - 1656
Pierre de Voyer, Vicomte d'Argenson	1658 - 1661
Pierre Dubois, Baron d'Avaugour	1661 - 1663
Augustin de Saffray, Sieur de Mézy	1663 - 1665
Daniel de Rémy, Sieur de Courcelle	1665 - 1672
Louis de Buade, Comte de Frontenac	1672 - 1682
Lefèvre de La Barre	1682 - 1685
Jacques-René de Brisay, Marquis de Denonville	1685 - 1689
Louis de Buade, Comte de Frontenac	1689 - 1698
Louis-Hector, Chevalier de Callières	1699 - 1703
Philippe de Rigaud, Marquis de Vaudreuil	1703 - 1725
Charles, Marquis de Beauharnois	1726 - 1747
Roland-Michel Barin, Comte de La Galissionière	1748 - 1749
Jacques Pierre de Taffanel, Marquis de la Jonquière	1749 - 1752
Dusquesne, Marquis de Menneville	1752 - 1755
Pierre de Rigaud, Marquis de Vaudreuil-Cavagnal	1755 - 1760

James Murray	1763 - 1768
Guy Carleton	1768 - 1778
Frederick Haldimand	1778 - 1786
Guy Carleton, Baron Dorchester	1786 - 1796
Robert Prescott	1797 - 1807
Sir James Henry Craig	1807 - 1811
Sir George Prevost	1811 - 1815
Sir John C. Sherbrooke	1816 - 1818
Duke of Richmond	1818 - 1819
Earl of Dalhousie	1819 - 1828
Baron Aylmer	1831 - 1835
Earl of Gosford	1835 - 1838
Earl of Durham	1838
Sir John Colborne	1839
Baron Sydenham	1839 - 1841
Sir Charles Bagot	1842 - 1843
Sir Charles T. Metcalfe	1843 - 1845
Earl Cathcart	1846 - 1847
Earl of Elgin	1847 - 1854
Sir Edmund W. Head	1854 - 1861
Charles Stanley Monck	1861 - 1867
Viscount Monck	1867 - 1868
Lord Lisgar	1868 - 1872
Earl of Dufferin	1872 - 1878
Marquis of Lorne	1878 - 1883
Marquis of Lansdowne	1883 - 1888
Baron Stanley of Preston	1888 - 1893
Earl of Aberdeen	1893 - 1898
Earl of Minto	1898 - 1904
Earl Grey	1904 - 1911
H.R.H. Duke of Connaught	1911 - 1916
Duke of Devonshire	1916 - 1921
Lord Byng of Vimy	1921 - 1926
Viscount Willingdon of Ratton	1926 - 1931
Earl of Bessborough	1931 - 1935
Lord Tweedsmuir of Elsfield	1935 - 1940
Earl of Athlone	1940 - 1946
Viscount Alexander of Tunis	1946 - 1952
Vincent Massey	1952 - 1959
Georges Vanier	1959 - 1967
Roland Michener	1967 -

PRIME MINISTERS OF CANADA

Sir John Alexander Macdonald	1867 - 1873
Alexander Mackenzie	1873 - 1878
Sir John Alexander Macdonald	1878 - 1891
Sir John Joseph Caldwell Abbott	1891 - 1892
Sir John Sparrow David Thompson	1892 - 1894
Sir Mackenzie Bowell	1894 - 1896
Sir Charles Tupper	1896
Sir Wilfrid Laurier	1896 - 1911
Sir Robert Laird Borden	1911 - 1920
Arthur Meighen	1920 - 1921
William Lyon Mackenzie King	1921 - 1926
Arthur Meighen	1926
William Lyon Mackenzie King	1926 - 1930
Richard Bedford Bennett	1930 - 1935
William Lyon Mackenzie King	1935 - 1948
Louis Stephen St. Laurent	1948 - 1957
John George Diefenbaker	1957 - 1963
Lester Bowles Pearson	1963 - 1968
Pierre Elliott Trudeau	1968 -

DOCUMENTARY SOURCES

Page No.	Doc. No.	
154	148	MacNutt, *New Brunswick*, pp. 150-151.
155	149	Craig, *Upper Canada*, pp. 52-53.
155	150	White, *Lord Selkirk's Diary*, p. 141.
156	151	Craig, *Upper Canada*, p. 53.
156	152	Sandham, *Ville-Marie*, pp. 91-92.
157	153	Guillet, *Great Migration*, p. 4.
158	154	*Ibid.*, pp. 35, 39, 40.
158	155	Beck, *Voice of Nova Scotia*, p. 34.
160	156	Lucas, *Durham's Report*, v. 2, pp. 255-256, 257.
160	157	Guillet, *Great Migration*, pp. 84, 15, 93.
161	158	Coyne, *Talbot Papers*, pp. 45-46, 48-49.
161	159	Guillet, *Great Migration*, pp. 3, 230-231.
162	160	Innis and Lower, *Documents . . . 1783-1885*, p. 45.
162	161	MacTaggart, *Three Years in Canada*, v. 1, pp. 196-200.
164	162	(a) Lucas, *Durham's Report*, v. 2, p. 148. (b) Lindsey, *William Lyon Mackenzie*, v. 1, p. 40.
165	163	Head, *A Narrative*, pp. 464-465.
165	164	*Ibid.*, pp. 108-109, 311.
166	165	*PAC Report*, 1923, p. 317.
166	166	White, *Lord Selkirk's Diary*, pp. 217-219.
167	167	Doughty and McArthur, *Documents . . . 1791-1818*, pp. 394-397.
167	168	*PAC Report*, 1883, p. 162.
168	169	*Ibid.*, pp. 160-162.
168	170	Doughty and Story, *Documents . . . 1819-1828*, p. 146.
169	171	De Celles, *Papineau*, pp. 67, 84.
171	172	(a) Kennedy, *Documents . . . 1759-1915*, p. 435. (b) De Celles, *Papineau*, p. 120. (c) Kennedy, *Documents . . . 1759-1915*, pp. 439-441.
172	173	De Celles, *Papineau*, p. 165.
172	174	*C.H.R.*, XVIII-1, March 1937, pp. 53-54.
173	175	Lucas, *Durham's Report*, v. 2, pp. 239-240.
173	176	Spragge, *John Strachan*, pp. 185, 182.
174	177	(a) Head, *A Narrative*, p. 35. (b) Smith, *Canada and the Canadian Question*, p. 111.
175	178	Kilbourn, *The Firebrand*, p. 103.
175	179	Lindsey, *William Lyon Mackenzie*, v. 1, pp. 178-179.
175	180	Kilbourn, *The Firebrand*, p. 95.
176	181	Lindsey, *William Lyon Mackenzie*, v. 1, p. 388: v. 2, p. 35.
176	182	*Ibid.*, v. 2, Appendix F, pp. 358-362.
177	183	*Ibid.*, v. 1, p. 41: v. 2, p. 292.
178	184	Chisholm, *Speeches of Joseph Howe*, v. 1, pp. 70-71.
179	185	MacNutt, *New Brunswick*, pp. 236-237, 249, 255.
180	186	Lucas, *Durham's Report*, v. 2, p. 198.
180	187	Hatton and Harvey, *Newfoundland*, pp. 86-87.
181	188	*PAC Report*, 1923, pp. 317, 318, 323-324.
183	189	*PAC Report*, 1928, p. 74.
183	190	Lucas, *Durham's Report*, v. 2, pp. 16, 22, 37, 53, 70.
184	191	*Ibid.*, v. 2, pp. 303-304, 307, 323-324.
184	192	*Ibid.*, v. 2, pp. 277-278, 279-280.
184	193	*Ibid.*, v. 2, pp. 281-282.
185	194	*PAC Report*, 1923, p. 328.
185	195	Lucas, *Durham's Report*, v. 2, pp. 288-289, 292-293, 294.
186	196	(a) Chisholm, *Speeches of Joseph Howe*, v. 1, pp. 216-217. (b) Garneau, *History of Canada*, v. 3, pp. 405-406.
186	197	(a) Smith, *Canada and the Canadian Question*, p. 112. (b) Scrope, *Lord Sydenham*, p. 143.
188	198	Lucas, *Durham's Report*, v. 2, pp. 149-150.
188	199	*Ibid.*, v. 2, p. 84.
190	200	Doughty and McArthur, *Documents . . . 1791-1818*, p. 396 f.
190	201	(a) Garneau, *History of Canada*, v. 3, p. 424. (b) Leacock, *Baldwin, Lafontaine, Hincks*, p. 70.
190	202	*Lafontaine Papers*, v. 5, PAC.
191	203	Kennedy, *Documents . . . 1759-1915*, p. 522.
192	204	Kaye, *Lord Metcalfe*, p. 412.
192	205	Kennedy, *Statutes, Treaties . . . 1713-1929*, pp. 478-479.
194	206	*Ibid.*, pp. 481-482.
195	207	Kaye, *Lord Metcalfe*, p. 418.
196	208	Walrond, *Earl of Elgin*, p. 40.
196	209	Foster, "The Montreal Riot of 1849", pp. 62-63.
198	210	Beck, *Voice of Nova Scotia*, p. 66.
198	211	Chisholm, *Speeches of Joseph Howe*, v. 1, p. 230.
200	212	Hatton and Harvey, *Newfoundland*, pp. 257-258.
200	213	*Ibid.*, pp. 388, 392.
201	214	Hind, et al., *Eighty Years'*, p. 705.
202	215	Beck, *Voice of Nova Scotia*, pp. 27-28.
202	216	Lucas, *Durham's Report*, v. 2, pp. 198, 199.
203	217	Hind, et al., *Eighty Years'*, p. 627.
204	218	MacNutt, *New Brunswick*, p. 350.
205	219	Innis, *Canadian Economic History*, pp. 116-117.
205	220	Hodgins, *Schools and Colleges in Ontario*, v. 2, p. 84.
206	221	Hind, et al., *Eighty Years'*, p. 538.
207	222	Ross, *Red River Settlement*, pp. 102-103.
207	223	*Ibid.*, pp. 375-376.
209	224	MacBeth, *The Selkirk Settlers*, pp. 80-81.
209	225	Ormsby, *British Columbia*, pp. 114-115.
213	226	(a) Careless, "George Brown". Cited in McDougall, *Our Living Tradition*, p. 45. (b) Underhill, "Some Aspects. . . .", p. 47.
214	227	Tassé, *Georges Cartier*, pp. 148-149, 151. (Trans. Larry M. Herstein).

Page No.	Doc. No.	
215	228	(a) *Conf. Debates*, p. 26.
		(b) Underhill, "Some Aspects....", pp. 48-49.
216	229	Skelton, *Tilloch Galt*, pp. 229-230.
217	230	Careless, *Brown of the Globe*, v. 1, pp. 317, 320.
217	231	Young, *Public Men*, v. 1, p. 371.
218	232	Walrond, *Earl of Elgin*, p. 100.
220	233	*Conf. Debates*, pp. 64-65.
220	234	*Ibid.*, pp. 98, 99-100.
221	235	(a) Whelan, *The Union*, pp. 27, 48.
		(b) *Conf. Debates*, pp. 107-108.
221	236	*Ibid.*, p. 251.
222	237	Wild, *Amor de Cosmos*, p. 36.
222	238	Whelan, *The Union*, pp. 51-52.
223	239	*Conf. Debates*, pp. 130, 132.
223	240	*Ibid.*, p. 107.
224	241	Waite, *Life and Times*, p. 317.
226	242	*George Brown Papers*, PAC. Cited in Waite, *Pre-Confederation*, pp. 216-217.
226	243	Whelan, *The Union*, pp. 29-31.
227	244	(a) Pope, *Memoirs*, v. 1, pp. 269-270.
		(b) *Conf. Debates*, p. 59.
227	245	(a) *Ibid.*, pp. 86-114.
		(b) *Ibid.*, pp. 694-695.
		(c) Waite, *Life and Times*, p. 122.
228	246	*Conf. Debates*, pp. 9, 922, 694, 510.
229	247	Waite, *Life and Times*, p. 156.
229	248	(a) New Brunswick Debates of the House of Assembly for 1866, p. 89. Cited in MacKirdy, *Changing Perspectives*, p. 217.
		(b) Waite, *Life and Times*, p. 212.
		(c) Fowke, et al., *Canada's Story in Song*, pp. 106-107.
230	249	Nfld., P.E.I., N.S., N.B., Assembly Journals, 1866. Cited in Waite, *Pre-Confederation*, p. 229.
231	250	Pope, *Memoirs*, v. 1, p. 313.
234	251	Trudeau, *Federalism*, p. 131.
236	252	MacKay, *The Unreformed Senate*, p. 1.
240	253	Russell, *Leading Constitutional Decisions*, pp. xiv-xv.
243	254	*Commission on Bilingualism and Biculturalism*, Book I, pp. 134-135.
244	255	Ollivier, *Canadian Sovereignty*, pp. 4-5.
247	256	Skelton, *D'Arcy McGee*, p. 539.
248	257	Pope, *Correspondence*, pp. 83-85.
249	258	Morton, *Begg's . . . Journal*, pp. 22-23.
250	259	*Ibid.*, pp. 257-258.
250	260	Pope, *Memoirs*, v. 2, pp. 59-60.
251	261	Morton, *Begg's . . . Journal*, pp. 225-226.
251	262	Warner, "Drang Noch Norden", p. 699.
252	263	Morton, *Begg's . . . Journal*, pp. 265-266, 270.
252	264	Begg, *The Creation of Manitoba*, p. 103.
253	265	Morton, *Begg's . . . Journal*, pp. 326-328.
255	266	Grant, *Ocean to Ocean*, pp. 340-341.
256	267	Journals of the Legislative Council of British Columbia, 1870, pp. 16-17. Cited in Brown and Prang, *Confederation*, p. 6.
257	268	Pope, *Memoirs*, v. 2, p. 148.
258	269	*Ibid.*, v. 2, pp. 93, 105-106.
259	270	*Ibid.*, v. 2, p. 113.
259	271	*Ibid.*, v. 2, p. 138.
260	272	Guillet, *You'll Never Die, John A!*, p. 52.
260	273	Buckingham and Ross, *Alexander Mackenzie*, pp. 348-349.
261	274	*PAC Pamphlets*, Vol. II, p. 8. Cited in Reid et al., *A Source-Book*, p. 308.
262	275	De Kiewet and Underhill, *Dufferin-Carnarvon Correspondence*, p. 410.
263	276	Buckingham and Ross, *Alexander Mackenzie*, pp. 665-666.
263	277	*H. C. Debates*, March 7, 1878, pp. 854, 858-859.
264	278	Secretan, *Canada's Great Highway*, pp. 99-100.
265	279	*Ibid.*, pp. 248-249.
265	280	Gibbon, *Romantic History*, p. 296.
265	281	*Ibid.*, p. 241. Citing from Robinson, Noel, *Blazing the Trail Through the Rockies*.
266	282	Sharp, *Whoop-Up Country*, pp. 204-205.
267	283	Andrist, *The Long Death*, pp. 333-334.
268	284	MacLeod, *Songs of Manitoba*, pp. 54-55.
269	285	Gibbon, *Romantic History*, pp. 285-286.
269	286	Needler, *Louis Riel*, p. 55.
270	287	*The Queen vs Louis Riel*, pp. 147-152.
271	288	Toronto *Evening News*, April 20, 1885. Cited in Bliss, *Documents*, pp. 195-196.
271	289	Rumilly, *Mercier*, pp. 263-265. (Trans. Larry M. Herstein).
272	290	Biggar, *Oliver Mowat*, v. 1, p. 428.
274	291	*Thompson Papers*, PAC. Cited in Brown and Prang, *Confederation*, p. 67.
275	292	Smith, *Canada and the Canadian Question*, pp. 268-269.
275	293	Pope, *Memoirs*, v. 2, pp. 253, 273-274.
277	294	(a) Wade, *The French Canadians*, p. 253.
		(b) Rumilly, *Mercier*, pp. 363-364. (Trans. Larry M. Herstein).
277	295	Pope, *Memoirs*, v. 2, pp. 335-336.
278	296	(a) *Ibid.*, v. 2, pp. 339-341.
		(b) *Ibid.*, v. 2, p. 280.
		(c) *Ibid.*, v. 2, pp. 343-347.
280	297	*Brandon Sun*, May 30, 1889. Manitoba Archives.
280	298	Manitoba Archives.
281	299	*H. C. Debates*, Jan. 15, 1896, p. 75.
281	300	(a) Skelton, *Laurier*, v. 1, pp. 470-471.
		(b) *H. C. Debates*, March 3, 1896, pp. 2758-2759.
		(c) *Ibid.*, March 3, 1896, pp. 2734-2736.
		(d) *Laurier Papers*, PAC, Series 'A' No. 5, 3739-4243. Cited in Reid et al., *A Source-Book*, p. 353.
285	301	Dafoe, *Laurier*, pp. 41-43.
285	302	Skelton, *Laurier*, v. 1, pp. 464-465.
286	303	Dafoe, *Clifford Sifton*, pp. 105-106.
286	304	Manitoba Archives.
287	305	Sifton, "The Immigrants We Want", p. 16.

BIBLIOGRAPHY

ABBREVIATIONS USED:
Canadian Annual Review   *C.A.R.*
Canadian Historical Association   *C.H.A.*
Canadian Historical Review   *C.H.R.*
Confederation Debates   *Conf. Debates*
Debates of the House of Commons   *H.C. Debates*
Public Archives of Canada   *PAC*

The authors wish to thank the publishers and authors who graciously granted permission to quote from some of the following titles:

"A British Secret Service Report on Canada, 1711." *C.H.R.*, 1-1, March 1920.

Adair, E. R., "A Re-Interpretation of Dollard's Exploits," *C.H.R.*, XIII-2, June 1932.

Adams, Arthur T., ed., *The Explorations of Pierre Esprit Radisson.* Minneapolis: Ross & Haines, Inc., 1961. Selections reprinted by permission of the publishers.

Allen, Ralph, *Ordeal By Fire. Canada 1910-1945.* New York: Doubleday & Company, Inc., 1961. Selections reprinted by permission of the publishers.

Andrist, Ralph K., *The Long Death: The Last of the Plains Indians.* New York: The Macmillan Company, 1964. Selections reprinted by permission of the publishers.

Atkins, Thomas B., ed., *Selections From the Public Documents of the Province of Nova Scotia.* Halifax: Charles Annand, 1869.

Bailey, Thomas A., ed., *The American Spirit: United States History as Seen by Contemporaries.* Boston: D. C. Heath and Company, 1963. Selections reprinted by permission of the publishers.

Ball, George W., *The Discipline of Power: Essentials of a Modern World Structure.* Toronto: Little, Brown & Co., 1968. Selections reprinted by permission of the publishers.

Beal, John R., *The Pearson Phenomenon.* Toronto: Longmans, Green and Company, 1964. Selections reprinted by permission of the publishers.

Beamish, Murdoch, *A History of Nova-Scotia.* 3 vols. Halifax: James Barnes, 1866.

Beck, Murray J., ed., *Joseph Howe: Voice of Nova Scotia.* Toronto: McClelland and Stewart Limited, 1964. Selections reprinted by permission of the publishers.

————, *Pendulum of Power.* Scarborough, Ont.: Prentice-Hall of Canada Limited, 1968.

Begg, Alexander, *The Creation of Manitoba: Or, A History of the Red River Troubles.* Toronto: Hunter Rose & Co., 1871.

Belkin, Simon, *Through Narrow Gates: A Review of Jewish Immigration, Colonization and Immigrant Aid Work in Canada (1840-1940).* Montreal: Canadian Jewish Congress and the Jewish Colonization Association, 1966.

Bemis, Samuel Flagg, *Jay's Treaty: A Study in Commerce and Diplomacy.* New Haven: Yale University Press, 1962.

Biggar, C. R. W., *Sir Oliver Mowat: A Biographical Sketch.* 2 vols. Toronto: The Musson Book Company, Limited, 1905.

Biggar, H. P., *The Early Trading Companies of New France.* Toronto: University of Toronto Library, 1901.

————, *The Precursors of Jacques Cartier 1497-1534.* Ottawa: Government Printing Bureau, 1911.

————, ed., *The Voyages of Jacques Cartier.* Ottawa: King's Printer, 1924.

————, ed., *The Works of Samuel de Champlain.* 6 vols. Toronto: The Champlain Society, 1922-1936. Selections reprinted by permission of the Society.

Bliss, J. M., ed., *Canadian History in Documents, 1763-1966.* Toronto: The Ryerson Press, 1966. Selections reprinted by permission of the publishers.

Bonenfant, Jean Charles, *The French Canadians and the Birth of Confederation.* C.H.A. Booklet No. 21. Ottawa: C.H.A., 1966.

Borden, Henry, ed., *Robert Laird Borden: His Memoirs.* 2 vols. Toronto: The Macmillan Company of Canada Limited, 1938.

Borden, Robert Laird, *Canadian Constitutional Studies.* Toronto: University of Toronto Press, 1922.

Bourassa, Henri, *La Conscription.* Montréal: Editions du Devoir, 1917.

Brebner, John Bartlet, *Canada, a Modern History*. Ann Arbor: The University of Michigan Press, 1960.

————, "Canadian Policy Towards the Acadians in 1751," *C.H.R.*, XII-3, September 1931.

————, *North Atlantic Triangle. The Interplay of Canada, the United States, and Great Britain*. Toronto: Ryerson Press, 1945.

————, *The Explorers of North America, 1492-1806*. Garden City, N.Y.: Doubleday, 1955.

British North America Act and Amendments, 1867-1943. Ottawa: King's Printer, 1943. Selections reprinted by permission of the Queen's Printer.

Brown, George W., *Building the Canadian Nation*. Toronto: J. M. Dent & Sons (Canada) Limited, 1958.

————, ed., *Canada*. Berkeley: University of California Press, 1955.

————, ed., *Readings in Canadian History*. Toronto: J. M. Dent & Sons (Canada) Limited, 1940.

Brown, R. C. and Prang, M. E., eds., *Confederation to 1949*. Scarborough, Ont.: Prentice-Hall of Canada Ltd., 1966.

Brunet, Michel, *French Canada and the Early Decades of British Rule 1760-1791*. The C.H.A. Booklet No. 13. Ottawa: C.H.A., 1965. Selections reprinted by permission of the association.

Bryce, George, *The Remarkable History of the Hudson's Bay Company*. London: William Briggs, 1900.

Buchanan, M. A., "A Spanish Account of New France 1608," *C.H.R.*, 1-3, September 1920.

Buckingham, William and Ross, Geo. W., *The Hon. Alexander Mackenzie: His Life and Times*. Toronto: Rose Publishing Company (Limited), 1892.

Burpee, Lawrence J., ed., *Journals and Letters of Pierre Gaultier de Varennes de La Vérendrye and his Sons with Correspondence Between the Governors and the French Court, Touching the Search for the Sea*. Toronto: The Champlain Society, 1927. Reprinted by permission of the Champlain Society.

Burt, A. L., *Guy Carleton, Lord Dorchester, 1724-1808*. C.H.A. Booklet No. 5, Ottawa: C.H.A., 1964.

————, *The Old Province of Quebec*. Toronto: The Ryerson Press, 1933. Selections reprinted by permission of the publishers.

————, *The Romance of Canada*. Toronto: W. J. Gage & Co., Limited, 1945.

Cameron, Margaret M., "Play-Acting in Canada During the French Regime," *C.H.R.*, X1-1, March 1930.

Campbell, P., *Travels in the Interior Inhabited Parts of North America in the Years 1791 and 1792*. Ed. H. H. Langton. Toronto: The Champlain Society, 1937.

Canniff, Wm., *History of the Settlement of Upper Canada (Ontario) with Special Reference to the Bay of Quinté*. Toronto: Dudley & Burns, 1869.

Careless, J. M. S., *Brown of the Globe*. 2 vols. Toronto: The Macmillan Company of Canada Limited, 1959. Selections reprinted by permission of the publisher.

————, *Canada, A story of Challenge*. London: Cambridge University Press, 1953.

————, "George Brown," in McDougall, Robert L., ed., *Our Living Tradition*.

Careless, J. M. S. and Brown, Craig R., eds., *The Canadians 1867-1967*. Toronto: The Macmillan Company of Canada Limited, 1967.

Chaput, Marcel, *Why I Am a Separatist*. Trans. Robert A. Taylor. Toronto: The Ryerson Press, 1961. Selections reprinted by permission of the publishers.

Charlevoix, P. F. X. de., *History and General Description of New France*. 6 vols. Trans. John Gilmary Shea. Chicago: Loyola University Press, 1870.

Chevrier, Lionel, *The St. Lawrence Seaway*. Toronto: The Macmillan Company of Canada Limited, 1959. Selections reprinted by permission of the publisher.

Chiel, Arthur A., *The Jews in Manitoba*. Toronto: University of Toronto Press, 1961.

Chisholm, Joseph Andres, ed., *The Speeches and Public Letters of Joseph Howe*. 2 vols. Halifax: The Chronicle Publishing Press, 1909.

Clark, S. D., *Movements of Political Protest in Canada 1640-1840*. Toronto: University of Toronto Press, 1959. Selections reprinted by permission of the publishers.

————, *The Social Development of Canada: An Introductory Study with Select Documents*. Toronto: University of Toronto Press, 1942.

Cleverdon, Catherine Lyle, *The Woman Suffrage Movement in Canada*. Toronto: University of Toronto Press, 1950. Selections reprinted by permission of the publishers.

Colden, Cadwallader, *The History of the Five Indian Nations of Canada*. 2 vols. New York: New Amsterdam Book Company, 1902.

Colvin, James A., "Sir Wilfrid Laurier and the British Preferential Tariff System," *C.H.A. Report*, 1955.

Cook, Ramsay, Ricker, John C., and Saywell, John T., *Canada, a Modern Study*. Toronto: Clarke, Irwin & Company Limited, 1963.

Corbett, Edward M., *Quebec Confronts Canada*. Baltimore: The Johns Hopkins Press, 1967. Selections reprinted by permission of the publishers.

Cornell, Paul G., *The Alignment of Political Groups in Canada, 1841-1867*. Toronto: University of Toronto Press, 1962.

————, *The Great Coalition*. The C.H.A. Booklet No. 19. Ottawa: C.H.A., 1966.

Cote, Ernest A., "Conclusion," in Van Steense, ed., *People of Light and Dark*.

Coupland, Reginald, *The Durham Report*. Oxford: Clarendon Press, 1945. Selections reprinted by permission of the publishers.

————, *The Quebec Act: A Study in Statesmanship*. London: Oxford University Press, 1925.

Courchene, David, "Address to the Fifteenth Annual Indian and Métis Conference," Winnipeg, March 24, 1969. Selections reprinted by permission of the author.

Cox, Joslin, ed., *The Journeys of Réné Robert Cavelier Sieur de la Salle*. 2 vols. New York: A. S. Barnes & Company, 1905.

Coyne, James H., ed., *The Talbot Papers*. Transactions of the Royal Society of Canada, 1909.

Craig, G. M., *Lord Durham's Report*. Toronto: McClelland and Stewart Ltd., 1963. Selections reprinted by permission of the publishers.

————, *Upper Canada, The Formative Years 1784-1841*. Toronto: McClelland and Stewart Limited, 1963.

Creighton, Donald, *Dominion of the North: A History of Canada*. Toronto: The Macmillan Company of Canada Limited, 1962. Selections reprinted by permission of the publishers.

————, *John A. Macdonald: The Old Chieftain*. Toronto: The Macmillan Company of Canada Limited, 1955.

—————, *John A. Macdonald: The Young Politician.* Toronto: The Macmillan Company of Canada Limited, 1952.

—————, *The Commercial Empire of the St. Lawrence, 1760-1850.* Toronto: The Ryerson Press, 1937. Selections reprinted by permission of the publishers.

—————, *The Road to Confederation: The Emergence of Canada, 1863-1867.* Toronto: The Macmillan Company of Canada Limited, 1964.

Crouse, Nellis M., "The Location of Fort Maurepas," *C.H.R.,* 1X-3, September 1928.

Currie, A. W., *Canadian Economic Development.* Toronto: Thomas Nelson & Sons (Canada) Limited, 1952.

Dafoe, John W., *Clifford Sifton in Relation to His Times.* Toronto: The Macmillan Company of Canada Limited, 1931. Selections reprinted by permission of the publishers.

—————, *Laurier: A Study in Canadian Politics.* Toronto: Thomas Allen, 1922. Selections reprinted by permission of the publishers.

Dawson, MacGregor E., ed., *The Development of Dominion Status, 1900-1936.* London: Oxford University Press, 1937.

—————, *William Lyon Mackenzie King: A Political Biography, 1874-1923.* Toronto: University of Toronto Press, 1958. Selections from King Diary reprinted by permission of J. W. Pickersgill.

Debates of the House of Commons.

De Celles, Alfred D., *Louis-Joseph Papineau.* Toronto: Morang & Co., Limited, 1909.

De Kiewet, C. W. and Underhill, F. H., ers., *Dufferin-Carnarvon Correspondence, 1874-1878.* Toronto: The Champlain Society, 1955. Selections reprinted by permission of the Society.

Dent, John Charles, *The Story of the Upper Canada Rebellion.* 2 vols. Toronto: C. Blackett Robinson, 1885.

Denys, Nicholas, *The Description and Natural History of the Coast of North America (Acadia).* Ed. and Trans. William F. Ganong. Toronto: The Champlain Society, 1908.

Desbarats, Peter, *The State of Quebec.* Toronto: McClelland and Stewart Limited, 1967.

Divine, Arthur A., "Miracle at Dunkirk," *Reader's Digest.* December, 1940. Selections reprinted by permission of the publishers. Copyright 1939 by Reader's Digest Ass., Inc.

Dominion-Provincial and Interprovincial Conferences from 1887 to 1926. Ottawa: King's Printer, 1951. Selections reprinted by permission of the Queen's Printer.

Dorland, Arthur G. *Our Canada.* Toronto: The Copp Clark Co. Ltd., 1951.

Doughty, Arthur G. and McArthur, Duncan A., eds., *Documents Relating to the Constitutional History of Canada 1791-1818.* Ottawa: King's Printer, 1914.

Doughty, Arthur G. and Story, Nora, eds., *Documents Relating to the Constitutional History of Canada 1819-1828.* Ottawa: King's Printer, 1935.

Downey, Fairfax, *Louisbourg: Key to a Continent.* Englewood Cliffs, N.J.: Prentice-Hall, Inc., 1965.

Du Creux, Francois, *The History of Canada or New France.* 2 vols. Ed. James B. Conacher, trans. Percy J. Robinson. Toronto: The Champlain Society, 1951-1952. Selections reprinted by permission of the Society.

Dunham, Aileen, *Political Unrest in Upper Canada, 1815-1836.* Toronto: McClelland and Stewart Limited, 1963.

Easterbrook, W. T. and Aitken, Hugh G. J., *Canadian Economic History.* Toronto: The Macmillan Company of Canada Limited, 1956.

Eccles, W. J., *Canada Under Louis XIV, 1663-1701.* Toronto: McClelland and Stewart Ltd., 1964.

—————, *Frontenac, the Courtier Governor.* Toronto: McClelland and Stewart Limited, 1965.

Economic Council of Canada: Fifth Annual Review: The Challenge of Growth and Change. Ottawa: Queen's Printer, 1968. Selections reprinted by permission of the Queen's Printer.

Ellis, Ethan L., *Reciprocity, 1911.* New Haven: Yale University Press, 1939.

Fairley, Margaret, ed., *Selected Writings of Mackenzie.* Toronto: Oxford University Press, 1960.

Finnie, Richard, *Canada Moves North.* Toronto: The MacMillan Company of Canada Limited, 1942.

Forsey, Eugene, "The Constitution: Whence and Whither," *Winnipeg Tribune,* "Century 1867-1967," week of February 13, 1967. Selections reprinted by permission of the author.

Foster, Josephine, ed., "The Montreal Riot of 1849," *C.H.R.,* XXX11-1, 1951.

Foulché-Delbosc, Isabel, "Women of New France (Three Rivers: 1651-63)," *C.H.R.,* XX1-2, June 1940. Selections reprinted by permission of the University of Toronto Press.

Fowke, Edith, Mills, Allan and Blume, Helmut, *Canada's Story in Song.* Toronto: W. J. Gage Limited, (1960). Selections reprinted from *Old-Time Songs of Newfoundland,* by permission of Gerald S. Doyle.

Fraser, Alexander, ed., *Fourth Report of the Bureau of Archives for the Province of Ontario, 1906.* Toronto: Warwick Bro's & Rutter, Limited, 1907.

Fregault, Guy, *Canadian Society in the French Régime.* The C.H.A. Booklet No. 6. Ottawa: C.H.A., 1956.

Garneau, F.-X., *History of Canada. From the Time of its Discovery till the Union Year (1840-41).* 3 vols. Trans. Andrew Bell. Montreal: John Lovell, 1860.

Gibbon, John Murray, *The Romantic History of the Canadian Pacific.* New York: Tudor Publishing Company, 1937. Selections reprinted by permission of the Bobbs-Merrill Company.

Gilchrist, William M., "About Our Untold Resources," in Van Steense, ed., *People of Light and Dark.* Ottawa: Queen's Printer, 1966.

Glazebrook, G. P. de T., *A History of Transportation in Canada.* Toronto: The Ryerson Press, 1938. Selections reprinted by permission of the Carnegie Endowment for Peace.

—————, *Canada at the Paris Peace Conference.* Toronto: Oxford University Press, 1942.

Gordon, Walter L., *A Choice for Canada.* Toronto: McClelland and Stewart Limited, 1966. Selections reprinted by permission of the publisher.

Graham, Gerald S., ed., *The Walker Expedition to Quebec, 1711.* Toronto: The Champlain Society, 1953. Reprinted by permission of the Society.

Graham, Gwethalyn and Chaput-Roland, Solange, *Dear Enemies.* Toronto: The Macmillan Company of Canada Limited, 1963. Reprinted by permission of the publishers.

Graham, Roger, *Arthur Meighen.* C.H.A. Booklet No. 16. Ottawa: C.H.A., 1965.

———, ed., *The King-Byng Affair, 1926: A Question of Responsible Government.* Toronto: The Copp Clark Publishing Company, 1967.

Grant, George M., *Ocean to Ocean. Sandford Fleming's Expedition Through Canada in 1872.* Toronto: James Campbell & Son, 1873.

Grant, W. L., ed., *Voyages of Samuel de Champlain, 1604-1618.* New York: Barnes & Noble, Inc., 1907.

Gray, James H., *The Winter Years.* Toronto: The Macmillan Company of Canada Limited, 1967. Selections reprinted by permission of the publisher.

Guillet, Edwin C., *The Great Migration—The Atlantic Crossing by Sailing-Ship Since 1770.* Toronto: University of Toronto Press. 1963. Selections reprinted by permission of the publishers.

———, ed., *The Valley of the Trent.* Toronto: The Champlain Society, 1957.

———, *You'll Never Die, John A!* Toronto: The Macmillan Company of Canada Limited, 1967.

Gundy, Pearson H., "Sir Wilfrid Laurier and Lord Minto," *C.H.A.* Report, 1952.

Hardy, Reginald H., *Mackenzie King. A Biography.* Toronto: Oxford University Press, 1949. Selections reprinted by permission of the publisher.

Harkness, Douglas S., "The Defence of the Free World—Canada's Role," *Canada Month.* VI-12, December 1966. Selections reprinted by permission of the author.

Harvey, D. C., ed., *Journeys to the Island of St. John or Prince Edward Island 1775-1832.* Toronto: The Macmillan Company of Canada Limited, 1955.

Hatton, Joseph and Harvey M., *Newfoundland, its History, its Present Condition, and its Prospects in the Future.* Boston: Doyle & Whittle, 1883.

Hawthorne, Harry B., ed., *The Doukhobors of British Columbia.* Vancouver: The University of British Columbia and J. M. Dent & Sons (Canada) Limited, 1955.

Head, Francis, *A Narrative.* London: John Murray, 1839.

Healy, W. J., *Women of Red River.* Winnipeg: Russel, Lang & Co. Ltd., 1923.

Henry, Alexander, *Travels and Adventures in Canada and the Indian Territories Between 1760 and 1776.* Ed. James Bain. Toronto: George N. Morang & Company, Ltd., 1901.

Hewitt, W. A., *Down the Stretch.* Toronto: The Ryerson Press, 1958. Selections reprinted by permission of the author.

Hind, H. Y. et al., *Eighty Years' Progress of British North America.* Toronto: L. Stebbins, 1863.

Hodgetts, A. B., *Decisive Decades.* Toronto: Thomas Nelson & Sons (Canada) Limited, 1960.

Hodgins, George J., *The Establishment of Schools and Colleges in Ontario, 1792-1910.* Toronto: King's Printer, 1910.

Hoffman, Bernard, *Cabot to Cartier.* Toronto: University of Toronto Press, 1961. Selections reprinted by permission of the publishers.

Holt, Simma, *Terror in the Name of God.* Toronto: McClelland Stewart Limited, 1964.

Horowitz, Gad, "On the Fear of Canadian Nationalism," *Canadian Dimensions,* IV, May-June 1967. Selections reprinted by permission of the publishers.

Howard, Joseph Kinsey, *Strange Empire: The Story of Louis Riel.* Toronto: Swan Publishing Co. Ltd., 1965.

Hutchison, Bruce, *Mr. Prime Minister, 1867-1964.* Toronto: Longmans Canada Limited, 1964. Selections reprinted by permission of the publishers.

Innis, Harold A., *Essays in Canadian Economic History.* Ed. Mary Q. Innis. Toronto: University of Toronto Press, 1962.

———, *The Fur Trade in Canada.* Toronto: University of Toronto Press, 1962. Selections reprinted by permission of the publishers.

Innis, H. A. and Lower, A. R. M., eds., *Select Documents in Canadian Economic History 1783-1885.* Toronto: University of Toronto Press, 1933. Selections reprinted by permission of the publishers.

Innis, Mary Quayle, *An Economic History of Canada.* Toronto: Ryerson Press, 1945.

Irwing, J. A., *The Philosophy of Social Credit.* Toronto: University of Toronto Press, 1945.

Jeffreys, Charles W., "The Reconstruction of the Port Royal Habitation of 1605-13," *C.H.R.,* XX-4, December 1939.

Jenness, Diamond, *The People of the Twilight.* New York: The Macmillan Company Ltd., 1928.

Johnston, Charles M., ed., *The Valley of the Six Nations. A Collection of Documents on the Indian Lands of the Grand River.* Toronto: The Champlain Society, 1964. Selections reprinted by permission of the Society.

Johnstone, Walter, *A Series of Letters Descriptive of Prince Edward Island. Travels in Prince Edward Island, Gulf of St. Lawrence, North America, in the Years 1820-1821.* Edinburgh: James Robertson, 1824.

Jones, Richard, *Community in Crisis: French-Canadian Nationalism in Perspective.* Toronto: McClelland and Stewart Limited, 1967. Selections reprinted by permission of the publishers.

Kaye, John William, ed., *Selection from the Papers of Lord Metcalfe.* London: Smith, Elder and Co., 1855.

Kennedy, W. P. M., ed., *Documents of the Canadian Constitution 1759-1915.* Toronto: Oxford University Press, 1918.

———, ed., *Statutes, Treaties and Documents of the Canadian Constitution 1713-1929.* London: Oxford University Press, 1930. Selections reprinted by permission of the Clarendon Press.

Kenton, Edna., ed., *The Jesuit Relations and Allied Documents.* Toronto: McClelland and Stewart, 1925.

Kerkkonen, Matti, *Peter Kalm's North American Journey.* Helsinki: Finnish Historical Society, 1959.

Kilbourn, William, *The Firebrand.* Toronto: Clarke, Irwin & Company Limited, 1960. Selections reprinted by permission of the publishers.

King, Joseph Edward, "The Glorious Kingdom of Saguenay," *C.H.R.,* XXXI-4, December 1950.

Knox, John, *An Historical Journal of the Campaigns in North America.* 3 vols. Ed. Arthur G. Doughty. Toronto: The Champlain Society, 1914. Selections reprinted by permission of the Society.

Labaree, Leonard W. and Bell, Whitfield, S., eds., *The Papers of Benjamin Franklin.* 11 vols. New Haven: Yale University Press, 1961-1967.

Lahontan, Louis Armand, *New Voyages to North-America.* 2 vols. Notes etc. Reuben G. Thwaites. Chicago: A. C. McLurg & Co., 1905.

Lamb, Kaye W., ed., *Sixteen Years in the Indian Country. The Journal of Daniel Williams Harmon 1800-1816.* Toronto: The Macmillan Company of Canada Limited, 1957. Selections reprinted by permission of the publishers.

————, ed., *The Letters and Journals of Simon Fraser, 1806-1808.* Toronto: The Macmillan Company of Canada Limited, 1960. Selections reprinted by permission of the publishers.

Lanctot, Gustave, *A History of Canada.* 3 vols. Toronto: Clarke, Irwin & Company Ltd., 1963-1965.

————, "The Elective Council of Quebec of 1657," *C.H.R.,* XV-2, June 1934. Selections reprinted by permission of the author, and of the University of Toronto Press.

————, "Was Dollard the Saviour of New France," *C.H.R.,* XIII-2, June 1924.

————, "The Noblesse of Canada," *C.H.R.,* 111-3, September 1922.

LaViolette, F. E., "The Japanese Canadians," *Behind the Headlines.* VI-2. Toronto: Canadian Institute of International Affairs, 1946. Selections reprinted by permission of the Institute.

Leacock, Stephen, *Baldwin, Lafontaine, Hincks.* Toronto: Morang & Co. Limited, 1912.

LeBourdais, P. M., *Nation of the North, Canada Since Confederation.* London: Methuen & Co. Ltd., 1953. Published in New York by Frederick A. Praeger. By permission of Frederick A. Praeger.

Lescarbot, Marc, *The History of New France.* 3 vols. Trans. W. L. Grant. Toronto: The Champlain Society, 1907-1911. Reprinted by permission of the Society.

Lindsey, Charles, *The Life and Times of William Lyon Mackenzie, with an Account of the Canadian Rebellion of 1837, and the Subsequent Frontier Disturbances, Chiefly from Unpublished Documents.* 2 vols. Toronto: P. R. Randall, 1862.

————, *William Lyon Mackenzie.* Ed. G. G. S. Lindsey. Toronto: Morang & Co. Limited, 1909.

Livingston, Ross W., *Responsible Government in Nova Scotia.* Iowa City: University of Iowa, 1930. Reprinted by permission of the publishers.

Lochner, Louis P., ed., *The Goebbels Diaries.* Garden City, N.Y.: Doubleday & Company, Inc., 1948. Selections reprinted by permission of the publishers.

Long, Dorothy E., "English Interest in the Fur-Trade of Hudson Bay Before 1670," *C.H.R.,* XIV-2, June 1933. Selections reprinted by permission of the Association.

Longley, J. W., *Joseph Howe.* Toronto: Morang & Co. Limited, 1909.

Lower, Arthur R. M., *Canada, Nation and Neighbour.* Toronto: Ryerson Press, 1952.

————, *Canadians in the Making: A Social History of Canada.* Toronto: Longmans, Green and Company, 1958. Selections reprinted by permission of the publishers.

————, *Colony to Nation: A History of Canada.* Toronto: Longmans, Green & Company, 1946. Selections reprinted by permission of the publishers.

————, *The North American Assault on the Canadian Forest: A History of the Lumber Trade Between Canada and the United States.* Toronto: Ryerson Press, 1938.

Lucas, C. P., ed., *Lord Durham's Report on the Affairs of British North America.* 3 vols. London: Oxford University Press, 1912.

————, *The Canadian War of 1812.* Oxford: Clarendon Press, 1906.

Lynch, Charles, Selections from the *Winnipeg Tribune,* June 29, 1968, and November 19, 1968. Reprinted by permission of the author.

MacBeth, R. G., *The Selkirk Settlers in Real Life.* Toronto: William Briggs, 1897.

Macfie, Matthew, *Vancouver Island and British Columbia.* London: Longmans Green Longmans. Roberts & Green, 1865.

MacInnis, Grace, *J. S. Woodsworth: A Man to Remember.* Toronto: The Macmillan Company of Canada Limited, 1953. Selections reprinted by permission of the publishers.

MacKay, Robert A., *The Unreformed Senate of Canada.* London: Oxford University Press, 1926. Selections reprinted by permission of the Clarendon Press.

Mackenzie, Alex., *The Life and Speeches of Hon. George Brown.* Toronto: The Globe Printing Company, 1882.

Mackenzie, Alexander, *Voyages from Montreal Through the Continent of North America to the Frozen and Pacific Oceans in 1789 and 1793.* 2 vols. New York: A. S. Barnes and Company, 1903.

MacKirdy, K. A., Moir, J. S. and Zoltvany, Y. F., eds., *Changing Perspectives in Canadian History.* Toronto: J. M. Dent & Sons (Canada) Limited, 1967. Selections reprinted by permission of the publishers.

MacLeod, Margaret Arnett, *Songs of Old Manitoba.* Toronto: The Ryerson Press, 1959. Selections reprinted by permission of the publishers.

MacNutt, W. S., *New Brunswick, a History: 1784-1867.* Toronto: The Macmillan Company of Canada Limited, 1963. Selections reprinted by permission of the publishers.

————, *The Atlantic Provinces: The Emergence of Colonial Society.* Toronto: McClelland and Stewart Limited, 1965.

MacTaggart, John, *Three Years in Canada: An Account of the Actual State of the Country in 1826-7-8.* 2 vols. London: Henry Colburn, 1829.

Maheux, Arthur, *French Canada & Britain, a New Interpretation.* Toronto: Ryerson Press, 1942. Selections reprinted by permission of the publishers.

Manning, Helen Taft, *Revolt of French Canada, 1800-1835.* Toronto: The Macmillan Company of Canada Limited, 1962.

Marriott, Anne, *The Wind Our Enemy.* The Ryerson Poetry Chap-Book. The Ryerson Press, 1939. Selections reprinted by permission of the author.

Martin, Chester, ed., *Canada in Peace and War.* Toronto: Oxford University Press, 1941.

————, "Confederation and the West," *C.H.A. Report,* 1927.

————, *Foundations of Canadian Nationhood.* Toronto: University of Toronto Press, 1955.

Massey, Vincent, *What's Past is Prologue.* Toronto: The Macmillan Company of Canada Limited, 1963. Selections reprinted by permission of the publishers.

Masson, L. R., *Les Bourgeois de la Compagnie Nord-Ouest: Original Journals, Narratives, Letters, etc., Relating to the North West Company.* 2 vols. New York: Antiquarian Press Ltd., 1960.

Masters, D. C., *The Coming of Age.* Montreal: The Canadian Broadcasting Corporation, 1967. Selections reprinted by permission of the C.B.C.

————, *The Winnipeg General Strike.* Toronto: University of Toronto Press, 1950.

Mathews, Hazel C., *The Marks of Honour.* Toronto: University of Toronto Press, 1965. Selections reprinted by permission of the publishers.

McArthur, Duncan, *History of Canada for High Schools.* Toronto: W. J. Gage & Co. Ltd., 1946.

McDougall, Robert L., ed., *Our Living Tradition.* Second and Third Series. Toronto: University of Toronto Press, 1959. Selections reprinted by permission of the publishers.

McDowell, Stan, "Where the 'Two Nations' Idea Began," *Winnipeg Free Press,* August 16, 1968.

McIlwraith, T. F., "Archaeological Work in Huronia, 1946," *C.H.R.,* XXVII-4, December 1946.

McInnis, Edgar, *Canada, a Political and Social History.* New York: Holt, Rinehart and Winston, 1959.

McL. Rogers, Norman, "The Abbé le Loutre." *C.H.R.,* XI-2, June 1930. Selections reprinted by permission of University of Toronto Press.

McNaught, Kenneth, *A Prophet in Politics: A Biography of J. S. Woodsworth.* Toronto: University of Toronto Press, 1959. Selections reprinted by permission of the publishers.

Meighen, Arthur, "The Issues As I See Them," *Maclean's Magazine,* September 1, 1926.

————, *Unrevised and Unrepented: Debating Speeches and Others.* Toronto: Clarke, Irwin & Company Limited, 1964. Selections reprinted by permission of the authors.

M'Gillivray, Duncan, *The Journal of Duncan M'Gillivray of the North West Company at Fort George on the Saskatchewan, 1794-95.* Toronto: The Macmillan Company of Canada Limited, 1929.

Minifie, James M., *Peacemaker or Powdermonkey.* Toronto: McClelland & Stewart Limited, 1965. Selections reprinted by permission of the publishers.

Morgan, Henry J., *Sketches of Celebrated Canadians, and Persons Connected with Canada.* Quebec: Rose & Co., 1862.

Morrison, Elting E., ed., *The Letters of Theodore Roosevelt.* 8 vols. Cambridge: Harvard University Press, 1951. Selections reprinted by permission of the publishers.

Morrow, Lloyd E., *Church Union in Canada: Its History, Motives, Doctrine and Government.* Toronto: Thomas Allen, 1923.

Morton, Arthur S., *A History of the Canadian West to 1870-71.* Toronto: Thomas Nelson & Sons Ltd., 1939.

————, "LaVérendrye. Commandant, Fur-Trader, and Explorer," *C.H.R.,* IX-4, December 1928.

Morton, W. L., ed., *Alexander Begg's Red River Journal and Other Papers Relative to the Red River Resistance of 1869-1870.* Toronto: The Champlain Society, 1956. Selections reprinted by permission of the Society.

————, *Manitoba: The Birth of a Province.* Altona, Man.: D. W. Friesen & Sons Ltd., 1965. Selections reprinted by permission of the publishers, and the Manitoba Record Society.

————, *The Critical Years: The Union of British North America, 1857-1873.* Toronto: McClelland and Stewart Limited, 1964.

————, *The Kingdom of Canada.* Toronto: McClelland and Stewart Limited, 1963.

————, *The Progressive Party in Canada.* Toronto: University of Toronto Press, 1950.

————, *The West and Confederation, 1857-1871.* C.H.A. Booklet, No. 9. Ottawa: C.H.A., 1958.

Mowat, Farley, *Westviking: The Ancient Norse in Greenland and North America.* Boston: Little, Brown and Company, 1965.

Muller, Charles G., *The Darkest Day: 1814.* New York: J. B. Lippincott Company, 1963. Selections reproduced by permission of the publishers.

Munro, William Bennett, ed., *Documents Relating to the Seigniorial Tenure in Canada, 1598-1854.* Toronto: The Champlain Society, 1908.

————, "The Brandy Parliament of 1678," *C.H.R.,* II-2, June 1921. Selections reprinted by permission of University of Toronto Press.

Murray, Jean E., "The Early Fur Trade in New France," *C.H.R.,* XIX-4, December 1938.

Myrand, Ernest, *1690, Sir William Phips Devant Quebec.* Montreal: Librairié, Limitée, 1925.

Neatby, Blair H., "Laurier and Imperialism," *C.H.A. Report,* 1955.

————, *William Lyon Mackenzie King, 1924-1932. The Lonely Heights.* Toronto: University of Toronto Press, 1963.

Neatby, Hilda, *Quebec: The Revolutionary Age, 1760-1791.* Toronto: McClelland and Stewart Ltd., 1966.

Needler, G. H., *Louis Riel.* Toronto: Burns and MacEachern, 1957. Selections reprinted by permission of the publishers.

New, Chester William, *Lord Durham's Mission to Canada.* Toronto: McClelland and Stewart Ltd., 1963.

Newman, Peter C., *Renegade in Power: The Diefenbaker Years.* Toronto: McClelland and Stewart Limited, 1964. Selections reprinted by permission of the publishers.

————, "English Understanding of French First Step to Unity: Pearson," *Toronto Daily Star,* December 24, 1966. Selections reprinted by permission of the author.

Nish, Cameron, ed., *The French Regime.* Scarborough, Ont.: Prentice-Hall of Canada Ltd., 1965.

————, ed., *The French Canadians, 1759-1766: Conquered? Half Conquered? Liberated?* Toronto: The Copp Clark Publishing Company, 1966.

O'Callaghan, E. B., ed., *Documents Relative to the Colonial History of the State of New York.* 11 vols. Albany: Weed, Parsons and Company, 1855-1861.

Odlum, Victor W., "The Gas Attack at Ypres," the *Winnipeg Tribune,* March 9, 1967. Selections reprinted by permission of the author.

O'Hearn, Peter J. T., *Peace, Order and Good Government: A New Constitution for Canada.* Toronto: The Macmillan Co. of Canada, Ltd., 1968.

Oleson, Tryggvi J., *Early Voyages and Northern Approaches, 1000-1632.* Toronto: McClelland and Stewart, 1963. Selections reprinted by permission of the publishers.

Oliver, E. H., ed., *The Canadian North-West: Its Early Development and Legislative Records.* 2 vols. Ottawa: Government Printing Bureau, 1914.

Ollivier, Maurice, *Problems of Canadian Sovereignty.* Toronto: Canada Law Book Company, Ltd., 1945. Selections reprinted by permission of publishers.

————, ed., *The Colonial and Imperial Conferences From 1887 to 1937.* 3 vols. Ottawa: Queen's Printers, 1954.

Ormsby, Margaret A., *British Columbia: A History.* Toronto: The Macmillan Company of Canada Limited, 1958. Selections reprinted by permission of the publishers.

Ouellet, Fernand, *Histoire Economique et Sociale du Québec 1760-1850.* Ottawa: Editions Fides, 1966. Selections reprinted by permission of publishers.

————, *Louis Joseph Papineau: A Divided Soul.* C.H.A. Booklet, No. 11. Ottawa: C.H.A., 1964.

Parkman, Francis, *Montcalm and Wolfe*. 2 vols. Toronto: The Musson Book Co. Limited, [1844].

————, *Pioneers of France in the New World*. 2 vols. Toronto: George N. Morang & Company Limited, 1899.

————, *The Conspiracy of Pontiac and the Indian War After the Conquest of Canada*. 2 vols. Toronto: The Musson Book Company Limited, [1870].

————, *The Jesuits in North America*. Boston: Little, Brown and Company, 1867.

————, *The Old Regime in Canada*. Toronto: The Musson Book Co. Limited, [1874].

Parliamentary Debates on the Subject of the Confederation of the British North American Provinces. Quebec: Hunter Rose & Co., 1865.

Penlington, Norman, "General Hutton and the Problem of Military Imperialism in Canada," *C.H.R.*, XXIV-2, June 1943.

Perkins, Bradford, ed., *The Cause of the War of 1812. National Honor or National Interest?* New York: Holt, Rinehart and Winston, 1963.

Phillips, Charles E., *The Development of Education in Canada*. Toronto: W. J. Gage and Company Limited, 1957. Selections reprinted by permission of the publishers, and of Cambridge University Press.

Pickersgill, J. W., The Mackenzie King Record, 1939-1944. Vol. 1. Toronto: University of Toronto Press, 1960.

Pohl, Frederick J., *Atlantic Crossings Before Columbus*. New York: N. W. Norton & Company, 1961.

Pope, Joseph, *Correspondence of Sir John Macdonald*. Toronto: Oxford University Press, [1921]. Selections reprinted by permission of the publishers.

————, *Memoirs of the Right Honourable Sir John Alexander Macdonald, G.C.B.* 2 vols. Ottawa: J. Durie & Son, [1894].

Porritt, Edward, *The Revolt in Canada Against the New Feudalism*. London: Cassell and Company, Limited, 1911.

Preston, R. A., "The Laconia Company of 1629: An English Attempt to Intercept the Fur Trade," *C.H.R.*, XXXI-2, June 1950.

Pritchett, John Perry, *The Red River Valley 1811-1849*. New Haven: Yale University Press, 1942.

Puech-Milhau, M. L., "An Interview on Canada with La Salle in 1678," *C.H.R.*, XVIII-2, June 1937.

The Queen vs. Louis Riel. Ottawa: Queen's Printer, 1886.

Quinn, Herbert F., *The Union Nationale: A Study in Quebec Nationalism*. Toronto: University of Toronto Press, 1963. Selections reprinted by permission of the publishers.

Rawlyk, G. A., ed., *Revolution Rejected, 1775-1776*. Scarborough, Ont.: Prentice-Hall of Canada Ltd., 1968.

Raymond, W. O., ed., *Winslow Papers, A.D., 1776-1826*. St. John, N.B.: The Sun Printing Company Ltd., 1901.

Read, D. B., *The Lieutenant-Governors of Upper Canada and Ontario, 1792-1899*. Toronto: William Briggs, 1900.

Reeve, G. J. and MacFarlane, R. O., *The Canadian Pageant*. Toronto: Clarke Irwin and Company Limited, 1951.

Reid, Allana G., "Representative Assemblies in New France," *C.H.R.*, XXVII-1, March 1946.

————, "The First Poor-Relief System of Canada," *C.H.R.*, XXVII-4, December 1946.

Reid, Stewart, McNaught, Kenneth, and Crowe, Harry S., eds., *A Source-book of Canadian History*. Toronto: Longmans, Green and Company, 1959. Selections reprinted by permission of the publishers.

Report of the Royal Commission on Bilingualism and Biculturalism. Book 1. Ottawa: Queen's Printer, 1967. Selections reprinted by permission of the Queen's Printer.

Report of the Royal Commission on Dominion-Provincial Relations. 3 Books. Ottawa: King's Printer, 1940. Reprinted by permission of the Queen's Printer.

Report of the Royal Commission on Price Spreads. Ottawa: King's Printer, 1935. Selections reprinted by permission of the Queen's Printer.

Report of the Royal Commission to Inquire Into Railways and Transportation in Canada. Ottawa: King's Printer, 1917.

Richards, P. M., "Mr. Howe's White Paper," *Saturday Night*, April 21, 1945. Selections reprinted by permission of the publishers.

————, Selection in *Saturday Night*, November 24, 1945, p. 8. By permission of the publishers.

Riddell, Walter, A., ed., *Documents of Canadian Foreign Policy 1917-1939*. Toronto: Oxford University Press, 1962. Selections reprinted by permission of the publishers.

Robinson, Percy J., "Some of Cartier's Place-Names 1535-1536," *C.H.R.*, XXVI-4, December 1945.

Ross, Alexander, *The Red River Settlement: Its Rise, Progress, and Present State*. London: Smith, Elder and Co., 1856.

Rothney, G.O., *Newfoundland: From International Fishery to Canadian Province*. C.H.A. Booklet, No. 10. Ottawa: C.H.A., 1959.

Rumilly, Robert, *Henri Bourassa*. Montréal: Les Editions Chantecler Ltée, 1953. Selections reprinted by permission of the author.

————, *Mercier*. Montréal: Les Editions du Zodiaque, 1936. Selections reprinted by permission of the author.

Russell, Peter H., ed., *Leading Constitutional Decisions*. Toronto: McClelland and Stewart Limited, 1965. Selections reprinted by permission of the publishers.

Ryerson, Egerton, *The Loyalists of America and Their Times: From 1620 to 1816*. 2 vols. Toronto: James Campbell & Son, and Willing & Williamson, 1880.

Sabine, Lorenzo, *Biographical Sketches of Loyalists of the American Revolution with an Historical Essay*. 2 vols. Boston: Little, Brown and Company, 1864.

Sack, Benjamin G., *History of the Jews in Canada*. Vol. 1. Montreal: Canadian Jewish Congress, 1945.

Sagard, Gabriel, *The Long Journey to the Country of the Hurons*. Ed. George M. Wrong, trans. H. H. Langton. Toronto: The Champlain Society, 1939. Selections reprinted by permission of the Society.

Sandham, Alfred, *Ville-Marie, or Sketches of Montreal Past and Present*. Montreal: George Bishop & Co., 1870.

Saturday Night, January 19, 1946. p. 3.

Saunders, R. M., "Coureur de Bois: A Definition," *C.H.R.*, XXI-2, June 1940. Selections reprinted by permission of the author, and of the University of Toronto Press.

Schull, Joseph, *Laurier: The First Canadian*. Toronto: The Macmillan Company of Canada Limited, 1965.

Scott, Frank and Oliver, Michael, eds., *Quebec States Her Case*. Toronto: The Macmillan Company of Canada Limited, 1966. Selections reprinted by permission of the publishers, of Claude Savoie, and Jean-Marc Léger.

Scrope, Poulett G., ed., *Memoirs of the Life of the Right Honourable Lord Sydenham, G.C.B. with a Narration of his Administration in Canada*. London: John Murray, 1843.

Secretan, J. H. E., *Canada's Great Highway: From the First Stake to the Last Spike*. London: John Lane the Bodley Head Ltd., 1924. Selections reprinted by permission of the publishers.

Select Standing Committee on Agriculture and Colonization, Minutes of Proceedings and Evidence and Report. Session, 1928. Ottawa: King's Printer, 1928. Selections reprinted by permission of the Queen's Printer.

Sharp, Paul F., *Whoop-Up Country: The Canadian American West, 1865-1885*. Minneapolis: University of Minnesota Press, 1955. Selections reprinted by permission of the publishers.

Shortt, Adam, ed., *Documents Relating to Canadian Currency, Exchange and Finance During the French Period*. 2 vols. Ottawa: King's Printers, 1925.

Shortt, Adam and Doughty, Arthur G., eds., *Documents Relating to the Constitutional History of Canada 1759-1791*. 2 parts. Ottawa: King's Printers, 1918.

Siegfried, André, *The Race Question in Canada*. London: Eveleigh Nash, 1907.

Sifton, Clifford, "The Immigrants We Want", *Mac-Lean's Magazine*, April 1, 1922. Selections reprinted by permission of the author's family.

Skelton, Isabel, *The Life of Thomas D'Arcy McGee*. Gardenvale, Que.: Garden City Press, 1925.

Skelton, Oscar Douglas, *Life and Letters of Sir Wilfrid Laurier*. 2 vols. London: Oxford University Press, 1922. Selections reprinted by permission of the publishers.

————. *The Day of Sir Wilfrid Laurier*. Toronto: Glasgow, Brook and Company, 1916.

————. *The Life and Times of Sir Alexander Tilloch Galt*. Toronto: Oxford University Press, 1920.

Smith, Henry C., *The Story of the Mennonites*. Newton, Kansas: Mennonite Publication Office, 1957.

Smith, Goldwin, *Canada and the Canadian Question*. Toronto: Hunter Rose & Company, 1891.

Smith, William, *Robert Gourlay*. Kingston: The Jackson Press, 1926.

Soward, F. H., *The Department of External Affairs and Canadian Autonomy, 1899-1939*. C.H.A. Booklet, No. 7., Ottawa: C.H.A., 1961.

Sparks, Jared, ed., *The Writings of George Washington*. 12 vols. New York: Harper Brothers, 1847.

Spell, L., "Music in New France in the Seventeenth Century," *C.H.R.*, VIII-2, June 1927.

Spragge, George W., ed., *The John Strachan Letter Book; 1812-1834*. Toronto: The Ontario Historical Society, 1946. Selections reprinted by permission of the Society.

Stacey, C. P., *The Undefended Border, the Myth and the Reality*. C.H.A. Booklet, No. 1, Ottawa: C.H.A., 1957.

Stamer, W., *The Gentleman Emigrant*. 2 vols. London: Tinsley Brothers, 1874.

Stamp, Dudley L., *A Regional Geography*. Part I, The Americas. London: Longmans, Green and Co., 1958.

Stanhope, Earl, *Life of the Right Honourable William Pitt*. 4 vols. London: John Murray, 1861.

Stanley, George F. G., *Canada's Soldiers, 1604-1954. The Military History of an Unmilitary People*. Toronto: The Macmillan Company of Canada Limited, 1954. Selections reprinted by permission of the publishers.

————. *The Birth of Western Canada: A History of the Riel Rebellions*. Toronto: University of Toronto Press, 1963.

Stavrianos, L. S., "The Rumour of Russian Intrigue in the Rebellion of 1837," *C.H.R.*, XVIII-4, December 1937.

Stefansson, Vilhjalmur, *My Life with the Eskimo*. New York: The Macmillan Company Ltd., 1913.

————, *The Friendly Arctic, the Story of Five Years In Polar Regions*. New York: The Macmillan Company Ltd., 1943.

Stoochnoff, John Philip, *Doukhobors as They Are*. Toronto: Ryerson Press, 1961.

Sulte, Benjamin, "The Captains of Militia," *C.H.R.*, 1-3, September 1920. Reprinted by permission of the Society.

Talman, James J., ed., *Loyalist Narratives from Upper Canada*. Toronto: The Champlain Society, 1946.

Tassé, Joseph, ed., *Discours de Sir George Cartier*. Montreal: Eusébe Senécal & Fils, 1893.

Thomson, Dale C., *Louis St. Laurent: Canadian*. Toronto: The Macmillan Company of Canada Limited, 1967. Selections reprinted by permission of the publishers.

Thorburn, Hugh G., ed., *Party Politics in Canada*. Scarborough, Ont.: Prentice-Hall of Canada Ltd., 1967.

Thwaites, Reuben Gold, ed., *The Jesuit Relations and Allied Documents*. 72 volumes in 36. New York: Pageant Book Company, 1959. Selections reprinted by permission of the publishers.

Trudeau, Pierre Elliott, *Federalism and the French Canadians*. Toronto: The Macmillan Company of Canada Limited, 1968. Reprinted by permission of the University of Toronto Press.

Trudel, Marcel, *Le Régime Militaire dans le Gouvernement des Trois-Rivières 1760-1764*. Trois-Rivières: Editions du Bien Public, 1952. Selections reproduced by permission of the publishers.

————. *The Seigneurial Régime*. C.H.A. Booklet, No. 6. Ottawa: C.H.A., 1956.

Tucker, Gilbert Norman, *The Canadian Commercial Revolution, 1845-1851*. New Haven: Yale University Press, 1936.

Tureck, Victor, *Poles in Manitoba*. Toronto: Polish Alliance Press Limited, 1967.

Tyrrell, J. B., ed., *David Thompson's Narrative of His Explorations in Western America, 1784-1812*. Toronto: The Champlain Society, 1916. Reprinted by permission of the Society.

————, ed., *Documents Relating to the Early History of Hudson Bay*. Toronto: The Champlain Society, 1931. Reprinted by permission of the Society.

————, ed., *Samuel Hearne's Journey from Prince of Wales Fort in Hudson's Bay to the Northern Ocean in the Year 1769, 1770, 1771, and 1772*. Toronto: The Champlain Society, 1911. Selections reprinted by permission of the Society.

Underhill, Frank H., "Some Aspects of Upper Canadian Radical Opinion in the Decade Before Confederation," *C.H.A. Report*, 1927. Selections reprinted by permission of the Association.

United Empire Loyalists' Centennial Committee, *The Centennial of the Settlement of Upper Canada by the United Empire Loyalists, 1784-1884.* Toronto: Rose Publishing Co., 1885.

Urquhart, Hugh M., *Arthur Currie, The Biography of a Great Canadian.* Toronto: J. M. Dent & Sons (Canada) Limited, 1950.

Van Steense, Maja, ed., *People of Light and Dark.* Ottawa: Queen's Printer, 1966.

Wade, Mason, *The French Canadians 1760-1945.* Toronto: The Macmillan Company of Canada Limited, 1956.

————, *The French Canadian Outlook: A Brief Account of the Unknown North America.* New York: Viking Press, 1946.

Waite, P. B., ed., *Pre-Confederation.* Scarborough, Ont.: Prentice-Hall of Canada Ltd., 1965.

————, *The Life and Times of Confederation 1864-1867.* Toronto: University of Toronto Press, 1962. Selections reprinted by permission of the publishers.

Wallace, Stewart W., ed., *Documents Relating to the North West Company.* Toronto: The Champlain Society, 1934. Reprinted by permission of the Society.

————, "The Beginnings of British Rule in Canada," *C.H.R.,* VI-3, 1925. Selections reprinted by permission of the publishers.

————, *The Growth of Canadian National Feeling.* Toronto: The Macmillan Company of Canada Limited, 1927. Reprinted by permission of the publishers.

Walrond, Theodore, ed., *Letters and Journals of James, Eighth Earl of Elgin.* London: John Murray, 1872.

Wapemoose, Joseph, "Thoughts of an Urbanized Indian," *Indian Confrontation,* March 1969. Selections reprinted by permission of the author.

Warner, Donald F., "Drang Noch Norden: The United States and the Riel Rebellion," *Mississippi Valley Historical Review,* March 1953. Selections reprinted by permission of the author.

Watkins, Ernest, *R. B. Bennett. A Biography.* London: Secker & Warburg, 1963. Reprinted by permission of Bellhaven House, Ltd.

Weaver, Emily P., "Nova Scotia and New England During the Revolution," *American Historical Review,* X, 1904.

Weld, Isaac, *Travels Through the States of North America and the Provinces of Upper and Lower Canada During the Years 1795, 1796, and 1797.* London: John Stockdale, 1799.

Whelan, Edward, *The Union of the British Provinces.* Toronto: Garden City Press, 1927.

White, Patrick C. T., ed., *Lord Selkirk's Diary 1803-1804.* Toronto: The Champlain Society, 1958. Selections reprinted by permission of the Society.

Whitelaw, W. M., *The Quebec Conference.* C.H.A. Booklet, No. 20. Ottawa: C.H.A., 1966.

Whitton, Charlotte, "Baby Bonus Plan Involves Waste and Duplication," *Saturday Night,* March 17, 1945. Selections reprinted by permission of the publishers.

Wild, Roland, *Amor de Cosmos.* Toronto: The Ryerson Press, 1958. Selections reprinted by permission of the authors.

Williams, Basil, *The Life of William Pitt, Earl of Chatham.* 2 vols. London: Longmans Green and Co., 1913. Selections reprinted by permission of Frank Cass & Co.

Willison, John, *Sir George Parkin, A Biography.* London: Macmillan and Company Limited, 1929.

————, *Sir Wilfrid Laurier and the Liberal Party.* 2 vols. Toronto: George N. Morang and Company Limited, 1903.

Willms, A. N., "Conscription 1917: A Brief for the Defence," *C.H.R.,* XXXVII-4, December 1956.

Wilson, Alan, *The Clergy Reserves of Upper Canada.* Toronto: University of Toronto Press, 1968.

Wood, William, ed., *Select British Documents of the Canadian War of 1812.* 3 vols. Toronto: The Champlain Society, 1920-1928. Selections reprinted by permission of the Society.

Wrong, George M., *Canada and the American Revolution: The Disruption of the First British Empire.* Toronto: The Macmillan Company of Canada Limited, 1935.

Wrong, George M., Martin, Chester and Sage, Walter N, *The Story of Canada.* Toronto: Ryerson Press, 1940.

Young, James, *Public Men and Public Life in Canada. The Story of the Canadian Confederacy Being Recollections of Parliament and the Press.* 2 vols. Toronto: William Briggs, 1912.

Young, Scott, "Pay-off in Oil," *Maclean's Magazine.* June 15, 1947. Selections reprinted by permission of the author.

Yuzyk, Paul, *Ukrainian Canadians: Their Place and Role in Canadian Life.* Toronto: Ukrainian Canadian Business & Professional Federation, 1967.

Zaslow, Morris. *The Defended Border: Upper Canada and the War of 1812.* Toronto: The Macmillan Company of Canada Limited, 1964.

INDEX

Grand Trunk Railway, 213, 216, 221,
    222, 323
  subsidizing of, 216
Grange, the, 298
Grant, G. M., 274
Great Britain:
  and Alaskan Boundary dispute, 308-10
  Canada and the Chanak affair, 354-55
  Canada and the Halibut
      Treaty, 355-56
  Confederation, encouragement of, 230
  economic slump after *1815*, 157
  and France's aims during the
      American Revolution, 110, 111
  and Imperial Preference, 303
  interim government (military) in
      French Canada after the
      conquest, 93-94
  and the Naval issue of *1909*, 310-11
  and problems of the conquest of New
      France, 91-95
  relations with the U.S. after the
      Civil War, 258
  urging of the Atlantic provinces to
      accept Confederation, 230
  see also England
Great Central Plains, extent of, 17
Green, Howard, 423
  on Canada's role in the Suez crisis, 415
  on the treatment of Japanese-
      Canadians during World War
      II, 385
Grey, Lord, 195, 199, 310
Greysolon, Daniel, 44
Groseilliers, Médard Chouart des, 35
  exploration of, 43, 44
  problem with the Governor in
      Quebec, 45
  service to the English, 45

H

Haliburton, Thomas Chandler, 201
Halibut Treaty, 355-56
Halifax, founding of, 82-83
Harkness, Douglas, 423
  on unification of the armed forces, 405
Harrison, S. B., 192
Harvey, Sir John, 199
Head, Sir Francis Bond, 176
  on the Family Compact, 165
  on the reformers, 165-66
  on William Lyon Mackenzie, 174
Hearne, Samuel, 140
  exploration, 141
  on the murder of Eskimos on the
      Coppermine River, 141-42
Heavener Rune Stone, 9
Hellyer, Paul, 405
Henday, Anthony, 50n, 140
  exploration, 141
Hepburn, Mitchell, 371-72
Herjulfsson, Bjarni, 9
Hincks, Sir Francis, 192, 213
Hochelaga, 14, 24
Homestead Act, 262
Howe, C.D., 373, 398, 401
  on accomplishments of the
      Department of Munitions and
      Supply, 373
  on production of war materials, 372
Howe, Joseph, 158, 198, 212, 229
  agitation for repeal of
      Confederation, 247
  criticism of subjection of Governors
      to the Executive Council, 198
  on his contribution to the
      encouragement of literary
      talent, 202

Howe, Joseph (*cont'd.*):
  on Lord Durham's Report, 186
  role in the Nova Scotia reform
      movement, 178-79
Hudson, Henry, 12
Hudson Bay waterways system, 19-20
Hudson's Bay Company, 96, 137, 145,
    156, 209, 253, 264
  amalgamation with the North West
      Company, 150
  comparison with the North West
      Company, 140
  and d'Iberville's expedition, 37, 80
  formation of, 36, 45
  geographical advantage of, 138
  and the Red River Settlement,
      146-50 *passim*
  and restrictive trade regulations re
      Red River Settlement, 207
  rivalry with the North West
      Company, 138-50 *passim*
  sale of lands to Canada, 248-49
  suggestions for dividends to
      employees of, 140
Hudson's Bay Railway, 344
Hughes, Sam, 317
Huntington, L. S., 260
Huronia, 61-62
Hurons, 23, 40, 41, 61
  death blow by the Iroquois, 34, 62
  as middlemen in the fur trade, 33-34
  reasons for conflict with the
      Iroquois, 24
  the use of steam baths, 25
Hutton, General Edward, 304, 306
Hydro-electric power, 296-97, 391
  development and use during the
      1920's, 328
Hydro-Electric Power Commission of
    Ontario, 296

I

Iberville, Pierre le Moyne d', 47
  expedition against the Hudson's Bay
      Company, 37
  exploits of, in Hudson Bay, 80
Ignatieff, George, 415
Immigration, 283
  and the B.N.A. Act, 239
  the Great Migration, 156-60
    reasons for, 157-58
  and the Land Companies, 160, 161
  Laurier's policy of, 287-90
  to Lower Canada, prior to *1815*, 156
  policy of the *1920's*, 326
  in Upper Canada prior to *1815*, 155
  views on non-Anglo-Saxon
      immigrants, 289
  to the West, 287-92
Imperial Conference:
  1921, 354
  1923, 356
  1926, 357-58
  and the Balfour Report, 357-58
Imperial Economic Conference, *1932*,
    362-63
Imperial Federation League, 274
Imperial War Conference, *1917*
  and Resolution IX, 352
Income War Tax Act, 323
Indians, 21-27
  area of settlement, 20-24
  culture of, 24-27
  Eastern Woodlands, 22
    linguistic classification, 22
    social and tribal organization, 22

Indians (*cont'd.*):
  effect of European goods, 26
  effect of the fur trade, 37
  family as basic unit, 25
  hostility toward Americans' westward
      expansion, 125
  land grant to the Six Nations, 118
  in modern society, 26-27
  Pacific Coast, 20-21
    social and tribal organization, 20-21
  Plains, 21-22
    social and tribal organization, 21
  religion, 25
  resist Christianization, 60
  St. Lawrence Valley, 23-24
    social and tribal organization, 23
  stoical outlook, 25
  values different from Europeans', 26
Industrial Disputes Investigation Act,
    301
Industry:
  automotive, 327-28
  and the Combines Investigation
      Act, 298
  founding of the Canadian
      Manufacturers' Association, 297
  growth of, 297-98
  pulp and paper, growth of, 328
Intendant:
  function of, in New France, 54
Intercolonial Railway, 273
  and the B.N.A. Act, 243
  completion of, 261
International Civil Aviation
    Organization, 412
International Control Commission, 416
International Court of Justice, 412
International Joint Commission,
    310, 422
International Labour Organization, 412
International Monetary Fund, 412
Internation Nickel Company, 388
International Nickel Company, 388
International Postal Union, 412
International Workers of the World, 330
Ireland: potato crop failure,
    1840's, 157-8
Iron Ore Company of Canada, 389
Iroquois Confederacy, 41
  annihilation of the Neutral and
      Tobacco Indians, 34
  the attack on Lachine, 79
  Champlain's expedition against, 34, 40
  defeat by Frontenac, 80
  destruction of Huronia, 34, 62
  dominance of the Ottawa River fur
      route, 34-35, 62
  expedition against, by
      Denonville, 78-79
  as middlemen in the fur trade, 33-34
  political development of the
      Confederacy, 24
  reason for conflicts with the
      Hurons, 24
  threat to New France, 34
  tribes of, 23
Ivens, Reverend William, 331, 332

J

Jay's Treaty, 125
  and the fur trade, 136-37
Jesuit Estates Act, 276-77
Jesuit Relations, 61, 62
Jesuits, 61, 92, 102
  accomplishments of, 61-62